T0348070

ECONOMIC DEVELOPMENT OF AFRICA,
1880–1939

CONTENTS OF THE EDITION

ECONOMIC DEVELOPMENT OF AFRICA, 1880–1939

GENERAL EDITOR
David Sunderland

ADVISORY EDITOR
Godfrey N. Uzoigwe

Volume 1
Agriculture: Non-Food and Drink

Routledge
Taylor & Francis Group

LONDON AND NEW YORK

First published 2011 by Pickering & Chatto (Publishers) Limited

Published 2016 by Routledge
2 Park Square, Milton Park, Abingdon, Oxon OX14 4RN
711 Third Avenue, New York, NY 10017, USA

Routledge is an imprint of the Taylor & Francis Group, an informa business

Copyright © Taylor & Francis 2011
Copyright © Editorial material David Sunderland 2011

BRITISH LIBRARY CATALOGUING IN PUBLICATION DATA

Economic development of Africa, 1880–1939. – (Britain and Africa)
1. Great Britain – Colonies – Africa – Economic conditions. 2. Great Britain –
Colonies – Africa – Economic policy. 3. Agriculture – Africa – History – 19th
century. 4. Agriculture – Africa – History – 20th century. 5. Industrialization –
Africa – History – 19th century. 6. Industrialization – Africa – History – 20th
century. 7. Economic development – Social aspects – Africa – History – 19th century. 8. Economic development – Social aspects – Africa – History – 20th century.
I. Series II. Sunderland, David, 1958–
325.3'41096-dc22

ISBN-13: 978-1-84893-063-6 (set)

Typeset by Pickering & Chatto (Publishers) Limited

CONTENTS

GENERAL INTRODUCTION

Among the many motivations behind Britain's scramble for Africa the most important were economic. It was believed that the continent would supply the raw materials and foodstuffs required by Britain's ever-expanding industries and population, furnish guaranteed markets for some of the goods produced by those industries, and provide investment opportunities and high returns for the large amount of capital unable to find employment at home.[1] There was also a wish to protect this supposed economic Eldorado from exploitation by other European powers, such as France and Germany, which were increasingly threatening Britain's dominance of the world economy. This general introductory essay, the thematic introductions and the sources reproduced in this collection examine the extent to which these goals were realized.

Governmental Contribution to Development and the Impact of External Shocks

The imperial government's attitude to its African colonies was one of *laissez faire*. It had little involvement in the economic development of the continent and, at least until the inter-war period, it was relatively unconcerned as to whether Britain economically directly benefited from its colonies. Over, the period, little finance was provided for development and Africa largely remained a free-trade area. However, although the government's reluctance to finance growth no doubt harmed development, its commitment to free trade probably promoted economic expansion, as did the construction of infrastructure, the introduction of a stable currency and a variety of other services.

Finance

The imperial government provided few funds for the administration of the continent. Colonial governments were expected to be self-financing, to balance their budgets and, if possible, to build up a small surplus. The British Treasury only paid the military and administrative expenses of new dependencies that had yet to develop revenue streams and, subsequently, provided non-repayable grants-in-aid. These had to be approved by Parliament and were given to those colonies unable to cover their administration costs or that had suffered a natural disaster or civil emergency and needed funds for reconstruction or relief.[2]

Nor was the imperial government willing to finance development. Except for a brief period from 1895 to 1903 when the then Colonial Secretary, Joseph Chamberlain, promoted the idea of constructive imperialism, the orthodox view was that economic growth should be funded by local administrations and the private sector.[3] The policy only slightly changed in the 1920s. High post-war unemployment and the fear of an imminent shortage of cotton required for the Lancashire textile industry prompted the imperial government in 1924 to provide a £3.5m loan for the construction of the Uganda–Kenya railway and, two years later, to make another £10m available for the further development of transport in East Africa and Palestine.[4] There were also calls by the Conservative MP and later Colonial Secretary (1924–9) Leo Amery in 1922 and the 1925 and 1928 East Africa Commissions for the creation of a Colonial Develop-ment Fund. This was eventually established in 1929 with the aim of aiding the development of agriculture and industry in the colonies and thereby fostering industrial expansion in the United Kingdom. The Fund was managed by the Colonial Development Committee, which considered schemes put forward by colonial governments and could advance in any one year up to £1m in the form of grants, loans or the payment of interest on loans raised elsewhere.[5]

Unfortunately, the amount of money available for distribution was deter-mined by Parliament and tended to fall in years of poor trade when colonial needs for finance were at their greatest. By 1940, MPs had permitted just £8m of expenditure, half in the form of grants, of which only £6.5m was actually spent.[6] Moreover, rather than the large-scale projects envisaged, most of the loans and grants were used to finance small-scale transport and public health schemes. The Colonial Development Committee lacked both ambition and a long-term strat-egy and colonial governments were reluctant to initiate innovative programmes. Naturally conservative, they feared that economic advancement would weaken their ability to rule and were influenced in this belief by the Colonial Office and the British government. Both feared that industrialization would break down traditional societies and also suspected that colonial development by increas-ing competition would ultimately damage the UK economy and would lead to political repercussions in Britain from those who interpreted industrialization as exploitation.[7] Nonetheless, Africa did relatively well out of the Fund. In total, the continent obtained £2.654m in grants and £1.653m in loans; the greatest beneficiary being Tanganyika, which obtained over £0.8m.[8]

The funds needed to administer and develop colonies came from revenues, the Crown Agents (CAs), and locally raised and guaranteed loans.[9] Revenues were raised via import duties and only to a lesser extent through taxation, as the widespread distribution and poverty of populations made taxes difficult to collect and the amount collectable relatively small.[10] Tariffs were calculated on an ad valorem basis and bore heavily on clothing and other consumer items. Taxation comprised flat rate hut or poll taxes, and, in some colonies, miscellaneous fees for grazing, dipping, the ownership of dogs, etc.[11] Non-payment resulted in imprisonment and prison labour, and, in some places, the burning of homes and crops.[12] British trading and mining firms paid UK tax, though a half share was returned to the colony in which the income was generated.[13] Both sources of finance were thus regressive and fell more on Africans than on Europeans, ensuring that the costs of providing the security and infrastructure from which British companies and investors benefited were borne by the ruled rather than the rulers.

The purpose of taxation, however, was not merely to raise revenue. Taxes forced Africans to enter paid employment and to migrate long distances to find work, and helped to keep employee remuneration low (high wages reduced the amount of time Africans had to work to pay off their tax obligations). They additionally encouraged cash cropping, contributed to the abandonment of domestic slavery and forced labour, and had moral and other benefits. Africans were released from their 'lives of sloth and idleness' and firmly placed on 'the path of civilization', and they could use part of the wages earned to purchase British imports.[14] The taxes were initially paid in labour or produce, but later, as the circulation of European currency increased, in cash, thus promoting further currency circulation and the attendant growth of trade.[15] Income tax was rare; given the existence of subsistence farming, it would have failed to force farmers onto the labour market.

The external finance provided by the CAs comprised loans and current account overdrafts and advances. The loans were either publicly issued, sold to private institutions in the London money market or obtained from the inter-colonial loan scheme or from the Bank of England and the London and Westminster Bank. From 1880 to 1939, £128.3m of African government colonial stock was publicly issued or sold on the London market, each loan having a lifespan of five to sixty years, after which it had to be repaid, and an annual interest charge of between 2.5 and 6 per cent of the loan's value (Tables 1 and 2). The majority were used to finance the construction of railways and harbours. Generally, the CAs issued comparatively low interest rate loans for which they charged relatively high prices. Colonial stocks had trustee status, i.e. they could be purchased by trusts, which increased demand, and investors were well aware that colonial government finances were supervised by the Colonial Office and that imprudent behaviour was therefore unlikely and the UK government would never allow a colony to default on its debts. The CAs also adopted a variety of strategies to ensure that there was great demand for issues. In the nineteenth century, for example, several months before a flotation was to occur they purchased the existing loan stock of the issuing colony for the colonial investment funds that they managed, causing the market price to increase and permitting them to set a relatively high price for the new loan.[16]

Table 1: Public Issues on the London Market, 1880–1939[17]

Period	Colony and year loan(s) issued	Total amount of issue (£m)
Nigeria		
1880–1913	Nigeria/Lagos/S. Nigeria (1905; 1908; 1911)	10
1914–39	Nigeria (1916; 1919; 1921;1927)	17.675
Nigerian total, 1880–1939		27.675
Gold Coast		
1880–1913	Gold Coast (1902; 1909)	2.035
1914–39	Gold Coast (1914; 1920; 1925; 1931)	10.833
Gold Coast total, 1880–1939		12.868
Other territories		
1880–1914	Sierra Leone (1904; 1913)	57.385
1914–39	Kenya (1921; 1927; 1928; 1930; 1936)	17.275
1914–39	Uganda (1932)	2
1914–39	Northern Rhodesia (1933)	1.097
1880–1913	Cape (1880; 1881)	3.5419
1880–1913	Natal (1882; 1884; 1885; 1888; 1889; 1881; 1893)	6.3685
1880–1913	Zanzibar (1901)	0.1
African total, 1880–1939		128.3104

Table 2: The Sale of Stock in the London Market to Institutions, 1914–39[18]

Colony and year loan(s) issued	Total amount of issue (£m)
Gold Coast (1935)	0.052
Nigeria (1922; 1930)	0.504988
Sierra Leone (1930; 1931)	0.3536
Northern Rhodesia (1931; 1932)	1.25
Uganda (1933; 1939)	0.85
Kenya (1933)	0.3056
Total	3.316

In addition to the loans issued and sold by the CAs, colonial administrations also issued guaranteed loans on the London market and floated their own issues on their own money markets. Guaranteed loans were floated by the Bank of England and were so called because the UK government guaranteed to repay the loan and pay the dividends if the issuer defaulted. They were generally issued when a loan without such a guarantee would fail or have to be offered at an excessively low price or high interest rate. During the period, three such loans were issued for Tanganyika and one for East Africa. Colonial administrations began to issue loans on their own money markets after the First World War. The practice was adopted where the colony possessed a local securities market, the proceeds were to be spent internally rather than on the purchase of goods from the UK, the money was required by public bodies, which were effectively barred from the London market, or when a UK flotation was likely to prove difficult because the colony was not regarded as creditworthy or the money was to be used for unremunerative purposes. The loans were relatively small with short lives, were largely bought by local banks and were issued by Kenya, Northern Rhodesia, Sierra Leone, Tanganyika and Uganda.[19]

The CAs' inter-colonial loan scheme was established in 1925 to allow borrowers that were unable to raise funds on the London market to obtain money.[20] The CAs created stock for the colony requiring finance and then sold it to one or more of the colonial investment funds under their management. The stock was not quoted on the market and recipients therefore faced no flotation expenses and could repay the loan at any time. From 1925 to 1939, Sierra Leone borrowed £0.67149 under the scheme in four loans and Nigeria obtained one £0.045m loan.[21] A number of colonies also obtained loans via the CAs from the Bank of England and the London and Westminster Bank (Table 3). The advances were short-term and, in return, the colonies paid the banks the ruling Bank of England interest rate.[22]

Table 3: Bank Loans from the Bank of England and the London and Westminster Bank[23]

Colony and year of loans	Amount (£m)
Bank of England	
Zanzibar (1899; 1901)	0.096
Uganda (1902)	0.242
Transvaal (1903)	2.515
East African Protectorate (1914)	0.15
London and Westminster Bank	
Cape (1880; 1881; 1882)	2.235
Nata (1880; 1884)	0.576
Gold Coast (1898; 1899; 1900)	0.095
Lagos (1898; 1899; 1900)	0.3345
Sierra Leone (1899; 1900)	0.143
Total	6.3865

The current account overdrafts and advances provided by the CAs to colonies were also relatively small and short-term. Each colony kept in London a current account that contained the unspent proceeds of any loans it had issued and the money it remitted to the UK to be used to pay for its transactions in the country, largely the purchase of supplies. The CAs allowed governments to run overdrafts on their own accounts and to obtain advances from other colonies' accounts. The overdrafts rarely exceeded £100, carried an interest rate and were usually repaid within the month. The advances were larger and were generally provided when a colony was unable to issue a loan on the London money market, either because the market was depressed or its credit poor.[24]

The imperial government's reluctance to invest in Africa was matched by private investors. The continent received only a small proportion of total British overseas investment; 13 per cent of the £4 billion invested overseas in 1914, and 21 percent of the £4.5 billion invested in 1938.[25] Reasons for this poor performance include the relative absence of plantation agriculture, adequate infrastructure, private capital markets and local demand; in the case of mining outside South Africa and the Rhodesias, the insignificance of the known deposits of the most important minerals; and government policy that was often inimical to inward investment – West African governments essentially forbade Europeans from acquiring land. After 1914, there was also relatively little demand for many of Africa's commodities and their prices were subject to wide swings.[26] Of the private capital invested, the vast majority found its way to South Africa and, to a lesser extent, Southern and Northern Rhodesia (Table 4). Deep-shaft mining generated heavy requirements for fixed capital and for railways, and, particularly in the inter-war period, industries to service and support the mines.[27] Not surprisingly, most of the money was invested in mining and trade and the investors were largely British nationals, though, as will be discussed below, after the First World War there was a significant inflow of American finance.[28]

Table 4: Private Capital Investment in British Territories, 1879–1936[29]

	Amount (£m)	Percentage of total British investment in African territories
South Africa and the Rhodesias	657.084	69.8
West Africa	116.73	12.4
East Africa	156.523	16.63
Miscellaneous	10.97	1.16
Total British territories	941.307	100

Trade

The imperial government's laissez faire view of empire extended to trade. Prior to the First World War and unlike her French colonial counterpart, Britain committed herself to free trade through a number of binding treaties. The Berlin Act of 1885 and the Brussels agreement of 1890 prohibited protective/differential tariffs in much of West Africa, British East Africa and Northern Rhodesia, and further freedom of trade was assured by the 1898 French treaty on West African trade, the 1918 Convention of St Germain and the commercial clauses attached to the 1919 mandates.[30]

As with the finance of the empire, however, Britain's commitment to this policy weakened in the 1920s and collapsed in the 1930s. In 1919 British customs duties on various empire goods including Rhodesian tobacco were reduced;

in the Gold Coast and Nigeria large export duties were placed on palm kernels (1919–22) and tin ore (1919–38) that were not destined for processing within the empire; and, among other countries, Kenya and South Africa introduced protective tariffs.[31] On the fall of commodity prices from 1929 there was a complete retreat from free trade. Britain introduced the imperial preference system, though it had little impact on African imports; colonial administrations increased and extended existing protective tariffs; and Kenya, Southern Rhodesia and South Africa established export subsidies. There was also a clampdown on the import of cheap Japanese textiles into Africa, which had begun to have an impact on the Lancashire clothing industry. In 1934, some West African territories imposed custom duties on Japanese textiles and Nigeria introduced a quota that fixed the maximum amount of such cloth that could be brought into the country.[32] The introduction of similar tariffs and quotas in East Africa was prevented by the pro-free-trade Congo Basin treaties to which Japan had acceded in 1919.[33]

By the end of the period Britain's proud boast of a free-trade empire was somewhat tarnished. In reality, of course, trade was never truly free. Colonial administrations diverted business towards British companies that were endowed with linguistic and institutional advantages not possessed by their foreign competitors, and all the goods imported for the use of colonial administrations were procured through the CAs, who placed almost all of their orders with UK suppliers.[34] Not surprisingly, therefore, Africa's trade was skewed towards Britain (Table 5). In 1900, 65.9 per cent of British Africa's exports flowed to the home country, though the extent of imperial dependence varied greatly. By 1937, the proportion had fallen to 39 percent, a reflection of the relative decline of the UK as a manufacturer, consumer and entrepôt country.[35] As for British imports into Africa, around 65.8 per cent of African imports came from the UK, though again there were great variations, and by the late 1930s the proportion had fallen to 44 per cent.[36] It should be noted, however, that African external trade was relatively small and was severely affected by the 1930s depression (Table 6) and that trade with Africa comprised only a small proportion of total British trade.[37] Nonetheless, the imperial power's relationship with Africa in the inter-war period undoubtedly softened the impact of slower economic growth; whilst at the same time masking economic decline and delaying the much-needed restructuring of the economy.

Table 5: Trade with Britain as a Percentage of Total Trade (annual averages)[38]

	West Africa		East Africa		Central Africa	
	Exports	Imports	Exports	Imports	Exports	Imports
1895–99	50.9	75.3	7.1	11	–	–
1915–19	70.6	77.1	29.1	22.2	64.7	47
1925–9	38.9	59.4	45.5	37.2	72.4	47.5
1935–9	44.1	46.7	32.2	34.1	49.3	44.9

Table 6: Average Annual Exports and Imports of British tropical Africa (£m)[39]

	West Africa		East Africa		Central Africa	
	Exports	Imports	Exports	Imports	Exports	Imports
1895–99	3.5	3.3	1.8	2.1	—	–
1915–19	18.2	15.3	7.8	10.4	5.1	3.5
1925–9	30.8	28.4	16.7	21.3	4.8	10.1
1935–9	23.3	24.1	17.3	18.9	13.4	12.6

Other Contributions to Development

In addition to their commitment to free trade, which on balance probably had a positive impact on development, the imperial and colonial governments further promoted economic growth through the construction of infrastructure and the introduction of stable currencies. The state built and operated most of the railways, harbours and roads of Africa; the private sector lacking the financial resources and will to become involved in projects that would not necessarily provide a return. As will be seen in the second collection of this series, such infrastructure opened up areas to capitalist economic activity, allowing entrepreneurs cheaply to transport produce to the new export markets and import capital goods, and freed labour that had previously been involved in head porterage for other duties.

The need for stable currencies arose from the failings of indigenous means of exchange – barter, credit, cowries, brass rods and gold dust. These were insecure and lacked universal acceptance and thus restricted the growth of trade, the development of a pricing system and the introduction of taxes.[40] To rectify these problems, the UK introduced imperial currencies into its territories – in West Africa sterling, in East Africa until the early 1920s the rupee; and, in South Africa and Rhodesia, the rand.[41] In West Africa, the spread of sterling was slow. Coins were relatively scarce, the lack of small denominations prevented its use for small purchases and its adoption was strongly opposed by the trading companies, who made large profits out of the barter system. Circulation then accelerated largely due to the activities of colonial administrations and the imperial government. Colonial authorities used sterling to pay the salaries of soldiers, administrators and the labourers building the railways and other public works; required taxes, court fees and fines to be paid in coin; publicized the use of sterling; in 1908, introduced smaller denomination coins – pennies and tenths of pennies; and passed ordinances that declared that indigenous currencies were no longer legal tender.[42] More importantly, the Colonial Office and the CAs encouraged the establishment of the Bank of British West Africa (BBWA). In addition to its other services, the BBWA imported and issued coin to customers, for which it received a fee of 1 per cent; sent back to Britain surplus and worn coin; and issued paper currency, removing the need for traders and administrators to carry around large amounts of heavy small denomination coin.[43]

By the early twentieth century, the majority of commercial transactions involved sterling. There were, however, concerns about the activities of the BBWA and the stability of the currency. The BBWA made large profits from the difference between the tender and the metallic value of the coins it imported and the fees it charged customers who wished to receive the coin. It was also reluctant to increase its costs by repatriating surplus and worn coins, and there were fears that it would overissue currency, leading to West African inflation, and, by forcing the repatriation of coins to UK, stoking British inflation. In 1912, therefore, a Currency Board for West Africa was established in London. Staffed by financial experts, this took over from the BBWA the import and issue of currency and ensured that the currency was convertible and backed by sufficient holdings of British government securities.[44]

As a large part of the region's trade was conducted with India and by Indian merchants, in East Africa and Somaliland the local denomination was the Indian silver rupee, which from 1893 was convertible to sterling at a fixed exchange rate. The currency proved eminently suitable until 1914 when Britain's abandonment of the gold standard caused the peg with sterling to be removed. Unfortunately, the price of silver and therefore the rupee then began to appreciate and, by early 1920, its exchange value had risen from 1 shilling 4 pence, the exchange rate that was fixed in 1906 and existed until 1914, to 2 shillings 10 pence.[45] The impact of this rise on the East African economy was devastating. Capital imports fell and those farmers and mine owners who sold their produce in London for sterling saw their receipts collapse by over 50 per cent.[46] Although imports were cheaper, other local costs and debts denominated in rupees had not changed and there was little scope for reductions in labour or wages. By March 1920, the situation had become so dire that it was decided to return to a fixed exchange rate and to set the rate at which the East African rupee could be exchanged for sterling at 2 shillings; to introduce a new sterling currency based on the florin coin, each of which was worth 1 rupee, i.e. 2 shillings; and, to oversee this new currency, to establish in London a Currency Board. In the event, the new exchange rate was set too high. Almost immediately after its establishment, the value of the rupee began to depreciate in terms of sterling. Calls from the commercial community for the florin to be devalued, however, fell on deaf ears and the region's currency remained overvalued.[47]

The Currency Boards established in West Africa (1912), East Africa (1920) and the Rhodesias and Nyasaland (1940) contributed much to the economic development of their regions. Board control of the issue of currency spared administrations the problems and risks of currency management and reduced the likelihood of overissue and inflation. More importantly, the Boards ensured that currencies were freely convertible into sterling at face value and thus facilitated British Africa's trade with the UK and strengthened the sterling area's economic and political standing.[48] On the distaff side, local administrations lost control of their own monetary policy, and, by linking currencies with sterling, the Boards tightened the trade relationship between Africa and Britain, which was not necessarily to the colonial advantage, and made African economies more susceptible to fluctuations in world market prices. The Boards also maintained a high ratio of reserves to currency liabilities, though there were great variations in the ratios retained. The West African Board achieved a target ratio of 100 per cent in 1926 and thereafter exceeded this figure; whilst the East African Board, more influenced by local interests, rarely attained a ratio of 50 per cent, and, in 1932, possessed a ratio of less than 10 per cent. All of these reserves were invested in the UK and generally in low-interest British government securities. Many argued that such funds if invested in the colonies themselves would have assisted economic growth and that their absence had a deflationary effect. Calls, however, for a change in investment policy were rejected; many colonies lacked efficient domestic money markets and African investments were risky.[49]

Of the other facilitators of development associated with the imperial state the most important was probably the establishment of peace. In pre-colonial Africa, inter-tribal warfare and invasions by tribes of other's territory disrupted trade and took up large parts of the lives of young males. British rule permitted Africans to invest for the future without fear that their efforts would be destroyed by raiders, freed males for wage employment and promoted cross-border trade. Other significant contributions include the alienation of land, the replacement of the multiplicity of indigenous legal jurisdictions with a uniform legal system, and better education and health. Land alienation, which is discussed below, permitted European settlement, and a uniform legal system facilitated regional trade, the formalization of trading relationships and the resolution of trade disputes. Education, which was partly financed through subventions from the colonial state, ensured that employees were literate, numerate and, more importantly, disciplined.[50] The provision of very basic medical services and the use of vaccinations, quarantines and the destruction of plague-infected dwellings improved the health and productivity of workers.[51]

External Economic Shocks

A major drawback of Africa's gradual absorbtion into the World commercial system was that its economies were subject to external commercial shocks, the three most important of which over the period covered by this collection were the First World War, the post-war recession and the 1930s recession. The First World War affected colonial economies in a number of ways. There was firstly the loss of German/French markets and imports, the former of which particularly damaged West Africa and the Gambia. Before the war, Germany had been a major importer of Gold Coast cocoa and had obtained respectively 80 per cent and 75 per cent of Sierra Leone's and Nigeria's palm kernel harvests; while France had taken 90 per cent of the Gambia's groundnut crop.[52] Some of the producers struggled to find new markets; Gold Coast cocoa exports fell from £2.5m in 1913 to £1.8m in 1918. Others successfully redirected their exports to Britain, with one of the main impacts of the war being an increase in the dominance of the West African export trade by British trading companies. Unfortunately, some UK firms took advantage of their new-found power. Traders in palm kernels colluded to keep prices low, with the result that, whilst prices rose in London, in West Africa they stayed static or even fell.[53] As for the loss of German and French imports, these were again largely replaced by British goods, entrenching UK firms in the African import trade, though in West Africa a proportion of the replacement products came from the United States.[54]

Trade was further impaired by the shortage of shipping and the related increase in shipping and insurance rates. The imperial government introduced controls on foreign trade and shipping space, which favoured the larger British trading companies and thus led to the disappearance of smaller African merchants, and, in West Africa, the German Woermann line and the French West African steamship service halted operations.[55] The resultant fall in exports affected those who produced for overseas markets and the collapse in imports led to price inflation, which particularly harmed African wage earners; in South Africa, Southern Rhodesia and elsewhere this stimulated the development of local industries manufacturing consumer goods, such as clothes, footwear and processed foods; and in the Gambia, whose main foodstuff was imported rice, it resulted in near-famine conditions.[56] The fall in both exports and imports also reduced local government revenues. Faced with the cost of maintaining large military forces, some raised import duties, adding to the general inflation, and others abandoned capital projects that on completion would have contributed to development.[57]

A further impact of the war was the loss of European and African labour. The absence of Europeans reduced production on settler farms and plantations and forced government trading posts and technical departments to close, though in West Africa there was some temporary Africanization of previously white occupations, such as the driving of railway engines.[58] Africans were recruited as soldiers, and, to a greater extent, as carriers and labourers. Their disappearance crippled the European agriculture and mining sectors and decimated subsistence farming, with Eastern Uganda descending into famine.[59] In some cases, the shortage of labour became permanent.[60] Conditions for both African soldiers and carriers/labourers were poor and food supplies minimal, and large numbers died from tubercolosis, dysentery and malaria. Those that survived and returned often brought with them smallpox, meningitis and plague and large numbers of Africans, enfeebled by the fall in real wages, succumbed to the 1918–19 influenza pandemic.[61]

The colonies obtained a foretaste of the fall in commodity prices from 1929 to 1933 in the summer of 1920 when the immediate post-war rise in prices, stoked by the release of four years of pent-up demand and monetary inflation, collapsed. Producers for export experienced a drop in incomes, but recovery was relatively swift.[62] This was not the case in the 1930s, partly because in many regions the fall in prices was exacerbated by other problems. Kenya in 1928–9 was ravaged by locusts, and, in 1931–4, by drought.[63] Tanganyika in 1930 suffered heavy floods.[64] Southern Rhodesia in 1931 had to cope with an outbreak of foot and mouth and the restriction of cattle exports to neighbouring countries.[65] The South African economy was damaged by droughts in 1930–1 and 1932–3 and its decision in October 1931 not to follow Britain's lead and abandon the gold standard. Until the end of 1932, when the government finally accepted its mistake, the country thus faced fierce competition from countries that had devalued.[66]

The fall in prices affected both Europeans and Africans. Large numbers of European farmers, who had often financed expansion through heavy borrowing, were ruined.[67] Many voluntarily or otherwise abandoned their farms. Others stayed, generally because their assets were unrealizable and creditors accepted the futility of foreclosure.[68] These farmers variously temporarily halted cultivation; reduced the acreage cropped; where possible, consumed their produce themselves; cut the wages of their African workforce; increased production, encouraged in Tanganyika by the local government's 'Grow More Crops' campaign; or switched crops.[69] In Kenya, where the area under cultivation fell from 644,000 acres to 502,000 acres from 1930 to 1936 and African wages dropped by 40 per cent, there was a movement away from the growing of maize to the rearing of cattle and the growth of pyrethrum.[70] As regards other European activities, the smaller expatriate trading companies went to the wall or were taken over by their larger competitors, which possessed the advantages of vertical organization and strong customer relationships.[71] Gold mining was little affected by the depression. Gold prices remained high and, on the abandonment of the gold standard by Britain and the USA and the greater use of actual rather than notional gold, they rose.[72] Other mining operations survived by forcing down wages.[73] Local governments faced with falling revenues and costly agricultural aid programmes, cut capital projects.[74]

The impact of the price collapse on Africans was uneven. Those farmers who had embraced cash cropping were badly affected, though most lacked the burden of debt carried by their European counterparts; wage labour faced unemployment and lower wages; and the general fall in incomes reduced the turnovers of African shopkeepers and entrepreneurs.[75] The responses of those most damaged by the recession were similar to those adopted by Europeans. Many farmers

halted cultivation for export and large numbers of African retailers and entrepreneurs went out of business, replaced in West Africa by Syrian and Lebanese
traders, who were more dependent on and therefore more favoured by the British
trading companies and local governments. Those who survived increased production, encouraged in Tanganyika and Kenya by local government initiatives,
or switched crops. A large number of Africans, however, escaped the recession
relatively lightly. Subsistence farming was unaffected by the fall in prices and
all Africans benefited from the drop in import prices, particularly those in East
Africa who were able to buy cheap Japanese imports.[76]

African Agriculture

African economic activity comprised agriculture and the production of various
crafts and the provision of waged labour. The latter roles are described in the
Labour Supply, Working Conditions and African Enterprise thematic introductions in Volume 5 of this collection. African agriculture took the form of
subsistence farming, the cultivation of foods wholly consumed by the families
that grew them, and cash cropping, the production and sale of goods for the
domestic or the export market. Subsistence farming occurred throughout Africa
and was the most common form of agriculture; in 1910 it constituted 90 per cent
of the Nigerian economy and 75 per cent of that of the Gold Coast.[77] Farmers
grew plantains, yams, cassava, rice and maize in West Africa and bananas, maize,
cassava and millet in East and Central Africa; selling any surplus in good years
in the local markets.[78] By comparison, cash cropping largely took place in West
Africa and Uganda, though it was also carried out, to a far lesser extent, in East,
Central and South Africa, and generally involved the growth of family foodstuffs
and a variety of export crops, such as palm fruits, coffee, cocoa and cotton.

West Africa

Explanations for the Development of Cash Cropping

The emergence of cash cropping in West Africa was related to the trade and the
environment of the region. There was a long history of trade between West Africans living in coastal areas and Europeans. On the abolition of the slave trade,
merchants turned to 'legitimate business'; British trading companies purchased
from Africans palm oil, ivory, ebony, red wood, peppers, gum and beeswax and
provided in return such goods as gin, tobacco and gunpowder.[79] The result of
such commerce was that Africans had developed political expertise in dealing
with and some trust of Europeans and had become familiar with and developed
a taste for European goods.[80] The British trading companies, meanwhile, wishing to protect their business interests and lacking the ability to adopt plantation

agriculture, vigorously opposed individuals and firms wanting to establish plantations in the area. The environment of the region was also favourable to cash cropping. Its climate was almost perfect for the cultivation of cash crops, some of which (for example palm fruits and groundnuts) had long been grown there.[81] It was not rich in minerals and therefore did not attract Western mining companies, and it was inhospitable to Westerners. Known as 'the white man's grave', its sweltering temperatures and the presence of malaria and other tropical diseases resulted in high Western mortality rates, though similar conditions elsewhere failed to discourage white settlement and, by 1900, disease could be more effectively controlled.[82]

The reasons why Africans so readily adopted cash cropping are complex and include the rise of consumerism, the availability of labour, and entrepreneurialism. The growth of consumerism obviously played a large part. Africans desired Western goods not only to improve their standard of living, but also to gain the status and authority associated with ownership.[83] Some commentators claim that the appearance of new goods made possible by the development of the steam ship from the 1850s and the construction of railways largely from the 1890s gave farmers an incentive to bring new land into cultivation and to substitute effort for leisure. Others argue that the main incentive was not new goods but a desire to buy more of the same products and the falling price of these imports, again caused by transport improvements, which for the first time brought them within the reach of large numbers of Africans.[84]

To engage in cash cropping, black farmers required additional labour, as production for the market involved an increase in the amount of land cultivated. It is argued that this extra labour was available either because in the pre-colonial era Africans preferred leisure over work, or, more likely, because subsistence agriculture required relatively little labour (and land) and there was therefore a surplus of both, a thesis termed the vent-for-surplus model.[85] However, the latter theory is subject to caveats. It assumes that cash cropping was a new phenomenon. In fact, even before the arrival of colonialism, African farmers had sold a proportion of their harvests to local towns and traders. Although the intensity of sales varied from region to region, it therefore appears likely that the labour surplus was not as great as once assumed.[86] The surplus labour was also not idle all year round. During the planting and harvesting of subsistence food crops all the workers available were fully employed. Farmers who began to cultivate cash crops, the planting and harvesting seasons of which clashed with those of domestically consumed vegetables and grains, therefore had to limit food cultivation. When world prices for the export crops were high, this decision made economic sense, as the cash earned from exports could be used to purchase food. Problems arose when export prices fell. When this occurred, farmers had insufficient food grown by themselves, could not buy in vegetables and grains, and therefore faced starvation.

In the forests and woodlands of the southern parts of West Africa and the East Coast and northern shores of Lake Victoria, this was not a great dilemma, as the main food crops (plantains and root vegetables) were grown all year round. But in other areas the cultivation of cash crops, particularly cotton, could lead to famine and African farmers were therefore reluctant to embark on their cultivation.[87]

Nonetheless, it appears likely that in certain parts of West Africa there was a surplus of labour available for the cultivation of certain cash crops. It is also possible that the returns from cash cropping improved the health of Africans, enabling them to work longer and harder, and that there was some reallocation of labour. In the southern areas of the Gold Coast, for example, farmers halted the cultivation of palm fruits and the collection of wild rubber to concentrate on coffee; in the Amansie district of the Gold Coast there was a movement away from gold mining; and it seems likely that railways and later lorries released to agriculture a large number of former head porters.[88]

A further explanation for the development of cash cropping is entrepreneurialism. It used to be believed that the impetus for commercial agriculture came from British missionaries and colonial governments.[89] Missionaries certainly played a role. They actively fostered the cultivation of cocoa, coffee and cotton, believing that their promotion of these crops would increase the prosperity of Africans and thus make Christianity more attractive and that cotton cultivation would suppress domestic slavery.[90] The impact of colonial governments is more controversial. Colonial authorities were well aware that the main source of their revenues were import duties, and, to a lesser extent, taxation and that these could be maximized by the expansion of exports, which by increasing incomes would facilitate the payment of taxes and boost the demand for imports.[91] The most obvious and easiest method of expanding external trade was through the promotion of African agriculture. The economic system necessary for cash cropping already existed, it would be difficult to attract white settlers into the region and the necessary seizure of land and introduction of forced labour would spark costly and bloody African opposition.[92]

Whether, however, colonial governments were the main movers behind cash cropping is arguable. Actions that facilitated the adoption of the practice include the non-alienation of land, taxation and the construction of a transport infrastructure. Unlike in the rest of Africa, West African governments acted against the sale of land to Europeans. In Nigeria, all land was deemed to belong to the local Africans; ownership in Northern Nigeria being vested in the governor as trustee, and, in Southern Nigeria, in the native tribes. A similar situation existed in the Gold Coast and Sierra Leone. To prevent Africans themselves selling territory to Europeans, a 1916 Northern Nigeria ordinance ruled that ownership titles were only valid if the governor had consented to the sale. In the Gold Coast, a 1900 ordinance restricted non-agricultural sales to five square miles and ruled that the sale had to be approved by the courts, and a 1916 order-in-council restricted sales of all land to one square mile and again made consent by the governor obligatory.[93] The result of these policies was that there was little scope for European economic activity, except in mining and trading. Meanwhile, taxation forced farmers to sell at least a proportion of their harvests to the outside world, and the construction of railways and later roads enabled produce to be quickly and cheaply moved to the coast and opened up to commercial farming large areas that had previously been cut off from the export market, though there is evidence that in some areas roads and bridges were built on the initiative of and by local people.[94]

Actions that probably had less impact were the encouragement and advice given to Africans to spur them to cultivate particular crops. Colonial agricultural experts neglected the role played in agriculture by women, instead directing their recommendations only to African males, and, more importantly, were often ignorant of local conditions.[95] Local growers therefore often ignored their advice. To take cotton as an example (more are discussed in the thematic introductions to this and Volume 2 of this collection), many Africans were well aware that its cultivation would have a negative impact on food supplies and could possibly result in famine and therefore simply refused to begin to grow or to increase the acreages they devoted to the crop.[96]

A far more important source of entrepreneurialism was the African community. Black farmers were both innovative and ready to take risks, and, faced with new market opportunities, they were more than willing to cultivate new crops and to adopt innovative methods of production.[97] There was also a sprinkling of entrepreneurs who moved into agriculture from other areas when they became aware that there were profits to be made. Examples include the Hausa merchants who financed the Northern Nigerian Kano groundnut sector and the Creole merchants/planters who pioneered cocoa farming in Lagos.[98] The efforts of these farmers and entrepreneurs were supported by African institutions and the high levels of social capital that existed in communities. In the Gold Coast, for example, the development of the cocoa industry by Akwapim and Krobo migrant cocoa farmers was facilitated by the Krobo (patrilineal) and Akwapim (matrilineal) group purchase of land and the willingness of the Akyem sub-chiefs to sell them this land.[99] The Akan distinction between the ownership of land and the ownership of property on that land encouraged other farmers to plant cocoa trees confident that their ownership of the plants would not be disputed.[100]

Nature of Cash Cropping

Cash croppers generally produced food to feed their own families, as well as goods for the market, and, in a minority of cases, supplemented their income through the manufacture of crafts, trade or wage employment.[101] There also existed a small number of gentry farmers – chiefs who operated large farms and used patronage and clientship to obtain the necessary labour or rented out their land to tenants over whom they had influence as regards the crops grown and the farming methods adopted.[102] The cash crops cultivated, described in the thematic introductions to this and Volume 2 of this collection, and the acreage devoted to them varied according the state of world prices. If prices fell, growers would reduce production, and, if the fall appeared to be permanent, they would switch to a more lucrative cash crop; on the decline of palm oil prices, for example, the palm fruit growers of the Gold Coast shifted to the collection of wild rubber and, when rubber prices collapsed, began to cultivate cocoa. As described in the Marketing of Produce thematic introduction in Volume 3 of this collection, the goods produced were sold to local towns and mines, either directly or through middlemen, or, if destined for the export market, to British-based trading companies.

Farms were generally small, though in Nigeria and the Gold Coast the size increased over time.[103] Farmers were excluded from the marketing of their produce and thus had little opportunity to accumulate large amounts of capital and their only sources of credit were European trading companies, co-operative societies, money lenders and pawning.[104] Although the African Banking Corporation and, from 1905, other West African banks were keen to offer credit facilities to African farmers and entrepreneurs, most European bankers were reluctant to lend.[105] Africans were unable to provide collateral for loans in the form of proof of land ownership, the result of the colonial authorities' refusal to introduce compulsory land titling, and the handling of large numbers of individually small transactions was costly. There was also a high rate of bad debts; a desire on the part of some bankers to protect the interests of British merchants, who were their main customers and, in the case of the Anglo-African Bank, their largest shareholders; and, in Kenya, the 1903 Credit to Natives Ordinance laid down that no credit of more than £10 could be advanced to an African without the approval of a district officer.[106]

The farms were worked by members of the farmer's family, though at the end of the farming year there was often some communal labour, each farmer helping his neighbour to bring in the harvest.[107] This source of labour was supplemented by slaves, semi-independent descendants of slaves, pawns and waged workers. Both domestic slavery and pawning, which involved people being used as security for a loan and their labour as the loan interest, were relatively common in West Africa.[108] Although slavery was forbidden by the colonial authorities, they turned a blind eye to the practice well into the twentieth century.[109] Gradually, however, such forced labour was replaced by waged workers. These were often smaller or relatively unsuccessful farmers, who supplemented their income through part-time employment, but increasingly were migrants from other areas of Africa.[110] By the late 1920s, migrant labour was a common sight on cocoa and cotton farms, the majority of workers being employed only during the harvest, after which they returned home.[111]

Settler Economies

Agriculture

Cash cropping was less prominent in the settler economies. The exception was Uganda, where, as in West Africa, there was a climate generally unattractive to white settlers; a rich African agricultural tradition; in Buganda, a strong ruling class that vigorously promoted peasant cultivation; and, as a result of treaties with the Banu, government recognition of indigenous customary land rights.[112] African farmers thus had security of tenure and it was difficult for prospective settlers to buy economically viable amounts of land. The post-war decimation of European agriculture also played a part. Of the 140 white settlers who by 1914 had established farms in the country, a large proportion failed to survive the immediate post-war recession and the collapse of cotton, rubber and cocoa prices. Unlike their Kenyan brethren, they received little support from the colonial government or commercial banks and faced relatively high transport costs and strong competition from African rivals, whose lower expenses and standards of living enabled them to withstand the crisis better. By 1921, over half of the land farmed by Europeans had been taken out of cultivation and, under pressure from the main trading companies in the region, the British East Africa Company and the Uganda Company, the government decided to back the agricultural sector that had proved its worth.[113] Africans were thus given free seeds and advice on the planting, growth and weeding of crops, and price controls were introduced.[114]

In the rest of East, Central and South Africa cash cropping was very much secondary to settler agriculture. As will be discussed, local colonial authorities grabbed large amounts of land, which they then sold off to white settlers. African farmers thus had to buy land; farm in the special areas reserved for them, known as native reserves; or squat on white farmers' land.[115] Unlike West Africa, the region had little history of commercial contact with Europe and no indigenous and therefore familiar cash crops, apart from the banana, which had a high weight-to-value ratio, was highly perishable, difficult to store and transport, and was cultivated far from the coast.[116] There was also competition for labour from the European mining industry, and it was difficult for African Savannah grain farmers to fit cash crops into the prevailing agricultural cycle without increasing the risk of famine at times of falling world prices.[117]

There was in addition government opposition to African cash cropping and policies were adopted that benefited white cash croppers, and made life dif-

ficult for their black counterparts and encouraged the African production of
grain crops for the domestic market, though whether these initiatives damaged
African agriculture is the subject of some debate.[118] There were a number of reasons for this antagonism. Settler cash croppers, who possessed great influence
over government decision-making, wished to protect themselves against African competition and there was a great need for cheap grain to feed those who
worked on the settler farms and the mines, At the same time, there were fears that
cash cropping would reduce African labour supplies and lead to overproduction
and result in famine, which in densely populated areas could lead to costly and
economically destructive discontent and even rebellion. There was also a belief
in Kenya that there were insufficient Africans (two million) to sustain a cash-
cropping sector and here and elsewhere that black farmers were too conservative
and lacked entrepreneurial abilities.[119] The latter view was almost certainly false,
though African social organizations and institutions were admittedly less conducive to commercial farming than those in other parts of the continent.[120]

As in West Africa, the majority of Africans grew only food crops consumed
by their own families. Such subsistence farming was tolerated by the colonial
authorities, as African males were not fully employed on their farms and were
therefore available for paid employment, and the foods grown supplemented
and allowed the payment of low wages.[121] Cash croppers produced goods largely
for the local market and, to a lesser extent, for world markets. Relatively few African farmers bought land and the practice was over time prohibited by colonial
governments; in South Africa in 1913, in Kenya in 1926, and in Southern Rhodesia, to a limited extent, in 1930.[122] Farming on the native reserves was similarly
discouraged. The reserves were too small to support African agriculture, which
was often based on shifting cultivation, and generally comprised poor-quality
land (in Southern Rhodesia tsetse-infected) which was distant from railways
and local markets.[123] Overgrazing led to soil erosion and a decline in productivity and those Africans who opted to remain on the reserves were often under- or
malnourished. In South Africa, the movement from farming to wage labour was
further encouraged by the 1884 Glen Grays Act, which restricted the size of
reserve farm holdings, banned the sale, rental or subdivision of reserve land, and
levied a labour tax on those who lived on the reserves but did not farm.[124]

At first, Africans who squatted on the land of white owners were welcomed
by their landlords.[125] There were broadly two types of squatter: sharecroppers
and tenants. The former, largely found in South Africa, provided their landlords
with a share of up to half of the output of the land they farmed.[126] Tenants, alternatively, paid rent in the form of labour, cash or produce, or a combination of
all three, and often additionally paid grazing and dipping fees.[127] Those who met
their rent in the form of labour generally agreed to work for their landlords for
a specified number of days per year, for which they received a wage, albeit lower

than that commanded by wage labourers.[128] Cash tenants, meanwhile, paid money rents, in some cases in South Africa and Southern Rhodesia to absentee landlords.[129] The system benefited both the white community and the tenants. For white farmers, squatting solved labour recruitment problems; allowed them to accumulate the capital needed to develop their farms into commercial concerns; in the case of sharecropping, permitted them to participate in the export of goods they did not themselves produce; and, if they were ranchers or plantation owners, ensured a supply of foodstuffs. Squatters could produce food for their families and the local/export market; were not always required to provide the specified amount of labour; and, in Kenya, could sometimes avoid the payment of government taxes and the labour demands of chiefs, who could compel native reserve inhabitants to perform work for no payment.[130]

The practice began to disappear in South Africa from the 1890s and elsewhere in the 1920s, as a result of the actions of European farmers and colonial governments. White farmers no longer needed the capital provided by their African tenants, who often represented an obstacle to intensive farming or a competitive threat.[131] In South Africa and Southern Rhodesia, there was also an increasing demand for cheap African workers from the expanding mining sector, in South Africa rising land prices and, in Kenya, a post-war shortage of labour. Settler farmers thus began to tighten tenancy agreements, forcing cash tenants to become labour tenants, and then, by increasing the number of days labour required, encouraging labour tenants to give up their farms.[132] Their actions were supported and supplemented by colonial governments, which sought to end squatting by legislative means. In Southern Rhodesia, Africans on European land who were not employed as labourers were in 1930 given six years to quit; in Kenya, Native Labourers Ordinances in 1918 and 1937 subjected squatters to increasingly onerous terms of employment; and, in South Africa, there were a number of laws that made squatting successively more difficult, culminating in the 1913 Native Lands Act, which ruled labour and cash tenancies illegal.[133] Inevitably, such actions were often defied by the squatters. In South Africa, resistance was sometimes violent, involving in 1924 the burning of European wheat stacks.[134] In Southern Rhodesia and Kenya, opposition was more peaceful and generally more successful. Many settler landlords still required the food and labour provided by squatters, and colonial administrations often failed to force squatters in breach of legislation off their farms, or, if they did so, to take action when the squatters drifted back.[135]

Move to Towns

The response of many in South Africa to the difficulties of rural life was to move to the towns, and, by 1911, one in eight Africans (500,000) lived in urban areas.

Most were migrants, though some made the towns their permanent home, bringing their families to join them.[136] Many obtained waged employment as bricklayers, builders, drivers and factory workers and as domestic servants and washer men serving the needs of the single white miners who resided in boarding houses, though employment in this area fell as European female immigration increased and the arrival of white families increased fears of rape. Others survived as hawkers, small-scale traders, herbalists, operators of Shebeens and, in the case of women, as prostitutes.[137] Perhaps inevitably, housing conditions were dire. There were insufficient bachelor hostels and few towns provided accommodation for African incomers. They thus rented rooms or backyard spaces in city-centre slums and, after these were condemned and demolished by the 1934 Slums Act, moved to new townships or squatted in large illegal shanty towns outside city limits.[138]

Away from South Africa, little such movement occurred. The largest urban areas in East Africa were Nairobi (with a population in 1938 of 65,000), Mombassa (60,000) and Dar es Salem (40,000); in Southern Rhodesia, Bulawayo and Salisbury; and, in West Africa, Ibadan (with a population in 1936 of 318,000), Lagos (167,000), Kaduna, Enugu, Kano and Port Harcourt.[139] Africans drifted to these towns when they lost their livelihoods elsewhere. The inter-war expansion of Bulawayo, for example, was related to the 1928 decision by South Africa to repatriate migrant workers, the collapse of the Mashonaland tobacco boom, and the 1930s recession. Most were migrants or temporary residents, living in overcrowded ghettos on the edge of urban areas and working on the railways, and in factories and shops, though some also obtained positions as domestic servants, clerks and mechanics. Those who failed to obtain permanent work survived through gambling, prostitution and theft.[140]

European Economic Activity

European economic activity comprised agriculture, trade, mining, manufacturing and banking. The latter three sectors are explored in the Mining, Industry and Trade, and Banking thematic introductions in Volume 4 of this collection.

Trading and Mining Investment

As already discussed, the majority of private capital invested in Africa was ploughed into trade and mining

Trading Investment

Many of the trading companies operating in West Africa had been involved in the slave trade and moved to so-called 'legitimate business' on the abolition of that trade in 1807. The companies were largely based in Liverpool, the port at the heart of the slave trade and close to the large Lancashire market for palm oil/other cash crops, though a significant number were operated from Bristol.[141] Over time and particularly in the inter-war period, the sector became more concentrated as large firms took over their smaller competitors. The new oligopolies gained economies of scale in the transportation of goods to and from the interior of the continent and in the procurement of the standardized goods that they sold to the African market.[142] They could also collude in the fixing of low export and high import prices and make agreements not to compete in each other's spheres of interest; on taking over their smaller rivals, cut costs by closing down poorly performing branches and sacking staff; and they were less affected by commodity price movements. Gradually, trade became to be dominated by such companies as the African and Eastern Trading Company, Lever Bros., G. B. Ollivant, the Niger Company, the Liverpool firm John Holt and Company, Manchester's Paterson Zochonis, the Cypriot A. G. Leventis, and, to a much lesser extent, the French firms Compagnie Francaise de L'Afrique Occidentale (CFAO) and Societe Commerciale de L'Ouest Africain (SCOA).[143] In 1929, two of these companies, Lever Bros. and the African and Eastern Trading Company, combined to form the United Africa Company (UAC), which handled over half of West Africa's trade. In the same year, Lever Bros., facing bankruptcy, merged with the Dutch margarine combine Van den Bergh and Jurgens to form Unilever.[144] By the 1930s, the general trade of British West Africa was therefore dominated by just seven firms, which belonged to the collusive organization the Association of West African Merchants. These were joined in the purchase of cocoa by the agents of the British chocolate manufacturers, largely Cadburys and Rowntrees, and by various interlopers; often Greeks, Levantines or North Africans, such as Saul Raccah, who in the late 1930s broke UAC's control of the Kano groundnut market.[145] Needless to say, the imperial government and local colonial authorities, champions of free trade, had little involvement in these organizational manoeuvres; colonial marketing boards only appearing after the Second World War.[146]

The early companies that traded in East Africa were newcomers to the region. Most had business links with India, Burma and Australia and began to operate in East Africa after the opening of the Suez Canal and the creation of the new steamship route between India and Europe.[147] Unlike their West African counterparts, they immediately established themselves inland. Cash crops were bought from middlemen, who purchased in return various consumer goods that they then sold to the African and European farmers from whom they had bought the crops. The vast majority of middlemen were Indians from the Punjab, Gujarat, Kathiawar and Critch, who possessed the necessary commercial skills and were willing to live more simply than Europeans.[148] Most established themselves in Zanzibar or other towns and later moved up country when they had acquired sufficient funds.[149] They were joined in the trade by Greek, Lebanese, Portuguese and South African merchants.[150]

As in West Africa, the external trade of the region was dominated by a few British trading companies. Before 1914, there were only two large firms operating in the area – Smith MacKenzie and the British East Africa Corporation, which was largely involved in the cotton trade. After the First World War, more international firms entered the sector, including Dalgety, Mitchell Cotts, the Uganda Company, A. Baumann, Twentsche Overseas and Leslie and Anderson. Such companies, however, were smaller and less vertically and horizontally integrated than their West African counterparts, tending to specialize along product lines and having little involvement in the retail trade. Returns were relatively small, as the companies had to deal with more sophisticated European farmers, some of whom formed marketing co-operatives, such as the Kenya Farmers Association, or, in the case of plantation owners, sold directly onto the world market through London brokers. In addition, the overall market was smaller, the retail sector dominated by low-cost Asian businesses and the growth of such firms was restricted by the economic nationalism and protectionist policies of settler communities and local governments.[151]

Chartered Companies

Three of the trading companies operating in Africa – the Royal Niger Company, the British East Africa Company and the British South Africa Company – obtained from the imperial government charters, which entitled them to act as the British government's agent in a particular region and gave them the right to acquire and administer territory and to levy taxes. For the imperial government, such charters ensured that vast swathes of the continent would be opened up to trade and commerce at very little expense to the British taxpayer; while the chartered companies hoped to use their new-found powers to maximize profits.[152]

The Royal Niger Company operated in West Africa and was founded by George Goldie. Faced with falling palm oil prices, Goldie in 1879 merged four of the trading companies operating in the sector into the United Africa Company. Wishing in 1881 to increase profits by moving inland and cutting out the African middleman, he then raised £1m and reorganized the company, renaming it the National Africa Company. He obtained his charter in 1886 largely because the imperial government feared that the French and later the Germans would dominate the trade of the region if there was no British presence. The charter gave his company, now retitled the Royal Niger Company, the right to make treaties along the Niger and Benue rivers and to levy taxes to cover its administrative expenses, but insisted that the region's trade remain free. In practice, the company negotiated treaties with the Sokoto, Gwandu and Nupe that essentially gave it a trading monopoly.[153]

The firm's downfall occurred in 1900. The British government, stung by criticism of the company's informal monopoly from other Liverpool traders and wishing to appease the French, removed its charter, paying it compensation of £865,000, three times its value.[154] Retaining its assets and renamed the Niger Company, the firm continued to operate successfully, expanding both its trading area and commercial activities; moving into tin mining in the Bauchi Plateau and Northern Nigerian peanut cultivation. These expansions, however, placed severe strains on its personnel, existing organizational structure and capital base, and in 1920 it was taken over by Lever Bros. Ltd as part of that company's attempt to gain direct access to the palm oil from which it produced its soap.[155]

The British East Africa Company was the brainchild of Sir William MacKinnon, the senior partner of the British merchant house MacKinnon MacKenzie and manager of the shipping line British India, who wished to expand his two business interests into new areas and ports. After unsuccessfully attempting to lease a stretch of the East African mainland opposite Zanzibar in the 1870s, he formed the East African Association, which was chartered and renamed the British East Africa Company in 1888. Fearful that Germany would control the trade of the region after its 1885 'occupation' of East Africa, the British government believed that a chartered East African Association was well placed to halt such expansion. The company traded in the region and the previous year had been assigned by the Sultan of Zanzibar the administration of his coastal territories north of the German-controlled regions and had been allowed to extend its influence into the interior.[156]

Given the right to tax, make treaties and acquire territories, the newly chartered company should have been a great success. In fact, it lost money. Undercapitalized, having initially raised only £250,000, it found that the vast territory that came under its control was devoid of established trade and excessively costly to administer. The final blow came in 1890 when the failure of Barings Bank and the disruption of the London capital markets meant that it was unable to raise additional finance. To reduce costs, it withdrew from Uganda, which was temporarily taken over by the Foreign Office, but in 1894 it accepted the hopelessness of the situation and sold its charter back to the imperial government for a mere £0.25m, equivalent to half of its costs.[157]

The third of the chartered companies, the British South Africa Company, was equally unsuccessful. It was founded by Cecil Rhodes, who had prospered from his interests in the South African diamond industry, and brought together or acquired a number of companies, including the Central Search Association and the Exploring Company Ltd. Its twenty-five-year charter, awarded in 1889, gave the company the territories of Ibengula and the power to make agreements with African rulers, to grant or distribute land, to establish banks and to form a police force (the British South Africa Police). In return, the company agreed to develop and allow free trade in the territory it controlled and to respect existing African laws.[158] In reality, armed with its charter the Company proceeded aggressively and bloodily to extend its sphere of influence. In 1890 a column of settlers led by 500 'policemen' marched into Mashonaland and, in 1893–4, war with the Matabele resulted in the company acquiring the sovereignty of Matebeleland, which it successfully retained in 1896–7 when the Matabele attempted to throw off British rule; the two new areas becoming Southern Rhodesia. The company then extended its authority into Bechuanaland in 1895; the British Central African Protectorate, in 1907 renamed Nyasaland; and into North East and North West Rhodesia, amalgamated in 1911 to form Northern Rhodesia.[159]

Although successful in terms of land acquired, the firm was a financial failure and in its early days was financed by Rhodes's mining company, the Goldfields of South Africa Ltd, and De Beers.[160] The mineral resources that it expected to discover in the two Rhodesias failed to materialize and administration and military costs exceeded revenue. The 8,000 original shareholders of the company thus obtained no return on their investment. In a forlorn attempt to increase revenues, the Company sought to lure more settlers into its territories, but its efforts failed to improve its financial situation, and in 1918 it cut back expenditure and public services and, as a result, faced demands for its removal. The post-war recession led to further losses, and an attempt in 1922 to transfer Southern Rhodesia to South Africa failed when the colony's settlers vetoed incorporation. The Company thus entered protracted negotiations with the British government that ended in it losing its charter, but gaining £2m in compensation and retaining its mineral rights, railways and real estate.[161]

Mining Investment

Where a mineral could only be extracted by means of deep-shaft mines, extraction in each territory tended to be dominated by just one or two firms, often holding companies that had interests in other African countries and elsewhere in the world and were able to manipulate world markets and prices, sometimes to the detriment of Africa.

In the South African gold mining sector, the rise of deep mining contributed to the development of a group system of ownership, whereby a large number of companies were owned by mining houses, effectively holding companies; in 1899, there were nine such mining houses, and in 1928, six.[162] Deep-shaft mining and the nature of the below-surface reefs required a great deal of technology and immense amounts of capital that could only be provided by such houses. Ores found below 100 feet were pyritic, i.e. contained sulphides and had to be expensively treated, and deep-shaft mining necessitated the employment of expensive skilled workers, who initially could only be found in Europe. As discussed in the Mining thematic introduction in Volume 4 of this collection, although cheaper black skilled labour then became available, white trade union power and the assertion of racial privilege prevented the mining companies employing these workers.[163] The group system also delivered administrative, technical and financial economies of scale and ensured that the companies cooperated with each other in the recruitment of labour. As demand for gold remained constant, there was additionally much cooperation between the mining houses themselves, which exchanged technological information and, through the Chamber of Mines, lobbied the South African government for special treatment.[164]

The first of the large mining houses was the Transvaal Gold Exploration and Land Company formed and financed by the merchant company Matheson and Company, which controlled the Pilgrim's Rest mines.[165] This firm was then eclipsed by Consolidated Goldfields and the Corner House Group. Consolidated Goldfields was established in 1892 and comprised Goldfields of South Africa Ltd, which had been established by Cecil Rhodes and Charles Rudd in 1887, and several other Rand companies. The new corporation was largely financed by the City of London and controlled by Rhodes, though his personal power gradually diminished as other mining properties were acquired and in 1895 its management structure was reorganized.[166] The company generally lagged behind Corner House. Its only successful operations were the Transvaal Robinson Deep and Simmer and Jack mines and the East Rand Sub Nigel mine, and it only attained real success in the 1930s when it took the lead in opening up the West Rand gold reefs in conjunction with the Anglo-American Corporation.[167] By this time it had become an international conglomerate dominating the Gold Coast gold mining sector and owning shares in gold mines in Australia, the United States, and Papua New Guinea, American power companies, Mexican and Trinidad oil and the American Telephone and Telegraph Company.[168]

Corner House was an amalgamation of twenty-six companies, including Wernher Beit and Company, H. Eckstein and Company, and the Central Mining and Investment Corporation, and was financed by the French, who owned 30 per cent of its shareholding in 1906, the British (16 per cent) and Germany (9 per cent).[169] The group expanded from outcrop to deep-shaft mining and, by 1902–13, produced more than 37 per cent of the Rand's gold. Its influence then declined, largely because the directors who succeeded the group's founders on their deaths lacked entrepreneurial flair.[170] Its place as South Africa's foremost gold mining house was taken by the Anglo-American Corporation, formed in 1917 by Ernest Oppenheimer with American finance from the Newmont Mining Corporation, J. P. Morgan and Company, and Guaranty Trust. The group in the 1930s cemented its position by expanding its operations into the goldfields of the Orange Free State and the East Rand.[171]

Unlike the gold industry, the South African diamond sector was controlled by just one company, De Beers Consolidated Mines Ltd. Formed in 1888 by Cecil Rhodes and financed by the Rothschild family and funds from France and Germany, the company sold its entire output to the London-based Diamond Syndicate and together the two groups took control of the world price of diamonds. Cracks in the monopoly began to appear in 1902 when the Cullinan mine was discovered and the owner sold its output to the independent diamond dealer Ernest Oppenheimer. Oppenheimer and his Anglo-American Corporation then acquired German mines in south-west Africa, negotiated purchasing agreements with non-South African producers, and established their own sales outlet, leading to the collapse of the Diamond Syndicate in 1925. Unable to compete with Oppenheimer, De Beers allowed him to take control of the company in 1929 and, in 1930, Oppenheimer formed the Diamond Corporation, which controlled both production and distribution and forced up the price of diamonds by restricting output.[172]

Mining outside South Africa was equally dominated by oligopolies and monopolies. From the early 1930s, the Northern Rhodesian copper sector was controlled by just two companies. The Rhodesian Selection Trust, part of the American finance house Selection Trust Ltd (1913), in which Ernest Oppenheimer was a major investor, operated the Mufulira and Roan Antelope mines. The Nkana-Kitwe and Nchanga mines, meanwhile, were owned by Rhodesian Anglo-American Ltd, a subsidiary of Oppenheimer's Anglo-American Corporation.[173] A further British company, Tanganyika Concessions, held a substantial stakeholding in the Union Miniere de Haut Katanga, the Belgium concessionaire that monopolized the Congo industry.[174] Selection Trust Ltd was also involved in the Sierra Leone diamond sector. In 1934, the Consolidated African Selection Trust (1924), another subsidiary, was given exclusive rights for a period of 99 years to prospect for, mine and dispose of the colony's diamonds on the pretext that a local diamond sector comprising a number of companies would be difficult to control. In return, the company was to pay income tax at the rate of 27 per cent on its profits, in addition to a small development fund, mainly for the Kono region. Creative accounting ensured that in the four years after mining intensified (1948–1952), the firm paid just £3 million to the government.[175] Five years earlier similar rights for the exploitation of iron ore had been given to the African and Eastern Trading Company, later part of the United Africa Company. To finance its operations, the company joined forces with the Northern Mercantile and Investment Corporation to obtain funds from the Colonial Development Fund. The two firms formed a third company, the Sierra Leone

Development Corporation, to which the African and Eastern Trading Company transferred its 99 years of rights at a significant profit.[176]

In Nigeria, from 1928 Associated Tin Mines Ltd, an offspring of Anglo-Oriental Trust of Malaya, had a virtual monopoly of tin mining, and, in Southern Rhodesia, the coal and chrome mining sectors were controlled by Sir Edmund Davis, an associate of Cecil Rhodes. Coal was mined by the Wankie Colliery Company, of which Davis was chairman and managing director. The colliery was almost wholly owned by the British South Africa Company, which in 1923 granted it exclusive prospecting rights to over 880 square miles of the country, effectively giving it a monopoly of the sector.[177] Chrome at first was mined by a number of individuals and companies, the largest of which was Davis's Bechuanaland Exploration Company. In 1908, Davis organized an amalgamation of all the participants, forming Rhodesia Chrome Mines Ltd, which in 1910 was given by the British South Africa Company, the company's second largest shareholder, prospecting rights to most of the remaining known copper belt. Davis subsequently acquired mines in India, the French chrome company, Le Chrome and its New Caledonia mines, and, in 1929, Rhodesia Chrome and Asbestos Company, which had begun to exploit new deposits in the Umvukwes region of the country, forming a new company, African Chrome Mines Ltd, better known as the Chrome Trust. Able to control the world market in the metal, Davis in the same year cut production in Southern Rhodesia by 80 per cent in an attempt to destroy a South African rival. Output only attained its previous levels in 1932 after the competitor had agreed to sell out to Davis.[178] A similar strategy was used in country's asbestos industry, which was dominated by the Rhodesian and General Asbestos Corporation, of which Davis was chairman and managing director and a major shareholder was the British South Africa Company. The company was a subsidiary of the international asbestos company Turner and Newell, which in 1929 agreed to cut Rhodesian production by two-thirds in return for an agreement from Russian miners not to dump their output onto the European market.[179]

Agriculture

European agriculture can be divided into settler and plantation farming. Settler farming comprised the small-scale growth of cereal crops and the rearing of stock by permanent settlers, generally with the help of a small number of African labourers. Plantation agriculture was undertaken by companies or individuals and involved the large-scale cultivation of high-value crops that necessitated the employment of large quantities of African labour usually managed by expatriate Europeans who eventually returned to their homes in Britain.[180] The crops cultivated are described in the thematic introductions to this and Volume 2 of this collection.

Settler Farming

At first, settler farming predominated. For the British South Africa Company, settler land grants were a cheap means of rewarding those who had helped to defeat the Ndebele and it believed that the Highlands of Central Africa would make an ideal home for British farmers and that white settlement would rapidly increase the traffic and profitability of the region's railways and have a civilizing influence on the local African population.[181] An attempt to speed agricultural development by attracting concessionaire companies into the region ended in disaster. Although by 1899 over nine million acres of prime land in Southern Rhodesia had been sold to such companies, few had begun cultivation, preferring to hold the land for speculative purposes.[182] In Kenya, meanwhile, the successful development of the Canadian prairies and the Australian outback appeared to indicate that the growth of grains and rearing of sheep would lead to greater prosperity than plantations, particularly as world prices for plantation produce were relatively low and the colony had a meagre labour supply. Moreover, settlers preferred to cultivate crops with which they were familiar; for the capitalist speculators who had purchased large amounts of land at low prices in the hope of selling it off later at a profit, settlers were essential to the success of their schemes; and concessionaire companies displayed little interest in investing in the region. The area was untried, poorly administered and possessed a less agreeable climate and soil conditions than South East Asia.[183]

To attract settlers the colonial authorities adopted a number of strategies, some of which are investigated in the European Settlement thematic introduction in Volume 3 of this collection. The most important was the alienation of land and its sale to incomers. Africans were given the alternative of moving to areas that had been reserved for their occupation (native reserves), squatting or becoming wage labourers.[184] The extent to which land was alienated was dependent on the chronology of annexation, geography and climate, and the extent of self-government; more land being siezed where annexation occurred relatively early, soils and climate were attractive to European settlement, and settlers possessed political autonomy. The process was most advanced in South Africa where it was held that Europeans could make the best use of the lands available, and, by 1931, 1.8m white settlers possessed 440,000 square miles and 6m Africans just 34,000 square miles.[185] Much territory was also alienated in the Rhodesias and Nyasaland. In Southern Rhodesia, there were successive divisions of land into European and African areas, culminating in the 1930 Land Apportionment Act. By 1931, white settlers occupied 48m acres and almost all of the territory within 40 km of the railways and over 900 metres, where temperatures were mild and rainfall adequate and reliable; whilst Africans possessed the remaining 28m acres.[186] In Northern Rhodesia and Nyasaland the situation from the African point of view was slightly better. By the 1930s, Europeans in Northern Rhodesia held just 8.75m acres, though, as in its southern neighbour, this comprised the most productive soils, all the territory along the railway line and the area around the large markets of Fort Jameson and Abercorn.[187]

In Kenya, official attitudes towards alienation changed over time. The Foreign Office policy of giving colonists only territory outside the outermost settlements of each tribe was abandoned at the turn of the century by the local governor, largely to ensure the profitability of the railway. In 1903, Europeans were granted Masai land around Lake Naivasha in the Central Rift Valley and, in 1904, some Kikuyu land to the north of Nairobi.[188] Thereafter, until the First World War, over 4m acres were seized from Africans and sold to Europeans on 99-year leases and, after 1915, on 999-year leases.[189] From 1930, however, the policy again changed and the government increasingly protected African land occupation, passing in 1930 and 1938 Native Land Trust Ordinances. By the mid-1930s, therefore, Europeans held 16,700 square miles, Africans 53,000 square miles and the Crown 99,000 square miles.[190] In Uganda and Tanganyika alienation was even more restricted. As already discussed, in Uganda most of Buganda was placed in the hands of local tribes, and in 1920 the local government banned the sale of land to Europeans. As a result, by 1930 Europeans held just 300 square miles out of a total area of 94,131 square miles. In Tanganyika, British action was circumscribed by previous German policies that had involved the alienation of 1.75m acres. Nonetheless, from 1923 all unalienated territory was declared 'public', i.e. the property of African communities, and Europeans were granted acreages only on restricted leases.[191]

Not all of the land alienated was bought or farmed by settlers. In Kenya large tracts were purchased by speculators through a process known as 'dummying', whereby individuals applied for land grants in the names of their friends, relatives, employees etc.[192] The land bought was held for a few years and then sold onto genuine settlers at a considerable profit; land values in the Rift Valley rose in the six years from 1908 to 1914 from 6 pence per acre to £1 per acre.[193] In Kenya and Southern Rhodesia, land was also occasionally bought to be used as collateral in dealings with the land bank or was rented out to Africans. In Southern Rhodesia in 1900, only 150 settler farms were in existence; the rest of the land being rented to 153,000 cash tenants (1913).[194]

Unfortunately, as discussed in the European Settlement thematic introduction in Volume 3 of this collection, settler farmers often struggled to survive. Over time, local governments thus found themselves with a European farming sector that was unable to compete either in the export market or even in the domestic market against African farmers who possessed the advantage of family labour, a relatively low standard of living, and had not had to purchase their land.[195] Colonial authorities were therefore forced to introduce policies that ensured the survival of settler agriculture and minimized African competition. In Kenya in the 1920s, for example, farmers received export subsidies; those who cultivated maize paid low, and, for the railway, uneconomic rail freight rates; and, from 1923, wheat and dairy producers were protected from goods grown elsewhere by import tariffs.[196] Generally Africans were either excluded from these policies or did not participate in the areas protected. They also faced other restrictions. In Kenya from 1916, Africans wishing to grow coffee and pyrethrum, the most lucrative crops, had to obtain licences that were never issued in the case of coffee and rarely granted for pyrethrum.[197] In Southern Rhodesia from 1934 they were prevented from cultivating tobacco, and in South Africa they were not permitted to obtain credit from the land bank and received no government marketing assistance.[198]

Government support of farming and the bias against African agriculture heightened from 1930 when the collapse of world commodity prices and, in South Africa, the adverse exchange rate, the country's adherence to the gold standard and a series of natural disasters threatened the very survival of white agriculture.[199] The help provided comprised, among other things, export subsidies, access to credit and the establishment of state marketing boards. Export subsidies were introduced in Kenya and Southern Rhodesia on cattle and beef, and, in South Africa, on maize and dairy produce – financed in Southern Rhodesia by the dipping fees paid exclusively by African ranchers and a slaughter levy. To ensure European farmers had access to credit and to prevent bankruptcy, in Kenya foreclosure on settler farms was prohibited, and, in 1931, a land and agricultural bank was established with a capital of £500,000 obtained via a government loan. The bank made mortgage loans of up to thirty years and at interest of 6.5 per cent for farm improvements, though until 1937 almost 40 per cent of the money advanced was used to pay off existing debt. In Southern Rhodesia, the government made cash payments into the existing land bank and placed a moratorium on debt repayments.[200]

Kenya, Southern Rhodesia, Northern Rhodesia and South Africa also all set up monopolistic state marketing boards. In Kenya, the boards covered wheat, maize, dairy products and various other crops; in Southern Rhodesia, tobacco, dairy products, pigs, maize and cotton; and, in Northern Rhodesia, maize and beef. In South Africa, the boards were regulated by the 1937 Marketing Act, which made the white farmer co-operatives the sole purchasers of a number of commodities.[201] Inevitably these organizations blatantly favoured white farmers. The Northern Rhodesian Maize Board paid higher prices for crops intended for export markets, and grown almost exclusively by Europeans, than for maize destined for the domestic market and greatly restricted the number of African farmers who could sell to the local market. The Cattle Board, meanwhile, made it illegal to sell livestock below prices at which African cattle were routinely sold.[202] Other help provided to settlers included in Southern Rhodesia and Kenya compulsory African livestock destocking and the sale of the cattle involved to white ranchers at arbitrary prices; the establishment in 1938 in Southern Rhodesia of the Cold Storage Commission, a public utility company that controlled the export of chilled and frozen beef; and, as described above, policies designed to reduce the number of African squatters.[203]

Move to Towns

One response to the poverty of agriculture was to move to the towns, which particularly occurred in South Africa, where urbanization was most pronounced. European migration was prompted by a combination of push and pull factors. Forces pulling people into urban areas were the growth of manufacturing and industry and a desire for a more interesting and exciting life. Push factors, apart from the difficulties of making a living from farming, included a decline in the size of farms caused by the Roman-Dutch inheritance law whereby each child obtained an equal portion of land and a combination of a rising population and a shortage of new land, the result of the closing of the frontier and the locking up of large tracts by mineral speculators. Farmers were also prompted to abandon their rural livelihoods by the destruction of cattle herds by Rinderpest in the 1890s, the 1897 drought, the British burning of crops during the Boer War, the spread of jackal-proof fencing, which hindered the movement of flocks owned by landless farmers, and the 1930s recession.[204] Those who left were largely poor Afrikaners. Unfortunately, migration generally failed to improve their standard of living. Most spoke only Afrikaans, possessed few saleable skills and faced competition for jobs from Africans. Confronted with both European and African suffering, the South African government largely sought to relieve the former. Laws were introduced that controlled the flow of Africans into urban areas and into particular sectors and leglislation was passed that maintained the differentials status of white and black wages.[205]

Plantation Agriculture

The great advantage of plantation production was that owners reaped economies of scale. In the cultivation of crops and the rearing of animals, these economies came from the specialization of labour, but were offset by the high costs of European management.[206] The real economies of scale derived from the processing of the harvested crops and plantation agriculture was therefore largely adopted in the cultivation of produce that was processed on or close to the farm. This was the case as regards flue-cured tobacco, sugar and sisal – sugar cane and sisal leaves being too bulky to be economically transported to distant processing factories – and also tea, which has to be treated within hours of picking.[207] Sugar had been grown on plantations in Natal and later coastal Zululand from the mid-nineteenth century.[208] Elsewhere, plantation agriculture only became popular after the First World War as a result of a rise in the price of some of the goods produced, greater British overseas investment, changing political conditions in tropical Asia that prompted a number of plantation companies to spread their risks and move into Africa, and a realization that English-style settler agriculture was unable to compete successfully in international markets.[209] Among other crops, sisal began to be grown on plantations in Kenya, Mitchell Cotts entering the sector in 1936; tea in Uganda, Nyasaland and Kenya, Brooke Bond beginning cultivation in Kenya in 1924; coffee in Kenya and Nyasaland; and sugar in Uganda, where the first plantation was established at Lugazi in 1922 by the Indian entrepreneur Nanji Kalidas Mehta.[210]

Conclusion

It is generally accepted that Britain's presence in Africa greatly benefited the British economy, though, as discussed, the returns were often not as great as tends to be assumed. The impact of British rule on Africans and African economies is more controversial. Nonetheless, it seems clear that West Africans gained more than those living in other parts of the continent.[211] The gains, however, were unequally distributed and were dependent on the crops grown; the amount of land cultivated; the social status of the farmer, chiefs benefiting more than peasants; and, within households, gender.[212] There is some evidence that a disproportionate amount of the additional work was undertaken by women. Other West Africans also benefited. There is evidence that the real wages of migrant workers in the Gold Coast and Uganda rose in the 1920s and 1930s, and the prosperity of the cash croppers no doubt trickled down via the multiplier effect to other sectors of the local economy.[213]

Africans living in East, Central and Southern Africa profited less from colonial rule, though it appears that greater gains were made in Kenya than in Southern and Northern Rhodesia or South Africa and there were great differences within and between regions.[214] Fewer farmers participated in cash cropping and those that were involved were less successful. The crops grown, particularly cotton, commanded lower prices and required greater labour inputs, which fell unequally on women, and the farmers were subject to discriminatory government policies.[215] Those Africans who lived on the reserves generally eked out a living and the large numbers driven into wage employment on settler farms and in European-owned mines had to tolerate poor and often physically harmful working conditions and earned low, and in some cases falling, incomes – the real wages of black gold miners in South Africa only began a sustained rise above their early twentieth-century levels in the 1970s.[216]

The impact of colonialism on development is equally contentious. The African economy was made dependent on the production and export of a relatively small range of primary products, the profitability of which was determined by world prices over which the continent had no control. The European companies that extracted and traded in these products made vast profits, the majority of which were repatriated to Britain; only a small amount of produce was processed locally; and there was little development of industry. Most goods, capital and skills were imported and Africans were prevented from becoming involved in manufacturing.[217] The export base of African colonies, however, was wider than in the rest of the empire and there were great variations in the width of that base. In the late 1930s, it was greatest in Nigeria followed by Kenya, South Africa and Southern Rhodesia, Nyasaland, the Gold Cost and Somaliland. Only Northern Rhodesia and the Gambia were largely dependent on a single commodity.[218] Likewise, the profits of expatriate firms involved in Africa were no higher than those operating in other high-risk environments. The cost of extracting minerals was relatively high and traders faced fairly steep inland transport and handling charges, middlemen profits and import tariffs.[219] British colonialism also bequeathed to the continent relatively efficient transport, financial and legal infrastructures, stable and freely convertible currencies and, as compared to French territories, a tradition of low taxation, openness of trade and exposure to world competition.[220] There was some growth of the African handicraft sector and the entrepreneurial skills learnt by cash croppers and others who became involved in the market economy as well as the education provided by missionaries and bought with the incomes and wages earned by Africans no doubt increased the human capital of the continent. On balance, therefore, Africa may have economically gained from British rule, though to a far lesser extent than Britain herself.

Editorial Note

To reduce source length, tables of contents, indices, sections not relevant to a topic, repetitions and illustrations have all been deleted. Omissions are marked by an ellipsis in square brackets ([...]). Original page breaks are marked by a forward slash (/).

Notes:

1.   P. Wickins, *An Economic History of Africa from the Earliest Time to Partition* (Oxford: Oxford University Press, 1981), pp. 295–8; G. Gachino, 'Industrial Policy, Institutions and Foreign Direct Investment: The Kenyan Context', *African Journal of Marketing Management*, 1:6 (2009), pp. 140–60.

2.   D. Sunderland, *Managing British Colonial and Post-Colonial Development: The Crown Agents 1920–1980* (London: Boydell & Brewer, 2007), p. 59. From 1900 to 1918, Nigeria, one of the largest recipients of these grants, received nearly £5m (E. G. Charle Jr,

'English Colonial Policy and the Economy of Nigeria', *American Journal of Economics and Sociology*, 26:1 (1967), pp. 79–82, on p. 81).

3. J. F. Munro, *Britain in Tropical Africa: Economic Relations and Impact* (London: Macmillan, 1984), pp. 23–4.

4. D. Meredith, 'The British Government and Colonial Economic Policy 1919–39', *Economic History Review*, 28 (1975), pp. 484–99, on pp. 485–6. By 1929, only £3.5m of East Africa and Palestine loans had been made (ibid., p. 486).

5. D. Meredith, 'State Controlled and Economic "Development": The Case of West African Produce during the Second World War', *Economic History Review*, 39:1, (1986), pp. 77–91; Meredith, 'The British Government', pp. 485–6; Sunderland, *Managing British Colonial and Post-Colonial Development*, pp. 59–60.

6. Sunderland, *Managing British Colonial and Post-Colonial Development*, p. 60.

7. Meredith, 'The British Government', p. 499; Meredith, 'State Controlled and Economic "Development"'.

8. Meredith, 'The British Government', p. 491. Nigeria received £325,453 in grants; Tanganyika £707,211 in grants and £95,683 in loans; Uangda £5,832 in grants; Northern Rhodesia £222,161 in grants and £262,000 in loans; and Nyasaland £756,101 in grants (ibid.).

9. The Crown Agents were a quasi-governmental organization that provided colonial administrations with external finance, managed their United Kingdom investments, purchased their supplies and, until the turn of the century, supervised the construction of their infrastructure. See D. Sunderland, 'Principals and Agents: The Activities of the Crown Agents for the Colonies 1880–1914', *Economic History Review*, 52:2 (1999), pp. 284–306.

10. In West Africa, customs duties made up roughly two-thirds of the total government revenue (A. G. Hopkins, *An Economic History of West Africa* (New York: Columbia University Press, 1973).

11. C. C. Wrigley, 'Aspects of Economic History', in A. D. Roberts (ed.), *The Cambridge History of Africa, Volume 7: 1905–1940* (Cambridge: Cambridge University Press, 1986), pp. 77–139, on p. 118; K. Deininger and H. P. Binswanger, 'Rent Seeking and the Development of Large Scale Agriculture in Kenya, South Africa and Zimbabwe', *Economic Development and Cultural Change*, 43:3 (1995), pp. 493–522.

12. M. Forstater, 'Taxation and Primitive Accumulation: The Case of Colonial Africa', *Research in Political Economy*, 22 (2005), pp. 51–64; J. McCracken, 'British Central Africa', in Roberts (ed.), *The Cambridge History of Africa, Volume 7*, pp. 602–48, on p. 605. In some regions, such as the Gold Coast, the obligation to pay taxes was not enforced until the late 1930s (J. F. A. Ajayi and M. Crowder, 'West Africa 1919–39: The Colonial Situation', in J. F. A. Ajayi and M. Crowder (eds), *History of West Africa*, 2 vols (London: Longman, 1974), vol. 2, pp. 514–41, on p. 530).

13. K. Ingram, 'Tanganyika: Slump and Short Term Governors, 1932–45' in V. Harlow, E. M. Chilver and A. Smith (eds), *History of East Africa, Volume 2* (Oxford: Clarendon Press, 1965), pp. 594–624, on pp. 614–15. Income tax was only introduced in Northern Rhodesia and Nyasaland from 1921 onwards; in Kenya briefly in 1920–2 and again in 1937; and in Nigeria from 1927, but not for companies until 1940 (Wrigley, 'Aspects of Economic History', p. 118).

14. Forstater, 'Taxation and Primitive Accumulation'; G. Kanyenze, 'African Migrant Labour Situation in Southern Africa', Paper presented at the ICFTU-Afro Conference on Migrant Labour, 15–17 March 2004.

15.   Governments also faced difficulties in selling the goods provided and payment in produce and labour was subject to moral hazard (C. Ehrlich, 'The Uganda Economy 1903–45', in Harlow et al. (eds), *History of East Africa, Volume 2*, pp. 395–475, on p. 401).

16.   Sunderland, *Managing British Colonial and Post-Colonial Development*, p. 15, 30; Charle, 'English Colonial Policy', p. 80. See also N. Ferguson and M. Schularick, 'The Empire Effect: The Determinants of Country Risk in the First Age of Globalisation, 1880–1913', *Journal of Economic History*, 66:2 (2006), pp. 283–312.

17.   Source: D. Sunderland, *Managing the British Empire: The Crown Agents for the Colonies 1833–1914* (London: Royal Historical Society and Boydell & Brewer, 2004), appendix, tables 2–3; author's database.

18.   Source: Sunderland, *Managing British Colonial and Post-Colonial Development*, pp. 42–3.

19.   Ibid., pp. 45–7, 53–4.

20.   Inability to raise finance was usually related to the colony's poor credit rating or the unremunerative nature of the project to be financed.

21.   Sunderland, *Managing British Colonial and Post-Colonial Development*, pp. 48–9. Sierra Leone obtained loans from the scheme in 1928, 1934 and 1938 and Nigeria in 1934 (ibid.).

22.   Sunderland, *Managing the British Empire*, pp. 322–3.

23.   Source: ibid., pp. 322–3.

24.   Ibid., pp. 193–4; Sunderland, *Managing British Colonial and Post-Colonial Development*, pp. 50–1. Although records for the whole period no longer survive, from October 1897 to November 1900 British East Africa borrowed £147,595 in nineteen overdrafts and advances and the Gold Coast £96,255 in thirteen overdrafts and advances (Sunderland, *Managing the British Empire*, p. 195).

25.   D. K. Fieldhouse, 'The Economic Exploitation of Africa: Some British and French Comparison', in P. Gifford and W. R Louis (eds), *France and Britain in Africa: Imperial Rivalry and Colonial Rule* (London: Yale University Press, 1971), pp. 593–662, on p. 637. It should be noted that all inward capital statistics are relatively inaccurate. The money brought by small settlers and traders was not recorded and only the South African government required larger companies to lodge accounts (ibid., p. 628).

26.   M. Havinden and D. Meredith, *Colonialism and Development: Britain and its Tropical Colonies 1850–1960* (London: Routledge, 1993), pp. 308–9; Fieldhouse, 'The Economic Exploitation of Africa', p. 637.

27.   Munro, *Britain in Tropical Africa*, p. 26. From 1870 to 1936, 42.9 per cent of the foreign investment in Africa was invested in South Africa (ibid.).

28.   Fieldhouse, 'The Economic Exploitation of Africa', p. 630. By 1936, 66.6 per cent of foreign investment in South Africa was in the gold mining industry (ibid.).

29.   Source: adapted from ibid., p. 655.

30.   Ibid., pp. 602–3.

31.   Ibid.; Wrigley, 'Aspects of Economic History', p. 114.

32.   Charle, 'English Colonial Policy', p. 83; Wrigley, 'Aspects of Economic History', p, 114. The quota reduced the living standards of Africans, who strongly opposed its introduction (Charle, 'English Colonial Policy', p. 83).

33.   A. D. Roberts, 'East Africa', in Roberts (ed.), *The Cambridge History of Africa, Volume 7*, pp. 649–701, on p. 687.

34. B. Ndoma-Egba, *Foreign Investment and Economic Transformation in West Africa, 1870–1930 with an Emphasis on Nigeria* (London; Lund, 1974), p. 100; Wrigley, 'Aspects of Economic History', p. 115. In 1938/9, the Crown Agents placed just £32,0000 of orders abroad (Sunderland, *Managing British Colonial and Post-Colonial Development*, p. 129). The goods purchased also tended to be overly expensive and their delivery was subject to long delays (D. Sunderland, '"Objectionable Parasites": The Crown Agents and the Purchase of Crown Colony Government Stores 1880–1914', *Business History*, 41:4 (1999), pp. 21–47.

35. Fieldhouse, 'The Economic Exploitation of Africa', pp. 650–1.

36. Ibid., pp. 647–9.

37. In 1914, Africa took only 6 per cent of Britain's exports (ibid., p. 626).

38. Source: Munro, *Britain in Tropical Africa*, p. 22.

39. Source: ibid., p. 20.

40. Ndoma-Egba, *Foreign Investment*, p. 30; Munro, *Britain in Tropical Africa*, pp. 19–20, 30, 249. Barter and credit also generated friction (Fieldhouse, 'The Economic Exploitation of Africa', p. 607).

41. Ingram, 'Tanganyika', p. 607.

42. Ndoma-Egba, *Foreign Investment*, pp. 31–2, 249.

43. A. E. Afigbo, 'The Establishment of Colonial Rule 1900–1918', in Ajayi and Crowder (eds), *History of West Africa*, vol. 2, pp. 424–84, on p. 470; Sunderland, *Managing British Colonial and Post-Colonial Development*, pp. 243–7; Ndoma-Egba, *Foreign Investment*, pp. 24, 30–2; J. M. Carland, 'The Colonial Office and the First West African Note Issue', *International Journal of African Historical Studies*, 23 (1990), pp. 495–502. Prior to the establishment of the BBWA, coins were imported by merchants (Sunderland, *Managing British Colonial and Post-Colonial Development*, p. 243).

44. Sunderland, *Managing British Colonial and Post-Colonial Development*, pp. 249–51; Ndoma-Egba, *Foreign Investment*, pp. 34–5; A. G. Hopkins, 'The Creation of a Colonial Monetary System: The Origins of the West African Currency Board', *International Journal of Historical Studies*, 3 (1970), pp. 101–32. See also J. B. Loynes, *A History of the West African Currency Board* (London: West African Currency Board, 1974).

45. Ingram, 'Tanganyika', p. 607; C. C. Wrigley, 'Kenya: The Patterns of Economic Life 1902–45', in Harlow et al. (eds), *History of East Africa, Volume 2*, pp. 209–64, on p. 234; Ehrlich, 'The Uganda Economy', p. 431.

46. Ehrlich, 'The Uganda Economy', p. 431. Cotton producers who could send their harvests to Bombay were unaffected by the appreciation (ibid., p. 432).

47. Wrigley, 'Kenya', p. 234; Ehrlich, 'The Uganda Economy', p. 432; W. T. Newlyn and D. C. Rowan, *Money and Banking in British Colonial Africa* (Oxford: Clarendon Press, 1954), pp. 25–71. In 1922, the florin was replaced by a shilling currency (Ehrlich, 'The Uganda Economy', p. 431).

48. Wrigley, 'Aspects of Economic History', p. 119; Fieldhouse, 'The Economic Exploitation of Africa', p. 608; Ingram, 'Tanganyika', p. 609.

49. Wrigley, 'Aspects of Economic History', pp. 119–20; Ingram, 'Tanganyika', p. 609.

50. Education was largely provided by missionary societies and was thus partly financed by UK Christian congregations (Wrigley, 'Aspects of Economic History', p. 134). However, in Nigeria in 1935 only 3.4 per cent of revenue was used to finance education, and in Kenya in 1946 just 2.26 per cent (W. Rodney, *How Europe Underdeveloped Africa* (London: Bogle l'Ouverture Publications, 1972).

51. Wrigley, 'Aspects of Economic History', p. 137; C. Ehrlich, 'Building and Caretaking: Economic Policy in British Tropical Africa, 1890–1960', *Economic History Review*, 26 (1973), pp. 649–67. Improvements in health were also associated with better diets, especially towards the end of the period, and the greater use of washable clothes. Both factors were related to higher incomes (ibid., p. 138).

52. M. Crowder, 'The 1914–18 European War and West Africa', in Ajayi and Crowder (eds), *History of West Africa*, vol. 2, pp. 484–513, on p. 503; D. C. Dorward, 'British West Africa and Liberia', in Roberts (ed.), *The Cambridge History of Africa, Volume 7*, pp. 399–459, on pp. 424–5.

53. Crowder, 'The 1914–18 European War', p. 505; Charle, 'English Colonial Policy', p. 88.

54. Dorward, 'British West Africa', p. 425.

55. Ibid., pp. 424–5. Many African merchants were forced to become agents of British firms (ibid., p. 427).

56. Crowder, 'The 1914–18 European War', p. 505; A. P. Walshe and A. D. Roberts, 'Southern Africa', in Roberts (ed.), *The Cambridge History of Africa, Volume 7*, pp. 544–601, on p. 562; A. D. Roberts, 'Introduction', in Roberts (ed.), *The Cambridge History of Africa, Volume 7*, pp. 1–23, on p. 17.

57. Dorward, 'British West Africa', p. 426; Crowder, 'The 1914–18 European War', pp. 505–6. In West Africa, the extension of the Sierra Leone railway and the construction of the Eastern Nigerian railway North of Nugu were abandoned (Dorward, 'British West Africa', p. 426).

58. Dorward, 'British West Africa', p. 427; Wrigley, 'Kenya', p. 233; Ehrlich, 'The Uganda Economy', p. 422.

59. Roberts, 'East Africa', p. 668. The situation in Uganda was exacerbated by the late 1917 drought (ibid., p. 668).

60. Africans were often not allowed to fight and were largely recruited as carriers/labourers. Over 30,000 served in south-west Africa, 17,000 in East Africa and 19,000 in France (Walshe and Roberts, 'Southern Africa', p. 561). In East Africa, 750,000 Africans were called-up, and in West Africa 25,000 served as soldiers and an unrecorded number as carriers/labourers (Roberts, 'East Africa', p. 667; Dorward, 'British West Africa', p. 424).

61. Roberts, 'Introduction', pp. 16–17; Ehrlich, 'The Uganda Economy', p. 422. In East Africa, 100,000 died (Roberts, 'East Africa', p. 667). In South Africa, influenza killed up to 200,000 Africans and the belief that it was spread by Africans contributed to demands for the racial segregation of towns (Walshe and Roberts, 'Southern Africa', p. 563; N. Worden, *The Making of Modern South Africa: Conquest, Segregation and Apartheid* (London: Blackwell Publishing, 2000), p. 48).

62. Wrigley, 'Aspects of Economic History', p. 132.

63. Wrigley, 'Kenya', p. 247.

64. Ingram, 'Tanganyika', p. 597.

65. I. R. Phimister, *An Economic and Social History of Zimbabwe, 1890–1948* (London: Longman, 1988), p. 172.

66. D. H. Houghton, 'Economic Development, 1865–1965', in M. Wilson and L. Thompson (eds), *The Oxford History of South Africa* (Oxford: Clarendon Press, 1971), pp. 1–48, on p. 25; Walshe and Roberts, 'Southern Africa', p. 583.

67. Ironically, it was generally the most progressive farmers who were worst affected (Houghton, 'Economic Development', p. 25).

68. Wrigley, 'Kenya', p. 248.

69. Ibid.; Phimister, *An Economic and Social History of Zimbabwe*, p. 173; Roberts, 'East Africa', pp. 688–9; Ingram, 'Tanganyika', p. 597; C. C. Fourshey, '"The Remedy for Hunger is Bending the Back": Maize and British Agricultural Policy in South Western Tanzania 1920–1960', *International Journal of African Historical Studies*, 41:2 (2008), pp. 223–62.

70. Wrigley, 'Kenya', pp. 248–9.

71. Dorward, 'British West Africa', p. 443.

72. Roberts, 'East Africa', p. 688; Walshe and Roberts, 'Southern Africa', p. 582; Ingram, 'Tanganyika', p. 597; Houghton, 'Economic Development', p. 25; Wrigley, 'Kenya', p. 250; Wrigley, 'Aspects of Economic History', pp. 90–1. The gold sector also benefited from technical improvements and the lower price of imported equipment (ibid.).

73. In Nigeria, the daily rates of tin miners fell from 1 shilling to 5 pence (Dorward, 'British West Africa', p. 444).

74. Walshe and Roberts, 'Southern Africa', p 582; Wrigley, 'Kenya', p. 248; Ingram, 'Tanganyika', p. 597. Government attempts to help European farmers are described below.

75. Wrigley, 'Kenya', pp. 250, 253; Ingram, 'Tanganyika', p. 597; Dorward, 'British West Africa', p. 443.

76. Wrigley, 'Kenya', p. 253; Dorward, 'British West Africa', pp. 443, 446.

77. R. Oliver and A. Atmore, *Africa since 1800* (Cambridge: Cambridge University Press, 2004), p. 149.

78. A. A. Boahen, *General History of Africa, Volume 7: Africa under Colonial Domination, 1880–1935* (London: Heinemann, 1985), p. 200.

79. G. Austin, 'Resources, Techniques, and Strategies South of the Sahara: Revising the Factor Endowments Perspective on African Economic Development, 1500–2000', *Economic History Review*, 61:3 (2008), pp. 587–624; Ndoma-Egba, *Foreign Investment*, p. 24; M. Lynn, 'British Business and the African Trade: Richard & William King Ltd of Bristol and West Africa, 1833–1918', *Business History*, 34:4 (1992), pp. 20–37.

80. Oliver and Atmore, *Africa since 1800*, p. 148.

81. Munro, *Britain in Tropical Africa*, p. 43.

82. D. Acemoglu, S. Johnson and J. A. Robinson, 'The Colonial Origins of Comparative Development: An Empirical Investigation', *American Economic Review*, 91 (2001), pp. 1369–401.

83. Wrigley, 'Aspects of Economic History', p. 127. The goods included bicycles, sewing machines and roofing materials, for example.

84. G. K. Helleiner, *Peasant Agriculture, Government and Economic Growth in Nigeria* (Homewood: Robert D. Irwin, 1966); R. Szereszewski, *Structural Changes in the Economy of Ghana, 1891–1911* (London: Weidenfeld & Nicolson, 1965).

85. Szereszewski, *Structural Changes*.

86. J. E. Inikori, 'Africa and the Globalization Process: Western Africa, 1450–1850', *Journal of Global History*, 2:1 (2007), pp. 63–86.

87. Munro, *Britain in Tropical Africa*, p. 43.

88. Ibid.

89. L. C. A. Knowles, *The Economic Development of the British Overseas Empire* (London: Routledge, 1928); A. McPhee, *The Economic Revolution in British West Africa* (London: Routledge, 1926).

90. Wickins, *An Economic History of Africa*, p. 268; S. S. Berry, 'Christianity and the Rise of Cocoa-Growing in Ibadan and Ondo', *Journal of the Historical Society of Nigeria*, 4:3 (1968), pp. 439–51; B. M. Ratcliffe, 'Cotton Imperialism: Manchester Merchants and

Cotton Cultivation in West Africa in the mid-Nineteenth Century', *African Economic History*, 11(1982), pp. 87–113.

91. G. Austin, 'African Economic Development and Colonial Legacies', *Revue International-ale de Politique de Développement*, 1 (2010), pp. 11–32.

92. Oliver and Atmore, *Africa since 1800*, p. 149.

93. Fieldhouse, 'The Economic Exploitation of Africa', p. 618.

94. Ehrlich, 'Building and Caretaking'; Munro, *Britain in Tropical Africa*, p. 45. P. O. Erim and J. O. Ajor, 'The Indigenous Factor in the Economic Development of Old Ogoja Province of Nigeria, 1930–1955', *Journal of International Social Research*, 3:12 (2010), pp. 155–63.

95. C. J. Korieh, 'The Invisible Farmer? Women, Gender, and Colonial Agricultural Policy in the Igbo Region of Nigeria, c. 1913–1954', *African Economic History*, 29 (2001), pp. 117–62; Austin, 'African Economic Development'; Ehrlich, 'Building and Caretaking'.

96. G. Carswell, 'Food Crops as Cash Crops: The Case of Colonial Kigezi, Uganda', *Journal of Agrarian Change*, 3:4 (2003), pp. 521–51. In Tanganyika from 1925 to 1945, the colonial government's demands that the Sukuma move from subsistence farming to cash cropping led to food shortages and chronic malnutrition (M. Little, 'Colonial Policy and Subsistence in Tanganyika 1925–1945', *Geographical Review*, 81:4 (1991), pp. 375–88).

97. Munro, *Britain in Tropical Africa*, p. 42.

98. J. S. Hogendorn, *Nigerian Groundnut Exports: Origins and Early Development* (Oxford: Oxford University Press, 1979).

99. P. Hill, *The Migrant Coffee Farmers of Southern Ghana* (Cambridge: Cambridge University Press, 1963).

100. Austin, 'African Economic Development'.

101. Munro, *Britain in Tropical Africa*, p. 47; R. M. A. van Zwanenberg with A. King, *An Economic History of Kenya and Uganda 1800–1970* (London: Macmillan Press, 1975), p. 64.

102. In Uganda, the development of this elite was checked by the land legislation of the 1920s, which constrained the growth of estate farming and gave tenants more security of tenure and fixity of rents (Munro, *Britain in Tropical Africa*, p. 46).

103. Wickins, *An Economic History of Africa*, p. 287.

104. Austin, 'Resources, Techniques, and Strategies'; C. U. Uche, 'Foreign Banks, Africans and Credit in Colonial Nigeria c, 1890–1912', *Economic History Review*, 52:4 (1999), pp. 669–91.

105. Uche, 'Foreign Banks'; M. P. Cowen and R. Shenton, 'Bankers, Peasants, and Land in British West Africa 1905–37', *Journal of Peasant Studies*, 19:1 (1991), pp. 26–58; A. Gächter, 'Finance Capital and Peasants in Colonial West Africa: A Comment on Cowen and Shenton', *Journal of Peasant Studies*, 20:4 (1993), pp. 669–80.

106. Uche, 'Foreign Banks'; Austin, 'African Economic Development'.

107. P. S. Nyambara, 'Colonial Policy and Peasant Cotton Agriculture in Southern Rhodesia, 1904–1953', *International Journal of African Historical Studies*, 33:1 (2000), pp. 81–111; Ndoma-Egba, *Foreign Investment*, p. 111.

108. G. Austin, 'Factor Markets in Nieboer Conditions: Early Modern West Africa c.1500–c.1900', *Continuity and Change*, 24 (Special Issue 1) (2009), pp. 23–53; T. R. Metcalf, '"Hard Hands and Sound Healthy Bodies": Recruiting "Coolies" for Natal, 1860–1911', *Journal of Imperial and Commonwealth History*, 30:3 (2002), pp. 1–26; B. Achi, 'The Gandu System in the Economy of Hausaland', *Nigeria Magazine*, 57:3–4 (1989), pp. 49–59.

109. Austin, 'Resources, Techniques, and Strategies'.
110. G. Austin, 'The Emergence of Capitalist Relations in South Asante Cocoa-Farming, c. 1916–1933', *Journal of African History*, 28:2 (1987), pp. 259–79; Wickins, *An Economic History of Africa*, p. 287.
111. Roberts, 'East Africa', p. 685; Ndoma-Egba, *Foreign Investment*, p. 123.
112. Zwanenberg with King, *An Economic History of Kenya and Uganda*, p. 60; P. F. B. Nayenga, 'Commercial Cotton Growing in Busoga District, *Uganda*, 1905–1923', *African Economic History*, 10 (1981), pp. 175–95; Wickins, *An Economic History of Africa*, p. 280; T. Taylor, 'The Establishment of a European Plantation Sector within the Emerging Colonial Economy of Uganda, 1902–1919', *International Journal of African Historical Studies*, 19:1 (1986), pp. 35–58; J. D. Fage, *A History of Africa* (London: Hutchinson, 1978), p. 397.
113. Roberts, 'East Africa', p. 683; Zwanenberg with King, *An Economic History of Kenya and Uganda*, pp. 60, 63–4.
114. Roberts, 'East Africa', p. 684.
115. Forstater, 'Taxation and Primitive Accumulation'.
116. Wickins, *An Economic History of Africa*, p. 279.
117. Munro, *Britain in Tropical Africa*, p. 58.
118. Mosley argues that in many areas government policy had little impact on agriculture and that elsewhere its main impact was to increase population pressures and that these pressures stimulated agricultural productivity (P. Mosley, 'Agricultural Development and Government Policy in Settler Economies: The Case of Kenya and Southern Rhodesia, 1900–60', *Economic History Review*, 35:3 (1982), pp. 390–408). Others disagree with this view (e.g. S. Choate, 'Agricultural Development and Government Policy in Settler Economies: A Comment', *Economic History Review*, 37:3 (1984), pp. 409–13).
119. P. Mosley, *The Settler Economies: Studies in the Economic History of Kenya and Southern Rhodesia, 1900–63* (Cambridge: Cambridge University Press, 1983); Wickins, *An Economic History of Africa*, p. 279; Zwanenberg with King, *An Economic History of Kenya and Uganda*, pp. 39, 60; E. Mandala, 'Feeding and Fleecing the Native: How the Nyasaland Transport System Distorted a New Food Market, 1890s–1920s', *Journal of Southern African Studies*, 32:3 (2006), pp. 505–24; Wrigley, 'Kenya', p. 213. In Kenya, the government additionally claimed that settler farming promoted conservation (A. F. D. Mackenzie, 'Contested Ground: Colonial Narratives and the Kenyan Environment, 1920–1945', *Journal of Southern African Studies*, 26:4 (2000), pp. 697–718).
120. C. A. Bayly, 'Indigenous and Colonial Origins of Comparative Economic Development: The Case of Colonial India and Africa', *BWPI Working Paper*, 59 (2008).
121. Much of the relatively small amount of farm work was completed by women and other family members.
122. Walshe and Roberts, 'Southern Africa', p. 548; Deininger and Binswanger, 'Rent Seeking'.
123. McCracken, 'British Central Africa', p. 605; Walshe and Roberts, 'Southern Africa', p. 551.
124. Walshe and Roberts, 'Southern Africa', p. 551; Deininger and Binswanger, 'Rent Seeking'.
125. In 1882, 55 per cent of Natal's African population lived as tenants on privately owned or Crown land. In the Transvaal in 1904, 50 per cent of Africans lived on European-owned land (Deininger and Binswanger, 'Rent Seeking').

126. Worden, *The Making of Modern South Africa*, p. 53; C. Youé, '"A Delicate Balance": Resident Labour on Settler Farms in Kenya until Mau Mau', *Canadian Journal of History*, 22:2 (1987), pp. 209–29. See also C. Youé, 'Black Squatters on White Farms: Segregation and Agrarian Change in Kenya, South Africa, and Rhodesia, 1902–1963', *International History Review*, 24:3 (2002), pp. 558–602.

127. P. S. Nyambara, '"That Place was Wonderful!" African Tenants on Rhodesdale Estate, Colonial Zimbabwe, c. 1900–1952', *International Journal of African Historical Studies*, 38:2 (2005), pp. 267–300.

128. Youé, '"A Delicate Balance"'.

129. Deininger and Binswanger, 'Rent Seeking'; J. Lambert, 'Africans on White-Owned Farms in the Mist Belt of Natal, c1850–1906', *Journal of Natal and Zulu History*, 10 (1987), pp. 32–50.

130. Worden, *The Making of Modern South Africa*, p. 53; Nyambara, '"That Place was Wonderful!"'; T. Keegan, 'The Sharecropping Economy on the South African High Veld in the Early Twentieth Century', *Journal of Peasant Studies*, 10:2–3 (1983), pp. 201–26; Youé, '"A Delicate Balance"'.

131. Nyambara, '"That Place was Wonderful!"'; Youé, '"A Delicate Balance"'.

132. Worden, *The Making of Modern South Africa*, p. 54; Roberts, 'East Africa', p. 677; Deininger and Binswanger, 'Rent Seeking'; J. Iliffe, 'The South African Economy 1652–1997', *Economic History Review*, 52:1 (1999), pp. 87–103.

133. McCracken, 'British Central Africa', p. 627; Deininger and Binswanger, 'Rent Seeking'; Youé, '"A Delicate Balance"'.

134. M. J. Murray, '"Burning the Wheat Stacks": Land Clearances and Agrarian Unrest along the Northern Middelburg Frontier, c. 1918–1926', *Journal of Southern African Studies*, 15:1 (1988), pp. 74–95.

135. Youé, '"A Delicate Balance"'. See also I. D. Ochiltree, 'A Just and Self-Respecting System? Black Independence, Sharecropping, and Paternalistic Relations in the American South and South Africa', *Agricultural History*, 72:2 (1998), pp. 352–80.

136. Houghton, 'Economic Development', p. 35; Walshe and Roberts, 'Southern Africa', p. 552.

137. Worden, *The Making of Modern South Africa*, pp. 46, 71; J. C. Martens, 'Settler Homes, Manhood and "Houseboys": An Analysis of Natal's Rape Scare of 1886', *Journal of Southern African Studies*, 28:2 (2002), pp. 379–400.

138. Worden, *The Making of Modern South Africa*, pp. 70–1. Well-known city-centre slums included District Six in Cape Town and Doornfontein in Johannesberg. Large shanty towns appeared on the Cape flats and at Hout Bay near Cape Town and at Cato Manor in Durban (ibid.).

139. Roberts, 'East Africa', p. 701; Roberts, 'Introduction', p. 17; E. Isichei, *A History of Nigeria* (London: Longman, 1983), p. 436.

140. Phimister, *An Economic and Social History of Zimbabwe*, pp. 152–3; Wrigley, 'Kenya', pp. 261–2; Roberts, 'Introduction', pp. 18–19.

141. Lynn, 'British Business'.

142. Wrigley, 'Aspects of Economic History', p. 115.

143. The African and Eastern Trading Company was formed in 1919 and comprised the African Association and a number of other firms trading in the region. The African Association was also an amalgamated company. Established in 1884, over the following five years it took over the majority of the British firms trading around the Niger. In 1889, one of these businesses, Miller Bros., left the Association and the resultant trade war between

this company and the Association continued until 1900 when they, along with the Company of African Merchants and the Niger Company, came to a pooling arrangement that stood well into the 1930s (J. Iliffe, *A Modern History of Tanganyika* (Cambridge, Cambridge University Press, 1979), pp. 429–30).

144. C. Wilson, *The History of Unilever*, 3 vols (London: Cassell, 1954–68), vol. 2, pp. 318–23; Wrigley, 'Aspects of Economic History', p. 116. Although Unilever theoretically could have set excessively low prices for the produce that it bought from African cash croppers, it failed to use this power, realizing that such actions would merely reduce demand for the products it imported into West Africa (Wilson, *The History of Unilever*, vol. 2, p. 319).

145. Wrigley, 'Aspects of Economic History', p. 117.

146. Ajayi and Crowder, 'West Africa', p. 529; R. Alence, 'Colonial Government, Social Conflict and State Involvement in Africa's Open Economies: The Origins of the Ghana Cocoa Marketing Board, 1939–46', *Journal of African History*, 42:3 (2001), pp. 397–416.

147. J. Darwin, *The Empire Project: The Rise and Fall of the British World System 1830–1970* (Cambridge: Cambridge University Press, 2009), p. 125.

148. Roberts, 'East Africa', p. 657. By 1911, there were almost 11,000 Indians in the East African Protectorate, 2,200 in Uganda and 9,000 in Zanzibar (Roberts, 'East Africa', p. 657).

149. Ehrlich, 'The Uganda Economy', p. 409; Roberts, 'East Africa', p. 657.

150. Munro, *Britain in Tropical Africa*, p. 28.

151. J. J. Jorgensen, *Uganda: A Modern History* (London: Croom Helm, cop. 1981), p. 139; Wrigley, 'Kenya', p. 240; I. R. Phimister, *Wangi Kolia: Coal, Capital and Labour in Colonial Zimbabwe 1894–1954* (Harare: Witwatersrand University Press, 1994); Wrigley, 'Aspects of Economic History', p. 117.

152. Darwin, *The Empire Project*, p. 126; Wickins, *An Economic History of Africa*, p. 301.

153. Darwin, *The Empire Project*, p. 127; Wickins, *An Economic History of Africa*, p. 301.

154. Darwin, *The Empire Project*, p. 127.

155. C. Newbury, 'Trade and Technology in West Africa: The Case of the Niger Company, 1900–1920', *Journal of African History*, 19:4 (1978), pp. 551–75; Wrigley, 'Aspects of Economic History', p. 116. Made at the top of the market, the purchase of the Niger Company almost led to the bankruptcy of Lever Bros. (Wrigley, 'Aspects of Economic History', p. 116).

156. Darwin, *The Empire Project*, p. 128; Wickins, *An Economic History of Africa*, p. 302.

157. Darwin, *The Empire Project*, p. 129; Wickins, *An Economic History of Africa*, p. 302.

158. Wickins, *An Economic History of Africa*, p. 302.

159. McCracken, 'British Central Africa', p. 602; Wickins, *An Economic History of Africa*, p. 302.

160. Phimister, *An Economic and Social History of Zimbabwe*, p. 8. The activities of Goldfields of South Africa Ltd and De Beers are discussed below.

161. McCracken, 'British Central Africa', p. 602; Wickins, *An Economic History of Africa*, p. 303.

162. R. V. Kubicek, 'Mining: Patterns of Dependence and Development 1870–1930', in Z. A. Konczacki, J. L. Parpart and T. M. Shaw (eds), *Studies in the Economic History of Southern Africa, Volume 2* (London: Frank Cass, 1991), pp. 64–78, on pp. 68, 73.

163. Wrigley, 'Aspects of Economic History', p. 90.

164. J. Teisch, '"Home is Not so Very Far Away": Californian Engineers in South Africa, 1868–1915', *Australian Economic History Review*, 45:2 (2005), pp. 139–60; P. Richard-

son and J. J. Van Helten, 'The Development of the South African Gold Mining Industry, 1895–1918', *Economic History Review*, 37:3 (1984), pp. 319–42.

165. S. D. Chapman, 'British-Based Investment Groups Before 1914', *Economic History Review*, 38:2 (2008), pp. 230–47.

166. Kubicek, 'Mining', p. 68; Teisch, '"Home is Not so Very Far Away"'.

167. In 1902–13 the company extracted only 11 per cent of Rand gold (Kubicek, 'Mining', p. 71).

168. A. P. Cartwright, *Gold Paved the Way: The Story of the Gold Fields Group of Companies* (London: Macmillan, 1967).

169. R. Hyam and P. Henshaw, *The Lion and the Springbok: Britain and South Africa since the Boer War* (Cambridge: Cambridge University Press, 2003).

170. A. P. Cartwright, *Golden Age: The Story of the Industrialization of South Africa and the Part Played in it by the Corner House Group of Companies, 1910–1967* (Cape Town: Purnell & Sons, 1968).

171. T. E. Gregory, *Ernest Oppenheimer and the Economic Development of Southern Africa* (New York: Arno Press, 1977); Chapman, 'British-Based Investment Groups'.

172. Wrigley, 'Aspects of Economic History', p. 89; S. Kanfer, *The Last Empire: De Beers, Diamonds, and the World* (London: Hodder & Stoughton, 1993).

173. L. J. Butler, *Copper Empire: Mining and the Colonial State in Northern Rhodesia, c.1930–64* (Basingstoke: Palgrave, 2007).

174. Wrigley, 'Aspects of Economic History', p. 93.

175. Dorward, 'British West Africa', p. 445; P. Greenhlagh, *West African Diamonds: An Economic History, 1919–83* (Manchester: Manchester University Press, 1985), p. 249; I. Smillie, L. Gberie and R. Hazleton, *The Heart of the Matter* (Ontario: Partnership Africa Canada, 2000), p. 40.

176. Dorward, 'British West Africa', p. 445.

177. Iliffe, *A Modern History of Tanganyika*, p. 430; Phimister, *An Economic and Social History of Zimbabwe*, p. 122. In 1925, the British South Africa Company held 70 per cent of the shares of the company (ibid.).

178. I. R., Phimister, 'The Chrome Trust: The Creation of an International Cartel, 1908–38', *Business History*, 38:1 (1996), pp. 77–89. The output reduction was also related to the worldwide fall in demand.

179. Phimister, *An Economic and Social History of Zimbabwe*, pp. 118, 119, 123.

180. Wrigley, 'Kenya', p. 216; Wrigley, 'Aspects of Economic History', p. 108.

181. McCracken, 'British Central Africa', p. 605; Oliver and Atmore, *Africa since 1800*, p. 157; A. Lester, 'Colonial Settlers and the Metropole: Racial Discourse in the Early 19th–Century Cape Colony, Australia and New Zealand', *Landscape Research*, 27:1 (2002), pp. 39–49.

182. Phimister, *An Economic and Social History of Zimbabwe*, p. 58.

183. Wrigley, 'Kenya', pp. 216–17; Fieldhouse, 'The Economic Exploitation of Africa', p. 637.

184. Austin, 'Resources, Techniques, and Strategies'.

185. Fieldhouse, 'The Economic Exploitation of Africa', p. 617.

186. Ibid.; Boahen, *General History of Africa*. See also M. Lundahl and D. Ndlela, 'Land Alienation, Dualism, and Economic Discrimination: South Africa and Rhodesia', *Economy and History*, 23:2 (1980), pp. 106–32.

187. Fieldhouse, 'The Economic Exploitation of Africa', p. 617; McCracken, 'British Central Africa', p. 625.

188. Wrigley, 'Kenya', pp. 227–8.

189. Boahen, *General History of Africa*, p. 500.
190. Fieldhouse, 'The Economic Exploitation of Africa', p. 617.
191. Ibid.
192. By 1915, 20 per cent of the alienated land was held by just five individuals or groups: the third Lord Delamere, who lived permanently in the region from January 1903; the Hon. Berkeley Cole and the Hon. Galbraith Cole, Delamere's brothers-in-law and the sons of the Earl of Enniskillen; Ewart Grogan, the first man to journey from the Cape to Cairo (1898–9), who arrived in May 1904 as a partner in a timber business; and the East African Syndicate (Zwanenberg with King, *An Economic History of Kenya and Uganda*, p. 37; G. Bennett, 'Settlers and Politics in Kenya up to 1945', in Harlow et al. (eds), *History of East Africa, Volume 2*, pp. 265–332, on p. 268). The remarkable career of Ewart Grogan is related in E. Paice, *Lost Lion of Empire* (London: Harper Collins, 2001).
193. Zwanenberg with King, *An Economic History of Kenya and Uganda*, p. 38.
194. Deininger and Binswanger, 'Rent Seeking'; Youé, '"A Delicate Balance"'.
195. This view is questioned by Mosley in *The Settler Economies*.
196. Nyambara, '"That Place was Wonderful!"'; Roberts, 'East Africa', p. 679; Munro, *Britain in Tropical Africa*, p. 28.
197. Zwanenberg with King, *An Economic History of Kenya and Uganda*, p. 40; A. F. D. Mackenzie, 'Betterment and the Gendered Politics of Maize Production, Murang'a District, Central Province, Kenya, 1880–1952', *Canadian Journal of African Studies*, 33:1 (1999), pp. 64–97.
198. Deininger and Binswanger, 'Rent Seeking'; Walshe and Roberts, 'Southern Africa', p. 551.
199. A. Minnaar, 'The South African Wool Industry and the Great Depression (1929–1934)', *Kleio*, 22 (1990), pp. 56–76; A. Minnaar, 'The Effects of the Great Depression (1929–1934) on South African White Agriculture', *South African Journal of Economic History*, 5:2 (1990), pp. 83–108.
200. R. M. Maxon, 'The Colonial Financial System', in W. R. Ochieng and R. M. Maxon (eds), *An Economic History of Kenya* (Nairobi: East African Educational Publishers, 1992), pp. 249–58, on p. 256; Wrigley, 'Kenya', p. 249; Nyambara, 'Colonial Policy'; Deininger and Binswanger, 'Rent Seeking'. South Africa also doubled its sugar tariff (Walshe and Roberts, 'Southern Africa', p. 582).
201. W. Beinart, *Twentieth-Century South Africa* (Oxford: Oxford University Press, 2001), p. 118; F. Wilson, 'Farming, 1866–1966', in Wilson and Thompson (eds), *The Oxford History of South Africa*, pp. 104–71, on p. 140.
202. Deininger and Binswanger, 'Rent Seeking'; McCracken, 'British Central Africa', p. 627. There were also meat marketing controls in South Africa (Walshe and Roberts, 'Southern Africa', p. 582).
203. Deininger and Binswanger, 'Rent Seeking'; I. R. Phimister, 'Meat and Monopolies: Beef Cattle in Southern Rhodesia, 1890–1938', *Journal of African History*, 19:3 (1978), pp. 391–414; A. S. Mlambo, 'The Cold Storage Commission: A Colonial Parastatal 1938–1963', *Zambezia*, 23:1 (1996), pp. 53–72.
204. Wilson, 'Farming', pp. 126–32; Houghton, 'Economic Development', pp. 25–6.
205. Houghton, 'Economic Development', pp. 25–6, 30–1; Deininger and Binswanger, 'Rent Seeking', p. 73; D. Duncan, 'Wage Regulation for African Workers 1918–1948', *South African Journal of Economic History*, 8:2 (1993), pp. 24–45.
206. On Tanganyika sisal plantations, for example, the labour force comprised field workers who were divided into clearers, who cleared new land of vegetation; planters, who

planted and replanted fields; cutters, who harvested the crop etc; and factory workers, variously involved in decorticating, drying, pressing and baling the fibre. The type of work performed was dependent on skill, age, gender and ethnicity. As regards field work, planting was undertaken by children, migrant Nyamwezi males harvested the crop, local males cleared mature fields and local women cleared immature fields. All worked in gangs of between ten and fifteen workers and were closely managed and monitored by several layers of supervisors and reporters, who constantly toured the fields and factories (H. Sabea, 'Mastering the Landscape? Sisal Plantations, Land, and Labor in Tanga Region, 1893–1980s', *International Journal of African Historical Studies*, 41:3 (2008), pp. 25–35).

207. Wrigley, 'Aspects of Economic History', p. 104.
208. See D. Lincoln, 'An Ascendant Sugarocracy: Natal's Millers-cum-Planters, 1905–1939', *Journal of Natal and Zulu History*, 11 (1988), pp. 1–39; C. A. Lewis, 'The South African Sugar Industry', *Geographical Journal*, 156:1 (1990), pp. 70–8; A. Graves and P. Richardson, 'Plantations in the Political Economy of Colonial Sugar Production: Natal and Queensland, 1860–1914', *Journal of Southern African Studies*, 6:2 (1980), pp. 214–29.
209. Wrigley, 'Kenya', pp. 220, 222, 223; Munro, *Britain in Tropical Africa*, p. 28.
210. Munro, *Britain in Tropical Africa*, p. 28; R. Kaplinsky, *Readings on the Multinational Corporation in Kenya* (Oxford: Oxford University Press, 1978); Fieldhouse, 'The Economic Exploitation of Africa', p. 636; Jorgensen, *Uganda*, p. 141.
211. Austin, 'African Economic Development'; S. Bowden, B. Chiripanhura and P. Mosley, 'Measuring and Explaining Poverty in Six African Countries: A Long-Period Approach', *Journal of International Development*, 2:8 (2008), pp. 1049–79.
212. Munro, *Britain in Tropical Africa*, p. 46; Nyambara, 'Colonial Policy'.
213. Bowden et al., 'Measuring and Explaining Poverty'.
214. Ibid.
215. Nyambara, 'Colonial Policy'.
216. Austin, 'African Economic Development'.
217. Wickins, *An Economic History of Africa*, p. 286; P. O. Ndege, 'Colonialism and its Legacies in Kenya', Lecture delivered during the Fulbright-Hays Group Project Abroad Program, 5 July–6 August 2009.
218. Wrigley, 'Aspects of Economic History', pp. 129–30.
219. Fieldhouse, 'The Economic Exploitation of Africa', pp. 637–8. For the profits of early palm oil traders, see M. Lynn, 'The Profitability of the Early Nineteenth Century Palm Oil Trade', *African Economic History*, 20 (1992), pp. 77–97.
220. J. A. Agbory, J. W. Fedderkez and N. Viegix, 'How Does Colonial Origin Matter for Economic Performance in Sub-Saharan Africa?', Working Paper 176 (University of Cape Town, Economic Research Southern Africa).

BIBLIOGRAPHY

Acemoglu D., S. Johnson and J. A. Robinson, 'The Colonial Origins of Comparative Development: An Empirical Investigation', *American Economic Review*, 91 (2001), pp. 1369–401.

Achi, B., 'The Gandu System in the Economy of Hausaland', *Nigeria Magazine*, 57:3–4 (1989), pp. 49–59.

Adebayo, A. G., 'The Production and Export of Hides and Skins in Colonial Northern Nigeria, 1900–1945', *Journal of African History*, 33:2 (1992), pp. 273–300.

Adler, G., 'From the "Liverpool of the Cape" to the "Detroit of South Africa": The Automobile Industry and Industrial Development in the Port Elizabeth-Uitenhague Region', *Kronos*, 20 (1993), pp. 17–43.

Afigbo, A. E., 'The Establishment of Colonial Rule 1900–1918', in Ajayi and Crowder (eds), *History of West Africa*, vol. 2, pp. 424–84.

Agbory, J. A., J. W. Fedderkez and N. Viegix, 'How Does Colonial Origin Matter for Economic Performance in Sub-Saharan Africa?', Working Paper 176 (University of Cape Town, Economic Research Southern Africa).

Aghalino, S. O., 'British Colonial Policies and the Oil Palm Industry in the Niger Delta Region of Nigeria, 1900–1960', *African Study Monographs*, 21:1 (2000), pp. 19–33.

Ahazuem, J. O., 'The Nigerian Coal Industry and the Dilemma of a Shrinking Market for Coal', *Transafrican Journal of History*, 17 (1988), pp. 139–51.

Ajayi, J. F. A., and M. Crowder (eds), *History of West Africa*, 2 vols (London: Longman, 1971–4).

—, 'West Africa 1919–39: The Colonial Situation', in Ajayi and Crowder (eds), *History of West Africa*, vol. 2, pp. 514–41.

Alence, R., 'The 1937–1938 Gold Coast Cocoa Crisis: The Political Economy of Commercial Stalemate', *African Economic History*, 19 (1990–1), pp. 77–104.

—, 'Colonial Government, Social Conflict and State Involvement in Africa's Open Economies: The Origins of the Ghana Cocoa Marketing Board, 1939–46', *Journal of African History*, 42:3 (2001), pp. 397–416.

Alexander, P., 'Challenging Cheap-Labour Theory: Natal and Transvaal Coal Miners, ca 1890–1950', *Labor History*, 49:1 (2008), pp. 47–70.

Alford, B. W. E., and C. E. Harvey, 'Copperbelt Merger: The Formation of the Rhokana Corporation, 1930–32', *Business History Review*, 54:3 (1980) pp. 330–45.

Anderson, D., 'Depression, Dust Bowl, Demography, and Drought: The Colonial State and Soil Conservation in East Africa during the 1930s', *African Affairs*, 83 (1984), pp. 321–43.

—, 'Stock Theft and Moral Economy in Colonial Kenya', *Africa*, 56:4 (1986), pp. 399–416.

Anjorin, A. O., 'Tin Mining in Northern Nigeria during the Nineteenth and early part of the Twentieth Centuries', *Odu*, 5 (1971), pp. 54–67.

Anon., *Social Statistics: Statistics of Wages and Industrial Matters and of Retail and Wholesale Prices, Rents and Cost of Living* (Pretoria: Bureau of Census and Statistics, 1919–22).

—, *Prices of Commodities in Kenya Colony, 1924 to 1930* (Nairobi: East African Meteorological Department, 1932).

—, *Steel in South Africa* (Cape Town: South African Iron and Steel Industrial Corporation, 1953).

—, *Bauxite* (New York: Society of Mining Engineers, 1984).

—, *Kenya's Sisal Industry* (Nairobi: Export Processing Zones Authority, 2005).

—, *BCLME Commercial Fisheries Rights Holder and Vessel Analysis*, BCLME Project LMR/SE/03/03 (2006).

Archer, S., 'Technology and Ecology in the Karoo: A Century of Windmills, Wire and Changing Farming Practice', *Journal of Southern African Studies*, 26:4 (2000), pp. 675–96.

Ash, C. B., 'Forced Labor in Colonial West Africa', *History Compass*, 4:3 (2006), pp. 402–6.

Atta-Mills, J., J. Alder and U. R. Sumaila, 'The Decline of a Regional Fishing Nation: The Case of Ghana and West Africa', *Natural Resources Forum*, 28 (2004), pp. 13–21.

Austin, G., 'The Emergence of Capitalist Relations in South Asante Cocoa-Farming, c. 1916–1933', *Journal of African History*, 28:2 (1987), pp. 259–79.

—, 'Resources, Techniques, and Strategies South of the Sahara: Revising the Factor Endowments Perspective on African Economic Development, 1500–2000', *Economic History Review*, 61:3 (2008), pp. 587–624.

—, 'Factor Markets in Nieboer Conditions: Early Modern West Africa c.1500–c.1900', *Continuity and Change*, 24 (Special Issue 1) (2009). pp. 23–53.

—, 'African Economic Development and Colonial Legacies', *Revue Internationale de Politique de Développement*, 1 (2010), pp. 11–32.

Austin, G., and C. U. Uche, 'Collusion and Competition in Colonial Economies: Banking in British West Africa, 1916–1960', *Business History Review*, 81:1 (2007), pp. 1–26.

Babatunde, A., 'The Development of Wage Labour in Agriculture in Southern Yorubaland 1900–1940', *Odu*, (37) (1990), pp. 29–48.

Baines, G., 'From Populism to Unionism: The Emergence and Nature of Port Elizabeth's Industrial and Commercial Workers' Union, 1918–20', *Journal of Southern African Studies*, 17:4 (1991), pp. 679–716.

Baker, C., *Seeds of Trouble: Government Policy and Land Rights in Nyasaland, 1946–1964* (London: British Academic, 1993).

Baldwin, R. E., 'The Northern Rhodesian Economy and the Rise of the Copper Industry', in Z. A. Konczacki and J. M. Konczacki (eds), *An Economic History of Tropical Africa, Volume 2: The Colonial Period* (London: Frank Cass, 1977), pp. 60–76.

Barnes, C., 'An Experiment with Coffee Production by Kenyans, 1933–48', *African Economic History*, 8 (1979), pp. 198–209.

Barrett-Gaines, K., 'The Katwe Salt Industry: A Niche in the Great Lakes Regional Economy', *African Economic History*, 32 (2004), pp. 15–49.

Bayly, C. A., 'Indigenous and Colonial Origins of Comparative Economic Development: The Case of Colonial India and Africa', *BWPI Working Paper*, 59 (2008).

Beachey, R. W., 'The East African Ivory Trade in the Nineteenth Century', *Journal of African History*, 8:2 (1967), pp. 269–90.

Beavon, K. S. O., and G. Elder, 'Formalizing Milk Production in Johannesburg: The Dissolution of White Petty Milk-Producers, 1908–1920', *New Contree*, 30 (1991), pp. 10–15.

Beinan, W., 'Soil Erosion, Animals and Pasture over the Longer Term: Environmental Destruction in Southern Africa', in M. Leach and R. Meams (eds.), *The Lie of the Land* (Oxford: James Currey, 1996), pp. 54–72.

Beinart, W., 'Transkeian Migrant Workers and Youth Labour on the Natal Sugar Estates, 1918–1948', *Journal of African History*, 32:1 (1991), pp. 41–63.

—, *Twentieth-Century South Africa* (Oxford: Oxford University Press, 2001).

Bennett, G., 'Settlers and Politics in Kenya up to 1945', in Harlow et al. (eds), *History of East Africa, Volume 2*, pp. 265–332.

Berman, B., *Control and Crisis in Colonial Kenya* (London: James Currey, 1990).

Berry, S. S, 'Christianity and the Rise of Cocoa-Growing in Ibadan and Ondo', *Journal of the Historical Society of Nigeria*, 4:3 (1968), pp. 439–51.

—, 'The Concept of Innovation and the History of Cocoa Farming in Western Nigeria', *Journal of African History*, 15:1 (1974), pp. 83–95.

Bienefeld, M. A., 'Trade Unions, the Labour Process, and the Tanzanian State', *Journal of Modern African Studies*, 17:4 (1979), pp. 553–93.

Bhana, S., and G. Vahed, *The Making of a Political Reformer: Gandhi in South Africa, 1893–1914* (New Delhi: Manohar, 2005).

Blench, R., *Traditional Livestock Breeds: Geographical Distribution and Dynamics in Relation to the Ecology of West Africa* (London: Overseas Development Institute, 1999).

Bloch, G., 'The Development of S. Africa's Manufacturing Industry', in Konczacki et al. (eds), *Studies in the Economic History of Southern Africa, Volume 2*, pp. 87–102.

Boahen, A. A., *General History of Africa, Volume 7: Africa under Colonial Domination, 1880–1935* (London: Heinemann, 1985).

Bond, P., 'A History of Finance and Uneven Geographical Development in South Africa', *South African Geographical Journal*, 80:1 (1998), pp. 23–32.

Bourret, F. M., *Ghana: The Road to Independence, 1919–1957* (Oxford: Oxford University Press, 1960).

Bowden, S., and P. Mosley, 'Politics, Public Expenditure and the Evolution of Poverty in Africa 1920–2009', *BWPI Working Paper*, 125 (July 1910).

Bowden, S., B. Chiripanhura and P. Mosley, 'Measuring and Explaining Poverty in Six African Countries: A Long-Period Approach', *Journal of International Development*, 20:8 (2008), pp. 1049–79.

Bozzoli, B., 'The Origins, Development, and Ideology of Local Manufacturing in South Africa', *Journal of Southern African Studies*, 1:2 (1975), pp. 194–214.

Bradford, H., 'Lynch Law and Labourers: The ICU in Umvoti, 1927–1928', *Journal of Southern African Studies*, 11:1 (1984), pp. 128–49.

Bradlow, E., 'Women at the Cape in the mid-19th Century', *South African Historical Journal*, 19 (1987), pp. 51–75.

Braithwaite, C. J. R., 'Depositional History of the late Pleistocene Limestones of the Kenya Coast', *Journal of the Geological Society*, 141:4 (1984), pp. 685–99.

Breckenridge, K., 'The Allure of Violence: Men, Race and Masculinity on the South African Goldmines, 1900–1950', *Journal of Southern African Studies*, 24:4 (1998), pp. 669–93.

Brown, K., 'The Conservation and Utilisation of the Natural World: Silviculture in the Cape Colony, c. 1902–1910', *Environment and History*, 7:4 (2001), pp. 427–48.

—, 'From Ubombo to Mkhuzi: Disease, Colonial Science, and the Control of Nagana (Livestock Trypanosomosis) in Zululand, South Africa, c. 1894–1953 ', *Journal of the History of Medical and Allied Sciences*, 63:3 (2008), pp. 285–322.

Bush, J., '"The Right Sort of Woman": Female Emigrators and Emigration to the British Empire, 1890–1910', *Women's History Review*, 3:3 (1994), pp. 385–409.

Butler, L. J., *Copper Empire: Mining and the Colonial State in Northern Rhodesia, c.1930–64* (Basingstoke: Palgrave, 2007).

Carland, J. M., 'The Colonial Office and the First West African Note Issue', *International Journal of African Historical Studies*, 23 (1990), pp. 495–502.

Carswell, G., 'Food Crops as Cash Crops: The Case of Colonial Kigezi, Uganda', *Journal of Agrarian Change*, 3:4 (2003), pp. 521–51.

—, 'Soil Conservation Policies in Colonial Kigezi, Uganda: Successful Implementation and an Absence of Resistance', in W. Beinart and J. McGregor, *Social History and African Environments* (London: Heinemann, 2010), pp. 131–54.

Cartwright, A. P., *Gold Paved the Way: The Story of the Gold Fields Group of Companies* (London: Macmillan, 1967).

—, *Golden Age: The Story of the Industrialization of South Africa and the Part Played in it by the Corner House Group of Companies, 1910–1967* (Cape Town: Purnell & Sons, 1968).

Chapman, S. D., 'British-Based Investment Groups Before 1914', *Economic History Review*, 38:2 (2008), pp. 230–47.

Charle Jr., E. G., 'English Colonial Policy and the Economy of Nigeria', *American Journal of Economics and Sociology*, 26:1 (1967), pp. 79–92.

Chauveau, J. P, 'Cocoa as Innovation: African Initiatives, Local Contexts and Agro-Ecological Conditions in the History of Cocoa Cultivation in West African Forest Lands (c. 1850–c. 1950)', *Paideuma: Mitteilungen zur Kulturkunde*, 43 (1997), pp. 121–42.

Chimwala, M., 'SA Company Ready to Launch Malawi Bauxite Project Feasibility Study', *Mining Weekly* (18 January 2009).

Chipungu, S. N., 'Locusts, Peasants, Settlers and the State in Northern Rhodesia, 1929 to 1940', *Transafrican Journal of History*, 15 (1986), pp. 54–80.

Choate, S., 'Agricultural Development and Government Policy in Settler Economies: A Comment', *Economic History Review*, 37:3 (1984), pp. 409–13.

Christopher, A. J., 'The Natal Land and Colonization Company in Colonial Times', *Natalia*, 4 (1974), pp. 49–54.

Clark, N., 'South African State Corporations: "The Death Knell of Economic Colonialism?"', *Journal of Southern African Studies*, 14:1 (1987), pp. 99–122.

Coleman, F. L., *The Northern Rhodesia Copperbelt, 1899–1962: Technological Development up to the End of the Central African Federation* (Manchester: Manchester University Press, 1971).

Cowen, M. P., and R. Shenton, 'Bankers, Peasants, and Land in British West Africa 1905–37', *Journal of Peasant Studies*, 19:1 (1991), pp. 26–58.

Critchley, M., *Sir William Gowers, 1845–1915: A Biographical Appreciation* (London: William Heinemann Medical Books, 1949).

Cross, T., 'Britain, South Africa and the entente internationale de l'acier: The Development of the South African Iron and Steel Industry, 1934–1945', *South African Journal of Economic History*, 9:1 (1994), pp. 1–12.

Crowder, M., 'The 1914–18 European War and West Africa', in Ajayi and Crowder (eds), *History of West Africa*, vol. 2, pp. 484–513.

—, 'The 1939–45 War and West Africa', in Ajayi and Crowder (eds), *History of West Africa*, vol. 2, pp. 596–621.

Darwin, J., *The Empire Project: The Rise and Fall of the British World System 1830–1970* (Cambridge: Cambridge University Press, 2009).

Davies, R., 'Mining Capital, the State, and Unskilled White Workers in South Africa, 1901–1913', *Journal of Southern African Studies*, 3:1 (1976), pp. 41–69.

Deininger, K., and H. P. Binswanger, 'Rent Seeking and the Development of Large Scale Agriculture in Kenya, South Africa and Zimbabwe', *Economic Development and Cultural Change*, 43:3 (1995), pp. 493–522.

Dickinson, P., 'M.C. G. Smith & Company Limited, 1910–1939', *Journal of Natal and Zulu History*, 12 (1989). pp. 35–52.

Dorward, D. C., 'British West Africa and Liberia', in Roberts (ed.), *The Cambridge History of Africa, Volume 7*, pp. 399–459.

Dumett, R. E., 'Obstacles to Government-Assisted Agricultural Development in West Africa: Cotton-Growing Experimentation in Ghana in the Early Twentieth Century', *Agricultural History Review*, 23:2 (1975), pp. 156–72.

—, 'Tropical Forests and West African Enterprise: The Early History of the Ghana Timber Trade', *African Economic History*, 29 (2001), pp. 79–116.

Dunbar, G. S., 'African Ranches Ltd., 1914–1931: An Ill-Fated Stockraising Enterprise in Northern Nigeria', *Annals of the Association of American Geographers*, 60:1 (1970), pp. 102–23.

Duncan, D., 'Wage Regulation for African Workers 1918–1948', *South African Journal of Economic History*, 8:2 (1993), pp. 24–45.

Dzahini-Obiatey, H., O. Domfeh, and F. M. Amoah, 'Over Seventy Years of a Viral Disease of Cocoa in Ghana: From Researchers' Perspective', *African Journal of Agricultural Research*, 5:7 (2010), pp. 476–85.

Edgecombe, R., 'Dannhauser (1926) and Wankie (1972) – Two Mining Disasters: Some Safety Implications in Historical Perspective', *Journal of Natal and Zulu History*, 13 (1990–1), pp. 71–90.

Edgecombe, R., and B. Guest, 'The Black Heart of the Beautiful Mountain: Hlobane Colliery, 1898–1953', *South African Historical Journal*, 18 (1986), pp. 191–221.

Egboh, E. O., 'British Control of the Forests of Lagos Colony and Protectorate, 1897–1902', *Journal of African Studies*, 6:2 (1979), pp. 88–97.

—, 'British Cotton Growing Association (BCGA): Enterprise in the Lagos Colony and Protectorate, 1902–1905', *Bulletin de L'institut fondamental d'Afrique noire. Serie B*, 41:1 (1979), pp. 72–99.

Ehlers, A., 'Trust Companies and Boards of Executors versus Banks: Aspects of the Battle for Corporate Trusteeship and Trust Business in South Africa up to 1940', *South African Journal of Economic History*, 22:1–2 (2007), pp. 22–50.

Ehrlich, C., 'The Uganda Economy 1903–45', in Harlow et al. (eds), *History of East Africa, Volume 2*, pp. 395–475.

—, 'Building and Caretaking: Economic Policy in British Tropical Africa, 1890–1960', *Economic History Review*, 26 (1973), pp. 649–67.

El-Darwish, M., *A New Series of Index Numbers of Wholesale Prices in Egypt, 1899–1929* (Cairo: Egypt Cotton Bureau, 1931).

Erim, P. O., and J. O. Ajor, 'The Indigenous Factor in the Economic Development of Old Ogoja Province of Nigeria, 1930–1955', *Journal of International Social Research*, 3:12 (2010), pp. 155–63.

Fage, J. D., *A History of Africa* (London: Hutchinson, 1978).

Ferguson, N., and M. Schularick, 'The Empire Effect: The Determinants of Country Risk in the First Age of Globalisation, 1880–1913', *Journal of Economic History*, 66:2 (2006), pp. 283–312.

Fieldhouse, D. K., 'The Economic Exploitation of Africa: Some British and French Comparison', in P. Gifford and W. R. Louis (eds), *France and Britain in Africa: Imperial Rivalry and Colonial Rule* (London: Yale University Press, 1971), pp. 593–662.

Flint, J. E., and E. A. McDougall, 'Economic Change in West Africa in the Nineteenth Century' in Ajayi and Crowder (eds), *History of West Africa*, vol. 2, pp. 386–93.

Forstater, M., 'Taxation and Primitive Accumulation: The Case of Colonial Africa', *Research in Political Economy*, 22 (2005), pp. 51–64.

Fourshey, C. C., '"The Remedy for Hunger is Bending the Back": Maize and British Agricultural Policy in South Western Tanzania 1920–1960', *International Journal of African Historical Studies*, 41:2 (2008), pp. 223–62.

Freud, B, *The Making of Contemporary Africa* (London: MacMillan Press, 1984).

Fry, R., *Bankers in British West Africa: The Story of the Bank of British West Africa Ltd* (London: Hutchinson, 1976).

Fyle, C. M., and A. Abraham, 'The Country Cloth Culture in Sierra Leone', *Odu*, 13 (1976), pp. 104–11.

Gachino, G., 'Industrial Policy, Institutions and Foreign Direct Investment: The Kenyan Context', *African Journal of Marketing Management*, 1:6 (2009), pp. 140–60.

Gächter, A., 'Finance Capital and Peasants in Colonial West Africa: A Comment on Cowen and Shenton', *Journal of Peasant Studies*, 20:4 (1993), pp. 669–80.

Gandhi, R., *Gandhi: The Man, his People and the Empire* (London: Haus Books, 2007).

Gilfoyle, D., 'Veterinary Research and the African Rinderpest Epizootic: The cape Colony, 1896–1898', *Journal of Southern African Studies*, 29:1 (2003), pp. 133–54.

—, 'Anthrax in South *Africa*: Economics, Experiment and the Mass Vaccination of Animals, c. 1910–1945', *Medical History*, 50:4 (2006), pp. 465–90.

Goucher, C. L., 'Iron is Iron 'til it is Rust: Trade and Ecology in the Decline of West African Iron-Smelting', *Journal of African History*, 22:2 (1981), pp. 179–89.

Graves, A., and P. Richardson, 'Plantations in the Political Economy of Colonial Sugar Production: Natal and Queensland, 1860–1914', *Journal of Southern African Studies*, 6:2 (1980), pp. 214–29.

Greenhlagh, P., *West African Diamonds: An Economic History, 1919–83* (Manchester: Manchester University Press, 1985).

Gregory, T. E., *Ernest Oppenheimer and the Economic Development of Southern Africa* (New York: Arno Press, 1977).

Guest, B., 'Financing an Infant Coal Industry: The Case of the Natal Collieries', *South African Journal of Economic History*, 3:2 (1988), pp. 40–60.

Gupta, D., 'South Asians in East Africa: Achievement and Discrimination', *South Asia*, 21 (1998), pp. 103–36.

Harlow, V., E. M. Chilver and A. Smith (eds), *History of East Africa, Volume 2* (Oxford: Clarendon Press, 1965).

Harries, P., 'Plantations, Passes and Proletarians: Labour and the Colonial State in Nineteenth-Century Natal', *Journal of Southern African Studies*, 13:3 (1987), pp. 372–99.

Harris, K., 'The 1907 Strike: A Watershed in South African White Miner Trade Unionism', *Kleio*, 23 (1991), pp. 32–51.

—, 'Rand Capitalists and Chinese Resistance', *New Contree*, 35 (1995) pp. 19–31.

Harrison, E., *History and Activities of Locusts in Kenya and Relative Costs of Destruction* (Nairobi: Department of Agriculture, 1929).

Hart, K., and V. Padayachee, 'Indian Business in South Africa after Apartheid: New and Old Trajectories', *Comparative Studies in Society and History*, 42:4 (2000), pp. 683–712.

Harvey, C., *The Rio Tinto Company: An Economic History of a Leading International Mining Concern, 1873–1954* (Penzanze: Alison Hodge, 1981).

Havinden, M., and D. Meredith, *Colonialism and Development: Britain and its Tropical Colonies 1850–1960* (London: Routledge, 1993).

Hay, A. M., 'Imports versus Local Production: A Case Study from the Nigerian Cement Industry', *Economic Geography*, 47:3 (1971), pp. 384–8.

Heap, S., '"We Think Prohibition is a Farce": Drinking in the Alcohol-Prohibited Zone of Colonial Northern Nigeria', *International Journal of African Historical Studies*, 31:1 (1980), pp. 111–34.

—, 'Before "Star": The Import Substitution of Western-Style Alcohol in Nigeria, 1870–1970', *African Economic History*, 24 (1996), pp. 69–89.

—, 'The Quality of Liquor in Nigeria during the Colonial Era', *Itinerario*, 23:2 (1999), pp. 29–47.

Helleiner, G. K, *Peasant Agriculture, Government and Economic Growth in Nigeria* (Homewood: Robert D. Irwin, 1966).

Hellermann, P. von, 'Things Fall Apart? Management, Environment and Taungya Farming in Edo State, Southern Nigeria', *Africa*, 77:3 (2007), pp. 371–92.

Heydenrych, D. H., 'Indian Railway Labour in Natal, 1876–1895: The Biggest Indian Work Force in the Colony', *Historia*, 31:3 (1986), pp. 11–20.

Higginson, J., 'Privileging the Machines: American Engineers, Indentured Chinese and White Workers in South Africa's Deep-Level Gold Mines, 1902–1907', *International Review of Social History*, 52:1 (2007), pp. 1–34.

Hill, P., *The Migrant Coffee Farmers of Southern Ghana* (Cambridge: Cambridge University Press, 1963).

Hinds, A. E., 'Colonial Policy and the Processing of Groundnuts: The Case of Georges Calil', *International Journal of African Historical Studies*, 19:2 (1986), pp. 261–73.

Hogendorn, J. S., *Nigerian Groundnut Exports: Origins and Early Development* (Oxford: Oxford University Press, 1979).

Hollett, D., *The Conquest of the Niger by Land and Sea: From the Early Explorers and Pioneer Steamships to Elder Dempster* (Abergavenny: P. M. Heaton, 1995).

Honey, M., 'Asian Industrial Activities in Tanganyika', *Tanzania Notes and Records*, 75 (1974), pp. 55–69.

Hopkins, A. G., 'The Creation of a Colonial Monetary System: The Origins of the West African Currency Board', *International Journal of Historical Studies*, 3 (1970), pp. 101–32.

—, *An Economic History of West Africa* (New York: Columbia University Press, 1973).

Houghton, D. H., 'Economic Development, 1865–1965', in Wilson and Thompson (eds), *The Oxford History of South Africa*, pp. 1–48.

Hughes, D. L., 'Kenya, India and the British Empire Exhibition of 1924', *Race and Class*, 47:4 (2006), pp. 66–85.

Hutson, J. A., 'An Outline of the Early History of the Tea Industry in Malawi', *Society of Malawi Journal*, 31:1 (1978), pp. 40–6.

Huttenback, R. A., 'Indians in South Africa, 1860–1914: The British Imperial Philosophy on Trial', *English Historical Review*, 81:319 (1966), pp. 273–91.

Hyam, R., and P. Henshaw, *The Lion and the Springbok: Britain and South Africa since the Boer War* (Cambridge: Cambridge University Press, 2003).

Iliffe, J., *A Modern History of Tanganyika* (Cambridge, Cambridge University Press, 1979).

—, 'The South African Economy 1652–1997', *Economic History Review*, 52:1 (1999), pp. 87–103.

Ingram, K., 'Tanganyika: Slump and Short Term Governors, 1932–45' in Harlow et al. (eds), *History of East Africa, Volume 2*, pp. 594–624.

Inikori, J. E. 'Africa and the Globalization Process: Western Africa, 1450–1850', *Journal of Global History*, 2:1 (2007), pp. 63–86.

Isichei, E., *A History of Nigeria* (London: Longman, 1983).

Jeeves, A. H., 'Over-Reach: The South African Gold Mines and the Struggle for the Labour of Zambesia, 1890–1920', *Canadian Journal of African Studies*, 17:3 (1983), pp. 393–412.

Johnson, D., 'Settler Farmers and Coerced African Labour in Southern Rhodesia, 1936–46', *Journal of African History*, 33:1 (1992), pp. 111–28.

Jones, G., 'Multinational Chocolate: Cadbury Overseas, 1918–39', *Business History*, 26:1 (1984), pp. 59–76.

Jones, S., 'The Apogee of the Imperial Banks in South Africa: Standard and Barclays, 1919–1939', *English Historical Review*, 103:409 (1988), pp. 892–916.

—, 'Origins, Growth and Concentration of Bank Capital in South Africa, 1860–92', *Business History*, 36:3 (1994), pp. 62–80.

—, 'Productivity and Profitability in an Imperial Bank in the Age of Imperialism: The Case of the Standard Bank of South Africa, 1902–1914', *Bankhistorisches Archiv*, 20:2 (1994), pp. 63–75.

Jorgensen, J. J., *Uganda: A Modern History* (London: Croom Helm, 1981).

Kanfer, S., *The Last Empire: De Beers, Diamonds, and the World* (London: Hodder & Stoughton, 1993).

Kanyenze, G., 'African Migrant Labour Situation in Southern Africa', Paper presented at the ICFTU-Afro Conference on Migrant Labour, 15–17 March 2004.

Kaplinsky, R., *Readings on the Multinational Corporation in Kenya* (Oxford: Oxford University Press, 1978).

Katz, E. N., 'The Underground Route to Mining: Afrikaners and the Witwatersrand Gold Mining Industry from 1902 to the 1907 Miners' Strike', *Journal of African History*, 36:3 (1995), pp. 467–89.

Keegan, T., 'The Sharecropping Economy on the South African High Veld in the Early Twentieth Century', *Journal of Peasant Studies*, 10:2–3 (1983), pp. 201–26.

Kennedy, D., *Islands of White: Settler Society and Culture in Kenya and Southern Rhodesia, 1890–1939* (Durham, NC: Duke University Press, 1987).

Kenyanchui, S. S. S., 'European Settler Agriculture', in Ochieng and Maxon (eds), *An Economic History of Kenya*, pp. 111–27.

Kieran, J. A., 'The Origins of Commercial Arabica Coffee Production in East Africa', *African Historical Studies*, 2:1 (1969), pp. 51–68.

Kitching, G., *Class and Economic Change in Kenya* (London: Yale University Press, 1980).

Knowles, L. C. A., *The Economic Development of the British Overseas Empire* (London: Routledge, 1928).

Kolia, W., *Coal, Capital and Labour in Colonial Zimbabwe 1894–1954* (Johannesburg: Witwatersrand University Press, 1994).

Korieh, C. J., 'The Invisible Farmer? Women, Gender, and Colonial Agricultural Policy in the Igbo Region of Nigeria, c. 1913–1954', *African Economic History*, 29 (2001), pp. 117–62.

Konczacki, Z. A., J. L. Parpart and T. M. Shaw (eds), *Studies in the Economic History of Southern Africa, Volume 2: South Africa, Lesotho and Swaziland* (London: Frank Cass, 1991).

Kramer, E., 'The Early Years: Extension Services in Peasant Agriculture in Colonial Zimbabwe, 1925–1929', *Zambezia*, 24:2 (1997), pp. 159–79.

Kubicek, R. V., 'Mining: Patterns of Dependence and Development 1870–1930', in Konczacki et al. (eds), *Studies in the Economic History of Southern Africa, Volume 2*, pp. 64–78.

Kuper, L., 'African Nationalism in South Africa 1910–1964', in Wilson and Thompson (eds), *The Oxford History of South Africa*, pp. 424–75.

Kynoch, G., 'Controlling the Coolies: Chinese Mineworkers and the Struggle for Labor in South Africa, 1904–1910', *International Journal of African Historical Studies*, 36:2 (2003), pp. 309–29.

—, '"Your Petitioners are in Mortal Terror": The Violent World of Chinese Mineworkers in South Africa, 1904–1910', *Journal of Southern African Studies*, 31:3 (2005), pp. 531–46.

Lambert, J., 'Africans on White-Owned Farms in the Mist Belt of Natal, c1850–1906', *Journal of Natal and Zulu History*, 10 (1987), pp. 32–50.

Lang, J., *Bullion Johannesburg: Men, Mines and the Challenge of Conflict* (Johannesburg: Jonathan Ball Publishers, 1986).

Lester, A., 'Colonial Settlers and the Metropole: Racial Discourse in the Early 19th-Century Cape Colony, Australia and New Zealand', *Landscape Research*, 27:1 (2002), pp. 39–49.

Lewis, C. A., 'The South African Sugar Industry', *Geographical Journal*, 156:1 (1990), pp. 70–8.

Lincoln, D., 'An Ascendant Sugarocracy: Natal's Millers-cum-Planters, 1905–1939', *Journal of Natal and Zulu History*, 11 (1988), pp. 1–39.

—, 'Flies in the Sugar Bowl: The Natal Sugar Industry Employees' Union in its Heyday, 1940–1954', *South African Historical Journal*, 29 (1993), pp. 177–208.

Little, M., 'Colonial Policy and Subsistence in Tanganyika 1925–1945', *Geographical Review*, 81:4 (1991), pp. 375–88.

Long, B. K., *Drummond Chaplin: His Life and Times in Africa* (Oxford: Oxford University Press, London, 1941).

Loynes, J. B., *A History of the West African Currency Board* (London: West African Currency Board, 1974).

Lumby, A., 'A Comment on the Real Forces in South Africa's Industrial Growth prior to 1939', *South African Journal of Economic History*, 5:1 (1990), pp. 1–9.

Lundahl, M., and D. Ndlela, 'Land Alienation, Dualism, and Economic Discrimination: South Africa and Rhodesia', *Economy and History*, 23:2 (1980), pp. 106–32.

Lynn, M., 'From Sail to Steam: The Impact of the Steamship Services on the British Palm Oil Trade with West Africa, 1850–1890', *Journal of African History*, 30:2 (1989), pp. 227–45.

—, 'British Business and the African Trade: Richard & William King Ltd of Bristol and West Africa, 1833–1918', *Business History*, 34:4 (1992), pp. 20–37.

—, 'The Profitability of the Early Nineteenth Century Palm Oil Trade', *African Economic History*, 20 (1992), pp. 77–97.

McClendon, T. V., '"Hiding Cattle on the White Man's Farm": Cattle Loans and Commercial Farms in Natal, 1930–50', *African Economic History*, 25 (1997), pp. 43–58.

McCracken, J., 'Planters, Peasants and the Colonial State: The Impact of the Native Tobacco Board in the Central Province of Malawi', *Journal of Southern African Studies*, 9:2 (1983), pp. 172–92.

—, 'British Central Africa', in Roberts (ed.), *The Cambridge History of Africa, Volume 7*, pp. 602–48.

McCulloch, J., 'Asbestos Mining and Occupational Disease in Southern Rhodesia/Zimbabwe, 1915–98', *History Workshop Journal*, 56:1 (2003), pp. 131–52.

—, 'Women Mining Asbestos in South Africa, 1893–1980', *Journal of Southern African Studies*, 29:2 (2003), pp. 413–32.

MacKenzie, A. F. D., 'Betterment and the Gendered Politics of Maize Production, Murang'a District, Central Province, Kenya, 1880–1952', *Canadian Journal of African Studies*, 33:1 (1999), pp. 64–97.

—, 'Contested Ground: Colonial Narratives and the Kenyan Environment, 1920–1945', *Journal of Southern African Studies*, 26:4 (2000), pp. 697–718.

MacKinnon, A. S. 'The Persistence of the Cattle Economy in Zululand, South Africa, 1900–50', *Canadian Journal of African Studies*, 33:1 (1999), pp. 98–135.

MacMillan, W. M., 'The Protectorates', in E. A. Walker (ed.), *The Cambridge History of the British Empire, Volume 7, Part 1* (Cambridge: Cambridge University Press, 1936), pp. 671–5.

McPhee, A., *The Economic Revolution in British West Africa* (London: Routledge, 1926).

Mafela, L., 'Colonial Initiatives and African Response in the Establishment of the Dairy Industry in the Bechuanaland Protectorate, 1930–1966', *Botswana Journal of African Studies*, 13:1–2 (1999), pp. 100–27.

Majuk, S. E., P. O. Erim and J. O. Ajor, 'Bakor Women in Pottery Production in Colonial South Eastern Nigeria', *Journal of International Social Research*, 3:11 (2010), pp. 416–20.

Makanda D. W., and J. F. Oehmke, 'Kenya's Wheat Agriculture: Past, Present and Future', *Staff Paper No. 95-54* (Department of Agricultural Economics, Michigan State University).

Mandala, E., 'Feeding and Fleecing the Native: How the Nyasaland Transport System Distorted a New Food Market, 1890s–1920s', *Journal of Southern African Studies*, 32:3 (2006), pp. 505–24.

Martens, J. C., 'Settler Homes, Manhood and "Houseboys": An Analysis of Natal's Rape Scare of 1886', *Journal of Southern African Studies*, 28:2 (2002), pp. 379–400.

Matthews, D., 'Serendipity or Economics? Tin and the Theory of Mineral Discovery, 1800–1920', *Business History*, 32:3 (1990), pp. 15–48.

Maxon, R. M., 'The Colonial Financial System', in Ochieng and Maxon (eds), *An Economic History of Kenya*, pp. 249–58.

—, 'Up in Smoke: Peasants, Capital and the Colonial State in the Tobacco Industry in Western Kenya, 1930–1939', *African Economic History*, 22 (1994), pp. 111–39.

—, 'Where Did the Trees Go? The Wattle Bark Industry in Western Kenya, 1932–1950', *International Journal of African Historical Studies*, 34:3 (2001), pp. 265–85.

Mazonde, I. N., 'Bordermanship – a Factor of Economic Differentiation among the Afrikaner and the English Settlers in the Tuli Block, Eastern Botswana', *Botswana Notes and Records*, 22 (1990), pp. 79–89.

Meredith, D., 'The British Government and Colonial Economic Policy 1919–39', *Economic History Review*, 28 (1975), pp. 484–99.

—, 'Government and the Decline of the Nigerian Oil-Palm Export Industry, 1919–1939', *Journal of African History*, 25:3 (1984), pp. 311–29.

—, 'State Controlled and Economic "Development": The Case of West African Produce during the Second World War', *Economic History Review*, 39:1 (1986), pp. 77–91.

—, 'The Colonial Office, British Business Interests and the Reform of Cocoa Marketing in West Africa, 1937–1945', *Journal of African History*, 29:2 (1988), pp. 285–300.

Metcalf, T. R., '"Hard Hands and Sound Healthy Bodies": Recruiting "Coolies" for Natal, 1860–1911', *Journal of Imperial and Commonwealth History*, 30:3 (2002), pp. 1–26.

Milburn, J., 'The 1938 Gold Coast Cocoa Crisis: British Business and the Colonial Office' *African Historical Studies*, 3:1 (1970), pp. 57–74.

Minnaar, A., 'Labour Supply Problems of the Zululand Sugar Planters, 1905–1939', *Journal of Natal and Zulu History*, 12 (1989), pp. 53–72.

—, 'The South African Maize Industry's Response to the Great Depression and the Beginnings of Large-Scale State Intervention, 1929–1934', *South African Journal of Economic History*, 4:1 (1989), pp. 68–78.

—, 'The Effects of the Great Depression (1929–1934) on South African White Agriculture', *South African Journal of Economic History*, 5:2 (1990), pp. 83–108.

—, 'The Great Depression 1929–1934: Adverse Exchange Rates and the South African Wool Farmer', *South African Journal of Economic History*, 5:1 (1990), pp. 31–48.

—, 'The South African Wool Industry and the Great Depression (1929–1934)', *Kleio*, 22 (1990), pp. 56–76.

Miracle, M. P., 'The Introduction and Spread of Maize in Africa', *Journal of African History*, 6:1 (1965), pp. 39–55.

Mlambo, A., 'The Cold Storage Commission: A Colonial Parastatal 1938–1963', *Zambezia*, 23:1 (1996), pp. 53–72.

—, *White Immigration into Rhodesia: From Occupation to Federation* (Harare: University of Zimbabwe Press, 2002).

Mlambo, A., and I. Phimister, 'Partly Protected: Origins and Growth of Colonial Zimbabwe's Textile Industry, 1890–1965', *Historia*, 51:2 (2006), pp. 145–75.

Moeti, M., 'The Origins of Forced Labor in the Witwatersrand', *Phylon*, 47:4 (1986), pp. 276–84.

Moodie, T. D., 'Maximum Average Violence: Underground Assaults on the South African Gold Mines, 1913–1965', *Journal of Southern African Studies*, 31:3 (2005), pp. 547–67.

Morapedi, W., 'Migrant Labour and the Peasantry in the Bechuanaland Protectorate, 1930–1965', *Journal of Southern African Studies*, 25:2 (1999), pp. 197–214.

Morgan W. B., and J. C. Pugh, *West Africa* (London: Methuen, 1969).

Morrell, R., 'Farmers, Randlords and the South African State: Confrontation in the Witwatersrand Beef Markets, c.1920–1923', *Journal of African History*, 27:3 (1986), pp. 513–32.

—, 'The Disintegration of the Gold and Maize Alliance in South Africa in the 1920s', *International Journal of African Historical Studies*, 21:4 (1988), pp. 619–35.

Mosley, P., 'Agricultural Development and Government Policy in Settler Economies: The Case of Kenya and Southern Rhodesia, 1900–60', *Economic History Review*, 35:3 (1982), pp. 390–408.

—, *The Settler Economies: Studies in the Economic History of Kenya and Southern Rhodesia, 1900–63* (Cambridge: Cambridge University Press, 1983).

Munro, J. F., 'British Rubber Companies in East Africa before the First World War', *Journal of African History*, 24:3 (1983), pp. 369–79.

—, *Britain in Tropical Africa: Economic Relations and Impact* (London: Macmillan, 1984).

Murray, M. J., '"Burning the Wheat Stacks": Land Clearances and Agrarian Unrest along the Northern Middelburg Frontier, c. 1918–1926', *Journal of Southern African Studies*, 15:1 (1988), pp. 74–95.

Mutowo, M. K. K., 'Animal Diseases and Human Populations in Colonial Zimbabwe: The Rinderpest Epidemic of 1896–1898', *Zambezia*, 28:1 (2001), pp. 1–22.

Nattrass, G., 'The Tin Mines of the Waterberg (Transvaal), 1905–1914', *New Contree*, 26 (1989), pp. 5–12.

—, 'The Tin Mining Industry in the Transvaal 1905–1914: Some Social and Economic Implications and Perspectives', *South African Journal of Economic History*, 6:1 (1991), pp. 91–120.

Nayenga, P. F. B. 'Commercial Cotton Growing in Busoga District, Uganda, 1905–1923', *African Economic History*, 10 (1981), pp. 175–95.

Ndege, P. O., 'Internal Trade in Kenya 1895–1963', in Ochieng and Maxon (eds), *An Economic History of Kenya*, pp. 201–22.

—, 'Colonialism and its Legacies in Kenya', Lecture delivered during the Fulbright-Hays Group Project Abroad Program, 5 July–6 August 2009.

Ndoma-Egba, B., *Foreign Investment and Economic Transformation in West Africa, 1870–1930 with an Emphasis on Nigeria* (London: Lund, 1974).

Nel, E., and C. M. Rogerson, 'Incipient Local Economic Development in the Eastern Cape, 1909–1947', *New Contree*, 37 (1995), pp. 1–9.

Newbury, C., 'Trade and Technology in West Africa: The Case of the Niger Company, 1900–1920', *Journal of African History*, 19:4 (1978), pp. 551–75.

Newlyn, W. T., and D. C. Rowan, *Money and Banking in British Colonial Africa* (Oxford: Clarendon Press, 1954).

Nindi, B. C., 'Labour and Capital in Settler Economy in Colonial Tanganyika', *Journal of Eastern African Research and Development*, 17 (1987), pp. 90–6.

Njoku, O. N., 'Some Thoughts on the Trust System in Eastern Nigeria', *African Development*, 5 (1980), pp. 37–49.

—, 'Colonialism and the Decline of the Traditional Metal Industry of the Igbo, *Nigeria*', *Itinerario*, 15:2 (1991), pp. 59–78.

Nwabughuogu, A. I., 'From Wealthy Entrepreneurs to Petty Traders: The Decline of African Middlemen in Eastern Nigeria, 1900–1950', *Journal of African History*, 23 (1982), pp. 365–79.

Nwaka, G. I., 'Cadburys and the Dilemma of Colonial Trade in Africa, 1901–1910', *Bulletin de l'Institut fondamental d'Afrique Noire. Serie B*, 42:4 (1980), pp. 780–93.

Nworah, K. D., 'The West African Operations of the British Cotton Growing Association, 1904–1914', *African Historical Studies*, 4:2 (1971), pp. 315–30.

—, 'The Politics of Lever's West African Concessions, 1907–1913', *International Journal of African Historical Studies*, 5:2 (1972), pp. 248–64.

Nyambara, P. S., 'Colonial Policy and Peasant Cotton Agriculture in Southern Rhodesia, 1904–1953', *International Journal of African Historical Studies*, 33:1 (2000), pp. 81–111.

—, '"That Place was Wonderful!" African Tenants on Rhodesdale Estate, Colonial Zimbabwe, c. 1900–1952', *International Journal of African Historical Studies*, 38:2 (2005), pp. 267–300.

Ochieng, W. R., and R. M. Maxon (eds), *An Economic History of Kenya* (Nairobi: East African Educational Publishers, 1992).

Ochiltree, I. D., 'A Just and Self-Respecting System? Black Independence, Sharecropping, and Paternalistic Relations in the American South and South Africa', *Agricultural History*, 72:2 (1998), pp. 352–80.

Ofcansky, T. P., 'Kenya Forestry under British Colonial Administration, 1895–1963', *Journal of Forest History*, 28:3 (1984), pp. 136–43.

Ogutu, M. A, 'The Cultivation of Coffee among the Chagga of Tanzania, 1919–1939', *Agricultural History*, 46:2 (1972), pp. 279–90.

O'Hear, A., 'Craft Industries in Ilorin: Dependency or Independence?', *African Affairs*, 86:345 (1987), pp. 505–21.

Okoye, C. U., and A. O. Okpala, 'The History of Community Banking and its Role in Nigerian Rural Economic Development', *Review of Black Political Economy*, 29:1 (2001), pp. 63–77.

Oliver, R., and A. Atmore, *Africa since 1800* (Cambridge: Cambridge University Press, 2004).

Olukoju, A., 'Slamming the "Open Door": British Protectionist Fiscal Policy in Inter-War Nigeria', *Itinerario*, 23:2 (1992), pp. 13–28.

—, 'Nigeria's Colonial Government, Commercial Banks and the Currency Crisis of 1916–1920', *International Journal of African Historical Studies*, 30:2 (1997), pp. 277–98.

Onyeiwu, S., 'Deceived by African Cotton: The British *Cotton* Growing Association and the Demise of the Lancashire Textile Industry', *African Economic History*, 28 (2000), pp. 89–121.

Paice, E., *Lost Lion of Empire* (London: Harper Collins, 2001).

Palmer, R., 'The Nyasaland Tea Industry in the Era of International Tea Restrictions, 1933–1950', *Journal of African History*, 26:2–3 (1985), pp. 215–39.

—, 'The Politics of Tea in Eastern Africa, 1933–1948', *Journal of Social Sciences*, 13 (1986), pp. 69–90.

—, 'Working Conditions and Worker Responses on Nyasaland Tea Estates, 1930–1953', *Journal of African History*, 27:1 (1986), pp. 105–26.

Phillips, S. T., 'Lessons from the Dust Bowl: Dryland Agriculture and Soil Erosion in the United States and South Africa, 1900–1950', *Environmental History*, 4:2 (1999), pp. 245–66.

Phimister, I. R., 'Meat and Monopolies: Beef Cattle in Southern Rhodesia, 1890–1938', *Journal of African History*, 19:3 (1978), pp. 391–414.

—, *An Economic and Social History of Zimbabwe, 1890–1948* (London: Longman, 1988).

—, 'The Chrome Trust: The Creation of an International Cartel, 1908–38', *Business History*, 38:1 (1996), pp. 77–89.

—, *Wangi Kolia: Coal, Capital and Labour in Colonial Zimbabwe 1894–1954* (Harare: Witwatersrand University Press, 1994).

—, 'Corners and Company-Mongering: Nigerian Tin and the City of London, 1909–12', *Journal of Imperial and Commonwealth History*, 28:2 (2000), pp. 23–41.

Phoofolo, P., 'Face to Face with Famine: The Basotho and the Rinderpest, 1897–1899', *Journal of Southern African Studies*, 29:2 (2003), pp. 503–27.

Pole, L. M., 'Decline or Survival? Iron Production in West Africa from the Seventeenth to the Twentieth Centuries', *Journal of African History*, 23:4 (1982), pp. 503–13.

Power, J., '"Individualism is the Antithesis of Indirect Rule": Cooperative Development and Indirect Rule in Colonial Malawi', *Journal of Southern African Studies*, 18:2 (1992), pp. 317–47.

Pratt, R. C., 'Administration and Politics in Uganda 1919–45', in Harlow et al. (eds), *History of East Africa, Volume 2*, pp. 476–541.

Ratcliffe, B. M., 'Cotton Imperialism: Manchester Merchants and Cotton Cultivation in West Africa in the mid-Nineteenth Century', *African Economic History*, 11 (1982), pp. 87–113.

Renne, E. P., 'The Production and Marketing of "Babban Riga" in Zaria, Nigeria', *African Economic History*, 32 (2004), pp. 103–22.

Reynolds, G., '"From Red Blanket to Civilization": Propaganda and Recruitment Films for South Africa's Gold Mines, 1920–1940', *Journal of Southern African Studies*, 33:1 (2007), pp. 133–52.

Richardson, P., 'The Natal Sugar Industry, 1849–1905: An Interpretive Essay', *Journal of African History*, 23:4 (1982), pp. 515–27.

Richardson P., and J. J. Van Helten, 'The Development of the South African Gold Mining Industry, 1895–1918', *Economic History Review*, 37:3 (1984), pp. 319–42.

Roberts, A. D. (ed.), *The Cambridge History of Africa, Volume 7: 1905–1940* (Cambridge: Cambridge University Press, 1986).

—, 'Introduction', in Roberts (ed.), *The Cambridge History of Africa, Volume 7*, pp. 1–23.

—, 'The Imperial Mind', in Roberts (ed.), *The Cambridge History of Africa, Volume 7*, pp. 24–76.

—, 'East Africa', in Roberts (ed.), *The Cambridge History of Africa, Volume 7*, pp. 649–701.

—, 'The Gold Boom of the 1930s in Eastern Africa', *African Affairs*, 85:341 (1986), pp. 545–62.

Rodney, W., *How Europe Underdeveloped Africa* (London: Bogle l'Ouverture Publications, 1972).

Rogerson, C. M., and M. da Silva, 'Urban Small-Scale Industry on the Witwatersrand: Emergence, Destruction and Revival', *African Urban Quarterly*, 4:3–4 (1989), pp. 349–60.

Ross, A. C., *David Livingstone: Mission and Empire* (London: Hambledon, 2002).

Sabea, H., 'Mastering the Landscape? Sisal Plantations, Land, and Labor in Tanga Region, 1893–1980s', *International Journal of African Historical Studies*, 41:3 (2008), pp. 25–35.

Sanderson, F. E., 'The Development of Labour Migration from Nyasaland', *Journal of African History*, 2:2 (1961), pp. 259–71.

Scott, R. 'Gowers of Uganda: The Public and Private Life of a Forgotten Colonial Governor', *Australasian Review of African Studies*, 30:2 (2009) pp. 1–22.

Sekgoma, G., 'The Introduction and Impact of Agricultural Policy in Sierra Leone, 1930–1939', *Trans-African Journal of History*, 17 (1988), pp. 172–85.

Shaw, G., *The Cape Times: An Informal History* (Cape Town: David Philip Publishers, 1999).

Sherry, S. P., 'History of the Wattle Industry in Natal', *Natalia*, 3 (1973), pp. 40–4.

Sherwood, M., 'Elder Dempster and West Africa, 1891–1940: The Genesis of Underdevelopment?', *International Journal of the African Historical Society*, 30:2 (1997), pp. 253–76.

Shokpeka, S. A., and O. A. Nwaokocha, 'British Colonial Economic Policy in Nigeria: The Example of Benin Province 1914–1954', *Journal of Human Ecology*, 28:1 (2009), pp. 57–66.

Slater, H., 'Land, Labour and Capital in Natal: The Natal Land and Colonisation Company, 1860–1948', *Journal of African History*, 16:2 (1975), pp. 257–83.

Smillie, I., L. Gberie and R. Hazleton, *The Heart of the Matter* (Ontario: Partnership Africa Canada, 2000).

Smit, J., 'Glass Bottle Manufacture in South Africa up to 1944', *Africana Notes and News*, 24:8 (1981), pp. 265–70.

Smith, F. H., '"What Happened to the Forests?" Policy towards Managing the Timber Resources in Kwazulu/Natal during the Colonial Period (1853–1910)', *New Contree*, 48 (2000), pp. 47–64.

Steele, M. C., 'The Economic Function of African-Owned Cattle in Colonial Zimbabwe', *Zambezia*, 9:1 (1981), pp. 29–48.

Steyn, P., 'Oil Exploration in Colonial Nigeria, c. 1903–58', *Journal of Imperial and Commonwealth History*, 37:2 (2009), pp. 249–75.

Stigger, P., 'The Land Commission of 1894 and Cattle', *Zimbabwean History*, 11 (1980), pp. 20–43.

Stocking, M. A., 'Relationship of Agricultural History and Settlement to Severe Soil Erosion in Rhodesia', *Zambezia*, 6:2 (1978), pp. 129–45.

Summers, C., *Colonial Lessons: Africans' Education in Southern Rhodesia, 1918–1940* (Oxford: James Curry, 2002).

Sunderland, D., '"Objectionable Parasites": The Crown Agents and the Purchase of Crown Colony Government Stores 1880–1914', *Business History*, 41:4 (1999), pp. 21–47.

—, 'Principals and Agents: The Activities of the Crown Agents for the Colonies 1880–1914', *Economic History Review*, 52:2 (1999), pp. 284–306.

—, *Managing the British Empire: The Crown Agents for the Colonies 1833–1914* (London: Royal Historical Society and Boydell & Brewer, 2004).

—, *Managing British Colonial and Post-Colonial Development: The Crown Agents 1920–1980* (London: Boydell & Brewer, 2007).

Swan, M., 'The 1913 Natal Indian Strike', *Journal of Southern African Studies*, 10:2 (1984), pp. 239–58.

Swindell K., and A. Jeng, 'Migrants, Credit and Climate: The Gambian Groundnut Trade, 1834–1934', *Journal of Agrarian Change*, 7:4 (2007), pp. 570–2.

Szereszewski, R., *Structural Changes in the Economy of Ghana, 1891–1911* (London: Weidenfeld & Nicolson, 1965).

Talbott, I. D., 'The Kenya Flax Boom', *Kenya Historical Review*, 2:1 (1974), pp. 59–66.

—, 'African Agriculture', in Ochieng and Maxon (eds), *An Economic History of Kenya*, pp. 75–91.

Taylor, T., 'The Establishment of a European Plantation Sector within the Emerging Colonial Economy of Uganda, 1902–1919', *International Journal of African Historical Studies*, 19:1 (1986), pp. 35–58.

Teisch J., '"Home is Not so Very Far Away": Californian Engineers in South Africa, 1868–1915', *Australian Economic History Review*, 45:2 (2005), pp. 139–60.

Tropp, J. A., 'Dogs, Poison and the Meaning of Colonial Intervention in the Transkei, South Africa', *Journal of African History*, 43:3 (2002), pp. 451–72.

—, 'The Contested Nature of Colonial Landscapes: Historical Perspectives on Livestock and Environments in the Transkei', *Kronos*, 30 (2004), pp. 118–37.

—, *Natures of Colonial Change: Environmental Relations in the Making of the Transkei* (Athens, OH: Ohio University Press, 2006).

Turrell, R., 'Diamonds and Migrant Labour in South Africa, 1869–1910', *History Today*, 36 (May 1986), pp. 45–9.

Uche, C. U., 'Foreign Banks, Africans and Credit in Colonial Nigeria c, 1890–1912' *Economic History Review*, 52:4 (1999), pp. 669–91.

Utzinger, J., Y. Tozan, F. Doumani and B. H. Singer, 'The Economic Payoffs of Integrated Malaria Control in the Zambian Copperbelt between 1930 and 1950', *Tropical Medicine and International Health*, 7:8 (2002), pp. 657–77.

Van der Laan, H. L., 'Marketing West Africa's Export Crops: Modern Boards and Colonial Trading Companies', *Journal of Modern African Studies*, 25:1 (1987), pp. 1–24.

Van Helten, J. J., and K. Williams, '"The Crying Need of South Africa": The Emigration of Single British Women to the Transvaal, 1901–10', *Journal of Southern African Studies*, 10:1 (1983), pp. 17–38.

Walshe, A. P., and A. D. Roberts, 'Southern Africa', in Roberts (ed.), *The Cambridge History of Africa, Volume 7*, pp. 544–601.

Waters, A. R., 'Change and Evolution in the Structure of the Kenya Coffee Industry', *History of Agriculture*, 1:4 (1974), pp. 81–105.

Webb, A., 'The Circumstances Leading to the Formation of the Natal Bank in 1854', *South African Journal of Economic History*, 4:2 (1989), pp. 78–90.

Welsh, D., 'The Growth of Towns', in Wilson and Thompson (eds), *The Oxford History of South Africa*, pp. 172–244.

Westcott, N., 'The East African Sisal Industry, 1929–1949: The Marketing of a Colonial Commodity during Depression and War', *Journal of African History*, 25:4 (1984), pp. 445–61.

Whitehead, A., 'Continuities and Discontinuities in Political Constructions of the Working Man in Rural Sub-Saharan Africa: The "Lazy Man" in African Agriculture', *European Journal of Development Research*, 12:2 (2000) pp. 23–53.

Wickins, P., *An Economic History of Africa from the Earliest Time to Partition* (Oxford: Oxford University Press, 1981).

Williams, C. B., 'Observations on the Desert Locust in East Africa from July 1928 to April 1929', *Annals of Applied Biology*, 20:3 (1933), pp. 463–97.

Willis, J., 'Demoralised Natives, Black-Coated Consumers, and Clean Spirit: European Liquor in East Africa, 1890–1955', *Journal of Imperial and Commonwealth History*, 29:3 (2001), pp. 55–74.

Wilson C., *The History of Unilever*, 3 vols (London: Cassell, 1954–68).

Wilson, F., 'Farming, 1866–1966', in Wilson and Thompson (eds), *The Oxford History of South Africa*, pp. 104–71.

Wilson, M., and L. Thompson (eds), *The Oxford History of South Africa* (Oxford: Clarendon Press, 1971).

Wiseman, C. C., 'Child and Youth Labour on the Nyasaland Plantations, 1890–1953', *Journal of Southern African Studies*, 19:4 (1993), pp. 662–80.

Witt, H., '"Clothing the Once Bare Brown Hills of Natal": The Origin and Development of *Wattle* Growing in Natal, 1860–1960', *South African Historical Journal*, 53 (2005), pp. 99–122.

Worden, N., *The Making of Modern South Africa: Conquest, Segregation and Apartheid* (London: Blackwell Publishing, 2000).

Wrigley, C. C., 'Kenya: The Patterns of Economic Life 1902–45', in Harlow et al. (eds), *History of East Africa, Volume 2*, pp. 209–64.

—, 'Aspects of Economic History', in Roberts (ed.), *The Cambridge History of Africa, Volume 7*, pp. 77–139.

Yager, T. R., *The Mineral Industry of South Africa* (Washington; US Geological Survey, 2007).

Youé, C., '"A Delicate Balance": Resident Labour on Settler Farms in Kenya until Mau Mau', *Canadian Journal of History*, 22:2 (1987), pp. 209–29.

—, 'Black Squatters on White Farms: Segregation and Agrarian Change in Kenya, South Africa, and Rhodesia, 1902–1963', *International History Review*, 24:3 (2002), pp. 558–602.

Zwanenberg, P. van, 'Kenya's Primitive Colonial Capitalism: The Economic Weakness of Kenya's Settlers up to 1940', *Canadian Journal of African Studies*, 9:2 (1975), pp. 277–92.

Zwanenberg, R. M. A. van, 'Aspects of Kenya's Industrial History', *Kenya Historical Review*, 1:1 (1973), pp. 45–61.

Zwanenberg R. M. A. van, with A. King, *An Economic History of Kenya and Uganda 1800–1970* (London: Macmillan Press, 1975).

AGRICULTURE: NON-FOOD AND DRINK

The non-food and drink goods cultivated can be split into those produced by Africans and those grown by Europeans.

African-Cultivated Crops

Non-food goods produced by Africans included palm fruits and groundnuts, cotton, timber, wattle, tobacco and rubber.

Palm Fruits and Groundnuts

Palm fruits and groundnuts were both produced for their oil. The cultivation of palm fruit (see Thomas, 'On the Oil Rivers of West Africa' (1872–5), *Despatches relating to the Sierra Leone Oil Palm Industry and the Establishment of Oil Palm Plantations* (1925) and *West Africa. Palm Oil and Palm Kernels* (1925), all below), in Nigeria, Sierra Leone and, to a lesser extent, the Gold Coast, was stimulated by the introduction of a regular steamship service between Britain and West Africa in 1852, which opened up new areas to the oil trade, and the increasing demand for palm oil in Europe.[1] The oil was the main ingredient in soap and candle manufacture; a lubricant for machinery, such as railway stock; and used in the processing of wool and the manufacture of tin.[2] Africans' response to this new demand was positive. Palm trees were indigenous to Africa and there was a domestic demand for the product, and growers were therefore not wholly dependent on the export market; the oil was used in cooking, the kernels as food and the fronds as building materials. At first, farmers simply harvested wild palm trees, but then began to plant the crop, which was grown in small plantations and tended by family labour, with the various tasks divided by gender. Generally, men climbed the trees and collected the fruits and women and children crushed the inner nut between stones to extract the kernels/oil.[3]

The sector reached its peak in the late 1850s/early 1860s, but then entered a long decline caused by a fall in prices. West African palm oil began to face competition from oils produced in Sumatra, Malaya and the Belgium Congo, petroleum oil from Pennsylvania, tallow from Australia and groundnut oil from India, the transport costs of which were lowered by the opening of the Suez Canal. The industry was partly helped by the development of the margarine industry, which used palm oil as a major ingredient, the use of crushed kernels as cattle cake, and the First World War. The military blockade of Germany, a major source of margarine, led to the growth of the British margarine industry and an increase in the demand for West African oil.[4] To guarantee supplies and to stimulate production, in Nigeria relatively low export duties were placed on palm kernels and, in 1917, their export to any country other than the UK was prohibited.[5]

Unfortunately, this upturn proved to be a mere respite. After the war and the resumption of normal supplies, prices again began to fall and the Nigerian industry was further damaged by the 1919 decision to introduce a large export duty on palm kernels that were not destined for processing within the empire. The policy was finally abandoned in 1922 as improper and on balance against British interests – by which time exports had fallen by 30 per cent.[6] Alarmed by the decline of the sector, the Nigerian colonial authorities in the 1920s and 1930s sought to stimulate cultivation. Farmers who had switched to the growth of other cash crops were encouraged to return to the cultivation of palm fruits by the sale of palm seedlings at token prices and, in the late 1930s, the Esan and Benin Native Administrations assisted and advised palm oil cooperative societies. There were also attempts to maximize crop yields through the establishment of nurseries, the employment of staff to advise farmers on the best methods of cultivation and the distribution of wire collars for the protection of seedlings.[7]

Groundnuts (see Middleton, *Report on the Ground-Nut Trade in Kano Province* (1924), below) were grown in the Gambia; from 1907 in the Northern Nigerian provinces of Kano and Katsina; and in Tanganyika. As with palm fruit, cultivation was encouraged by the existence of a domestic market and a large European demand from Britain, France, Germany and Portugal; the oil being used in the manufacture of soap, candles, cooking oil and later margarine. Other factors that stimulated production included, in the Gambia, the presence of the river Gambia, which allowed harvests to be easily transported to the coast, and the adoption by farmers of various strategies to reduce the likelihood of famine at times of depressed world prices. These included the rotation of the crop with millets and sorghum, the growth of rice along the banks of rivers and in other locations where the cultivation of groundnuts was not suitable, and the importation of rice. In Nigeria, cultivation was spurred by the arrival of the railhead at Kano in 1911, the need for Hausa traders to diversify the goods they traded and the tendency for cotton farmers to switch to groundnuts, which were more reliable than and not as dependent as cotton on the export market. The crop was grown on small farms tended by the farmers' families, though in the Gambia migrant labour from Upper Senegal was often employed. Tasks were again segregated by gender, with women concentrating on the drying and decortication of the nuts.[8]

Cotton

Cotton was grown throughout British Africa, but was most dominant in Uganda, where it was cultivated in Buganda, Busoga and, by 1914, in Teso, where by 1925 it contributed 93 per cent of that country's total exports. Elsewhere, in West Africa (see Penzer, *Cotton in British West Africa, including Togoland and the Cameroons* (1920), below) it was produced in the Gold Coast and Northern Nigeria, and, in East Africa, in Southern Rhodesia, Tanganyika, Nyasaland and Kenya (see *The Cotton-Growing Industry in Uganda, Kenya, and the Mwanza District of Tanganyika* (1925), Addison and Jefferys, *Cotton Growing in Southern Africa and the Rhodesias* (1927) and Simpson, 'British Central Africa Protectorate. Report on the Cotton-Growing Industry, 1905', all below).[9] The impetus for its growth came from the Lancashire cotton textile industry, which was heavily dependent on the American cotton crop and wished to diversify its sources of supply. American exports of raw cotton were disrupted by the American Civil War and the First World War, and from 1918 there were fears that the rise of the American textile industry would permanently curtail the amount of raw cotton available for Lancashire. The industry's response to the problem was the British Cotton Growers' Association (BCGA). Founded in 1902 by the Lancashire Chamber of Commerce and various Liverpool merchants, the BCGA sought to initiate the growth of cotton in the British colonies, choosing Africa over India because it was believed that the continent had the potential to produce a higher quality fibre.[10]

To achieve its aims the BCGA variously supplied seeds to African farmers, and in Uganda to chiefs, who were ordered to ensure that it was planted by peasants under their authority; established buying centres; built and operated ginneries; sold at low prices or gave away half-gins; and purchased the cotton produced at guaranteed prices. Its efforts were assisted by the Empire Cotton Growing Association (1919), a quasi-governmental organization that advised the British government on the best means of promoting the growth of the crop, and in Uganda by the Uganda Company, an organization established in 1903 by T. F. V. Buxton, the president of the Anti-Slavery and Aborigine Protection Society, to spread Christianity through commerce.[11]

The attempts to encourage cultivation had mixed results. In West Africa there was little enthusiasm for the crop. Growth entailed the sowing of seeds at regular intervals, the periodic thinning of plants, constant weeding, and rapid and careful harvesting to avoid spoilage. It therefore absorbed a great deal of labour, particularly during planting, which reduced the manpower available for the cultivation of food crops. If harvests were poor or markets were bad, farmers therefore faced near starvation.[12] More importantly, the ecology of the Savannah areas of West Africa meant that cotton could not be grown as efficiently as elsewhere and growers rarely received a good return for their crop, which in

Southern Nigeria was additionally prone to damage by insect pests and disease. Prior to 1920, Northern Nigerian farmers sought to reduce the risks involved in cultivation by inter-planting their cotton plants with other early crops that were picked before the cotton was harvested.[13] Generally, however, growers resisted the blandishments and demands of the BCGA, and by 1914 most officials accepted that the Nigerian scheme had failed.[14]

Cotton proved more popular in East Africa. Although farmers in the Lango district of Western Uganda were at first reluctant to grow the crop, preferring sim sim (sesame), most Ugandan farmers eventually embraced cotton. The area possessed ideal soil and climatic conditions; cotton could easily be grown along-side bananas, the cultivation of which required little labour; and from 1929 the amount of cotton produced per acre greatly increased, due to the sowing of new higher yielding varieties and the greater use of ploughs and migrant workers.[15] Theoretically, the crop should have been equally successful in Southern Rhodesia and Kenya. Both colonies had suitable soil and climatic conditions and colonial authorities that supported the development of the sector. In fact, production was disappointing. In Kenya, farmers preferred to concentrate on maize and sim sim, the growth of which was easier, and, in the short term, more profitable. In Southern Rhodesia, cotton again had to compete with the cultivation of food-stuffs, the varieties grown proved unsuitable, there were problems with pests and disease, and there was no organized marketing system. There was also opposition to African cotton cultivation from the settler community, who believed that it would reduce the supply of labour, particularly in the tobacco-growing regions; compete with their own cotton sector; and that African lackadaisical farming methods would increase the number of and lead to the spread of pests. South Rhodesian native cotton growth, however, enjoyed something of a renaissance from the 1930s, when, wishing to divert peasants from the major white settler crops, the colonial government aggressively promoted cultivation and in 1936 established the Cotton Research and Industry Board to act as ginners and to purchase cotton at fair prices.[16]

Timber and Wattle

African production of timber was most significant in the Gold Coast and Southern Nigeria (see Oliphant, *Report on the Commercial Possibilities and Development of the Forests of Nigeria* (1934), below), where mahogany, Sapele wood and Iroko were the main species grown, and to a lesser extent in Uganda (see Nicholson, *The Future of Forestry in Uganda* (1929), below).[17] In the Gold Coast, the sector expanded rapidly from the early 1890s owing to the growing popularity in Europe of mahogany furniture and interior decoration. Until the 1920s, the industry was dominated by Africans, who, unlike their European competitors, could move to new areas at relatively short notice, had better access to labour willing to travel long distances, and could harvest the timber with fewer complications from local people.[18] Thereafter, European companies gained the upper hand, benefiting from their superior capital resources, greater use of technology, access to railways and shipping services and expert knowledge of European prices.[19]

Throughout West Africa a major problem faced by the industry was deforestation caused by traditional rulers leasing timber rights to contractors who felled all fully grown trees before moving onto the next forest. Colonial government attempts at conservation were met by protests from European timber and shipping interests, traditional rulers, African entrepreneurs and, in the Gold Coast, the Aborigines Rights Protection Society.[20] Government conservation methods were also at first relatively unsuccessful. The natural and artificial regeneration schemes adopted by the Southern Nigerian Forestry Department, whereby some trees were cut back to encourage the growth of others or new woods were planted, not only failed to regenerate forests, but were also expensive and administratively cumbersome. More successful was the Taungya system introduced in the late 1920s. Under this regeneration method, native forest reserve land was cleared for farming and trees then planted about sixteen feet by sixteen feet apart between the 2-acre plots. After one or two years, farming of the plots ceased, trees were planted on the plots and a further area of forest reserve cleared and planted with trees/farmed. The system ensured that the planted trees flourished, it having been noted that saplings grew best on abandoned farmland and when they had adequate access to sunlight, and, more importantly, had the support of African farmers, who gained from being given each year or two a portion of good forest land.[21]

An agricultural sector related to forestry was the growth of wattle, a species of acacia. This was grown by Africans in the Central Province of Kenya from the 1920s and, by 1932, 30,000 acres were devoted to its cultivation (see Leckie, *The Growing of Wattle and Production of Wattle Bark in Kenya* (1932), below). The rise of the sector was related to the expansion of the European tanning industry, which used juice extracted from wattle bark for the tanning of leather, and, in the 1930s, by the Kenyan government's promotion of the sector. Cultivation was particularly appropriate to peasant growers as there was little European competition, owing to the low prices paid for the bark, and the trees required little land or maintenance, and, being leguminous, fixed nitrogen into the soil, aiding its fertility. The wood could also be used for building, firewood and the manufacture of charcoal, and producers were therefore not wholly dependent on the export market. Prior to 1932, the bark was sold to the Asian-owned firm Premchand Raichand and Company and thereafter to the Natal Tanning Extract Company, a subsidiary of the Forestal Land, Timber and Railways Company, a London-based firm that also had wattle interests in South Africa and controlled the production of quebracho extract, another tanning agent produced in Argentina and Paraguay. Unfortunately, in 1936 the company, fearing overproduction and a fall in world prices, forced the Kenyan government to halt the planting of new wattle trees, threatening to reduce the price of the South American quebracho extract to below that of Kenyan wattle if it refused to comply with their demands. The result was that for the following two years no new trees were planted and many Africans left the sector.[22]

Other Crops

Other less significant cash crops cultivated by Africans were tobacco, rubber and, to a lesser extent, indigo (see Moloney, *West African Produce (Indigo &c.)* (1890), below). Tobacco was grown in the Lilongwe and Dowa areas of Nyasaland, where, in 1929, 47,500 Africans were involved in the sector, and, in the 1930s, in the Bunyoro and West Nile districts of Uganda (see *Report of the Tobacco Advisory Committee* (1936), below).[23] An attempt in the 1930s by the Kenyan government to promote cultivation, in order to increase revenues and limit cigarette imports, failed, largely because Africans were unwilling to abandon the profitable growth of foodstuffs.[24] Rubber was produced in Nigeria and the Gold Coast (see Holland, *Rubber Cultivation in West Africa* (1901), below) and largely collected from wild rubber trees. The expansion of the trade was related to the increased European demand for rubber; the fact that little capital, skill or expensive equipment was needed to begin cultivation; and the fall in palm oil prices, which prompted many palm fruit growers to enter the industry. Unfortunately, the rubber sector eventually went the way of palm fruit cultivation. Trees were recklessly tapped and destroyed, and, from the late 1890s, rubber began to be produced on Malayan plantations that was not only cheaper than the West African product, but also better quality.[25]

European-Cultivated Goods

The non-food goods produced by Europeans included tobacco, timber and wattle, sisal and various animal by-products.

Tobacco

Tobacco was cultivated in Mazoe in Southern Rhodesia, and, to a lesser extent, in the Central Province of Nyasaland, Tanganyika and Northern Rhodesia and South Africa (see *Report on the Tobacco Industry* (1924), below).[26] The industry established itself in the early 1900s, stimulated by the expansion of the British and South African markets; from 1919, the relatively low UK tariffs placed on African, as opposed to American, tobacco; and, in Nyasaland, the 1915 extension of the local railway.[27] In Southern Rhodesia, the industry grew from 1909 to 1913, but then suffered a setback caused by a fall in prices. The sector survived and boomed in 1926–7, but then again collapsed when world prices fell and South Africa introduced import quotas (1930). The industry, however, again pulled through helped by government purchases of unsold crops and the UK and Southern Rhodesia's departure from the gold standard, which gave the colony's product an advantage in Britain over American competition.[28]

Timber and Wattle

Timber was largely cultivated in South Africa and Kenya. As with the African industry, over-exploitation and a fear that global timber supplies were close to exhaustion led to the introduction of conservation measures. Forestry departments were established, cutting restrictions introduced, and Africans were excluded from woodlands and, in the Cape from the 1920s, encouraged to meet their wood needs from the acacia trees grown on colonial plantations.[29]

Wattle trees were cultivated in Natal from the 1860s and, from 1903, in Kenya, where the wood was initially used as fuel for the local railway.[30] In Natal, the wattle was grown by individuals and companies, such as the Town Hill Wattle Company and the Clan Syndicate, and from the First World War the juice began to be extracted from the bark before shipment, thus reducing shipping costs. Output fell in the 1920s and 1930s partly due to the collapse of world prices, but mainly because growers failed to thin trees, which resulted in reduced yields. By the war, however, education by the local agricultural department and the cooperative Wattle and Timber Growers' Association had caused yields to rise and the industry had again returned to profitability.[31]

Sisal

Sisal, used for the manufacture of rope, was found in Tanganyika and in Kenya (see Rutherford, *Sisal in Kenya* (1924), below), where it was grown from 1893, and was Tanganyika's main export (accounting for 40 per cent of total exports in 1921–3) and Kenya's second-largest export. In both countries, the crop was a replacement for agricultural products that had failed to conquer or had lost their export markets – wool, meat and dairy goods in Kenya and rubber in Tanganyika – and, able to tolerate semi-arid conditions, was grown in areas that were good for little else.[32] Inevitably, farmers were hit by the fall in world prices, which dropped in the mid-1920s, but then recovered only to collapse by more than 50 per cent from 1929 to 1931. In Tanganyika, many small producers went to the wall, their farms taken over by concessionaire companies, the non-payment of wages led to strikes, and the discharge of workers resulted in a renaissance in African farming.[33]

Livestock

Livestock goods produced included mohair and ostrich feathers, both of which came from South Africa, and skins and head trophies from the hunting of wild animals.[34] Ostrich farming emerged in the 1860s, when excessive hunting had caused the number of wild animals to decline, and peaked from the 1870s to the 1890s due to the fashion for feathered hats. Production then fell back, only to peak again in the inter-war period owing to improved breeding and farming methods reducing costs.[35] The hunting of animals other than ostriches continued well into the twentieth century and occurred throughout Africa (see Speight, 'Big Game Hunting in South Africa' (1926), below). It was largely the preserve of settlers and professional hunters who shot wildlife for sport and to supply the international hide, trophy and ivory trade. African involvement was usually restricted; Cape officials in the 1880s and 1890s systematically poisoned and shot the dogs of African hunters, and, in 1918, the Nyasaland government limited African ownership of guns. Over time, European hunting was also confined. The wanton and indiscriminate slaughter of wild animals, some endangered, led to an international outcry and the inter-war establishment of game departments and the introduction of regulations designed to limit the species and number of animals that could be shot.[36]

Other Crops

Other goods produced included: pyrethrum, an insecticide-yielding daisy cultivated in Kenya in Upper Kiambu, Nakuru, Nandi, the Aberdares and Mount Elgon that needed little capital investment and yielded a large profit margin; flax, again grown in Kenya, though the sector collapsed during the 1920s; cotton, cultivated unsuccessfully by white farmers in Southern Rhodesia, and, in the interwar period, in Uganda; and rubber, produced by plantation companies from 1900 in Kenya and Uganda (see Lyttelton Gell, *The Rubber Industry in the British South Africa Company's Territories* (1900), below). In the former colony, low yields rapidly led to the decline of the sector, but in Uganda, the industry remained relatively successful until the mid-1920s, after which production dwindled.[37]

Notes:

1.   M. Lynn, 'From Sail to Steam: The Impact of the Steamship Services on the British Palm Oil Trade with West Africa, 1850–1890', *Journal of African History*, 30:2 (1989), pp. 227–45; P. Wickins, *An Economic History of Africa from the Earliest Time to Partition* (Oxford: Oxford University Press, 1981), p. 270. In 1934–8, Nigeria supplied 29.7 per cent of total world exports of palm oil (ibid., p. 272).
2.   M. Lynn, 'British Business and the African Trade: Richard & William King Ltd of Bristol and West Africa, 1833–1918', *Business History*, 34:4 (1992), pp. 20–37.

3. Wickins, *An Economic History of Africa*, pp 270–1; B. Ndoma-Egba, *Foreign Investment and Economic Transformation in West Africa, 1870–1930 with an Emphasis on Nigeria* (London; Lund, 1974), pp. 22–3.
4. Lynn, 'British Business'; G. Austin, 'Factor Markets in Nieboer Conditions: Early Modern West Africa c.1500–c.1900', *Continuity and Change*, 24 (Special Issue 1) (2009), pp. 23–53; Wickins, *An Economic History of Africa*, pp. 131, 271; Ndoma-Egba, *Foreign Investment*, p. 24.
5. A. Olukoju, 'Slamming the "Open Door": British Protectionist Fiscal Policy in Inter-War Nigeria', *Itinerario*, 23:2 (1992), pp. 13–28.
6. E. G. Charle Jr, 'English Colonial Policy and the Economy of Nigeria', *American Journal of Economics and Sociology*, 26:1 (1967), pp. 79–92; C. C. Wrigley, 'Aspects of Economic History', in A. D. Roberts (ed.), *The Cambridge History of Africa, Volume 7: 1905–1940* (Cambridge: Cambridge University Press, 1986), pp. 77–139, on p. 114.
7. S. A. Shokpeka and O. A. Nwaokocha, 'British Colonial Economic Policy in Nigeria: The Example of Benin Province 1914–1954', *Journal of Human Ecology*, 28:1 (2009), pp. 57–66; D. Meredith, 'Government and the Decline of the Nigerian Oil-Palm Export Industry, 1919–1939', *Journal of African History*, 25:3 (1984), pp. 311–29.
8. K. Swindell and A. Jeng, 'Migrants, Credit and Climate: The Gambian Groundnut Trade, 1834–1934', *Journal of Agrarian Change*, 7:4 (2007), pp. 570–2; Wickins, *An Economic History of Africa*, p. 271; Ndoma-Egba, *Foreign Investment*, pp. 110–13, 121; A. D. Roberts, 'East Africa', in Roberts (ed.), *The Cambridge History of Africa, Volume 7*, pp. 649–701, on p. 671; C. Ehrlich, 'Building and Caretaking: Economic Policy in British Tropical Africa, 1890–1960', *Economic History Review*, 26 (1973) , pp. 649–67. See also A. E. Hinds, 'Colonial Policy and the Processing of Groundnuts: The Case of Georges Calil', *International Journal of African Historical Studies*, 19:2 (1986), pp. 261–273.
9. Roberts, 'East Africa', pp. 655, 683; K. Deininger and H. P. Binswanger, 'Rent Seeking and the Development of Large Scale Agriculture in Kenya, South Africa and Zimbabwe', *Economic Development and Cultural Change*, 43:3 (1995), pp. 493–522; J. McCracken, 'British Central Africa', in Roberts (ed.), *The Cambridge History of Africa, Volume 7*, pp. 602–48, p. 607; R. M. A. van Zwanenberg with A. King, *An Economic History of Kenya and Uganda 1800–1970* (London: Macmillan Press, 1975), p. 40.
10. P. S. Nyambara, 'Colonial Policy and Peasant Cotton Agriculture in Southern Rhodesia, 1904–1953', *International Journal of African Historical Studies*, 33:1 (2000), pp. 81–111; E. O. Egboh, 'British Cotton Growing Association (BCGA): Enterprise in the Lagos Colony and Protectorate, 1902–1905', *Bulletin de l'Institut fondamental d'Afrique noire. Serie B*, 41:1 (1979), pp. 72–99; S. Onyeiwu, 'Deceived by African Cotton: The British Cotton Growing Association and the Demise of the Lancashire Textile Industry', *African Economic History*, 28 (2000), pp. 89–121.
11. Wickins, *An Economic History of Africa*, p. 280; Nyambara, 'Colonial Policy'.
12. Nyambara, 'Colonial Policy'; G. Austin, 'Resources, Techniques, and Strategies South of the Sahara: Revising the Factor Endowments Perspective on African Economic Development, 1500–2000', *Economic History Review*, 61:3 (2008), pp. 587–624; R. E. Dumett, 'Obstacles to Government-Assisted Agricultural Development in West Africa: Cotton-Growing Experimentation in Ghana in the Early Twentieth Century', *Agricultural History Review*, 23:2 (1975), pp. 156–72.
13. Ndoma-Egba, *Foreign Investment*, p. 134.

14. K. D. Nworah, 'The West African Operations of the British Cotton Growing Associa-tion, 1904–1914', *African Historical Studies*, 4:2 (1971), pp. 315–30.

15. Zwanenberg with King, *An Economic History of Kenya and Uganda*, p. 60; Austin, 'Resources, Techniques, and Strategies'; Ehrlich, 'Building and Caretaking'; Roberts, 'East Africa', p. 655.

16. Wickins, *An Economic History of Africa*, p. 280; Roberts, 'East Africa', p. 656; Nyambara, 'Colonial Policy'.

17. P. von Hellermann, 'Things Fall Apart? Management, Environment and Taungya Farm-ing in Edo State, Southern Nigeria', *Africa*, 77:3 (2007), pp. 371–92.

18. C. B. Ash, 'Forced Labor in Colonial West Africa', *History Compass*, 4:3 (2006), pp. 402–6.

19. R. E. Dumett, 'Tropical Forests and West African Enterprise: The Early History of the Ghana Timber Trade', *African Economic History*, 29 (2001), pp. 79–116.

20. D. C. Dorward, 'British West Africa and Liberia', in Roberts (ed.), *The Cambridge His-tory of Africa, Volume 7*, pp. 399–459, on p. 410; E. O. Egboh, 'British Control of the Forests of Lagos Colony and Protectorate, 1897–1902', *Journal of African Studies*, 6:2 (1979), pp. 88–97.

21. Hellermann, 'Things Fall Apart?'.

22. H. Witt, '"Clothing the Once Bare Brown Hills of Natal": The Origin and Develop-ment of Wattle Growing in Natal, 1860–1960', *South African Historical Journal*, 53 (2005), pp. 99–122; R. M. Maxon, 'Where Did the Trees Go? The Wattle Bark Industry in Western Kenya, 1932–1950', *International Journal of African Historical Studies*, 34:3 (2001), pp. 265–85.

23. Roberts, 'East Africa', p. 696; McCracken, 'British Central Africa', p. 626.

24. R. M. Maxon, 'Up in Smoke: Peasants, Capital and the Colonial State in the Tobacco Industry in Western Kenya, 1930–1939', *African Economic History*, 22 (1994), pp. 111–39.

25. Wickins, *An Economic History of Africa*, p. 274.

26. R. E. Baldwin, 'The Northern Rhodesian Economy and the Rise of the Copper Industry', in Z. A. Konczacki and J. M. Konczacki (eds), *An Economic History of Tropical Africa, Volume 2: The Colonial Period* (London: Frank Cass, 1977), pp. 60–76, on p. 61; J. F. Munro, *Britain in Tropical Africa: Economic Relations and Impact* (London: Macmillan, 1984), p. 53; Nyambara, 'Colonial Policy'; B. C. Nindi, 'Labour and Capital in Settler Economy in Colonial Tanganyika', *Journal of Eastern African Research and Development*, 17 (1987), pp. 90–6.

27. McCracken, 'British Central Africa', pp. 606–7; Munro, *Britain in Tropical Africa*, p. 53; J. McCracken, 'Planters, Peasants and the Colonial State: The Impact of the Native Tobacco Board in the Central Province of Malawi', *Journal of Southern African Studies*, 9:2 (1983), pp. 172–92.

28. McCracken, 'British Central Africa', pp. 606, 625, 627; Deininger and Binswanger, 'Rent Seeking'; W. Morapedi, 'Migrant Labour and the Peasantry in the Bechuanaland Pro-tectorate, 1930–1965', *Journal of Southern African Studies*, 25:2 (1999), pp. 197–214.

29. J. A. Tropp, *Natures of Colonial Change: Environmental Relations in the Making of the Transkei* (Athens, OH: Ohio University Press, 2006); C. M. Rogerson and M. da Silva, 'Urban Small-Scale Industry on the Witwatersrand: Emergence, Destruction and Revival', *African Urban Quarterly*, 4:3–4 (1989), pp. 349–60; K. Brown, 'The Con-servation and Utilisation of the Natural World: Silviculture in the Cape Colony, c. 1902–1910', *Environment and History*, 7:4 (2001), pp. 427–48; T. P. Ofcansky, 'Kenya

Forestry under British Colonial Administration, 1895–1963', *Journal of Forest History*, 28:3 (1984), pp. 136–43; F. H. Smith, 'What Happened to the Forests?' Policy towards Managing the Timber Resources in Kwazulu/Natal during the Colonial Period (1853–1910)', *New Contree*, 48 (2000), pp. 47–64. Africans relied on the forests for wood for building huts and livestock kraals, for fighting sticks and the performance of rituals, and for medicinal herbs and roots. In the Cape until the 1920s Africans continued to use the forests secretly or by taking advantage of the policy differences between government departments and individual officials (Tropp, *Natures of Colonial Change*).

30. Witt, '"Clothing the Once Bare Brown Hills of Natal"'; Maxon, 'Where Did the Trees Go?'.

31. S. P. Sherry, 'History of the Wattle Industry in Natal', *Natalia*, 3 (1973), pp. 40–4.

32. Zwanenberg with King, *An Economic History of Kenya and Uganda*; Roberts, 'East Africa', pp. 689, 693; N. Westcott, 'The East African Sisal Industry, 1929–1949: The Marketing of a Colonial Commodity during Depression and War', *Journal of African History*, 25:4 (1984), pp. 445–61; Wrigley, 'Aspects of Economic History', p. 103.

33. H. Sabea, 'Mastering the Landscape? Sisal Plantations, Land, and Labor in Tanga Region, 1893–1980s', *International Journal of African Historical Studies*, 41:3 (2008), pp. 25–35.

34. Wool production is discussed in Volume 2 of the collection.

35. Wickins, *An Economic History of Africa*, p. 283.

36. McCracken, 'British Central Africa', p. 609; J. Tropp, 'Dogs, Poison and the Meaning of Colonial Intervention in the Transkei, South Africa', *Journal of African History*, 43:3 (2002), pp. 451–72; R. W. Beachey, 'The East African Ivory Trade in the Nineteenth Century', *Journal of African History*, 8:2 (1967), pp. 269–90.

37. S. S. S. Kenyanchui, 'European Settler Agriculture' in W. R. Ochieng and R. M. Maxon (eds), *An Economic History of Kenya* (Nairobi: East African Educational Publishers, 1992), pp. 111–27, on p. 121; C. C. Wrigley, 'Kenya: The Patterns of Economic Life 1902–45', in V. Harlow, E. M. Chilver and A. Smith (eds), *History of East Africa, Volume 2* (Oxford: Clarendon Press, 1965), pp. 209–64, on p. 250; Roberts, 'East Africa', pp. 684, 696; I. D. Talbott, 'The Kenya Flax Boom', *Kenya Historical Review*, 2:1 (1974), pp. 59–66; T. Taylor, 'The Establishment of a European Plantation Sector within the Emerging Colonial Economy of Uganda, 1902–1919', *International Journal of African Historical Studies*, 19:1 (1986), pp. 35–58; Nyambara, 'Colonial Policy'; J. F. Munro, 'British Rubber Companies in East Africa before the First World War', *Journal of African History*, 24:3 (1983), pp. 369–79.

W. N. Thomas, 'On the Oil Rivers of West Africa', *Proceedings of Royal Geographic Society*, 17:3 (1872–5), pp. 148–55.

2. *On the Oil Rivers of West Africa.*
By W. Nicholas Thomas, Esq., r.n., f.r.g.s.[1]

The oil rivers on the West Coast of Africa may be described as one enormous delta, with the chief rivers, Benin, Niger, Brass, New Calabar, Bonny, Ossobo, Old Calabar, and Cameroons, from which is derived the enormous trade employing so many magnificent steamers on the coast of Africa, trading with Liverpool and Glasgow.

Very early on the morning of the 4th March I anchored off the mouth of the River Bonny, and at 7.30 a.m. I proceeded over the bar into the river in a small steamer, anchoring not far from the hulk of the African merchants about noon.

The English merchants who trade with the natives have wisely adopted the greatest precautions to preserve their health in this climate so dangerous to Europeans, and therefore, instead of living on shore, amidst the swamps by which the native town is surrounded, they reside in large hulks (many of them formerly large East Indiamen) moored in the centre of the river. There were some 14 or 15 of them to be seen, and, from the comfortable way in / which most of them were fitted up, there was evidently no expense spared by the proprietors to render living on board quite as desirable as the extraordinary nature of the place permits.

The River Bonny or Boni was one of the first rivers the Dutch, English, and Portuguese were acquainted with in this portion of Africa. From the sixteenth to the present century it was the favourite mart of the slave-ships, when the exportation of human beings was a legalised traffic, and the amount of slaves transhipped seldom came to less than 16,000 per annum. Most of these slaves were natives of the Eboe country; the remaining part were of the Allakoo country. Fairs for the purpose were held every five or six weeks at several villages on the banks of rivers and creeks in the interior, and large canoes, carrying 120 men, were employed in the navigation.

The entrance to the Bonny presents a broad expanse of water, consisting of the mouth of the Bonny to the eastward, and the New Calabar to the westward. The entrance to the River Bonny is very intricate, but our ship carried 24 feet of water over the bar. On entering the river, low, marshy banks, covered with mangrove bushes, were seen on either side, and on the starboard side the town of Bonny, ruled over by King George Pepple and Oko Jumbo,[2] with other chiefs, &c. The country surrounding this town is low and marshy, consequently it is always unhealthy to Europeans. After seeing several of the hulks, I went on shore to view the town.

There is, of course, no proper landing-place; but, as the water is very shallow and the beach muddy, our boat's crew had to carry us some distance before we reached *terra firma*. The huts of the natives are built in the usual style of wicker-work covered with mud, and roofed in with palm-leaves and rushes. There is no furniture inside, with the exception of a few wooden stools, some mats, and raised seats made of mud. Crockery-ware and cooking utensils are placed in prominent places, to beautify and ornament the general appearance of the hovel.

Passing from the beach towards the town I went to the Jew-Jew-house (spelt also Dju-Dju, and Ju-Ju),[3] the temple of the religion of these poor heathen, and it proved a sight I shall never forget. It is fact admitting no denial, that at the present moment cannibalism is practised amongst the natives of the Bonny, and is not by any means confined to the interior of the country. Certainly, from time to time, various treaties for the abolition of this fearful custom have been made with the natives, more especially of late years; but there exists no doubt that now and then the horrible practice is / resorted to by the conquerors, who satisfy their hunger by eating the bodies of their enemies.

The Jew-Jew house was a building not very large in extent, built of bamboo wicker-work, roofed and covered with mud, in the same way as the other houses. The door was fastened; but from a sort of window I could look inside, and see the horrible contents of this house of religion.

On ledges, completely round the interior, and in numbers sufficient to cover the walls completely, were ranged hundreds of human skulls; and in the centre of the room was an altar, built of the same horrible materials, to form a sort of table, at the foot of which were placed the offerings to the unknown deity or Jew-Jew. It is almost impossible adequately to describe the creeping sensation of horror on first gazing on such an extraordinary scene. From every nook and corner of the building, the hollow grinning aspect of a human skull met the eye, and the different lines of light and shade pervading the place, converted it at once into a scene ghostly sepulchral. The skulls also, to add to the horror of the display, showed unmistakeable traces of fire.

They were the remains of hundreds of poor creatures, whose flesh, to judge from the marks on the skulls, had been either boiled or roasted, to gratify the ogre-like appetite of the natives.

The gifts at the foot of the altar were valuable. I saw a magnificent tusk, beautifully carved, and there were many other native treasures. Many descriptions of crockery-ware appeared as offerings, and I am given to understand that plates,

&c., with intricate patterns on both sides, are bound to be devoted as offerings to the Jew-Jew.

From the Jew-Jew house I walked through the filthy town, to what is termed the Palace of the Head Chief, 'Oko Jumbo.'

I was received by that worthy in the native costume, which may be at once described by stating that the only thing presented in the way of dress is a cloth round the loins. He spoke English very well, and is a most powerful and muscular man. He entertained me with some excellent Madeira, and, surrounded by his slaves and workmen, who were building him another palace, he was most affable and humorous. The palace he is now building promises to be a very good stone house, but the place inhabited at present is nothing more than an ordinary negro hovel, although answering to the name of palace.

I may here remark that the actual King of the Bonny is George Pepple, a negro educated in England, but eschewing all interest in native affairs; he lives chiefly in retirement, so that most of / the wealth and power of the Bonny country is vested in Oko Jumbo.

Returning from that chief's house, I may narrate, as a curious circumstance for Africa, I met a young negro lad nearly naked, reading a well-known work on mathematics, and I asked him why he read it, and how he came to be possessed of such a work. I learnt that he was a son of Oko Jumbo, and had recently arrived from England, where he had received a superior education.[4]

That evening I slept on board one of the merchants' hulks in the river. During the night there was a fearful tornado, – the wind blowing with great force, accompanied by vivid lightning and an enormous quantity of rain. The wind blew so fiercely that at one time the river was converted into one broad sheet of foam.

It continued to rain all night, but early on the morning of the 5th of March I steamed away for the River New Calabar, and at 9 A.M. passed a small outlying reef, called Breaker Island, which, with the reefs surrounding, must, no doubt, be rapidly increasing in dimensions, owing to the amount of deposit from the Rivers Bonny and New Calabar.

I consider it very desirable that the whole of this portion of the coast should be re-surveyed, as it has not been surveyed for very many years. The latest corrections received are by Navigating-Lieutenant Langdon for the year 1867.

On entering the New Calabar River, the shore on each side presented a very picturesque appearance. There is a small bar at the entrance, easily passed by the mail-steamers. The surrounding country is extremely flat and marshy, but large trees and high shrubs extend right down to the water's edge, making penetration into the interior a work of some difficulty.

There are about ten or twelve hulks of the merchants, moored at the mouth of the river, which, from time to time, has borne the most deadly character, and carried off numbers of Europeans, whose bodies, attacked with the fell fever of Africa, have succumbed to its debilitating effects, and are now lying buried in the sand on the banks of the river.

The Rio Real is another name for the River New Calabar. The river is broad, and presents banks clearly defined on each side. The native town of New Calabar is about 8 miles further up than the merchants' hulks, and I anchored off there at 2 P.M. Tuesday is the Sunday of the natives here, and I embraced a favourable opportunity to proceed on shore, and endeavour to gain some information in reference to their religious ceremonies.

Captain Hopkins, H.B.M.'s Acting Consul, accompanied me, and / we paid a visit to King Amochree II., at his tumble-down mud-hut or palace. It was with some difficulty that we effected a landing at the town, owing to the immense amount of mud in which it is built.

It forms, with stakes driven in the mud all around it, a description of stockade, thus preventing enemies from landing without raising an alarm. To attempt to describe the filth and dirt, mixed with the mud in the streets of this town, would be impossible. You might almost see the poisonous malaria arising as you walked along, and feel it as you drew each breath.

By the banks of the river I saw a number of war-canoes, capable of having thirty men paddling on each side. In the centre sits the king or chief personage, and a rusty old gun is secured with matting, rope, &c., at the bows of the canoes; more dangerous, I should think to those who have the courage to fire it than to the enemy.

Some of the guns were of American make, others of very obsolete English patterns. The canoes, worked by sixty men, proceed with considerable speed, and present (with the chief on a daïs in the centre) rather an interesting sight.

On landing, I walked through the muddy paths, on each side of which were the mud-huts of the staring natives. On arriving at the house of King Amochree, he received us very cordially, and we sat some time with him. He is a fine, well-built man. He was well dressed, and had enormous bracelets of solid ivory on each wrist, very heavy and unpleasant to wear, I should think. Round his neck he had a very handsome necklet of large coral beads, intermixed with gold. He produced brandy-and-water, and the palmwine or tombo, the latter only to be liked when a sufficiently acquired taste for soap and water is obtained.

Hearing the sound of gongs, I asked if there were any Jew-Jew ceremonies going on, and learnt that Tuesday being their Sunday, it was a great occasion for the furtherance of religion with them. Having obtained permission, we repaired to the Jew-Jew house, which was almost of the same dimensions I have mentioned in regard to the house at Bonny Town. On entering we were received by the high priest, or head Jew-Jew man, who presented an extraordinary appearance. He was a tall, muscular man, with handsome features and enormous breast;

his colour was completely of a yellowish tinge, and he was quite naked, with the exception of a waistband. His head was shaved completely on the right side, and on that side, all down his body to the centre, he was covered with chalk or some white substance. An assistant was with him, and / they took a goat offered by one of the congregation, and, having cut its throat, permitted the blood to flow into a small hole dug in the mud of the floor, preparatory to fire being used to burn the sacrifice.

Ever and anon various gongs and bells were beaten in the hut by some natives; but we particularly noticed that there existed a restraint in practising their religion before us, and that when we entered they appeared to cease all demonstration until we were gone. The congregation consisted of the principal chiefs of the tribe, and there were no women present.

These men above referred to were worshipping with their tumblers by their side, and as their religious ardour overpowered them they imbibed various potations of their much-loved palm-wine, or the never-failing rum. As we entered they all rose to receive us, and placing chairs for us, offered us a similar refreshment, which we sipped only. I sat down by the side of a modern Hercules, who could speak a little English. This worthy was decorated with a wig of red hair, which he wore over his own wool, and I need only say that nothing more studied could have the more added to his natural ugliness. Some of the chiefs had on black wigs over their wool, and this gave them a sort of Indian look. I learnt afterwards that to possess a wig, and to wear it well, was considered by these chiefs as quite a Piccadilly or Rotten Row adornment, because they had observed, 'white man he do the same.' The portion of the Jew-Jew house above the head Jew-Jew man, and near the portion which I suppose ought to be described as the altar, was covered with an enormous number of wooden dolls for children, suspended to the wall, intermingled with penny looking-glasses and enormous wooden idols, very ugly and very badly painted.

On my asking my native friend the reason of this gorgeous display, with which I appeared much gratified, he replied with infinite gusto that 'it was to make pretty for Jew-Jew;' and when I asked him whether 'they were praying for peace or for war,' he at once replied 'peace' – a matter very desirable for them, with a number of British men-of-war at hand, I should consider. There were numerous offerings of ivory (very valuable tusks), rum, palm-wine, and the neverfailing plates and crockery, &c., to propitiate their deity. All the time we were inside the Jew-Jew house a number of, horrible and very ancient native women, nearly naked, were outside yelling one of their Hymns (Ancient and Modern, I suppose – with a good deal of the former), and from time to time clapping their hands and uttering the wildest cries. Now and then one old hag, more hideous and toothless than the rest, advanced to me and performed various extra-ordinary / and by no means graceful dances for my edification, or else that I might give her something by way of a 'dash.' This attention on the part of this interesting female I acknowledged by bowing, at what appeared to me appropriate intervals, as, not understanding a word she said, I was not calculated to be capable of expressing much sympathy with her in her song.

Having seen all it was possible to see in the New Calabar River, we took boats and embarked on board our steamer. As we passed the stockades or walls of the town in our boats, we perceived numerous sacrifices to Jew-Jew. On the fishing-stakes many live fowls were attached as sacrifices, and left to die there, as some propitiation to the native deities.

From New Calabar River I proceeded to Fernando Po, an island so well known as to need no description from me. I have been particular, however, to minutely describe all I saw in the Jew-Jew houses of the natives, for I am given to understand that it is only on very rare occasions that Europeans have had opportunities of viewing the celebration of the extraordinary rites.

On the 7th March I left Fernando Po and went to Ambas Bay, on the mainland, situated at the southern base of the Cameroons Mountains, which tower up to the enormous height of 13,760 feet (the highest peak). The peak, however, that is closest to Ambas Bay is called Mongo M'Etindeh, and is only about 5000 feet high. The Cameroons Mountains have been well explored, and are reported to be covered with the most luxuriant verdure, and that there exists magnificent soil in the valleys amongst the range.

There are three islands in Ambas Bay, which add much to the picturesque nature of the scenery. I think, however, that the sea must be washing away some portion of the islands, which are very small, although inhabited by fishermen.

I landed at Ambas Bay, where fresh provisions are to be procured after a little difficulty.

There are some Sierra Leone men who are colonists here, but they do not appear to make the place thrive very well. The natives from the surrounding country visit them at times from the neverending bush. I saw a few of them: they are short, insignificant-looking negroes, with their heads completely shaven.

From Ambas Bay I went up the River Bembia towards the River Cameroons, anchoring off King William's Town, Bembia. I landed in the cool of the evening; but found it impossible to take a walk, as there was no penetrating the interminable forest. The heat also was very oppressive, and the wind, coming over the low and marshy banks of the river, anything but healthy. During the / night we were pestered with myriads of flies and winged ants which repaired on board, attracted by the light. The day after, we returned to Fernando Po.

In conclusion, I may remark that, in my experience of travel (in North America, Central America, the West Indies, &c.), I have never been so thoroughly impressed with the fatal nature of climate to Europeans as during this recent cruise in the west African rivers. Sooner or later the seeds sown during exposure must reap a harvest on the frame of the white man, too often resulting in death, and in verifying the oft-quoted passage:–

> 'Where the fever hot and damp,
> Shed by day's expiring lamp,
> Through the misty ether spreads
> Every ill the white man dreads, –
> Fiery fever's thirsty thrill,
> Fitful ague's shivering chill.'[5]

Despatches relating to the Sierra Leone Oil Palm Industry and the Establishment of Oil Palm Plantations (Freetown: Government Printer, 1925).

SIERRA LEONE.

Despatches

relating to the

Sierra Leone Oil Palm Industry

and the

Establishment of Oil Palm

Plantations. /

Enclosure to Despatch Sierra Leone No. 416 dated 25th September, 1925.

No. 2.

C.L.F. 258351/1925.

LANDS AND FORESTS DEPARTMENT,

FREETOWN, SIERRA LEONE,

8th September, 1925.

Sir,

Sierra Leone Oil Palm Industry.
Establishment of Oil Palm Plantation in Sierra Leone.

Report of
Colonial Office
Committee.
I have the honour to submit, as instructed in M.P. 1474/25, my views on the Colonial Office Report on 'Palm Oil and Palm Kernels' (No. 10 of 1925), and on the correspondence forwarded under cover of the Secretary of State's despatch No. 128 of the 30th April, 1925, in so far as the subject matter affects Sierra Leone.

Observations on
Report by Lands
and Forests Staff.
2.   A copy of the Colonial Office Report and the correspondence referred to has been circulated to the Agricultural Chemist, the Provincial Superintendents of Agriculture and the Assistant Conservators of Forests and I attach hereto copies of the replies received:–

  (*A*) Minute by the Agricultural Chemist (Dr. F. J. Martin).
  (*B*) Minute by the Provincial Superintendent of Agriculture, Northern Province (Mr. R. R. Glanville).
  (*C*) Minute by the Provincial Superintendent of Agriculture, Central Province (Mr. J. D. Fisher).
  (*D*) Minute by the Acting Conservator of Forests (Mr. D. G. Thomas).

This memo
confined to
consideration of
Colonial Office
Report and
correspondence
relating thereto.
3.   I am engaged on a special memorandum on the Sierra Leone Oil Palm Industry, which has however been unfortunately much delayed and interrupted through pressure of routine work and absence on leave of the larger number of my European assistants. I propose therefore to confine this memorandum to the consideration of the recommendations of the Secretary of State's Committee, and to the correspondence referred to in paragraph, 1 and of the minutes referred to in the preceding paragraph. In other words I propose here to deal only with the more immediately urgent and practical steps it is desirable to take in Sierra Leone and to leave the more scientific aspects of the problem to the special memorandum referred to.

The Eastern plantation menace.
4.   The Committee draw attention to the danger confronting the West African palm oil trade by the competition of the Dutch West Indies, Malay, etc., where the oil palm, under scientific cultivation by experienced and careful European planters, is producing not only superior oil and kernels, but also on a far more prolific scale than the wild and uncultivated oil palm of West Africa. It is estimated that in the course of fifteen years the East Coast of Sumatra will export more palm oil than West Africa's pre-war record. If this prediction be realized,

and judging from the development of the plantation rubber industry during the last thirty years, it is not unlikely that it will be, it is obvious that it must adversely affect the West African palm oil trade if steps are not immediately taken to improve the quality and increase the quantity of palm oil and kernels produced in and exported from West Africa. The fact that plantation palm oil and kernels from the East, may be placed on the market at a substantially lower price than West African palm oil and kernels, shows that the 'Sumatra menace' is no bogie, but a serious one to be faced.

5.   That it may prove a serious menace to Sierra Leone trade is obvious when we consider that palm produce forms the backbone of the trade of the country. The total value of domestic produce exported from Sierra Leone in 1924 was £1,510,353, of which palm produce represented £1,189,527. I give hereunder the figures for the last 10 years, showing the relative values of palm produce to the total value of domestic produce exported, which can leave no doubt as to the importance of the oil palm industry in the trade and commerce of Sierra Leone:– / *Relative values of total domestic and palm produce exports.*

	Total exports domestic produce. £	Total value palm produce exported £
1915	852,751	549,704
1916	1,101,846	734,327
1917	1,276,434	904,893
1918	1,221,225	716,885
1919	1,869,669	1,307,122
1920	2,405,556	1,524,883
1921	1,080,588	692,777
1922	1,069,803	784,189
1923	1,347,115	1,071,442
1924	1,510,353	1,189,527

6.   It is argued that there is an unlimited market for palm oil and that the production of plantation palm oil on a large scale in the East will not seriously affect the West African trade. If however plantation palm oil and kernels are placed on the market at lower prices than at present produced in Sierra Leone it cannot but reflect on the prices locally. We all know how a drop in the value in palm kernels affects trade in this country, and I fully concur in the necessity for the introduction of improvements as suggested in paragraph 8 of the Committee's report.

7.   It might now be convenient to summarise the Committee's principal recommendations embodied in paragraphs 8–11 of the Report:– *Lines for propaganda amongst African growers.*

(*a*) That all possible steps should be taken to teach the Africans to improve the present condition of the existing trees by cleaning the heads and opening up the bush, and to demonstrate to them the result of such improvements.

(*b*) That the African should be encouraged to create blocks of palm trees by planting up bare patches where the forest trees are scattered.

(*c*) That the destruction of oil palm trees for the manufacture of palm wine should be restricted as far as it is practicable.

(*d*) That communal plantations might be encouraged where the conditions are suitable.

(*e*) That avenues of oil palms might be planted along the roads.

(*f*) That adequate inducements should be offered to attract private enterprise to erect mills.

Mechanical production of palm oil.

8.   With regard to (*a*) steps have already been taken to interest the chiefs and people to improve their oil palm stands. I would however suggest that when the Provincial Commissioners come to Freetown next month a round table conference should be held in order to determine the policy which should be adopted in the Provinces in respect to the lines of propaganda referred to in (*a*), (*b*), (*c*), (*d*) and (*e*) of paragraph 7. It may be mentioned that I proposed, some time ago, that the boundaries of chiefdoms, wherever practicable, might be delimited by planting a belt of oil palms, and that the custom of leaving a 66 foot belt of bush on the sides of Protectorate roads might be gradually replaced by a belt of oil palms of approved varieties. The latter project is provided for, to some extent, in the re-afforestation and roadside planting scheme foreshadowed in connection with contemplated extra-ordinary expenditure for the next few years of my department. To carry out the recommendations enumerated under (*a*) – (*c*) in the preceeding paragraph will require intensive propaganda which will necessitate the active co-operation of the political, agricultural and forestry officers, it is therefore that I suggest a round table conference should be held to consider fully how far these proposals can be applied under the conditions obtaining in the three respective Provinces of the Protectorate.

Round table Conference with Provincial Commissioners.

Encouragement of palm oil extraction mills.

9.   In regard to (*f*), the question of the establishment of mills or factories is an important one, and while I consider the proposal should be given every encouragement, we should, I think, consider carefully the reasons why the experiment of Messrs. Lever Brothers in Sierra Leone made between 1912 – 1915 proved a failure.[1] I attach, as appendix 'E,' a short resume of Messrs. Lever Brothers' attempt to establish a mill at Yonnibanna. They applied for the concession in 1912, but it was found it could not be granted under existing ordinances and the Palm Oil Ordinance No. 7 of 1913, was then enacted and the concession made. The West African Oil Company, to whom the concession was subsequently transferred, had the mill / established and ready to start work early in 1914, and

a mono-rail laid down to Small Magbassa, a distance of ten and a-half miles. The first difficulty occurred apparently over the price to be paid for the fruit. The company offered 30*s*. per ton and the chiefs wanted 60*s*. per ton. The price ultimately accepted was 30*s*. per ton for fruit delivered at the factory, deductions being made for fruit delivered at the mono-rail according to distance from the mill. Apparently insufficient fruit was forthcoming and the second year, with the approval of the Government, the firm employed labourers to cut and collect the fruit, paying 1*s*. 6*d*. to the labourers per fifteen heads delivered on the mono-rail, and 3*d*. per fifteen heads to the owners of the palms through the headmen, which works out at roughly 1 ½*d*. per head. The company failed to get sufficient fruit and in December, 1915, it closed down. A perusal of the papers on this subject show that failure was due to the following causes:–

(*a*) Low price paid for the fruit (1 ½*d*. per head).

(*b*) Disinclination of the native to carry palm heads long distances (at 1 ½*d*. per head, it is obvious they could not be carried far in a country where the rate of labour is 9d. per day).

(*c*) Inadequacy of transport facilities from palm areas to factory.

(*d*) Antagonistic attitude of small traders who persuaded the natives against supplying the company.

(*e*) Inability of the natives to appreciate advantages of disposing of the palm fruit – loosing the pericarp oil[2] which he requires for domestic use and the palm nuts which provides employment for his wife and children in their spare hours. Palm kernels form the current bank account of the native – he draws on his stock in hand when he requires funds.

10.   It was ten years ago the Yonnibanna mill closed down and the conditions which obtained then have not materially changed. It is true that advances have been made on palm oil extraction machinery but the same local difficulties exist. In my opinion the palmeries of this country are not sufficiently continuous, or the palm areas are not sufficiently stocked with palm trees, to permit of them being worked on plantation lines and the fruit dealt with in a central mill. The existing palmeries contain a large number of unproductive palms and varieties which yield very little pericarp oil. The necessary preliminary to the establishment of mills is the improvement of the palmeries. It is essential:– *Improvement of palmeries first necessity.*

(*a*) To cut out old unproductive palms and replace them with good oil-yielding varieties.

(*b*) To remove the bush and clean up the heads of the palms.

(*c*) To fill up vacant areas with palms of good varieties.

(*d*) To eliminate the thick shelled varieties which yield little pericarp and replace them with good oil-yielding varieties.

11.   I recommend that a suitable palm area should be selected in each of the three provinces to commence with, where the paramount chief would be well disposed to the establishment of a central mill, and that the palm stands should be improved as suggested in the preceding paragraph. When this has been done the establishment of a mill might be considered, but I think it would be imprudent to do so before, as I feel we should only be inviting failure. I suggest this proposal should be put on the agenda of the conference proposed in paragraph 8 for the consideration of the Provincial Commissioners.

12.   It might be of advantage to here consider the relative values of the local oil palms as sources of oil. The Agricultural Chemist has examined fruits of the local varieties and a Nigerian variety under cultivation at Njala and gives the following results:–

Variety of Palm.	Pericarp.	Shell.	Kernels.	Per cent oil in Pericarp.	Per cent oil in whole fruit.
(*a*) Nigerian	71	18.6	10.4	45.9	32.6
(*b*) Togboi	74	24	2	66.5	49.2
(*c*) Henoi	47	36.5	16.5	50.1	23.5
(*d*) Kpolei	58	29	13	38.5	22.3
(*e*) Kawei	20	64.4	15.6	47.5	9.5
(*f*) Jiakeye	22	57	21	39.7	8.8

These figures indicate that, with the exception of the Togboi variety, the Nigerian oil palm is superior as a source of oil; and that the superiority of the Togboi variety, as a source of pericarp oil, is counterbalanced by its low percentage of kernels which is negligible. These results should however not be regarded as conclusive, a further series of tests will be made in due course. It should be borne in mind that the Nigerian fruits examined are from cultivated palms, and the native fruits from uncultivated palms and that the latter might also, under cultivation, show increased yields of the pericarp. On the other hand the Nigerian fruits examined were collected from very young palms and it may be expected that with age the size of the racemes and quality of the fruit may improve. The Togboi variety moreover is comparatively rare and it may be difficult to obtain seed in large quantities for plantation purposes. The varieties are tabulated in order of merit and it will be noticed that the two last in the list, Kawei and Jiakeye, although they yield a fairly high percentage of kernels, contain high percentages of shell and very low percentages of pulp or pericarp. It is desirable therefore that these varieties should be replaced by superior oil-yielding varieties such as *a, b, c,* or *d.*

13.   I would most strongly urge the desirability of concentrating attention on the best palm areas in the Protectorate and of the importance of their improvement and development, as far as possible, on plantation lines, and that such areas should be protected from damage by fires. In my opinion the damage caused by

fires every year in Sierra Leone is very much greater than the damage caused by the tapping of palms for wine. The 'shifting' system of cultivation followed in Sierra Leone is very prejudicial to the oil palm industry. The bush is allowed to grow for three, four, five or six years, according to the area of land available for farming, and is then burnt over. The young palms in that bush had not commenced to bear generally, being overgrown with thick bush, and occasional ones that had commenced to bear, are usually so inaccessible that the heads are not collected. The bush is burnt and the palms are scorched and receive a serious set-back to their growth and development. It is only when the palms get their crowns well above the bush that they commence to bear, so whereas under cultivation palms may commence to bear at four or five years, or even at a younger age, it is often that, under natural conditions, subject to damage from fires, they do not commence to bear until they are six, seven, or in many cases eight years or more old. If the bush in which palms occur is 'brushed' twice say in six or seven years, the palms receive two very serious checks in their growth before they reach the bearing stage, and even palms well above the height of the bush often get a serious scorching at a much later age, which seriously affect their productivity. I think it is very doubtful if, under existing conditions, the crop of palm oil and kernels reaped in Sierra Leone, form one-tenth of what it should be were the palms protected from damage by fires. It is therefore, in my opinion, desirable to concentrate on the best palm areas and improve and develop same on plantation lines, protecting them from damage by fire.

14. It will be of interest here to record certain data respecting the Nigerian oil palms under cultivation at Njala. The fruits referred to in paragraph 12 were collected from five year old palms. The plantation was laid down in 1920 from seedlings raised in 1919. At the end of 1922 the condition of the plantation was as shown below under 'A' and the condition at the end of 1923 was as shown under table 'B.', and at the end of 1924 as shown under table 'C.' Some of the palms commenced to bear at 2 ½ years from date of sowing the seed.

Nigerian Oil palm plot at Njala.

'A.' – 1922.

Area.	Number of Trees	Number Flowering.	Fruiting Number	Number of Heads.	Average Number Heads per Tree.
4.44 ac.	336	91	40	278	6.9

'B.' – 1923.

Area.	Number of Trees	Number Flowering.	Fruiting Number	Number of Heads.	Average Number Heads per Tree.
4.44 ac.	336	89	189	1,779	9.4

'C.' – 1924

Area.	Number of Trees	Number Flowering.	Fruiting Number	Number of Heads.	Average Number Heads per Tree.
4.44 ac.	334	18	292	4,083	13.9 /

It is unfortunate that we have no plantations of native varieties corresponding in age with the Nigerian one so that a comparison could be made. There is little doubt however that the native varieties will, under cultivation, commence to bear as early as the Nigerian variety. The only cultivation the Nigerian plot has had up to date is cutlassing the grass and weeds between the rows and ring-weeding around the palms. Of all the crops under cultivation at Njala, none have created so great an interest with the various chiefs and natives who have visited Njala from all parts of the Protectorate than the Nigerian oil palms. They have

Early yields from Nigerian palms. all expressed amazement to see the palms bearing so young and all have been eager to obtain seed nuts to plant in their chiefdoms. A comparison of this paragraph with the preceding one will, I think, make it quite clear that, under natural conditions obtaining with the oil palm in this country, several years of production are usually lost and that the productivity of palms in later years is seriously affected from time to time through farm or bush fires and general neglect. It will be seen from table 'C' that at the end of five years 292 out of 334 of the Nigerian palms were bearing and that these carried 13.9 racemes per tree, or an average of twelve heads per palm for the whole plantation. It is true that the heads are always small at this age, but they cost little to collect as compared with trees ten years and more in age, which involve climbing.

Plantation area represented by wild palms in Sierra Leone. 15.   The Acting Conservator (Mr. D. G. Thomas) in paragraph 4 of his minute (Appendix D) gives an interesting calculation based on the export of kernels, as to the area the palmeries of Sierra Leone would cover, assuming the production of fruit is equivalent to a plantation output of 3 ½ tons per acre and that the kernels form 15 per cent. of the fruit. He calculates that the area would be 113,419 acres or 177.2 square miles or 0.65 per cent. of the total area of Sierra Leone. Even assuming the production is only half of that estimated it will be seen that the total area of land that should be under oil palms is 1.3 per cent. of the total area of the country, a very small area for the principal and most important industry of the country which forms the principal occupation of the people.

Plantations versus wild palm stands. 16.   It is obvious that some time must elapse before the uncultivated palm groves, growing under natural conditions, could be improved and planted up to approach anything like plantation conditions, even were the owners enthusiastic to do so, and it is further obvious that until the production is brought up to something approaching plantation output, and the acreage is sufficient to supply a mill, the establishment of an extraction plant would not be justified. It should be borne in mind that however efficiently natural palm groves are improved by a process of elimination, of weeding out, replanting and cultivation, such natural palmeries can never approach the productivity of a plantation where the palms have been carefully raised from selected seed of good varieties and have received careful cultivation year after year and been protected from the damaging effect of fires and the palm wine tapper.

Government model oil palm plantation. 17.   It is my opinion, and that of the officers of my department, that oil palm plantations should be encouraged in Sierra Leone and that the government should lead the way by establishing a model plantation, the objects of which would be:–

(*a*) To prove that an oil palm plantation is a paying proposition.

(*b*) To test and prove on a commercial scale the relative values of the different varieties of oil palms.

(*c*) To form an object lesson for the chiefs and natives of Sierra Leone and others who may wish to establish oil palm plantations.

I have already pointed out in paragraph 5 that the exploitation of the wild oil palm constitutes the backbone of the trade of the country. It is obvious that the establishment of oil palm plantations on scientific lines and the provision of mills for the extraction of the oil would so much increase the importance of and stabalize the industry in Sierra Leone that I need put forward no further plea for approval to the establishment of a government plantation.

18.   Early in the present year I instructed the Agricultural Chemist to examine the existing literature and the various and numerous minute papers on this subject and to carry out tests as to the relative values of the indigenous palms and I now attach as appendix 'F' a copy of a memorandum he then submitted entitled 'Oil Palms in Sierra Leone.' This useful memorandum forms a précis of valuable information about the oil palm and its products and gives the results of his analyses of the indigenous varieties, information as to the improvement of wild palm stands, and deals at length with the question of the establishment of oil palm plantations, as well as with trials made with the Culley Depericarper[3] and Nutcracker. /

(margin note: Agricultural Chemist's report on oil palms in Sierra Leone.)

19.   Specimens of the fruits of the indigenous varieties, with the exception of Kpolei which had not then been collected, were submitted to the Director of Kew for determination for the purpose of correlating them with the varieties grown in the Gold Coast and Nigeria. Since Dr. Martin wrote his memorandum, a report from Kew has been received which states that, although the material submitted was scarcely sufficient to admit of accurate determination of the varieties, or to correlate them with varieties from the Gold Coast and Nigeria, it is suggested that they are probably as follows:–

(margin note: Sierra Leone varieties similar to those in other parts of West Africa.)

'Kawei' – *Elacis guineensis* var. *communis*. chev. f. *dura Becc* or the 'hard-shelled nut.'

'Henoi' – *Elacis guineensis* var. *communis*, f. *tenera* 'soft-shelled' or 'thin-shelled variety.'

'Togboi' – *Elacis guineensis* var. *gracilinux,* chev. the 'shell-less' or 'soft-nut.'

'Jiakeye' – *Elacis guineensis* var. *communis*. f. *dura Becc.*

Kawei is therefore the 'hard-shelled' nut similar to the common type in the Gold Coast, Nigeria and other parts of West Africa.

Henoi is the 'soft-shelled' or 'thin-shelled' variety which is similar to Abobo-be in the Gold Coast and is found, although scarce, all along the West Coast. The Imperial Institute reporting on Abobo-be sent from the Gold Coast in 1909 states:–

> '... it is obvious that 'Abobo-be' is superior to all the other Gold Coast varieties with the exception of the seedless kind in yield of palm oil and at the same time gives a high yield of kernels and further the shells being thin the nuts are easier to crack.'

Togboi is the 'shell-less' or 'soft-nut.' This is similar to the 'seedless' variety found in the Gold Coast and at other parts of the West Coast. It is rare.

Jiakeye appears to be the same type as *Kawei,* the 'hard-shelled ' nut.

It will therefore be seen that we have in Sierra Leone types similar to those found in other parts of the West Coast. The 'seedless' variety (*Togboi*), yields the most valuable fruit, followed by the 'thin-shelled' varieties (*Henoi* and *Kpolei*).

'Hard-shelled' or 'Thickshelled' varieties most common in West Africa.

20.   It has been erroneously reported that in Sierra Leone 'only one variety of oil palm occurs and that it is of the ordinary type having thick-shelled nuts. As is generally the case the fruits even on the same tree show considerable variation and different names are given by the natives to the fruits at different stages of growth.' The Director of Kew reports that the greater part of the commercial supplies throughout West Africa are drawn from the fruits of the so-called *forma dura* or 'hard shelled' nut which under var. *communis* may perhaps be regarded as the typical form (Kew Bull. Add. series ix. page 735). The pericarp may vary in thickness and yield of oil; but the nuts usually afford a good supply of kernels.

Suitable varieties to plant confirmed.

21.   I have diverted from paragraph 17 so as to furnish further confirmatory evidence as to the values of the different varieties given in paragraph 12. It is now quite clear that there is no longer any doubt as to the varieties which should be tested commercially on the proposed Government plantation.

Agricultural Chemist's Memorandum.

22.   I would now draw attention to paragraphs 24 – 29 and (Section A) of the Chemist's memorandum (Appendix F). Dr. Martin's original proposal was to plant up vacant areas in forest reserves. The majority of reserves however are situated on very hilly lands and there would be a difficulty in getting continuous areas of any appreciable size, and the hilly nature of the land would render the collection of the fruits and their transport to a central mill difficult and expensive. I am therefore of opinion that Mabang would prove a more suitable locality for the first oil palm plantation; there is ample unoccupied land available there and its proximity to Freetown would facilitate visits being made by interested persons. Moreover I propose that the scheme would be supervised by

an Assistant Conservator of Forests resident at Mabang. Dr. Martin's scheme is that the Government should acquire a long lease of about 20,000 acres of land and to plant up a 1,000 or 2,000 each year. I do not however consider that we should acquire more than 5,000 acres of land and that we should not, in the first instance at least, plant up more than 2,000 acres, which should be ample for demonstration purposes. I visited Mabang with the District Commissioner, Sembehun and Dr. Martin in March last and provisionally selected the land and have since established a nursery of oil palms of the *Henoi* variety there with the approval of the Provincial Commissione. /

23.   The following is a rough estimate of the cost of bringing this plantation into bearing. I have not dealt with the cost of the installation of a mill as this might be done by a private firm under the supervision of and with a working arrangement with this department. There would, I think, be no difficulty in getting a private firm to put up a depericarping plant. However, it might prove advisable for the Government to do so from an experimental point of view, that is however a matter which could be settled later on. {Estimate of cost of plantation.}

ESTIMATE.

	£	£
1926 – Nurseries and clearing and holing 1,000 acres	2,500	
Buildings, tools, etc.	500	
		3,000
1927 – Clearing and holing 1,000 acres and planting 2,000 acres	2,600	
Weeding 1,000 acres	1,000	
Buildings, tools, etc.	400	
		4,000
1928 – Upkeep, plantation and buildings, tools, etc.	2,250	2,250
1929 – Upkeep, plantation and buildings, tools, etc.	2,250	2,250
1930 – Upkeep, plantation and buildings, tools, etc.	2,250	2,250
1931 – Upkeep, plantation and buildings, tools, etc.	2,250	2,250
Total		£16,000

24.   The probable cost per acre to bring this plantation into bearing is about £8 and it is not likely that this will be exceeded, as it is proposed to grow catch crops between the palms for the first few years which it is hoped will reduce the expenditure. Dr. Martin has in Section 'A' of his memorandum (Appendix 'F'), given full details of the probable yields, and estimates that we should, under average conditions, obtain a crop of from £20 to £30 per acre in value, and very much more, should the palms under cultivation here, bear as heavily as they do in Sumatra. {Returns per acre from plantation.}

25.   With regard to the inducements which the Committee consider desirable in order to attract private enterprise to erect mills, as stated in paragraph 16 of the Colonial Office report, and dealt with at some length in the concluding part of the report, I am in general agreement, but I do not think they err on the side {Mill concessions, exclusive transport rights, and contracts}

of liberality. The question of the exclusive right to mechanical transport is an important one. Rapid transport facilities from different centres of the concession to the mill is essential to the success of any such undertaking wherever it may be located. The transport of palm fruits by aerial ropeways may be considered where the lie of the land is appropriate for such a method of transport. The question of contracts with the natives is a matter which I propose to leave to the political officers, I need only observe that it is necessary a mill owner should have a guarantee that he will have the output of the area over which he is granted collecting rights, but I anticipate there will be many objections to contracts with chiefs for the supply of fruit over which the peasant owner has definite rights.

Approval to estab-
lish plantation
sought.
26.   I conclude in recommending most strongly the establishment of a Government oil palm plantation at or near Mabang. I can conceive of no worthier object on which to spend a little of the surplus funds of the Colony, than in the Government itself setting forth to demonstrate what can be done to improve and develop on scientific lines the principal industry of the country, so that it may continue to remain, in spite of menaces from the East, a source of wealth to the natives, the merchants and the Government. I therefore seek His Excellency the Governor's approval and sanction to the expenditure outlined in paragraph 23 of this memorandum.

I have, etc.,

M. T. DAWE,
Commissioner of Lands and Forests. /

Appendix 'A'
CH. 135/8/24.

APPENDIX A

From the Agricultural Chemist,
To the Honourable Commissioner of Lands and Forests.

26th May, 1925.

I have read the documents forwarded with your C.L.F./1286/50/1925 of 20/5/1925 with great interest and I submit herewith my observations.

2.   The view expressed by the Committee, (although not endorsed and in fact disputed by Nigeria) that the oil palm plantations of Sumatra are a serious menace to the West African interest is, in my opinion, sound. Nigeria (*see* para. 6 (iv) of letter of C.S. Nigeria) is apparently under the impression that the expansion

of the areas in British Malaya and Sumatra are rigidly restricted owing to the limited areas of suitable soil. There are however many countries other than those named with suitable climates and I think it has yet to be proved that the oil palm is very restricted in regard to the nature of the soil in which it will thrive. If therefore the Nigerian Government belittle the effect of outside competition on account of lack of suitable soil in tropical countries I think they have but little real basis for their opinion.

3.   It appears to me that the attitude of Nigeria is not so much that the findings of the Committee were wrong, but that the policy of the Nigerian Government would not allow that Government to carry them out, and that as a consequence they are prepared to exploit a certain alternative scheme despite the fact that a similar scheme had already failed in Sierra Leone.

4.   The Committee recognized the great difficulty of collecting oil palm fruits in the bush and the labour involved in its collection, they do not state however that the labour involved in collecting the wild fruits is much greater in the aggregate than the labour required to produce the same amount of fruit on plantation lines, and herein lies the menace of Sumatra to the present unorganised production of palm oil in West Africa.

5.   With regard to methods of improving the natural stands of oil-palms the recommendation in paragraph 8 has already been put forward by me and demonstration centres have been started in the Southern Province. The recommendation in paragraph 9 has already been put forward by you.

6.   The Committee have considered the introduction of machinery and the terms under which private companies might be induced to put up plants on the West Coast. These terms are stated in paragraph 16 and with these I am in agreement so long as it is stated in 16 (*e*) that such conditions only hold while the area is being properly exploited.

7.   It being generally understood that at the present time modern methods of extraction by machinery can only be carried out by European firms at great expense, the obtaining of such supplies of fruit as will keep a factory going becomes the crucial point on which the success of the introduction of such machinery depends. This fruit could be supplied by any of the following methods:–

(*a*)   By a plantation of suitable size under European control.

(*b*)   By an African owned plantation of suitable size.

(*c*)   By fruit being brought in by natives from the surrounding bush provided the bush were sufficiently rich in oil palms.

In my opinion *(b)* may not be looked for for many years and *(c)*did not prove successful in Sierra Leone. The reason for the non-success of *(c)* is, I think that by carrying the fruit to the factory the men are depriving their own women of a job and their own supply of palm oil disappears since it is doubtful if the factory would undertake local retail; *(a)* is then left as the only means by which a factory can be supplied with fruit.

8.   A plantation under European control can be run either –

   (*a*) By the Government as already suggested in my 'Notes on Oil Palms' forwarded with Ch. 83/8/1924 of 28/2/25, /

   (*b*) By a European firm, in which case a long lease of a suitable area of land is indispensable. I should like to see the area that such a firm could acquire increased under suitable terms to 10,000 acres.

9.   In the case of 8 *(a)* above I do not suggest that the Government should run the oil extracting plant but only produce the plantation. Where the plantation is produced the rights of oil extraction from the fruit can be leased at a rate profitable to all parties concerned.

10.   I think that where there is any difficulty or feeling with regard to the land passing into the hands of Europeans the Government as representative of the people should procure (lease or buy) the land and establish plantations with the aid of native labour, European capital only coming in to put up machinery, housing and transport with reference to the extraction plant. In this way the minimum amount of land would be acquired by Europeans. In this connection it may be pointed out that the costs of producing such a plantation is only about one-third the cost of the amount required for the erection of factory, houses, machinery, transport, rent, etc. which would be necessary in connection with a large oil extracting plant.

11.   My opinion therefore is that the Government should encourage to the utmost the establishment of plantations on the lines suggested by the Committee and that greater facilities be given for the establishment of plantations. In the meantime and until such time as European companies come forward to assist Sierra Leone, the Government should start a plantation of its own and on a sufficiently large scale to attract the attention of European firms as soon as the trees come into bearing.

   F. J. MARTIN,
   Agricultural Chemist, Division of Research.

APPENDIX 'B'

No. P.S.N. 39/14/1925.

From Provincial Superintendent of Agriculture, Northern Province, To The Honourable The Commissioner of Lands and Forests.

26th May, 1925.

I have the honour to acknowledge receipt of your letter No. 1286/50/1925 and enclosures of the 20th May, on the question of the best means of increasing and improving the oil palm products of this country.

2.　This question has attracted so much attention recently that any proposals must of necessity be, for the most part, a repetition of what has been suggested already.

3.　If it is true that European owned or leased plantations are for the moment infeasible and undesirable in Sierra Leone, then it would seem that the best results are to be gained by attention to the following among other points.

4.　*Establishment of New Plantations.* – The establishment of new plantations – on approved lines – in suitable areas, where the oil palm is now scarce or non-existent and the planting up of unused ground in the oil palm areas.

　　If fresh areas are to be planted up it is desirable that the native should know which is the best variety to plant.

　　I understand that the Agricultural Chemist is carrying out comparative tests, in this connection.

　　Field tests seem very necessary to provide data on the yields of the oil and kernel per acre as apart from the yield per weight of fruit.

　　Only, selected fruits from the best variety would be used on the proposed plantations. /

5.　*Improvement of existing palm area.* – Much could be done to increase the present yield of oil palm products by the judicious thinning and cleaning of existing blocks of trees. Many blocks are over-grown and the palms are covered with creepers and ferns.

6.　*Experimental and Demonstration Plots.* – It will be difficult to induce the natives to take the steps mentioned in paragraphs 4 and 5, unless we can first show him concrete examples of instances where definite benefits and financial profits have followed the adoption of improved methods of cultivation.

　　This will necessitate the formation of experimental plots at central points under the control of the department of Lands and Forests.

7.   *Introduction of up-to-date machinery.* – The setting up of large mills may not be advisable at the present time, but I believe a wider introduction of small oil extracting and kernel cracking machines would result in a considerable and comparatively rapid increase of output of oil palm products, as the present methods are both wasteful and tedious.

To familiarise the native with the benefits to be obtained by their use, the Government might loan suitable plant to some of the more enterprising chiefs in the oil palm areas.

After due trial many would probably wish to obtain their own mills. The mills might be communal and a small percentage of the value of the produce handled charged, to go towards the cost and upkeep of the machinery.

8.   *Tapping for Palm Wine.* – Great damage is done as a result of this practice. Not only is the tree's vitality greatly impaired by the process, but frequently the incisions made so weaken the trunk that eventually the crown is blown down.

9.   *Education.* – Every opportunity should be taken to impress upon the students in the various schools and colleges the great value of the oil palm industry to the country and how this value may be enhanced by developing and exploiting the industry on more scientific lines. Many of the children now at school will eventually be chiefs and men of position and will consequently have an opportunity of putting what they learned into practice.

Anything which will tend to raise the standard of living will do much to encourage this and other forms of agricultural development.

R. R. GLANVILLE,
Provincial Superintendent.

APPENDIX 'C'

P.S.C.52/28/1915.

FROM PROVINCIAL SUPERINTENDENT OF AGRICULTURE, CENTRAL PPROVINCE, TO THE HONOURABLE THE COMMISSIONER OF LANDS AND FORESTS.

1st June, 1925.
OIL PALM QUESTION IN WEST AFRICA.

I have the honour to acknowledge receipt of your letter No. C.L.F.1286/50/1925 of the 20th ultimo, with attached report and correspondence relative to the above subject.

2.   In the development of this industry I consider that first place should be given to the active propaganda by European officers of this department and by

political officers. Political officers are in a strong position to further the work since they are in close touch with the chiefs, and their words naturally carry more weight than do those of the officers of any other department.

This propaganda should be directed towards explaining to chiefs and their headmen the following points on which a memorandum of instructions might be drawn up (note that only chiefs owning palm oil bush where transport facilities are satisfactory should be dealt with):–

(*a*) To point out to the natives the unsatisfactory condition of their wild oil palms. /

(*b*) How their oil palms can be improved without a great deal of labour by setting aside definite areas of lands bearing oil palms on which farming should be prohibited; by clearing the bush and all other growth from these areas leaving only the palms, and by pruning and cleaning these palms.

(*c*) The rapid strides in production of high grade oil being made by foreign countries particularly in the East.

(*d*) The result of carrying out the improvement in (*b*), namely increased production of fruit of better quality – more kernels and more palm oil at a smaller cost of labour and transport.

(*e*) What will be the effect on the trade of this country and therefore on the welfare of many of its inhabitants if they fail to carry out these improvements.

(*f*) To enlighten them on the poor quality of the pericarp oil as produced by their native methods and the waste of oil involved in the process as compared with the method of extraction by oil-mill machinery. Machines can produce double the quantity of oil of the quality which is desired.

(*g*) The possible effect on the Sierra Leone palm oil trade when Liverpool merchants find they can procure better oil elsewhere, and probably at a lower cost.

3.   In immediate furtherance of the propaganda scheme as above outlined, I would suggest that chiefs be encouraged by provincial officers of this department to set aside a suitable block of palm bush for improvement under the guidance of these officers. In the first place a block of twenty acres in the chiefdom might be selected or alternatively ten acre plots in two or more sections of the chiefdom if the latter plan is more desirable from the labour point of view, and also dependent on the distribution of oil palms in the chiefdom. These palm areas would then be surveyed by the Agricultural or Forestry officer, the bush and grass cleared and the palms thinned out regularly and as nearly as possible to sixty palm trees per acre.

Old and useless palms to cut out. Palms to be pruned and thoroughly cleaned. The bush to be kept cleared and stumping carried out where palms are interfered with. The bare patches them to be planted up with seedlings of proved good varieties. e.g. '*Henoi*,'

The palms on such areas under improvement would require to be taken into the ownership of the chief but the person or persons who formerly had the right to cut fruit from these trees should be in a position to claim some form of compensation from the chief for loss.

4.   In addition to this, chiefs where transport facilities are satisfactory or are likely to become so in the near future should be asked to lay down plantations of oil palms of a good variety. This to be done under the guidance of officers in this department. Plantations of ten to twenty acres might be made in the first place. There should not be much difficulty in getting the chiefs to make plantations. A good number of chiefs I know are keen to do so. Most chiefs who have seen the small plantation of Nigerian palms at Njala have been impressed and several of them have asked for seeds of that variety to plant in their chiefdoms.

5.   Nurseries of a good type of oil palm should be made throughout the country as close as possible to the areas to be improved and to the plantation sites. One nursery at least, should therefore be made in each chiefdom concerned in the scheme otherwise transport of seedlings to the plantation would prove a very big undertaking.

6.   The question of the establishment by the Government of a large plantation, of say, 1000 acres, should be considered. I believe such an undertaking would soon prove of value in the propaganda programme. A small mill could later be put in as an experiment.

7.   The exploitation of this and other West African industries by private enterprise is a subject which has called forth much discussion recently. The Government of Nigeria has stated that the recommendations of the Committee appointed by the Secretary of State are distasteful to that Government insomuch as / they involve the reversal of the policy of the Government in respect of land tenure by natives. It is understood that the same view is taken by this Government. Government should not itself undertake the establishment of oil mills throughout the country since the production of palm oil is such a highly technical business. If however. as the Nigerian Government has suggested, the leading commercial bodies in England who are interested in this trade would associate to establish mills throughout British West Africa in the manner effected by the British Cotton Growing Association in regard to the establishment of cotton ginneries, a big step would be made towards solving the problem. Such an association working with a certain amount of support by Government would, I feel sure, be regarded favourably by the natives and might therefore look forward with some hope of success.

J. D. FISHER.
Provincial Superintendent of Agriculture.
SAIMA,
LAY CHIEFDOM,
KONNO DISTRICT.

APPENDIX 'D'

DIVISION OF FORESTS.
FREETOWN

2nd June, 1925.
OIL PALM QUESTIONS IN WEST AFRICA

SIR,

I have the honour to reply to your letter C.L.F. 1286/58/25, of the 20th instant asking for my considered views on the possibilities of the development of the palm oil and kernel industry in Sierra Leone.

2.   The problem resolves itself into a choice between two policies, that of encouraging individual or communal cultivation and practically excluding the capitalist, or of allowing the latter to assist in the cultivation under safeguards. I will first endeavour to indicate how native cultivation can be developed.

(1) *The Prevention of tapping for wine.* The yield of palm fruit is greatly diminished by the tapping of the trees for palm wine. This occurs mostly in the vicinity of all large towns and generally through the prohibition area of the north. This attack on the oil palm could be reduced by encouraging the formation of plantations of *raphia vinifera* Local laws against tapping the oil palm would then have a chance of being obeyed, and the valuable piassava industry would receive an impetus.

(2) *Tending of palm stands.* By instructive propaganda on the care of young palms some good might be accomplished, but the results of the efforts of several political officers during the past ten years in this direction is disappointing.

It is perhaps unreasonable to expect the native to diligently cut his way through thorns, sword grass and drives of black ants in order to clean and tend young palms, a profusion of which flourish naturally around him.

(3) *Planting by Natives.* This would go much farther towards solving the problem. It is, however, difficult to think of a suitable system that would greatly affect the position. Under the instructions of Government the native chiefs would readily take to planting. For example, nurseries could be started in every chiefdom under the direction of officers of the Provincial Administration and the Division of Agriculture much in the same way as the cocoa industry is being fostered, however, there is a difference in the cash yield per acre between the two crops, cacao being the more valuable and this crop does not call for an expensive installation of machinery to prepare it for market nor a regular daily yield. Again, a native's principal concern in life is his rice crop, and he knows that rice does not thrive on land well stocked with oil palms; the small black roots of this tree form a dense network for several yards around and robs other crops of their food. /

3.   Thus, although the numbers and yield of the oil palm could be increased by the three methods outlined above, I fear that the efforts would be so scattered and spasmodic that only the fringe of the problem would be touched. Again, with the natural increase of population the tendency is to cut down the palms in order to provide more farm land, and in hungry years, which occur in every three or four the cabbage of the young palm is the standby for many months of the year and great destruction is done. In brief, I consider in the present state of advancement the native himself cannot be brought to grapple with this problem within the time available. Sumatra has already a start of fourteen years and it is claimed that in another fourteen years it will exceed the pre-war output of oil from West Africa. Therefore the time factor is all important and it seems clear that the only policy is the formation of oil palm plantations. This solution is now widely accepted by those concerned with the problem whether their interest is commercial, official or academic, but there seems to be much misconception of what the policy means. As is perhaps natural on so wide a subject, many who have given their authoritative opinions appear to be only partly informed, this often leading them to devote much time to attacking bogeys which they have themselves erected or at least pointing out obstacles to the suggested policy which do not exist in this country.

It is possible for Sierra Leone to have its oil plantations on such terms as will satisfy the legitimate requirements of the capitalist, and at the same time, neither alarm nor cause hardship to the native proprietors. If it is made clear to the native that the land for plantation is being leased for only a term of years and if the negotiations are carried out by officers who know the native mind, his habits and customs and is therefore sympathetic, there should not arise any but very minor difficulties of local interest.

4.   A point liable to be overlooked is that only about a tenth or less of the area of the country is cultivated in any one year, the remainder is fallow except for a proportion that may be regarded for present purposes as permanently unproductive. The appositeness of this appears when it is calculated what area of plantations would yield the present output of oil palm products. On account of the large domestic consumption of palm oil (its export is decreasing), it is difficult to arrive at the quantity of this commodity produced, but in the case of kernels, the export figures give a basis for calculation. The year 1923 was a record year and 59,545 tons of kernels were exported form Sierra Leone. At the yield of 3½ tons of fruit per acre (the Sumatra figure is 2 ½ to five tons per acre) and of fifteen per cent. of kernels from the fruit this export total could be produced on a plantation area of 113–419 acres.

= 177.2 square miles.
= Approximate area of Tonkoli Forest Reserve.

= 0.65% of the total area of Sierra Leone.

= A circle with a radius of 7 ½ miles.

= A rental value of £5,671 per annum at 1*s*. per acre. (The value of the 1923 export of kernels was £968,787).

There are as yet no figures to show what yield per acre could be expected in Sierra Leone (it would be interesting to weigh the crop from a well stocked acre of natural palms) but even if the yield were half that indicated above, viz., only 1¾ tons per acre, the area required for plantations would be only 1.3% of the total area of Sierra Leene to yield all the kernels and more than the palm oil exported in 1923. This is a very small proportion of the total area of the country to be devoted to its main source of wealth and it leaves over 90 per cent. of the country under the unfettered control of the native proprietors on which they could be encouraged to copy the methods of cultivation demonstrated on the plantations, and send their quota of fruit to the factories, thus, in the course of time private or communal palmeries would supply the bulk of the fruit.

5.   One of the fears expressed is that the population would be converted from peasant cultivators into wage earners. This danger will not materialise if foreign controlled plantations are limited in total area. It may be observed that there is available now an ever-increasing number of labourers who cannot or who will not cultivate their own farms as long as they can earn daily or monthly wages from a European. Many of these are ex-soldiers who, having lived in barracks for a number of years are disinclined to bury themselves in some remote village. /

There is again the problem of the up-country native who for some criminal offence is sent to gaol for a short term. He may not be of a criminal type, but being disinclined after release to return to farming he takes to casual labour in the trading centres, and is liable to get into bad company and bad ways. It would be very desirable if these two types of potential labour could be retained on the land, and employment under an European is the only thing that will attract them.

6.   Another matter that may be lost sight of is that the native of Sierra Leone has been living on his capital as represented by the one-time virgin and fertile forest tracts. The last of this wealth is in sight and the end is now being seen not only by trained European observers but also by the more intelligent tribal rulers. Therefore if the admirable and proper care of native rights is carried so far beyond what is just and reasonable to all parties, as to make the formation of plantations impossible, it may be found that in a few generations the land of which we are the trustees and which we have guarded with such superlative care will be deserted by our proteges, or they will be existing on it only in the condition of squalor and poverty that can now be observed in certain parts of the country. It will be seen therefore that a little more Government interference is not only justified but is a

matter of duty. It must be recognised that the economic conditions of the people are changing very rapidly and that the spread of popular education is also going to affect their habits and customs, so the vision of a land of prosperous peasant cultivators is liable to remain a vision while the reality will be an awakening and partly educated mass which has been allowed to fritter away its natural heritage in the land and which will be discontented with those who brought it to this condition. It must be remembered also that the price of the oil must fall, for whether the supplies from the British Colonies will be able or not to affect the market in the future it is evident that the other nations are not going to allow their 'estates' to lie fallow. Thus, there will be over-production and the story of the manner in which rubber prices fell from 12*s.* to 6*d.* per lb. will be repeated, and the native producer no longer contributing to the world supplies.

7.   I may not have been expected to touch upon anything controversial, but it was inevitable that I should do so, as no amount of care and skill in execution would make a badly conceived scheme a success. My conclusions are that Government should, with the least possible delay, bring into being 100,000 acres of plantations scattered through the country in blocks of 5,000 – 10,000 acres, not leaving out the middle and upper reaches of the large rivers and the grassfields of the north. Whether this work and cost of formation be best borne by Government, public and private companies, or by an association similar to the British Cotton Growing Association I am not qualified to judge, but it is the immediate duty of Government to appoint a survey party consisting of a political officer and, say a forest officer, both possessing a minimum of five years experience of this country to select sites suitable and obtainable for the formation of oil palm plantations. They should be given precise instructions, especially in the point of reporting on the means by which any villages existing in suggested plantation areas could be moved by negotiation and where in the same neighbourhood the disturbed occupiers would be able to obtain their accustomed livelihood. Particular attention might be directed to be paid to those areas administered as Protectorate but which are really Colony and in which the acquisition of land for plantations might present fewer problems.

8.   I add as a postscript a note on the closely allied subject of domestic food supply.

I have, etc.,
D. G. THOMAS,
Acting Conservator of Forests.
THE HONOURABLE
THE COMMISSIONER OF LANDS AND FORESTS,
SIERRA LEONE. /

P.S. Bound up closely with all development is the increase of domestic food resources. This I know is receiving attention, but, for instance, the survey of swamp areas entrusted to the existing officers of the Agricultural and Forestry Divisions to be undertaken in the course of their other duties will not yield much definite information for years. I would advocate the appointment of a special officer with civil engineering qualifications who would inspect first, all the swamps along the banks of some of the large rivers and who would put up schemes for their reclamation and the control of the water inundating them, and who would be able to carry out such schemes himself. By suitable negotiations the occupiers removed from the oil palm plantations could be brought on to these reclaimed lands. Further, it is my opinion that it would not be undesirable for Government to crop such reclaimed land for a short term of years to pay for cost of reclamation, the produce going to supply public establishments like military and court messenger barracks, gaols and public works such as road and railway building, thus relieving the competition for upland rice.

D.G.T.

APPENDIX 'E'

RESUME OF MESSRS. LEVER BROTHERS ATTEMPT TO ESTABLISH AN OIL EXTRACTING INDUSTRY IN SIERRA LEONE.

In 1912. Messrs, Lever Brothers applied for permission to erect an oil-extracting plant in Sierra Leone and for certain exclusive rights inside a defined area. These exclusive rights included the sole right of putting up extraction plant inside the defined area and the sole right to construct railways and tramways (actually they used a mono-rail) for transporting fruit in that area.

2.   It was decided that no concessions such as those contemplated by Messrs. S. S. 417/1912 Lever Brothers could be granted under the existing ordinances and consequently an ordinance, No. 7 of 1913 'An Ordinance to make provision for the grant of exclusive rights for the erection of mills for the extraction of oil from palm fruit,' was passed. Under this ordinance a concession was granted to Messrs. Lever Brothers, the details of which are set forth in the file SS 417/1912.

3.   The gist of the concession was:–

(*a*)   the grant of a lease of 20 acres of land for 21 years on payment of a rent of £60 a year as a site for erection of factory, etc;

(*b*)   permission to dam a river and construct water works;

(*c*)   such exclusive rights as are mentioned in the Palm Oil Ordinance No. 7 of 1913 in a defined area;

(*d*)   the sum to be spent during the first year to be not less than £15,000.

L. N. 174/1912   4.   After the granting of the concession, Messrs. Lever Brothers transferred their rights to the West African Oils Company, Limited, which was apparently a subsidiary company.

L. M. 385/1912   5.   Permission to proceed with the erection of the necessary plant was accorded on 2nd November, 1912.

L. M. 70/1913 D.   6.   Subsequently in May 1913, permission was granted for the Company to
C. R. 55/1913   lay down a mono-rail subject to the condition that no mono-rail should be laid down on existing paths and roads used by the public except with the permission of the District Commissioner. About ten-and-a-half miles of mono-rail were laid down extending from Yonnibanna to Small Magbassa.

7.   The question then arose as to whether the mono-rail should be allowed to cross the Government Railway, and, under a grant of Easement, this was allowed, subject to gates being erected at the crossings (such gates to be tended by Sierra Leone Railway officials and paid for by the West African Oils Company, Limited), and to the Sierra Leone Government Railway having precedence on all occasions. /

D. C./R.55/1913   8.   Permission was granted in October 1913 for the West African Oils Company, Limited, to erect factories and trading stations at such points where their mono-rail touched or passed near towns.

R.8./1913   9.   A private siding was built for the Company at Yonnibannah and the Company was charged £60 a year rent.

S. S. 66/1914   10.   The West African Oils Company, Limited, apparently had all their arrangements to start work complete by the early part of 1914, and the then Governor (Sir E. M. Merewether) inspected the factory in March, 1914. From his report it appears that the buildings consisted of:–

     Three large sheds, one as store for palm kernels, one for plant, one as store for palm fruit; two bungalows for staff; one office.

11.   The West African Oils Company, Limited had not started work then as they had a difficulty in obtaining fruit. The local chiefs wanted £3 a ton and the firm were only willing to offer 30/- a ton.

12.   The difficulty of obtaining sufficient fruit supplies was attributed by the District Commissioner, Ronietta, to two causes:–

     (*a*) antagonistic attitude of small traders (who also persuaded the native against supplying the Company);

     (*b*) the natives were doubtful of the pecuniary advantage of disposing of their fruit in the raw state.

13.   The chiefs ultimately accepted 30/- a ton for fruit at Yonnibanna, deductions being made for fruit delivered on the mono-rail, according to the distance from the factory. For instance, fruit was 11*d*. a bushel at Yonnibanna and 8*d*. at Small Magbassa, 10 ½ miles distant. The records do not say if the 'bushel' refers to 'fruits' or 'heads,' but in view of the subsequent prices paid 'per head,' the bushel obviously refers in this case to 'fruit.' It would be pretty well impossible to measure mature heads satisfactorily by a bushel measure. The prices at Yonnibanna were 11*d*. bushel and 30/- a ton, so that 30/- could either be paid for 1 ton of fruit or 32 ¾ bushels. From this, it can be assumed that in Messrs. Levers' estimation, 32 ¾ bushels weighed 1 ton and that a bushel of ripe palm fruit weighs between 68 and 69 lbs. This obviously varies with the state of ripeness of the fruit and has not been checked.

14.   The Company were unable to obtain sufficient fruit and the following year D.C./R.19/1915 the Manager suggested and put into practise with the consent of the Government the following method of collection. The firm employed labourers to cut and collect the fruit paying as follows:–

⅕*d*. to the labourers per 15 heads delivered on mono-rail and 3*d*. per 15 heads to the owners of the bush through headmen.

15.   This works out at just under 1 ½*d*. a head, of which the owner of the oil palms gets 1/5th of a penny.

16.   In December, 1915, Messrs. Lever Brothers announced their decision to close down. There is no doubt that this decision was arrived at through failure to obtain sufficient fruit at a reasonable price, i.e. 30/- a ton or 1 ½*d*. a head. The District Commissioner Ronietta, suggests that one of the causes of this failure is the disinclination of the natives to carry palms heads long distances.

ADDENDUM.

17.   In 1919 a further application for a concession under Ordinance No. 7 of S. S. 92/1919 1913 was made.

18.   In connection with this Governor Wilkinson suggested that grants of monopoly were unnecessary as areas available were plenty (22nd April, 1919).

19.   Lord Milner's decision 30th July, 1919 '...... it is not desirable to grant any more exclusive rights for the erection of depericarping machinery in that Colony (Sierra Leone).' /

APPENDIX 'F'

FROM THE AGRICULTURAL CHEMIST, TO THE HONOURABLE COMMISSIONER OF LANDS AND FORESTS.

1st March, 1925
OIL PALMS IN SIERRA LEONE.

The fruits of the oil palms, *Elaeis guineensis,* have been used from time immemorial for the extraction of oil, and all along the West Coast of Africa the industry is pursued with more or less intensity depending upon other agricultural attractions. The methods employed in the extraction of the oil are crude and wasteful and result either in a poor quality of oil or a low percentage extraction. Of recent years there has been an ever increasing demand for palm oil and palm-kernel oil and improved methods involving the use of machinery have been invented to increase the yield and improve the quality of produce from oil palm fruit. Simultaneously with the demand for palm oil there have been investigations into the position and possibilities of the oil palm areas in West Africa with a view to increasing out-put. Unfortunately for the ease and security of West Africa the cultivation of oil palms has now started in Sumatra and the East Indies. These palms are cultivated on plantation lines and naturally give a better economic return than the wild products of the West Coast. What therefore was a comfortable life for oil-producing colonies may shortly become a struggle for existence.

2.   These facts have not escaped the attention of various governments in the past and conferences innumerable have been held to grapple with this question.

3.   In 1887 the Gold Coast Commission appointed to consider the promotion of economic agriculture in the Gold Coast reported as follows:–

> '... The tree prefers a moist soil, flourishing in the warm, damp valleys, where it grows in extensive forests. It has never been made the object of systematic cultivation, but, as far as can be ascertained, it begins to bear in its fourth or fifth year, increasing till its fifteenth, and continues to bear at least sixty years. It produces from four to seven bunches of 'nuts every year. At the 'fatness' of the nuts (i.e. the amount of oil contained in the fibre) differs greatly accordingly to soil, the quantity of oil varies from three gallons per year in a moist soil to one gallon in dry. These nuts have a fibrous covering which contains the famous palm oil. Three varieties of the tree are distinguished, having orange, red, and black nuts respectively, the first giving the finest oil but small kernels, the others less oil but larger nuts.'

4.   In 1982 an Anglo-French Boundary Commission was appointed and to this Commission a botanist and a geologist were attached. The Colonial Office

issued a report of the botany and geology of the district of Sierra Leone traversed and from that report the following information was extracted (K.B. 1893 p. 168).

'The export of palm oil and kernels forms by far the largest part of the West African Export trade. The following figures are given by the *Sierra Leone Gazette*:–

–	1888	1889	1890
	£	£	£
Palm oil	12,285	11,379	13,599
Palm kernels	97,177	105,963	107,827

The tree is more abundant further down the West African coast, and appears to prefer alluvial, often marshy ground near the sea. It particularly seems to thrive on the rich soil of the mangrove accumulations. There are large numbers of these trees in the Mahela district, where a factory once existed, and there are also a considerable number up the Scarcies river, and in the lower part of the Limba district. It grows also on low sand-stone or gneissose hills, but probably does not produce so much in such places as on the low lying rich alluvials. The palm is propagated from the off-shoots that appear at its base, and these are said to begin to bear in the second or fifth year, and are in full bearing about the tenth to fifteenth year; they continue producing for sixty years. A single tree / yields from one to three gallons of palm oil. This would be a profit of from 2*s*. to 6*s*. a tree per annum. The palms require no care, and are not, apparently, attacked by any injurious insects. The preparation of the oil is of a very rough and makeshift character: the fruits are thrown into a tank and left till decomposition begins; they are then boiled, and afterwards pounded in a mortar. Probably twenty-five per cent. of the oil is lost in preparation.'

5. The report of the botanist seems to be a little inaccurate as to the method of propagation of the oil palm and equally so in supposing that only 25 per cent. of the oil is lost in preparation.

6. It is only comparatively recently that more than one variety of oil palm has been recognised in Sierra Leone for as recently as 1909, in a despatch of the Acting Governor to the Secretary of State the following paragraph occurs:–

'The Agricultural Superintendent reports as follows:– 'So far as I am aware the oil palm as it occurs in this Colony cannot be divided into distinct varieties.' This statement is supported by Dr. Maxwell, the District Commissioner of the Railway District, who states that there may be differences in the thickness of the shell, but in no case has he seen what would be considered as a thin-shelled kernel.'

VARIETIES OF OIL PALMS IN SIERRA LEONE.

7.   Five different kinds of oil palms have been recognized in Sierra Leone and these with their various characteristics are shown in the following table:–

Local Name.	Size of Fruit.	Pericarp.	Shell.	Kernel.
Kawei	Large	Thin	Thick	Large
Henoi	Medium	Medium	Rather thinner than medium	Medium
Jiakeye	Large	Thin	Medium	Rather larger than medium
Kpolei	Large	Thick	Rather thinner than medium	Rather larger than medium
Togboi	Small	Thick	Soft and thin	Small, negligible

8.   These fruits have been sent to Kew for identification and they have also been examined here in the laboratory. The report from Kew has not yet been received but the results of analysis which are exceedingly interesting are given below:–

Local Name.	Amount Pulp per cent.	Amount Nuts per cent.	Per cent. Oil in Pericap.	Per cent. Kernels in Nuts.	Per cent. Oil* in Fruit.	Per cent. Kernels in Fruits.
Kawei	20	80	47.5	19.4	9.5	15.6
Henoi	47	53	50.1	31.0	23.5	16.5
Jiakeye	22	78	39.7	27.0	8.8	21.0
Kpolei	58	42	38.5	31.0	22.3	13.0
Togboi	74	26	66.5	8.5	49.2	2.0

*   Indicates pericarp oil.

9.   A glance at the table shows at once the great difference in value between the various types of fruits – Kawei and Jiakeye are obviously inferior to the others, Togboi is obviously the best and Henoi and Kpolei are very similar.

10.   Unfortunately we do not know the yield per acre of these varieties but we do know that whereas Kpolei and Togboi are very rare, Henoi is quite well known and is found growing well in some parts of the Protectorate. There has been some doubt expressed as to whether Togboi will germinate successfully but until this has been definitely tried it would be unwise to assume that because the kernel is small it is infertile. /

11.   A variety of oil palm (name unknown) was imported from Nigeria and sown at Njala; this is doing well and information as to the yield and composition of the fruit will be forthcoming by the end of the season.

12.   The question as to what is the best variety to grow is still not definitely settled, but we do know this – Henoi is a good type of palm, it contains 23.5 per cent. pericarp oil and 16.5 per cent. Kernels, also it grows well in Sierra Leone and seed is easy to obtain. This is therefore a sound variety to propagate. Togboi and Kpolei are also good types but for the next few years it will probably be impossible to obtain a large amount of seed of these varieties.

13.   A further point must be borne in mind with regard to the composition of the fruits examined – these fruits were all from wild palms found in the bush; it is highly probable that if grown under plantation conditions the yield of pericarp oil and kernels from the varieties examined would be higher than is the case when grown under bush conditions.

DEVELOPMENT OF THE OIL PALM INDUSTRY IN SIERRA LEONE.

14.   The two chief products of the oil palms are pericarp oil and kernel oil. Pericarp oil is prepared by the natives on the spot and the kernels are sent to Europe and the oil is there expressed. It is therefore obvious that the value of the oil palm depends on the value of the oil plus the value of the kernels after taking into consideration the labour involved in obtaining each of these products.

15.   The analyses of the five varieties of oil palm show that Togboi is the most valuable and that Henoi and Kpolei are also very good types, so that in any schemes for the increase of oil palm products in Sierra Leone these varieties may be taken as suitable for propagation.

16.   At the present time the oil palms are usually found in the bush surrounded by undergrowth, the stems covered with parasitic growths and the oil palms frequently overcrowded. No cultivation of the oil palm has yet been attempted either in the form of establishing plantations or cultivating wild palm stands.

INCREASING THE OUTPUT OF OIL PALM PRODUCTS.

17.   In the past, reports on the oil palm industry in Sierra Leone indicate reserves of oil palm areas not yet utilised on account of insufficient population (K.B. 1909 p. 169 – report of Acting Governor of Sierra Leone) and although it is quite probable that much material is wasted this may be due not so much to the sparse population as to the difficulty of collection. To collect the fruit it is often necessary to hack a way through the undergrowth for some distance, climb very high palms to cut the fruits and subsequently transport the heavy bunches to a village centre where the oil is extracted from the pericarp. Also palm trees struggling for existence against the undergrowth with their stems often covered with parasitic growths give a small yield as compared to palms grown on plantation lines and this means that many trees have to be climbed to collect enough fruit for oil extraction: often the amount of fruit on a tree is so small that it is not collected.

18.   There are several methods of increasing the output of oil palm products:–

   (1) By laying out new plantations.
   (2) By planting wherever possible the variety of palm which gives the best return in pericarp oil and kernels.
   (3) By bringing the wild palm forests under cultivation.

The Cultivation of Wild Palm Stands.

19.   A lot of work has been done and recorded showing the possibilities of wild stands of palms under cultivation. At Peki Blengo in the Gold Coast (B.I.I. 1920, XVIII, 213) an area of five acres of a palm forest was cleared by cutlassing, there was no soil cultivation, but the stems of the trees were 'dressed', 398 trees were left standing for the first year and thinning was carried on from year to year with the results given below:–

> 1915 – 398 trees gave 171 bunches weighing 3,222 lb.
> 1916 – 357 trees gave 222 bunches weighing 4,355 lb.
> 1917 – 327 trees gave 534 bunches weighing 12,639 lb.
> 1918 – 281 trees gave 629 bunches weighing 17,790 lb. /

20.   The above figures show an increase in yield of nearly 500 per cent, in four years, by just cutlassing the undergrowth, thinning out and dressing the trees.

21.   Other experiments at Bingerville, Ivory Coast (B.I.I. 1922, XX, 229) were started in 1918, and in 1922 had already shown the good effect of clearing the ground and thinning and pruning the trees. As a result of these operations at Bingerville the 1923 records (B.I.I. 1924, XXII, 74) show that the average weight of palms heads was over 11 kilos (25lb, nearly) and the produce of 40 hectares was 93 tons of fruit (nearly a ton an acre) and a heavier yield is anticipated for 1924.

22.   The following methods were therefore suggested for increasing the output of oil palm products:–

(1) Demonstration plots to be established in the palm oil areas, these plots to be cleared of undergrowth, thinned and the trees dressed.

(2) As soon as the beneficial results of these operations are obvious the chiefs in the surrounding districts should be encouraged to carry out these operations in their own villages and each village might be required to clear an area corresponding to the size of the village, for example at the rate of ten palms for each male adult, the palms to be thinned leaving 60 to 90 trees an acre.

(3) The establishment of nurseries for the distribution of seedlings at the rate of two seedlings for each acre of cleared palm forest, that is, enough to renew a plantation once in every 30 years.

(4) Simultaneously with the above, experiments will be carried out to determine if there is a more suitable type than Henoi, Kpolei or Togboi but until such variety is found these types should be planted.

23.   A number of these demonstration plots have already been started (*see* Section A for instructions) and if they are successful, and there is no reason to

suppose they will not, it will perhaps be possible to induce every chief and sub-sequently every village in the oil palm areas to cultivate the natural stands of oil palms in the manner described, thereby greatly increasing the amount of oil palm products and at the same time reducing the labour required to obtain them.

THE ESTABLISHING OF OIL PALM PLANTATIONS.

24.   However attractive the cultivation of wild palm stands may be it lacks one feature essential to the economic treatment of the fruit. In order to make the most of the fruit it is necessary that up-to-date methods of oil-extraction and nut cracking be used and this is not very possible where the oil palm plots are scattered over the whole of the country as they will be in the case of cultivated wild palm stands, so that while the cultivation of natural stands should materially increase production there is another method, namely, the establishment of oil palm plantations on a large scale which should give an even better return for the labour involved.

25.   For some unknown reason everybody has shied at the idea of laying down oil palm plantations in Sierra Leone. This I think is due to the fact that the palm is actually in the bush and the fruit has only to be collected. This is true, but the labour of collecting the fruit and bringing it into a centre for disposal is greater than that involved in the running of a plantation and it is for this reason and this reason alone that the Sumatra plantation may become a deadly menace to our palm oil trade.

26.   Oil palm plantations must be established. There is plenty of land in the Protectorate suitable for this project which is at present under low bush. The elimination of the low bush and the laying down of plantations and the cleaning up of the land during this process should go far to eliminating the tsetse-fly in such areas. The Conservator of Forests is of the opinion that oil palm plantations would have a more beneficial climatic effect than would 'deserted farm areas' and 'low bush' areas that it is proposed to replace; therefore the interests of humanity and animal life would be served by such plantations.

27.   With respect to the variety to be planted, recent investigation has shown that Henoi which grows well in this country is a very good type while Togboi if it can be successfuly germinated is a fruit even more valuable. There is no need therefore to delay on the score of unsuitable varieties. /

28.   Section A shows a scheme for the establishment of oil palm plantations by the government. The scheme shows the probable cost of planting 1,000 acres a year and their probable value when they come into bearing. The collection of the fruit and the cost of running an oil-extraction plant are not considered as it is

thought that the running of the plant could be best undertaken by a private firm and the collection of fruit and the keeping clean of the plantations when they come into bearing could best be done by settling native families on small (say 10 acre) blocks of plantation. A somewhat similar scheme with cotton is now being run by the Sudan Government in the Blue Nile Province, Sudan, to the mutual benefit of the Government (who supply the water) the Sudan Plantations Syndicate (who collect and gin the cotton, and supervise the crop), and the native cultivators (who grow the cotton).

29.   Owing to the existing laws of Sierra Leone which prevent private individuals from easily acquiring large areas of land in the Protectorate (5,000 acres is only a comparatively small plot of land) it is up to the Government to acquire the land either on long lease or purchase, and initiate and control the oil palm enterprise. As soon as we have one to two thousand acres of bearing plantations and more coming on we shall have no difficulty in disposing at a profitable rate of the rights of oil extraction in such areas. Furthermore the settling of natives on government land will be a guarantee of security for the results of their labours.

INTRODUCTION OF OIL PALM MACHINERY.

30.   The introduction of machinery into the oil palm industry as a means of increasing production has not been overlooked. Two kinds of plant are available, one the big plant housed in a factory and dealing with immense quantities of fruit and the other the hand plant, portable, but only capable of dealing with small quantities of fruit. The principle is the same in both cases: first, the removal of the pericarp and the subsequent expression (or centrifuging out) of the oil, and secondly, the drying and cracking of the nuts. With regard to the large size plants these can only be run by experienced men and require large quantities of fruit, say 3,000 tons a year, to run them profitably. Such an amount of fruit is at present not easy to collect in Sierra Leone, where communication and transport are often very difficult. Where palms are not cultivated, the distance from which the fruit has to be brought and the high cost of transport renders big plants a questionable proposition. Under plantation cultivation however 2,000 acres should produce sufficient fruit and consequently if the extraction plant were in the centre of a plantation block, not more than a mile from any part need be traversed in order to reach the factory. A dissertation on the economic aspect of large plants is given by Barnes in a special Bulletin of the Agricultural Department, Nigeria 1924, entitled 'Chemical Investigations into the products of the oil palm' (page 61).

31.   Hand power plants are not yet in use in Sierra Leone, but recently, Messrs Culleys Expressor's Coy, have presented us with a complete expression plant including a nut cracker. This plant has been tested and found to work fairly satis-

factorily although perhaps it does not do all that Messrs. Culley's claim for it. A European with some knowledge of mechanics would probably work it successfully but it is doubtful if it could be recommended for native cultivators. This refers to the depericarper and a description of preliminary tests with this machine will be found in Section C. The nut cracker produced by the same firm is however a somewhat different proposition, it is easy to work and works very well and is recommended for use in the Protectorate: an account of tests with this machine will be found in Section D. If this or any other suitable nut cracking machine becomes popular in the Protectorate, the increase in palm kernel exports should be considerable. Steps are being taken to popularise nut cracking machinery.

SUMMARY.

32.   There are five known varieties of oil palms in Sierra Leone; they are Kawei, Henoi, Jiakeye, Kpolei and Togboi.

33.   These varieties have been analysed and from their percentage composition are arranged in the following order for value of fruit – Togboi, Henoi, Kpolei, Jiakeye and Kawei. Kawei is the common type and Henoi is found fairly frequently. The other types are rare.

34.   Two methods of increasing the output of oil palm products are suggested:–

   (1) The cultivation of wild palm stands.
   (2) The laying down of oil palm plantations.

The second method is likely to give the better return. /

35.   The introduction of oil palm machinery has been considered. The value of big plants until plantations have been established is problematical: small hand plants probably require the supervision of men more used to machinery than are likely to be found in the Protectorate. The small nut cracking machine made by Messrs. Culley is regarded as fairly successful.

SECTION A.

ESTABLISHMENT OF OIL-PALM PLANTATIONS.

36.   *Suitable Areas.* – Probably any district in which oil palms grow would be suitable provided that such areas were not poor as regards soil or swampy during the rainy season. The areas that it is proposed to utilise are 'low bush' and 'abandoned farm' areas. Such areas exist in some of the forests reserves but are small and not continuous probably not more than 1,000 to 2,000 acres being available in any one spot. A more suitable and much larger area is said to exist at Mabang. As

Mabang is within easy reach of Freetown and near the headquarters of the Conservator of Forests, this locality would probably meet our requirements. It has two advantages, one, as a demonstration plantation being easily accessible by the railway, and the other, it is under the direct supervision of the Conservator of Forests.

37.   *Varieties to Plant.* – For the greater part of the area, Henoi should be planted, This is a good type of oil palm and grows well in this country. Small blocks of Kpolei and Togboi should also be planted as these are valuable types although the seed is difficult to obtain: we should then be able to compare yields of these varieties under plantation conditions.

38.   Proposed Plantations. – The present proposal is to plant 1,000 acres a year (or 2,000 if possible) in the Mabang area. This will involve:–

   1.   The establishing of a nursery or nurseries capable of turning out 100,000 seedlings a year for each 1,000 acres to be planted. The area of the nursery should be about eight acres and it is proposed to grow the palms in the nursery until they are eighteen months to two years old. This decreases the cost of plantation and gives the young palms a better chance of survival on transplanting than would be the case if they were planted out at one year old. They will be germinated in beds and then planted out in the main nursery in rows 3' x 1' apart, where they will remain until about two years old. The present staff of the Forestry Department is able to cope with this work, and the nursery should be started at once.

   2.   The brushing and planting of 1,000 acres of land in 1927 (if the nurseries are started forthwith) and subsequent years. The cost of such brushing is estimated at from £2 to £2 10*s*. an acre, the former being the estimate of the Director of Agriculture and the latter that of the Conservator of Forests. The sum of £2,000 to £2,500 would have to be budgeted for in 1927 for this purpose. In subsequent years £1 an acre, or £1,000 a year. would have to be allowed for keeping the land clean. As the oil palm starts to bear at five[1] years and the young plants are one to two years old when transplanted they will be three to four years in the the plantation before they start to bear, so that the total cost of cleaning before the oil palms come into bearing is about £3 to £4; the total cost of nursery, planting, clearing and annual cleaning should amount to about £6 to £7 an acre by the end of five years when the palms come into bearing. As the plantation grows older the cost of annual clearing becomes less.

39.   *Yield of Fruit.* The yields of fruit given in Sumatra are:–

5th to 8th year	96 lb. a tree
10th to 15th year	209 lb. a tree
20th to 22nd year	132 lb. a tree

40. Assuming a price of £40 per ton for palm oil and £25 a ton for kernels, the return per acre in Sumatra is estimated at £26 10s. in the fifth year and £39 when in full bearing. /

41. For Sierra Leone, suppose we calculate on the basis of sixty trees an acre, we get the following yields:–

5th to 8th years	2 ½ tons per acre
10th to 15th years	5 tons per acre
20th to 22nd years	3 ½ tons per acre

and taking the analysis given for Henoi on page 48 and assuming an 80 per cent. extraction under up-to-date methods for pericarp oil and 90 per cent. for kernels recovered we get the following figures per acre the value of pericarp oil being taken as £40 a ton and kernels as £21 a ton:–

Year.	Palm Oil.	Palm Kernels.	Total Value.
	£	£	£
5th to 8th	18	8	26
10th to 15th	36	16	52
20th to 26th	26	11	37

42. This is a very high value for the annual produce and perhaps the yields given above are too high to be expected in Sierra Leone, at half the above yields the crop would still be valuable.

43. At Peki in the Eastern Province of the Gold Coast a yield of 2 ½ tons an acre was recorded on plot 1, and 1 ½ tons an acre on plot 2, in 1923 – 1924 (Report on the Agricultural Department of the Gold Coast April 1923 – 1924). This is not much to go on but it shows that 2 ½ tons an acre can be produced on the West Coast. Other trustworthy details of oil palm crops have not yet been found.

44. The records this year at Njala should materially assist us in forming an opinion of the probable yield of fruit in young plantations, and although no figures have yet been received the crop is reported to be a heavy one.

45. *Probable value of the crop.* From the figures given above we could I think reckon on a crop of from £20 to £30 an acre in value, and if oil palms under plantation conditions here, bear as heavily as they do in Sumatra then this figure should be considerably increased.

46. In any case if for an outlay of about £7 we can get an acre of plantation yielding £20 worth of products annually, these plantations should be established forthwith.

SECTION B.

REPORT ON TRIALS CARRIED OUT WITH CULLEY'S DEPERICARPER AND OIL EXPRESSING MACHINES.

47.   The palm fruit used in these trials was chiefly Kawei although a certain amount of Henoi was also used.

PREPARATION OF THE FRUIT FOR DEPERICARPER.

48.   A great amount of difficulty was experienced in getting the pericarp into a soft state suitable for the depericarper. The method suggested by Messrs. Culley of standing tins containing the fruit in boiling water for an hour was found unsuitable as even after two hours standing the fruit was not hot and consequently not soft. The fruit thus treated when put through the machine came through with most of the pericarp still adhering to the nuts. /

49.   The fruit was then placed in a native basket and dipped in boiling water for fifteen minutes; this treatment introduced a small amount of water but softened the pericarp to such an extent that most of the pericarp was removed.

50.   The details of this trial were as follows:–

Weight of fruits taken	90 lb.
Weight of nuts after depericarping	71 ½ lb.
Weight of pericarp removed	18 ½ lb.
Percentage of pericarp removed	20%

51.   The amount of pericarp removed was greater than that recovered; about four to five pounds being lost either in the interior of the machine or clinging round the drum of the depericarper. The amount of pericarp was insufficient for the oil press to be used efficiently and only about 2 lb. of oil were recovered.

52.   A further trial was made and in this case the fruit was placed in a petrol tin and a little oil and water placed in the tin which was then covered and stood on a fire. This treatment was about as effective as placing the fruit in a basket in boiling water and also introduces a small amount of water.

53.   The details of the experiment were as follows:–

Weight of fruit taken	75 lb.
Weight of nuts after depericarping	54 ½ lb.
Weight of pericarp removed	20 ½ lb.
Weight of pericarp recovered	16 ½ lb.
Weight of pericarp lost in the machine	4 lb.
Percentage of pericarp removed	22 per cent.

54.   With the aid of a block of wood as a filler it was possible to use the oil-press and the results obtained were as follows:–

| Weight of pericarp taken | 16 ½ lb. |
| Weight of oil recovered | 8 ½ lb. |

55.   This is a very high percentage of oil (just over 50) to be recovered from the pericarp but in this respect it must be remembered that the fruit had been some time in transit and the pulp was in a very dry condition previous to the start of the experiment the proportion of oil to pericarp being higher than in the normal moist state. For this reason the free fatty acids of the oil were not determined as these were probably very high in the fruit as received.

REMARKS ON THE WORKING OF THE MACHINE.

56.   The depericarper has one great disadvantage, and that is, the toothed drum must be constantly cleaned if all the pericarp is to be removed from the nuts; this is necessary for about every 100 lb. of fruit. Up to the present we have had no break ages but whereas it would not be difficult for a European to replace broken parts I do not think that even the educated native would do it since the educational system in vogue in this Colony runs rather to the teaching of the classics and the scriptures than the mechanical sciences and ideas relating to mechanical contrivances are therefore not inculcated in the native mind.

57.   The oil-press works very well and is simple in construction and manipulation.

SECTION C.

REPORT ON A TRIAL WITH CULLEY'S NUT CRACKING MACHINE CARRIED OUT ON 11TH FEBRUARY, 1925.

58.   One thousand nuts of the type known as Kawei were counted out and used for this trial. These nuts were very large with exceedingly thick shells, providing a test of great severity. /

59.   The whole of the nuts were fed into the machine in just over 2 ½ minutes, the machine being worked by the mechanic attached to this department. During this short time, he had to change feet once on account of the hard work involved.

60.   Of 1,000 nuts 876 were cracked by one passage through the machine (i.e. there were 12.4 per cent. uncracked). On passing these 124 through the machine 108 were cracked (i.e. there were 13 per cent. uncracked). From the whole 1,000

nuts only 9 kernels were broken, or less than 1 per cent., and of these about half had the appearance of being previously defective.

61.   The weight of the nuts was 18 ¾ lb., the weight of the whole kernels 3 ½ lb., and the weight of the broken shells 15 lb. This left ¼ lb. for the broken kernels and unrecovered broken shells.

62.   The percentage of kernels recovered to nuts was 18.7 per cent., and this may be compared with 19.4 per cent. which was the amount obtained by cracking an entirely different sample of Kawei nuts in the laboratory.

F. J. MARTIN,
Agricultural Chemist, Division of Research.

West Africa. Palm Oil and Palm Kernels. Report of a Committee Appointed by the Secretary of State for the Colonies, September, 1923, to Consider the Best Means of Securing Improved and Increased Production (London: HMSO, 1925).

WEST AFRICA.
PALM OIL AND PALM KERNELS.

Report of a Committee appointed by the Secretary of State for the Colonies, September, 1923, to consider the best means of securing improved and increased production.

To the Right Honourable J. H. THOMAS, M.P.,[1]
His Majesty's Secretary of State for the Colonies.

SIR,

1.   In September, 1923, your predecessor, the Duke of Devonshire, approved the appointment of a Committee to consider the best means of securing improved and increased production of palm oil and palm kernels in West Africa by better methods of cultivation and preparation. The inquiry was made at the request of the Joint West African Committee of the Liverpool, London, and Manchester Chambers of Commerce[....]

2.   The merchants and others interested in the British West African Colonies, who suggested this inquiry, had in view the admittedly wasteful collection and non-collection of oil palm fruits in those Colonies, the laborious native methods of manufacturing palm oil and palm kernels and the rapid progress being made on the oil palm plantations in Sumatra, Malaya, etc. In the course of their experience they have seen the development during the past 30 years of the rubber plantations of the East, and during the course of such development have seen the forest rubber industry of West Africa / practically eliminated as a factor in the world rubber market. In the 10 years ending 1900 rubber from the West Afri-

can Colonies represented an important share of the world's rubber production. To-day to all intents and purposes there is no forest rubber produced in British West African Colonies. This has resulted from the competition of rubber plantations in other parts of the world, and it is thought that, unless steps can be taken to introduce up-to-date methods of cultivation, transport and manufacture, the palm oil and kernel industry in the British West African Colonies may in course of time suffer in the same way as the West African rubber industry.

3. In view of the evidence taken before previous committees bearing on the oil palm industry in British West Africa, particularly before the West Africa Lands Committee in 1912–13 and the Edible Nuts Committee, 1915–16,* the detailed memoranda as to recent developments already in existence and the particular information possessed by some of its members, the Committee did not consider it necessary to call witnesses and take oral evidence. It first considered the latest available reports as to the cultivation and working of the oil palm plantations in Sumatra and elsewhere. The first commercial exploitation of the oil palm in East Sumatra was started in 1911, and in four years 6,500 acres had been planted. The war intervening, planting ceased, so that by 1st January, 1917, only 6,500 acres were under cultivation, but from that time onwards there has been a steady development, and the acres planted on the East Coast of Sumatra alone are as follows:–

1st January, 1917	6,500 acres.
1st January, 1918	8,500 acres.
1st January, 1920	17,100 acres.
1st January, 1922	28,000 acres.
1st January, 1923	30,000 acres.

There are also a few plantations in the Malay States and Cochin China which scarcely exceed 5,000 acres in all. The plantations in the East may, therefore, be calculated to embrace between 35,000 and 40,000 acres, which, according to the official publication of the Sumatra planters, will be increased to 100,000 acres in the next ten years, and it has been publicly claimed that within 15 years the East Coast of Sumatra will export more palm oil than West Africa's prewar record output.

4. The oil palm industry in the Dutch East Indies has the great advantage of the extremely well planned and carefully organised association of planters known as the Algemeene Vereeniging van Rubber-planters ter Oostkust van Sumatra (usually referred to as the A.V.R.O.S.) with which are associated gentlemen of high scientific attainments. Every stage of the planter's art receives the most minute investigation and research. From time to time the results achieved in the labora-

---

* Cd. 8248.

tories and experimental fields of the A.V.R.O.S. are published, and the planters are thereby kept in the closest touch with every stage of discovery and development concerning the planting and cultivation of palm trees, and the methods of producing palm oil and kernels. /

5.   No less than 62 estates situated in Java and Sumatra are reported as having started plantations of oil palms. The production of oil in 1922 in these districts amounted to 3,800 tons, and this will be largely exceeded during 1923; it is confidently expected to reach a figure of 20,000 tons in 1930. Moreover, it is stated that this oil can be put upon the European markets at a substantially lower price than West African oils. The development of this new industry which has been started upon scientific plantation lines, with an available and good supply of trained indentured labour, whilst the fruit is treated by modern mechanical processes, is clearly a serious danger to the long-established palm oil and kernel trade of West Africa.

6.   The Committee considered the steps which are being taken elsewhere in West Africa to meet this threatened competition. In the volume *Memoires et Rapports sur les Matieres Grasses*, Tome II, issued by the Institut Colonial de Marseille in 1922, there is a very full and interesting account of the position in French West Africa. It appears that in 1919 Dr. G. Van Pelt was commissioned to make a careful investigation into the steps that should be taken to enable palm produce from the French West African Colonies to compete with Sumatra. His conclusions were that unless prompt steps were taken the palm products industry in the French Colonies would diminish and finally disappear; that mechanical power mills for treating the produce of the palm trees were essential; and that although the working of the forest palm trees should be undertaken where possible regular plantations of the best type of palm trees were essential. Full details are given of the existing experimental mills in French West Africa and of the difficulties they have experienced in obtaining regular supplies of fruit from the natives, while the later papers in the volume show that since the date of Dr. G. Van Pelt's report in 1919 substantial advance has been made by the establishment of a central station at Bingerville in the Ivory Coast for the investigation of all aspects of the problem. As regards the Belgian Congo, from a report by Monsieur Edmond Leplae, Director-General of Agriculture in the Belgian Colonial Office, which is included in 'Record' Handbooks No. 1, Oil Palms and their Fruit, printed by Griffith and Company, Limited, in 1922, and from a paper read by Mons. Beckers before the Colonial Conference held at the School of Engineering, Liège University, in June, 1922, it appears that the Belgians are reasonably confident that the palm products industry in the Congo will be able to meet the competition from the East. The Belgians claim that oil palms cultivated in the Congo have up to the present produced an equal

quantity and as good quality of fruit as the Sumatra trees. Plantations of palms have been started by Europeans, the largest of which is now about 5,000 acres. Much research has been devoted to the best varieties of palms to plant. But what is more important is the great advance that has been made in working the natural palmeries in the Congo. As compared with plantations these are at a disadvantage owing to the palms being more widely scattered and of different ages. On the other hand the initial costs of a plantation are avoided, and these natural palmeries cost very little as the State which owns the land leases large areas for only a few centimes per hectare as rent. Production / can be quickly increased as the natives learn to look after the trees, by clearing away under-growth and cleaning the heads of the palms. The natives are also encouraged to plant up bare patches in the natural palmeries, so as to concentrate the palms and reduce transport to a minimum. Mills for treating the fruit have been erected with the latest machinery and mechanical transport facilities. Difficulties were experienced owing to the comparative scarcity of native labour in the best oil palm areas, but it is understood that these difficulties are gradually being surmounted. In view of the prospective competition from the East attention is now being directed towards the reduction of the cost and difficulty of steamer and railway transport from the Haut-Congo. The best oil palm areas in the Congo are at an average distance of 1,000 to 1,500 kilometres from the sea.

7.   The oil palm industry in the British West African Colonies does not have to contend with such transport difficulties, or, except in the Gold Coast, such comparative scarcity of native labour, as are met within the Haut-Congo, but on the other hand in those Colonies little progress has been made in the industry. The fruit is collected by natives from forest trees which are to a large extent uncared for. Much of the fruit is not gathered at all, and only a comparatively small amount of fruit is obtainable without the laborious process of climbing the trees with slings round the climber's body. The palms are scattered and transport of the fruit and oil is a heavy charge. The oil is extracted from the pericarp[2] of the fruit by native methods which are wasteful of labour, and in most cases produce an inferior oil with a high content of free fatty acid. Moreover, the amount of oil obtained by these native methods is from 8 to 10 per cent, of the weight of the fruit, whereas more than double that amount can be obtained with efficient power-driven machinery. It is impossible to estimate the difference in cost of production by native methods compared with machinery, but it can be readily understood that collecting the fruit by motor and rail transport instead of head carriage may alone give the machinery product an all important advantage. Collection and extraction by the present methods are so laborious that the industry depends essentially on an abundant supply of cheap native labour. Such an industry must be very sensitive to any decrease in the price of the product,

and it must tend to diminish as the general progress of a colony offers alternative uses for labour. It is not surprising that it has languished in the Gold Coast, and its position in Nigeria cannot be regarded as secure. And yet the natural oil palm forests which exist in Nigeria, the Gold Coast and Sierra Leone should, if properly worked and developed on scientific lines, be an important source of wealth and prosperity to the native communities, the merchants and the local Governments.

8.   The Committee is satisfied that unless important improvements are promptly introduced there is grave danger of the palm products industry in British West Africa being seriously affected by the development of plantations equipped with mills in Sumatra and elsewhere. It is true that certain steps have been taken by the Agricultural Departments in the British West African Colonies to / investigate the oil palm, and the most recent reports by those Departments have been carefully considered. But it is felt by the merchants there is a danger of too much attention being devoted to the chemical and botanical aspects of the problem to the neglect of more immediately urgent practical steps. Whilst it is very desirable that the best varieties of oil palms for plantation purposes should be determined and the best native methods of manufacturing palm oil and any possible improvements thereof ascertained, it is most important that all possible steps should be taken to teach the Africans to improve the present condition of the existing trees by cleaning the heads and opening up the bush, and to demonstrate to them the result of such improvements, *i.e.*, that they would obtain a much larger yield of fruit at a less cost of labour and transport from an equal number of trees. The Africans should also be encouraged to create blocks of palm trees by planting up bare patches where the forest trees are scattered. And the destruction of oil palm trees for the manufacture of palm wine should be restricted as far as is practicable.

9.   The Committee suggest that intensive propaganda on these lines should be undertaken by agricultural, forestry, administrative and other officials. Communal plantations might be encouraged where the conditions are suitable, and avenues of oil palms might be planted along the roads. It is not desirable that such propaganda should be delayed until a time when the undesirability of allowing this important industry to decay becomes apparent.

10.   But while the Committee attaches the greatest importance to propaganda on these lines, it is satisfied that such methods by themselves are not sufficient. Without the introduction of modern machinery for removing the oil and kernels from the fruit, it will not be possible for the oil palm industry in British West Africa to increase to any extent, or in the near future to compete with plantation products from the East. The Directors of Agriculture in the Gold Coast

and Nigeria are agreed that the introduction of such machinery is essential. It follows that either the local Governments must themselves establish mills with suitable machinery or they must offer adequate inducements to encourage private persons to establish them.

11.   The Committee has not considered in any detail the question of the establishing of mills by the local Governments, but there are obvious objections to Governments undertaking such industrial and commercial enterprises. The Committee is of opinion that this necessity should be avoided by adequate inducements being provided to attract private enterprise to erect mills, as the establishment and management of a palm oil mill is a highly technical business proposition.

12.   In a consideration of the inducements which might be offered to private enterprise, it is useful to consider what has been attempted in the past. No steps of any importance have been taken in Nigeria, which from the oil palm industry point of view is by far the most important and promising of the British West African Colonies, but in Sierra Leone and the Gold Coast a tentative step was taken by / the enactment of the Palm Oil Ordinances of 1913. These Ordinances made it possible for the Governor, if he was satisfied that the consent of the tribal authorities had been obtained, to grant to an individual the exclusive right to erect a palm oil mill within an area not exceeding a circle with a ten miles radius and for a period not exceeding twenty-one years. At the expiration of twenty-one years the Governor might renew the grant for such further period not exceeding twenty-one years and upon such terms and subject to such conditions as he thought fit. It was hoped that such a partial monopoly for a limited period would be sufficient inducement to persons with the necessary capital to erect palm oil mills.

13.   Numerous applications were made for grants under these Ordinances, particularly in Sierra Leone, and in one case a mill was actually erected. The mill, however, was not successful, and the numerous grants which had been taken out were allowed to lapse. The chief reason for the failure appears to have been the impossibility of securing a regular supply to palm fruit to the mill. It is clear that if a palm oil mill is to be run in an economic way it must be assured or an adequate regular supply of fruit at a reasonable price. But under the 1913 Palm Oil Ordinances the mill owner was wholly dependent on the natives of the district for the supply of fruit, and it is stated that even a good price would not secure a regular supply. Apart from the fact that no fruit would be brought to the mill while the natives were observing festivals, funeral customs, etc., the African of the farming class is not accustomed to regular work, and having brought in a supply of fruit and received a good price therefor he will undertake no further work for days or weeks at a time. The mill owner was not permitted either to hire labour and collect the fruit himself, paying a royalty to the native owners

of the trees, or to enter into a contract with the native owners that they would deliver a certain quantity of fruit to the mill and in the event of their failing to do so that he should be at liberty to hire labour and collect the deficiency. Subsidiary causes for the failure may have been that the palm fruit in Sierra Leone is not so rich in pericarp oil as in Nigeria and the Congo, that the power-driven machinery was not so efficient as it is now, and that the period of twenty-one years for which monopoly rights were definitely granted was not sufficiently long to induce the grantee to embark on an expensive programme of planting new palms and training the natives to improve the existing palms in the area round his mill. Moreover, he had no assurance that his mill would benefit by any such improvements, as the natives of the district might not collect any extra fruit that was grown, and new palms might be destroyed at any time by the natives in the exercise of their rights of shifting cultivation.

14.   But although experience has shown that the inducements offered in 1913 for the erection of mills were inadequate, it must be noted that many objections were raised against the policy. It was urged that it was unjust and impolitic to grant exclusive rights for the use of power-driven machinery over a large area for a period of twenty-one years; that the native owners of the oil palms in a large area would receive for their fruit only the price which the mill owner / cared to offer instead of the possibly higher price that would have resulted from competition; and that the natives of the area were prevented from combining to erect mills and so dealing with their palm fruit in the most efficient way.

15.   It may be admitted that the last objection is really theoretical. In the ten years since 1913 no natives have in fact combined to erect mills, and it seems probable that for some time to come only European capital and enterprise can provide such mills. The other objections are those which can be urged against any monopoly, but it is generally admitted that some partial monopoly may be necessary in the initial stages to establish a new industry. The Committee is satisfied that the erection of mills as rapidly as possible is most desirable in the interests of the palm products industry, and that experience shows that substantial inducements are necessary to secure their erection. It is possible that without exclusive rights mills might, in the course of time, be erected in British West Africa, but the Committee is satisfied that without exclusive rights there is no prospect of sufficient mills being erected in the near future to enable the West African oil palm industry to compete on anything like equal terms with palm oil from Sumatra. But the Governments which grant exclusive rights must have the power to see that such rights are not abused, and it must be remembered that the ultimate aim is not a number of isolated monopolist mills but an adequate number of mills to deal with the fruit available, operating in healthy competition. The interests of the native owners of the soil and palms are paramount and must be preserved, but it

is in their interests that up-to-date machinery and methods should be introduced in time to cope with the threatened competition from Sumatra and elsewhere, a competition which they can of themselves neither foresee nor guard against.

16.   The inducements which the Committee considers desirable in order to give reasonable prospects of success appear to be the following:–

> (*a*) the person who undertakes to erect a pioneer mill should be given all possible assistance in acquiring a suitable site on freehold or long leasehold terms;
>
> (*b*) he should be protected for a certain period against any rivals erecting a mill within a certain area;
>
> (*c*) he should, if he so desires, be able to acquire a plantation area for cultivating oil palms, so as not to be entirely dependent on the natives for bringing sufficient fruit to his mill;
>
> (*d*) he should be given facilities for making legally binding contracts with the natives for collecting fruit from specified areas;
>
> (*e*) he should be given exclusive rights for the use of mechanical transport for collecting oil palm fruit within a certain area.

17.   As regards the site for the mill, bungalows and stores it is unnecessary to emphasise that it should be freehold or long leasehold, / The grantee should be given a definite period in which to install his machinery and commence the manufacture of palm oil in accordance with the terms of his agreement. Thereafter should he, without sufficient cause, cease to manufacture on a reasonable scale, his grant of exclusive rights within the area would be subject to forfeiture, but in that event he would be entitled to remove all his machinery, buildings and plant, whether portable or fixed to the soil.

18.   As regards the period for which protection should be granted, there is considerable difference of opinion. The period fixed in the Palm Oil Ordinances of 1913 was twenty-one years with the possibility of renewal for a second similar period. On the one hand it is understood that the Nigerian Government considers that twenty-one years is too long a period for the definite grant of monopoly rights, quite apart from any question of renewal, as it is impossible to see what developments may take place in twenty-one years, and it is urged that it would not be equitable to grant to an individual the sole right for that period of dealing with the palm fruit in a certain area by machinery. In this connection it may be noted that the Committee on Edible and Oil-Producing Nuts and Seeds of 1915 observed that 'A new factor in the situation will arise if any of the smaller (*i.e.*, hand-driven) machines, now in the experimental stage, prove commercially practicable by which it is hoped that natives will be able to make palm oil of good quality' (p. 20 of Cd. 8247). On the other hand it is urged that the period

of twenty-one years is inadequate and that it should be extended to forty-two years in order that the grantee may have adequate inducement to improve the palms in the area served by his mill. It is urged that no mill owner is going to incur the expensive pioneering work of getting the natives to plant new palms in the bare spaces and cultivate the existing palms so as to improve their yield if at the end of twenty-one years a rival may be permitted to establish a mill in the area and take advantage of all the pioneering work which has been done. It must be borne in mind that from congested, untended wild palm bush very little fruit of value is obtained; that wild palms up to fifteen or twenty years of age respond to treatment and will give increased yields if systematically pruned and cleared; and that while properly cultivated new palms begin to bear at about five or six years from the seed they are in full bearing from about their 12th to 40th years. If a mill owner has systematically spent a reasonable sum annually on developing an area within a radius of seven miles of his mill, at the end of twenty-one years the production from that area will be so great and so convenient for working, owing to the reduction of transport costs by the concentration of the palms, that a rival might prefer to establish a mill in that area and compete with the existing mill rather than to start in a fresh area where there would be no mill to compete with, but where heavy annual expenditure would be necessary on improving the area, on transport, and on educating the native to sell his palm fruit instead of the products thereof. The rival mill would hope to reap the benefits of the years of pioneering work already done, but it appears improbable that such intensive competition would be in the interest of the industry or the native owners of the palms. The latter might obtain some benefit / at first in increased prices for their palm fruit, but the mills would find it increasingly difficult to carry on and to meet the competition of palm oil from the Sumatra plantations. In a very short time either one mill would have to close down or the mills would be driven to agree to a fixed price for fruit considerably lower than either would be able to offer, if operating alone. Moreover, the risk of such intensive competition might deter capitalists from erecting mills.

19.   An illustration of the evil of undue competition under some-what similar conditions has been given by the Nigerian Director of Agriculture. An agricultural circle in the Punjab, India, of which he was in charge, consisted of two distinct areas irrigated by two canals, of which one was comparatively old, the other newly opened. The old area was badly overstocked with cotton ginning factories, and the number was still being increased. The procedure was that a new factory would be opened, fierce competition would ensue for a week or two, then, since there was not enough cotton for all, a pool would be formed, or the existing pool extended to include the newcomer. Sometimes agreement was reached before the new ginnery started work at all. Under the pool rules only a

limited number of gins were allowed to be worked, and for the privilege of working the owners paid to the owners of the idle gins an amount sufficient to cover interest on capital, upkeep, etc., and a sufficient inducement to make them prefer to have their gins idle rather than enter into competition. At the same time none of the reputable ginners would come forward to set up ginneries in the new area, although that area was the most promising field for their operations. In the end the difficulties were met by the Government preventing the erection of more ginneries in an area than was necessary to ensure adequate, but not excessive, competition.

20.   It takes twelve years under plantation conditions for an oil palm to come into full bearing, and it would be possible to plant up and improve only a few hundred acres each year. If there were a prospect of fierce competition at the end of twenty-one years, it would be impossible for a company to obtain from the investing public the capital necessary to bring a wide area up to full bearing or to undertake the expenditure of the large sum of money necessary, even if the money were available. With a view to meeting the coming competition from Sumatra the Committee is impressed with the importance of making such expenditure on development of the large area not only possible to the mill owner but clearly desirable, and has, therefore, decided to recommend that the period for which exclusive rights for the erection of power-driven machinery should be granted should be twenty-one years, as laid down in the 1913 Palm Oil Ordinances, with the certainty of renewal for a further period of twenty-one years on the same terms unless it is proved to the satisfaction of the High Court that the mill owner has not developed the area within which he holds exclusive rights for the use of power-driven machinery in accordance with the terms of his agreement or is not purchasing at a reasonable price all the fruit brought to his mill by the natives of the area. It appears to be essential that the decision as to what constitutes reasonable development / and a reasonable price should rest with the judicial authorities and not with the executive, as otherwise there will not be sufficient security to justify the raising and expenditure of the necessary capital.

21.   The question of the area over which exclusive rights to erect power-driven machinery should be granted and the area which the grantee should be allowed to acquire for plantation purposes depends upon what is considered the economic size of a mill and upon what production of palm fruit per acre can be expected. The size of mill depends to a great extent on the price paid for the fruit and received for the oil and kernels. The larger the mill which can be regularly supplied with fruit the more cheaply it should be possible to produce oil and kernels. In an article in the Annual Bulletin (1922) of the Nigerian Agricultural Department the Director of Agriculture discusses the prospects of a mill treating 6,000 tons of fruit per annum. His figures have been criticised on the

ground that the average purchase price per 100 lb. of fruit works out at over 3s. instead of 2s. to 2s. 3d., and that the sum of £2,000 allowed for European supervision, native clerks, engineer and labour is quite inadequate. We have also been informed that no profits are in fact being made, nor have been made, by mills established in Nigeria, Dahomey, Togoland, the Gold Coast, the Ivory Coast and Sierra Leone. In his evidence before the West African Lands Committee in January, 1913, Mr. Smart stated that in his opinion the minimum size of mill, with prospects of being a financial success, was one treating 10,000 tons of cleaned palm fruit per annum. He is now inclined to the belief that owing to increased cost of wages and materials 25,000 tons should be considered the minimum. We are informed that in the Dutch East Indies even larger mills than that are contemplated, but in the East Indies the plantations are concentrated and connected up with mechanical transport, so that one mill will be able to deal with the output from several plantations. In the Congo the five mills of the S. A. Des Huileries du Congo Belge each work about 12,000 tons of fruit a year. In the paper by Mons. Beckers, referred to in paragraph six, it is stated: 'It is uneconomical, generally speaking, to erect a mill for a fruit output of less than 10 tons per day, if reasonable control of all operations is exercised. Such a mill will deal with the fruit from a circle of good natural palmery of some two kilometres radius; but in practice labour conditions involve cropping over a much larger area.' The question is a difficult one, but it is not clear to some of us why a mill dealing with from 6,000 to 10,000 tons of fruit per annum should not be an economic proposition in British West Africa.

22.   As regards area it is even more difficult to draw any hard and fast lines. A given area which might pay in one district, by reason of a plentiful supply of good palms, might not pay to work in a more hilly and remote district, even with the same quantity of palm fruit available. Also the various superficial areas carry widely varying quantities and qualities of palms, and have varying prospects of obtaining fresh fruit by water transport, or otherwise, from adjoining areas. Still, certain general conclusions may be arrived at. The Africans will not, as a general rule, carry the fruit further than four or five miles unless canoe transport is available. It follows / that if an individual is granted the sole right of erecting powerdriven machinery within a circle of seven miles radius there is little danger of the fruit within five miles of his mill being carried to a rival mill, if the use of mechanical transport for the purpose is restricted to the mill owner. Accordingly we are agreed that the area which was specified in the 1913 Palm Oil Ordinances, viz., a circle of a radius of ten miles, was unnecessarily large. The grant of exclusive rights over such large areas might tend to hinder development.

23.   But while we recommend the reduction to a seven mile radius of the area specified under the 1913 Palm Oil Ordinances we consider that the grantee

should be allowed, if be so desires, to acquire an agricultural concession within the area for the cultivation of palm trees on plantation lines, so that he need not be entirely dependent on the natives for bringing fruit to his mill. The area of such a concession might perhaps be such as would supply one-third of the fruit required by the mill, while two-thirds would have to be purchased from the natives of the surrounding district. It seems probable that from such a concession developed on plantation lines with about sixty palms to the acre a production of two tons of fruit per annum per acre could eventually be reached. In Sumatra from four to five tons of cleaned fruit per acre have been obtained. On this basis a mill dealing with 10,000 tons of fruit would require an agricultural concession over a minimum of 1,600 acres, while a 6,000 tons mill would require a minimum of 1,000 acres. In the early years after the acquisition of a plantation area the fruit collected from it would not approximate to two tons per acre, although the palms already on the area would yield increased crops in response to cultivation and clearing.

Moreover, in any area acquired for plantation purposes, there would be some tracts unsuitable for intensive cultivation. After careful consideration we consider that if the mill owner is prepared to undertake the necessary expenditure on clearing and planting he should be allowed to acquire in any one district a plantation area not exceeding a maximum of 5,000 acres. The area would have to be acquired from the native owners on a long lease, say 99 years, adequate compensation by way of rent or otherwise being given for the palms already on it and for the renunciation by the Africans living in the district of their rights to hunting and shifting cultivation over it and of residence on it. Conditions requiring the lessee to spend a reasonable sum annually on development and planting should be strictly enforced, but the mill owner should be allowed to lease the area and commence clearing and planting before he actually erects his mill.

24.   We have considered the objections which have been urged against European-owned plantations in West Africa, and agree generally that the ideal arrangement in British West Africa is that the palms should be cleared and cultivated by their native owners, who should collect the fruit and sell it to the central mill. Overhead plantation costs will thereby be avoided which should be an important factor in competition with the Dutch planters in the East. But we are satisfied that such plantations of palms, as we suggest / above, are justified if they are a necessary inducement to Europeans to erect mills, and that they would provide valuable object lessons to the natives of the surrounding districts in the proper care of their palms. Other advantages of such plantations would be (*a*) reduction of manual labour in transport, (*b*) saving in height of trees to be climbed, and (*c*) less damage to fruit in collection as the bunches will not be dropped to the ground.

25.   The Committee are also of opinion that it would be an important additional inducement for the erection of power-driven machinery if it were possible

for the mill owner to acquire collecting rights in certain circumstances over a wider area than that covered by his agricultural lease. It should be legal for him to enter into contracts with the natives of particular areas under which they would undertake to supply a quantity of fruit to the mill at a specified price. In the event of the natives failing to fulfil their contract the mill owner should be free, but not obliged, to hire labourers and collect fruit up to the total specified in the contract, subject to a payment to the native owners of the oil palms by way of royalty. Such contracts would have to be subject to Government approval and supervision in order to prevent abuses. There should be no attempt to force the natives of any area to sign such a form of contract or to renew such a contract on the same or similar terms when it had expired. Care would be necessary in fixing the period of the contract, the quantity of fruit to be brought in, the price to be paid, and the amount of the royalty in the event of default, but it is felt that with goodwill on all sides such details might be arranged on a mutually satisfactory basis, and that some such arrangements would be most beneficial to the West African industry in meeting the Sumatra competition, as it would tend to eliminate the great waste which occurs in West Africa owing to the non-collection of fruit and would aid the mills in securing regular supplies.

26.　　As a last inducement the Committee wish to emphasise the importance of mechanical transport. A mill owner should be encouraged to lay down a monorail and/or decauville system to connect his mill with the producing areas and/ or to employ motor transport both in his leased agricultural area, if he acquires one, and in the wider area of natural palm forest in which he has the exclusive right to erect power-driven machinery for treating the palm fruit. If fair advantage of mechanical transport is taken in an oil palm area, only one-tenth the manual labour will be required in producing the palm oil and kernels. After careful consideration the Committee has decided to recommend that the mill owner should be given the exclusive right to use mechanical transport for the purpose of collecting oil palm fruit in the area within seven miles of his mill in which he has the exclusive right to erect power-driven machinery. No obligation should be put upon the mill owner to carry passengers or goods for third parties. An exception would, however, be necessary in favour of the native owners of palms in that area. It would not be equitable to deprive those owners of the right to use, say their own motor transport, to collect the fruit from their palms and carry it to whatever market they chose, but care would be necessary to prevent such natives becoming nominal owners of motor transport under the control of competing firms. /

27.　　It is felt that this grant of the exclusive right to use mechanical transport for the purpose of collecting oil palm fruit is one which may be misrepresented, but on the other hand it appears to be most important if the mill owner is to undertake large expenditure on development in the area served by his mill.

Without such a grant it is clear that once the mill owner has brought a part of the area served by his mill into full bearing by himself clearing the bush and planting new palms or by encouraging the natives to do so, a rival might establish a mill or fruit collecting station just outside the seven mile radius from the original mill and obtain the benefits of the mill owner's expenditure by sending a fleet of motor lorries into the developed area. No mill owner can be expected to incur the necessary expenditure on development if he is liable to receive no return owing to a competitor collecting the fruit by motor transport. On the other hand it is not proposed that ordinary trading activities in the area within seven miles of the mill should be interfered with in any way. Any genuine trading store in the area would be allowed to use motor transport for removing palm oil and kernels brought to the store by natives of the area, but it would not be permissible for rivals to purchase palm fruit. What the Committee aim at is an extensive area round each mill covered with blocks of palms properly spaced and cultivated, but trading, mining, farming or other rights in the area must not be interfered with, except on the mill owner's plantation or mill site. Moreover, as the sole justification for this grant of the exclusive right to use mechanical transport for fruit collecting purposes is to encourage the mill owner to develop the area within seven miles of his mill, that grant would be liable to revocation at any time if it appeared that the mill owner was not expending a reasonable sum on such development. Expenditure on the leased plantation area would, of course, not count for this purpose. The decision as to what constitutes reasonable expenditure should rest with the judicial authorities.

28.   To give effect to the Committee's recommendations a certain amount of legislation will be necessary. In all the Colonies legislation may be required to make possible contracts of the nature contemplated in paragraph 25. In Sierra Leone the Palm Oil Ordinance (No. 7 of 1913) is still in force. Section 3 should be amended to reduce the area from a circle with a ten mile radius to a circle with a seven mile radius, and the following definition of mechanical power which is taken from the Gold Coast Ordinance should be inserted in section 2: 'Mechanical power means machinery worked by steam, electricity, water power or internal combustion engines, and does not mean machinery worked by hand.' Section 3 would require to be altered to provide for the renewal of the grant for a second period of twenty-one years. In Sierra Leone an Ordinance has recently been passed (No. 13 of 1922) which permits the grant of agricultural concessions not exceeding 5,000 acres, if used for the sole purpose of the cultivation of the oil palm on scientific and commercial lines, and provides that such concessions need no longer be validated by the Concession Court. The interests of the natives are safeguarded by a proviso that only one such grant shall be made in any one chiefdom – a proviso which incidentally would serve as / an additional protection to

the mill owner who obtains such a concession near his mill. It is felt, however, that while the main purpose of the agricultural concession not exceeding 5,000 acres must be the cultivation of the oil palm, the growing of a certain amount of foodstuffs or other subsidiary crops on the concession should be permissible.

29. The construction of light railways or tramways in Sierra Leone is governed by the Proprietary Railways Ordinance (No. 30 of 1909). Clause 3 of that Ordinance, after prohibiting the construction of any railway without a licence, contains the following saving paragraph: 'Nothing in this section shall prevent a landowner or a concession holder from constructing without such licence and working a railway within the limits of his land or concession, to be used exclusively in connection with the development of his land or with the exercise of the rights granted by the concession, as the case may be; provided that be comply with any directions that may be given him in writing by any inspector appointed under this Ordinance with a view to ensuring the safety of the general public and of persons using or working the railway.' Under that section the mill owner could construct light railways within the area of his agricultural concession, but to extend such railways into the wider area served by his mill he would have to obtain way-leaves from the chiefs or other landowners in accordance with the procedure laid down in the Proprietary Railways Ordinance. It would be necessary to pass legislation to enable the mill owner to acquire the exclusive right to use mechanical transport for fruit collecting purposes in the area within seven miles of his mill.

30. In the Gold Coast the Palm Oil Ordinance (Chapter 97 in the Revised Edition of the Ordinances) is similar to that in Sierra Leone and the remarks already made as to the amendments that would be required apply, except that the definition 'mechanical power' already appears in the Gold Coast Ordinance. The position under the Proprietary Railways Ordinance (Chapter 110 in the Revised Edition) is also the same as in Sierra Leone, and similar action would be necessary. The acquisition of an area for plantation purposes is more difficult in the Gold Coast. A lease for purely agricultural purposes need not go through the Concessions Court, but it is understood that unless the acquisition of an area has been validated by the Concessions Court, the grantee has no sufficient security to justify expenditure on development and planting, as his title may be upset at any time. On the other hand sub-sections (6), (7) and (8) of section 11 of the Concessions Ordinance provide that no concession shall be certified as valid (*a*) unless the Court is satisfied that the customary rights of the natives are reasonably protected in respect of shifting cultivation, collection of firewood and hunting and snaring game; (*b*) if it grants or purports to grant rights to collect natural produce, other than timber, to the exclusion of natives, or (*c*) if it grants or purports to grant rights to remove natives from their habitations within the area of such concessions. It is clearly impossible to develop an oil palm

plantation (*a*) if any native has the right to come into the area to grow crops or snare game; or (*b*) if a native can come in and collect the fruit of the trees / which have been planted or improved by cultivation on the ground that such fruit is 'natural produce'; or (*c*) if it is illegal to induce any natives living within the proposed plantation area to remove their habitations outside it. The Gold Coast Concessions Ordinance was not drafted with a view to the development of limited areas by intensive cultivation, and contemplates the grant of areas not exceeding 'in the case of land in respect of which rights to cut timber or to collect rubber or relating to other products of the soil are conferred twenty square miles.' It is not generally desirable that any natives should be permitted to give up their rights to farm, hunt or collect natural produce over so large an area as twenty square miles. An ordinance might be enacted in the Gold Coast on the lines of the Sierra Leone Ordinance No. 13 of 1922, with the necessary amendment to permit the growing of foodstuffs, and other subsidiary crops, but that would not meet the difficulty that in the Gold Coast a concession which has not been validated by the Court does not give sufficient security of title. Probably the simplest course would be to amend the Gold Coast Concessions Ordinance to provide that sub-sections (6), (7) and (8) of section 11 shall not apply to the grant of an area not exceeding 5,000 acres, if made for the primary purpose of the cultivation of the oil palm on scientific and commercial lines. The Court would have to be satisfied that the conditions of the concession were such as in point of fact to secure that the area would be developed on those lines, and that it would cause no hardship to the natives of the district to permit them to give up their rights of collecting fruit, of hunting and of shifting cultivation over and residence in the area in question. It has also been suggested to us that arrangements should be made to enable an individual to obtain a sound title much more quickly and at less expense than is at present practicable in the Gold Coast, particularly by some representative of the Government being present when the lease is explained to and signed by the grantors.

31.   In Nigeria the position is quite different from the Gold Coast and Sierra Leone. No ordinance similar to the 1913 Palm Oil Ordinances of these two Colonies has been passed, and it might be difficult to pass such an ordinance at the present time, even if it included the amendments which we have indicated as desirable in the Gold Coast and Sierra Leone Ordinances. On the other hand the Nigerian Government is anxious to encourage the erection of power-driven mills in order to meet the competition from Sumatra and would be prepared to give a reasonable measure of protection against undue competition. It is probable that the requisite legislation would prohibit any person from erecting a power-driven mill for treating oil palm fruit without a licence from the Government and give Government power to regulate such mills so as to prevent their

operations being conducted in ways contrary to the interests of the native population or of agricultural production. The Government when issuing a licence to any individual would give him protection from competition for a reasonable period by undertaking that it would not license a competitor to establish a mill within a certain distance. There might also be a general undertaking that licences would only be issued to allow of a reasonable degree of competition, and not out of all proportion to the amount of produce available, / and that if an individual has expended reasonable sums on increasing the production of palm fruit from an area during his protected period, he will be given every opportunity to provide adequate milling facilities for the requirements of that area at a reasonable price before a licence is granted for the establishment of a rival mill in the neighbourhood. If the Nigerian Government decides to proceed on some such lines, it is most desirable that the decision as to whether the mill owner has undertaken reasonable development and is providing adequate milling facilities should rest with the judicial and not the executive authorities, and that the protection granted both as regards area and period should be not less than in the Gold Coast and Sierra Leone. It is possible that the Governments of Sierra Leone and the Gold Coast might prefer to legislate for some such licensing system rather than to amend the 1913 Palm Oil Ordinances.

32.   In Nigeria there is no Proprietary Railways Ordinance and apparently no legislation is necessary to enable any person to construct a light railway on land owned by or leased to him, or on any other land with the consent of the owner thereof. The Railways Ordinance (Chapter 110 of 1923 Revised Edition of the Ordinances) applies only, to railways 'for the public carriage of passengers, animals or goods.' Legislation would, however, be necessary to enable the mill owner to acquire the exclusive right to use mechanical transport for palm fruit collecting purposes in the area within seven miles of his mill.

33.   Again, as regards the lease of a plantation area for cultivating palms, the position is quite different in Nigeria from that in the Gold Coast or Sierra Leone. There is no court which has to validate concessions and it is not desirable that such a procedure should be established. The individual would apply for an agricultural lease either of crown land under the Crown Lands Management Ordinance or of native land under the Native Lands Acquisition Ordinance, By Rules made under the Crown Lands Ordinance (page 516, Volume III of 1923 Revised Edition of the Ordinances) no agricultural lease of Crown lands will be granted in respect of an area of more than 1,200 acres, but on the other hand a second area may be leased to the same individual once the Governor is satisfied that two-thirds of the area already held by such lessee is under cultivation. No lease will ordinarily be granted for a term exceeding 45 years, and the follow-

ing special covenants on the part of the lessee shall, unless expressly varied or excepted, be implied in every agricultural lease:–

'(*a*) To pay such compensation as may be fixed by the Governor or his authorised agent for disturbance of natives in their use or occupation of the land.

'(*b*) During the first two years of the term of the lease to expend on cultivation and clearing a sum at least equivalent to five shillings per acre of the total area demised.

'(*c*) To bring the cultivatable portion of the land demised under cultivation at the rate of one-eighth of such land in each of the first eight years of the term of the lease, and thereafter to keep in cultivation the whole of the cultivatable portion of the area of the lease to the satisfaction of the Governor.' /

It is also provided that

> 'When natives are at the date of the lease occupying any part of the land demised, the compensation to be paid to them by the lessee for improvements and disturbance will be assessed by the Governor or his authorised agent, as soon as conveniently may be after the date of the lease, and such native shall have the option either:–

(i) to vacate immediately the land and receive the compensation assessed, or

(ii) to remain on the land until the lessee requires them to vacate or they desire to vacate the land, and on vacating the land to receive from the lessee the compensation assessed as aforesaid.'

34. The conditions under which a lease of native land might be acquired for agricultural purposes under the Native Lands Acquisition Ordinance are not so clearly defined (Native Lands Acquisition Regulations, Chapter 89, Volume III of Revised Edition of Ordinances), but it is understood that generally speaking the Governor, whose consent is necessary, would require conditions similar to those in the case of a lease of crown land. There does not, however, appear to be any legal bar to the lease of an area of native land not exceeding 5,000 acres, and the Committee wish to point out that there would be objections to limiting the initial lease to 1,200 acres with the possibility of extension later, as the most suitable land over which to extend might be acquired and held for a rise in price.
[...]

RIDER BY MR. SMART.

I am of opinion the foregoing inducements to capitalists should be considered the irreducible minimum, and that it would pay the African very much better immediately to give such greater inducements as will more quickly (before

Sumatra, etc., establish a lead) attract ample capital to develop the industry. Probably ten years hence it will be too late to offer inducements which might be ample, if offered now. Over restrictive conditions will appeal, if at all, only / to capitalists now in the African Trade, which will so limit developments as seriously to prejudice the African whose interests should be considered before all others, £50 per acre is about the cost of creating an Oil Palm Plantation and a charge of £10 per acre is probably a low estimate to plant up and improve large palm areas to anything approaching plantation standards. In round figures the latter means £1,000,000 to improve only one seven mile radius area. There are hundreds of such areas available, and those now in the West Africa Trade may not be willing or able to develop more than a small percentage of them. It is therefore necessary quickly to attract other capitalists of the right class by offering the maximum possible inducements.

LEWIS A. SMART.

H. H. Middleton, *Report on the Ground-Nut Trade in Kano Province*, Sessional Paper no. 41 (Lagos: Government Printer, 1924).

SESSIONAL PAPER
No. 41 of 1924.
Paper laid on the Table of the Legislative Council.
SUBJECT:
Report on the Ground-Nut Trade in Kano Province by Mr. H. H. Middleton,[1]
Resident;
with
Memorandum by Mr. W. F. Gowers,[2] *C. M. G.,*
Lieutenant-Governor of the Northern Provinces. / /
[...]

MEMORANDUM BY HIS HONOUR THE LIEUTENANT-GOVERNOR.

This report is a most interesting and valuable one. As Resident of Kano I was in touch with the export ground-nut trade from its inception, and judged in the light of considerable knowledge and experience of this Province Mr. Middleton's careful deductions and conclusions may, I consider, be accepted with confidence.

2.   With reference to the statistics in paragraph 6 of the report it may be noted that the ground-nut crop in 1921 was a bad one, and even if there had been keen competition in buying, and high prices offered, it is probable that considerably less than the normal quantity would have been available to meet the export demand. I feel no doubt that the conclusion in paragraph 8 is correct. In paragraphs 31 and 32 and 34 Mr. Middleton points out that the ground-nut crop requires a heavy rainfall in the early part of the season. The total rainfall recorded at Kano in 1922 during the months of May, June and July was 8–98 inches, whereas the average rainfall for these months at Kano, taken over 14 years (statistics in *Nigerian Handbook*) was 15–29 inches. This fact appears to me to corroborate almost conclusively Mr. Middleton's opinion that the total

crop for that year was little more than sufficient to supply the requirements of the native community.

3.   I do not feel quite able to go so far as Mr. Middleton when he says in his paragraph 9 that the fluctuations in the cultivation of ground-nuts are 'almost entirely' due to the export trade. That this is a very important factor I readily admit also that the export trade is almost entirely responsible for the steady increase in production from 1913 to 1920. But my personal opinion is that the peculiarly suitable climatic conditions in 1923, following as it did a year when the climatic conditions were peculiarly unsuitable were a more important factor, as compared to the intelligent anticipation of events before they occurred, than the report admits.

4.   In paragraph 17 Mr. Middleton estimates the total crop of 1923 at 80,000 tons. In 1918 I estimated the total production at the same figure (p. 37 of the Gazetteer of Kano Province). The present report seems to confirm the accuracy of that estimate since it referred to a year next the apex of the gradually ascending curve of production from 1913 onwards which, as indicated in paragraph 5, probably reached its highest point with the crop of 1919.

5.   On the general question of the profits made by the middlemen and the proportion of the export price which reaches the actual producer the report indicates a state of affairs which may be regarded as satisfactory. The profits of the middlemen cannot be regarded as exorbitant, and the exporting firms have evidently cut down their profit to the smallest reasonable proportions.

W. F. GOWERS,
14th May, 1924. /

REPORT ON THE GROUND-NUT TRADE IN KANO PROVINCE.

A. – EXTENT OF CULTIVATION, ETC.

As is well known, there is scarcely a town or hamlet in the whole of Kano Province in which some attempt is not made – in a greater or lesser degree – to cultivate ground-nuts. That degree depends primarily on suitability of soil and secondly, to a certain extent, on nationality as I find that in Districts where Beri-beri[3] and Mangawa[4] preponderate one almost invariably sees a greater proportionate number of ground-nut farms while the reverse is the case in Fulani[5] areas. This becomes more noticeable the further one goes from Kano itself.

2.   Within a 10 mile radius of Kano City I estimate that 40% of the farmers grow nuts while in the rest of the Emirate the cultivation of this crop is, generally speaking, more extensive in the North and West. Two notable exceptions to this, however, are the Districts of Kura and Wudil which lie South of Kano and are second and third on the list of last year's ground-nut growers with returns showing that 38% and 36% respectively of the adult male population cultivated this commodity. Gworzo heads the list with 40% with Dawaki ta Tofa fourth (32%). In Dambarta, Fogolawa, Karaye and Dawaki ta Kudu the percentage was 25 while the lowest producers in proportion to the male population were Tudun Wadda (6%), Birmin Kudu (8%). Dutsi (8 ½%) and Jafun (9%).

In the following Emirates the Districts mentioned are the chief growers:–

KATAGUM:– Udubo, Galadima, Tsokwa and Azare in all of which the population is largely composed of Beri-beri.
JEMAARI:– Dogon Jeji.
MISSAU:– Dambam (where there is a considerable number of Kerri-kerris).
HADEJIA:– Sarkin Arewa, Madaki, Sarkin Bai and Sarkin Dawaki.
DAURA:– Kaura, Murka, Yarima and Sarkin Bai.
KAZAURE:– Yarima.
GUMEL:– Sarkin Bai.

3.   Katsina Emirate is not, and never has been, an important ground-nut producing area, and though it grows enough (and no doubt more than enough) for local consumption, it has never seriously catered for the export trade. Only in the North-east have farmers planted hitherto with a view to meeting the demand outside their own and immediate environment. In this Emirate the ground-nut has to compete with an ever increasing cotton cultivation and the Emir is of opinion that some Districts have already reached the limit of their capacity for exportable produce if they are to maintain their independence as regards local food supplies. Although, of course, the ideal soils for cotton and ground-nuts are very different, there is no doubt that, if there were no demand for the former, the peasant would attempt to cultivate the latter as soon as he realised that there was a possibility of turning his produce into hard cash.

4.   From and including 1913 until 1920 there was undoubtedly a small but steady annual increase in the cultivation of ground-nuts, producers who were already growing this commodity extending their acreage while others began then to sow for the first time. Between those years the curve only showed a downward tendency in 1914 when the sowing season synchronised with the famine resulting from the previous year's drought and, in consequence, the population concentrated most of its agricultural energies on the production of cereals.

5.   For this gradual increase the export trade, which first showed signs of becoming important during the winter of 1912/13, is entirely responsible. /

The curve reached its highest point in 1920, immediately after the 'boom' season of 1919/20, and it was after the disastrous slump of the ensuing season that farmers found themselves saddled with large surplus stocks of ground-nuts which they were unable to realise except at an absurdly low price. The situation was further aggravated by the fact that large numbers of peasants – relying on the scale of nuts for securing sufficient means to purchase their food supplies for themselves and their families – had by this time so reduced their cultivation of cereals for the sake of ground-nuts that they were no longer self-supporting in this respect and were now faced with the problem of rising food prices and little or no money with which to buy. The natural result was a very considerable falling-off in the cultivation of ground-nuts in 1921.

6.   I have unfortunately no figures to show what proportion of the total exported from Nigeria during those years was actually bought in Kano but the average annual purchases from this Province from 1917 to 1920 were considerably over 40,000 tons, while, during the twelve months from October, 1921 to September, 1922, only 24,560 tons were railed by the Kano and of these at least 8,000 tons belonged to the 1920 and the 1921 crop, therefore, little more than 16,000 tons actually reached the European market and during the following season (from October, 1922 to September, 1923) the total amount railed from Kano was 16,622 tons.

7.   As far as I have been able to ascertain (and in obtaining these figures I am indebted to the Agents of certain European firms) the average price per ton paid by the Kano exporters during each season since the first year that Nigeria began to eater for the home markets is approximately as follows:–

Season.	£	s.	d.
1912–13	5	10	0
1913–14	9	10	0
1914–15	5	0	0
1915–16	4	15	0
1916–17	8	0	0
1917–18	10	0	0
1918–19	11	10	0
1919–20	34	0	0
1920–21	–		
1921–22	10	10	0
1922–23	12	0	0
1923–24	14	15	0

8.   As regards the 1922 crop and the shortage of supplies for export opinion has been divided. In some quarters it has been alleged that native traders and

middlemen bought large quantities in the villages and held up the stocks in the hopes of cornering the market and obtaining a big price later on. Personally, however, I have seen no justification for this view and my own opinion is that the nuts were not there – or rather that the total crop was little more than was sufficient to supply the requirements of the native community. Had a better price been offered earlier in the season. I have no doubt that the consumers would have been willing to part with a reasonable proportion of the store which they had reserved for their own use but, at the average price ruling at the time, they preferred to retain what was necessary to meet the normal internal demand. I am also firmly convinced that the stocks of ground-nuts reserved for local consumption in this Province are, at the moment, actually less than they were twelve months ago. The average price has been considerably higher and therefore the producer has been willing to sell a greater proportion of his harvest.

In addition to this the cereal crops of 1923 were very much better than those of the previous year and therefore the internal demand for ground-nuts as food is not so great.

9.   But, apart from the fact that the 1922 harvest was by no means a good one, the actual acreage under ground-nuts had been reduced and everything points to the fact that the fluctuations in the cultivation of this commodity in recent / years are almost entirely due to the export trade. In saying 'almost entirely' I use the words advisedly as there is no doubt that some farmers are partly guided by climatic conditions. Those (and they are in the majority) who sow their nuts a month or more after the corn have, by that time, been able to form some opinion as to the possible success or otherwise of their cereals and, in the latter case, may abandon their original intention of sowing ground-nuts in favour of increasing their staple food supplies.

10.   If my study of the question has led me to correct conclusions, it is now necessary to explain why the cultivation of ground-nuts was so greatly increased in 1923. That the increase over the previous years was very considerable in almost every district throughout the Province is an indubitable fact and in my personal interviews with farmers in every Emirate I have been struck by the large numbers who are known to have sown ground-nuts for the first time last season or to have started again after a lapse of three years.

11.   In view of the comparative slump of the last two seasons one might have expected that the cultivation would have been reduced almost to pre-export level but, for some reason or other, farmers were universally under the firm conviction that there was a certain prospect of a big buying season a-head. This conviction was not confined to agriculturists in the immediate vicinity of Kano but was spread to the very confines of the Province and in such distant places

as Azare, Hadejia and Daura. The statement was confirmed by all classes of the community, – from the Emirs themselves downwards.

12.   As to how the rumour started or whence it emanated is largely a matter of conjecture. It has even been suggested that the native is by nature a gambler and – in staking on even chances – is a believer in the theory that, if black has turned up twice running, the odds are in favour of red winning at the third spin. A more plausible explanation, however, is the fact that at least one big firm started to buy very late in the season last year and that, for such nuts as they were able to obtain, they paid an average of over £14 per ton. This being so, it may be wondered why the supply was not greater but it must be remembered that sowing began early and at the end of the ordinary buying season the native traders had already left the villages so that, even if the owners had been willing to sell at that price, there would have been the difficulty of getting them to Kano.

13.   In addition to the rumoured prospect of a revival in trade, farmers also had the incentive of peculiarly suitable climatic conditions which helped to decide the question for those who were hesitating.

14.   The successful result of the 1923 crop and the high average price paid during the recent buying season have combined to imbue farmers with a determination to cultivate an even greater quantity of ground-nuts in 1924 and I anticipate that, while the crop will be more evenly distributed and there should be very little risk of individual producers repeating their mistake of 1920, the actual amount sown during the forthcoming season will surpass all previous 'records.'

15.   I must frankly confess that I have approached the question of estimating the total crop with no small diffidence and misgiving. Some years ago, after twenty-one months of continuous assessment work, I essayed to work out the total annual yields of all agricultural products in Hadejia Division and it was only when I came to the question of ground-nuts that I felt any real uncertainty as to the correctness of my facts and figures and, with specific reference to that crop, I wrote in my Annual Report for 1918:– 'How much of this is available for export must remain pure conjecture. At any rate my own attempts to work it out by *known* figures have proved an utter failure.' /

16.   I originally intended to base my estimate for the whole Province on returns (for which all Divisional Officers have been asked) showing the number of farms under ground-nut cultivation separately for the last two years. By taking the average acreage and yield per acre, one would thus be able to arrive at an estimate not only of the total crop but also – by deducting the tonnage known to have been sold for export – of the amount retained in the Province for local consumption. Such returns, however, – being compiled so long after the harvest – would probably be far from reliable and I finally decided that a safer method would be

to endeavour to find out what proportion the amount actually bought in Kano for export this season bears in relation to the total crop.

17.   I recognise that this method, too, is not very satisfactory as, even if we could ascertain exactly what percentage of his crop each farmer sells, we still have to take into account the fact that the local markets and the internal trade have also to be supplied. The conclusion at which I have arrived is that approximately two-thirds of the total crop in the Province has actually reached the export market and, if this hypothesis is correct, the 1923 harvest produced, in round figures, 80,000 tons. The amount purchased in Kano itself during the season is 56,000 tons, while an additional 3,000 have been bought at stations on the line (practically all at Maidobi), making a total of 59,000 tons. From this, however, I have had to deduct the estimated quantity imported from Bornu and French Territory and I have no hesitation in saying that this did not amount to more than 5,000 tons at the very outside, thus leaving the total home-grown tonnage available for export at 54,000.

18.   I have estimated that the increase in cultivation in 1923 over that of 1922 was at least 25% and the yield per acre was probably 20% better. This gives a total of about 53,000 tons from the 1922 crop – a figure which, after deducting the 16,000 odd tons sold for export, brings us very near the estimated average of 40,000 tons for pre-war years.

B. – METHOD OF CULTIVATION.

19.   The most suitable soil is that known as 'jigawa' – of a light sandy nature with quick drainage – the next best being 'jangargari,' a slightly heavier but friable reddish earth. With the exception of Gumel and Hadejia Emirates (where 'jangargari' only occurs in a very small area of the latter) both types are found throughout the Province, but there is almost everywhere a preponderance of 'jigawa.'

20.   Generally speaking it may be taken as a practically invariable rule that ground-nuts are never cultivated on the same area in two consecutive years and it is usual to allow not less than two seasons to elapse before sowing with this product again. In the interval cereals are grown although. in thinly populated districts where there is plenty of room for agricultural development, the average farmer will always prefer to break new ground and it may be several years before he sows ground-nuts on the same site again. The only exceptions to the rule mentioned are the small plots (cultivated chiefly by women) in, or round, the compounds where manure is plentiful.

21.   Near Kano where land is valuable and is extensively manured, most farmers who grow mixed crops divide their farms into sections and it is not uncommon to find a farm of 2 or 3 acres carrying guinea corn, maiwa, cassava and ground-

nuts at the same time. But in every case a strict rotation of crops is observed and, where grown. 'maiwa' (Pennisetum Spicatum) usually follows immediately after the ground-nut.

22.   Where a man possesses two or three farms he either grows ground-nuts separately or mixes them with cereals sown in lines at right angles to the ridges (Hausa 'Gichiye.') The latter method is especially noticeable in Gumel Emirate but the cereals in this case are very sparsely sown and at large intervals. At the same time, the tendency for the one-farm cultivator to grow nuts more or less at haphay and amongst his other crops is annually increasing. /

23.   I was interested to learn from the Emir of Daura that the local farmers have in the past left the cultivation of ground-nuts almost entirely to women.

24.   The crop is grown on ridges about 2 feet 6 inches apart and 9 inches to 12 inches in height, the seeds being sown 15 inches to 18 inches apart. Two kernels are generally sown in each hole at a depth of about 2 ½ inches, the top soil being merely brushed back lightly with the foot. In Katagum Emirate however, I was informed that only one kernel is usually sown at a time.

25.   The nuts are sown either at the very beginning of the rains at the same time as millet or a month or so later. In the former case in a normal year the crop is ready for harvesting in three-and-a-half or four months while that sown later (which is more commonly the case) takes approximately five months to ripen. The latter generally gives better results and produces a larger nut.

26.   In both cases the plant appears above the ground in five or six days and begins to propagate by shooting out the nut-bearing tendrils in about a month. It is at this stage that the farm is hoed and this is almost universally, the only occasion that the crop undergoes the process of 'noma.' As far as I know, the Katagum farmers are the only cultivators who 'noma' the ground-nut crop more than once, though it may be necessary to pull up the grass and weeds round the plants from time to time.

27.   There are two methods of harvesting the crop, in both cases the plants being first dug up with the hoe. In order to separate the nuts from the plants the more common practice is to collect the plants bodily (stalks, nuts and all) and pile them in heaps until quite dry and brittle. They are then beaten with light sticks until all the nuts are detached and the final separation is subsequently effected by winnowing in calabashes.

28.   The other method is to detach the nuts on the spot by hand and then dry them separately; this is invariably done near Kano as it involves less damage to the rest of the plant for which, when dried ('Harawa'), there is always a ready sale as fodder, the price being roughly ¼d. per lb. If the 'Harawa' is spoilt by subse-

quent rain or is not required as fodder it is frequently used as manure by being scattered over the farm and burnt.

29.   Gleaning ('Kala') by women and children is a common practice and generally well repays the efforts of the gleaners.

30.   Only two distinct varieties of ground-nut are found in this Province, viz.: 'Yargari' and 'Bagwariya,' of which the former is by far the more common and the more popular. Although much smaller than the 'Bagwariya' it is said to contain a considerably greater percentage of oil, and oil-extractors will always refuse to buy the other variety. The shell contains one, two, or three kernels – being known as 'Mairakumi' when it has three owing to its resemblance to a camel's back in shape. The 'bagwariya' (also called 'Mai-lemo' or 'Babarbaria') almost invariably contains two kernels and can be distinguished by the longitudinal lines with which the shell is scored or 'keeled' instead of the net-like pattern of the 'Yargari;' the terminal of the nut is also slightly hooked. This variety is better known in Zaria, and in Kano Province is only found to any extent in Jafun and Dambarta Districts of Kano Emirate.

C. – CLIMATIC EFFECT ON CROP.

31.   Although the ground-nut requires a heavy rainfall to begin with, when once it has had a fair start it is an exceedingly hardy plant and is affected far less than cereals by long periods of drought. The effect of drought is to prevent the full development of the kernel but the period / would have to be very protracted to ruin the crop altogether and, generally speaking, the actual yield probably seldom varies more than 25% from year to year, as a direct result of climatic and meteorological conditions. This remark, however, only applies to crops which are grown on land suitable for the purpose, *i.e.*, jigawa or jangargari, and, if the farmer chooses to speculate by planting on heavy soil, which retains the moisture or is liable to become waterlogged, he runs the risk of losing the entire crop in the event of an excessive rainfall. In this case the roots simply rot.

32.   The conditions required for the very best results are fairly heavy rain the first month, moderate and evenly distributed rain for the next three months and plenty of sunshine with only a few showers during the last month. The plant can stand any amount of heat and sun.

33.   Its greatest enemy is a mauve-flowered parasitic weed known as 'kudduji' (striga senegaleusis) which is only too common on land that has become sterile through over-cultivation and lack of manure. The presence of this weed is said to account for a reduction in yield of as much as 50% and even 60%.

34.   Lack of rain – especially during the first month after sowing – is apt to encourage the ravages of the termite and of its larger neighbour, the 'zaggo,' and it is owing to the depredation of these pests rather than to the actual lack of moisture that a drought in the early days may ruin 30% of the crop. Finally, there is a small whitish grub, locally known as 'Soki,' which is also liable to cause damage to the new roots by attacking the terminals before the nuts have formed. It is said to occur more frequently during drought and may be found in any kind of soil but it is not particularly common and the actual damage done by it rarely amounts to more than 1%.

35.   The crop can, of course, be improved by the use of vegetable or animal manure but, except in the immediate vicinity of Kano, all the manure that a farmer can obtain is generally reserved for his cereal crops.

36.   I have made extensive enquiries from growers as to the actual number of nuts which one would expect to find on one plant and the reply is almost invariably from 50 to 100, with the additional information that as many as 300 to 400 are occasionally found. It is difficult, however, to reconcile these numbers with the information that is generally given as to the total yield in proportion to the amount actually sown and it is doubtful whether the average grower has ever taken the trouble to count. Some years ago I personally counted the nuts on plants as they were being harvested and, as far as I remember, from 50 to 60 would have been a fair average. This figure, too, is more in consonance with the statements of the growers as to the total yield which, if those statements are to be believed, is about twenty-fold of the amount sown. I have frequently endeavoured to prove to farmers that the total yield as compared with the amount of seed sown must bear some relative proportion to the average yield per plant but they remain unconvinced and refuse to be shaken from their original statements. Several, however, have endeavoured to conciliate me by qualifying their figures with the explanation that the women and children pick a lot of the nuts before harvest and by reminding me that the efforts of the gleaners would be bootless if nothing were left behind.

37.   From information recently supplied me by Divisional Officers and from that culled from Assessment Reports I have had to modify the opinion I formed some years ago as to the average yield per acre. At one time I held that 550 to 600 lb. of decorticated nuts would be a conservative estimate but I doubt if this can be taken as a fair average and 400 to 450 lb. is probably nearer the mark. Under the best conditions and on extensively manured farms I believe that a ton of nuts could be grown from 2 ½ acres (or nearly 900 lb. per acre) but such a harvest is extremely rare. /

38.   I endeavoured to obtain definite statistics of last season's crops (mostly mixed) on a group of 165 farms near Kano which had been measured by the Revenue Survey Department but, as both the Emir and the Village Headmen admitted, the statements made by the farmers were obviously wrong and the figures therefore useless. This, however, was only to be expected as the 'talaka' is always suspicious of questions connected with his income and accurate data can only be obtained by personal investigation at the time of harvesting.

D. – LOCAL DEMAND AND CONSUMPTION.

39.   If my estimate of the total crop is correct the amount left to meet the local demand within the Province is 26,000 tons. Before we can deal with the question of actual consumption, however, we have to deduct the amount to be set aside as seed for the coming year. On this point, at least, I have had almost invariably the same replies from growers in all the Emirates I have visited and I find that most farmers – in order to be on the safe side reserve from 7 ½% to 10% for this purpose.

40.   We may therefore take it that not less than 6,000 tons of last season's crop are being kept for seed, leaving 20,000 tons for local consumption amongst a population of 3 ½ millions – or 13 1b. per head. This I believe to be very much below the average and means that the supply for this year will not be commensurate with the *normal* internal demand but, while admitting that I may have under-estimated the total crop for 1923, I have already given it as my opinion that the stocks now in the hands of the farmers and consumers are less than they were a year ago, when the price offered by the Kano firms was lower and the harvest of cereals had not been so good. According to my estimate for 1922 there were some 37,000 tons left to provide for local needs within the Province and this may, I think, be taken as a very fair average of the consumption.

41.   In the appendix to this Report I have recorded briefly the methods employed for extracting both the edible oil and the so-called 'black oil' which is used as an illuminant and also by leather workers and boot makers for softening skins. This latter, however, is not now a very common commodity as, owing to the fact that the edible oil can be used for all purposes (giving actually better results with skins) and also that those who can afford to illuminate their houses are using kerosene to an increasing extent, the demand is extremely small and I doubt whether the whole output accounts for more than 2% of the nuts locally consumed.

42.   As will be seen from the appendix, the solid residue of the nut after the edible oil has been extracted is used for food and the 'kulli' is by far the commonest form in which ground-nuts are eaten. It is therefore quite impossible to differentiate between the requirements for edible oil and for food, and any

estimate of the proportions used for each purpose would be pure guess-work and would therefore, I submit, be of absolutely no value.

43.   Only a very small proportion of the nuts is eaten raw and, next to the 'kulli-kulli,' the favourite method is to have them fried and salted; in this form they are known as 'Motsin gemu' (literally – beard-wagging) and it is thus that one sees them set out on mats in small heaps in every way-side market. I have never known the price (½ per heap) to vary and this is regulated solely by the quantity contained in each heap. The nomenclature though not an important point, is amusing as, to the native mind, the wagging of the human beard is similar to the wagging of the canine fail and its expressive of pleasure.

44.   As far as I am aware the only other forms in which the nut is eaten without extracting the oil are known as 'Alandeya' and 'Kwoddo' respectively. To pre-pare the former, which has the appearance of a small dough-nut, / the raw nut is crushed into a paste, rolled into a ball and then lightly fried in ground-nut oil; 'kwoddo' also consists of ground-nut paste which is mixed with the boiled leaves of the 'Dunya or 'Dinya' tree.

45.   Beyond the comparatively small quantity used as an illuminant, as hair-oil and as a leather-dresser and in the manufacture of soap the cooking-pot has exclusive claim on all the edible oil produced. The number of native dishes in which it is used for frying purposes would fill a small cookery-book but I will content myself here with enumerating only a few of the commonest items of food so prepared:–

> *Weina:*– A small round cake made from the flour of millet, guinea-corn, rice, pea-nut (gujia) or cassava.
> *Finkaso:*– A fritter made with alkalmma flour.
> *Tsatsaffa:*– A fritter made with guinea-corn flour.
> *Kosei:*– A small cake of crushed beans.
> *Jan Karago:*– Balls of pea-nut (gujia) paste boiled in ground-nut oil.
> *Taliya:*– Macaroni made of alkamma flour, rolled in the palm of the hand.
> *Tsutsa:*– As its name suggests, is similar to vermicelli and is made in the same way as Taliya but is rolled between the thumb and fingers.
> *Dindi-kwollo:*– Fried potato.

46.   Most householders buy their oil in minute quantities at a time and it is generally sold in a small calabash ladle (akoshi), the price varying with the cur-rent price of the raw produce. The extraction of oil, which is done exclusively by women, is skilled labour and, when a grower requires oil, he takes his raw nuts to the professional extractor and either pays a small fee in cash or – as is the more usual practice – allows her to take a percentage of the result.

E. – INTERNAL DEMAND AND THE EXPORT TRADE.

47.   This subject has already been partially dealt with both directly and indirectly in other sections of the report and it is only necessary to add here a few notes on the general aspect of the question.

48.   Briefly it may be stated that the native is willing (up to a certain point) to sacrifice the internal demand to the requirements of the export trade provided *(a)* that the price offered is sufficiently attractive and *(b)* that he has ample food supplies of other kinds (*i.e.*, cereals, cassava and beans) for his needs. To many peasants ground-nuts and ground-nut oil are luxuries which they are willing to forego if the abstention is made worth while.

49.   The export trade, therefore, regulates the price of this commodity until the surplus stock is exhausted, after which the local market then takes charge of the situation and may even demand a higher price than the exporter can afford to pay. Distributed, as the produce is, over such a large area and in such small quantities, it is not easy to understand how the local trade appreciate the dividing line between surplus stocks and internal requirements – more especially in view of the fact that the daily demand in each individual market throughout the year is extremely small as compared with that of the export trade which accounts for so large a proportion of the crop in four or five months. In addition to this there is always a certain number of farmers who sell their entire crop during the buying season and who, in consequence, have to purchase fresh supplies of seed later on.

50.   There is no doubt, however, that the petty traders and retailers are always fully alive to the position and, as they are in direct touch with both the internal and the external trades, they have the advantage (over producer and buyer alike) of knowing whether immediate sale to the exporter or deferred transactions in the local markets will eventually show a better profit. /

51.   While the majority of farmer-growers sell the whole of their surplus stock at once, there are still others who are less impulsive and who, at the end of the harvest, are content to sell only a sufficient quantity of nuts wholesale to enable them to pay their taxes and to clear off any other liabilities that may be outstanding. Their remaining surplus stocks (*i.e.*, those which they do not require for their own consumption and for seed) they store for the time being and take their cue as regards subsequent disposal from the retail dealers.

52.   During a big buying season like that which has just ended the effect of the export trade of ground-nuts on the cost of living generally is remarkable and it is worth while recording that the price of cereals in Kano was higher during December and January (usually the cheapest months in the year) than it was in

March when the buying had slackened off and local trade began once more to resume its normal course.

F. – THE GROUND-NUT TRADE.

53.   The tracing of the various methods and stages by which the nuts pass from the producer to the exporting firm forms a most interesting and absorbing study. The details, however, are so variable and so intricate that it is difficult to know where to begin and, for the sake of clearness, I have finally decided to risk the obvious 'hysteron proteron' and start with the ultimate buyer.

54.   Although some exporters (notably the Syrians) are willing to deal personally with small quantities at a time and so get into direct touch not only with the petty trader but also with the producer himself it is obvious that the big European firms, each of whose purchases amount to several thousands of tons in one season, could not provide the necessary staff to supervise the weighing, paying and bagging of odd donkey-loads and small consignments and they are therefore compelled to buy the produce wholesale.

55.   To this end the exporter has three courses open to him and generally he makes use of all three, viz.: (i) direct purchase from the middleman (Hausa, Arab, Yoruba, Syrian and even Sierra-Leonean); (ii) A temporary agreement with a native 'agent' to whom he advances money and who makes his headquarters at one of the big buying markets on a main road, and (iii) direct purchase from natives or others to whom he advances money and assigns a buying site on the firm's own premises. In a few instances, firms have rented plots in the Produce Market in their own name for the accommodation of these 'agents.'

56.   In every case the exporter first issues – generally on loan – to all these classes a supply of bags, in which the produce is to be finally shipped and sold in the European market. Twine for sewing up the filled bags is also supplied at the same time and in this way actual handling by the firm is reduced to a minimum. The size of these bags is invariable and, when full, each weighs approximately 180 lb. For purposes of rough calculation for freight, etc., 12 ½ bags equal one ton.

57.   Strictly speaking the three classes from whom the Kano firm buys should all be described as middlemen but, whereas the middleman in class (i) uses his own capital and is free to sell where he likes, those of classes (ii) and (iii) are under an obligation to the firm from whom they have received advances of cash. The practice of advancing money to such men is still common but, with few exceptions, the amounts so advanced are small and it is satisfactory to note that the tendency to hand over large sums of money to unknown persons without any security has considerably diminished since 1921, while increased reliance is being placed in the middleman with capital. /

58.   The past season has been noteworthy for the number of contracts which have been placed by the firms with these middlemen for the delivery of so many tons at a fixed price. Contracts for consignments of 100 and 200 tons at a time are now comparatively common and I know of one instance where a contract of 1,000 tons was made and the nuts were delivered within three weeks. Such a transaction enables one to realise the enormous amount of ready cash which some of the wealthier native and Arab traders have at their command and to appreciate the desire of the more important European firms to exclude the 'man of straw' and to increase their business with the native capitalist.

59.   These middlemen have a wide scope for their activities and each one is gradually extending his business connexion not only in the immediate proximity of Kano City but also in the outlying Districts and neighbouring Emirates. Most of them have their headquarters in the native town and many also possess plots in the Syrian quarters or in the 'Sabon Gari' while, during the height of the ground-nut season, they rent plots in the Produce Market in addition. As a rule they have a certain number of permanent assistants and employees to whom they entrust money for the purpose of procuring nuts in the more important districts and mainroad markets, such as Bichi (Katsina Road), Dambarta (Daura Road), and Gaya (Azare and Borna Road) where they buy from the actual producer or the petty trader and send in their purchases by camel transport. These markets not only tap the main trade routes to Kano but are also useful centres for the locally produced crops.

60.   It is interesting to note that while the Syrians and the wealthy Kano traders (who work alone) usually remain in Kano and do all their outside business through paid employees, the Arab, Yoruba and Coast middlemen frequently club together (each, of course, with their own kind) and work in partnership. One partner stays in Kano not only to carry on the local buying but also to supply the necessary funds to the others who are stationed in outlying markets and who send their purchases direct to him for final disposal to the exporting firms.

61.   In Kano Emirate it has long been customary for the Native Administration to issue permits to all middlemen, agents and their employees who wish to establish themselves in the outlying buying markets during the ground-nut season. Those who are not natives of Kano or ordinarily resident within the jurisdiction of the Kano Native Courts have to sign a declaration that they will submit to the local Native Authorities and will consider themselves amenable to the discipline of the local Courts.

During the past season 228 such permits have been issued and of the applicants ten were Arabs, five Yoruhas, five natives of Sierra-Leone and the remainder Hausas. The officials of the District Administration, however, are not very strict about this rule and there must have been a large number of persons who were allowed to trade in this way without permits.

62.   By having two or three business places at Kano itself the middleman also gets into personal touch with the ever-increasing number of growers and petty traders who prefer to come to Kano direct and this gives him an opportunity of extending his regular clientèle. Whereas a few years ago the majority of petty traders and farmers who came to sell their produce in Kano arrived with no particular objective and merely wandered round seeking the best price they could obtain, there is now an annually growing tendency for them to go direct to one of the middlemen whom they know and of whom they have now become regular customers. But every year brings a crowd of hitherto perfect strangers and I am afraid that I cannot hold the middleman and his paid agents guiltless of employing touts and 'runners' for the purpose of rounding up the new-comers. /

63.   The class of middleman whom I have described as an 'agent' of the European firm and to whom the latter advances money is generally more restricted in his business activities. He may rent a plot for the season in the produce market but otherwise he possesses no business premises of his own and is usually to be found in the district markets and villages. He, too, in many cases is able to collect a small clientele with the assistance of his touts and the same remark applies also to members of the third class who carry on business actually on the firm's premises. Amongst this class one finds a number of ex-cooks and other retired domestic servants – both Yoruba and Hausa – and it has been alleged to me that they are the worst offenders in the employment of touts and are in the habit of making use of ex-soldiers and ex-constables for this purpose. I know of no concrete instance of this and I merely record a statement to which I can readily give credence in view of the fact that there are still many 'talakawa' whom the owner of an imposing row of medal ribbons would have little difficulty in persuading to obey his behests. Were such cases numerous, however, we should no doubt hear more about them.

64.   During this last season several of the Arab and Kano middlemen, as well as the native 'agents' of European firms, have gone further a-field than in previous years and both Daura and Hadejia, for instance, have now become quite important buying centres. Hitherto the ground-nuts from Hadejia Emirate and South-western Bornu were exported chiefly from Yalo Market (near the Hadejia-Kano boundary) by local or Kano petty traders but the greater part of the business has recently been transferred from Yalo to Hadejia itself which is now in direct touch with the Kano trade. This has the beneficial result of stimulating competition and so securing a better price for the producer.

65.   In the course of my report I have several times mentioned the 'petty trader' and, before proceeding further it may be as well to explain more precisely my

meaning of the term in connexion with the ground-nut trade. The real 'middleman' is the wholesale dealer or broker who actually supplies the Kano firms – as described in a preceding paragraph – while the 'petty trader' is the middleman between the 'middlemen' and the producers. He owns his own transport (donkey or pack-oxen) and his chief business lies in the villages and hamlets and in the smaller or more distant markets to which the 'middleman' proper and his employees have not yet penetrated. Generally he buys his nuts in small quantities and in an undecorticated condition, pays for their decortication on the spot and transports them to Kano or the nearest buying market in the 'teke,' or native leather sack. On arrival he sells to the 'middleman' who, in his turn, sells to the European firm.

66.   There is a very large number of these petty traders in Kano City and, while a few of them do occasionally deal direct with the exporter, the majority transact their business almost exclusively through the middlemen. The local petty trader in the outlying Districts and Emirates generally prefers 'small profits and quick returns' and deals with some middleman in the nearest buying market to his own village. At the same time the number of those who come from a distance direct to Kano is annually increasing.

67.   We now come to the question of prices and profits and of the amount which the actual producer receives. This last depends on three main factors, viz.: (i) the ruling price in Kano, (ii) the distance from Kano and (iii) the amount of competition in the locality where the producer sells.

68.   As regards (i) I am told that never in the history of the Kano ground-nut trade has the price fluctuated so frequently as during this last season. During the boom of 1919–20 the fluctuations were considerably greater in amount but the price generally remained fairly steady for a week or so at a time whereas the recent changes have been of daily occurrence. During the first two or three days of November / the price per ton was little more than £9 but a fortnight later had risen to £13 and, before the end of the month, as much as £14 15s. 0d. had been paid. Between the middle of December and the middle of January prices ranged from £14 15s. 0d. to £15 15s. 0d. (this latter being the highest recorded during the season as far as I have been able to ascertain) and from that time began to drop again until, a month later, £13 5s. 0d. was reached. After that, buying slackened off and by March 10th, when I began my investigation, firms were either refusing to buy at all or were offering £12 10s. 0d. to £12 15s. 0d. only.

I have been told (but here again I merely record a statement which I have no means of verifying) that the Syrian exporters were chiefly responsible for the high prices paid in December and January. They were willing to risk a gamble in order to maintain their connexion with the middlemen and continued for some time to offer slightly higher rates than the other firms who were compelled to follow them.

69.   In ascertaining the average price for the whole season I have received the greatest assistance from several Agents of the larger European firms who not only gave me such information as I required but, in some cases, even allowed me access to their books. I have, therefore, little fear of contradiction in stating that the average price paid for the 59,000 tons bought in this Province was £14 15s. 0d. per ton which puts the total amount expended in the purchase of ground-nuts at £870,000.

70.   How much of this sum actually reached the pockets of the farmer-grow-ers it is almost impossible to calculate with any hope of reasonable accuracy and, even though one collects voluminous data and statistics (as I have done) from the producers themselves, one has to remember that these are merely the uncorroborated statements of individual natives (based on purely approximate weights and measures) and also that the actual dates of the transactions would have to be known to enable one to obtain any clear idea as to the profits made at the various stages.

71.   To begin with, however, I propose to take two extreme cases and will assume that on each occasion the market price on the day that the nuts reach Kano is the season's average, *i.e.,* £14 15s. 0d. per ton.

   (*a*) Where the producer decorticates his own nuts at home, transports by his own donkeys and sells direct to the exporter himself. In this instance he would probably be paid at the rate of about £14 per ton – or not very much more than he would receive from a middleman in the produce market, But such cases are extremely rare as, in the first place, there are still comparatively few farmers outside a radius of one day's journey who actually bring their own nuts to Kano. Secondly, those who do come gen-erally prefer to do their business with the middlemen in the City, the produce market or the Syrian trading sites. Thirdly, even if the farmer does bring his produce direct to the Kano firm, he seldom has an oppor-tunity (as I have previously pointed out) of dealing with the European himself but has to complete the transaction through one of the native 'agents' located on the premises.

72. (*b*) At the other extreme is the farmer who lives some 120 miles away – in Katagum Emirate, for instance. He takes his undecorticated nuts to the nearest village market where he finds a local petty trader waiting to buy. It is not, however, etiquette for the latter to purchase direct and the cor-rect procedure is to secure the services of a 'Mai-aunia' – a lady whose profession it is to measure the produce and do the bargaining. The latter

receives no money but takes a small quantity of the produce (probably averaging not more than / 2%) as her fee for the part she has played in the transaction, this fee being taken from the farmer before payment. The trader then has to have the nuts decorticated and when he has obtained from various farmers (or even local retailers) all he requires – which depends on the number of donkeys he possesses – he starts off towards Kano. About half-way he begins to meet the middlemen's touts and one of them eventually persuades him to follow him to Geya (about 34 miles from Kano) where he introduces him to his employer. To the latter the petty trader sells his consignment which is immediately bagged and eventually goes by camel to the middleman's partner in Kano.

73.   Still assuming that the Kano price is £14 15s. 0d. per ton and working backwards from the exporter to the producer, the following account gives a very fair idea of the various stages of the transaction and of the profits made at each:–

	£	s.	d.
Transport from Geya	1	2	0
Middleman's expenses for touts and labour (bagging, etc.)	0	8	0
Middleman's net profit	1	5	0
Decortication	0	10	0
Petty Trader's expenses on road	1	6	0
Petty Trader's net profit	2	15	0
	£ 7	6	0

To this we have to add the value of the produce – say 4/- – taken by the 'mai-aunia,' the farmer-grower thus obtaining £7 5s. 0d. per ton as against £12 paid at Geya.

74.   It should be pointed out that the petty trader's expenses depend largely on the number of donkeys he has at his disposal and I have in this case taken him as the owner of two, which is a fair average. In order to deal with one ton of nuts, therefore, he would have to make six or seven journeys to Geya – each of nine days there and back – and his food for himself and his boy would cost him about 4s. per journey. By the time he had rested his beasts and collected a new consignment of produce between each journey, he would scarcely be able to cope with more than one ton during the whole season and so his profit, though it looks large as compared with that of the middleman, is not really very considerable and reduces itself to a few shillings each trip.

75.   Between these two extremes there are, of course other means by which the nuts might reach Kano. The petty trader from Katagum, for instance, might pass straight through to Kano and so cut out the transport charges and the middleman's expenses, though he would not generally secure the latter's profits as the produce would still have to go through a middleman's hands before reaching the exporter. The producer himself on the other hand, might (and frequently does if

he owns, or can burrow, a donkey) have his nuts decorticated at home and himself take them to Geya, in which case he would obtain the £12.

76.   During the height of the season when the competition both in Kano and in the District buying markets is at its zenith, producers who take the trouble to come themselves to any one of these markets can always obtain so fair a price from the middlemen that most of them find it is really hardly worth their while to bring their small consignments any further and they would in the end make very little more than the actual cost of transport. /

77.   I should add here that farmers and petty traders rarely travel alone if they have to go any distance and they generally form small caravans under the conduct of one man whom they unanimously select and who is called the 'madugu.' These 'Madugu' are always chosen from amongst those who have personally had dealings with the Kano traders and middlemen before and they are valuable assets in helping to extend the latters' clientèles. In time they become recognised professional conductors and receive from the middlemen a small commission on each donkey-load of produce in the caravans which follow them.

78.   I have already mentioned the advantages that have accrued to the Hadejia farmer through the recent stimulus of competition and I can illustrate this by concrete figures. During the 1917–18 season (with the Kano price *averaging* £10) the very highest rate paid at Yalo market (90 miles from Kano) was £2 15s. 0d. and, even when over £40 was being quoted during the 'boom' year, the Hadejia farmer was lucky if he got £5. This year, however, the District Officer assures me that in Hadejia town (110 miles from Kano) the price actually reached £10 per ton, whereas in Azare, which is only 10 miles further away from Kano but where there is at present little or no competition, I doubt whether the producer has at any time received more than £7 10s. 0d. per ton.

79.   The 3,000 odd tons that have been purchased at Madobi have been mostly brought to the exporters through the agency of Yoruba middlemen, many of whom are permanently resident there and who seem to enjoy what almost amounts to a monopoly in the ground-nut trade in that locality.

80.   I have been at some pains to work out an estimate of the net profits obtained by middlemen and have discussed the question, at some length with several of the more important Arab and native traders both in Kano and in the outlying markets. The best time for them is just before the buying season starts seriously and immediately after the harvest when farmers are in urgent need of ready cash to pay their taxes and are willing to sell a large proportion of their produce at once without waiting to see whether prices are likely to increase. At the same time such purchases by the middleman are somewhat speculative as no one can tell with any certainty beforehand what course the export trade will take.

One of the Arab buyers in Dambarta, for instance, told me that he had been able to secure a few tons of nuts during the early days of November at an average of £7 per ton and by the time they reached Kano they fetched £12. With transport and expenses at about 30s. this meant a clear profit of £3 10s. 0d. per ton.

81.   Such profits, however, are not secured for more than a few days and are soon cut down by competition and by the producer's knowledge of prevailing prices. As long as prices rise the middleman is perfectly safe but, directly the Kano buying shows signs of slackening off and prices begin to drop, his profits are reduced until, at the very end of the season, they practically vanish altogether. By that time the producer is not as hard up as he was and sees no reason why he should sell his nuts at a reduced rate, so it is the middleman who chiefly suffers.

82.   Another Arab buyer at Dambarta allowed me to see the record of his transactions, showing the number of bags that he had sent to Kano and the actual amount of cash which had passed through his hand. His total purchase was 185 tons and his expenditure (including freight, labour and his own living expenses) £2,500 or £13 10s. 0d. per ton. At that time he and his partner in Kano had not balanced their final accounts but, assuming the produce to have been sold at the average of £14 15s. 0d. the net profit would be £1 5s. 0d. per ton. A Sierra Leone trader at the same market bought 48 tons at a total cost of £12 5s. 0d. per ton which gives him a clear profit of £2 10s. 0d. per ton. Again, one of the biggest native traders in Kano City while admitting that / he sometimes made well over £2 per ton, stated that he had actually lost £55 on one contract of 100 tons and this statement was subsequently confirmed by the firm to whom the nuts were delivered. Another case that might be quoted is that of an Arab in Hadejia who had bought 220 tons at an average of £9 16s. 0d.; to this must be added the cost of freight to Kano (£32s. 6d.) and labour, etc. (say 5s.), bringing the total cost per ton to £13 3s. 6d. per ton. The net profit should therefore have been £1 11s. 6d. per ton.

83.   I have specially chosen the above examples because I think that my informants on these occasions were being perfectly candid as to their transactions and I look upon them as reliable persons who – provided that their names were not mentioned – were willing to help and to give accurate information. Taking the whole season through I have come to the conclusion that the average clear profit made by the middlemen must have been about 25s. per ton. Several well-known European traders would, I believe, join issue with me on this point and would place the middleman's profit at less than £1 but my experience is that generally speaking the exporter does not concern himself with the history of the produce he buys and is usually quite ignorant as to its place of origin. The middlemen, too, would hardly be likely to confess to the full extent of their profits in discussing the question with their patrons who are also, in a way, their rivals.

84.   The middleman's expenses are not usually very heavy; they depend to a great extent on whether he uses touts or not and, in the ordinary way, should not exceed 5s. per ton. Producers or petty traders, therefore, dealing direct with the middleman or agent of the exporting firm should be paid at the current Kano rate *less* 30s. per ton (*i.e.,* 25s. profit and 5s. expenses) and less the transport charge according to the distance.

85.   A detail of the trade which is not without interest is that connected with weights and measures. Every locality has its own special method of calculating produce and, in replying to questions, farmers and traders will always quote in terms of 'kwaria', 'kwando', 'bufu', 'teke', 'kiskirri', 'mangalla', etc., etc., and all these bags, sacks, baskets and calabashes have to be reduced to tons, the difficulty being increased by the fact that even the basket (or whatever the local measure may be) varies in size between one district and another. In Kano itself, however, even the middleman almost invariably uses the ordinary heavy weighing machine and incidentally it may be noted here that during November an Inspector under the Weights and Measures Ordinance examined all the machines then in use.

86.   But there is another method of calculation which has become increasingly popular amongst middlemen and native traders both in Kano and in the outside buying markets and that is measurement by the bucket. The particular bucket used for this purpose is of European origin and is invariable in size, holding 36 lb. of decorticated nuts or exactly one fifth of a bag. In most of the outside markets prices are exclusively quoted at so much per bucket and so widely known is the measure becoming that it may in time form a useful basis of calculation even for internal trade. Meanwhile its name has already penetrated to distant villages where the utensil itself has not yet been seen and I shall be surprised if the official dictionary now in course of preparation does not contain the word 'Boketi.' At present the opinion of the vendors as to the relative merits of the bucket and the weighing machine seems to be divided but one Missan trader whom I met in Azare confided to me that he preferred the latter. His objection to the bucket was that the whole of the contents of his leather sacks had to be emptied out before the produce could be measured and an offer made by the purchaser. If the offer did not come up to expectations the owner was left with the alternative of collecting his scattered produce, repacking his sacks and going elsewhere or of accepting a price which he thought was inadequate. With the weighing machine, on the other hand the sack was merely thrown on to the scale and the price quoted at once. /

87.   Katsina seems to be the only place which has so far definitely adopted a recognised and universal measure for ground-nuts and this is a small metal bowl (also of European manufacture) which holds 2 lb. of decorticated nuts and is

known as 'Dan Uku tarro' (*i.e.*, '3 for 3d.' the local price at the time of its introduction being ½d. per lb.) The Emir told me that vendors and purchasers in the
Katsina market now refuse to transact business with any other form of measure
and it is a pity that some larger vessel was not originally adopted as the sale of a
ton of nuts by this means must require the employment of an unnecessary vast
amount of labour.

88.   Except for the purpose of meeting the demand in Kano City, for which
there is a large number of resident petty traders who cater specially, the internal
ground-nut trade is purely local and is almost exclusively retail.

By 'local' I mean that each town and village market taps only the produce
grown in the hamlets from which that particular market is most accessible.
Very small quantities change hands at a time and the retail traders are generally
women who are also professional oil-extractors. Petty traders do undoubtedly
buy to a certain extent when the nuts are cheap and hold for a later rise but, as
a rule, their storage capacity is limited and the amounts held by the individual
comparatively small. Business in the local markets is practically confined to
undecorticated nuts.

89.   It should be added that a few tons of undecorticated nuts are exported
annually from this Province not only to Jos and Kaduna and elsewhere in Nigeria but also to Accra. Such as it is, the trade with the last named town is in the
hands of one or two Gold Coast natives resident in the Kano 'Sabon Gari.'

G. – TRANSPORT.

90.   While privately-owned donkeys and, to a very much smaller extent, oxen
are employed by both growers and petty traders to transport the nuts not only
from the villages to local District markets but also from the latter to Kano, I estimate that nearly 50% of this season's purchase was brought in by camels. Soon
after the buying season begins the Asbenawa flock over the border from French
Territory with their camels and continue to ply regularly between Kano and the
big buying markets, where they are exclusively employed by the Arab, Yoruba,
Coast and Hausa middlemen, until the stocks are exhausted. It would be interesting to know how many thousands of camels have actually been employed for this
purpose in the Province during the past season but unfortunately I was too late to
be able to form even a rough estimate and, as far as I know, no figures are available.

91.   The chief advantage of camels is that each can carry two full bags comfortably (and some even three) while owing to its bulky shape and lack of 'give' when
properly filled, a bag is an awkward and almost impossible load for a donkey. For
the transport, therefore, of all the nuts bought and bagged ready for export by the
middlemen from the outlying markets, the trade is dependent entirely on camels.

92.   The early arrivals from French Territory always take full advantage of their opportunities and keep their transport charges high until other competitors come into the field. The first caravans began to arrive this season during the early days of November and it was not until towards the end of that month that the charges become fixed in each market. These remained conslant until after the middle of February when buying began to slacken off and the rates became further reduced. From Dambarta for instance, (32 miles from Kano) the rate per ton in November was 25s. for the next 2 ½ months 22s. and by the middle of March had dropped to 14s. It may also be noted here that the camel drivers invariably insist on full payment before accepting the freight. /

93.   Although the transport rates from all markets roughly equi-distant from Kano are the same, the actual rate per ton-mile does not remain constant, the tendency being for the rate to decrease as the radius increases.

   This is shown in the following table:–

Miles from Kano.	Lowest.			Highest.			Fixed rate during height of season.		
	£	s.	d	£	s.	d	£	s.	d.
10	0	9	6	0	9	6	0	9	6
12	0	12	6	0	12	6	0	12	6
18 to 23	0	12	6	0	19	0	0	18	0
32 to 35	0	14	0	1	5	0	1	2	0
40	1	2	0	1	11	6	1	8	0
Katsina 100	2	3	6	3	2	6	2	16	6
Hadejia 110	3	2	6	3	2	6	3	2	6

94.   The regular hire of donkey transport is confined to the carriage of nuts from the Native City (3s. per ton) and the Produce Market (1s. per ton) to the Canteen and also from the South of the Emirate where camel transport is not used beyond a distance of 20 miles from Kano. Owing to this and to the fact that they can operate from stations on the Railway line, middlemen make little use of the markets in the Southern Districts and all the nuts that reach Kano from the South are bought by petty traders and agents and are transported in native leather sacks by donkeys. Hire of the latter works out at approximately 1s. per ton per mile.

95.   In addition to the cases enumerated in the preceding paragraph, donkeys are frequently hired from friends by growers and petty traders but such arrangements are purely private and there are no recognised or fixed rates.

H. – Palm-oil.

96.   It may be stated definitely that the local consumption of ground-nut oil is in no way affected by the importation of palm-oil. Only a comparatively small quantity of the latter is brought into this Province (chiefly by Yorubas) and it is not used for the same purposes as ground-nut oil. A few of the wealthier natives

of Kano City and Katsina use it in the preparation of 'miya' (a thick soup which, when so prepared, is almost a 'palm-oil chop,' – otherwise it is chiefly applied externally as an unguent or embrocation and even in the outlying Districts it is eagerly sought as a cure for rheumatism, etc. A large proportion of the amount imported is purchased by Native Foreigners. In price it is about 30% more expensive than ground-nut oil and is generally sold at 1s. per (whisky) bottle in the Kano Market where the same amount of ground-nut oil can be purchased for 9d. on an average.

I. – DECORTICATION.

97. This is done exclusively by women by means of the wooden mortar ('Turmi') and pestle ('Tabariya'). Only a small quantity is poured into the mortar at a time and the nuts are then pounded ('sussuka') with the pestle until all the shells have been broken and the kernels separated. Although it looks very simple, a certain amount of skill is required to break the shells without crushing the kernels.

98. The contents of the mortar are then turned into a calabash and winnowed ('shika') by pouring from one calabash to another until all the shell has been blown away.

99. Two women invariably work one mortar between them, taking it in turns to beat and winnow. By careful weighing and timing I have worked out that two women will produce one ton of decorticated nuts in rather less than 27 hours, at a fee of from 8s. to 10s. between them. This / fee is almost invariable and the difference is accounted for by the variation in measure in the different localities, *i.e.*, so much is paid in one place per 'teke' (leather sack), in another per basket, in another per calabash and so on and it is noteworthy that the fee actually works out at slightly less per ton in Kano City than in some places 100 miles away.

100. When properly dried the kernel weighs exactly 70% of the undecorticated nut while the bulk of the latter is approximately 2 ½ times as great.

101. Decortication by hand ('bare') which takes four times as long, is *only* employed when the kernels are required or sowing.

J. – KANO PRODUCE MARKET.

102. Ever since 1920 the more important European firms, backed by the Kano Chamber of Commerce, have been agitating for the abolition of the Township Produce Market which was established in the earlier days of the trade at their own request. A little over a year ago the Chamber was 'still unanimously of opinion that no useful purpose is served by the continuance of this Market, which is

mostly the resort of undesirables who have no real stake in the business of the Township.'

It was, however, pointed out that of the twenty-three plots taken up in February. 1923, only two were occupied by 'small speculative and migratory middlemen' the remaining tenants being well-known local traders.

103.   During the past season the question was again raised but the Government eventually decided that the Market should remain open for the present, the chief objection to its abolition being the loss to the Township revenue and the difficulty that the Native Administration might experience in enforcing its prohibition against the erection of booths in the immediate vicinity of the Township boundary.

104.   It is not within the province of the present report to discuss the ethics of the question but I consider that my enquiry into the trade would not be complete without some estimate as to the extent to which the Produce Market is used and as to whether the volume of trade which passes through it is decreasing or increasing. Unfortunately, owing to the lateness of the season, my personal visits to the Market gave me little or no first-hand information and my deductions are based chiefly on the result of enquiries made not only amongst the European merchants but also amongst the more important African traders who have other business premises besides these market plots.

105.   To begin with, the number of plots rented last December (the busiest month of the season) was forty-seven as compared with fifty-five during the corresponding month of 1922. Although the actual difference is small it must be remembered that there were far more people engaged in the trade this year and that the tonnage dealt with was three and a half times greater than during the previous season. Further evidence of the waning popularity of the Market is forthcoming from the wealthy native traders who say that their customers are now coming direct to their houses in the City in increasing numbers. As long as the Produce Market is permitted to remain, middlemen will, in self-defence, continue to rent plots in it, but I am equally certain that the proportionate volume of trade therein will annually decrease. /

106.   My estimate of the distribution of this last season's ground-nut business is as follows:–

Bought in Produce Market	25%.
Bought by middlemen in other Emirates and District buying Markets	45%.
Bought in the City, Trading plots and the Native Reservation	30%.

I may be accused of exaggerating the percentage bought in the outside markets by middlemen and despatched to Kano ready for export by camel transport but I have gone into the question very carefully and am convinced that there is an increasing tendency on the part of middlemen, brokers and agents to enlarge their sphere of operations and to bring the export market nearer to the producer.

K. – TOUTING AND OTHER OFFENCES.

107.   Touting, though still prevalent, has shown distinct signs of diminution during the past season and, at any rate, has been accompanied by fewer instances of violence and intimidation than was the case three or four years ago when complaints against acts of this nature were becoming alarmingly frequent. Unless there is a direct complaint of active molestation one hears very little about these touts in Kano itself and my information on the subject generally has been obtained chiefly from farmers and petty traders in the neighbouring Emirates. It is difficult to find a single man who has not, while travelling towards Kano with ground-nuts, been accosted at some part of his journey by these parasites.

108.   It is a common practice for the latter to offer money or food to the traveller by way of binding him to a contract but this trick is now too well known to deceive any but the most ignorant and credulous of the 'talakawa' and there are occasions when the intended victim himself assumes the role of villain. One 'madugu' informed me with great pride that he had deliberately accepted 1s. from a tout but that, as he had already definitely decided upon his destination and had a fairly strong party with him, he had merely thanked the donor on reaching the pitch of the latter's employer and passed on his way. As a rule, too, it is only necessary for the owner of the nuts to mention the name of the firm or broker whom he intends to patronise in order to avoid further molestation.

109.   Nevertheless, isolated cases of violence do still occur and two men were sentenced to six months and three months respectively in the Station Magistrate's Court in December for assaulting a farmer who refused to follow them with his donkey load of ground-nuts. In the same Court a Syrian was fined 30s. for assaulting a native middleman during an argument as to who had the prior right to purchase ground-nuts brought in by a certain farmer. Another case was a complaint by a Syrian that a native trader in the Syrian quarters had taken produce intended for the Syrian. Before the case came before the Court, however, the nuts had been returned to the owner and the defendant was discharged with a caution.

110.   Only three other complaints were brought before the Station Magistrate's Court in connexion with touting but in no instance could the touts be found. One of these was a particularly bad case and is worth recording. Complainant, the European agent of a Trading firm, alleged that the touts of another firm had seized by violence and taken to the latter firm ground-nuts intended for the complainant. The owner who sent the ground-nuts to the complainant's firm owed them money and wished to have the value of his produce written off

against his debt. Unfortunately the touts could not be identified. I was especially interested in this case because it coincides so exactly with a story told me at Daura by a petty trader of that town that I have no doubt that it is the same / man. This trader had for some time been personally transacting business with a Kano firm, buying salt and selling ground-nuts, but on this occasion he sent his brother and the latter was forcibly taken to another firm by touts and the nuts were weighed and paid for by one of the native middlemen located on the firm's premises. According to the brother's statement he first complained to the European agent who merely said that it was not his concern.

111.   I do not know the name of the defendant firm but the case raises the question as to how far the Manager of a firm is legally responsible for the acts of persons engaged in business on the firm's premises though not actually employed by them. Were I satisfied that any particular firm was in the habit of knowingly permitting such acts to be committed, I should personally have no hesitation in informing the Emir and allowing the Native Administration to take such steps as it could to warn the Districts with a view to organising a boycott.

112.   In the Kano Native Courts two touts were sentenced to one year's imprisonment each for using violence while another was imprisoned for one month for attempted intimidation.

113.   Adulteration of ground-nuts is rare and only two persons charged with this offence were brought before the Supreme Court during the recent season. One native trader was fined £10 while in the second case the accused was found not guilty.

114.   In the same Court three persons were fined in December last, for buying nuts elsewhere than in the Produce Market or other authorised place and five persons were convicted for a similar offence in the Native Courts and sentenced to one day's imprisonment each.

L. – Conclusion.

115.   It is almost superfluous for me to record the fact that the representatives of all the Kano firms have complained bitterly of the delay in evacuating this year's ground-nut purchases by rail. The problem is not an easy one and there is much to be said for both sides but meanwhile the future of the trade depends very considerably on the successful solution of the difficulty. Several buyers who have, between them, accounted for more than half of this year's tounage have already stated definitely that they will not purchase a single bag during the next season unless some arrangement can be made whereby the produce can be shipped home in reasonable time.

116.   The trouble is, of course, that the prices in the home markets are continually fluctuating and, whereas at the actual time of purchase a margin is allowed for a certain amount of profit at the current price, a subsequent fall in the home market reduces the profits to zero and, if the fall continue delay in evacuation may be the direct cause of a definite loss to the buyers. Brokers at home are naturally unwilling to offer contracts until they know that the produce has been shipped and even were they willing to do so the firms out here are unable to accept contracts for fear that lack of transport may prevent delivery by the date agreed upon.

117.   Every firm has apparently a different estimate of the total expenses and charges incurred – over and above the actual purchase price – in transferring a ton of nuts from the vendor in Kano to the buyer at home and from several I have obtained the details of these estimates. The lowest I have seen is £8 15s. 9d. and the highest £10 5s. 7d., the chief difference between these particular two being the item for 'Establishment Charges' which was put down as 1s. in the former and £1 in the latter. I rather suspect, however, from the low average prices said to have been paid by this firm that the £1 includes various commissions paid to the / 'madugu' and others which would normally be entered as part of the actual purchase price. Most firms estimate these additional expenses at about £9 and, if they paid an average of £14 15s. 0d. for the produce, the total cost per ton is therefore £23 15s. 0d. The loss of interest on capital between purchase in Kano and delivery in England *is* not, of course, included.

118.   This was the price (£23 15s. 0d.) that was being quoted in Liverpool towards the end of February for consignments then afloat but from that date the quotations began steadily to fall and it seems, therefore that the stories one hears of actual losses on the season's total business are not without foundation. The prospect of still further delay in clearing the consignments caused several firms to deliberate whether it would not be advisable to hold up their stocks either in Lagos or Kano in the hopes of a later rally in the home market. At the former, however, they would run the risk of serious deterioration while the retention of the stocks in Kano would merely add to the congestion during the following seasons.

119.   I do not quite know how the Nigerian nuts compare with those from all other parts of the world but I have been told by a dealer at home that at any rate they are inferior in quality to the Sudan variety. Unless their quality is at least up to the standard of other nuts imported into the European Market it seems essential that the Nigerian crop should be allowed to take advantage of its geographical position to supply the home demand *before* the crops from the East are due to arrive.

120.   On the other hand it is obvious that the Government must be given some reasonably accurate estimate of the tonnage with which the railway will be called upon to deal in good time to allow of the necessary arrangements being made. I am told that it was estimated during the summer of 1923 that the forthcoming season would result in the purchase of 25,000 tons but I understand that this estimate was as unauthoritative as it has subsequently proved to be inaccurate and misleading. Had the estimate been correct the whole of the crop to be exported would have been evacuated in reasonable time as over 28,000 tons had been railed by the end of March. Of this amount the railway dealt with 27,360 tons (or 6,840 per month) between December 1st and March 31st.

121.   As regards next season's prospects many of the leading merchants have let it be widely known that, if the nuts are forthcoming at such price as they may be prepared to offer and if they can assure themselves that the produce can be railed without undue delay, Kano will be prepared to buy 100,000 tons. All farmers within 100 miles of Kano are aware of this announcement in so far as its apodosis is concerned but they cannot appreciate how much depends upon the fulfilment of the condition as regards the railway. Given even a normally good harvest, therefore, I believe that the nuts will be there ready to meet the demand when it comes and that the forthcoming season will be an important one in the history of the ground-nut trade. Meanwhile, in order to put that trade on a surer footing and to secure for it a more permanent success than it can hope to attain as long as the present annual fluctuations, both in price and in demand continue, it is our duty to warn the producers that they must be prepared to accept a lower rate than that which governs the market in 'boom' years, and it is the duty of the merchants to come to some agreement amongst themselves with a view to keeping the price steady. I fully appreciate the fact that the local trade is at the mercy of the home markets, but if we could be assured that, in normal years, the Kano firms would be prepared to purchase, say, 80,000 tons at £10 to £12 per ton, I think there would be little difficulty in maintaining the supply.

H. HALE MIDDLETON.
Resident.
30.4.24. /

APPENDIX A.

Method of Extracting Edible Oil.

(i)   Decorticated nuts poured into earthenware cooking pot and roasted to a golden brown colour. They have to be stirred the whole time to prevent burning.

(ii) Spread on a mat till cool.

(iii) Rolled ('murje') under a stone on the mat in order to detach the red skin in which the kernel is enclosed.

(iv) Crushed ('dakka') in a wooden mortar ('turmi') with pestle ('tabariya').

(v)   Ground between grinding-stones.

(vi) Returned to mortar and boiling water poured over. Then stirred ('tuka') with a species of 'swizzle-stick' ('muchia') into a thick paste.

(vii) Paste transferred to flat stone placed in slanting position and the oil is then squeezed out ('markadda') and runs down into a calabash spoon ('akoshi').

(viii) Oil boiled, and ready for consumption, except for a small deposit ('kwonkwoni') which settles at the bottom and can be used as an illuminant.

The residue of the paste after the oil has nearly all been squeezed out is then mixed with salt and baked; the resulting 'kulli-kulli' (or 'kwalli-kwalli') being the most popular form in which ground-nuts are eaten. It is generally made into rings or small round biscuits not unlike our macaroons in appearance.

The whole process of oil extraction takes about seven hours and I carefully weighed out 30 lb. of nuts in order to discover the proportions of oil and kulli-kulli and also to ascertain the profit made:–

Raw materials.	Weight.	Value.	
	lb.	s.	d.
Ground nuts	30	3	0
Wood			4
Salt			½
Total cost		3	4½

Result.	Weight.	Value.	
	lb.	s.	d.
Edible oil	4½	2	7½
Kulli-kulli	20	1	10
Kwonkwoni	½	0	1½
Total	24¾	4	7 /

APPENDIX B.

Method of Extracting 'Bekkin Mai' or Lamp Oil

(i) to (v)   As in A, but roasted on the fire rather longer.

     (vi)   Turned into a cooking pot and stirred while boiling water is gradually poured in.

    (vii)   The pot is kept gently rocking over a fire and the oil gradually forces its way to the surface; when cool it is poured off and ready for use.

Here too the residue is made use of and is moulded into 'briquettes' for lighting fires. The 'briquettes' are the same shape and size as the sun-dried and bricks used for building, weigh 3 lb. each and are sold for ½ d.

N. M. Penzer, *Cotton in British West Africa, including Togoland and the Cameroons* (London: Federation of British Industries, 1920).

Federation of British Industries[1]

INTELLIGENCE DEPARTMENT

COTTON
IN BRITISH WEST AFRICA
INCLUDING
TOGOLAND AND THE CAMEROONS

BY
N. M. PENZER,[2] B.A., F.R.G.S., F.G.S.,

with an introduction by
The Rt. Hon. THE VISCOUNT MILNER[3]

P.C., G.C.B., G.C.M.G.
His Majesty's Secretary of State for the Colonies
[...]

Special Introduction
By LORD MILNER

THE necessity for the development of the supply of raw materials from within the British Empire can hardly be over-estimated. Although it is now many years since Mr. Joseph Chamberlain first pointed out what boundless possibilities our Colonies offered, and what little advantage had been taken of them, it still needed the late War to awake us to the great importance and potentialities of our Colonies. Practically all the Colonies under direct Imperial control are, from a European point of view, backward countries. We must look upon ourselves as trustees and take every opportunity to develop to the fullest extent the natural resources of these countries.

Opportunities for the increased production of raw materials within the Empire exist on every hand. There are many Colonies, three or four times as big as the British Isles, whose natural resources are still practically untouched. This is the case in every Continent. The minerals of such countries as Nigeria, the late German Colonies in East and West Africa, and further east in Burma, have hardly been exploited at all, while new regions capable of producing oils and fats and cotton are still being discovered.

This being the case, it is plainly of great importance to collect in a handy and comprehensive form all that is known up to the present of the resources in raw material of any of our Colonies.

The Federation of British Industries has realised the necessity for collecting such information, and is issuing short memoranda on various important raw materials in different parts of the British Empire. One such memorandum has already been issued dealing with Rubber in Malaya. A second, dealing with Cotton in West Africa, is now offered to the public. The information contained in it relates not only to the British Colonies in West Africa, but to the late German Colonies, Togoland, and the Cameroons. As in the case of 'Rubber in Malaya' a fairly / complete bibliography has been added. The importance of a good bibliography is self-evident, and I trust that the F.B.I. will continue to make this a feature of any further memoranda which it may issue.

Our manufacturing industries at home are in constant need of raw materials. This is peculiarly the case with cotton; indeed the world is threatened with a great shortage of this staple, and in many other industries the amount of raw material required is increasing day by day. The demand is great, not only in our own country, but on the part of our Allies, and our late enemies as well. They all look to the British Empire to supply them, and it is obviously of the first importance that we should meet their demand to the utmost of our power. The United States, our principal creditor, is at the same time a great customer for raw materials, which our Colonies can supply. The significance of this fact, as a factor in re-establishing the balance of trade between the United States and the Empire, can hardly be over-estimated. But when dwelling upon the great potentialities of the Empire in this respect, we must always bear in mind that a vigorous policy of development is necessary if we are to realise them. British capital must be forthcoming for this purpose, and especially for equipping the Colonies with adequate means of transportation, roads, railways and ports.

For these reasons I feel that the F.B.I. is doing a work of national importance in directing the attention of its members to those areas within the Empire from which an abundant supply of raw materials of the greatest value can be derived. /

COTTON
IN BRITISH WEST AFRICA

Section I

HISTORICAL SKETCH

FROM time immemorial Africa has been one of the homes of the Cotton Plant. The first record we have of African cotton is through the pen of a Moor, Al Hassan Ibn Mahommed al Wezaz al Fusi, better known as Leo Africanus.[4] Born at Granada in Spain in 1494, he explored the basin of the Niger, was captured by pirates and sold into slavery, but obtained his freedom from Pope Leo X. on his accepting Christianity. In his famous 'Description of Africa' he mentions that cotton was grown in what we now call Nigeria. In describing the Kingdom of 'Ghinea' (Guinea) he tells us that it 'extendeth two hundred and fiftie miles along the Rieur of Niger, and bordereth vpon the Ocean Sea in the same place, where Niger falleth into the saide sea. This place exceedingly aboundeth with barlie, rice, cattell, fishes, and cotton: and their cotton they sell vnto the merchants of Barbarie, for cloth of Europe, for brazen vessels, for armour and other such commodities ... the inhabitants are clad in blacke or blew cotton, wherewith they couer their heads also: but the priests and doctors of their law go apparelled in white cotton.'

The cotton plant grows wild in Nigeria, Gold Coast, Senegal, Angola and other parts of West as well as East Africa. The cotton tree (Eriodendron anfractuosum) producing the 'Kapok' of commerce, is to be found throughout Tropical West Africa, and the 'bombax' (B. reflexum and Buonopoz), producing a similar floss to 'Kapok' also occurs commonly in West Africa.

Although India is the supposed birthplace of cotton manufacture, the inhabitants of the Western and Southern coasts of Africa made cotton garments long before they were imported into the country. The beauty of the colours and design of the native cotton dresses have frequently been commented on by the early explorers. In the neighbourhood of Sierra Leone, Liberia, Lagos, the island of Fernando Po, and in the interior of Africa, cotton has, for centuries, been manufactured. From Macpherson's 'Annuals' it appears that cotton, woven on the 'coast of Guinea,' was imported to London from the Bight of Benin, in the year 1590. /

The Beginning of the British African Cotton Trade

The first voyages of the British to Benin and Guinea Coast were made by two vessels sailing from Portsmouth in 1553; in 1618 an African Company was formed, not originally with the object of trafficking in slaves, though in 1631 it degenerated into this, and the slave trade was carried on in British vessels.

Owing to the large demand for cotton robes created by the Mahommedan races who live there, Northern Nigeria has been the centre of the cotton industry. The cotton was ginned by hand, or by very primitive means, spun into yarn and woven on very simple looms into the so-called 'country cloths,' that is to say, narrow strips of cloth which have to be sown together to make cloths of any size. These stuffs are very durable, and are ornamented by the use of dyed yarns. What was not needed for local requirements was exported by river and caravan as far north as the Mediterranean.

Kano used to be the great cotton market, and bought up all the cotton from the neighbouring countries. The prices paid at Kano were often twice as great as what was paid for cotton at Liverpool.

Mr. Thomas Clegg, a Manchester merchant, was the first to carry on profitable trade with West Africa. He encouraged the natives to grow cotton and hoped by giving them employment to discourage the slave traffic, as well as to increase England's supply of raw material.[5] His experiment was first confined to the district round Sierra Leone, and was afterwards extended to the interior cotton fields, and the residences of the chiefs about Abeokuta. In 1851 he imported 285 lbs. of cotton, by 1853 the imports had risen to 37 bales, whereas in 1859, 3,500 bales were imported. (100 to 120 lbs. a bale).

Mr. Macgregor Laird also took great interest in the cotton producing possibilities of the country. In 1857 he tried to establish trading stations on the river Niger, but his enterprise was not successful owing to the bad climatic conditions, and to native opposition.[6]

By 1860 Lagos had become the largest cotton port of West Africa. Formerly it had been a slave mart, but the traders were dispelled by Commodore Bruce, and it became an open port for legitimate commerce. The country round is well adapted for the growth of cotton, and the Yoruba inhabitants of the district are enterprising and skilled in local trade, while the Hausa is, as is well known, the travelling merchant trading between Nigeria and the Mediterranean.

In January, 1901, Mr. Benjamin Crapper pointed out to the Oldham Chamber of Commerce the dangerous position of the Lancashire cotton trade.[7] The failure of the American cotton / crop, on which England was almost entirely dependent for her raw material, would be disastrous to the industry. Such an event could be avoided by the establishment of cotton growing in different parts of the world, preferably in the British Colonies, so as to render the industry more or less independent of American supplies. A committee appointed by the Oldham Chamber of Commerce to consider the question reported in November, 1901, that various parts of the Empire were suitable for the cultivation of cotton for the Lancashire trade.

British Cotton Growing Association Formed

At a meeting of representatives of various Chambers of Commerce, held in February, 1902, a committee was appointed to discuss the matter, and in May of the same year, at a dinner of West African merchants, held in Manchester, the British Cotton Growing Association was formed. It was formally inaugurated on June 12th, 1902, at a meeting of the various bodies interested, with a guarantee fund of £50,000. The late Sir Alfred Jones, who had already sent out 10 tons of American seed to West Africa on his own account, was elected President.

Experts were at once dispatched to various parts of the Empire to investigate, and it was soon realised by the General Committee of the Association that it would have to extend its original scheme of experimental and research work, if the enterprise were to be a success, and undertake the entire supervision of the industry. Its funds, however, were found to be inadequate for its purposes, and the Guarantee Fund was raised to £100,000.

In 1904, owing to unfavourable climatic conditions, the American crop was a small one, being only 10,124,000 bales, which was much short of the world's requirements, and this enabled speculators to 'corner' the crop, the most notable being Mr. Sully, who was known as the great wheat operator. Naturally, with a shortage of American cotton, the American mills were the first to get supplies, and Lancashire and the outside mills had to take what was left, which was too little to go round. This necessitated working short time, with the result that there was considerable anxiety and some distress amongst the operatives. It was therefore decided to reconstitute the Association on a permanent basis, with a capital of £500,000, and to apply for a Royal Charter, which was finally sealed on August 27th, 1904. The Association did not expect any profits from its work for some time – it was indeed stipulated that no dividends should be paid for 7 years – as pioneering work would be necessary for a considerable period, and consequently some difficulty was found in raising the capital. /

The Association consists of spinners, manufactures, merchants, shippers, and representatives of the various industries and Labour bodies connected with the cotton trade.

It has received assistance from the Government in the way of monetary grants, given firstly from the local Governments on the condition that the Association should spend an equal amount on cotton growing and experimental work, and latterly by the Imperial Treasury on condition that the money should be spent in special districts approved of by the Government, which recognised the value of the work undertaken both in developing the resources of the colonies and in giving the Government the benefit of its experience in all matters where its advice can be of use.

Some of the islands of the West Indies, whose finances at one time were dependent upon Imperial grants, became very prosperous owing to the work of the Association.

Cotton is now the chief product exported from Uganda and the second largest in Nyasaland, while in Nigeria a large proportion of the revenue of the country is derived from cotton.

The Empire Cotton Fields

The principal Empire cotton fields are India and Egypt (which are the producers of several million bales of cotton), the Sudan, Nigeria, Uganda, Nyasaland, and the West Indies, all of which have now passed the experimental stage, and the Association's work now consists in developing these countries, and is therefore concentrating its efforts upon them.

The lack of Agricultural Departments in West Africa from which particulars as to the areas suitable for cotton, etc., could be obtained was a great handicap to the work of the Association, as all information of this sort had to be collected by the Association itself before any start could be made. This meant the expenditure of a great deal of money and waste of time, which would otherwise have been avoided. British West Africa comprises about 450,000 square miles, a very large area to investigate, and the population is about 20,000,000.

The first step taken by the Association was to send out to all the West African colonies a number of American planters, who reported that cotton of fair quality grew wild, and that a certain amount was grown for local consumption in some districts. A great difficulty in the way of development in West Africa is the climate, which makes it impossible for Europeans to work there without long and frequent intervals of leave; the cost of passages to and from England is consequently heavy, and as the salaries paid are high, the Association found it difficult to work large plantations economically. For this reason, and because the natives work better on their own land than they do on European plantations, it was decided to encourage and assist the natives to grow their own crops, rather than to start large plantations under English management. /

The Establishment of Model Farms

It requires three or four years' work to discover whether exotic varieties of cotton are likely to flourish in a new country, and which particular areas are most suitable to the different varieties; therefore in 1904 an agreement was made with the Government to establish model farms for the purpose of experimenting with different varieties of seed, and ultimately distributing the varieties found most suitable, the cost of which was to be borne by the local government. The Association undertook to buy all seed cotton offered for a period of three years, at a minimum price first of ¾d. and later of 1d. per lb., and to send experts to travel round the country and encourage the natives to grow cotton. Later, this agreement was modified, the Association taking over the experimental work at the plantations, in return for a grant of £6,500 per annum from the Governments of Sierra Leone, Lagos, and Southern Nigeria; the Association was to spend £10,000 annually in experimental work in each of the three colonies.

Plantations, from a commercial point of view, did not pay, but the results of the experiments made were valuable. It was found that it was better to start with local varieties of cotton than to distribute exotic seed which had not been established; if the local varieties were unsatisfactory in quality they could subsequently be replaced by American or Egyptian seed, which could, after a certain number of years, be established so as to give good results. Some of the best results were obtained from Upland American seed.

The Association, finding it was unwise to distribute exotic seed, endeavoured to improve the local varieties by selection; this was done in bulk at the ginneries. Samples were sent home from each lot of cotton, and instructions sent out to reserve certain lots for sowing purposes, and to destroy or ship home the seed from undesirable cotton. This method, though unscientific, has proved very satisfactory in Lagos; the Association control and bear the cost of the distribution of seed.

There was at first a very great variation in the quality, and the cotton was difficult to sell; its usual price being about one penny per pound below Middling American. Efforts made by the Association to improve the quality by selection, by having the ginneries in their own hands, resulted in the African cotton showing considerable improvement during the last few years, and it is sold to-day at prices ranging from 'Pass' to one halfpenny per pound on Middling American. Unfortunately the ginning outturn of West African cotton is only 27 per cent.: in other words, it requires 3 ¾ lbs. of seed cotton to yield 1 lb. of lint. The yield per acre was also low. An effort was therefore made to try and establish a variety of cotton which would give the grower a larger production per acre, together with a larger percentage of lint. With this aim in view / steps have been taken by the agricultural authorities in Northern Nigeria, under the supervision of Mr.

Lamb, the Director. At first a few bales were produced, the seed of which next season was distributed, and so on, until in 1918 over 2,000 bales of excellent cotton have been grown in Northern Nigeria. This cotton gives a lint percentage of about 30 per cent., has a larger production per acre, and is worth to-day about two pence per pound on Middling American, which enables the Association to pay the grower one halfpenny per pound more for his seed cotton than for the native variety. Another disadvantage of West African native cotton is that it is rough and harsh with a brown colour; it is, however, very strong, and were it a bit longer and whiter, there would not be the same necessity for its improvement. At the moment all hope lies in the further extension of the exotic variety, as this is just the class of cotton required by Lancashire, and has the most ready sale.

The local Governments of the West African Colonies subsequently decided to take over the experimental farms, and the Imperial Government undertook to pay the Association a grant of £10,000 per annum, for a period of three years, ending March 31st, 1913. Later, this was extended to March 31st, 1916; the grant was given on condition that the Association raised £150,000 additional capital, and maintained two ginning and buying stations in the Gold Coast (Labolabo and Tamale), one in Southern Nigeria (Illushi), three in Northern Nigeria (Lokoja, Zaria and Kano), and one in Nyasaland (Port Herald). The Association also promised to distribute seed free of charge in these Colonies, and Lagos, and to allow their staff to give up part of their time to missionary work; the cost of distributing seed is considerable, amounting in 1913 to £1,700 in Lagos alone.

In the early days of the war, and before the issue of paper money, various Government departments set about in rather a panicky manner to cut down what appeared to them unnecessary expenditure, *i.e.* expenditure not giving an immediate return; consequently the grant was not renewed. A deputation from the Association, however, interviewed Mr. Bonar Law,[8] the then Colonial Secretary, to request the Government to make a grant of £1,000 if only to show that the authorities were continuing their sympathy with the movement. This £1,000 was given for one year only.

An agreement was entered into with the large number of merchants established in West Africa to purchase all cotton offered on account of the Association, who were thus saved the expense of a special staff for buying cotton. The Banks have also been of great assistance to the Association, for thereby it has been possible to obtain all the cash required. This is an important consideration, for all cotton has to be paid for in cash. /

The chief difficulty in the way of the Association in Africa is the inadequate means of transport. The dryer lands in the Interior are the most suitable for cotton; as a rule, the rivers are too low to be of use at the time when they are most needed for the transport of the cotton to the coast, and until the Colonies are opened up by railways, cotton growing cannot, in the opinion of the Association, be really successful. Much has already been done in this direction, and a new railway is now in course of construction. African railways pay well, and the direct and indirect benefits of railway construction to the Colonies are enormous.

The first saw ginning factory was erected at Ibadan in 1905, and the Association found it far more economical to erect large ginneries than small ones. The lint when conveyed in lightly-pressed bales to a central baling factory, was often stained and damaged, but when efficiently packed at the ginnery by a hydraulic baling press, it is far less easily damaged; it is, of course, impossible to have a powerful hydraulic press at each small ginnery. It is more expensive to convey the seed cotton long distances to the large ginneries than to have small ones established in many places, but, on the other hand, it is cheaper to handle the larger well-pressed bales turned out by the large factories.

In the Association's ginneries, the cotton is conveyed automatically by pneumatic feed to the gins, of which there are four in each battery and two batteries in a ginnery. There are seventy saws in each gin; from the gin the cotton is taken to the press, which turns out eight bales of 400 lbs. of lint cotton per hour and about 12,000 bales in the season. The weight of the bales is regulated by an electric attachment so that it is absolutely accurate. The bales measure 80 cubic feet to the ton weight; this gives a density of 28 lbs. per cubic foot. The standard weight of 400 lbs was adopted because bales of a heavier weight are more difficult to handle.

Two or three four-cylinder gas engines of the vertical type, each of 100-h.p., are generally used; the gas is obtained from cotton seed, which has little value owing to the high freight home, whereas coal or oil would be very expensive. The cotton is usually stored unginned for a short time after picking, as this is said to improve it.

The seed is conveyed to hoppers, where it is weighed automatically as it is stacked. The Association erected as an experiment a small oil-mill plant at Ibadan for the purposes of extracting the oil from cotton seed; but it was found that there was no local demand for the cake or the oil. It was found more economical to ship the seed for sale to English crushers. /

On the whole, the work of the Association in West Africa, apart from Nigeria, has not been altogether a success. In Gambia the natives preferred to grow ground nuts rather than cotton; the heavy rainfall makes Sierra Leone unsuitable, and in the Gold Coast cocoa was more profitable to the natives than cotton. Nigeria is now the only British Colony in West Africa in which cotton is grown successfully.

The Southern Provinces have so far been the most satisfactory in view of the fact that Northern Nigeria has only recently been opened up by a railway;

the Southern Provinces also are rich in the palm oil trade and no large quantity of cotton can ever be expected from them. It is more from Northern Nigeria, which has an area capable of growing several million bales of cotton, that the Association expects its best results.

When war broke out and the price of American cotton slumped to fourpence per pound, the Association was faced with a very serious problem. They felt, however, that the time had arrived when they should take their courage in both hands, and they therefore guaranteed a buying price to the natives, which in spite of getting a reduction in railway freight from the Government and also from the Steamship Company, was likely to show them a serious loss; but this price was such as to encourage the natives to continue to grow cotton. Fortunately, the market conditions at home improved and the Association's losses were not so great as were at one time feared. Great credit is due to the West African merchants who are the Association's buying agents, for the loyal way in which they came forward and assisted them during this very trying period. In Northern Nigeria considerable quantities of cotton are used locally and there have been recently times when the local consumption was so great that the spinners and weavers could afford to pay a higher price for the cotton than the Association. This, however, is mainly brought about through the difficulty in obtaining European goods both on account of the shortage and to the high prices for same. /

Section II

NIGERIA

(a) General

NIGERIA was formerly under separate administrations, but on January 1st, 1914, it was known under the comprehensive title of 'The Colony and Protectorate of Nigeria,' and was divided into two groups of provinces, the northern and the southern, each under a Lieut-Governor appointed by the King, and subject to the Governor-General, by whom the whole country is governed.

Nigeria is bounded on the north by French West Africa, on the south by the Gulf of Guinea, on the east by the French Equatorial Africa and Cameroons, and on the west by Dahomey.

The area is roughly 335,000 square miles, and the population estimated at 18,000,000.

The rainfall is very variable, ranging from about 28 ins. in the Northern Provinces to over 150 ins. in the Delta Region. The rainy season extends from April to October, and in the Southern Provinces the rainfall gets lighter after July.

The average temperature in Southern Nigeria is 78'5 deg., and that of Northern Nigeria is 80 deg. In the winter a hot dry wind called 'Harmattan' blows across Nigeria from the Sahara, bringing with it fine dry dust, which produces a hazy atmosphere. The adverse influence of this wind on the crops is shown by the fact that should it begin when the rainy season closes and continue blowing, the size of the crop will be very greatly lessened.

Much has been written upon the climate of Nigeria, especially on unhealthiness of the Southern Provinces, due to the prevalence of the most malignant form of malaria and of black-water fever.[9] Of recent years, however, since the mosquito-borne character of malaria has been better understood by Europeans inhabiting Tropical Africa, and the importance of mosquito-net precautions and quinine prophylaxis better realised, it has become evident that Europeans can live in Nigeria, as in other malarial regions of West Africa, for lengthened periods without greatly suffering in health, if at all, provided facilities for travel and recuperation are allowed at intervals.

The most important river of Nigeria is the Niger which flows roughly southeast throughout the whole of the Protectorate. It is joined about 250 miles from its mouth by the Benue which rises in the Cameroons. The Niger is navigable as far as Jebba, while most of its tributaries are navigable for their / entire length in wet weather. The river Cross in the south-east corner of Nigeria, although only small as compared with the Niger, is very important since it carries a very large amount of trade to Calabar. In the wet months it is navigable as far as the (1914) German frontier.

The North of Nigeria is well adapted for wheeled transport and there are a number of good roads; also motor transport routes from Kano to Katsena, and Zaria to Sokoto and Ibadan to Oyo.

The Railways are inadequate for the needs of the country. The chief line runs from the Port of Lagos to Jebba and from thence to Kano. There is a branch line from Baro which joins the railway just north of Zungeru; another line runs south-east of Zaria to Bukuru. There is a line from the new Port Harcourt to the Udi coalfields. The war, however, postponed any further development.

A small quantity of cotton is now being produced in the Abakaliki district, about 30 miles east of the Udi coalfields. It is probable that a ginnery will be erected when the railway from Port Harcourt to Udi has been extended further inland.

The chief ports of Nigeria are Lagos, Forcados and Port Harcourt, Lagos, the most westerly of these, is the terminus of the main line of the railway. The port has recently been improved on, and it is used by ocean-going steamers. Forcados lies on an effluent of the Niger, the channel is so small that at some seasons of the year it can only be used by small steamers. Port Harcourt is a new port built round a natural harbour formed by the Bonny river, thirty-eight miles from the sea.

The cotton growing part of Nigeria is mostly confined to those districts which are in communication with the railway, rivers and the coast.

The best cotton growing area may, however, be found in part of Western Sudan and the Chad regions. The soil is specially adapted to its cultivation, and two cotton crops could probably be harvested a year, one by irrigation and one in the rainy season. An extension of the railway from Kano to Lake Chad would open up extensive additional cotton-growing areas in the Chad area.

(b) Methods of Cultivation and Varieties of Cotton

THE native methods of cultivation vary considerably. The cotton is grown in some places as an annual crop, in others it is left in the ground for three years, and again in some places it is left till the crop is so small that it is not worth harvesting and the plantation is then abandoned. /

Cotton and yam are sometimes grown in conjunction. The former can be planted when other crops are well on to maturity and it matures when other crops are harvested, which ensures to a certain extent the popularity of its cultivation.

The planting season is from the middle of June to the end of July. The land is first carefully prepared, then the cotton is planted in ridges, every hole fifteen inches apart, with five seeds, in thinning reduced to three, in each hole. The rows are three or four feet apart, according as to whether the cotton is American or native, and the land is kept clean by weeding or cultivation four or five times during the season. The picking begins in November or December and may continue as late as April or May.

In 1888 the Niger Company sent samples of indigenous cotton to England, and these were found to be of rough but useful staple.

The Upland, Sea Island and Egyptian varieties of cotton seed have been tried in Nigeria; the most successful of these is the American Upland, which is similar to the native variety.

In 1913 an American variety of seed, known as 'Allen's Long Staple' was experimented with on the Government plantations near Zaria. In 1914 this variety was distributed to the growers for cultivation, and was found to give a larger yield and ginning out-turn than the native variety, and the British Cotton Growing Association was able to pay 1 ½ per lb. for the seed cotton, while the native cotton was only worth 1 per lb.

Since then good progress has been made in extending the cultivation of American long staple cotton in the northern cotton districts.

In 1918, 311 tons of this seed were distributed by the Agricultural Department, and 2,000 bales of long staple cotton were purchased. The seed cotton was sold for 2 ¾d. per lb., so that the whole crop represented the sum of £27,000 in the hands of the native growers, mostly in the Zaria province.

Even the native spinner is beginning to prefer long staple cotton to the native variety, and the local weaving industry has been using more cotton of local production, being stimulated thereto by the higher prices realised by manufactured cloth. Owing to these facts it has been noticed that the number of bales of cotton brought in for sale does not increase in proportion to the seed distributed.

The result of the introduction of 'Allen's Long Staple' has therefore been proved most successful. At the Maigana Experimental Farm work is being continued with a view to the improvement of the local strain of Allen cotton by selection, so that the yield may be increased, and the quality of the staple improved.

The efforts of the B.C.G.A. and the Agricultural Department to secure uniformity and prevent hybridising have been furthered / by legislation, which prohibits the growing of any other variety of cotton in the districts into which 'Allen's' has been introduced, and in which all seed required by the natives is distributed free.

Since the introduction of 'Allen's Long Staple,' the quantity grown by the natives in 400 lb. bales is:–

> 1914\11   1915\24   1916\121   1917\433   1918\855

The Agricultural Department of the Southern Provinces has specialised in a medium stapled Upland known as 'Georgia,' which was distributed on a small scale in the Oyo Province. Owing, however, to the apathy of the farmers, the experiment met with but little success, and in 1917, the plant was tried at Meko, at which place, so far, reports are good.

(c) The Local Industry

THE local cotton industry is very important, as it has been estimated that about 70 per cent., or perhaps even more, of cotton produced in Nigeria is not exported but used for local consumption. It is bought by the natives, men, women, and children, and in the Kano bazaars it is a rare thing to see anything but native-made cloths worn. It is grown by the natives, spun by their wives, and again woven by themselves. Some of the cloths are of very fine texture and beautifully woven. At present Lancashire only sends very second-rate cloth to West Africa, and if a large trade is to be done with the natives a far finer cloth should be sent out, otherwise it can bear no comparison with their own production, which is far more durable and of much better quality than the imported stuff. Nigerian woven cotton (generally known as 'Kano cloth') of a special type of weaving, in strips 18-in. to 2-ft. wide, is extensively used by Europeans for their clothes. If, as time goes on, railways become largely developed in Nigeria, and

Northern Nigeria is opened up and brought into closer touch with the coast, there will be a competition between machine-made cotton and the hand-made cotton of the natives. It is fairly probable that in this case the native industry will in time be killed, although this time is far distant owing to the great extent of the local industry and the cheapness of production. The prices of Kano would then fluctuate with those of New Orleans and other large cotton centres. At present Northern Nigeria is quite self-contained and has a civilisation of its own, and whether such a state of things would be for the general good of the Colony is hard to say. With the native industry lost, as the native indigo and other industries have been lost, the natives would have to rely more and more on the imported articles. /

The total quantity of cotton grown at present in Nigeria has been estimated at between 100,000 and 150,000 bales of 400 lbs.; this is more likely to be an under-estimate than an exaggeration.

(d) Transport

THE great drawback to the cultivation of cotton in Nigeria is the distance between the plantations and the markets. Most of the population live at very remote distances from the existing railways and the rivers, and the 2d. per lb. of seed cotton which is offered the farmers only pays them if they are within a day's reach of the market, not if they have to carry their crops on their heads for a hundred miles or so.

This grave difficulty of transport accounts for the non-realisation of the brilliant future which had been predicted for cotton growing in Nigeria.

At the present moment the farmer only plants about a hundredth part of an acre with cotton, instead of devoting a far larger portion of his land to its cultivation, as he would do if the markets were more accessible, for he is always most anxious to grow any saleable crop.

Thus it will be realised that the question of improving the means of transport, and establishing sufficient markets, is one of far reaching importance.

Railways and roads take years to build and involve heavy expenditure. The cheapest form of transport would be by canoe, but the carrying capacity is very small. Where unnavigable streams exist, pack-donkeys are substituted. This is at present the almost universal method of transport.

The necessary markets cannot be established, nor can the transport be organised without Government assistance, and it is suggested that native administrations should undertake this work, the expenses to be borne by them, as they have ample resources to draw upon.

(e) Diseases and Pests

THE following is a list of the chief diseases and pests affecting the cotton plant. It must, however, be borne in mind that different diseases and pests seem to affect the plants in different years. Thus, in one year a disease that is very common hardly occurs at all two years afterwards.

(1) DISEASES

Leaf Curl:

This disease is confined to native cotton, foreign and hybridised varieties being immune. It manifests itself by intumescences which occur on the under side of leaves, due to local access of spongy parenchyma. In severe cases infected plants are sterile and in all cases the flowering is restricted. The plants have not been known to recover. /

Anthracnose:

Native cottons are susceptible to anthracnose (Colletotrichum Gossipii). American cotton and hybrids are very little subject to this disease. There is doubt as to the Nigerian anthracnose being the same as the American fungus. The first symptoms of the attack are on the bolls, which show a small reddish brown spot, depressed slightly in the centre. Seedlings and stems are liable to attack, but in Nigeria the leaves are immune. In plants otherwise healthy and strong the disease makes no progress.

Areolate Mildew:

Areolate Mildew (Ramulari Areolate) is common on American cotton, but rare on the native kinds.

Cotton Rust:

This is known as Uredo Gossypii. It is an enemy to the American varieties of cotton, but attacks also the other kinds.

(2) PESTS

Leaf Pests:

The cotton plant is attacked at an early stage by the larva of a small Tineid moth, still unidentified. The cotyledons are also attacked, in which case the vitality of the plant is impaired.

A species of Tetranychus, which bears a resemblance to the 'red spider,' is found later in the season in great numbers on the under side of leaves.

Early in the season the Cotton Aphides are abundant, but their activities are checked by their natural enemies – ladybirds.

In some seasons the leaf-rolling Pyralid caterpillar (Sylepta Derogata) occurs, but parasites keep him also in check.

The short-horned grasshopper, determined as Catanitops vittipes, is the worst pest attacking leaves. It is a black and green insect, the nymphs of which appear in great swarms in November and strip the foliage off entire plants.

Cotton Stem Pests:

Great damage is caused by the larva of a small green metallic looking beetle. It is a stem-borer and is, as yet, undetermined. Though the plant may survive the attack, its vitality is permanently impaired.

Another stem-borer comes from the larva of an Aegerial moth, possibly of the Eulophonotus species.

Pests attacking Roots:

Roots are attacked by the larva of a Lamellicorn beetle. The symptoms are a gradual withering of leaves, a premature opening of the bolls and the ultimate death of the plant.

Insects attacking Bolls:

There are four species of boll-worm. The first and commonest is the red boll-worm (Diparopsis Castanca), the larva of a nocteid moth. The eggs are found at the base of the bract, not more than two or three on a boll; they are also laid on young leaves.

The second species comes from the larva of the nocteid moth – Earras liplaya.

The third from the Tineid moth, Pyroderces simplex.

The fourth probably belongs to the Genus gnorimoschima. These do not attack unopened bolls.

Cotton Stainers:

The Pyrrhocorid bug, Dysderais superstitiosus, attacks developing bolls early in the season.

The mixed cultivation of cotton decreases the spread of insects. The hybrid cotton planted between belts of maize is relatively free from cotton pests as compared with that grown in open fields. /

Section III

THE OTHER BRITISH COLONIES

(a) Gold Coast
(b) Sierra Leone
(c) Gambia

(a) The Gold Coast

THE Gold Coast consists of the Colony itself, and of the two Dependencies of Ashanti and the Northern Territories. It has a coast line of 370 miles on the Gulf of Guinea and the total area is estimated at 82,000 square miles. On the west it is bordered by the French colony of the Ivory coast, on the north by French Sudan, and on the east by Togoland.

The climate is hot and moist, especially in the coast regions. In the interior the temperature is high, the humidity less and the country more open.

From December to March the 'Harmattan' blows, and in March the rainy season begins which lasts till November.

About 70 per cent. or 80 per cent. of the country is covered with forests which have been divided under the four main types of rains, monsoon, swamp and savanna forests. The most open part of the interior is in the north-east.

Of the many tribes inhabiting the Gold Coast, the most important are the Fanti, the Ashanti, the Accra, the Apollonians, and the Akimand.

The British first took Koromantine in 1618, and in 1672 the African Society built forts along the coast. It was not, however, till 1874 that the British Government formed the Gold Coast Colony, and in 1894 the first Resident was appointed.

Agriculture is the main occupation of the natives in the interior, the most important industry in the coastal regions being that of the cultivation of cocoa.

Some experiments have been made in the cultivation of cotton in this region, first by the Government, then by the British Cotton Growing Association, but they were not considered sufficiently good to justify further expenditure. It was found that cocoa and other crops were more profitable to the natives in the districts where transport facilities were good, and where they were bad it was not profitable to cultivate cotton. /

The natives of the Gold Coast do not, as a whole, appear to realise the value of cotton for cultivation. They make mats of woven grass and cloth by beating out strips of the fig-tree bark. The development of the industry has been retarded by the importation of finished cotton cloths from Europe.

The outer northern boundary of the dense forest region, and the Krepi country, east of the Volta river, are the only parts in which cotton is systematically cultivated, although scattered patches of the plant may be found near most villages. The inhabitants of the forest region are a mixed people, some of whom probable introduced cotton from the north, where it is a recognised field crop. The origin of cotton growing among the Krepi tribes is unknown.

In the middle of the last century an attempt was made to cultivate cotton for export, but it was a failure. The Government of the Gold Coast in 1903 started a plantation in the Krepi country at Anum, this was subsequently transferred to Labolabo, on the east bank of the Volta, as this was considered a better site. Native and American cotton was planted, and the natives were encouraged to grow cotton by an understanding that their crops would be purchased at 1d. a pound. This promise, however, could not be carried out, for no adequate arrangements were made to store and gin it. A great deal of it was taken to Togoland by the natives, who found that they could sell it there at a fair price. An arrangement was then made with a local firm to gin the cotton and prepare it for shipment, but the financial loss entailed was found to be heavy. The Government then asked for the assistance of the British Cotton Growing Association, who, in 1906, sent up three hand gins to Labolabo. Shortly after this the Association took over the whole plantation, and the Government paid it an annual grant to assist working.

Although in 1907 a steam power ginnery was set up, and the natives brought more cotton to Labolabo than they had hitherto done, it was reported that a considerable amount of cotton still went to Togoland, where the price was slightly higher than that paid by the Association.

From the ginnery the cotton was taken in native canoes to Amedika, and from thence in small steamers, which would not have been able to navigate the rapids between Labolabo and Amedika. The cotton had to be specially packed for the canoes, in which the cost of carriage was 20s a ton.

In 1909 the sphere of activities was transferred to the northern territories and an agricultural station was established at Ramale. Little success was, however, met with and the yield was small. In 1915 the enterprise was abandoned. /

Varieties of Cotton

There are three varieties of cotton cultivated in the forest region, of which the 'green seed' is the commonest. Its lint is long stapled and almost white, but it does not yield heavily. The lint of the 'Volta' variety is creamy-white and the seed dark brown or black without any fuzz, except for a small brown tuft at the apex which has a sharp spike. The third kind, usually known as the 'kydney' variety, has dark brown seeds adjoining one another, forming a conical mass from which it is difficult to separate the individual seeds.

These three types are similar in form to the Sea Island and Egyptian cotton. Though they have possibly come from the same original stock, they differ in habit from the American and Indian plants; they grow from seven to ten feet from the time of planting, and the stem near the base is often thicker than a man's wrist, and they appear to do best in sandy loam containing much humus. The bolls ripen continuously from January to April, and as many as 200 bolls are often produced in one season, but if left for a second season the bolls are much smaller in size.

The varieties of American cotton tried at Labolabo did not flourish; though they generally produced a good crop in the first year, they were more liable to the attacks of insects, and did not, as a rule, germinate the second year. They were more difficult to cultivate than the local varieties, and therefore not so suitable for native cultivation. Attempts to establish a cross between American and local cotton were not successful.

There is no gin in use for native work, and the lint is pulled off the seed by hand.

The Krepi sow the seed in rows on the tops of ridges, which sometimes have maize growing at the sides. On the northern limits of Ashanti, however, the cotton is usually grown alone. No system of rotation has been observed, although cotton is probably planted immediately after the yam crops in the early years of cultivation.

The 'seed bugs,' three species of which are found, do great damage to the cotton. As soon as the bolls are open they infest the lint and feed on the juices they suck from the seed. The cotton is placed in the sun as soon as it is picked, in order to drive the seed bugs out, as the seed is often rendered unfertile by them. The 'cotton stainer' is also found, it punctures the unopened bolls and damages the lint by a yellowish stain.

(b) Sierra Leone

The Colony and Protectorate of Sierra Leone are bounded on the east by Liberia, and on the north and west by French Guinea. /

The population of the Colony is about 77,000, and that of the Protectorate is estimated at a million. The area of the whole country covers about 34,000 square miles.

The Colony owes it birth to philanthropists, who sought to alleviate the lot of negro slaves, and a large number were sent to Sierra Leone in 1772, and in 1787 this number was enlarged by discharged negroes who fought in the American War of Independence.

The mortality was very great, and the population did not increase perceptibly until after 1807, when slave trading became illegal, and slaves captured by British vessels in neighbouring seas were brought to Freetown.

The most important Protectorate tribes are the Mendis, Timanis, Limbas, Sherbros, Port Lokkos, Sosoos, Galinas, Konnos and Vais.

At one time great hopes were entertained of the development of the native cotton industry of Sierra Leone, but the difficulties encountered by the British Cotton Growing Association in their attempts to establish cotton growing for export on a large scale were found to be insurmountable. The heavy rainfall (150–180 inches per annum), local inefficient method of cultivation, and disinclination on the part of the natives to adopt better ones, all contributed to the non-success of this venture.

A ginnery had been erected at Moyamba, but not enough cotton was produced to keep it employed. A large plantation was then made near it, and native, as well as exotic plants put in; at one time the crop looked most promising, but with the advent of the heavy rains the whole crop was ruined, labour was expensive and finally the work had to be abandoned.

The native method of cultivation is to mix the seeds with those of other crops and scatter them broadcast on the field, which has previously been lightly tilled.

The cotton yields crops for two seasons, but the second one is generally very inferior. There are three varieties of native cotton known respectively as 'Quondi,' 'Fandiwah,' and 'Dooli.' The best results were obtained from the variety which furnishes cotton of a pale cream colour about an inch long. A ginning station was erected, but owing to a recurrence of unfavourable conditions the exports were very small, especially as most of the cotton was used to supply native looms.

(c) Gambia

Gambia is the most northerly of the British West African possessions. It consist of a narrow tract of land which follows the course of the Gambia river for a distance of 250 miles. The / territory extends for about 3,619 square miles, the population of the colony comprises 13,456 inhabitants, that of the Protectorate is approximately 76,948.

The Gambia is inhabited by the Mandingo, Foulah Joloff, and Jolah tribes. The country is, on the whole, sparsely populated, and the people are careful cultivators of their land.

Cotton is grown chiefly by the Mandingoes and the Jolahs, to make the yarn for their native looms. The strips of cloth they weave are called 'pagns,' and are sewn together and made up into gowns.

The Mandingo cotton compares favourably with 'middling American,' although it is not so white or silky as the latter. It is grown as a mixed crop and produces cotton for two seasons.

The Jolah cotton is short-stapled and woolly, and although it is whiter than the Mandingo variety, it would be much more difficult to bring it up to the European standard.

The failure of the British Cotton Growing Associations' attempt to develop this industry in Gambia, can be attributed to the same causes as the failure in Sierra Leona. The natives, who were not familiar with modern methods of cultivation, found that they could get a better price for their cotton by selling it locally, than by disposing of it to the Association. Labour was scarce, and the natives preferred their old industry of ground nuts.

In 1890 an attempt was made to grow Egyptian seed in Gambia, but an experiment was a failure. /

Section IV

THE LATE GERMAN COLONIES

(a) Togoland

(i.) *Geographical and General*
(ii.) *Historical*
(iii.) *Varieties*
(iv.) *Statistics*
(i.) *Geographical and General*

THE former German Colony of Togoland is situated on the Northern coast of the Gulf of Guinea. Its frontage on the Gulf extends for 32 miles only, but it stretches inland for nearly 350 miles and has an average width of 130 miles. It is bordered on the West by the British Gold Coast, on the North by the French colony of Upper Senegal and Niger, and on the East by the French colony of Dahomey.

Togoland is divided into two triangles by a range of mountains which begins and ends beyond the frontiers, thus forming two distinct areas – the North-western consisting of lowlands drained by the rivers Oti and Kulukpene, and the South-eastern, low-lying coastal regions, and an interior plateau.

With the exception of the Kara and Kerang rivers, which rise on the Eastern side of the chain, all the rivers of the colony, the Volta and its many tributaries, rise in the Central Range.

Transport and intercourse are made difficult by impassable hills and swollen or deep-cut rivers.

The geological formations in the East of the colony consist of gneiss and granite, whilst further West are gneiss and limestone, with considerable quantities of quartzite on the Western border.

The soil of Togoland is not very fertile. The best is found in the river valleys and at the foot of certain mountains, especially the Agu Mountain, South of Misahöhe.

In Central Togo the maximum rainfall is in September. This is followed by three months of intense heat. The water supply is dependent on the rains, perpetual drought making some parts of the colony uninhabitable. /

Lome is the natural port of Togoland, and before the war there was direct communication with Hamburg.

The native population consists mainly of Sudan negroes, who have the reputation of being almost the best labour obtainable in Africa. The native population is estimated at about 1,000,000.

In 1913 there were 368 whites in Togoland, of which the large majority were Germans.

(ii.) Historical

THE German flag was hoisted at Lome in 1884 by Dr. Gustav Nachtigall, the German Consul-General for West Africa.[10] A series of disciplinary expeditions between that date and 1890 firmly established German dominion over that small, but hitherto independent, strip of country.

Since then the Germans have spared neither trouble nor money in developing the colony to the utmost. An excellent postal and telephone service was installed, railways and roads were built, schools and colleges were started. A large wireless had just been completed at Kamina when the war broke out.

Shortly before the beginning of the 20th century, the Germans, realising the disproportion of the world's cotton supply to the needs of the world, and resentful of their entire dependence for that commodity on the U.S., determined to endeavour to start a supply within their Empire.

Togoland appeared to them to offer very special opportunities for the cultivation of cotton, as it was densely populated and the natives were excellent agriculturists, well accustomed to growing cotton for their own use.

In 1900 the German Colonial Economic Committee determined to send out an expedition to Togoland to report on the most favourable districts for cotton growing, and to find out what machinery, &c., would be needed, and to make all the necessary recommendations. The services of an American expert, Mr. James N. Galloway, were secured, and he undertook to remain some years in the country to superintend the beginning of the industry.

As the fields and lands in Togo belong to the natives, it was decided from the beginning that cotton growing should be established as a native industry, and four coloured men, all of them experienced and educated cotton growers, were sent out from Alabama in 1900 to show the natives how to work.

The first station was opened in Towe, where 100 acres were cleared. Cotton growing was afterwards taken up by the Imperial stations at Misahöhe. Ho, Kpandu, Kete Kratchi, Atakpame and Soko. /

In 1904 the Colonial Economic Committee transferred its experimental station and school from Towe to Nuatjä, in Southern Togo, under the management of an American called John Robinson. The course was a three years' one, and when it was finished, the students, who were selected from different districts, returned to their native districts, where they were granted 20 acres of land each. This grant was subsequently discontinued, as it was found that the land was not used to its best advantage. In 1908 the Togo Government purchased the Nuatjä College from the Colonial Economic Committee, and since then all kinds of agricultural work, besides cotton growing, have been taught there.

The Germans hoped that under Government protection the cotton industry would be developed into a national pursuit. Not only would the natives become economically dependent on the Fatherland, but Germany even entertained the hope of eventually becoming independent of the United States for her supply of cotton. That these hopes were a great deal too optimistic, the Germans themselves finally realised, and in 1914 Moritz Schanz, on behalf of the Colonial Economic Committee, announced that cotton growing in Togoland was not capable of much further expansion.

(iii.) Varieties

NEARLY every locality in Togoland produces a different kind of cotton. The following are the most important indigenous varieties.

Two varieties of Gossypium Punctatum:–

(1) A variety with hairy seed, which is tall growing and has but a small yield, the bolls of which mature quickly. It flourishes along the coast and is able to withstand droughts.
(2) An up-country variety.

The Sokode cotton, belonging to G. Punctatum: similar to American Upland.

The Togo Sea Island cotton (G. Religiosum): a variety with bare seeds. Successful results from it have been obtained in the Upland districts, round Agu, Misahöhe and Atakpame.

The Kpandu cotton: a Hybrid of G. Peruvianum and G. Barbadense, with bare seeds which close up in a ball.

An indigenious variety which grows in the Mangu districts.

The Germans have made many attempts by hybridising the different varieties. One of their most successful experiments was made in Southern and Central Togo, where the Coast variety (G. Punctatum) crossed slightly with American Upland (G. Hirsutum) and Togo Sea Island, gave satisfactory results. /

The American variety, Russel Big Bolls (G. Hirsutum) was imported from the States. It yields more than the indigenous cotton, though the production is inferior to that in the States.

Egyptian seed has also been tried, but without success.

The authorities finally came to the conclusion that the most suitable kinds of cotton for cultivation were: south of Togoland, indigenous Sea Island cotton; in Central Togo, American Upland; in Northern Togo, an East India variety.

(iv.) Statistics

EXPORTS OF COTTON FROM TOGOLAND 1902–1911.

Year.	Cotton Bales. (550 lbs.)	Year.	Cotton Bales (550 lbs.)
1902	80	1906–7	1,205
1903	128	1907–8	1,691
1904–5	519	1908–9	2,300
1905–6	857	1910	1,859
		1911	2,071

In order to convince the natives that it was to their interest to grow cotton, the Colonial Economic Committee guaranteed them a fixed purchase price. In 1910 they received 3 ¾ per pound of lint brought to the coast. Cotton was also bought at all the Central buying agencies.

The average price obtained for Togo cotton in Germany in 1911–1912 was 6d. ½ kg. (1 lb. 1 oz.), whilst cotton seed yielded £6 to £6 10s. per metric ton.

The sea freight was 12s. per bale of 550 lbs. from Togo to Bremen.

(b) Cameroons

THE Cameroons form the north-western corner of the great Central African plateau. They have an area estimated at 306,000 square miles with a coast line of 220 miles and a population of 3,611,000. They are bordered on the north-west by Nigeria, on the north-east, east and south by French Equatorial Africa and Belgian Congo (in part), and on the west by the Bight of Biafra.

The country is naturally divided into the Cameroon plateau in the north, the coastal region, divided into two by the 13,000 feet high Cameroon Mountain, the Sanga lowlands between Wesso and the river Congo, the hill country of Adamawa and the Lake Chad basin.

The chief indentations are the Rio Muni and Monda Bay in the south, and the best natural harbour of the West African coast is in the five-mouthed Cameroons estuary. /

The temperature is highest in the north and lowest in the south. The rainfall varies greatly; it is heaviest on the coast, the western side of the Cameroons is one of the rainiest regions of the world, between 400 and 430 inches of rain falling during the year.

The south of the colony is covered with tropical evergreen forest, in the north are savanna regions.

Wild cotton and rice grow in the Chad basin, but the proportion of plantation products is small.

The bulk of the population consists of Sudan and Bantu negroes. Cameroon is certainly not a white man's colony and its development must depend on the capacity of the native population.

This colony was annexed by Germany in 1884. Sir Harry Johnston arrived as British Consul in the country on the same mission five days after it had been accomplished by Dr. Gustav Nachtigall. Most of the natives who were most anxious to belong to Great Britain, resented German domination, and it was only after a considerable amount of bloodshed that German influence was finally recognised over the whole country in 1902.

The Germans discovered that a large part of the country, consisting of primeval forest, a zone of oil palms and the rain-swept coast district was hopeless for cotton growing purposes, but they found that the highland districts of the interior seemed to be well adapted for its cultivation. Native cotton growing has long existed at Bamun and Balilande in Adamawa, and as far as Lake Chad.

The German Colonial Economic Committee proposed furthering cotton growing by provision of seed, ploughs, cotton gins and premium on Government stations, but until more railways had been built they did not think it worth creating a Cotton Growing Association similar to that in Togo.

The Kolonial Wirtschaftliche Gesellschaft began work in 1905 at Garua, which can be approached by the River Benue. The Imperial residence at Garua distributed cotton among the Mohammedan tribes as well as the heathen ones, and offered a reward of 2s. for 44 pounds of seed cotton.

The first cotton growing trials were undertaken at Bamun and Balilande to discover the best planting season. This was found to be between May and June. Native Bamun seed was used and experiments were also made with American and Togo seed. Trials were likewise made at the station of Yoko in Central Cameroon with Togo and Californian seed, the Togo seed giving the best results. Another trial station was erected at Geb and Kuti in 1912, and an agricultural station was established at Pittoa, near Garua. /

Cotton is cultivated on a large scale by the natives south of Lake Chad, and in the alluvial district of the Benue Valley. The soil and climatic conditions are very favourable, and the district is inhabited by a dense population of intelligent natives, who work at a low price. When means of communication are established, by the extension of the Baro-Kano Railway, there are great tracts of land, similar to those of Nigeria waiting to be cultivated.

A continuation of the Duala-Monenguba Railway would open up wide districts of the highlands, which are equally suitable for cotton growing.

A valuation in Germany of native cotton grown in North Cameroon, at Alkassim, shows it to be equal to fully middling Texas. /

Section V

THE LAKE CHAD DISTRICT

SO very little is known of the geography of the Lake Chad area, and still less of the possibilities of successful cotton cultivation, that it is well worth giving a short general survey of the geography and history of the area, especially as a large portion of the South-eastern shores of the Lake have recently been added to the British Empire. It is unnecessary to emphasize the desirability of the British Empire being less dependent on American cotton and of growing as much as possible in her own Colonies. As has been shown in the foregoing pages, the British Cotton Growing Association has done much to attain these ends, but experts consider that there is good reason to believe that the Chad area would be the best cotton growing area in West Africa, both in regard to its soil and irrigation facilities.

Lake Chad lies approximately between 12° 50' and 14° 10' N., and 13° and 15° E. It forms approximately the centre of an immense depression where the soil is mostly of the same type as that found between the Blue and White Niles in the Sudan; that is to say, black cotton soil. The natives *do not* however use the patches of black cotton soil, which occur extensively in the province for cotton planting; they plant in the other soils. This fact requires study and elucidation. The lake is divided into four different zones:–

(A) The dried up zone:
(B) The marshy zone:
(C) The navigable zone
(D) The lagoon zone.

(A) When visited by the French Commission in 1908 the dried up zone extended North of the parallel passing by the Komadugu-Yobe. The appearance presented by this district is that of a vast plain, extending up to the limits of the horizon and with no supply of water on its surface. In places there are pools not yet completely dried up and on the islands thus formed thinly populated Buduma villages exist. To the east it is nearly impossible to detect where the lake ends and the Kanem country begins. In all this district cattle are abundant and thrive well, while big game is frequently met with. /

(B) The marshy zone covers about one-third of the lake. It consists of muddy and opaque water in which grow masses of grass and reeds, but so rapid are the hydrographic changes in this area that in 1908 it was nearly dry, when four years before it had been a vast expanse of open water from 3ft. to 6ft. deep.

(C) The navigable zone fluctuates periodically, and is situated roughly in the south-east corner of the lake, starting from British Bornu on the west shore of the lake at Seyorom Baga. Going eastward there is an expanse of open water covering an area of from 16,000 to 20,000 acres bounded all round with forests of ambach. Proceeding eastwards the forest closes, leaving only a small channel about two miles long. Once this is got through, the most navigable part of the lake appears, which is roughly just within the new French territory.

(D) The zone of Lagoons is situated all along the east and north-east shores of the lake. The Lagoon-channels are of varying depth and breath, and intersect one another in all directions, penetrating into the interior and ending in chains of ponds or in independent basins.

From a general point of view Lake Chad is the shallowest lake in the World. It covers an area of 10,000 square miles, and its shores are very ill-defined, for owing to its gentle slope even the wind is sufficient to cause a submersion or emersion of considerable tracts of soil. The waters of the lake are renewed chiefly by its affluents which are the Shari, the Komadugu-Yobe, and numerous watercourses of the late German Bornu. Besides this, about one-tenth of the water of the lake is renewed by atmospheric precipitation. The losses of the lake are due to evaporation and infiltration. The amount of loss by each is very hard to calculate, but there is no reason to suppose that the lake is likely to disappear within the present geological age.

If the provisional agreement of March 4th, 1916, with regard to the Division of the Cameroons between the French and British is definitely ratified, and nothing of importance added in the Lake Chad District, nearly half of the coast line of the lake will fall to the British – that is to say from Bosso at the extreme north-west corner of the lake nearly to the delta of the Shari.

Round the circumference of the lake is a belt of very rich soil varying from 5 to 10 miles in breadth, which is inundated annually by the lake. The annual rise occurs usually in November, the maximum flood being reached in January. It is in this latter month that the natives plant their crops, including cotton, and the lake recedes in February and March. The rainfall is very small, but the cotton ripens about September. The total area suitable for cotton growing is about 200 miles and falls within both British and French territory. Two of the richest areas are at the estuary of the Komadugu, and in the southern corner of the lake near Dikoa and Gulfei. /

The conditions of Chad prevail east, and are continued in another inundated area similar to Chad called Fittri, which is a closed lake fed solely by the local rains. It is not saline, and has an average depth of about 5 feet and is estimated at being 50 feet higher than Chad. The inhabitants of this region are sedentary Baulalas, who are chiefly occupied in the cultivation of millet any cotton. The cotton of this region has been famous for mand years, and in native estimation is considered far the best in the Sudan belt. It has never been exported owing to lack of transport, but the Germans state that certain native cotton grown at Alkasim near Chad was equal to Middling Texas. If this statement is correct it would probably apply equally to all the cotton grown round Chad and Fittri, and with the railway completed from Kano to the lake, the future of the Chad area as a cotton growing centre would be assured. For many years the whole of the western shore of Chad has been a game reserve, and at the present moment the elephants are so numerous that cultivation is at a discount. It has never been scientifically studied from the agricultural point of view, but all kind of crops grow there, including wheat and barley in profusion.

From the labour point of view the conditions of the Chad area are similar to those of the Chausa and Tornba country, for the natives being by nature semi-nomadic are readily attracted by an industry which shows a chance of gain. The great economic difficulty of the country is to keep the people in it; there are so many better opportunities for profit outside the Chad region. At present the natives go as far afield as Kano, Southern Cameroons, Lagos and the Anglo-Egyptian Sudan, in search of work. If a permanent industry were once established in Bornu it would keep the greater proportion of this roving population at home. Cotton cultivation in this area would not have to compete with other and, perhaps, more paying industries, as is the case in other parts of Nigeria. In some respects it would even be a new industry to the natives, or at any rate an industry which would be carried on without detriment to other productions, such as ground nuts or palm oil.

It is as well to remember that the climatic conditions of Bornu are totally different to those of the west coast of Africa, or even of the Hausa Country, and more closely resemble those of Wadai and Kordofan in the Anglo-Egyptian Sudan. In the south of Bornu the average rainfall is between 20 inches and 30 inches a year, and in the northern part it rarely exceeds 16 inches a year. The temperature is at its lowest in January, and averages 75° F. around Fort Lamy, while in April it is over 91° F. A temperature of about 120° F. is often reached at mid-day in the hot season.

As regards the possibilities of a paying railway to Lake Chad, the southern corner of the lake is, undoubtedly, the point to make / for. Quite apart from the possibilities of a large cotton export not only from Bornu, but from the friendly and allied territories to the east, the southern corner of Lake Chad is, from the broad commercial point of view, the dominating centre of the whole of the trade of North Central Africa – serving an area as far east as Darfur, as far south as the upper affluence of the Congo, and as far north as the regions of Tibesti and Borku. From the southern corner of the lake, south, east and north, towards the regions mentioned the roads are good and supplies plentiful; water also is sufficient.

The general trend of the trade is thus naturally towards the west, and not the east, not only for these reasons but ethnologically and socially. That is to say Wadai and all the countries west of it belong to the Chad area, not to the Nile area. A railway terminus at the southern corner of the lake would thus become a supplying centre for the whole of this vast region. It would also, very probably, be a welcome assistance to the French Government of the Territoire Militaire, which is so far distant from the coast that it has had, and still has the greatest difficulties in securing necessary stores, material, etc.

Historical

LAKE Chad is supposed to have been known by report as early as the time of Ptolemy (A.D. 130) but was not seen by white men till 1823, when it was reached from Tripoli by the British Expedition under Dr. Oudney, accompanied by Captain Clapperton and Major Denham,[11] when the lake was named Waterloo. It was visited again in 1850, 1855 and 1870. and was not investigated in any detail until the latter date. In 1890 to 1893 its shores were divided by treaty between Great Britain, France and Germany. From that date the French have taken more trouble to explore the lake and its surrounding country, than either the Germans or the British. It was not until 1900 that communication between Algeria and Chad was opened. A British force, under Colonel Morland, visited the lake at the beginning of 1902, and in May in the same year the Germans reached it from the Cameroons for the first time. Detailed surveys were made by French officers the following year, and in 1905 Lieut. Boyd Alexander further explored the lake, and finally in 1907/8 a larger expedition under Captain Tilho made lengthy studies of its hydrography, fauna and flora, and published a complete series of maps and four thick volumes of explanatory matter.

On March 4th, 1916, the provisional agreement between the French and British with regard to the eastern boundary of the Cameroons was drafted, and after the Armistice was signed the Council of Four asked France and Great Britain to draw up an / agreement on the same question to be submitted afterwards for ratification to the League of Nations. This was done on June 28th, 1919, when it was agreed that the final line of demarcation between the French and British Territories would not differ sensibly from that which was fixed by the provisional agreement. An extension of the British zone was conceded by France in the region of Bornu, and in return the frontier was adjusted further south so as to leave entirely in French territory the road constructed by the German administration from the coast towards Lake Chad.

The Aborigines of the Chad Basin were, as far back as native tradition and record goes, of similar type to the Hill Pagans, who now live on the Bauchi Plateau. About 1000 A.D. these Pagans were driven West by a very tall type of negro called Kotoko, which is still surviving on the Southern shores of the Lake. These people, known as the 'Sos' in the Bornu records, drove the Aborigines out of the country and spread North as far as the Komadugu and West as far as Karnu.

From about 800 A.D. Arab tribes began to sweep into Africa. They over-ran Tripoli and Fezzan, and coming South began to fuse and intermarry with the Hamatic Berbui inhabitants of the Tibesti and Kanem region. From an amalgamation of Arabs, said to be of the Yemenite origin with some Tubu or Teda mother stock, sprang a race of kings commonly called the Sefawa, who began to reign over Kanem about 900 A.D. Kanem, which was in alliance with the Hafsite Dynasty of Tunis (founded in 1336) grew powerful in the four succeeding centuries, and the natives of Kanem began to raid Bornu to the West and drive the 'Sos' South and West.

On the heels of the Kanem conquest of Bornu there followed a large influx of Arabs and Hamites, so that the negro of Bornu was replaced by a cattle and sheep owning population. In addition to the ownership of animals, the power of Bornu was built up of slave trading from the tribes to the South.

In about the thirteenth century the power of Bornu extended practically from the Niger to the Nile. Then followed a period of civil war. In the seventeenth century, again Bornu was much the most powerful state in the Sudan.

Like all monarchies founded on Oriental despotic ideas, the ruling classes became greatly demoralized, and in 1810 the rising Fulani powers in the West gained the upper hand, and on the Fulani retirement, a Fezzani Marabout was able to seize the reins of government and dominate the whole Chad region. From him is descended the present Shehu of British Bornu, who still rules as much of Bornu as lies within British territory under the protection of the Government of Nigeria. /

Section VI

The Future of Cotton Growing in British West Africa

AS regards Gambia, Sierra Leone and the Gold Coast, it seems most unlikely for reasons given elsewhere, that there will be any revival of the industry. There will, of course, always be a native industry, but this being entirely local will in no way affect the cotton production of West Africa from a British point of view. Great expectations are entertained regarding Nigeria, but these can only be realised if the three great wants of the country are properly attended to: they are as follows:–

(1) Roads
(2) Railways
(3) Agricultural Departments.

(1) *Roads:* The roads of Nigeria are at present far from adequate, and although in text books a road is often described as being a good motor road, for more than half its course it is nothing more than bush track.

In the Southern provinces there are many roads in the region of Abeokuta which should be made suitable for motor traffic. At present such a road only exists between Abeokuta and Aiyetoro.

From a cotton growing point of view, motor roads suitable for waggons and heavy traffic should be made from Oshogbo to Illesha and Ife. Two further roads are necessary in this district: one from Abuja to Minna on the railway and the other from Abakaliki to some point on the Southern section of the Eastern railway, perhaps at Enugu.

In the North-west district of Nigeria there are a few good roads, but owing to the importance of this district for cotton growing, it is most essential that Sokoto should be linked up permanently with both Zaria and Kano by good roads. It has been suggested that Sokoto should be joined by a railway to either Zaria or Kano, but recent evidence of the importance of the Chad district tends to show that a railway from Kano to the Southern shores of Lake Chad would be even more profitable. More will be said of this scheme in the next sub-section.

It is not only the main roads like that suggested from Sokoto to Kano which require attention, but the construction of numerous subsidiary roads entirely for the use of the natives, which would be made from all villages within a reasonable distance of either a railway station or a main road.

(2) *Railways*: Although the necessity for roads is very great, motor transport is not always an economical method, and / it has been suggested that light railways of a similar pattern to those in use in Egypt would, in many cases, be not only more economical but more effective. Experiments with such light railways would best be made in the Southern provinces where they would act merely as 'feeders' to the main roads or the trunk lines.

As regards the development of the main railway system, as was mentioned in the introduction to the section on Nigeria, one of the first railways to be completed will probably be that from Udi to Kaduna. Another line has been suggested from Udi via Yola to Maidugari, but it would seem to be of greater importance to join up Kano with Lake Chad: the line would run from Kano via Katagum to Maidugari, thence to Dikoa (now British) Northeast to Ngala, which is now practically on the new boundary between Nigeria and the new French Cameroons. From Ngala it would probably be sufficient to construct a light railway right to the shores of Chad.

(3) *Agricultural Departments:* The importance of a far greater development of agricultural departments, not only in Nigeria but in practically all our Crown Colonies, cannot be over estimated. In the case of Nigeria it must be remem-

bered that it is practically entirely an agricultural Colony, and that the revenue is entirely dependent upon the development of such industry, and that fact alone should surely make agriculture one of the first considerations in dealing with the question of Administrative Departments.

The Agricultural Department opened its first experimental seed farm at Maigana on the Zunguru-Bauchi line, and in the southern provinces a plantation for growing improved Georgia seed has been opened at Meko. So far both have been a success, but a far larger number of similar farms should be started at the earliest possible date at the most important points in the cotton district of Nigeria. There should be one at Oyo and Iseyin, in the Oyo district of the Southern Provinces; at Abuja and Zungon-Katab, south of Kaduna; in the Sokoto district in the extreme north-west; and at Maidugari or Dikoa in the Chad region. The east centre should have its own Resident Agriculturist who should experiment with different seeds, plants, etc., and try various methods of growing them, and make a special study of soils, manures, etc., suitable to the district served. There would naturally have to be a small but capable staff of scientists under the direction of a highly paid Director, which would include entomologists and mycologists. It has been suggested that the whole department should be under the direction of a first-class man, and that the *modus operandi* should be similar to that employed in the Imperial Department of Agriculture in the West Indies. The necessity of the mycologist cannot be over-estimated, for as in the case of the rubber tree, unless the causes and cures of every disease and pest are scientifically studied, there is always a serious danger of contagious disease starting, and an entire plantation destroyed. /

As regards the Cameroons and Togoland, little can be said now that we know the probable division of those late German Colonies. On Saturday, June 28th, an agreement was drawn up between representatives of the British and French Governments, by which France obtains Lome (the capital of Togoland), and the Misahöhe and Atakpame railways, and Britain is ceded part of the northern district where the tribes are naturally attracted to the British Gold Coast. This means that as far as cotton is concerned the British do not score in respect of Togoland, for, as was explained in the section on that Colony, all the cotton growing centres are in the districts of Kete-Krachi, Atakpame and Misahöhe.

With regard to the Cameroons, [...] the area of the Provisional Agreement of March, 1916, will probably fall permanently to the British, namely a strip of country from Yola to the coast between Buea and Duala, and a small but important piece formed roughly by the triangle Dikoa, Keroua, Kutelaha. This latter area shows promise of being one of the most important cotton areas in the whole of north-west Africa.

The new Anglo-French boundary runs through an important cotton district between 5° and 6° N. lat., starting on the coast between Buea and Duala, and runs N.N.E. near Lum, where it curves north-east to Bare, and continues in the same direction to Kutum which is about 38 miles north of Fumban. After Kutum the boundary runs slightly E.N.E. to Songolong, and then north-east near Banjo to Sambolabo, when it continues N.N.E. past Kontscha to a point on the old boundary about 34 miles south of Yola. Here the line follows the old boundary until it reaches Bama, where the new British Chad district begins. Fumban can be taken roughly as the centre of cotton growing in the Cameroons, and although this is now French territory, the cotton area runs west and south-west across the boundary to places such as Bare, Mbo, Dschang, Bagam, Bana, etc. At present the British will be dependent upon the railway which runs from Duala and is now a French possession. It is obvious therefore that the only immediate developments that can be made are to improve the roads leading from all the cotton districts, to the boundary where the railway starts.

Empire Cotton Growing Corporation, *The Cotton-Growing Industry in Uganda, Kenya, and the Mwanza District of Tanganyika* (London: Guildford and Esher, 1925).

THE COTTON-GROWING INDUSTRY IN UGANDA, KENYA, AND THE MWANZA DISTRICT OF TANGANYIKA / [...]

Introductory

THE extension of cotton-growing in Uganda during the past twenty years has been a remarkable development in Central Africa. That it has been brought about in spite of the fact that the people are not naturally good agriculturists or particularly hard workers, and that it has included the construction of an admirable and most exceptional road system through a difficult country intersected with marshes, compels a high admiration for the combined work of the administration, the Agricultural Department, and the Public Works Department of the Protectorate.

[...]

To understand the industry with any degree of thoroughness, / and to grasp the reasons which have caused it to develop along certain lines, obviously requires more study and more knowledge than it was possible to give and acquire in a few weeks. I can only record impressions and make suggestions for what they are worth, and it is for those on the spot to say whether such suggestions are practicable or possible. [...]

Before going into any details I will summarize my impressions very briefly. They are as follows:

Uganda has now won for herself a secure and definite position among the cotton-growing areas of the world; she is producing nearly 200,000 bales of good cotton, and can produce considerably more. In my judgment it is probably desirable that this position should at the present time be consolidated and made secure before attempting any further extension of area. I believe that this can be done by studying how the present acreage can be made to produce more cotton of better and more uniform quality by the application of science and the gradual introduction of improved agricultural methods.

Although it would not be difficult to increase the acreage, it seems to me that development on such lines would intensify both labour and transport difficulties. Moreover, although the Protectorate is singularly blessed in its climate and in the absence of any serious pests, it would not be prudent to count on these conditions being permanent. For reasons which I will touch on later, a mere increase of acreage might make the crop more liable to pests, and quite apart from this possibility, it should be remembered that at present Uganda is almost a one-crop country, and that insurance by scientific safeguards and the development of productive and pest-preventing rotations are of the utmost importance.

For these reasons I suggest that the most immediate need is a further strengthening of the scientific side of the Agricultural Department.

[...]

THE GENERAL AGRICULTURAL AND COTTON POLICY OF THE PROTECTORATE

[...]

The policy of the Director of Agriculture is as follows:

(a) The production of cotton shall be increased to the fullest extent in any locality where there is a sale for it.

(b) The quality of the cotton shall be improved and the yield increased.

(c) The Agricultural Department shall ensure that, by means of the rotation of crops, an increasing cotton supply shall carry with it an increasing food supply.

(d) The Department shall do everything possible to bring the grower and the ginner into direct contact.

(e) The Department shall, by means of regulations strictly enforced, keep down pests and diseases.

It will be observed that this policy, formulated in 1923, is in no way inconsistent with what I have suggested, except that the Director then intended to increase the acreage under cotton. This he has since done successfully, and I think that for the moment at all events a halt might be called as far as this particular is concerned.

With regard to the improvement in quality and increase in yield, the Director does not give details regarding the actual methods by which these desirable ends may be achieved, but I shall touch on them at some length in subsequent pages of this report.

I need hardly say that I am in the fullest agreement with the remaining points of the Director's policy, although it is possible that the means that I have suggested may not be identical with those which he has in mind.

A memorandum outlining the Government's policy was issued in April, 1924. As this deals primarily with the marketing of / cotton, it will be more convenient to deal with it under that part of this report which deals with buying and marketing.

THE ESSENTIAL UNITY OF THE DIFFERENT PARTS OF THE COTTON-GROWING INDUSTRY

It is perhaps gratuitous to state that there are several links which make up the chain that binds the growing industry with the spinning and weaving industry in Lancashire and elsewhere, and that it is not always easy to distinguish where the problems of growing end and those of spinning begin. In other words, there are many links, but they are all of the same chain.

I am not sure that this is everywhere recognized in Uganda, for there are some who would be prepared to allow unrestricted and almost unlimited competition between the ginners by allowing them to erect factories wherever they wished. In my opinion this would result in serious over-capitalization of that part of the industry which provides the cash for the grower, and might lead to failures and loss of confidence, which would be most unfortunate. I was glad to learn, just as I left East Africa, that the Cotton Control Board of Uganda have recommended that the number of ginneries should not be increased for the present unless it is proved that any are required in new areas. This should ensure a reasonable amount of cotton to each ginnery and a consequent reduction in overhead charges, which I understand are heavy. Additional ginneries, which would be unnecessary even if the crop were considerably larger, would moreover complicate the transport question and intensify the labour difficulty. They would also make it harder to supervise buying, and would make it increasingly difficult to inspect the actual ginning. Such inspection seems to me essential, and I would urge the administration to give Ginnery Inspectors every possible facility to inspect ginneries for cleanliness before the buying season starts, so as to ensure that if there is any of last season's seed in stock for fuel purposes, it is properly stored and will not be mixed with the seed of the coming season. There should also be frequent inspection during the season, so that not only can bad ginning be stopped at once, and licences withdrawn, if necessary, but so that Inspectors can give advice and assistance to ginners should they ask for either. In this way much could be done for the reputation of Uganda cotton, for I know from personal experience that at some ginneries good cotton was being ruined by inefficient ginning. My opinion regarding the importance of, and necessity for, better and more uniform ginning was strengthened by my subsequent visit to India. The question seems to deserve special consideration in Uganda, because the cost of transport from there is so high that it is essential that the cotton bales exported should contain a minimum of waste material, dirt, etc. (In this connection see Appendices I. and II.)

Transport

Another most essential link in the chain is transport. So far as interior communications go there are comparatively few difficulties in Uganda. The roads are excellent, and there is a most efficient and well organized Government transport service, which ensures that the prices charged by commercial transport services are reasonable.

The only suggestion I have to make is, that during the period when seed is being distributed to the growers, a considerable amount of transport should be placed at the service of the Agricultural Department, in order to ensure that seed from the best areas is distributed throughout the country in good time for sowing. To distribute seed from bad areas in order to save transport is a wholly false economy. Further reference is made to this matter on pages 159 and 160 below.

I have already referred to the good road system in Uganda. The country is fortunate in having abundance of laterite gravel, which makes an admirable road surface. The roads, however, are not heavily metalled and have not deep foundations. I am of opinion that 'half-track' vehicles, if they prove successful in Nigeria or elsewhere, might well be introduced in Uganda, as they should save a good deal of the cost of maintenance of roads. The Albion lorry with paraffin fuel is, according to the Director of Transport, the most satisfactory form of lorry, and if the Albion chassis could be fitted with half-tracks instead of rear wheels, it might be convenient, as there are many mechanics in Uganda who thoroughly understand the engine.

It is proposed to convert the molasses from a sugar factory, situated between Kampala and Jinja, into commercial alcohol, and the manager told me that he felt confident that, as soon as the plant arrived, he could produce 20 gallons an hour and sell it for about 2s. a gallon. If this can be done it will be of immense advantage to road transport in Uganda, and the Corporation will no doubt await with interest the report on this fuel.

The real difficulties begin at the lake ports. It was calculated that the total export of lint and cotton seed in the season 1925–26 would amount to over 47,000 tons, and that, as a great deal of this would come via Lake Kioga ports, down the Busoga Railway to Jinja and thence across Lake Victoria, and would, therefore, be rehandled several times, the total amount to be dealt with at the / different ports in Uganda would be nearly 55,000 tons. At the same time a very large quantity of material for the new railway was to be imported at Jinja and Mjanji. It will thus be realized that the problem is a very difficult one. Mr. C. N. Felling, General Manager of the Uganda Railway, wrote to me on this point, and stated that, while admitting that delays had occurred on the lakes

during last season, cotton had arrived at Kilindini faster than it was exported.*
He doubted, however, *whether the transit of cotton to the coast would ever be really satisfactory until the railway is through to Mbulamuti (on the Busoga Line)*, and said that there was no doubt that there were serious difficulties ahead of the railway this season. The principal of these was labour shortage, and although the Uganda Government were doing their best, the labour supplied was 'raw' and of very poor quality. At Kisumu there was serious shortage when Mr. Felling wrote (January, 1925), because no voluntary labour was obtainable and the Railway and Marine Department had to depend on convicts. Unless more labour became available, further delays and congestion were unavoidable. There was no shortage of rolling stock, but a number of cranes which had been ordered had not been delivered in East Africa, and a steamer ordered in January, 1924, had not yet been delivered in England.

All the lake piers that I have seen were very deficient both of labour-saving devices and of weather-proof storage, and almost everything had to be man-handled by labour which Mr. Felling rightly described as raw. It seemed to me that much might be done by more efficient organization of that labour, and that possibly it might have been wise to postpone the import of railway material until at least Kismu, Jinja, and Mjanji piers had been improved. This, however, is a matter on which I am reluctant to express a more definite opinion, as I did not have time or opportunity to discuss it with those who could give me full information.

Even when the new railway is completed there will be considerable traffic on both lakes for many years to come, and although Jinja and Mjanji will lose much of their importance as ports, money spent on the immediate equipment of these ports would probably not be wasted, as part at least of that equipment could be transferred to other ports such as Bukakata or Mwanza or the ports on Lake Kioga.†

Another point which occurred to me as worthy of consideration was whether it would be advisable to delay the transport of cotton seed for a few months after the bales of lint had begun to move down to the coast. Seed is not a high priced commodity and could afford to wait for a time. At present no preference is given to lint over seed, and in fact the latter is often moved first because it is easier to handle. The Director of Agriculture has recently forbidden the exportation of seed cotton from any port of the Teso district situated on the shores of Lake

---

* The B.I. boat on which I travelled to India carried 1,500 bales of cotton. This, the captain told me, was a record amount of cotton for this season of the year, in spite of the fact that the cotton season had opened a fortnight later than usual. He also told me that his company were prepared to put on an extra boat during the cotton season, but that they hitherto had had some difficulty in finding out whether it was required.

† The conditions this year (1925) and the congestion at the lake ports have been worse than ever, and demand immediate attention.

Kioga, in order to reduce the bulk transported on that lake, and it might be possible to go a step further and to delay the export of seed from the Protectorate until most of the lint had left the country. Considerable previous notice should be given of such a step which obviously presents considerable difficulties.

The ideal, of course, would be to convert the seed into oil in Uganda. I understand that there is no great demand either for the oil or for its by-products in Uganda or Kenya, and that the oil would have to be exported. The practical difficulty is said to lie in the matter of containers, which would have to be imported. Possibly this difficulty may be overcome when the new railway is built, as it might be practicable to pump the oil direct from the factory into special trucks and from the trucks into steamers alongside the new Kilindini pier.

THE AGRICULTURAL DEPARTMENT

In order to understand the present functions of the Agricultural Department, and any desirable extensions to it, it is necessary to explain briefly the administrative system of the Protectorate. Uganda is governed by the Governor, assisted by various technical departments, and by the Secretariat which co-ordinates their work. There is also an Executive Council consisting of a few heads of departments and a Legislative Council made up from heads of departments and a certain number of unofficial members. On this Council the Government have at present a permanent majority.

The Protectorate is divided up into large areas called Provinces, each of which is in the charge of a Provincial or Senior Commissioner, while the Provinces are subdivided into districts under District Commissioners. The districts are further subdivided into counties and the counties into *gombolalas*, or village groups, which are the smallest administrative units in Uganda. The counties and *gombolalas* are administered to a very large extent by native chiefs, who are practically salaried civil servants, and can be changed if they are unsatisfactory.

It will be readily understood that the men whose words and / influence most readily reach the natives are the District Commissioners, and to a very large extent the development of cotton-growing is due to them. Hitherto, owing to the shortage of Agricultural Officers, it has not been possible to attach one to each district. As these officers became available they were sent to the areas where they were most needed. For instance, in the Eastern Province there were only four of them a few months ago. At the moment of writing, however, the arrival of students from the Empire Cotton Growing Corporation[1] has made it possible to increase this number to eight. Although the exigencies of leave will shortly reduce the number to five, this will mean that the Agricultural Department, without denuding other areas of its officers and without depending solely on the administration, will be able to exert a continuous influence on the agriculture of the Province which, as far as cotton is concerned, is at present the most important in the Protectorate.

These officers depend very largely for the success of their efforts on the support and co-operation of the District Commissioners, and I have found that everywhere this co-operation is a very real and close one. It depends, however, on personal relations more than on any organized or systematic division of responsibilities.

The headquarters of the Department are at Kampala, where in addition to the Director, Assistant Director, and clerical staff, there are entomological and mycological officers who have been lately reinforced by a chemist and another officer who were students of the Corporation. There is not at present, however, any laboratory, and the facilities for scientific work are therefore very few.

At Kampala also there is the recently constituted Cotton Control Board, consisting of the Chief Secretary, who is *ex-officio* Chairman, the Attorney-General, the Provincial Commissioners of the Eastern Province and of Buganda, two representatives of the ginners, one of the Chamber of Commerce, and the Kabaka (King of Buganda). The Assistant Director of Agriculture has hitherto acted as Secretary, but I understand that in future an officer of the Department will officiate as permanent Secretary to the Board. The principal functions of this Board are the selection of central markets and consideration of applications to erect ginneries. It also acts in an advisory capacity to the Governor on all matters relating to the cotton industry.

There is also the Serere seed selection farm in charge of Mr. Harper, who has worked, at first with very slender equipment, at plant selection in the Eastern Province since 1911. He has done a great deal for Uganda cotton in the face of difficulties which, to a less sanguine and persevering personality, must have seemed wellnigh insuperable. It was not until 1919 that the Cotton Excise Tax provided funds to build and equip an experimental station at Serere, where there are now, in addition to experimental plots, about 200 acres under N17 cotton, which is the type lately selected as most suitable for the whole Protectorate. Serere is therefore a seed farm as well as an experimental station. It is dealt with at greater length on pages 156–8.

For a country which depends wholly on agriculture for its prosperity, the expenditure on the Agricultural Department can hardly be called excessive. I understand that the Director proposes not only to increase the personnel of the Department, but has allocated a sum of £7,500 for the building of laboratories in the immediate future.

At places like Surat and Dharwar in the Bombay Presidency, where the local type of cotton is being improved by selection, and where experiments in plant breeding are being carried out, the staff of the farm usually includes a botanist, an entomologist, and a mycologist, with one or two assistants each, and a farm manager. At Lyallpur and Coimbatore, which are Agricultural Colleges as well as experimental stations, the staff working on cotton includes at least one British officer in addition to the above. In Africa, where at present there are no qualified native assistants, such experimental stations must be relatively more expensive, but they are even more necessary because there are not, as is the case in India, various other scientific stations to which reference can be made.

The Existing System of Agricutlture

The Baganda, who are remarkable among African natives for their intelligence, are not, however, agriculturists by tradition or instinct. They live mainly on bananas, which are not annuals, are easy to grow and, in Uganda, practically free from diseases. The original heavy work of clearing the ground of elephant grass is done by the men, but all subsequent cultivation and weeding of the bananas is done by the women. In this part of the Protectorate, therefore, there is practically no rotation of crops, and if the natives want to grow more cotton or to grow it on fresh ground, they clear a fresh patch. There is at present no difficulty about this as only a small proportion of the land is under cultivation.

In the Eastern Province bananas are grown to a lesser extent, and the natives depend more on millet, sweet potatoes, and ground nuts, crops which need more regular and systematic cultivation. The people are perhaps somewhat harder workers and easier to influence than the Baganda, but not so intelligent. In both areas /

they did not in the past grow more than was necessary for their own consumption, and, in the case of millet eaters, to fill the grain stores, which are their famine reserves.

It is therefore no small achievement to have induced them to grow a crop which they 'cannot eat,' but it will be obvious that twenty years have not been sufficient to create a class of instinctive though uneducated agriculturists, such as is found in India, Egypt, and other places where agriculture has been an industry for generations. The natives of the Protectorate are probably uniformly bad judges of the cotton they grow, and very few of them have opportunities of seeing how improved cultural methods might increase yield per acre or the number of bolls per plant. *Their seed is given to them, and therefore, apart from other reasons, practically none of them recognize the value of pedigree stock.* I came across only one instance of a man who had obtained seed from a chief in another part of the country (an illegal transaction in any case). He brought the resultant seed cotton to a ginnery which I happened to visit (and where fortunately it was kept separate), and it proved on examination to be both short and uneven in staple, but probably prolific in flower and fruit.

Mr. Howard, in his book on 'Crop Production in India,' writes: 'The average cultivator rarely devotes much attention to the seed he sows. He is too poor to pay the necessary premium for improved seed.' This is even more true of Uganda, but it is not poverty so much as ignorance which prevents the cultivator from realizing the importance of good seed. In India the cultivator at least pays something for the seed he sows, and there are indications that in some areas he is learning the value of and paying the premium for improved seed.

That the yield per acre is on the whole small is probably partly due to poor cultivation, though there are other contributory causes. The spacing of cotton seemed to me wide, and the few plots which I measured had not much more than one plant per square yard. I suggest that this is a subject which is worthy of investigation and experiment.

Tree stumps are probably another cause of the low yield, as they must rob the soil of much of its nourishment. The natives do not like the work of removing them with a stump-jack, and it is worth enquiry whether it is possible to introduce some simple form of jack, as until the ground is thoroughly cleared it will be impossible to plough effectively. I suggest that it might be worth the consideration of the Corporation to offer to Uganda an efficient stumping machine equipped with tractor and engine complete, or even to undertake stumping on a large scale.

It is at present too early to foresee what will be the effect of ploughing and of deeper cultivation. At first the results may seem disappointing, but the opinion of those best qualified to judge is that in the end it will lead to better crops.

In a country like Uganda, where it is impossible to get accurate acreage figures, except at a prohibitive cost, and where the estimates of the Agricultural Department are bound to be based on calculations which cannot be wholly reliable, it would be unwise to lay too much stress on figures of yields. I think, however, that the Department have made as accurate an estimate as is possible and practice of the crop of 1923–24, and I include it herewith as illustrating the variations in yield in different parts of the Protectorate.

District.		Population.	Tax-Payers.	Total Acreage.	Area Acreage Per Tax-Payer.	Total Crop (Tons).	Average Yield Per Acre (Lbs. of seed Cotton).
Buganda	Mengo	331,991	70,115	70,000	–99	18,293	585–610
	Entebbe	155,553	34,054	16,370	–48	3,121	426–450
	Masaka	147,981	25,873	10,000	–38	2,519	564–754
	Mubende	139,228	24,374	10,866	–44	1,567	323–379
Eastern Province	Teso	200,000	50,000	68,000	1–36	9,500	313
	Busoga	222,000	57,000	61,000	1–07	15,500	566
	Bugishu	190,000	38,180	21,210	–55	2,350	247
	Bugwere	150,000	30,100	57,560	1–91	9,150	278
	Lango	206,150	50,000	45,000	–90	8,500	428
	Budama	129,250	20,000	45,000	2–25	2,800	138*

* It is believed that the apparently very low yield in the Budama district was due partly to an over-estimate of acreage.

The figures for the total crops were:

Province.	Total Crop (Tons).	Average Yield per Acre (Lbs. of Seed Cotton).
Buganda	25,500	511
Eastern Province	47,800	328

It will be noted that were it not for the Busoga district of the Eastern Province, where conditions of climate and soil are very similar to those of Buganda, the yield per acre in the Eastern Province would have been considerably smaller.

I was unable to get any figures or even records of experiments showing the result of manuring, which, save in the form of green manuring, is hardly a practicable proposition at present. I believe that lime of poor quality can be obtained near Tororo, and it might / be worth while to carry out some experiments with it. The difficulty at present, however, is for agricultural officers to find the time and labour to carry out experiments even on a small scale.

A characteristic feature of agriculture in Buganda is the small irregularly shaped fields generally surrounded by elephant grass. This is the case to a much less extent in the Eastern Province, but even there the fields are very small. This form of cultivation, while difficult to supervise and making accurate estimates of acreage impossible, has the advantage of getting the maximum amount of shelter for the crop, and probably is a factor in making the Uganda crop as a whole practically free from serious pests. The fields are without ridges, and I saw no instances of ridge-planting in Buganda or the Eastern Province. It seems, however, to be a common practice in the cultivation of ground nuts in the Bukoba district of Tanganyika, where the annual rainfall is about seventy inches and much heavier than in Uganda.

Another matter about which the people have much to learn is picking. I refer later to the question of grading by the grower (see page 162). In no case did I see a native using two bags, one for dirty and one for clean cotton. They either put the cotton into a small basket, or, as is more frequently the case, they clasp the cotton to their greasy breasts until they have as much as they can hold, and then walk to their basket and put it in. Any sorting that is done is carried out in the native huts after picking.

To improve methods of agriculture and cultivation is, of course, primarily the work of the Department reinforced by the administration, but there is a third influence which might be brought to bear, and that is general education. At present education in the Protectorate depends on the different bodies of missionaries rather than on the Government, and there is, so far as I am aware, no co-ordinating body and no general, or what might be called national, system of education.

Since Uganda is dependent primarily on agriculture for her prosperity, and the great majority of her people are directly, if intermittently, engaged in agriculture, it would seem desirable to train the natives as a whole in simple agriculture and to select the best qualified as superintendents under the chiefs in every *gombolola*. Admittedly this will be a very slow process, and it may be necessary to maintain existing agricultural schools as a short cut to the desired end, but even such schools should be fitted into the general scheme, and they should not aim too high. They might even serve as the *nuclei of gombolola* or county national schools.

The question as to whom such native superintendents shall be responsible is an arguable one. Some authorities urge that they should be directly employed by and responsible to the Agricultural Department, but in most cases these men derive their authority from, and work through, the chiefs. A multiplication of salaried and uniformed native officials in Uganda unfortunately may mean multiplied opportunities for petty tyrannies and peculations. These opportunities a chief is better able to frustrate than is a white official.

For higher types of native agriculturists, and particularly for native assistants in the laboratories, etc., of the scientific side of the Agricultural Department, there is the native Training College of Makerere,[2] which will be in close touch with and in near proximity to the projected laboratory and plantations at Kampala. The Director of Agriculture has asked me whether the Corporation could see their way to making a grant of £250 per annum to the Department to enable him to give scholarships to students at Makerere, and I gladly submit this request, which I have already acknowledged. I have asked him to let me know whether he wishes to modify it when he has had an opportunity of discussing it with the newly appointed Director of Education, who by now will have reached Uganda.

SEED SELECTION AND DISTRIBUTION

Before touching on existing methods of selection and distribution I will quote the report of Mr. Jackson, with whom I visited more than fifty per cent. of the ginneries of the Eastern Province. He writes as follows:

'To treat the Province as a whole in the first place, the general average of the cotton is good, with occasional lapses due to bad ginning or deteriorated seed.

'In Busoga, which is considered to produce the best cotton in the Eastern Province, the average condition of the lint appears to be good, the staple is about 1 ³/₁₀ inches and strong, the cotton is a little leafy, with not much stain, and is usually of a good but rather creamy colour. Busoga has a good cotton-growing soil, and the land as a rule is well looked after and cultivated. There is some irregularity in the seed, as at one ginnery the staple was uneven and at two others the cotton was harsher than the average.

'In Bugwere, Budama, and Bugishu the cotton in comparison is poor: the best staple I could find was good 1 ⅛ inches, but the greater part is, at the outside, no better than 1 ⅛ inches. Three ginneries had 1 ⅛ inches staple, four had good 1 ⅛ inches, one was irregular, chiefly 1 ⅛ inches, with some 1 ⅛ inches among it, and one was barely 1 ⅛ inches. The cotton was only of medium / strength, weak at times, without much stain or leaf, and generally of a creamy tinge. This comparative shortness and irregularity is due, I am informed, to seed deterioration. Seed from this area has been supplied to the growers for a considerable number of years without any mixture of fresh seed from better localities, and consequently there has been deterioration.

'Teso shows a considerable improvement on Bugwere, etc., possibly because Serere is close to Soroti, the administrative headquarters of the district. The staple is generally 1 ³⁄₁₆ inches, with occasionally good 1 ⅛ inches and full 1 ³⁄₁₆ inches. It is fairly strong, comparatively free from leaf and stain, and of a good but slightly creamy colour.

'This, however, is the only district in the Province where I have seen any nep. In one ginnery this was due entirely to faulty saw-gins, as there was no trace of it in the seed cotton. At another factory, with roller-gins, there was a certain amount visible in the seed cotton which, of course, showed up much worse in the lint.

'In Lango I was unable, through lack of time, to see as much cotton as in other districts, but what I did see both in the fields and in the ginneries appeared to be fairly good. The staple was generally full, 1 ⅛ inches to 1 ³⁄₁₆ inches, fairly strong, and, where well ginned, almost free from leaf or stain. Colour slightly creamy.

'The cotton on the whole appears to be of sufficient quality to help to fill the gap caused by the shortage of 1 ³⁄₁₆ inches American. Where it is below that standard it should be capable of improvement by scientific methods.'

It should be noted that, as the buying season in Buganda did not open until the middle of February, Mr. Jackson had not much opportunity of examining the cotton there: it is, however, safe to assume that throughout Buganda the cotton is very similar to that grown in Busoga.

The Corporation have already had Mr. Wood's report on seed selection at Serere and Mr. Harper's comments on this report. I am not competent to offer more than a general opinion on this question, but I would remind the Corporation that Mr. Wood was convinced that, by careful selection, a cotton more suited to the different parts of Uganda than any grown at present could be evolved, and that proper provision for seed selection should form a strong feature of the programme of the Agricultural Department. Mr. Wood did not define what he meant by a cotton more suited to the country, but I have no doubt that he meant something similar to what I have in my mind – viz., a cotton suited climatically to Uganda, of fairly compact growth, which, throughout the area, would produce a larger number of bolls with uniform staple of 1 ³⁄₁₆ inches.

The present type of cotton grown in the Protectorate is a variety of Nyasa-land Upland, known as N32, which was distributed in Serere county in 1921 and throughout Uganda in 1922. Presumably, it is this cotton which forms the basis of the crop which I have seen. I counted the bolls on a very large number of plants and the average was about twenty. It should be remembered that there was an exceptional amount of rain in January, 1925, and there may have been more boll-shedding than usual. This will not be known until the end of the season, when it will be possible accurately to calculate the number of bales exported. My impression is that there is a strong strain of the original Sunflower cotton in Uganda, and that the present crop is not yet pure – that is, that there is an admixture of types and some cross-fertilization. At present this mixture has had no very serious effects, but it is bound in time to lead to lack of uniformity and deterioration.

I noticed on more than one occasion markedly different types in the fields which I was inspecting, and in all ginneries there was a distinct proportion of naked and green fuzzed seed mixed with the ordinary white fuzzed seed. The contrast between the ordinary Uganda seed and the very uniform quality of the seed of the various types of pure line selections in India was most remarkable.

Mr. Harper is now developing another Nyasaland variety (N17) which produces good cotton of 1 3/16 inches staple, and under good cultivation should have about fifty to sixty bolls. This has been tested at the experimental station and is now being grown as a seed crop, preparatory to issue in the segregated area of Kadunguru (2,000 acres) next year. Serere is therefore, as already mentioned, a research and experimental station and, on a small scale, a seed farm. For the ginning of special cotton Mr. Harper has to depend on the goodwill of neigh-bouring ginners. I consider that a small gin for the main crop and a miniature gin for the botanist are essential, and that the former be set up at Serere without delay. I was able to obtain a small hand-gin for the botanist through the kindness of a member of the Indian Central Cotton Committee.

As regards the 'segregated area,' arrangements have been made to have the cotton grown there ginned at the Kadunguru ginnery. It seems to me that there are the following weak points about this arrangement:

(a) It will be difficult to ensure that no other type of seed is grown in the area. If more than one type is sown it will be impossible to enforce either careful picking in the field or to prevent mixture of seed cotton after picking. /

(b) It is impossible to ensure that the whole crop will be taken to Kadunguru ginnery, for there are four other ginneries and one central market within comparatively easy reach of the natives in that area.

(c) The purity of the seed will depend on the seed cotton being kept sepa-rate before ginning, on the Kadunguru ginnery being thoroughly cleaned before the crop of N17 is ginned, and on there being no subsequent mixture of seed in the seed store.

(d) Finally there is a possibility of seed being mixed during the process of distribution.

Before putting forward any alternative suggestions, I will touch briefly on the question of treating Uganda and other parts of the Lake Basin as a 'one variety cotton community.' While hoping that this may be practicable, I am bound to admit that there are, even to the untrained eye, considerable differences in soil and vegetation, and that seed, all supposed to come from the same source, suffers different degrees of deterioration in the Budama, Bugwere, and Bugishu districts of the Eastern Province, in the Kavirondo area of Kenya, and in the Mwanza district of Tanganyika. I am not prepared to say whether this deterioration is due to physiological response to environmental conditions or to unsystematic distribution, but am inclined to believe that both causes have led to this result. In any case, I would strongly advise the establishment of trial grounds where seed of unquestioned pedigree can be tested in several different areas, and, if necessary, of seed-farms which can be treated as depots of pure seed for as many areas as are proved to require their own type in order to ensure the best results. These seed-farms should be of such a size that the Agricultural Department can produce directly a large volume of seed.*

I suggest that the Botanical Section of the Agricultural Department be strengthened and be established at a central research farm, which, for reasons mentioned hereafter, should be at Kampala. Further, as in botanical work continuity is absolutely necessary, I think there should be at least two botanists and possibly more if my suggestions with regard to Tanganyika and Kenya are accepted.

The number of experimental plots and eventually of seed-farms must depend on the experiments and recommendations of the botanical staff. It will probably prove convenient that Serere with its equipment should remain as it is, and I recommend that it should be equipped with a small ginnery which can deal with its own crop and possibly with that of the segregated area also, but that it should be a seed-farm rather than an experimental station.

The experimental plots and seed-farms would presumably be in the charge of agricultural officers who, with the assistance of the administrative staff, would decide to which chiefs and natives-the pure seed should be distributed in order to widen the circles in which pure seed was sown and so to increase the supply available for further planting.

Whether every seed-farm can have its own small ginnery must depend on the administration. It may not be possible to achieve this arrangement immediately,

---

*   My opinion as to the necessity for large seed farms has been confirmed by what I saw in India.

but it is essential if the farms are to be sources of really pure seed, and, as such, is an ideal to aim at for the future; nor do I think it extravagant in view of the great possibilities of the Lake Victoria Basin,* and the fact that a well-managed seed-farm ought to pay for itself, even if the seed is distributed free to cultivators. I hope that for this area, where, geographically and agriculturally, conditions are almost uniform, it may be possible for one Botanical Section to carry out all the research and experimental work in connection with cotton, and that every agricultural officer in the area may be in close touch with the Central Cotton Botanical Section. Throughout the whole area it will be possible to conduct experiments and make observations, and agricultural officers in the field will form a valuable reinforcement to the Botanical Section. They can collect individual plants which show promising characteristics, or can even carry out trials in bulk selection, provided that they keep the Botanical Section informed, as there are dangers in having a number of selectors working independently. There is little doubt that much can be done for the Lake Victoria area by skilled selection, the possibilities of which have not yet been exhausted, but it is to be hoped that no attempt will be made to introduce a constant succession of new varieties which would merely bewilder the cultivator (*vide* Howard, A., 'Crop Production in India').

DISTRIBUTION. – Plant breeding and selection are, however, only preliminary steps in the production of a pure crop, and are useless unless combined with a systematic organization for seed distribution. In Uganda the Government requisition free of cost such seed as they require from the ginneries and distribute it gratis to the native growers.

If a system of plant breeding and selection such as I have outlined were adopted, some special arrangements would have to be made to ensure separate ginning of the seed cotton of selected / natives and the storing and packing of the seed for further distribution. It would seem desirable to have seed for sowing packed in bags marked with the name of the ginnery from which it came, so that its source would be known to agricultural officers. Anything in the nature of haphazard distribution is undesirable, and to distribute seed from an area merely because it is conveniently situated may prove a very false economy. Well-distributed seed-farms will remove the temptation to distribute in a haphazard fashion and will eliminate many difficulties, but the essential factor is the goodwill and co-operation of the ginners concerned. There is little doubt that the Uganda Government can count on this assistance from a large proportion of the ginners in the Protectorate, but if they are to help intelligently and perhaps to keep a register of natives selected to grow cotton for seed, they must be taken into the confidence of and receive full instructions from the Department. It might also

---

*   Even exclusive of Kavirondo, where for various reasons, it may not be possible to grow a large quantity of cotton.

be worth consideration whether it would be mutually advantageous to register those ginners to whom pedigree seed cotton would be taken for ginning, and to grant them licenses on favourable terms in return for their assistance in recording and checking the list of natives who grow such cotton.

Finally, I think that it is time to consider the desirability and possibility of making a small charge for sowing seed. I feel sure that under the present system a considerable quantity is wasted or burned, because the natives do not appreciate what they get for nothing. If this is done with pedigree seed it will add materially to the length of time it takes to increase the area on which it is grown. I realize that such a step cannot be taken precipitately, but that it will have to be taken some day I am convinced, and it might be well to start some judicious propaganda on the subject.

Buying and Marketing

The policy of the Government is that of free competition for the purchase of seed cotton, modified only to the extent of preventing an excess of buying facilities where there is free competition, and of imposing such safeguards as may be considered necessary for ensuring the protection of the cotton from deterioration when bought. The Government do not intend to restrict the activities of middlemen in buying centres, nor will they intervene in regulating prices. The 'five-mile radius' between ginneries and central markets is accepted as a guiding principle to be applied as far as circumstances permit in the future.

At present there are two systems of buying in Uganda. In the Eastern Province, any cotton not bought at ginneries is bought at central markets, where there may be a large number of small stores, each buying on behalf of different ginneries or middlemen, who re-sell to the ginneries. In Buganda, cotton is bought at the ginneries and at numerous scattered buying posts. This system is to be abolished in the near future, and central markets are to be established as in the Eastern Province.

There has been, and still is, very considerable difference of opinion as to whether the middlemen are desirable and necessary. The Government have come to the conclusion that they serve a useful purpose. It is held that a well-placed market enables the natives to sell their cotton without having to carry it for great distances, that markets prevent a ring among the ginners and ensure a fair price to the natives, that they obviate delays in the disposal of cotton, and, above all, that the natives like the system, as it allows them to take their cotton from store to store and to bargain for the best price.

Ginners, as a whole, do not like markets, many of which are situated within the five-mile radius, and which necessitate their employing agents and constructing stores at one or more markets, and thus add to their overhead charges directly, as well as indirectly, by diverting cotton from the ginneries. They also complain that the small middleman can build a cheap wattle and daub store and keep seed cotton in it practically as long as it suits him, while at the ginneries they are compelled to keep their cotton in expensive rat-proof stores.

I have listened to arguments on both sides and I have seen many of these markets in my desire to arrive at an unprejudiced conclusion. On the whole I consider that central markets and buying by middlemen are not essential for the good of the industry or of the native, save in exceptional circumstances where ginneries are few and distances excessive.

It should be remembered that long distances have hitherto been no hardship to the natives, who are born travellers, and who think nothing of walking thirty miles to sell to a man who is known and trusted. Their readiness to walk these long distances is, however, diminishing.

The danger of a ring among ginners is not serious. As a rule there are too many men competing, and the competition is too keen for rings to be formed. Many ginners have admitted to me that there are irregularities in cotton buying, but those of which I have been told are invariably aimed at rival ginners and are not in any way harmful to the natives. The natives themselves have been grow-ing cotton for a sufficient number of years to know with some accuracy what is a fair price, and quite apart from other things, it would not pay any ginner to cheat them. The most / successful buyers are men who live amongst them for a considerable part of the year, and who are known to pay fairly and promptly. I doubt whether markets save much time in the disposal of cotton, and of thirty-two markets now in the Eastern Province I know of eight that I believe could be abolished without inflicting any hardship on the natives.

On the other hand, I admit that it is hardly likely that I should have been told of any irregularities affecting the natives adversely. That it may be possible to cheat them is quite likely, because, in spite of considerable shrewdness, they have a congenital predilection for a deal which savours of some dishonesty. For instance, there are cases where they prefer to sell to a buyer who pays 18s. per 100 lbs., and gives them 2s. or even 1s. 6d. *backsheesh*, than one who pays a fixed price of 20s. On the whole I am inclined to think that, if the native is cheated, it is more likely to be at markets or scattered buying posts, where supervision is difficult and most of the buyers are agents who are small men whose standard of honesty is not high.

That the natives themselves like the system of scattered buying posts and markets must carry some weight, but it does not necessarily follow that what the native likes is best either for himself or for the cotton-growing industry. The bad construction and temporary nature of the stores have been in themselves an inducement to theft by the natives.

Administratively, and from the point of view of the reputation of Uganda cotton, markets and buying posts are undesirable. There are, of course, many trades where middlemen are essential. They would be necessary in Uganda if the Government had adopted a policy of few and large ginneries. But there are over ninety ginneries in the Eastern Province alone, and the middleman seems hardly necessary either in the interests of the ginner or of the native, as the former can supply all the capital that is necessary to give the latter immediate cash for his crop, and there is, as I have said, little danger of rings being formed. If there were, it would always be possible for the Government to open markets or even to allow buying posts until the ring was broken.

Generally speaking, the middleman is not as interested in the reputation of Uganda cotton as is the ginner, and where his agent is an uneducated Indian or African, it is not likely that the natives are made to grade their cotton. I visited one market where the agent of a ginning firm was unable to obtain cotton, because while he insisted on grading by the growers, other agents, acting for middlemen, bought any cotton that was offered to them. Up to the present the Administration have found themselves unable to compel grading by legislation or regulation, as is done in other places. They admit its desirability, and the growers have been told that it is advisable. The Administration hold that 'economic factors are bound to operate, inducing the grower to grade his cotton in self-interest.' It appears more likely, however, that, so long as the native of Uganda can find a buyer who will take his cotton mixed and save him the trouble of grading, he will sell to that man in preference to one who makes him separate what is dirty and stained from his clean cotton. Failing legislation in this matter, the Government must depend on the co-operation of both ginners and middlemen.

Another administrative objection to markets or posts is that it is difficult, if not impossible, to trace the source of the seed and the area in which cotton has been grown. If only one variety were grown, and if that variety did not deteriorate, this would not matter, but in Uganda as everywhere else the ideal to aim at must be a constant stream of pure seed flowing outwards from seed farms, and periodical changes of variety. It is, therefore, convenient if the cotton grown in any area is for the most part ginned in that area, and it will probably prove necessary to abolish markets in the vicinity of seed-farms, because there must be no temptation for the natives to take their pedigree seed cotton to any place other than a recognized and approved ginnery in order to indulge in the haggling and bargaining which is so dear to their hearts. In the event of a serious pest, such as necessitated some form of control, they would probably all have to be closed down, at all events as a temporary measure.

From a transport point of view markets are undesirable, and, as has been stated, it has been found necessary to forbid the export of seed cotton from Lake Kioga ports in order to facilitate the transport of lint.

As regards ginning, I have attached as appendices two notes by Mr. Jackson on this subject. Generally speaking, I am in full agreement with the views he has expressed, but we both feel that we were not long enough in the country and have not had sufficient experience to justify our including these notes in the report itself.

JAPANESE PURCHASE OF UGANDA COTTON. – The Corporation have already received reports on this subject through the Department of Overseas Trade, and I know their views on the subject. I have discussed the question at some length with H.M. Trade Commissioner, but I see no practicable method of diverting the destination of cotton. So long as the present lack of shipping facilities to England exists, so long will a large proportion of cotton go to Bombay, which is a very good market, and to which there is a regular fortnightly service of steamers. I am in hopes that, / when the new harbour works are completed, and it is possible for cargo steamers to call without the risk of being delayed for ten days to a fortnight, more cotton will come direct to Liverpool. There is, however, little doubt that the Japanese are demanding a steadily increasing amount of good quality cotton, and while the Japanese market and prices are good, cotton will certainly go there. In this connection I draw your attention to Appendix III., which is an extract of a letter from the Bombay Uganda Company.

THE COTTON TAX. – The Government policy is to maintain the tax for the present. If prices drop considerably they have stated that it may be necessary to reduce the tax or to make it graduated. It is now generally realized that some form of taxation is necessary to enable the Government to meet the expenses of development, and that the existing tax does not press heavily on the natives or on the industry.

It is also agreed that it would pay the natives well to grow cotton at a price of about 15s. to 18s. per 100 lbs., and that it might perhaps have ensured a steadier if less sensational course for the industry if it had been possible in the first instance to calculate a graduated tax on some such basis of price. A portion at least of the tax could then have been set aside to stabilize prices, so that not only could the tax be remitted, but a bonus could, if necessary, have been paid to the growers. I think that it is likely that, if the price of cotton continues to fluctuate in future years, it is bound to make the natives regard cotton-growing as a speculation rather than an investment, and that for their sake it is desirable to try and stabilize prices. Apart from this, I am informed that the overhead expenses of the Uganda Government are about 10s. per bale, including the cost of new roads, upkeep of present roads, extra administrative services, transport of cotton seed, etc. It is therefore only just that the tax should be maintained.

Before leaving the subject of marketing, there is one aspect of the case which is perhaps worthy of consideration – namely, the moral effect on the native of all this competition for his produce. Every safeguard that can be devised ensures that he gets full material benefit from his cotton, and, if it were possible to draw up the balance-sheet of a native cultivator, it would probably be found that his profits at present prices are relatively very considerable, while his responsibilities as a landholder (as in Buganda) or as a tenant of the Crown (as in the Eastern Province) are small. The seed for his land is selected for him and supplied to him by Government at no cost to himself.

That he works as hard as he does and cultivates so much land reflects the greatest credit on the past efforts of the Administration and of the agricultural officers, and that he will continue to work for the sake of those luxuries which he so much appreciates is undoubted. A heavy slump in the price paid for his cotton would almost certainly reduce for a season or two the number of bales exported, but until some more paying crop is introduced, the production of cotton in steadily increasing quantities is assured. But the native in the cotton-growing areas of the Protectorate is at present very far from being hard worked, and for various reasons he gives a diminishing amount of labour for works of public utility, even when they are of direct advantage to himself. This point is dealt with under the heading of Labour. All around him he sees keen competition for his cotton, and there is no doubt in my mind that there is a certain amount of bribery and corruption to induce him to sell his cotton in certain quarters. This cannot have a good effect on him, nor is it conducive to commercial morality. It induces a gambling spirit throughout the country, and at present there are few signs of thrift among the population generally. It is too late now, and there are too many vested interests, to make any radical alterations in the administrative system of the Uganda cotton trade, but it is probable that if, for a term of years, the Government had exercised an even closer control, and had themselves bought the cotton from the natives, or had grouped all buying within an organization which they could influence, such measures would have had considerable administrative advantages. Prices could have been stabilized and profits could have been diverted towards general development and education. The natives would not have been so rich it is true, but they would have been very reasonably prosperous, and the dangers to them of getting rich too quickly would have been obviated.

Labour

It is almost universally agreed that there is a serious shortage of labour in both Kenya and Uganda. There are many reasons to account for this. In the past when production was small, labour was cheap, and probably more than was necessary was employed. African labour is not efficient, and there is a very natural temptation to employ a superabundance rather than go to the trouble of training and organizing it.

Both in the Colony and in the Protectorate production has increased greatly among white settlers and planters and also among the natives themselves. There are, in addition, railway extensions and harbour works. This necessity for more labour has synchronized with the abolition of forced labour, and in Uganda, with a sudden access of wealth among the landholders and tenants of the cotton-growing areas.

There are some who say that a policy of developing native smallholders is hopelessly antagonistic to the development of a wage-earning / class. Others assert that, if the natives are made to work on their own land, many of them will prefer to hire themselves out, and in any case that the taste for luxuries which has been developed during recent years will force them to earn money either on their own *shambas* or in the employ of another man. But there is no doubt that in Uganda labour for hire is not popular. It is said that the reason for this is that in the case of *Kasanvu*, or so-called forced labour, the natives were not looked after sufficiently well. Generally speaking, however, this form of labour was no hardship. It was a system which the natives themselves thoroughly understood, and which had been in existence for many years, probably for many centuries. Its abolition, therefore, was a dislocation of the established order of things, and the African, who is many hundreds of years behind our civilization, does not understand such changes, and may be demoralized by them in the same way that children may be demoralized by a lack of consistency in those in charge of them.

The natives are now being told that they must all work, either on their own land or for hire. This is admirable in theory but difficult to put into practice. At the present time, so far as I can understand the situation, the Protectorate is divided into producing and non-producing areas, and the natives from the latter – *i.e.*, the Ankole and the West Nile natives, are being recruited to carry out public works in Buganda and the Eastern Province. In view of the fact that there are considerable numbers of natives in the latter area who could work on the new railway without hardship to themselves or injury to the cotton crop, I cannot help thinking that any large importation of labour from other parts of the Protectorate may make it more difficult as time goes on to get them to work anywhere but on their own *shambas*. These are not large enough nor do they grow sufficient variety of crops to occupy men for more than a few months in the year. I do not imply that the natives of Africa are lazy, but, like most other people, they only work hard enough to supply their own wants. The high prices that they have been paid and the simplicity of their wants enable them to live comfortably with very little hard work.

Obviously, forced labour once abolished cannot be revived. I gather, however, that District Commissioners and chiefs still have powers to call out labour. It seems undesirable to throw the responsibility of deciding whether such labour is essential or not on District Commissioners, and that, to ensure uniformity, this should be decided by Provincial Commissioners on instructions from the Governor.

For instance, in a cotton-growing area a certain quota of labour is essential for every ginnery. It is for the District Commissioner to provide that labour. It is evident that a certain amount of pressure may be required, especially towards the end of the season, when most natives have been paid for their cotton, but provided that the work entails no hardship and does not prevent the men from sowing their crops, it would not be resented.

It is said that at present some of the best administrative officers are specially employed on labour recruiting duties in order to ensure that the labour for the new railway should be available. At the risk of touching on a subject which is outside my purview, I suggest that the machinery for recruiting such labour should, as far as possible, be included within the province and the district in which it is required, and that the Native Labour Department should be one of inspection to ensure good housing, good feeding, and proper medical attendance, etc., for the labourers.

In including the Labour Question in this report, it may seem that I have gone beyond my duty to the Corporation, but the effects of cotton-growing on the labour supply, and of the labour difficulty on the cotton-growing industry, are so important, and cotton-growing has so often been attacked as the main and principal cause of the shortage of labour, that I felt bound to go into the question.

In my opinion, this shortage is the result of many factors, of which I have enumerated the most obvious. I believe that the difficulties of labour can be overcome, but that some pressure, which, however, should become less and less as time goes on, will be necessary. Above all, economy of labour in every possible direction, more labour-saving devices, further training, and better organization are essential.

Suggested Reorganization of the Agricultural Department of Uganda

Broadly speaking I suggest that the present Agricultural Department should be grouped in three main sections under the Director. Each section to be in charge of an Assistant or Deputy Director. These sections to be:

1. Administrative or Agricultural.
2. Commercial.
3. Scientific or Research.

The Administrative Section to deal with all questions of administration within the Department, and to be responsible for all agricultural officers in the field and for all co-ordinating duties between the three sections and other Government Departments.

The Commercial Section to be responsible for all questions / connected with the distribution of seed, buying, grading by growers, and grading by government (which could perhaps be carried out best at seaports), ginning, including the inspection of ginneries (which sub-section I recommend should be strengthened in order to be effective), marketing and transport, so far as the Agricultural Department is concerned with them.

It is axiomatic that commercial questions do not fall within the sphere of the Agricultural Department as such, and that the primary work of the Department 'is completed when it has pointed the way to obtain the maximum amount of pure cotton, and it is only directly concerned with the subsequent disposal of the produce in as far as it may be necessary to protect the seed supply required for sowing and to ensure by this a condition of purity.*

Uganda, however, has not reached the administrative stage when such commercial questions can be handed over by the Agricultural to any other Department, and I therefore recommend the formation of a section within it to deal with the subjects I have mentioned and with any other commercial questions that may arise. With this end in view I have suggested to the Director of Agriculture, and I understand that he has approved my suggestion, that Mr. Morgan of the Department should visit the United States to study the question of marketing there. I strongly recommend that the Corporation should make a grant to enable Mr. Morgan to pay this visit, which I believe would be of interest and value both to the Uganda Administration and to the Corporation.

The Scientific Section to include botanical, entomological, chemical, and mycological sub-sections, and possibly an agronomist for field testing, cultural methods, design of implements, etc. This section to deal with all scientific questions concerning agriculture in Uganda, and to act in an advisory capacity in the Lake Victoria area and elsewhere, if the Governments of Kenya and Tanganyika so desire.

I understand that the Director of Agriculture has included in his estimates the sum of £7,500 to build a laboratory near Kampala and in the immediate vicinity of Makerere College. I hope that this laboratory will be equipped so as to include the botanical sub-section, which for many reasons I think should be grouped with the other sub-sections, and should have its main research farm at Kampala, and not at Serere. Kampala, although perhaps not the most convenient centre, is at least more convenient than Serere, and can be reached without very great difficulty or delay from any part of the lake. Moreover, some social

---

*   'Report on the Maintenance and Improvement of the Quality of Egyptian Cotton,' by Dr. H. Martin Leake, 1920, pp. 13, 14.

and intellectual amenities are essential if men are to do good research work, and it would be convenient if the Government botanists were in close and frequent touch with other people as well as their mycological and entomological *confrères*. I do not suggest that this section should undertake work that could be carried out at the Amani Institute if it were decided to find the personnel and apparatus necessary to carry out general tropical agricultural research at that place. Amani, however, is not suited for a cotton experimental station, and is inconveniently situated for conferences such as I suggest in the following paragraph. In my opinion, therefore, experimental and scientific work on problems of local importance connected with cotton should be done in Uganda.

I think it would be of the greatest advantage to all concerned if an East African Cotton Conference, at which lectures could be given and discussions take place, were held at Kampala at least once a year. Both ginners and agricultural officers could state their problems and their difficulties, and exchange their opinions informally as well as in the lecture room.

Finally, I put forward for consideration the question of giving agricultural officers some administrative status. This does not mean that I suggest that they should have administrative duties, because I think that even now too much of their time is occupied in visiting ginneries and cotton markets.

The administrative officer, however, is the man who counts in the eyes of the natives. The most junior has all the power and prestige of the District and Provincial Commissioners behind him, and it is known that his instructions must be obeyed and can be enforced. The agricultural officer is relatively a new-comer, and in the mind of the native, although he is a Government official, he is primarily concerned with *Shambas*. As I have said, the co-operation between administrative and agricultural officers in Uganda is remarkable; they never seem to encroach on each other's duties, and there is no amateur interference by an administrator who happens to be an enthusiastic but uneducated agriculturist. This harmony, however, depends on personal relations rather than on clear definition of duties, and I have not seen it laid down anywhere that the agricultural officer is the Provincial or District Commissioner's technical adviser. This would not mean any diminution in the authority of the Director of Agriculture, to whom naturally his subordinates would look for guidance in matters of policy, and on whom they would depend for promotion or transfer. It would mean, however, a closer linking up of administration and agriculture, and this seems desirable, since Uganda is a purely agricultural country, and since in the past / agriculture has been developed largely by the efforts of administrative officers. Further, I would change the title 'Agricultural Officer' to 'District Commissioner' or 'Assistant District Commissioner' (Agriculture); and I think that, when they had experience of the country and where the circumstances rendered it desirable, agricultural officers should be given some of the powers of administrative officers. Also I recommend that the administrative and agricultural offices should always be adjacent – as is actually the case at many but not all administrative headquarters. To ensure continuity it might be convenient to group them in pairs, so that when one went on leave the other would be able to carry on his work. This would avoid the necessity of changing a man's area on his return, and thus wasting his personal and local knowledge.'

APPENDIX I

The following is a note by Mr. Jackson on the ginneries which he saw in the Eastern Province:

'It is necessary to divide these ginneries into two categories, European and Indian, as I found distinct differences dependent on the management. 'European ginneries are on the whole well built, and the machinery generally well looked after. Both saw and roller gins are used, sometimes in the same ginnery, but the lint from each is kept and baled separately very carefully. Seed cotton openers are used in all roller-ginneries. Platts' gins are used almost universally; the hydraulic presses are made by John Shaw, Ltd., and the seed cotton cleaners by Platts. Hand-feeding of gins is universal, as the automatic feeder does not appear to be popular. I was told that these feeders do their work perfectly and save labour, but that the resultant ginning was not so good because there was no one watching each gin who could call for the ginfitter when necessary, as is the case when there is a boy to every gin. They are, moreover, rather expensive.

'The motive power is very varied. Producer gas, steam, and oil engines are all used. The steam pressure is about 100 lbs.; this relatively high pressure is being necessitated by the small boiler. The ginneries are built of corrugated iron, and are usually of two stories. Linter gins are not used.

'The cotton stores are built on a brick foundation usually extending about three feet above the ground to ensure they are rat-proof, and have concrete floors.

'In some ginneries in Teso and Lango the seed cotton is picked over by hand as it travels on a long creeper-lattice, and the ginned cotton is again hand-picked before baling. Where this is done the lint is remarkably clean and free from impurities.

'The Indian ginneries vary considerably, but none that I have seen come up to the European standard. Generally speaking, the construction is the same, but the standard of workmanship is lower.

'Roller gins are almost universally used, and a cleaner is installed in practically all Indian ginneries, but often it does only half the work it should owing to lack of attention. The gins are generally in fair mechanical condition, but some were ginning badly on account of bad setting and careless feeding. (I saw only one Indian ginnery fitted with saw-gins. There a very fair seed cotton was being ruined by bad ginning. The lint was full of neps, crushed seed, and broken fibre.)

'In no Indian ginnery did I see the cotton picked over. The ginners appeared to work on the principle that everything had been paid for, and that therefore everything possible must be ginned in order to swell the output.

'In making these remarks I should like it to be understood that I saw only about fifty ginneries in the Eastern Province, and that I did not have an opportunity of discussing this question with the Ginnery Inspector.'

APPENDIX II

The following is a note by Mr. Jackson on the respective merits of saw and roller gins for Uganda cotton:

'The question which is the better type of gin to be used for Uganda cotton is at present very much disputed, but, in my opinion, it all turns on the care and maintenance of gins. I have seen both saw and roller gins working in the same ginnery on identical cotton, and the lint from the saw-gin far excelled that from the roller-gin in grade, while the staple was identical in strength and length. I consider that this is due to the fact that the saw-gin once properly set will run for a very long time without being touched, while the roller-gin requires attention at short intervals if it is to do its best work.

'The saw-gin gives a more uniform appearance to the lint and appears to clean it of a certain amount of leaf, while the roller-gin produces a rather patchy-looking lint if the cotton is at all stained.

'Where the ginning is bad, the lint from the roller-gin is the better. The worst that can happen is that whole or crushed seed is plentiful in the lint, while a badly set or blunt saw-gin will not only let broken seed through, but will nep and tear the staple terribly.

'In the average ginnery the saw-gin appears to give the better result; the lint is regular in appearance, cleaner and equal in staple to the roller-ginned lint; the production is about four times greater than the roller-gin, and the gin requires less attention.

'Where the best ginning is obtained, and where the seed cotton is picked over, I consider that, although the saw-gin gives a lint of apparent equality to the roller-gin, yet the roller-gin will / give a better spinning cotton, simply because the fibre has been handled far more gently, and not beaten about at all; but the highest point of ginning has only been reached by a few firms in Uganda, and the average is far below them.

'One might say that saw-gins are better looked after than roller-gins, simply because people realize the harm they can do if not in perfect order, while roller-gins are allowed to work badly because their potentialities for harm are not realized.'

APPENDIX III

Extract of a letter from the Bombay Uganda Company, Ltd., dated Soroti, January 15, 1925:

'Foreign Competition and Need for More Definite Values for Uganda Cotton in England

'In confirmation of our conversation when we had the pleasure of a visit from you at our Rappayi factory, I wish to point out that ginning companies in this country who ship their cotton to Liverpool have no satisfactory basis on which they can depend during the cotton buying season when in competition with buyers shipping to foreign countries.

'At the commencement of the current season, Japanese firms were buying lint cotton in full pressed bales from Indian ginneries at the rate of Sh. 1–06 per lb. lint delivered at Jinja pier, Uganda, the buyer paying the Uganda cotton tax and all expenses onwards. These contracts were placed when Mid-American was quoted at 13d. per lb. in Liverpool, which value, after taking into consideration all other export charges till sold in Liverpool, is equivalent to 270 points on, whereas firms shipping direct to Liverpool cannot depend on receiving an average of 200 points on.

'During the latter half of 1924 Uganda cotton was fetching 400 points on, but we have no guarantee that when the cotton reaches Liverpool these points quoted during our buying season will remain at that value, and if we endeavour to compete in price for seed cotton with the Japanese firms, our basis of buying rests on an absolute gamble, and if we risk buying in the hopes of securing a higher average of points on, our chances are that we are more likely to lose on our purchases than otherwise.

'From reports which we have been receiving this week from our cotton buyers, it is evident that the Japanese firms, working in conjunction with two or three Indian companies, are paying prices in the Eastern Province which Liverpool shippers cannot touch with any degree of safety, and although it is apparent that Liverpool and Manchester want Uganda cotton, and have been complaining about lack of supplies, last season the Japanese exported from Uganda close upon 50,000 bales, and it seems to me that this quantity will be considerably increased this year unless the British companies take the risk in the hope that, whatever the position of Mid-American cotton may be in Liverpool, they may still secure the points on quoted during our buying.'

KENYA

Kavirondo

Thanks to the kindness of Mr. Holm, Director, and Mr. Harrison, Assistant Director of Agriculture, I had an opportunity of visiting Kavirondo, which is one of the two areas in which cotton is grown in Kenya.

Kavirondo is a native reserve, and lies north and south of the Uganda railway. The cotton is grown chiefly in the northern area. I visited ginneries at Malakisi (B.C.G.A.), Wamia (Folkes and Hilton), Sio (Captain Gordon Small), Asembo (B.C.G.A.), Kisumu (British East African Corporation), and Kibos (an Indian ginnery). No cotton was being ginned at any of these factories. At Malakisi the press was being awaited; Wamia appeared to be far from finished; at Sio Captain Small was ready to begin, and had bought about 600,000 lbs. of seed cotton; at Asembo only 50,000 lbs. of seed cotton had been bought; at Kisumu the Corporation were too busy pressing half-pressed bales from Uganda to deal with the small amount of cotton they had bought, and at Kibos there was a fair amount of cotton, but ginning had not begun when I was there.

The system of buying adopted in Kenya is that only a ginner or a person appointed by a ginner may buy seed cotton. Generally speaking, the five-mile radius is applied rigidly except in a township, where any ginnery may establish a buying store. It will be seen, therefore, that the middleman pure and simple has been eliminated, and that competition has been minimized by practically giving ginneries a monopoly in their own areas. It is not quite clear why this principle should not apply in a township, and I should be inclined, in the present stage of development, to abolish this exception.

While making every allowance for the difficulties of ginneries, I was disappointed to find that two of them which seemed to be very well placed were not ready to start work. The B.C.G.A. ginnery at Malakisi will, it is true, take only a short time to complete, but the Wamia ginnery, for which the site was allotted, so I understand, about two years ago, was not nearly completed. The manager of this ginnery had died of blackwater fever only a short time before my visit, and no doubt the difficulties of transporting the necessary machinery via Mjanji in present circumstances are considerable. It occurred to me that the residence for the manager could with advantage be situated on higher and more healthy ground about a mile away from the ginnery. /

As regards the actual buying of seed cotton, my impression was that everywhere this might be carried out in a more systematic fashion. Natives seemed to be allowed to crowd in around the buyer, and there was no attempt to construct a sort of 'pen' through which they could file past the buyer and his scales to the entrance of the seed cotton store. This principle is adopted at the best ginneries in Uganda, and I believe it saves much time and confusion.

In the northern part of North Kavirondo the cotton appeared well culti-vated and clean, far more so than in the southern part of the area. This is due to the northern tribes being more industrious and better workers than in the south.

Mr. Jackson reports on the cotton as follows:

'The general average of the cotton is short, the staple being 1 to 1 ¹⁄₁₆ inches, irregular, generally rather weak, of a good colour and picked fairly clean. This holds good for the whole district, with the exception of the area round Kisumu, which has produced a cotton about good 1 ⅛ inches staple, medium strength, and fairly regular. I am informed that the seed of this cotton was obtained at Busoga, while that of the rest was sent from Mbale. If this is correct, the dif-ference is at once explained, as the difference between the Busoga and Mbale cottons is very great.'

If the present seed were the best that could be supplied from Uganda, I should be very doubtful whether Kavirondo could be regarded as a favourable cotton-growing area, but I am convinced that the best that Uganda can produce has not yet been tried there. The samples of seed which I examined had a considerable proportion of mixed seed among them. In my report on Uganda I have dealt at some length with the question of seed selection and distribution, and have rec-ommended that the scientific staff in that Protectorate should be strengthened, and should act in an advisory capacity to Kenya as far as cotton is concerned. I need not therefore touch on this question except to say that a mere redistribu-tion of cotton seed from what is now grown in Kavirondo is highly unlikely, in my opinion, to produce good cotton. I believe, however, that by experiment and trial very much better cotton can be grown, and I recommend that no con-siderable extension should be attempted until further trials have been made. With the present labour shortage it seems hardly desirable to divert the supply of labour from the settlers, who are also growing crops of which the world is in need, especially if the cotton grown by natives is not going to help to overcome the shortage of American 1 ³⁄₁₆ inches.

Another point on which experiment seems to be needed is the possibil-ity of growing cotton in South Kavirondo. The difficulty here lies in the facts that the natives are said not to be good or industrious agriculturists, and the country is without good communications. It is possible that the Administration might like to try to develop this area, with the assistance of some company to which a monopoly could be given on some such lines as I have recommended for Tanganyika. There would be no temptation, however, to sink money in such an enterprise until it was proved that good cotton in reasonably large quantities could be grown there by the natives.

The Coastal Area

Another area of Kenya in which cotton might be grown is in the neighbourhood of the coast and in the Tana Valley. The natives of these districts are very backward, not very hardworking, and have few material wants. It would, therefore, be a work of some difficulty to induce them to grow a crop which they cannot 'eat,' and will require hard work and considerable propaganda. Both the administrative and the agricultural staff are keen to undertake this. Unfortunately time did not allow me to visit these districts, and Mr. Jackson was only able to see a few small samples. He reports as follows: 'The samples varied considerably in staple, giving respectively good to full 1 ⅛ inches, medium strength, good 1 ⅛ inches, medium strength, 1 ⅛ inches below medium strength, and 1 ¹⁄₁₆ inches below medium strength. It is impossible to give any just account of this cotton without seeing a good deal more of it, but the two best samples appeared to be very fair spinning cotton and well worth persevering with if the natives can be persuaded to grow it.'

Here again will be seen the necessity for experiment and trial. The coastal natives are very backward, and their development would, I believe, be welcomed everywhere in Kenya. But it will be a slow business. I hope that the agricultural officer at Mombasa may be allowed, before long, to visit Uganda, to study conditions there and obtain seed for trial plots.

If the Administration decide to persevere in their attempt to develop cotton-growing on the coast, it will be necessary to make some special concessions to the firm or individual undertaking the ginning. The amount grown will be very small probably for some years, and a factory to buy the cotton and gin it will be essential. The ginning of very small quantities is not a very paying proposition. /

Tanganyika

My experience in Tanganyika was limited to two short visits to Bukoba (on the west shore of Lake Victoria), and to three and a half days in Mwanza.

I was fortunate in being able to accompany Mr. Kirby, Director of Agriculture, to Mwanza, and was present at an interview he had with the representatives of the ginneries near that place. Both he and Mr. Turnbull, the Senior Commissioner, gave me every possible help, and I should like to take this opportunity of thanking them for their kindness.

I had hoped to meet the acting Governor, Mr. Scott, but unfortunately he was not able to make the trip he had intended, and I had not the time to go to Dar-es-Salaam.

In the above circumstances I was able to see very little, and make the following report with some reserve, as I may have formed false impressions.

Mwanza

Mwanza district has hitherto been mainly a ground-nut producing area. Provided that the food supply is not affected by cotton, I see no reason why very considerable quantities should not be grown between Mwanza and Tabora and in other subdistricts of the Lake Basin. The ground nuts and cotton could perhaps follow one another in rotation. Indeed, the prospects of a good rotation of crops seem better here than in Uganda, as the people, who are grain eaters, appear to be good and hard-working agriculturists. It is difficult to get accurate statistics of population, but there are said to be over a million people in the areas between Mwanza and Tabora. This vague figure is to a certain extent borne out by the number of people to be seen working in the fields near Mwanza, and in any case there are no complaints of shortage of labour.

In this district the cotton is sown about December and the early part of January, and the buying season commences in August and September. I saw no cotton in the field and was able to visit only one ginnery.

The following is Mr. Jackson's report on the cotton seen at the Nyanguge Ginnery (B.C.G.A.), about twenty miles east of Mwanza:

'What little cotton I have seen was of fair quality. The staple is about 1 ⅛ to good 1 ⅛ inches, and the A quality cotton was of excellent grade, being remarkably free from leaf and with no trace of stain. The staple is of medium strength. This good grade is mainly due to the fact that the natives grade the cotton themselves before selling. Unfortunately, in the case of Mwanza cotton, second quality is also the lowest grade, and includes everything which is not A.* Thus the B cotton may be of any grade from a little leaf and stain to useless, unsaleable, immature and dirty cotton.'

At present there are no serious cotton pests in Mwanza, but in September, 1924, the Government entomologist was at Kahama, and advised that any movement of cotton from that district should be prohibited except back to the Central Railway, where the seed originated, because there was danger of pink boll worm, which might spread into the clean Mwanza and Shinyanga areas. He also visited Mwanza, and inspected some raw cotton brought from Kahama, but found no trace of pink boll worm. Orders were given, however, that all Kahama seed was to be kept separate and destroyed.

He also advised that 'Hindi' cotton, which has been grown by the Wanyamwezi tribe for many years, must be subject to ordinary cotton rules and regulations. The pink boll worm was found to be breeding profusely in 'Hindi' cotton round Tabora, and he ordered all plants to be uprooted and burnt. This semiwild cotton acts as a breeding ground for pests and as a source for cross-

---

*   Elsewhere in Tanganyika the cotton is in three grades, A, B, and C.

pollination and degeneration. Isolated cotton bushes were also found by the entomologist and reported as being objectionable.

I believe that a great deal could be done to improve the quality of Mwanza cotton. The area has hitherto been dependent on seed supplied by ginneries in Uganda without much reference to the area in which the cotton is grown. At the Nyanguge ginnery, in a handful of seed I found that most of the seed was heavily fuzzed and white, but there was a considerable admixture of naked and green-fuzzed seed.

Unfortunately I was not able to visit Ukerewe Island, but I understand that the cotton there grows well and that the soil is very good. There is only one ginnery there, and I believe that this island might be turned into a segregated area on a large scale, and could supply seed for the whole of the Mwanza area. This would, of course, depend on the type of cotton being tried and found successful in the other areas on the same lines as I have indicated in my report on Uganda. In any case I hope that it will be possible for agricultural officers to work in the closest touch with the botanical and scientific sub-sections of the Uganda Department of Agriculture.

The great difficulty as regards development seems to lie in the / fact that Mwanza is so cut off from the administrative head-quarters of the territory. The distance to Tabora is about 180 miles, and the road is a bad one. In fact, it is impassable for motor-cars during the rains. The transport question is further complicated by considerable areas being infested with tsetse fly. The natives own very large herds of cattle, and I was told that a very large percentage of them are infected, and that consequently if an attempt is made to work them or if grazing fails – even for a short time – they die in large numbers.

There are two fortnightly steamer services round the lake, one steamer comes from Kisumu via the eastern and one via the western ports. It takes about a week to reach Kisumu from Mwanza via Bukoba and the Uganda ports and about two days via the Kavirondo ports.

At Mr. Kirby's interview with the ginning community in Mwanza, various points were raised in connection with the buying of cotton. Undoubtedly there has been considerable dissatisfaction among the merchants over the system and changes of system in the past. Some of the complaints which I heard at Mwanza seemed to me somewhat captious, and did not make allowance for a very shorthanded administrative and agricultural staff. On the other hand, the cotton-growing industry cannot flourish or expand without ginneries, and it is not clear that their difficulties are always realized by the Government. Last year I understand that about 4,000 bales were exported from nine ginneries, and as some of the companies had to pay very high prices for their sites, their profits were not likely to have been very large.

Hitherto the policy in Tanganyika has been to hold auction markets where fairly large quantities of cotton are put up to auction amongst the various bidders. This policy was adopted in order to ensure a fair price for the natives, as competition is not as keen as is the case in Uganda. Each market lasted for two or three days, and involved the presence and superintendence of an agricultural officer. Obviously this system cannot be continued beyond a certain time, because, when production increases, agricultural officers cannot spare time to attend these markets, and the Director of Agriculture has stated that probably the same system as obtains in Uganda – namely, that of central markets, will be adopted. He also proposes to adhere to the 'five-mile' policy, and to allow no market within five miles of a ginnery. I suggest that in a new area this radius is too small. Ginneries are essential to the cotton-growing industry, and when that industry is in its infancy it seems desirable that they should be ensured, so far as is possible, a reasonable amount of cotton. To have to carry his cotton for ten miles is no great hardship to a native, and if markets were established every twenty miles – *i.e.*, every market and every ginnery to have a radius of ten miles, it would, I think, be sufficient in the present stage of development. Transport is such a difficulty that, for the present, the natives must be encouraged to carry their produce for themselves as far as possible. What is required is that the markets should be well organized, so that they will become recognized trade centres. Their sites should be carefully chosen in areas where there is a considerable population and amount of cultivation, with a good supply of water, and on routes which it is desired to develop. If this view is correct, it will probably be necessary in the first instance for administrative officers to give them a good deal of supervision, and if such supervision is to be effective, there cannot be a large number of markets – as there would be if the five-mile policy were adopted.

The obvious risk of having ginneries or markets twenty miles apart is that there might not be sufficient competition to ensure a fair price to the natives for their cotton. To a certain extent this risk would be obviated by having agents from different ginneries at the same market. It might also be possible for the local administration to fix a minimum price for the three grades of cotton after consultation with the ginning firms in Mwanza. It is said that a minimum price will probably become the maximum one, but the experiment might be worth trying for a season.

TRANSPORT. – But the great need of this area is a better road system. Roads are required both for such ox transport as is available and for motor transport. I hope that steps will shortly be taken to lay out main roads, and that the road reserves will be sufficiently wide to admit in most places of two tracks, one for motor vehicles and one for ox transport, because the latter will cut up even well-made roads with a surface of laterite gravel.

The most pressing requirements of the roads are culverts and bridges, and I suggest that it might be possible to obtain help in this matter, so far as the Mwanza and Bukoba areas are concerned, from the Public Works Department of Uganda, whence stores could probably be conveyed more cheaply and easily than from Tabora.

BUKOBA

At Bukoba I only stopped for three hours on two occasions. The lake boats do not remain here longer than they can help as the anchorage is exposed to the prevailing wind, and the holding ground is bad. Several attempts have been made to build a pier, but it has always been washed away, and there is now only shelter for barges and open boats. This is unfortunate, because during 1924 the native coffee crop was 3,535 tons, worth £234,000, and / the area will probably some day produce a considerable quantity of tropical agricultural products. Some fourteen miles south of Bukoba, however, is Lubembe Bay, which, so far as can be judged from the chart, and a short personal visit, would afford an excellent and well-sheltered anchorage, and is actually nearer to the centre of production than is Bukoba. I understand that the Government are considering the question of changing the station to this place. Hitherto, cotton has not been grown with any success in Bukoba, but I believe that there is no agricultural officer available, and there have been no systematic experiments.* It is quite likely that cotton has been tried in the wrong situations. It is said that the samples of cotton were good, but I was not able to see any. At Bukoba the average annual rainfall is about 70 inches, and it is evident that cotton cannot be grown in the immediate vicinity of that place. The climate is reported to be much dryer farther inland, and the average rainfall at Nzaza (now in Belgian territory), 85 miles from the lake shore, and about 110 miles S.W. of Bukoba, is about 32 inches. The Senior Commissioner, Mr. Brett, believes that there are several areas in which cotton could be grown. While hoping that further experiments may be tried, I do not expect that there will be any large production of cotton from these areas, which are not densely populated and where there is already some shortage of food crops.

Bukoba is even more isolated than Mwanza. The only communication southwards, other than native tracks, is by lake with Mwanza. There is a road northwards to Uganda, which is passable for motor vehicles in dry weather, but I understand that it needs a considerable amount of money to be spent on it to make it fit to carry traffic throughout the year.

---

*   About 65 tons of seed cotton were exported from Bukoba in 1925. An agricultural officer was appointed to the area shortly after this report was written.

Suggestions as to a Possible Method of Development

It will be evident that Mwanza, and probably Bukoba, will repay development, but that a very considerable capital expenditure is needed before these areas can produce much.

The Tanganyika Government, with a very great area to administer, can afford only very gradual development, and I suggest that it might be worth the while of the Imperial Government to consider whether it would be practicable and expedient to encourage the formation of a large development company and to give that company a monopoly of some description in the Mwanza area, including in it the territory as far south as the central railway. The area in which the company had a monopoly could be extended if desired to other parts of the Lake Basin. The procedure that I suggest would be to buy out existing interests, and to pay them in cash or debentures, carrying a fixed rate of interest. The necessary capital would consist largely of such debentures, and to encourage the interest of existing companies, both in Tanganyika and Uganda, I would give to the debenture-holders first rights to establish new or buy up existing ginneries on the termination of the monopoly.

The monopoly must be limited in its duration. I imagine that it would be permissible, under the terms of the mandate, only if introduced for administrative reasons and for a term of years, the question of extension of the period to be considered at the end of each term, but in no case should it be continued beyond a certain maximum.

The interest to be paid on the capital should be fixed at not less than 8 per cent., any profits over to go to a sinking fund, or to be expended on further developments within the area in consultation with the Administration.

The natives' rights in their land would, of course, remain unchanged. Any land reclaimed from the tsetse fly area would be divided between the company and the natives on terms to be settled with the Government.

The advantages of such a scheme seem to me that development could proceed in a steady and systematic fashion. Ginneries of economic size could be built as and where necessary, and with a large amount of capital money could be spent on transport and communications. Above all, the fight against the tsetse fly could be waged on a big scale, and probably with economic advantages to the company and to the natives themselves.

It may well be asked whether such a monopoly would be good for the natives, and whether it is not more to their advantage to continue the existing competition and the resultant high prices for their produce. To my mind it would be to their advantage to get a stabilized price, and one on which they could count from year to year. As I have stated in my report on Uganda, fluctuating prices teach the natives to regard cotton as a speculation and not as an investment, and to encourage backward and undeveloped people to gamble on their agricultural produce is not in their best interest. To lay stress on their getting the maximum price for such produce is, in my opinion, to take a short view of what is good for them, and in some cases it is competition which has made merchants and middlemen profiteers of their ignorance. It is obvious that a stabilized price might mean large profits when cotton was scarce, but it might also mean a loss in other years. The profits would go back to the natives in the shape of education, / agricultural training, communications, and an ever-increasing area free from tsetse fly.

I do not propose to elaborate details which must be matters of further consideration by experts if the Corporation accept the principle of my proposal and recommend it as practicable to the Government.

There is, however, one point which I wish to emphasize, and that is, should the principle be accepted and the experiment tried, it is desirable that a certain amount of self-government be granted to the area concerned. It will be difficult, if not impossible, for a large development company to 'carry on' if they are subject to the same restrictions and regulations as are necessary in the case of small companies, and if constant reference must be made to Dar-es-Salaam.

J. S. Addison and H. C. Jefferys, *Cotton Growing in Southern Africa and the Rhodesias* (London: Empire Cotton Growing Corporation, 1927).

EMPIRE
COTTON GROWING
CORPORATION[1]

COTTON GROWING
IN
SOUTHERN AFRICA
AND
THE RHODESIAS.

REPORT ON A TOUR UNDERTAKEN IN SOUTHERN
AND CENTRAL AFRICA BY THE DIRECTOR, MR. J. S.
ADDISON, AND MR. H. C. JEFFERYS, APRIL-JUNE, 1927.

LONDON

1927 /
[...]

INTRODUCTION.

The objects which the Executive Committee of the Corporation had in front of them when they decided to send a small deputation to South Africa were to obtain reports on (1) on the progress that was being made by the staff of the Corporation in the Union, Swaziland and Rhodesia, (2) the prospects of cotton growing in those areas generally, (3) the prospects of two properties in which the Corporation are specifically interested.

[...]

Since its formation the Corporation has been interested in cotton-growing in South Africa. In 1923 Mr. G. F. Keatinge made a comprehensive report on the cotton-growing possibilities of the country, and expressed a favourable view of the prospects.[2] Consultations took place with General Smuts and other leading members of his Government who were in London on business connected with the Imperial Conference of 1923, and General Smuts assured the Executive that they could rely on the co-operation of the Union Government in any measures that were taken.

A change of Government occurred shortly afterwards in the Union of South Africa, and General Hertzog succeeded General Smuts as Prime Minister: but the political change has made no difference in our relations with the Government or the Department of Agriculture.

As a result of discussion between General Smuts and the Director, and of an interview between the former and the Executive, the services of Mr. Milligan, formerly Agricultural Adviser to the Government of India, and of Mr. F. R. Parnell, formerly Economic Botanist to the Government of Madras, were secured. Mr. Milligan took up his duties in June 1924, and Mr. Parnell in August 1924. They have worked indefatigably ever since, and their staff has been augmented from time to time as the exigencies of the work demanded. In a sense they began this work at an unfortunate moment, at the very top of a boom in the price of raw cotton, and after one or two / favourable seasons. These two factors combined had made those directly engaged in cotton-growing in South Africa somewhat lose their heads, and a number of undertakings came into being unduly heavily capitalised, and with but poor prospects of ultimate success in normal times and with normal prices. The imported varieties of cotton which proved satisfactory so long as insect pests remained dormant, turned out to be unsuited to a large portion of the cotton area and it became apparent that if foundations were to be securely laid, the question of the supply of seed must be vigorously tackled. As a result of consultation between Mr. Milligan and the Department of Agriculture, a new plant-breeding station was established at Barberton, for Low Veld conditions, where Jassid* has proved a limiting factor in cotton growing.

To summarise the state of affairs existing in April 1927, when your deputation arrived, the main plant-breeding station at Barberton had been fortunate enough to secure several Jassid-resisting strains, one of which (Z-1) had been multiplied for distribution in the event of its proving otherwise satisfactory. Mr. Wood, formerly Principal of the Agricultural College, Coimbatore, represented the Corporation in Swaziland, while Mr. Parsons, with the assistance of Mr. E. M. Keatinge, was in charge of a sub-station at Magut, in Zululand, which is the scene of operations of the well-known Candover Estates Ltd. The Corporation were also paying the salaries of three junior officers in the Divisions of Entomology and Chemistry.

In addition, the Corporation had acquired a large interest in the Premier Cotton Estates Ltd., on the Crocodile River in Portuguese East Africa, and a smaller interest in Cotton Plantations Ltd., which owns properties both in Portuguese East Africa and in Swaziland, so that it may be said to be in vital touch with the industry over the Low Veld area which stretches from Delagoa Bay wellnigh to Durban.

In addition it had acquired a controlling interest in The Spelonken Syndicate, a cotton-growing enterprise in the Northern Transvaal, so that Mr. Milligan did not lack opportunity of familiarising himself with the Middle Veld and its problems.

Finally, the Corporation had decided to assist in the training of students both in South Africa and overseas. It had offered Studentships tenable at The Imperial College of Tropical Agriculture, Trinidad, to promising South African graduates. Four South African graduates have completed their special training at the College and have entered or shortly will be entering the service of the South African Government. All four did well at Trinidad, and the South African Department of / Agriculture reports favourably on the capacity of the first two scholars of whom they are now in a position to form a considered judgment.

The above is a conspectus of the position in the Union of South Africa when your reporters arrived at Cape Town on April 4th, and were met by Mr. Milligan. The situation as a whole could not be described as particularly encouraging. Prices had dropped sharply, American Middling at Liverpool being quoted at

---

*   A small insect which attacks the leaves of the plant, causing them to turn brown and leading to cessation of plant development, boll shedding and the production of weak lint in a proportion of the bolls which ripen. The species found in South Africa is Empoasca facialis.

about 7d. An unparalleled drought had persisted for over a year in the Northern Transvaal and throughout the greater part of the Low Veld country, the visitation extending from the Crocodile River into Northern Zululand. The Low Veld had suffered severly, and the Middle Veld even more so.

With these general impressions in their minds your reporters started on their tour of inspection under Mr. Milligan's guidance. The tour consisted of visits to a few of the Middle Veld cotton growing areas, notably Louis Trichardt and Rustenburg, and a long continuous tour in the Low Veld from Barberton to Durban via Lourenco Marques, Stegi, Swaziland, Zululand and Natal.

Speaking broadly, the Middle Veld includes those districts where the elevation is from 2,500 feet to 4,000 feet, but no sharp line of demarcation is possible; the Rustenburg-Waterberg Tract falls within this area. On account of the total failure of the early rains large areas had not even been planted. The only consolation to be got from a visit to these areas was the fact that with the possible exception of kaffir corn, cotton had stood up to the unprecedented conditions much better than anything else, and had been the last crop to go out.

Spelonken Cotton Syndicate. – Louis Trichardt was visited from 17th to 19th April, and Mr. C. R. MacGregor, Manager of the Syndicate, conducted the party round the Syndicate's two farms, Town Lands and Una.

The Town Lands Estate. – This farm had received only about 14 inches of rainfall this season up to the date on which it was visited. In spite of this comparative drought the cotton was standing up well, the stand being fairly good and the height of the trees from 18 inches to 2 feet. But for pests, it appeared capable of giving from 600 to 800 pounds of seed cotton per acre. The appearance of the fields here was a striking demonstration of the power of the cotton plant to resist drought, when cultivation is intelligently performed. Closer examination revealed the fact that a very poor crop of cotton was to be anticipated, as pests were doing great damage to the developing bolls.

Jassid, Aphis and both the Bollworms, American and Sudan, were all present. The foliage of the plants indicated that Jassid / had materially affected their growth and strength. Though the Jassid in this area has not been considered a serious pest towards the West of Louis Trichardt, it will undoubtedly prove to be so in the Eastern areas. The Sudan Bollworm is probably the most serious pest in this district, being particularly dangerous to late sown cotton, i.e., cotton sown after 15th November. In years of late rains when cotton cannot be sown before this date, other crops may have to be substituted.

The variety of cotton grown at present is Improved Bancroft, from seed developed at Rustenburg. This strain has been recently developed and has had no chance of showing its qualities owing to the drought.

Very serious efforts are being made here to control the Sudan Bollworm, two methods being practised:–

(a) By hand picking of 'flared' squares. Before bolls are formed small larvæ enter the bud or square, very shortly after the entry its presence can be detected at a glance by the appearance of the bud, these 'flared squares' are hand picked, and in this way a number of larvæ are destroyed.

(b) By catching the moths. Boys are employed to walk through the cotton, the moths take to the wing and the boys proceed to catch them. A boy goes through one acre per day and this is repeated every fourth day. If continued throughout the whole season the cost works out at about £1 to 25s per acre. In conjunction with this method, about 5 per cent. of the cotton area will be left for ratoon, being used as a trap, in which early moths are to be caught.

It is hoped that something useful will come out of these experiments in Boll-worm control.

The Una Estate – Though a comparatively short distance from the Town Lands, this farm has a very different and considerably smaller average rainfall. To the date of our visit, the rainfall had only amounted to 6.76 inches since October last. Consequently, as was only to be expected, the cotton crop was a failure. Though germination had been better than was to have been expected, plants only reached a few inches high before moisture gave out, although they were still alive and occasional plants managed to produce a boll. Not only the cotton, but also millets and ground nuts were a failure though the latter were producing a very small crop. Maize was a complete failure.

The Una Estate is typical of a large tract in North-West Transvaal where the climate appears suitable for cotton, although the average rainfall is decidedly on the low side. The great value of this estate is / to try-out what cotton can do on a light rainfall, when the best methods of dry farming cultivation are practised. If the experiment should prove successful, a large area would be opened up for cotton growing. It is very evident that both the Town Lands and Una Estates are well managed and economically run. In the future both may prove most useful as areas on which to multiply up new pure lines of cotton for the distribution of good seed.

At Louis Trichardt there is a ginning factory consisting of a battery of four Dobson & Barlow saw gins, the power being supplied by a suction gas plant driving a Crossley twin 60 H.P. engine, the press being of the high density type. The space for seed cotton appeared rather on the small side and inconvenient for dealing with any considerable quantity. Within reason, the greater the number of even running bales that can be produced, and this entails thorough preliminary sorting, the better the chance of securing the full market value.

THE TOBACCO AND COTTON EXPERIMENTAL STATION, RUSTENBURG.

The work being carried out here covers a broad field of agriculture, tobacco and cotton being the two chief crops, but legumes, millets and maize all come in for a share of the experimental work. The Staff Manager and Tobacco Expert is Mr. L. J. Henning and the Cotton Research Officer, Mr. A. R. Pullen, while other members of the staff are doing research on Entomology and Mycology.

By agreement between the Ministry of Agriculture and Mr. Milligan, it was arranged that while Mr. Parnell at Barberton undertook to work on cottons suitable for the Low Veld, Mr. Pullen was to work on cottons suitable for the Middle Veld and Western Transvaal generally.

At the time he started work, Jassid was not considered a serious factor in the Western Transvaal. Consequently Mr. Pullen set to work on the improvement of the old Bancroft strain, which had proved fairly successful in former years, with the object of improving the staple and promoting early maturity. In this he has had considerable success and he has strains of Bancroft possessing very attractive staple.

Subsequent experience has shown that Jassid, at any rate in some years, is present in sufficient numbers materially to affect the crop. The extent of its damage, however, has to be proved experimentally, by comparing Jassid-resistant strains with the local Improved Bancroft. Although it may prove that even over this area, Jassid-resistant types are desirable, it must be remembered that early maturity is at present the main consideration. /

This season sufficient rain for sowing was late in coming, so on the date of our visit, though the cotton plants were fairly developed and had the necessary framework for a 600 to 800 lbs. crop, possibly not more than 200 to 300 lbs. would mature before cold weather checked development. Of the pests, Sudan Bollworm was active and doing somewhat serious damage, Jassid was fairly numerous and evidently having a deleterious effect.

A great deal of work is being done on tobacco, including breeding and selection. Of more interest to cotton growers, numerous crops to rotate with cotton are being tried out, in addition to the effect of manures on the cotton crop.

The Experimental Station is also being used as a training centre for farm apprentices; there are always 35 to 40 in residence, and they do most of the farm work. The course covers three years and is intended for men who wish to take posts as foremen, as well as for those who will go into farming on their own account.

There is a ginnery at Rustenburg which serves a considerable area.

THE PLANT BREEDING STATION, BARBERTON.

General survey of the work done. – The party reached Barberton on 22nd April. The first glance at Mr. Parnell's plots gave everyone a pleasant shock. The contrast between strains resistant and susceptible to Jassid was very marked. The latter showed the same characteristics as the cotton which we had previously seen – stunted trees 1 to 2 feet high, red, discoloured foliage, crinkled leaves and dried up bolls – the work of the Jassid – from which a crop of, say, 200 lbs. of seed cotton per acre, was the utmost for which one could hope. There were some extreme cases where different strains of cotton were evidently going to give no produce whatever.

In contrast to this sorry sight, the resistant strains showed up, green, bold and strong, with every appearance of health and vigour, carrying sufficient green bolls to give 1,000 lbs. of seed-cotton per acre. Since the rains were late, sowing was delayed and at the time of our visit the yield of the resistant strains depended upon a favourable warm late autumn and freedom from an early snap of frost. The impression was immediately gained, that the Jassid as a pest in this area, was defeated, and the more the plots were examined in detail the more sure did this feeling become.

During our journey south through Swaziland, again and again we came across test plots of Barberton Jassid resistant strains, chiefly selections from Zululand Hybrid. In every case the results obtained at Barberton were confirmed, as regards resistance to Jassid, though naturally, for other reasons, the prospective crop was variable as to yield. /

A full account of Mr. Parnell's work is to be found in the Corporation's publication 'Reports from Experiment Stations, 1925–26.' It is sufficient to describe here something of what we saw of the 1926–1927 crop. It is important to mention that this season has been one of exceptionally low rainfall, a total of only 14 inches having fallen. Further, sowing rains were late and this delayed planting beyond the date when good results are usually anticipated. Another important point is the fact that the Jassid attack, although not so severe as in the two previous years, was sufficient to show up differences in resistance amongst the selections.

Jassid-resistant strains have been selected from Cambodia, Bancroft, Uganda and Zululand Hybrid. So far no immediately useful strain has been developed from the Cambodia. Although the majority of the Cambodia selections are highly resistant to Jassid, they do not come up to the desired standard as regards staple and they are deficient in other characteristics. Last year's selections have given some better types; they failed at Barberton but matured at Candover. It is, however, remarkable to note that resistant strains have been selected from each of the other three parent varieties found in the country. It now remains to Mr.

Parnell to determine which of his numerous promising strains is going to give the best financial return per acre in each of the different cotton-growing areas. Much experimental work, over a number of years, is required, before definite decisions can be arrived at.

Of the strains which shewed up as very promising at the time of our visit, 22nd to 25th April, the following should be mentioned:– B.179 and 180 (Bancroft) also Andrews Bancroft; several different re-selections of Z-1 (Zululand Hybrid) and U-4 (Uganda). The last named is a particularly promising line; the plant is somewhat small, but stiff and upright in growth, carrying bolls close to the main stem, and seems capable of maturing and opening a large number of bolls in a year of low rainfall. The staple is also quite good, 1 ⅛ to 1 ³⁄₁₆ ins. in length and apparently nice and strong.

Since our visit the crop has been picked, and the results have shewn up a number of different strains. A series of photographs, included at the end of this report, which were taken by Mr. Parnell just before the first picking took place, demonstrate the success achieved better than words can describe. Some small plots of the best strains have actually given a yield representing nearly 1,000 lbs. seed-cotton per acre whereas practically nothing could be picked from plots growing the strains most susceptible to the Jassid.

After completing our journeyings through the cotton-growing areas, we are forced to the conclusion that the immediate success of the cotton-growing industry in South Africa depends very largely upon the work of the Barberton and Rustenburg Stations. Had it not been for the / success seen at Barberton, it is probable that we should have left the country with a very unfavourable view of the prospects of cotton-growing. Instead, we have the most decided impression that cotton can and will be grown in South Africa on a gradually increasing scale. It is clear that much work remains to be done to prove this impression and to tackle the other difficulties which are obvious, such as the pests other than Jassid, namely different Bollworms and the Stainer bugs. To this must be added the problem of discovering suitable crops to work into a rotation with cotton.

Requirements for future work. – Mr. Parnell has, to all intents and purposes, so far carried on the work at the Station himself, for he has had little continuous assistance, whilst the equipment of the Station is of the most simple order. In fact many would describe it as lacking essentials.

The time has now come when the Barberton Station should be made an up-to-date Plant Breeding and Experimental Station, fully equipped with laboratories and the necessary apparatus, a fireproof room for files and important lots of cotton seed, stores, a useful power ginning plant, as well as quarters for staff. Additions to the staff must be arranged for in accordance with the programme of work to be decided upon. There is also scope for work on the remaining insect pests, which will doubtless appear more important when the Jassid is eliminated from the list of pests.

No mention has yet been made of the fact that Barberton is not only a Plant Breeding Station but also, to a certain extent, a Seed Farm. The area of cultivated land is being increased to 500 acres which gives scope for multiplying up new strains in the preliminary stages. It is further an Experimental Station, much useful work already having been done more particularly in the direction of testing out possible rotation crops.

SWAZILAND.

(April 28th to May 3rd).

Bremersdorp Experimental Station. – At Bremersdorp a small area of land has been taken over by the Corporation and is run as an Experimental Station, under the management of Mr. Wood. The site here is not very suitable for the purpose, being on a heavy slope and the soil rather poor and sandy; it was the best that could be obtained at the time and is conveniently situated for the work. Several rotation crops were being tried, but there had been insufficient rain to give really significant results; still good indications were obtained as to the comparative value of various crops in dry seasons.

The cotton plots were most interesting for, although grown under severe conditions owing to poor soil and lack of sufficient moisture, / the Jassid-resistant strains were standing up green and carrying a fair number of bolls. There was, however, rather a severe attack of Bollworm and many bolls were drying up from this or other causes. The Z-1 selections were evidently going to produce a useful, even a paying, crop. Later Mr. Wood was able to inform us that from these selections he had actually picked an average of 500 lbs. of seed cotton per acre.

Local Farms. – In the neighbourhood of Bremersdorp several farmers have tried out the Barberton strains of Z-1 with very satisfactory results, their general remark is:– 'Give us seed of these Jassid-resistant types and we can grow cotton at a profit.'

Particular mention should be made of three farms which are multiplying the new Barberton strains. These belong to Mr. Lewis, Mr. Wallis and the Swaziland Development Corporation.

Mr. Lewis's Farm. – Mr. Lewis had been supplied with seed of three strains, namely, Z-1 (Bulk), Z-5 and Z-25. It should be explained that Z-1 (Bulk) is the original strain which Mr. Parnell got out, and is the only one sufficiently advanced to allow of the planting of any considerable area. It is not claimed that it is particularly uniform, and it is not so nice a plant nor so good a cropper as the re-selections known as Z-5 and Z-25. However, it serves its purpose as an advance guard. Mr. Lewis had made the most of the seed supplied; he had sown only 4 lbs. of seed per acre, at distances of about 3 feet between the rows and 2 feet between holes sowing by hand and using two seeds per hole. This compares with about 25 lbs. of seed per acre using a planting machine. Bollworm attacks in February had been severe and flared squares had been picked three times. At the time of our visit, there was very little sign of this pest.

The Z-1 (Bulk) was producing a crop, but it contained quite a number of plants which were severely damaged by Jassid. It had, however, already given a picking of about 200 lbs. and carried many bolls which were likely to open. The contrast between Z-1 (Bulk) and the other two re-selections was remarkable; neither Z-5 nor Z-25 shewed signs of damage by Jassid, the trees were stronger and of rather better shape, carrying many more bolls which looked likely to open. The staple also appeared nicer, longer and more regular. About 400 lbs. per acre had already been picked and at least as much again seemed probable.

A neighbouring field of cotton sown with Uganda seed was inspected. This field was badly damaged by Jassid and had the appearance of suffering from drought, while Z-5 and Z-25 were healthy and still flowering. As a guess one might hope for 400 lbs. of seed cotton per acre from this field. It should be mentioned here that according to Mr. Parnell's experiments, the Uganda variety has the / greatest resistance to Jassid of all the old varieties grown in South Africa, though this resistance is slight compared with the new selections.

Mr. Wallis's Farm. – Mr. Lewis's farm had left a pleasant impression on account of its neatness and good farming. The appearance of the Z-selections was much the same on Mr. Wallis's farm, except that they were stronger. In fact, the plants grown from Z-5 and Z-25 were rather too strong and full of leaf, standing shoulder high and touching across the rows; they looked like giving a crop of 700 to 800 lbs. per acre. Mr. Wood subsequently informed us they had picked rather over 900 lbs. The field of Uganda growing beside the Z selections showed severe damage from Jassid, the plants being very red and shrivelled in appearance and having ceased to make growth, while the Z's were still flowering.

Swaziland Development Corporation Farm. – On this farm, managed by Mr. Stapelton, other plots of Z selections were being grown. The resistance to Jassid was just as marked and there was every prospect of 700 to 800 lbs. per acre on the Z-5 and Z-25 plots. Uganda growing in an adjoining field, looked like yielding quite a fair crop. It was, however, badly damaged by Jassid and the yield must have been seriously reduced in consequence. The staple of the Z re-selections was markedly superior to that of the Uganda.

That the area round Bremersdorp can grow useful crops of cotton seems clearly demonstrated. Progress will take place when sufficient seed of resistant strains is available, but it will take two years or more to supply the full demand. There are serious difficulties in the way of cotton growers here; the cotton is ginned at the Bremersdorp ginnery and from there has to be transported in bales on ox carts to railhead at Goba, and railed to Lourenco Marques. Transport is therefore troublesome and expensive. Another factor which retards the expansion of cotton growing in this area is the high price usually commanded by maize. Natives, though well provided with land, do not grow sufficient food crops for their requirements and, owing to the high cost of transport, Swaziland farmers can usually rely on a much higher price for their maize than that ruling in the Union. For instance, maize in Swaziland has recently been worth £1 per bag. The advent of the railway to the Swaziland side of the Pongola River and the inauguration of a motor transport service will, it is expected, tend to encourage importation of maize from the Union and reduce prices. For this reason Swaziland farmers are anxious to develop crops other than maize, such as cotton. Another drawback to maize growing, and one which probably affects native-grown cereals generally, is rooi-broom, a root parasite which is difficult to eradicate and seriously reduces yields. /

Cotton Plantations Ltd. (Ingwavuma Estate). – By arrangement with the Company, Mr. Wood has taken over an area of land and laid out a number of experimental plots, covering the questions of time of sowing, spacing, and the effect of phosphatic manures on the cotton crop, using Uganda seed. Owing to the excessively dry season, however, useful results are hardly to be anticipated; only a few pounds of seed cotton will open as the plants were dryingup. The stand was very poor and irregular. Jassids were making their presence felt and doing much evident damage.

A selection of Mr. Parnell's strains was being tried out here. Unfortunately, over the whole area of the plots the stand was very poor, in many patches plants were few and far between owing to bad germination through lack of moisture. It is, therefore, useless to make comparisons. In spite of the severe drought, many of the resistant strains were still making growth, some flowering vigorously and developing bolls, though many bolls appeared to be drying up.

Particular mention should be made of the Barberton U-4 strain, it was seen standing up to the drought in a remarkable manner, exhibiting resistance to Jassid and producing quite a fair number of bolls, which were sound and appeared likely to open.

The cotton belonging to the Company was badly damaged by drought, although the yield was higher than at Changalane.* The Company is alive to the necessity of finding other crops to grow in rotation with cotton. Difficulties were at first experienced as regards an adequate water supply for man and beast,

*   [...] The Company have two estates, one in Swaziland and one in Portuguese East Africa.

but arrangements have now been made for a sufficient supply by a pump, delivered through a pipe-line.

Southern Swaziland. – So far as temperature goes Southern Swaziland comes within the possible cotton growing area; the question of rainfall distribution is more doubtful. A few settlers are to be found between Ingwavuma and the Pongola railhead. Visits were paid to two, Mr. Boast and Mr. Inglis. Here in each case the cotton and other crops were practically a failure through drought. Mr. Inglis was trying a small area of tobacco which, in spite of the dry season, may pay expenses.

This district is very badly supplied with water, and no profitable farming is possible until each farmer has his own water supply near at hand; many who at present are making a courageous struggle carting water several miles, will probably gradually drop out, unless assistance can be provided by sinking bores. The / Corporation have done something in the matter, but energetic measures by the Authorities are also required in the same direction.

[...]

ZULULAND.

(May 3rd – 11th).

The party crossed the Pongola River on May 3rd, where they were met by Mr. R. Rouillard (Chairman and Managing Director, Candover Estates), Mr. A. Colenbrander (Estate Manager, Candover Estates), Mr. E. H. Powell (Field Husbandry Officer, Natal and Zululand), Mr. F. S. Parsons (E.C.G.C. staff), and a representative body of farmers. Magut was made a centre for four days, during which time we toured Northern Zululand, where a considerable area of cotton is grown, and the Candover Estates are situated. In the Eastern part of this district numerous settlers have had to give up their lands on account of the drought conditions of the past two seasons, having had insufficient capital to carry them over a bad time. / The drought has been particularly severe in the area adjoining the Pongola River and crops are practically a failure this season. Nearing Magut conditions improved and cotton was giving a small crop.

Candover Estates. – On these Estates the cotton had the appearance of a possible yield of anything up to 300 or 400 lbs. of seed cotton per acre in places, but the average of the Estate would be much less than this.

Fields were seen overgrown with weeds, which had sprung up after the last rain as it had not been thought advisable to cultivate and keep weeds down, the crop being considered too poor to warrant the expense. Up to the present cotton has been practically the only crop grown, but the management have now arrived at the conclusion that other crops must be grown in rotation and the risks spread.

The cotton had been badly infested with Jassid and the impression was gained that, had Jassid-resistant seed been available, the rainfall was probably sufficient to have produced a profitable crop this season. In the same neighbourhood we saw trial plots of Mr. Parnell's strains, and the sight of these plots bore out this impression.

Two farms belonging to private owners were visited, on both of which some plots of Z-1 selections had been grown. The stand in each case was very poor, due to lack of moisture at planting time and consequent bad germination. The seed that had germinated, however, had given rise to trees which were of good size, green and full of vigour, carrying a fair number of bolls which were expected to open. With a full stand a heavy yield would have been obtained. Before leaving South Africa we were informed that over 500 lbs. per acre had been picked on one of the farms.

The Corporation's Experimental Station, Candover. – Mr. Parsons, with the help of Mr. E. M. Keatinge, is devoting a great deal of attention to trying out alternative crops, much valuable information having already been obtained. There was a remarkable collection of varieties of beans, also maize and sorghums. A number of experiments were also being carried out on cotton, bearing on conservation of soil moisture, phosphatic fertilisers, etc. Owing to the dry season, many of the experiments have failed, or can give no reliable information.

Several Barberton strains of cotton are being tried out. Mr. Parsons is growing some of the Barberton Cambodia re-selections. Some of these appear to be developing on promising lines.

The Experimental Station gave the pleasing impression of being very well run and the experimental work most carefully carried out, and although it is a great disappointment to the neighbouring farmers that the dry season has interfered with much of the work, valuable information with regard to the comparative drought-resistance of different crops and different varieties of these has been obtained.

Mr. Parsons is also collecting some valuable data on the wild plant hosts of the Spiny and Red Bollworms. /

NATAL.

(May 9th – 11th.)

The party proceeded south across the Mkusi River to Empangeni. In this district, especially round Ntambanana settlement, a considerable area of cotton is being grown, estimated by Mr. Powell at about 4,000 acres. Here the climate and rainfall have been favourable and a good crop is assured. On Mr. Brighton's farm we saw a crop of the Uganda variety which should certainly pick 1,200 lbs. per acre, and we saw other fields giving as much or more.

Mr. G. M. Robinson's farm, New Venture, was visited on 10th May, when we saw some cotton of excellent quality, both Watts Long Staple and Rustenburg Improved Bancroft, the staple of both being vastly superior to that of Texas Middling, being about 1 ¼ in. and nice and fine. Mr. Robinson is a well-known cotton grower, and chief prizewinner in the South African Shows. The bulk of his cotton had already been picked; he expected to average something over 600 lbs. per acre.

A visit was paid to the estates of the N'Kwaleni Valley Cotton Company, Ltd., where an area of about 2,500 acres was under cotton. Two varieties had been planted, Watts Long Staple and Griffin. Up to the present, cotton has been practically the only crop, part of the area being now under cotton for the fourth year in succession. The management is now considering the advisability of introducing some other crop to work into a rotation.

Though this season has been a good one, Jassid has done quite appreciable damage, and we saw a field of Griffin ratoon, in which the pest had seriously reduced the yield. The manager of the Company informed us that as soon as he could obtain seed of a Jassid-resistant strain he wished to try it, as he was of opinion that it would give a better return per acre than his Watts Long Staple, which is not a heavy cropper. He thought the average yield over the estate this season would be about 500 lbs., though it might reach 600 lbs. per acre. With better cultivation these results would be improved upon.

Though this is the most favoured cotton-growing area in the Union, extension is hampered by the shortage of labour and its comparatively high cost. A native labourer is paid £2 per month and in addition receives his food, which amounts roughly to a further 10s. per month. These costs cannot, however, be taken as typical of other parts of the Union. Many farmers who have a good cotton crop this year, are finding difficulty in obtaining sufficient pickers. We saw fields white with cotton which evidently should have been picked two or three weeks before, but the number of pickers at work was very small. /

This was, however, largely due to some form of epidemic. From Bremersdorp to Durban insufficiency of labour, more particularly for picking, puts a check on the rate of expansion of cotton growing. It seems, however, that women and children are more and more coming into the fields just for the picking season; if they will only take up this idea, the position will become more hopeful than ever.

Native Reserves. – There appears to be no immediate prospect of natives taking up cotton growing in the reserves. No doubt there are large areas suitable for cotton growing, but at present the native is too well off to bother his head about growing a crop for sale. He is satisfied to cultivate small areas of 'gardens' from which he obtains vegetables and grain sufficient for his own small requirements; besides, he has his cattle which represent his wealth.

Overstocking of the reserves with cattle, and economic pressure may cause him to increase his cultivated area, and farm better. This is more likely to come about through imitation of the white settler, for if he sees the white farmer making money out of farming, he may be more inclined to try and do the same. From what we were told on several occasions, it seems that the sale of small ploughs to natives is very much on the increase, which seems to indicate that a move is being made in this direction. Some people have stated that they have noticed a vast improvement of late years in the style of cultivation and yield of crops in the native 'gardens.'

The Natal Native Trust, under the Native Affairs Department, runs a small cotton-growing scheme. This year they have some 50 to 60 acres of cotton doing quite well, according to Mr. Powell, who says that they seem very pleased with the results.

GINNERIES IN SOUTH AFRICA.

During the course of our tour several ginneries were visited. In general these were modern efficient installations consisting of a battery of three or four gins of 70 to 80 saws each, with suction feed automatically regulated, and a high density press.

Certain complaints have in the past been received from Liverpool regarding the work of the ginneries. In the first place damage had been done to the staple by bad ginning, causing 'cutting' and 'nepping.' The trouble was traced to ginneries using gins which had not been set to deal in a proper manner with South African cotton. It was understood that the necessary modifications and adjustments have now been made, and no further trouble is expected in this direction.

The second complaint concerns 'false packing,' a number of consignments having been found to contain 'false packed' bales. The Union Government has taken this matter up very seriously and all ginneries have been warned that this is a very serious defect, and / fully advised that this is completely prevented if farmers see that each wool pack is filled with the same grade of seed cotton.

With one or two exceptions, ginneries are not supplied with sufficient floor space to allow all the cotton of a fairly large ginning lot to be emptied from the wool packs, and conveniently and thoroughly sorted before ginning.

THE UNION COTTON GRADING OFFICE, DURBAN.

This office is in the charge of Mr. Homewood, who explained the system of grading in the Union. It appeared that this side of the business was very well run. The greatest precautions are taken to insure correct grading and prevention of irregularity, the Grading Office receives three samples of cotton taken from each bale, during the time it is being pressed at the ginnery. Naturally this involves a great deal of trouble and labour. It is to be hoped it will be possible to modify the system, when the total crop of the country becomes much larger, and ginneries, with more experience, turn out more regular lots of cotton.

MARKETING IN DURBAN.

The Cotton Exchange. – The Cotton Exchange is the official Sale Agency of the Co-operative Societies, and is not, as might have been understood from its title, a public market where private owners of cotton expose their samples for sale to prospective buyers.

Private Sales. – Arrangements are, however, made for private owners to sell their cotton in Durban. They submit samples to the Union Grader in the usual way, and sale is effected on the basis of his report. The private owner appoints an agent to transact the business for him. A grower in Rhodesia finds no difficulty in selling cotton on sample in Durban, provided he complies with the Union regulations.

It seems to the advantage of the Union and also Northern and Southern Rhodesia to build up a sound cotton market at Durban.

SOUTHERN RHODESIA.

(May 21st – June 11th.)

After three days' rest in Pretoria, Southern Rhodesia came up for review, and the deputation, accompanied by Mr. Milligan, arrived at Bulawayo on 21st May and were met by Major Cameron, who is responsible for the work of the Corporation in that country. The recent history of cotton growing here resembles that in the Union. The expectations formed were perhaps greater and the reaction more severe. High prices and favourable, if not very large, returns caused a violent boom in 1923–24, and when Major Cameron took up his / duties some 60,000 acres were under the crop. He preached caution and good cultivation in vain, the crash in prices and the failure of the seed supply rapidly caused a diminution in area. No time was lost in setting up a seed station under the charge of Mr. Peat, at one time a holder of a Corporation Studentship at the Imperial College of Tropical Agriculture, Trinidad. Mr. McKinstry, likewise a graduate of the College, has recently been added to the staff, and the work of evolving suitable strains is being undertaken in good earnest. Nothing has been left undone by the Government of the country to assist the industry, and an exceptionally intelligent, if small, farming community have co-operated with a will. Southern Rhodesia is fortunate in possessing an extremely capable Minister of Agriculture, and his whole

Department which is at a high level of efficiency, has welcomed Major Cameron as one of themselves. It is fortunately an established fact that cotton is by far the best rotation crop at present within the knowledge of the maize grower, while the value of the seed as cattle food and as a supplementary tobacco manure is very fully recognised. No rapid progress is to be expected till some success has attended the seed-selection work, but the great majority of maize growers in the areas suitable for cotton have no intention whatever of discontinuing the cotton crop. The country is well provided with ginneries. The difficulties that have to be overcome are in the opinion of your reporters greater than in the Union, and several years' work is essential before definite opinions as to ultimate prospects can be confidently expressed. Prospects are, however, quite sufficiently good to warrant a steady prosecution of the work.

THE COTTON BREEDING STATION, GATOOMA.

This Station, visited from 22nd – 24th May, is most conveniently situated within two miles of Gatooma, which is on the railway line between Bulawayo and Salisbury, and in a district which from average rainfall and climatic conditions should be suitable for cotton. The Station was only started two years ago. Bush had to be cleared and land stumped and broken; the present crop is therefore only the second on the oldest land, while much is now carrying its first crop. Normal crop results this season could therefore hardly be expected.

For the early stages of a Station of this nature it is well equipped in the way of buildings and the Laboratory is provided with sufficient apparatus for present requirements. There is no power ginning installation, but until cotton growing has developed more than at present, the hand gins now used are sufficient. The Southern Rhodesian Ministry of Agriculture takes a very keen interest in the Station and pays a liberal share of the total cost. /

The total area of land amounts to about 500 acres, of which 180 are ploughed. It is intended to break and cultivate a further 70 acres, to bring the total arable area up to 250 acres. The soil is fairly typical of the district, and covers the usual variations found, some being of rather a poor nature.

In general, the cotton crop this season is very disappointing; though the rainfall has been moderate, but perhaps somewhat badly distributed, cotton plants have made very poor growth and appear stunted. The Jassid attack has been particularly heavy, and this is generally accepted as being the cause of the dwarfed or stunted appearance of the cotton trees; indeed, strains which appeared comparatively resistant last season, are seen to be severely damaged this year. It was noticed, however, that certain selections of Cambodia were standing up to the Jassid and were, in fact, practically untouched.

A few plants of Z-1. (Bulk) from seed supplied from Barberton were seen growing, but many of these were damaged by Jassid. No deductions must, however, be drawn from this, as the seed, when supplied two years ago, was not intended to be anything but a mixture from comparatively resistant plants, to be grown as a test and to see if any plants shewed a useful degree of resistance. As a matter of fact, a few plants were observed which shewed considerable resistance, and were opening several well-developed bolls. The staple from these was quite useful in length, strength and fineness – a great contrast to the staple of most other varieties which was short, rough and weak. It was subsequently observed that this season the staple of the cotton throughout Southern and Northern Rhodesia with a few exceptions, possesses these same unfortunate characteristics.

A walk through Mr. Peat's plots made it very clear that the first step towards developing cotton growing in Rhodesia is to develop Jassid-resistant strains. When this has been accomplished, then the true relative importance of the other pests may be determined, namely, various Bollworms, and boll rot apparently introduced into the green boll by the Red Stainer bug.

The Gatooma Station does not as yet show the same progress towards producing a Jassid-resistant cotton as the Barberton Station, but some promising strains were to be seen, which look hopeful. It may be found that the problem here is more difficult than in the Low Veld area of the Union and Swaziland.

The Gatooma Station is not confined to work on cotton only; selection of maize is being carried out, and much experimental work is being done which covers other crops, testing possible rotation crops and other most useful lines.

The General Cotton Crop. – The delegation toured through the chief cotton-growing districts of Southern Rhodesia between May 21st and / June 11th, namely, the Gatooma area, the Mazoe Valley, and the Lomagundi district of which Bindura is the centre. Major Cameron accompanied us throughout the tour in Southern Rhodesia, and Mr. Milligan was with the party till June 3rd, when he unfortunately had to return to Pretoria.

In general terms the cotton crop throughout Southern Rhodesia this season is a financial failure, only two or three fields were seen which were producing a crop sufficient to cover costs of production. The cotton had the same stunted, dried-up and shrivelled appearance which was noticed at the Gatooma Station. Everywhere the Jassid attack had been particularly severe; there were fields, however, in which the cotton plants had retained enough vigour to produce bolls sufficient to yield 400 to 600 lbs. of seed cotton per acre, but with few exceptions boll rot was so prevalent that practically every boll was attacked and had produced little, if any, useful cotton, having dried up before the cotton hairs had fully developed.

Another cause of the failure of this year's crop may be boll shedding. In many fields there appeared to have been a heavy loss from shedding when the bolls were about ½-inch in diameter. Many of these bolls appeared to have been punctured by a bollworm, probably the Spiny Bollworm, but this did not appear to be the only cause of the shedding.

Some mention may be made of the exceptional crops seen. Near Gatooma, on the Carfax Estates managed by Mr. Henderson, a field of useful cotton was found; a fair crop was open, and a yield of from 400 to 500 lbs. of seed cotton seemed likely, though the staple was rather poor.

The best crop of cotton seen in Southern Rhodesia was on Mr. Thornton's farm in the Bindura district. In one field patches looked like giving some 800 lbs. or more of seed cotton per acre; in fact, over the whole 150 acres growing on the farm, it appeared reasonable to hope for about 600 lbs. per acre. Indeed, sufficient bolls were being carried to produce at least 1,000 lbs., but such a large proportion of the bolls were attacked by boll rot that the damage done must amount to nearly 50 per cent. On Commander C. R. Townsend's farm near Shamva, some cotton was seen grown from seed obtained from Natal and treated with sulphuric acid by the African Explosives Company. The stand was very poor, but quite a few bolls were opening, and the staple seemed the best we had seen in Southern Rhodesia. Here, however, as elsewhere, the boll rot was very prevalent.

It is very clear that the farmers in Southern Rhodesia desire most earnestly to establish the cotton-growing industry. They are fully alive to the limitation of maize as their main stand-by, tobacco is not every man's crop, and the present extremely high profits from tobacco are not expected to last indefinitely. They want, therefore, / a good cash crop to work in rotation with maize, and cotton fits this position admirably.

Throughout Southern Rhodesia, as already mentioned, cotton is regarded as a rotation crop for maize, and all declare that maize grown after cotton gives three to five (sometimes even more) bags per acre more than when grown after maize, no fertiliser being applied to either the maize or cotton. It is further declared that maize grown after cotton gives a better crop than after bare fallow. Whatever the reason may be, all farmers are so definite in their declaration of the value of the cotton crop to the succeeding maize crop, that one is forced to accept their opinion. Again, cotton provides very useful grazing for stock after the crop has been picked, and the seed is a very good cattle food, giving excellent results when used for finishing off fat oxen. When not required for this purpose, it is a most satisfactory manure for mixing with phosphates, and we were told that it gave excellent results when used in this way for tobacco.

Seed Supply: Pests. – For the present the prospects of cotton growing in Southern Rhodesia are not so favourable as in parts of the Union. Farmers cannot be expected to grow cotton, until successful crops can be produced on the Gatooma Station. The problem is first to produce Jassid-resistant strains and when this has been done, as doubtless it will, then it must be proved that the Bollworm and the Red Stainers will leave sufficient crop to mature to give the farmer a profitable return for his outlay and trouble. The Red Stainer may prove to be the most important pest, once the Jassid has been defeated by producing resistant strains. Immediate work on the Stainer, and the boll rot it conveys, is of the highest importance in both Southern and Northern Rhodesia, as well as in the Low Veld of the Union, Swaziland and Portuguese East Africa. Just how far the various boll rots are a limiting factor, is at present unknown, but the damage done is certainly very serious.

It is evident that the present cotton crops in Southern Rhodesia will produce very little seed suitable for sowing next season, not only because the strains grown are so susceptible to Jassid, but also for the reason that the Jassid damage is so great that very poor germination of the seed is to be expected. Since many farmers are determined not to give up growing cotton entirely and wish to grow small areas of 20 to 30 acres each, it was decided that Major Cameron should get in touch with Mr. Powell and endeavour to obtain a small quantity of cotton seed from the good and healthy crops of Natal, and issue this to farmers who cared to apply for small quantities. This arrangement was made on the distinct understanding that no guarantee or even recommendation was given by the Corporation's Staff; in fact, it was pointed out to growers, that as regards resistance to pests, this Nata seed was not likely to be superior to the local seed. It was suggested that the quantity of Natal seed should be limited to 50 tons. /

Ginneries. – A visit was paid to each of the three ginneries in which the Southern Rhodesian Government, the British Cotton Growing Association and the Corporation are all equally financially interested. These are at Hartley, Bindura and Lomagundi. Each of the ginneries had applied to the Government to grant them temporary relief from payment of interest on the loan. The Minister of Agriculture, Mr. Downie, had replied that he was prepared to forego the interest on the Government share for a year or two, and hoped the other two partners would do the same. When at Salisbury, Mr. Downie requested Sir James Currie to use his influence with his Corporation to act in the same manner, and Sir James announced to the Directors who met your reporters at each of the ginneries, that he was in complete agreement with the Minister and would use his influence with his Corporation and recommend the same treatment, while he was hopeful that Sir William Himbury would take a line similar to his own.

NORTHERN RHODESIA.

(June 12th – 17th)

From Bulawayo your reporters proceeded to Livingstone in order to gain some insight of the possibilities in Northern Rhodesia. The problems are much the same as in Southern Rhodesia, but the general standard of farming is not so high, and the governing machine of a more elementary type. As in Southern Rhodesia a beginning was made on the crest of a boom, and the reaction has been correspondingly severe. About fifteen months ago Sir Herbert Stanley, the last Governor of the country, invited Mr. Milligan to visit the country and report to him on its possibilities, and on the policy that ought to be followed. Mr. Milligan's report was the subject of consideration both by the Governor and the Colonial Office, and it was finally adopted. His main recommendation lay in the proposed establishment of a joint experimental, agricultural, and veterinary station at Mazabuka, midway between Livingstone and Broken Hill.

The appearance of the cotton on the few farms visited was very much like that in Southern Rhodesia, and the same general remarks apply, with perhaps greater force. The crop this year is equally a failure, or even worse; the causes are apparently the same. Many farmers see clearly the desirability of growing cotton, but they cannot be expected to continue growing the crop at a loss. No development of cotton growing can be brought about until strains can be introduced or developed which produce a profitable crop, under what are evidently severe conditions. The causes of the failure of the cotton crop appear to be due to pests, rather than / to unfavourable climatic conditions and rainfall, but very little is really known about cotton growing in this country, and at least five or six years' work on selection and experiment is necessary, before prospects can be discussed. At present a supply of suitable seed is non-existent in the country.

Mazabuka Station. – This Research Station will not only deal with all the different agricultural crops now grown in the country, but also with crops of possible utility. There will be a Veterinary Research Branch, to deal with the diseases of animals. Two young and capable officers have been put in charge, and the control is in the hands of Mr. McEwen, formerly in the service of the Corporation in Tanganyika and Nyasaland. The veterinary side of the work is in charge of Mr. MacDonald. Both these officers will be responsible to the Secretary for Agriculture. Every one concerned is both keen and capable, and much turns on the results of their labours during the next five years.

A large area, some 27,000 acres, has been reserved for the station from which to take up as much land as may be deemed necessary. At present some 300 acres have been cleared and stumped, of which about 200 acres have been ploughed. Agricultural work will commence next season, though everything will not be in full swing till the following season. There has been considerable delay in deciding upon a suitable site, and so far little progress has been made in the erection of buildings.

Plans have been drawn up for a very extensive and well equipped institution, and the estimated amount of money required has been promised.

GENERAL NOTE.

To sum up the prospects of cotton growing in the Union of South Africa, Swaziland, Portuguese East Africa, and Northern and Southern Rhodesia; with the exception of a certain number of Companies, for the immmediate future cotton will only be grown in comparatively small areas, by white settlers. They will use it as a rotation crop, provided they can make a profit. It is generally agreed that the cotton crop is most desirable for the prosperity of the agricultural community wherever the climate is suitable; besides being an exportable cash crop, it serves many other useful purposes. The actual out-of-pocket expenditure, exclusive of manures, required to bring the crop to maturity is about 25s. per acre, varying a few shillings more or less in different districts. To this must be added the cost of picking and wool packs, say 3s. to 4s. per 100 lbs. of seed cotton. A 500 lb. crop, therefore, should not cost more than about £2 5s. 0d. / per acre to put in bag on the farm, or a cost of round about 3 ½d. per lb. of lint. About 2 ½d. to 3d. per lb., according to district, should cover costs of ginning, transport and sale charges at Durban. A small profit thus remains to the grower who can produce 500 lbs. of seed cotton per acre and sell the lint in Durban at 8d. per lb.

When strains of cotton are distributed which produce this average crop, extension of the cotton area will immediately follow, provided that American Middling is quoted at a minimum price of 8d.

Even though growers could shew a considerable profit per acre. extension of the cotton area must develop somewhat slowly for several reasons, the chief of these being the difficulty of obtaining pickers. This work, to be done economically, must be carried out by women and children. They are not in the habit of going out to casual work, but no doubt the demand for their services and the good pay which will be offered will gradually entice them out of their kraals in increasing numbers as has been the experience in other countries.

In spite of these difficulties it must be remembered that the possible cotton growing area is so vast and the settlers are so numerous, that though each farmer only grew an average of 50 acres, the total crop would be sufficiently large to make a welcome addition to the world's supply. We feel confident that many districts will shortly be producing successful crops.

Suggestions have been made that the future of the cotton growing industry in the Union lies in the development of irrigation schemes. To this we would add a note of warning. In the first place irrigation offers security against drought only – it offers none against insect pests which at present constitute the chief menace to cotton growing in South Africa. Secondly the yield of the Barberton

Jassid-resisting types, under irrigation, has yet to be proved. Since other crops than cotton must be grown in rotation, experience is required as to the yields which can be expected under irrigation from a variety of crops, including winter crops such as wheat and other grains.

Further, it must be pointed out that irrigation schemes often prove rather costly, possibly from say £8 to £16 per acre for the barrage and the main distributing channels. To this must be added the cost of the smaller distributing field channels, which in many cases will be quite considerable, with a continuous charge for maintenance, since the slope of the land is frequently too heavy to permit easy and even distribution of water to growing crops. Neither the general run of farmers nor the natives have had any experience of irrigation, and perhaps this accounts for the fact that few if any of the irrigation schemes, which are at present functioning, can shew a profitable return on the outlay. Experiments with pumps should precede ambitious schemes and the scientific agriculturist as well as the engineer should be consulted at every stage. /

CONCLUSIONS AND RECOMMENDATIONS.

In the previous chapters an attempt has been made to give a general account of the activities of the Corporation in the countries visited. Your reporters now feel it incumbent on themselves to attempt to formulate an appreciation of the prospects of the industry. These prospects indubitably exist, and the work of the past few years has been fully justified. There can be no question whatever as to the advisability of its continuance. By the end of another five years the situation will have clarified and much that is now merely promising will either have failed to mature or been translated into actuality. They feel they would be failing in their duty if they did not put on record the remarkable work that has already been accomplished.

In the Union, Mr. Milligan during a period of marked political disturbance appears to have acquired and retained the confidence of every section of the community. To this the present Minister of Agriculture testified without reserve. It was impossible to move about the country and not feel that the same statement may safely be made as regards the farmers. This confidence in the ability of your staff to extricate them from their technical difficulties was very marked, and will not be misplaced. This is not the place in which to praise or eulogise the qualities which have secured them their position, but the Corporation have every reason to feel proud of the qualities of the staff, senior and junior alike.

System of Land Tenure. – Taking South African conditions as they exist, it may be confidently predicted that the day of the large scale company is not yet over. Its function is to provide the necessary initial capital. The most efficient economic unit, however, for actual productive purposes is probably the farm of about 1,200 acres. Of this about half must be reserved for grazing. The ox, entirely grass fed, will remain for many years the cheapest form of power in South Africa in regions uninfested by fly and 600 acres is ample for an arable farm with cotton figuring prominently among the rotations. To enable it to compete profitably with other crops a return of from 500 to 600 lbs. of seed cotton to the acre is essential, and if Jassid and Bollworm can be successfully tackled these figures can be largely exceeded.

Native Cultivation. – On account of the competition of other crops and the demand for native labour for mining and industrial purposes, no substantial progress can be hoped for from native cultivation till fairly considerable production is attained. A yield of 100 lbs. of seed cotton per acre and the dedication of most of the crop to the Red Bollworm may lead to something in Nyasaland where the average agricultural wage is about six shillings per month plus food, but only / on the condition that the country remains unprovided with communications.*

Irrigation Possibilities. – These are quite considerable in many portions of the Low Veld and on the Orange River, provided the subject is handled with sufficient caution and patient experiment, pending the adoption of any particular scheme. If any attempt be made to hurry or rush matters disappointment and failure will inevitably ensue.

Southern Rhodesia. – No rapid progress can be expected until further development of seed breeding work has taken place. Gatooma will of course occupy the prominent place but in close co-operation with the whole system. Major Cameron, the representative of the Corporation, has earned the respect of the excellent local Department of Agriculture and of the whole farming community. The value of cotton as a rotation crop for maize will ensure its survival till Gatooma has had time to function, but till that happy day arrives no great progress can be looked for.

Northern Rhodesia. – The same remarks apply here. Mainly following the suggestions made to Sir Herbert Stanley by Mr. Milligan during his visit to the country, a large experimental station is being started at Mazabuka. It is in thoroughly good hands, and it must be given time. Mr. Salter, who represents the Corporation, can only hope to keep the industry alive till the initial seed difficulties are overcome. His duties are extremely arduous, involving most difficult and trying travelling, and he has confronted them with the utmost pluck. He too has gained the confidence of the farming community; but in the main that com-

---

*   It may be mentioned that, in a recent letter to the Director, Mr. Ducker indicates, however, that considerably greater yields have been obtained at the Experimental Station, in Nyasaland some 200 lbs. of lint per acre having been harvested from some plots of over 2 acres in extent.

munity does not attain to the proficient standard of Southern Rhodesia, and the Government is sorely crippled by lack of funds.

Nyasaland. – It is to be regretted that time did not permit a visit to Zomba and an inspection of Mr. Ducker's work there.

As regards practical proposals. –

I. It would be advantageous if Mr. Milligan could make an annual visit to all the centres – Zomba, Mazabuka and Gatooma – in addition to the Union chain – Barberton, Magut and Bremersdorp – so that they are fully cognisant of one another's results.

II. It would be desirable for those engaged in actual plant-breeding work outside the Union to make a periodical visit to Barberton at least every two years, and annually if time permits. /

III. The station at Barberton ought to be reasonably equipped including housing for the staff at a cost of approximately £12,000, and an adequate staff provided for it. The additional cost of such staff need not be large.

IV. The other Corporation stations in the Union ought to be regarded as supplementary to Barberton, not as independent of it, and in addition to carrying out local investigation ought to devote themselves to testing out and developing the Barberton results.

V. The crop rotation work which Mr. Parsons has started at Candover ought to be vigorously prosecuted.

VI. A first-rate Entomologist, if he can be procured, administratively responsible to Mr. Milligan, ought to be appointed and entrusted with the task of making a general conspectus of the problems of Stainers and Bollworms as they exist from Zomba southwards.

The total expense of these proposals need not be great, and if they are put through without delay and matters are allowed to develop naturally, the position of the Corporation as a force in the development of cotton growing in Southern Africa will be greatly enhanced.

VII. It is much to be hoped that the predominant say that the Corporation exercises in the cultivation programmes both at Spelonken and at Premier may continue. Such control renders possible experiments with large scale cultivation, which would not be practicable under any other conditions.

Your reporters desire to put on record their appreciation of the kindness and hospitality they experienced in all the areas visited. From General Kemp, representing the Union Government, and his officials, from Sir John Chancellor, the Governor of Southern Rhodesia, the members of the Cabinet among whom might be instanced Mr. Downie, the Minister of Agriculture, and his principal officers, and to the British South Africa Company Limited. They were likewise most hospitably entertained by Mr. Goode, the officer administering Northern

Rhodesia in the absence of Sir Herbert Stanley, and by Mr. Mullineux, who was in charge of the Mazabuka district. Equal kindness was experienced from the farmers in all parts of the country.

The Corporation has much to be proud of in the quality of its officers, and of the confidence they have won for themselves among all sections of the community.

Your reporters conclude by again recording their opinion that the prospects of success are certainly good enough to justify what has been done in the past, and that the future is full of hope provided that there is no relaxation of effort.

S. Simpson, 'British Central Africa Protectorate. Report on the Cotton-Growing Industry, 1905'. CO 879/89/3.

African
No. 792

BRITISH CENTRAL AFRICA PROTECTORATE.
REPORT ON THE COTTON-GROWING INDUSTRY.

By Mr. SAMUEL SIMPSON.
Colonial Office,

November, 1905. /

[...]

It is many years since Dr. Livingstone tried to bring before the notice of the world the possibilities existing in British Central Africa for the production of cotton.[1] In his travels he came across numerous villages whose inhabitants both grew and wove their own cotton in a primitive fashion, and to this day various indigenous cottons are found scattered about the country.

It is only, however, during the last two or three years that this district has taken up the subject of cotton-growing in earnest. This may be attributed to many reasons. During the last dozen years numbers of British planters had been at work, but had relied solely upon coffee. This crop had done remarkably well, and realised big prices for a time. Its cultivation was simple, and the mere tyro could be assured of a certain amount of success. Then came disease, crops failed, and prices fell, due to over production elsewhere, and the folly of any country, relying solely on one crop was plainly evident in the general depression which followed.

New crops were required, and the state of the home cotton market influenced the minds of planters in the direction of cotton-growing. Speculation in cotton had inflated prices so much that the British Cotton Growing Association had come into existence, and were prepared in every way to foster the growth of cotton in new districts. Seeds of various kinds were distributed, and cash advances were made to planters of recognised standing. Thus larger areas were planted than would otherwise have been possible, and the alluring price of the commodity held out hopes of balancing the losses of the lean preceding years. /

The movement has not been so successful as it might have been, but its progressive state is evident when the exports for the last three consecutive years are taken. They read as follows:– £3, £1,778, and £6,941. Still more would have been accomplished had the planters known more thoroughly the answer to the many varied and vital questions which continually face those embarking on a new undertaking.

Very diverse opinions prevailed as to the varieties of cotton to cultivate, when to sow, and how to deal with the crop.

An attempt has been made in this report to clear up obscure points, and to suggest lines of progression for future efforts, in the hope of putting the industry on a sound basis.

Soil.

This varies greatly according to district. In the river valleys and the low shores of the lake, rich alluvial soils are found. These are eminently suited for cotton growing. In the highlands the predominant surface soil is red clay, but there are large patches of sandy soils as well as those of a heavy black character.

Generally, on the mountain sides the soil is too thin for agricultural purposes, and fit only for forestry. The question of success in cotton growing does not depend upon soil. The plant grows well in most soils, the best being a lightish loan with a heavier sub soil.

Standing water in the soil is detrimental, whilst vigorous growth cannot be expected in very light sandy soils.

Climate.

The region suitable for cotton may be concisely described as that lying between lines drawn about 40 degrees on each side of the Equator, and the whole of this Protectorate lies well within these limits.

The whole question of cotton growing is one of climate, and it is on this pivot that everything turns. Because of this tables have been included showing the rainfall and temperatures, so that easy comparison may be made with two of the largest cotton-producing countries of the world – the United States of America and Egypt.

India produces more cotton than Egypt, but the quality of the bulk of the crop is such that it is unsuited to the requirements of the British manufacturer.

Rainfall.

[...]

Table No. 1 [not included] shows the annual rainfall in inches for the last four years in the Lower and Upper Shire and Highland districts. It will be noticed how variable are the results shown. The year 1903 was much below the average whilst on the other hand the following year was much above it.

In the districts about Lake Nyasa the records have not been kept continuous enough to warrant their insertion in this table.

Everything, however, points to an average rainfall of about 65 inches per annum throughout the whole region of the lake. The year 1904 was some inches below the average.

Tables Nos. 2, 3, and 4 [not included] show the distribution of the rainfall over the various months of the year. They clearly illustrate that the wet and the dry season are definitely defined.

This is a great boon to cotton growers, as the crop can ripen and be gathered in the dry period. /

Temperature.

Cotton is sown after the cold season in America and Egypt, and in both countries about the same month.

This fact must be taken notice of if the conditions are to be compared, and it should also be noted that places with the same mean temperature may not be equally favourable for plant life, because the maximum and minimum are different, and the extremes in temperature have always more influence with a crop than the mean.

Some of the places in British Central Africa cannot be thoroughly compared because of the absence of maximum and minimum thermometers.

The minimum temperature generally occurs about 5 a.m., and the maximum at about 3 p.m.

It is seen that readings at 7 a.m. and 2 p.m. make the mean maximum temperature lower than in reality, and the mean minimum temperature higher than it actually is, and also in some districts the maximum and minimum temperatures are not recorded.

Notice Cultivation.

Every encouragement has been given to foster the industry amongst the natives by the authorities. Both this year and the previous one upwards of twenty tons of seen have been distributed free of charge to native cultivators in the various districts. Good results have been obtained in some places, especially in the Upper Shire District. Last sowing season reliable seed could not be obtained, and this year's crop has suffered in consequence.

It is essential to ensure success that the seed distributed should be of the best and grown under European supervision.

If the seed produced in the native gardens is utilised for the production of next season's crop a good quality of native-grown cotton cannot be put on the market.

Their gardens are very small, and cultivation is exceedingly primitive, so that in a couple of years the seed would be badly mixed, and the plant would have deteriorated. Like most African peoples, the natives are not enthusiastic cotton growers. Their food plants maize and cassava, grow luxuriantly, and they see no reason to exert themselves by growing cotton. Besides, their wants are few and very easily satisfied. An extra inducement which should inspire the natives to put forth greater efforts in connection with the cotton-growing movement, is the fact that a good market is close at hand. Various companies pay ready money for all seed cotton brought to their stores. The price given is one penny per lb. in all districts except on the Lake, where the price has been fixed at three farthings. As a rule the produce is not fully ripe nor so clean as it might be, but with increased experience in the growth and handling of the crop, these defects will be remedied.

Before the introduction of cheap manufactured cotton goods, the natives themselves grew considerable areas of the staple for local use; and there is every reason to hope that under efficient guidance they are capable of producing a large quantity of good cotton suitable for export.

Labour.

This is both plentiful and willing, but it is not very efficient. However, it is cheap, but because of this should not be wasted. On some plantations during the sowing season a shortage may occur, but this should never happen with a little foresight. The native is getting more willing to work for longer periods, especially where decent housing is provided during the wet season.

This acts beneficially in more ways than one for the planter. A raw native turns out very indifferent work, but this improves after one or two months. If, therefore, they can be kept for longer periods, they use a hoe to better advantage.

Planters should get all land cleared and the soil turned over before the rains, so that at the first opportunity they are able to sow the seed and employ all available labour to the cultivation of the crop.

Very few implements are used except the hoe. Besides, the natives are unaccustomed to draught animals, so that it will be many years before ploughs or similar implements are much in evidence.

In clearing land, perhaps, the native is seen at his best.

Wages vary from 4s. per month in the highlands to 6s. per month on the river. /

The introduction of tillage implements will be a slow and tedious process; and the wooded nature of the country would make the cost of removing all the stumps almost prohibitive. Then there are comparatively few cattle in the country, which, in some districts, is under the domination of the tsetse fly. In the highlands numbers of oxen are used fro transport work, and even if it were possible to use them in the cultivation of the soil, the native would be found extremely backward in the handling of a team in the open field.

Transport.

This will ever be a heavy item for all products in the Protectorate. The country possesses no seaboard for a natural outlet, and is hemmed in on every side by other territories. Nearly everything has to be carried long distances by manual labour to the river, put into barges, transhipped at Chinde, and probably at Beira, before it gets on a homeward-bound steamer.

During the whole time it is ever at the mercy of a cotton's two most deadly enemies – fire and water.

The best time for carrying produce is in the cold dry season. But lately during that period the river has been so abnormally low that it is useless for transport work over a good proportion of its length.

Then the cost of removing agricultural produce at the proper season becomes almost prohibitive. The railway is in process of construction, but it will be some years yet before it is of sufficient extent to warrant its use as a medium for carrying the bulk of the country's exports and imports.

Incalculable benefits would be gained if the river could be kept navigable as far as Katungas during the whole year. At the present time it costs about three farthings per lb. to get produce to the home markets.

Land Companies.

Several companies are large holders of land. In an undeveloped country this has many distinct advantages, because they can carry out projects which no independent planter dare attempt. Thus they add to the common weal.

In choosing their assistants, however, they should insist on a thorough agricultural training, and allow, them a freer hand in carrying out the work on the plantations. It is impossible to direct any farming operations from home, and when distinct orders are given, such as the date on which to sow the seed of any crop, the whole thing becomes ludicrous, as the climatic conditions may be suitable for the operation in one place, whilst five miles away if the seed were sown disaster would result.

Also it is as well to remember that knowledge of local conditions affecting plant life accumulates year by year in any particular district. This can never be fully taken advantage of if all the work be directed form a home office.

Cottons in British Central Africa.

Time has been too limited for the making of a collection of the indigenous cottons, but there are doubtless two or three which grow wild in the bush. The plants of all the introduced varieties grow well in every part of the Protectorate, but in some districts the maturing period is too short to allow the finer varieties as at present constituted, to ripen a crop sufficiently large to make them economically successful.

The following cottons are of most commercial interest:– *Gossypium sherbaceum* has been cultivated by the natives for a long time, but there is at present very little in the country.

Gossypium barbadense is found on the shores of the Lake; it has probably been introduced by Arabs in recent times.

Gossypium perunianum was introduced about a dozen years ago. It is called 'Kidney' cotton because its seeds adhere together, in shape somewhat like a kidney. The plants are perennial, and give a good yield of a marketable product. Its fibre is white.

During the last three years quantities of Egyptian, Upland American, and Sea Island seed have been brought into the country. /

On the lower levels the Abbassi thrives best, and gives the highest yield. Sea Island grows well. The Affifi does not appear to be so much at home, as it loses its natural silkiness very readily. It is, however, worth persevering with as its colour enables it always to find a ready market.

Yannovitch should only be sown under the best conditions.

Ashmouni cotton is being tried. This variety is admirably suited to the hot climate of Upper Egypt. It is a smaller plant than Affifi, and its fibre is shorter and not so brown. These facts are to some extent balanced by its producing a heavier yield in a hot climate.

It has also not been accustomed to such a thorough system of cultivation as that given to the other varieties of Egyptian cotton.

On the poorer soils, the kidney cotton is a useful one to cultivate. There is a ready sale for its produce, and it remains down five or six years, with a pruning at the end of each season, so that its growth needs little labour.

In the highlands in favoured situations American cotton can be sown. These ought to be quick ripening varieties from the northern part of the United States cotton lands. The varieties grown on the red clays of Arkansas might be specially suited for growth in this country.

Some early varieties grown in America are the King, Mascot, Toole, Meredith, Garrard, Nancy Hanks, Dickson and Deering.

On specially favoured plantations small areas of Abbassi may be planted.

Steps are being taken to introduce quick-ripening varieties from other countries, in the hope of establishing a variety exactly suited to the soil and climate of the highlands.

Method of Cultivation.

The land should be cleared before the rains, the trees and grass being burnt on the spot. The soil should then be turned over by a fork with a long handle used and fashioned like a hoe. The better the soil is aerated the more likely has the young delicate plant a chance of making a good and early start.

Cotton is a deep-rooted plant, so that the deeper the cultivation the better.

Open drains are essential to carry off the heavy rainfall. These also provide a bigger feeding area for the plants, and in time of drought make them less independent of outside sources of water.

In America maize is the first crop grown on newly broken land, and in this country such a practice of growing some other crop before the cotton was planted is wise and to be highly recommended.

Time of Sowing.

The climatic conditions, being so well defined into a wet and dry period, leave no alternative but to sow the crop as early as possible at the beginning of the rains.

This allows the ripening and gathering of the crop to be undertaken in the dry season. Under normal conditions this should be in December, but in some years it might be November, or even as early as October.

Method of Sowing.

This should be done on the ridge. In some years in the Port Herald district, where the rainfall is low, better results would follow by sowing on the flat, so that the loss by evaporation is reduced to minimum.

Distance apart of the Ridges.

This varies according to soil and varieties cultivated. In the highlands from 3 to 3 ½ feet is an average distance, with the plants 15 to 18 inches apart in the rows. If the soil is very rich four feet will not be too great a distance between the ridges.

On the lower levels, on rich soil, where the plant is grown for the first time, the ridges may be put five feet apart, whilst on the lighter soils three feet would be ample. Distance apart should be regulated by the size the plants attain, as it is difficult to lay down any definite instructions on this point.

Sowing the Seed.

This should be sown on the top of the ridge. The seed is cheap and should be used liberally. An early stand of plants is thus ensured. /

Thinning.

This should be done on a wet day when the plants are about six inches high, the two best plants being left.

Re-sowing.

As soon as the plants are visible above the soil, the blanks should be filled up by means of seed soaked overnight. Transplanting cotton is a useless waste of time.

Hoeing.

This should be done continually, as long as the workers can get between the rows without damage. It keeps down weeds, and, by breaking the surface soil, conserves the moisture. In America they believe that two such hoeings are equal to one rain.

Topping.

This is not always necessary except when the plants grow too much wood. It however hastens the ripening of the crop, which is a great consideration in all countries with a short growing season.

Harvesting.

When the crop is ripe picking should commence. If the boll is not properly opened the fibre is weak, because the natural twist which gives strength and is so desirable has not been developed. Different varieties of cotton should be kept separate as well as the early, middle, and late pickings. Spinners avoid buying mixed cottons, and then only give the price of the worst sample.

The cotton must be freed from bits of broken leaf and rubbish during picking, and stored in a clean place. When the cotton is fully riper the bolls will be open and the cotton can be extracted without the employment of force.

Ginning.

Freshly picked cotton is easy to gin, but before the operation it should be well sunned. This allows insects to escape, and makes the cotton of a more silky texture.

Egyptian cotton merchants after ginning always add a little water by means of a sprayer at a temperature of 170° F. This keeps the strength of the fibre which has become heated in ginning.

The cotton is then thoroughly mixed and taken to the presses. Too much water spoils its colour and causes permanent injury.

Gins.

Through the agency of the British Cotton Growing Association a sufficient number of gins have been introduced into the country for the present output. There are both hand and power machines, chiefly of the roller type, for long stapled varieties.

Baling.

For this country it would be well to adopt a standard size and weight of bale. The making of small bales suitable for carrying by one or two men is not to be recommended. Each small bale entails a lot of work, such as pressing, packing, weighing, and marking. Besides, many of the presses introduced are entirely unsuited for dealing with such a valuable commodity as cotton. A central baling establishment is indispensable on the river, so that transport becomes easy for heavy weights.

The standard size of American bale is 54 inches long, 27 inches wide and 16 inches thick. It weight about 500 lbs, with a density of about 35 lbs, to the cubic foot. The Indian bale is the densest, being about 40 lbs, to the cubic foot. It weighs about 400 lbs. The Egyptian able is the largest, weighing about 740 lbs., whilst the Peruvian and Brazilian only average about 200 lbs, each.

The Sea Island cotton is baled like a packet of hops, with no iron bands, each weighting about 400 lbs. /

Oil Presses.

No machinery for extracting the oil from the cotton seed has, up to the present, been imported. This would be a step forward, because other valuable oil-producing seeds can be grown, such as the ground-nut, sesame, and castor oil.

Even for manurial purposes cotton seed is far better after the oil has been extracted.

Frequency of Cotton-Growing.

On some soils in America cotton is grown year after year, the land simply lying fallow from the end of one season tot he beginning of the next. Generally in the Sea Island district, cotton is grown every alternate year, so that the land remains fallow one year and carries a crop the next.

In Egypt, under a perfect system of rotations, cotton is grown every second year, or, more often, once every three years.

Distance from a market precludes the making of a workable rotation for this country, and thus we are hindered from taking advantage of the manifold benefits which a good system of rotation of crops would bring in its train.

However, more diversified system of cropping should be encouraged, and no planter should confine his energies solely to any one crop.

Ratooning Cotton.

By this a meant the cutting down of the cotton stalks, and allowing the roots to remain, so that a crop is produced in the coming season. Under ideal conditions with good varieties of cotton this 'cutting down' is a bad practice; the reason being that these cottons have been treated as annuals for a considerable time, and the plants have adapted themselves to that period of growth.

Disease and insects are kept under far better if, after the crop is picked, all stalks, roots, and rubbish remaining in the fields be destroyed by fire.

The quality of the produce is generally not so fine form cut down crops as that grown direct form seed.

For this season, however, it is recommended that all cotton on the lower levels which was planted early, and produced a good crop, should be uprooted and burnt. Cotton planted in those districts about March, which has made little growth, might remain uncut.

All American cotton, wherever planted last season, should be cleared out, as well as those field of Egyptian cut back last year.

In the higher lands, where Egyptian seed was sown with obvious failure, what remains should be cleared out and burnt.

In other places where a certain amount of success has been attained, the plats may be cut back, and ought to produce a paying crop next year.

Manuring.

Cotton needs manure, but in this country a careful study of this question has not become imperative, as most of the land is newly broken up. Liberal dressings of farmyard manure are beneficial. The seed of cotton contains most of the valuable ingredients taken from the soil, so that if this is returned the fertility of the soil is kept up to some extent.

Irrigation.

In places where an expensive system of irrigation can be installed the venture would be profitable, as the crop could then be planted from four to six weeks earlier than under normal conditions and its growing period thereby lengthened.

Production of Seed.

This subject is of vital importance to all interested in economic plant life. Especially is this the case in new countries where seed merchants and seed farms do not exist.

Indigenous varieties of all crops must be improved, whilst the very many exotic varieties introduced must be acclimatised and adapted to the peculiar conditions / of soil and climate which prevail in their new surroundings. Many methods for the attainment of this end have been fully described in Annex A.

Insects.

The cotton plant has many enemies in this country, which can hardly be wondered at when the comparatively small area under cultivation is considered. Most of the land is covered with scrub, where numerous insects live and propagate without any restraining influence whatsoever.

After the land is cleared these insects quite naturally make their home amongst the plants which have been substituted for their natural habitat.

The most troublesome at present are the boll-worm *Heliothis armiger*, the Stainer *Dysdercus* and the green fly *Aphilidoe*.

A leaf miner has also been observed, as well as kind of borer, whilst locusts, which sometimes visit the country, would find the cotton plant tasty feeding, although they refuse to eat the foliage of the coffee plant.

It has been thought advisable to deal at length with the above pests, and fuller information is given in Annex B.

Rats and squirrels do a little damage by eating the seed when the crop is ripe.

The outer husk which is left thus passes through the gins. Instances have been seen where game has attacked the foliage, but these are rare and can be neglected.

Cost of Cultivation.

The following has been given as a reliable estimate of the cost per acre to grow cotton. All the items included have been taken from actual figures:–

Clearing land, European supervision, cost of seed, sowing, and subsequent cultivation	£1	10	0
Harvesting	0	3	0
Ginning an baling a crop of 230 lbs	0	13	0
Freight, Blantyre to Liverpool, and insurance	0	14	4
Brokers' commission and discount	0	3	0
Dock charges, porterage from wharf, &c.	0	2	6
Interest on capital	0	3	0
	£3	8	10

For cultivation in subsequent years, the land will not have to be cleared, and a more thorough working of the soil can be given. The question of manuring will also come in for consideration, which will ensure a higher yield.

On the river the freight will be less, but labour is dearer. On the other hand a far bigger and better quality of crop can be raised in that region than in the Highlands. Statistics regarding the yield per acre in the different districts are not available, but it will be seen that in the Highlands an average of 2 cwts. of lint would give a profit whilst double that quantity is not too much to hope for on the lower levels.

Capital.

Some may perhaps inquire as to how much capital is needed for one desirous of becoming a planter in this country. £2,000 would enable a man to get a good start, and the more thorough his previous agricultural experience the better he will find his way about. Especially so if his observations have been undertaken in tropical or sub-tropical countries, where the same or similar crops are cultivated. A good house and bodily comfort are absolute necessities.

Little can be done the first year, but with such annual crops as cotton an immediate return results. With coffee three years must elapse before the first crop is harvested. Over one hundred Europeans are at present engaged in agricultural pursuits in the country.

Land.

Land is cheap, varying in price from 5s. to 10s. per acre. It may also be rented on a long lease at from 6d. to 1s. per acre, with sometimes the option of purchase within a certain number of years. /

Private estates in the country comprise 786,502 acres, of which only 32,809 are under cultivation, 5,190 acres have gone back from cultivation, 591,776 acres are in its natural condition and 156,727 acres are occupied by natives resident on estates.

Other Crops.

Coffee has been the staple product of the country for years, and does well when planted and cared for on the right soils. Tobacco-growing has been taken up in earnest, and the industry is full of promise. This may also be said of fibres. Tea is grown in one district and chillies thrive in all parts. The production of rubber, especially in the Lake region, is worth attention. Most tropical plants, such as sugar cane, are at home in the country, but the cost of transport stops production unless the market value is at least fourpence per lb. at home.

Cattle flourish in the Highlands and on the plateaux, and are reared with little trouble and expense.

[...]

The Importance and Necessity of Seed Selection.

With an account of Methods adapted to all Crops.
By SAMUEL SIMPSON, Cotton Expert to British Central Africa Administration.

Many and varied are the conditions under which agricultural practice is carried on. Plants are as dependent on food and air for existence as animals, and the more highly specialised the plant, the greater the need for care and attention.

Never should we forget that by subjecting plants to high cultivation for our own ends, we have made them constitutionally more delicate.

Besides, we have upset the balance of nature by establishing hundreds of thousands of plants, of the same order, at the same stage of growth in close proximity. Therefore when insect pests and fungoid diseases begin to work in our midst, they have every chance to play havoc.

All crops as at present cultivated have undergone great development under the guidance of man, so that there is ever present the tendency to degenerate or revert to their original condition.

This inclination is counteracted by growing the plants in a suitable soil and climate under good cultivation, but most of all by careful selection of the seed. This fact should be firmly impressed upon the minds of all those interested in economic plant life, as it cannot possibly be overestimated.

In many countries we have large numbers of trustworthy seed-merchants whose very existence depends upon being able to supply customers with proved seeds for every kind of crop. Very often something really excellent is brought out. This is named and put on the market at a fancy price.

In this country seedsmen in the ordinary way are non-existent, so that each planter is thrown more or less on his own resources for the supply of seed for the various crops. This in itself is a blessing in disguise, provided the present indifference and inaction gives place to strenuous efforts being made by each and all for the production of good seed. The older agriculturists talked loud and continually about the desirability of often changing the seed. This undoubtedly had many advantages, and under the old order usually increased returns were obtained by its adoption.

The reason, however, is not far to seek. These farmers of olden times grew crops year after year without any idea of saving the best of the crop for the following season. They expected the yield to dwindle, unless plenty of cultivation was put into the soil, and this supplemented by ample dressings of manure.

But the remedy was at hand. They could purchase approved seed for their whole area at almost a moment's notice. They understood thoroughly what they were doing, and were far-seeing enough to take into full consideration the conditions under which the purchased seed had been grown.

A later generation of farmers, whilst convinced of the advisability of changing the seed, did not do it quite so often, and they worked under a different system. They bought the best seed obtainable in sufficient quantity to sow an area, the crop from which would give seed to plant up what was required in the following year.

This newly introduced seed was grown on the best land and given every chance. It is an excellent practice in many ways. The outlay for seed is relatively small, whilst one year's growth in the district accustoms the plant to that particular soil and climate. Also, if the yield is in any way unsatisfactory, that variety can be discarded, and a fresh one substituted at a minimum of loss. When the live-stock question was under discussion, every one acceded that the introduction of new blood of the best kind into the herd was absolutely essential if vigour and stamina were to be maintained. But then it was acknowledged that the best animals were bred on the spot, and could not be purchased at any price. This was because care had been taken in the selection and mating of the animals.

This idea ought to be carried into the domain of plant life. A frequent change of seed may be highly desirable and profitable under some conditions, but it is ridiculous and unsatisfactory in every way for a grower to change his seed year by year.

Ample proof has been given over and over again that in any particular district seed can be produced by selection, which for vitality, immunity from disease, and crop-production qualities, far excels that of any variety suddenly dumped down from outside sources. /

The older growers exercised no care whatever regarding their seeds, so that the manifold advantages of changing the seed were, in their particular case, very evident.

Cotton is the crop in which we are at present most interested, but the methods to be described are applicable to every crop under cultivation. For the production of high quality and big yields, failure can be the only result if the best seed be not sown, no matter how good the cultivation or liberal the manuring.

We are all cognisant of the methods adopted to improve, or even to keep up to standard, any herd of animals. The weak and puny are eliminated, and quality is the one aim kept in view. The advantages are evident, even to the man in the street.

Carry this conception into the plant world, and it will be seen that if any variety of plant is to be kept vigorous, we must try to keep the scraggy weaklings from propagation. This is our only hope if we wish paying crops.

Below are some of the methods at present adopted for improving crops, many of which can be carried out by the ordinary farmer.

(1) Reserve the best part of the crop for seed.

(2) We may keep back for seed purposes the biggest and best developed seed from the whole crop.

(3) Spontaneous types or sports may be found differing completely from the other plants. If these have superior qualities the seed should be treasured and carefully planted out next growing season.

(4) By raising plants from seeds instead of from buds.

(5) By raising plants from seeds instead of underground stems.

(6) By cross-fertilisation or hybridisation.

(1)　The Saving of the Best Part of the Crop for Seed.

The commonest way adopted is to reserve a certain area for seed purposes. This is given full opportunities for good development, and the resulting crop is kept back entirely for next season's sowing.

Another method, and no less commendable, is to go over the growing crop and note any particular areas of great promise. The seed from the selected portions is carefully set apart for next year's crop.

But neither of the above is sufficient if we wish to progress on the right lines.

For example, we wish to develop varieties of cotton which, above all its other qualities, must be an early ripener. What system should we adopt to attain that end? We must collect the early ripening bolls, and after ginning this cotton by itself, reserve the seed for the propagation of the crop.

That this is sound and efficacious has been demonstrated times without number. Perhaps the best object lesson in this respect is to be found in a careful study of Sea Island cotton which to-day stands pre-eminent. Long ago when cotton seed was first introduced into that district it failed to give a crop in its first season.

The plants died down, but in the spring of the next year grew up and managed to ripen a few bolls before the end of the second season. The seeds from these were again planted with great care.

The method was assiduously followed up until to-day we find the Sea Island cotton ripening its crop in one season. And not only so, but, in the meantime, the length, strength, and fineness of the product have been enormously improved, so that now-a days it is unequalled on the market.

Perhaps a more homely illustration will add weight to what has preceded. The progenitor of such diverse plants as the turnip, cabbage, cauliflower, kohlrabi, &c., was one and the same, growing in its natural habitat on the sea-shore. But man stepped in and by persistent and continued guidance has evolved totally different plants. Root development has given us the turnip, a collection of flowers the cauliflower, whilst the cabbage is merely an accumulation of leaves.

It needs no epicure to distinguish them when cooked for the table, or one deeply versed in horticulture to label them whilst growing in the garden. Their characteristics are so definite and distinct. But take the seeds of the above plants and an expert would come to grief in his attempt at classification.

The reason for this being that the efforts of cultivators have been directed to making modifications in the plants themselves, and have overlooked or neglected the seed entirely. /

If we wish to select seed from our cotton crop let us be certain that the plants now growing are from pure seed and not mixed in any way.

Egyptian seed at the present time is far from pure. You cannot buy pure Affifi seed and be certain that no other varieties are present. This is easily accounted for.

In Egypt large ginning factories have been established where different varieties of cotton are dealt with.

Mixing of seed can easily take place, either at the gins, or in the riddles where the seed is separated if required for sowing purposes, the small and broken seeds being rejected. Thus after one variety of cotton has been through the machinery, unless great care is taken to clean up all the seed, mixing follows when the next kind is being dealt with.

It must also be remembered that much mixing takes place on the farm, where two or even more varieties are often grown. This mixing may take place in picking or by being put in the same store. In re-sowing for blanks mistakes are also prevalent, a different variety being used to the one originally sown.

Also a certain amount of crossing takes place when different varieties are grown near each other.

Can we wonder then that seed is often badly mixed, because, if growers take no pains to keep the varieties separate, no amount of care at the ginning factories can produce pure seed.

For seed purposes the ideal condition is for each grower to gin his own seed. In Egypt this system has not been followed, with the result that mixed seed is found everywhere.

Even to-day a big percentage of seeds belonging to an old native variety, called Hindi, is found in every consignment of Egyptian seed. Both plant, seed, and fibre are readily recognised. Needless to say, it was found in all the British Central Africa plantations, and its true value and significance have been pointed out to all cotton growers.

The plant is hardy, grows like a bush, with plenty of promise as regards fruit. Its leaves are smoother and more circular than the other varieties. The bolls are divided in four sections. Egyptian and Sea Island cottons have three only. Its fibre is white, very short, and the lint is practically filled with seeds. This can easily be demonstrated by taking a ripe boll and pressing it between the fingers. The seeds are black, rather triangular and are provided with a sharp point. The lint leaves the seed entirely, whilst a tuft always remains on true Egyptian seed.

The plants should always be uprooted when recognised. If it matures, the cotton should be ginned and sold separately, and none should ever be kept for seed purposes. This is very essential or otherwise with its prolific and hardy qualities in a few years plantations would be filled with this rubbish, and growers would be happy under the mistaken assurance that they were growing Egyptian cotton.

In America some years ago whole fields of young cotton were destroyed by the wilt disease. Some observant planters noticed that occasionally a plant remained. These they reared and persevered with until now disease-resisting varieties are on the market, and what promised to be dire calamity to the planting interest has been averted.

Perhaps if the coffee plant had been taken in hand in the same way, different results would now be seen in the Highlands. Everything points to the fact that coffee with careful selection could be made to flourish on the heavily impregnated iron soils, which are so abundant in this country.

Investigators at the present time are devoting their energies in many directions. Many are working to establish and fix a type of cotton plant which will ripen its bolls at the same time. This is to lessen the expense of picking, which in many places constricts the area, and diminishes profits. If this object is successful, it is hoped to bring forward machinery to take the place of the slow and laborious drudgery of hand-picking.

It is well known that the seed of American cotton as a rule is covered with short lint. This occasions great difficulty in ginning by the roller gin, in fact, in that country the saw gin is in universal use. This gin breaks and twists the fibre so that its value is very much lessened.

They are selecting lint-free seed from ordinary plants and even crossing the existing varieties with smooth-seeded varieties like Egyptian. In this way they hope to develop an Upland cotton which can be easily ginned by the roller gin and / so increase its market value. Strenuous efforts are also being made to develop early ripening varieties of cotton. These are for cultivation in the northern districts where the growing season is short. It has also been found that to counteract the ravages of the boll-weevil, early ripening varieties are the planters' only hope, where the pest is troublesome.

A comparatively simple method of selection, which could be undertaken by everyone, is as follows:– Train six or eight men to distinguish healthy well-developed trees from the others. Before the general area is picked, send these men to gather the crop from the trees thus fitted for seed production. Well-branched and not spindly or leggy trees should be chosen. If possible, the pickers should know something about quality, yield, and early ripening. If under careful supervision, the seed from the cotton thus gathered will give results far superior to that from the general crop.

Another way is to purchase a small quantity of the best seed and give it every care, reserving the resulting seed for the general area under cotton the next year.

(2) The Keeping Back FOR Seed Purposes OF THE Biggest AND Best Developed Seeds.

The keeping back for seed purposes of the biggest and best developed seeds from the whole crop is a step in the right direction. But it does not go far enough. It, however, ensures that the seed contains a supply of nourishment sufficient to give the young plant a good start in life, and to tide it over any early struggles for existence.

(3) Spontaneous Types of Sports.

Spontaneous types or sports frequently occur in plant life. These differ greatly from the surrounding plants, and if the qualities of the product are in any way superior, the type should be propagated and tended until it becomes fixed. Sports result chiefly from natural crossing in the field or from the influence of soil, climate, and cultivation on that particular plant.

Most of the Egyptian varieties of cotton have been developed from plants such as these found by observant cultivators.

It is said that a single oat plant found growing in a potato field in Scotland was the original of the popular potato oat which at one time had such a wide vogue.

Methods 4 AND 5.

Methods (4) and (5) may be taken together. They are of great use to the scientist and horticulturist. New varieties of potatoes are raised from seed instead of planting the tuber, whilst date palms are raised also from seed instead of planting the suckers.

In grafting we take the bud from one tree to another to work out our own ends in the improvement of the produce.

(6) By Cross-Fertilisation OR Hybridisation.

Our greatest hopes in plant development are focussed on this method. An ordinary planter could not be expected to carry it out, so little space will be devoted to it. Just as breeders of live-stock will cross a Shorthorn bull with a native cow, so plant breeders develop hybrids from two different plants. In this way they hope to combine and fix the best qualities of both plants in a single specimen.

In every part of the world much work is being done on this method of plant improvement, as its possibilities are so great. Even the good properties of some weeds are being utilised, and it needs little imagination to picture what might be accomplished by systematic and judicious plant breeding. In America crosses are being tried between Sea Island and the Upland cottons, and also with the Egyptian varieties, whilst in India the native varieties of cotton are being crossed with the better exotic varieties.

In great Britain a wonderful work has been done on this subject with grasses and cereal crops.

It has been thought advisable include an abstract of an article which gave full details of the methods adopted by the best growers of Sea Island cotton.

This description was from the able pen of Professor Herbert H. Webber, the Physiologist in charge of the Laboratory of Plant Breeding, U.S.A. Department of / Agriculture, and the summary printed below is taken from the Khedivial. Agricultural Society's Journal, and was written by George P. Foaden, Esq., Secretary of the Society.

'In the selection of seed for cotton we have two primary objects in view, viz., same time is quite possible, though we think that the main object in view can be accomplished by growing in the first place the very best seed obtainable, and then selecting seed from the heaviest yielding plants, provided the quality of those plants is equal to the best standard of that variety. In the system of selection adopted by Sea Island planters most distinctive results have been obtained. For example, one grower's ideal has been to obtain heavy yields with but a secondary regard for quality and this has been quite successful, the grower's cotton being known in the market as that from heavy yielding plants but whose quality is not extra.' Another planter again has selected for quality only, and though yield has been to a certain extent sacrificed, yet his cotton is sold for a much higher price. Thus starting with the same seed, two different ideals may be reached according to the wish of the particular grower.

'As a rule, however, our primary object is to increase the yield, and while striving to obtain this we have to see that we do not sacrifice quality and other desirable characteristics, but keep them at least up to the best standard.

'An area of the variety under consideration is planted with the best seed obtainable, and should possess a good soil and be thoroughly cultivated and manured in order to obtain a good development of the plants, and consequently ideal conditions for making selections.

'Just before the first picking, when some of the lower bolls are well open on all of the plants, the field should be gone over and every plant examined with reference to the productiveness, number and size of bolls, vigour and shape of plant, earliness, & c.

'It is desirable to mark more plants than are expected to be used, because, in going over and comparing the plants the first time, it is ordinarily found difficult to carry the characters desired in mind with sufficient accuracy to enable a careful judgment to be made. Therefore some fifty of the plants should be first marked and numbered, so that these can be more carefully examined a second time and the number reduced possibly one-half or more. The permanent numbers should be placed only on the plants which are finally selected. Before each picking, a careful man should go over the field and pick the cotton from each plant in sacks numbered to correspond with the numbers on the plants, in order that the different pickings from the same plant may be kept together. Later on, after the close of the picking season, the seed cotton from each individual plant can be more carefully compared and weighed, and any of the plants which are found to have fallen below the standard in production or in any other important feature should be rejected. The remainder should be ginned, care being taken to have the gin thoroughly cleaned out before beginning the process, so that the seed from the selections will not become mixed with ordinary seed. After ginning each individual plant, the seed should be carefully picked up and replaced in the numbered sack, so that all of the seed from the same select individual will be retained by itself.

'In describing the method of procedure, it is much clearer to base the explanation on the assumption that only one plant is chosen which will make our explanation more clear, and what can be done with one plant can be done with any number. Twenty-five or more are selected in practice.

'*Second Year's Selection* – The seed of the individual plant selected the first year is planted the second year. Each cotton plant yields from 500 to 2,000 seeds, and therefore 500 or more seedlings will probably be produced from each plant. When these plants reach the proper stage of maturity, the entire progeny should be examined to see whether the plant selected the first year has shown strong transmitting power. If a large percentage of the progeny possesses the desired qualities in a marked degree, showing that the transmitting power is fairly strong, several selections of the best plants should be made from among them. If, on the other hand, the transmitting power has been weak, the qualities for which the plants were selected not having been transmitted, the entire progeny should be discarded. The possibility of having to discard the entire offspring of a select individual is the principal reason for urging that a number of selections be made the first year instead of only one or two. The specially selected plants of this second generation should be carefully examined with reference / to the particular qualities desired, and a single plant finally selected which is superior to all of the others. The seed of this individual should be preserved separately, and handled exactly in the same way as the selection made the first year. The seed from the remaining plants produced by the single individual selected the first year should be ginned separately in order to avoid mixing, and retained to plant a seed patch of about five acres the third year, in order to obtain sufficient seed of a selected the first year sufficient seed will be obtained to plant five acres the third year.

'*Third Year's Selection* – The seed from the plant selected the second year is planted by itself the third year. Just before the first picking, all of the progeny should be examined, as in the second generation, to determine the strength of the transmitting power. If the progeny as a whole are found to have inherited the characters of the plant selected the second year, a few of the very best plants should again be selected and marked as previously. These should be more carefully examined, as in the above instances, and a single superior plant finally selected. The seed of the remaining individuals from the same number as the one selected, which will be about 500 in number, should be retained to plant a seed patch the fourth year to give sufficient seed to plant a general crop the fifth year. The seed obtained in the third year from the seed patch of five acres planted from the progeny of the selection of the first year will this year furnish sufficient seed for the general crop the fourth year.

'*Fourth Year's Selection.* – The seed from the specially selected plant of the third year is planted by itself and marked plainly to distinguish it from other selections, as in the previous year. From the 500 or more seedlings resulting, a particularly fine individual is again selected for further breeding, as in the preceding years, the same care being taken to determine the transmitting power to see that this is up to the standard. The other plants grown from the individual specially selected in the third year will this year give sufficient seed to plant a five acres seed patch the fifth year. The seed used to plant the general crop the fourth year is that from the seed patch of the third year, grown from the unselected plants of the second year, and thus the general crop the fourth year is derived directly from the plant selected the first year, and so on through succeeding generations. [...]

'*Necessity of Selecting more than One Plant.* – It is highly important in practice to select more than one excellent plant, as it not infrequently happens that a very fine plant is found having poor transmitting power, so that the progeny will be even / below the general crop of the year preceding. It is impossible in a short article to lay out a general plan which will fit all cases. If the plantation is of moderate size, a sufficient number of individual plants could be selected each year, so that instead of [a] five acres seed patch [...], the entire plantation could be planted the third year. According to this scheme, five plants selected the first year would in third year plant 25 acres, and if 20 plants were selected the first year, they would plant 100 acres. It is thus within possibilities, on a moderate sized plantation, to select enough plants each year to plant the general crop from select seed the third year. [As regards] the method of selection pursued by planters of Sea Island cotton on James and Edisto Islands [...] 'after the selection work has commenced, special selections are made each year from the small areas of very select seed, and that the main area is continually grown from seed descending from a single selected individual plant. Consequently in this system, the selection of the individual plant each year year is considered. In practice, however, a grower selects several plants each year from which to breed. It is seen, therefore, that the quality must improve year by year, and this has gone on with Sea Island planters until a very high standard of excellence has been reached. The writer in fact was informed that 40 or 50 dollars per 100 lbs. were sometimes obtained for the finest grades of cotton from such selected plants when ordinary Sea Island was selling for half this price. We are quite aware that such a system of selection is entirely beyond what can be expected in Egypt, but it has been given here to indicate to Egyptian cultivators what steps are taken not only to keep up, but to improve the staple of Sea Island cotton. If such a system cannot be realised in this country by individual growers it should be put into practise on their behalf, this is to say seed areas should be set apart for the purpose and the grain placed at the disposal of careful cultivators who would in their turn produce seed for general use.'

'B'

Insect Pests OF Cotton.
By Samuel Simpson, Cotton Expert to British Central Africa Administration.

Much of the information given below has been obtained from the excellent publications of the United States of America Department of Agriculture.

The Cotton Bollworm.
Heliothis Armiger.

This insect is indigenous over an extremely wide range, and can vary its food plants in an extraordinary degree. It feeds on cotton, maize, tomatoes, tobacco, peas, beans and numerous other plants.

The Egg. – The egg is yellowish white in colour and nearly round. It is laid on all parts of the plant, and hatches in about a week.

The Larva. – When newly hatched it is darkish green in colour, and walks like a looper.

It begins feeding at once on the leaves, crawling from one to the other, until a young bud or boll is found, into which it bores. During this early wandering existence, the insect may be destroyed by arsenical poisons. When it enters a bud or young boll, it feeds on it; the boll dies, and the insect passes on to another. One larva is thus capable of destroying a score of young bolls.

As the insects increase in size, they begin to vary greatly in appearance. Full-grown worms may be found of almost every intermediate stage of colour between light green and dark brown. They may be unstriped or unspotted, or they may possess dark stripes or black spots. These colour variations are not caused by different food, since different colours occur in specimens feeding upon the same plant. The larger worms as a rule feed on the larger bolls, whilst the newly developed larva confines its attention to the young bolls near the top of the tree.

The larger worms are great cannibals. They feed on the smaller ones even when there is an abundance of plant food. In two to four weeks the larva attains full growth. /

The Pupa or Chrysalis. – When full grown it enters the ground to transform, generally making an oval cell of particles of earth, remaining in this condition from one to four weeks.

The Adult Insect. – This has a varying colour from a dull ochre-yellow to a dull olive-green. Its wings expand about one and a half inches. The fore wings have a rather dark band near the tip, and the hind wings are also bordered with a darker band. The wing veins are lined with black, and the fore wings have also several dark spots. There is a great variation in these markings, and they are intensified in some individuals and almost lacking in others. The moth flies normally about dusk, but, when it is at rest, the fore wings are slightly open. When disturbed it flies with a low quick darting motion. It feeds on nectar secreted by flowers, and lays on the average about 500 eggs.

Number of Generations. – The usual time occupied by the insect in its transformations from egg to adult is forty days. The number of annual generations is generally five, but may vary according to climatic conditions. The early generations feed on maize, tomatoes, &c., but, when the maize has become too hard for appropriate food, the moths fly to cotton which at the time is' carrying young bolls.

Hibernation. – It has few natural enemies as it is not easily found when feeding in the interior of the cotton boll or other plants.

REMEDIES.

Lights for Trapping Moths. – These have often been recommended, but are of little avail on large areas.

Poisons. – When the young larvae are found on the leaves arsenical poisons have been found useful. Paris green, which is a chemical compound of arsenic, copper, and acetic acid, has been found the best. It may be applied either dry or as a spray.

When applied as a powder, it is better to mix it with air-slaked lime, so that it can easily be seen if the work has been thoroughly done. One pound of Paris green with six pounds of lime is a good proportion. This is sufficient for one acre, and should be applied in dry weather when the dew is on.

If used as a spray, equal weights of Paris green and quicklime should be used. The mixture should be made up and allowed to stand from 6 to 10 days before being used, and should be stirred every day. This allows the arsenic and lime to combine, thereby rendering it harmless to the leaves, whilst it still acts as a stomach poison.

One pound of Paris green is sufficient for 200 gallons of water. The Paris green, to have its greatest effect, should be extremely fine.

It should be remembered that it remains in suspension in the water, and the larger the particles the more rapidly do they sink to the bottom. When using, it should be constantly stirred.

London purple is an insecticide which may be used in an exactly similar manner.

If a crop be treated with either of the above preparations it will greatly assist in keeping down other insect pests.

Trap Crops – The cotton planter will find by far the most efficacious preventative of bollworm damage in the intelligent handling of trap crops. This suggestion is an old one. When planting cotton, leave vacant strips of five rows for every twenty-five of cotton. In these five rows, at the earliest possible time, plant one row with maize. Do not plant too thickly as a minimum number of plants is desired. During the silking period frequent careful examinations must be made as to the number of bollworm eggs.

As soon as no more fresh eggs are found each morning the silk ends of the corn should be cut away and burned, or fed to stock, in order to destroy the young worms and eggs. A few eggs may also be found upon the leaves of the plants, and since no more growth is to be made the plants should be cut and destroyed. Then three more of the rows should be planted. Upon these rows very large numbers of eggs will be laid, but they should be allowed to mature in order that the natural enemies which parasitize the eggs and prey upon the larvæ may not be destroyed.

The crowded condition of the worms in these rows will induce cannibalism to such an extent that the number of worms reaching maturity will be reduced to the minimum, / and these can well be allowed to escape if their natural enemies are saved thereby. To trap these escaping individuals, however, the fifth and last row should be planted so that they will be silking about the time this brood of moths are issuing. This last row should be carefully watched, and destroyed as soon as it appears that no more eggs are being deposited.

If the first two plantings of maize are well managed, the earlier broods of the bollworm will be so reduced in numbers that the third planting may be dispensed with. Also, the maize produced by the second planting ought to be sufficient to pay for the expense of cultivation and for the sacrifice made by growing maize instead of cotton.

It is quite unnecessary to plant up the whole of the cotton area as above: if five acres for every 100 be treated with trap maize the crop of the entire plantation may be protected.

It is also advisable to plant about a dozen yards with maize where the clearing borders on unbroken land. Where cut-down crops are being grown patches of maize must be planted if it is desired to protect the cotton crop. Clean farming is a great help because harbouring weeds are destroyed, and when the land is turned over in the cold season the pupa is killed by the cold, or destroyed by birds and insects.

THE STAINER.

Dysdercus.

This red bug or cotton stainer does considerable damage to cotton bolls, particularly those which have opened.

This insect, in its earlier generations, damages the bolls by puncturing them and sucking the sap, causing them to become diminutive or abortive. Later, however, they enter the open bolls, puncture the seed, and damage the fibre by their yellowish excrement. These stains are indelible, and greatly depreciate the value of the cotton on the market.

The best remedy against this species is suggested by the fact that in the cold season it will collect in numbers on piles of cotton seed, which can then be used as traps, and the insects destroyed by the application of hot water. When cotton, which contains stainers, has been picked, it should be left in the sun for a couple of days. The insects will then leave, and thus no further damage is done when the cotton is being ginned.

THE GREEN FLY.

Aphididae.

These are the well known plant-lice, made familiar to all agriculturists by their presence on every variety of plant.

Their life history is thrillingly interesting. Here we have the most striking apparent exception to the general rule that insects are developed from eggs; and yet, perhaps, the exception is more apparent than real.

At all events, parthenogenesis, or reproduction without the intervention of a male, occurs normally in a large percentage of the species. Of course there are many differences in life habits, but, as a rule, the plant-lice winter in the egg stage; but this is subject to many exceptions, especially in the warmer parts of the country.

As soon as there is a trace of reviving vegetation, these eggs hatch. The insect that now appears is wingless, and usually remains so, but grows rapidly by sucking the plant juices, and soon begins to produce living young. All the young born by this mother are, like herself, without sex; that is, they are neither males nor sexually-developed females.

The rate at which they are born varies, but as many as eight living young have been observed within a period of twenty-four hours from one specimen; and it is not unusual to find, early in the season, a single large louse surrounded by a group of from a dozen to twenty, or even more, small specimens. The rate of growth also varies depending upon the weather; indeed weather conditions early in the season frequently determine the question of whether or not certain species are to become injurious later on. A warm moist temperature favours their development, and reproduction goes on at a rapid rate. Correspondingly, cold wet weather checks development, and may even destroy a large number, especially of the young. /

Plant-lice in their younger stages are exceedingly susceptible to sudden changes of temperature and at almost any time in the season a sudden drop of fifteen to twenty degrees, accompanied by rain, will prove fatal to a great proportion of them. But assuming that all is favourable, the young that were first brought forth are in turn ready to reproduce in five or six days, and they also form little colonies. This method of reproduction continues as long as food is plentiful, and the weather mild. Experimentally reproduction of this kind has been, continued for several years in succession, without any tendency to develop sexed individuals or to produce eggs.

At almost any time after the first generation specimens may become winged, and these fly to other localities, forming new colonies wherever suitable food is found.

In this way they spread and though they may have started from a single favourable locality, yet, in the course of a few weeks, they may cover hundreds of acres.

Exactly what determines the formation of wings in some specimens and not in others is unknown. It is proved, however that the progeny of a single individual is variable the specimens are equally without sex, and are all viviparous, or bring forth living young. As the season advances, reproduction become less rapid. Plants tend to dry up, the supply of sap becomes less plentiful, until, with the approach of cold weather, plant growth ceases entirely.

It now becomes necessary to provide for the continuation of the species during the cold season, and sexed forms are developed. The males are usually winged, and appear a short time before the females which differ by the lack of wings, and are of small size compared with the normal sexless form.

Pairing takes place as soon as the female is mature, and in a few days afterwards eggs are laid.

In many instances the egg supply is exceedingly small; indeed there may be only one maintained by the female. Even this may remain within the body of the parent, which simply dries up, the skin shrivelling around, and forming a protection to the ovum.

More usually several eggs are produced, and these are of a large size when compared with the insect lays them.

The eggs vary greatly in colour: sometimes they are yellowish, but more often green or black. They are placed in sheltered situations on plants, and are very resistant to insecticides, it being only possible to destroy them by means of the most caustic mixtures. There are, however, many exceptions to this general life history.

Where the regular food-plant dies down after one season, the insect passes the cold season on some other plant, and migrates to its former host when the conditions become favourable.

Aphididae damage the plants by pumping an enormous amount of sap from the leaves, and they also interfere greatly with the proper respiration of the plants by crowding thickly on the under surface of the leaves. As they live by suction, stomach poisons like Paris green are useless. Spraying with tobacco juice is one of the best remedies. Another good insecticide for green fly is a mixture of soap, paraffin, oil, and water in the following proportions:–

Hard soap (shaved fine)	½ pound.
Paraffin oil	2 gallons.
Water (preferably soft)	1 gallon.

Dissolve the soap in boiling water and add to the paraffin oil; and churn the mixture until it becomes creamy in appearance. Dilute this with ten times its volume of water, and apply to the crop by means of a sprayer.

In dealing with all insect pests, the earlier the remedy is applied the more likely is the operation to be successful. Besides over a small area the work can be more thoroughly done, an the expense is small.

Moreover, attempt must be made to clean-out the pests at the weakest stage in their existence, and it must be remembered that stomach persons should be applied only when the insects have biting mouths.

LEAF MINERS.

These seldom do much damage and can easily kept in hard by the application of Paris green as described in the section dealing with the bollworm. /

THE BORDER.

This insect can never do the same damage to cotton as it does to coffee. The cotton plant is a quick grower, and, if its presence be observed, the plants may be uprooted and burnt.

SURFACE CATERPILLARS.

These are sometimes troublesome to all crops when newly planted. Nothing but a good clean system of agriculture will keep them within limits.

LOCUSTS.

Acridium.

When swarms settle on a plantation they should be driven off by calling out the neighbouring villages. A terrific noise, persistently kept up by the beating of drums and old tins, will generally suffice to clear them off. Fires on the windward side are very efficacious. When eggs are deposited these should be hoed up, gathered and destroyed. If young ones appear, they are easily driven out into an open drain where dry grass is fired. They are then destroyed.

F. M. Oliphant, *Report on the Commercial Possibilities and Development of the Forests of Nigeria,* **Sessional Paper no. 7 (Lagos: Government Printer, 1934).**

NIGERIA
SESSIONAL PAPER
No. 7 of 1934.
Paper laid on the Table of the Legislative Council.

SUBJECT:
Report on the Commercial Possibilities and Development of the
Forests of Nigeria

LAGOS
[...]

INTRODUCTION.

The following report describes an investigation, carried out on the recommendation of the Empire Timbers Committee[1] of the Department of Scientific and Industrial Research, into the commercial possibilities and development of the forests of Nigeria. The deliberations of the Committee upon the means of increasing trade in Empire timbers had shown the primary need to be a much closer liaison between the producing interests in the exporting colonies and the marketing and using interests in the United Kingdom. The Committee suggested that this liaison might be best established by the appointment of a special officer, trained in timber technology and acquainted with the commercial requirements of the British market, who should visit the colonies concerned. The Committee realised that, with the need for economy, it was not the moment to propose the creation of a new post the value of which had not been proved by results. In view however of the great desirability of taking immediate advantage of the present favourable opportunity for the development of Empire trade and neglecting no step to this end, the Committee suggested that an officer might be borrowed from the staff of the Forest Products Research Laboratory[2] and sent on a mission to Nigeria and the Gold Coast, by way of proving as soon as possible the value or otherwise of the proposal. It was suggested that two months should be spent in Nigeria and one month in the Gold Coast. The Empire Marketing Board undertook to provide the cost of transport to and from the colonies concerned, and of subsistence during residence therein, the Governments of Nigeria and the Gold Coast being asked to provide the cost of travel within their territories. The Department of Scientific and Industrial Research agreed to the proposal, and accordingly I was seconded to the Empire Marketing Board as from 30th November, 1932, on which date I sailed for Lagos, arriving on 15th December.

My terms of reference were:–

> 'To confer with the local Government and Forest authorities on matters connected with the commercial development of their timbers, to get into touch with the commercial interests concerned, and to assist in establishing effective co-operation between all parties.'

In respect of Nigeria, the provisional programme drawn up for me by the Forest Department contemplated a tour throughout the whole of the principal forest districts of the Southern Provinces from the vicinity of Ibadan in the west to, and including, the Cross River district and the British Cameroons in the east. After experience of the demands of the task, gained during the initial three weeks, I had regretfully to omit the Cross River district and the Cameroons from the programme and to confine my tour to the forest districts at present under exploitation, in order to allow adequate time for a thorough inquiry into the commercial possibilities of some forty or more different timbers in these districts and for becoming sufficiently well acquainted with the various official and trade interests concerned and with the conditions affecting the scheme of development that I had in mind.

Throughout my journey I met with unfailing and unstinted help from all those whom I met. Without that help this report / could not have been prepared. I cannot in this introduction hope to acknowledge individually all the kindnesses which I received; but I should be failing in gratitude if I did not mention in particular the pains taken by His Excellency the Governor to assure to me the best possible facilities for my necessarily rapid survey and the more than generous spirit in which all members of the public services, with whom my journey brought me in contact, gave effect to His Excellency's wishes. The excellent travelling arrangements made for me by the Forest, Public Works and Marine Departments, the very thorough plans made in advance by the Director of Forests for inspections and for contacts with individuals, and the courtesy and whole-hearted assistance of the Logging officials of the United Africa Company, especially in felling and preparing timbers for my inspection, enabled me not only to cover some 3,500 miles by motor car and launch but to use my time to the full and accomplish, as I believe, what I set out to do. I must certainly record a special debt to the Director of Forests and to the Director of Public Works, and to Mr. W. McLaren, the Timber Superintendent for the United Africa Company in the Ondo and Sapele districts, and, also, my appreciation of the assistance rendered by the Works Manager of the Public Works Department Sawmill at Ijora.

F. M. OLIPHANT.[3]
[...]
26th April, 1933. /
[...]

PART I.
THE GENERAL POSITION.

1.   The position in Nigeria, so far as the potentialities are concerned, is extremely encouraging. All the factors exist, or could be made to exist, necessary to make the forests of that Colony a valuable source of revenue.

2.   Out of 233,000 square miles of forest clad country, 53,000 square miles consist of merchantable forest from which timber for export can be obtained, which is either accessible now or will become accessible following development of transport facilities. Large areas of other forest are at present available for everyday domestic needs and local trade. But the amount of forest reserved is very far from being satisfactory, either from the domestic or the export point of view, for establishing a permanent trade of any value. Fortunately there is still time – though it should be done with the utmost speed – to make the position secure. The subject is discussed with figures, in a later paragraph.

3.   The forests contain a wide variety of valuable timber species. Given an adequate policy of conservation, and adequate methods of manufacture and use, supplies of the important species should be sufficient for the needs of the domestic market and a considerable export trade in perpetuity.

4.   As a future source of supply of hardwoods to the United Kingdom, it is no exaggeration to say that Nigeria is one of the most important of Empire countries. Moreover, there appears to be an increasing demand from continental Europe, the present volume of exports to that region being, it is stated, only slightly below that to the United Kingdom. Almost all other hardwood-producing countries have either destroyed the bulk of their forests for agricultural purposes or have over-exploited them without reference to a sustained yield. India and Burma are exceptions, but all the Indian supplies, with the exception of a small export from the Andamans,[4] are consumed domestically, while Burma's exports are practically all teak.

5.   Mahogany is the most important timber exported from Nigeria. One of the Nigerians species is a very excellent substitute for British Honduras mahogany, to which the best 'Lagos' mahogany especially approximates. There has been no effective conservation of supplies in British Honduras, and export markets are depending more and more on African supplies. Development of the Amazon region might render this dependence less, and there is also competition from Peru and other south and central American states, but there seems no reason why, with proper organisation, Nigeria should not successfully compete against these supplies. At present, Nigeria's foremost competitor in the hardwood market is the United States. The value of the hardwoods, unmanufactured and manufactured, imported into the United Kingdom annually is about 9 ¼ million pounds, of which the United States is responsible for over five million. But America, though she does now possess a forest service, acknowledges that she is over-cutting her forests, and it is probable that her supplies for export will become increasingly shorter and more costly, at / least unless and until supplies come forward from the Amazon region, which the Americans are reported to be definitely developing. Such an advance in price consequent on shortage has already taken place in American black walnut, to Nigeria's advantage. The largest export from the United States is oak, the rival of mahogany for furniture, the biggest single outlet. But there are signs that fashion is swinging back to mahogany, a change that would be expedited by an advance in the price of oak. Nigeria has substitutes also for the so-called 'soft-hardwoods' of America and possesses most of the utility and decorative species now exported by the French.

6.   Essentials to the efficient exploitation of forests are:–

  (*i*) The adequate conservation of the forest areas, to maintain a perpetual yield, including the education of the inhabitants to see that this is to their own advantage.
  (*ii*) An exhaustive knowledge of the character and composition of the forest areas, including the botanical identity of the species and the quantity of each.
  (*iii*) Means for making an assessment of the utilisation value of the timbers.
  (*iv*) Efficient logging and extraction from the forest.
  (*v*) Efficient protection of logs and timber from deterioration before and during shipment.
  (*vi*) Economical freight rates; ocean, coastwise and rail.
  (*vii*) Efficient sawmills.
  (*viii*)A domestic trade as the foundation for an economical and sure export trade.

(*ix*) The closest co-operation between Political Officers Forest Officers, officials of the timber companies, and, in the investigation of the timbers, of
the Public Works, Post and Telegraph and Railway services.

(*x*) Efficient liaison between the producer and his markets.

7.   With regard to the first and most important essential, namely forest conservation, the position is so far favourable in that, as already stated, ample forests still
exist; but I am informed that, at this date, there are serious political difficulties
in the way of securing adequate reservation. There is nevertheless a strong hope
that, with wider official appreciation of the need, means will be found whereby
these difficulties may be overcome. The subject is treated more fully in Part II
of this report. With regard to the other essentials, some are already in effective
existence, some exist but need developing, while circumstances are promising
for the establishment of the remainder. In technical staff and facilities needed
for development, Nigeria is very fortunate. She possesses an able and enthusiastic Forest Service, including a well-staffed research branch. The excellent work
at the Experimental Station at Sapoba[5] is invaluable to the future of Nigerian
forestry, whether for purposes of protection or exploitation. It may well prove
to be the means of solving the difficult problem of shifting cultivation, of which
more is said later in this report. At this station, also, a large volume of authoritative information upon the botanical identity of West African species has been
collected, which has already proved of service in the commercial exploitation
of timbers. The research staff of the Forest Service also includes a Utilisation
Officer, in charge of timber development, and a Wood Seasoning Officer, both
trained at Princes Risborough. The Wood Seasoning Officer is stationed at Ijora,
at the sawmill and wood workshops of the Public Works Department, where he
has an experimental timber-drying kiln at his disposal. /

The Public Works Department's Sawmill at Ijora is extremely well organised
and equipped, extensive exploratory work on the domestic and export value of
various native timbers has been in progress for some time past, and the Department is entitled to the highest credit for their enterprise and for the results
achieved. Prior to these investigations, American pitch pine was the staple timber for Government work and was imported in large quantities: the amount
now used by the Public Works Department is negligible. Similarly, as a result of
these investigations, the Railways have been able to make increasing use of native
timbers, and the same does or will apply to the Marine Department. A considerable sum of money has thereby been kept within the Colony. Not only has
the domestic trade been widened, but, by these practical trials of native timbers
and the excellent standard of sawing and seasoning, the possibility of a material
expansion of the export trade has both been enhanced and made more immediate. Timber exporting interests, and indeed probably domestic traders as well,

do not sufficiently realise how much they owe to the Public Works Department, in the saving of time and money and in the forward position in which the trade has been placed.

8.   On the trade side, the circumstances are most fortunate. The Timber Manager for the United Africa Company in the Ondo and Sapele areas, is not only extremely efficient and progressive in his logging and shipping methods, but is only too eager to co-operate in investigative work, better methods of marketing, and in securing permanent liaison with the other interests concerned. The Manager for United Africa Company in the Degema area is equally ready to co-operate. Both these officials have in the last few months instituted experiments in sawmilling, the one at Koko, the other at Degema, for the domestic market, and these may well prove to be the starting point not only of an increased trade but of placing it on a much more secure foundation. At the same time, an English-trained native carpenter and cabinet maker has recently returned to the Koko district and has inaugurated what appears to be a rapidly increasing business in furniture making, the article being distributed by canoe to various parts of the country. A good domestic market is the foundation of a stable export trade. In most cases it is, so to speak, the bread and butter, the export trade being the jam. Another interesting line of progress consists in the successful experiments made by the United Africa Company's Manager in the Sapele district in treating logs of obeche with various preparations to eliminate stain, decay and splitting during the passage of the log from forest to ship. The situation is undoubtedly one of great promise.

9.   In concluding this summary of the general position, it is necessary to make a few remarks on the subject of forest conservation for timber supply, apart from its conservation for protective, climatic reasons. Nigeria is in the happy position of still possessing adequate areas of commercial forest, but, as already stated, the position is by no means secure. A very few years' further delay will put it in jeopardy, and the necessary additional conservation is a matter of great urgency. The Director of Forests estimates the present rate of forest destruction throughout the country at 1,000 square miles a year. A comparison with India in conservation is instructive.

	India.	*Nigeria.*
Total, forest clad	251,468 sq. miles.	233,000 sq. miles.
Reserved	101,639 " "	14,000 " "
Protected	8,557 " "	} 14,000 " "
Unclaimed	141,272 " "	218,800 " "
Per cent. conserved	44%	6.3% /

The leading aim of forestry for exploitation purposes is to secure a sustained yield in perpetuity. A forest is very easily and speedily destroyed. More often than not it does not replace itself- at least so far as the valuable species are concerned – unaided, and then only if further destruction of the young growth is prevented and the crop tended over a long period. Repeated destruction of the young growth usually results in waste land, unproductive either for forestry or agriculture. A period of eighty to 100 years is probably required in Nigeria for trees to grow to maturity fit for exploitation as timber. It is thus only too easy to destroy forests at a far greater rate than they can be replaced. A felled area, if left to itself, may appear to the uninitiated to be reproducing another crop. Too often the new crop consists only of weed species of trees. By far the most powerful agency in bringing about this forest destruction is the pernicious system of shifting cultivation, the evil effects of which may be seen all over Nigeria, embracing large areas, in some cases containing little but weed species of trees, in others nothing but coarse grass, while in others erosion from lack of soil protection has disclosed the hare rock or created deep ravines in the sand. Unfortunately, it is the common experience of forest officers that these facts, and still more, the causes of them are seldom realised until too late, and that the forest officer is looked upon as an alarmist. Noteworthy exceptions are provided by India and Burma, who have indeed set an example to the rest of the Empire. The financial results have amply justified their policy. Examination of the figures for India shows that in the fifty-five years from 1864 to 1919, the surplus of revenue over expenditure had increased nearly twelve fold, and that during the last five years of the period it averaged over £1,000,000 per annum, without counting the value of forest produce given away free or removed by rightholders. From Burma, the export of teak to the United Kingdom alone is just under £1,000,000 per annum. The forestry development in these two countries originated in the efforts of a few individuals from 1827 onwards, culminating in the vigorous forest policy laid down by Lord Dalhousie in 1855. Nevertheless, from that date task early years of the Forest Department, in their unpopular task were marked by strenuous opposition, not least from Government district officials, many of whom neither appreciated the potential value of the forests nor the harm that would follow their destruction. A small book by Professor R. S. Troup, C.I.E., D.SC F.R.S., late of the Indian Forest Service, now Professor of Forestry and Director of the Imperial Forestry Institute, Oxford, entitled 'The Work of the Forest Department in India' is very instructive on the history of events in India, the conditions making for success, and the results achieved. It would repay perusal by Political Officers stationed in forest districts. Considering the power vested in the Political Service of Nigeria in connection with forest conservation, it is of the utmost importance that these officers should have a thorough understanding of the objects of the measure.

PART II.
FOREST CONSERVATION.

THE WHOLE SUBJECT OF CONSERVATION URGENTLY NEEDS FRESH SCRUTINY.

Proportion of forest under conservation.

10.   The proportion of controlled forest is no more than 6.3 per cent of the total forest area of 233,000 square miles, or 3.8 per cent of the total land area of 368,000 square miles (excluding the Cameroons). This means a reservation, including all types of forest – for export timber, protection, grazing, and so forth – of / only 14,170 square miles. Excluding forest areas which can be exploited for domestic consumption, there are 53,000 square miles of merchantable forest which are accessible now or will become accessible with the development of transport facilities, and suitable for the supply of timber for export. The merchantable forest capable of sustaining an export trade is therefore about 22.7 per cent of the total forest area. Up to date only 9,518 square miles, or less than 18 per cent of it, have been reserved. The Government's expressed policy provides for a forest reservation for the country as a whole equivalent to twenty-five per cent of the *total land* area, *i.e.*, a reservation of 90,500 square miles, but according to the Director of Forests this seems to have been interpreted as meaning an equal spread of twenty-five per cent, apportioned to each district of the country. Practically, this is manifestly unsound. The 50,000 square miles of forest accessible for export contain by far the best and most valuable stands of high forest in the country, capable of supporting a large, permanent domestic and export trade, representing a large potential revenue. The ideal is of course to reserve it all. The Director of Forests states that reservation of the area, which is still intact, could be increased to the neighbourhood of eighty per cent without disturbing the amenities of the local inhabitants. Delay will both imperil the position and create unnecessary difficulties in satisfying the local villagers' requirements. The greatest effort should be made to preserve this forest, as both a national and imperial asset.

Settlement of Reserves.

11.   The present procedure for the constitution of reserves appears to be unnecessarily cumbersome and conducive to prolonged delays. Moreover, there is evidence to show that the delay and the system under which preliminary proclamation is made in many cases actually hasten forest destruction. The Director of Forests states that preliminary proclamation has often merely served to

announce that areas of excellent forest land are still unreserved, whereupon shifting cultivators, on whom there is at present no restriction during preliminary proclamation, have immediately started operations therein. Eventually, during the long delay before settlement is begun, destruction has proceeded so far that constitution in the original form has been found to be impossible, and the area has been wholly or partially abandoned. No rights should be allowed to accrue after preliminary proclamation, and the area should at once rank as protected forest. The matter has been discussed with the Director of Forests and the following simplified and more speedy procedure is suggested.

(*i*) The Conservator, after consultation with, and with the approval of the Resident, shall select the site of the proposed reserve and prepare a preliminary plan.

(*ii*) This plan to be submitted with the reserve report to the Director of Forests through the Senior Conservator concerned, a copy at the same time to be sent to His Honour the Lieutenant-Governor along with a copy of the Resident's formal approval.

(*iii*) Preliminary proclamation then to take place. By this preliminary proclamation, the area becomes 'protected forest', *i.e.*, land in which no new rights can be acquired and in the high forests of which no acts of destruction are permitted. This does not affect existing farm land within the area.

(*iv*) Settlement to be initiated three months afterwards, and completed as soon as possible. (Comments on the Reserve Settlement Officer's duties are made in a later paragraph.) /

(*v*) Copies of the Reserve Settlement Officer's judgment to be sent to the Senior Conservator of Forests and Resident for their formal approval, duplicates being sent to His Honour and the Director of Forests by the Resident and Senior Conservator respectively.

(*vi*) Appeals to be heard by the Resident concerned during the ensuing six months, after which there shall be no further appeal. In exceptional cases an extension may be made up to two years, as at present, but in the meantime the area is to be protected as if reserved.

(*vii*) Final proclamation to follow immediately formal approval of the judgment is given by His Excellency the Governor.

12.   Under the present system, an agreement is drawn up and the signatures of a number of people, who in many cases do not afterwards prove to be the actual owners, are obtained. Any alterations have to be so signed, and, as the delay is often considerable, a fresh agreement may have to be negotiated owing to alterations in personnel. If the procedure suggested above were followed, it would normally be possible to reserve an area in a little more than one year; and during that time, the area, being protected, would not be subject to the

numerous attempts to establish claims for farming that invariably follow, it is stated, preliminary proclamation under the present system. In connection with the question of farming, the Director of Forests states that thousands of square miles in Nigeria have been cleared for temporary agriculture, for which they were quite unsuitable and should have been left as forest. Such areas are now not only waste land but in many cases their subsequent erosion has led to serious damage such as the silting up of rivers or the formation of desert country. Protection forests are not however within the scope of this report, but the matter needs close attention. A further consequence of the delay in creating reserves is that subsequently a reserve has to be selected in a situation which is by no means the most suitable economically.

Reserve Settlement Officer.

13.   After discussion with the Director of Forests, the following suggestions with regard to the Reserve Settlement Officer's duties are submitted. As soon as possible, and not more than three months after the preliminary proclamation of a reserve the Reserve Settlement Officer should cause to be posted in all courts and other public places a notice containing –

(*a*) a copy of the preliminary proclamation.
(*b*   stating that no further rights can be acquired and that the forest is now protected.
(*c*) explaining the consequences that will ensue when the area is reserved.
(*d*) fixing a period within not less than one month from the date of the notice, when the Settlement Court will be held, fixing the times and places thereof, and requesting everyone who has claims or rights with regard to the area to be present with such evidence as they possess for the support of such claims before the Settlement Court.

This information should also be broadcast as widely as possible within the area by word of mouth. The Reserve Settlement Officer should take down in writing particulars of all claims and rights, recording all evidence obtained. The Reserve Settlement Officer may allow or reject all claims either partially or wholly. /

Claims dealing with shifting cultivation.

14.   With regard to all claims except those dealing with shifting cultivation and farming rights the present methods appear to be satisfactory. After consultation with the Director of Forests, the following suggestions are made for dealing with claims to cultivation. The Reserve Settlement Officer should record for each village –

(1) the number of claimants (*i.e.*, adult males);

(2) the areas owned by the village and available for farming *outside* the limits of the proposed reserve.

(3) the area claimed by the village within the reserve.

(4) the total area necessary for farming purposes, basing the estimate on five to ten acres per adult male. depending on the district.

Provided such claims are admitted, be should then excise areas from the limits of the proposed reserve, sufficient as far as possible to allow for the exercise of the rights, taking into consideration however the lands held under (2) and the actual requirements under (4) above. In such excisions, obviously lands already farmed should be the first to go in preference to high forest. High forest should be excised only if no other lands are available and the purpose of the reserve is not stultified. The Reserve Settlement Officer should hear in mind that his fundamental purpose is to prevent the destruction of forests and create reserves, not to allocate forest land for farming. It is of course understood that allocation should be on the generous side, guided by humane considerations rather than by rule of thumb. The Political Officer's difficulties are also fully realised, in convincing the people of the wisdom of the measure. An increased allowance of not more than ten or twelve per cent might be made for possible increase in population. This will probably be found ample for many years, since. as there will be an enforced limit put to extensive temporary cultivation, more intensive permanent cultivation is likely to take its place. For a considerable period at any rate, this should probably more than counterbalance the legitimate demands made on land through increased population, and in addition will in itself be of great technical and political value. In the case of isolated areas upon which claims are allowed, the Reserve Settlement Officer should have power to effect an exchange and/or to create enclaves and/or compulsorily negotiate to extinguish rights with or without monetary or other compensation according to the value and extent of the right. The judgment should detail the final boundaries of the reserve enclaves, right areas, and so forth.

Sanctity of Reserves.

15. Forestry implies permanent woodland, and hence reserves which must be free from interference, except for the legitimate operations of silviculture and exploitation, in perpetuity. Lacking reserves, no amount of prohibition or restriction of felling can effect more than a temporary postponement of final destruction. Moreover, even the removal of commercially valueless species may adversely affect adjacent valuable species through the removal of shelter and soil protection. Forestry is usually unpopular and its objects and value are seldom understood. It is inevitable that complaints will be received from the local inhabitants and that many of them will have no real justification. Here is where

it is essential that Political Officers concerned shall have full appreciation of the requirements of forestry and of its value not only as a source of revenue but to the ultimate welfare of the inhabitants. Without this knowledge, they are likely to be unduly influenced / by these complaints. The Director of Forests states that cases occur where serious attempts are made to unreserve large areas of forest. In addition to minor excisions, one of these attempts was successful in freeing from reserve a large area of high forest in the most important timber district of the country, in spite of strong protest from the Director of Forests. The importance of conserving these forests cannot be too strongly urged: and it is obvious that some finality is necessary. Moreover, forests are not an asset solely for the benefit of the existing generation; they belong equally to succeeding generations. In the case of Nigeria, the forests exploitable for export purposes are also an Imperial asset.

Enforcement of the Forest Ordinance.

16.   The Forest Reserves in Nigeria are held under conditions which allow rights to the local inhabitants such that there is no interference with their every-day life and legitimate occupations. In non-reserved areas there is also no undue restriction, free grants of timber being allowed for all domestic and private occu-pational needs. The only restriction imposes a check on those people who would exploit the forests for commercial purposes in a manner detrimental to the forests themselves. However, from details supplied by the Director of Forests, it appears clear that unjustified complaints by the local inhabitants have been allowed to cause considerable relaxation in the application of the Forest Ordinance, which in fact should be tightened considerably. Indeed the Ordinance itself would seem to require some amendments should direction of increasing the powers of the European and Senior African officials. It is suggested that such amendments should include the granting of powers to European Forestry officers –

(*i*)   to compound offences;

(*ii*)   to seize and sell, destroy or allocate to Government use forest products illicitly obtained, the onus of proof being on the possessor of the forest produce;

(*iii*) to take any steps considered advisable by the Conservator to improve for-est land whether reserved or not whether by means of planting, thinning, or cutting out of mature, over-mature or dead stock, such stock to be sold on permits in the usual way or otherwise disposed of as the Director of Forests may prescribe.

At present the powers possessed by a Conservator of Forests in Nigeria appear to be below those possessed by considerably more junior officers in other parts of the world. For the wording of the amendment, reference is invited to the appropriate section of the Indian Forest Act.[6]

Issue of permits and granting of licences.

17.   Whether the area is or is not a reserve, it is urged that the final opinion as to whether permits should be issued, or whether silvicultural operations should be undertaken for the improvement of the forest, should lie with the Director of Forests. It is just as much part of a Forest Officer's duty if possible to prevent forests areas from becoming over-mature and much reduced in value as it is to prevent their destruction in other ways. Yet in many cases the inhabitants appear to be allowed great power in frustrating this work, with very little effort being made to explain and insist on the wiser course. There is no doubt also that cases have occurred and do occur where the owners refuse to allow trees to be felled because they expect a bribe in addition to the legal royalty. A case in point came to notice in the Degema district where permits have been refused to the logging company because the reputed owners have objected, notwithstanding that these / objections have been entirely unsupported by reasons or explanations. The illicit reason became clear during the discussion. The Director of Forests states that to some extent the same situation exists with regard to licenses. It is manifestly bad policy to prevent the exploitation of an over-mature area, and every effort should be made to secure that it is exploited. The provisions of the Forest Ordinance are certainly not harsh, and the Director of Forests is of opinion that the political risk of firmer enforcement is often magnified. He is of the opinion that, over considerable parts of the country, the fines are so small that it appears to pay the delinquent to take the risk of being found out.

Surveys and Descriptions.

18.   Considering the small staff of the Forest Service compared with the area of forest, it is remarkable that so much botanical and stock-taking survey work has been accomplished. There is however no exact knowledge of the commercial quantities of the various exploitable timbers, knowledge which is vital to final management including the regulation of exploitation for the maintenance of a sustained yield. The first questions to which a timber importer, proposing to deal in a new timber, requires an answer concern the extent, availability and regularity of the supply. Botanical identity is equally important, for in many cases a mixture of similar species, the one good and the other bad, has jeopardised the commercial future of the good timber. For the demands of aeroplane work, as in the exact identity of the various mahoganies, it is essential. It goes without saying that it would not be possible immediately to carry out enumeration surveys sufficiently detailed for the preparation of the necessary intensive working plans of all the forests of the country. But it is vital that an immediate

beginning should be made with linear or group enumerations, dealing with a percentage of average forest, throughout all the existing exploitable reserves. The data so collected will be invaluable to the Working Plans Officer and at the same time ensure that over-exploitation does not take place in the immediate future. This work has been more or less limited to one or two small areas near Sapoba, carried out by Mr. Kennedy, and has ceased through lack of funds. Only when such work is complete can an economic scheme of management be drawn up. The Director of Forests states that a few years ago, a beginning was made by the appointment of several African Forest Surveyors and an Assistant Conservator who was given special training in surveying and enumeration survey work. The African staff has now been retrenched and the Assistant Conservator returned to his ordinary duties. It is also understood that inadequate transport allowances limit travelling to the equivalent of three months in the year. Constant travelling is essential to efficient forestry work and a thorough first-hand knowledge of the forests, neither of which can be obtained from an office or from native Forest Guards stationed in the areas concerned. The result is that much general work preliminary to survey, which could be carried out by Assistant Conservators, is woefully behindhand. On the general question of finance, forestry work, unlike most other kinds, involves a plan extending over a period of years ahead, and interruption may result in much loss. An adequate and steady policy is essential.

Shifting Cultivation.

19.   Reference has already been made to the evils attendant upon shifting cultivation, the greatest danger which the forests have to meet. The rapidity and extent of the disappearance of / valuable high forest over wide areas of the south-west of Nigeria is a sufficient instance. Unfortunately, the problem of staying this danger is as difficult as it is urgent. In Chapter 5 of their book *West African Agriculture* by the Director of Agriculture, Mr. O. T. Faulkner, and Mr. J. R. Mackie of his staff, the authors discuss the difficulties and state:

'The problem of replacing shifting cultivation by permanent is therefore one of finding a supply of manure. But it must be noted that any manure or any new system of farming to provide for manuring, must be more profitable than shifting cultivation. However primitive the old system may be, or however objectionable, because it involves the destruction of forest or the use of an excessive area of land, the farmer cannot be expected to give it up in favour of a new system which yields a less return for the same amount of labour'.

The authors consider that mixed farming can provide a solution in the Northern Provinces, where cattle can be raised and land is not in general scarce; and 'green manuring' in the south-western Provinces. But, for the poor and over-populated soils of the Delta, they state that no solution has yet been found, the peculiarities of the soil, including its high acidity, in that region rendering 'green manuring' unprofitable or often impossible. This problem, the authors state, is being closely studied. Artificial manures have proved unprofitable owing to cost, and the authors do not consider that these offer any general solution to the problem of obtaining permanent in place of shifting cultivation. Pending a solution, much forest destruction will take place. The intensity of measures of control and of investigations designed to solve the problem must take account of the great rapidity with which this destruction proceeds and the value of the capital so destroyed. On the subject of the rotation of crops, the authors say:

'It may be mentioned that Europeans frequently seem to attach an exaggerated importance to crop rotation, and to think that by simply rotating crops the native farmer can avoid the necessity of shifting cultivation. This is not true: a series of crops grown regularly in rotation will eventually exhaust the soil just as surely as the growing of the same crop year after year unless the rotation in some way provides for a supply of 'manure' in some form or other. Moreover, as already shown, the native farmer does already practise the rotation of crops.'

All foresters, certainly, must be aware of the necessity for manuring in the rotation of crops but it may well be, as was my own case, that they are not aware of the difficulties presented in Nigeria. It is highly desirable that there should be close co-operation in such matters between the two Departments. It is always possible that the investigations of one Department may shed light on problems of the other.

20.   A method which is meeting with very successful results in Nigeria, in re-establishing the forests over destroyed forest land or land which has become too impoverished for agriculture, is the system variously known as *chena* or *taungya* plantations, a system of forming plantations by growing young trees along with temporary field crops. The success of this scheme in the Sapoba area is remarkable, and it has appealed so much to the local population that requests to come into the scheme have latterly had to be refused owing to the impossibility of supervising the work with the staff available. The natives themselves plant the trees, and in that area a small reward is given for the best three areas. / The cost of establishing these plantations has been less than one quarter of the cost of ordinary methods. *Chena* plantations have also been successfully established at Olokemeji, and, it is stated, in the Ogba reserve near Benin, the Ossomari and Akpaka reserve, Onitsha circle, and in the north. Since my return to England, I have had the advantage of a discussion with the Agricultural Adviser to the Colonial Office. He points out that the partiality for high-forest land for farming is due not only to the fertile virgin soil and the difficulty of manuring but also to the excessive weed growth that must be controlled on other areas. When the forest is cleared, a clean soil is secured. In clearing, the stumps of trees and shrubs are left, so that, when the land is eventually allowed to go fallow, it becomes a

fallow of secondary bush rather than of grass and weeds, and, moreover, is free of weeds when the land is again cleared. Passing reference to this fact is made in *West African Agriculture*. The value of *chena* plantations in this connection is obvious. They might well be given a place of greater importance in forestry development. It is these considerations that lead to the suggestion of co-operation between the Departments of Agriculture and Forestry. Mention may here be made of the successful anti-erosion work in the Enugu district, which is likely to result in the reclamation of now useless land. The existing work is being maintained, but cannot be extended owing to lack of funds.

21.   Before leaving the subject of conservation, the greatest stress is again laid upon the value of Nigeria's forests as a source of revenue; the fortunate position that she is still in, seeing that, alone among the majority of other countries, she is still in possession of ample forest land; and the urgent need of conservation to retain this position. Finally, stress is again laid on the need for Political Officers, in whom so much power in these matters is vested, to have a thorough understanding and appreciation not only of the climatic value – which to some extent is now appreciated – of these forests, but of their great value in revenue, as the source of an increasing domestic and export trade. The average value of timber and forest products exported annually during the past five years, 1927 to 1931, was:– timber, £255,000, minor forest products, £80,000. It may not be so generally known that the total value of timber and forest products domestically consumed and exported must, according to statistics collected by the Director of Forests for the next Imperial Forestry Conference, at a conservative estimate be of the order of £2,750,000 a year. This does not of course include the value of cultivated or semi-cultivated crops such as rubber, palm oil and the like.

PART III.
EXPLOITATION.

A. Assessing the Utilisation value of Timbers.

Preliminary Investigations.

22.   A great deal of exploratory work can be done, and some must be done, before applying to Princes Risborough for tests. With the facilities available in Nigeria, it will often be possible to carry out locally all the preliminary investigations needed before the timber can safely be offered to the export market. The principle should certainly be to carry the investigation as far as possible locally, before applying for tests at home. Tests at Princes Risborough will be those for which specialist knowledge and equipment are not available locally, for example, strength tests, durability tests with reference to United Kingdom / conditions,

certain special problems in seasoning, machining and finishing, special tests for the home consumer, conditioning of trial shipments, and the like. A good example is provided by *Celtis,* a genus containing several very similar species, some or all of which may be of considerable value for export. It is for Nigeria to determine the exact botanical identity of each species; practical means by which the logger may distinguish them; the possibility of keeping the timbers free from stain before and during shipment, whether in the log or as sawn timber; their seasoning qualities, and, by practical trials, their probable uses. Princes Risborough has already given advice on the prevention of stain, and in the final stage would carry out exhaustive tests to determine definitely the value of the timbers for the purposes suggested, including strength tests, and possibly seasoning and conditioning tests with special reference to the British market, and would arrange for commercial trials.

23.   Work on this basis will have several advantages. It will prevent much unnecessary work being thrown upon Princes Risborough, allow its programme to be concentrated, and add to the scope and speed in placing new timbers on the market. Given that the present willing co-operation of the timber firms is maintained, it will put an end to the deplorable practice of sending new species on consignment to export markets, unaccompanied by any information as to the character or possible uses of the timber. This practice cannot be too strongly condemned. A good timber may be sold to a purchaser who buys it for a use to which it is not suited, he may not understand its seasoning or machining requirements, the timber may arrive stained, and so forth, resulting in the ruin, often for many years, of the prospects of the timber on the market.

District Forest Officers and Logging operations.

24.   It is highly important that Forest Officers in districts where logging operations are in progress should not only co-operate sympathetically with the logging officials in matters in which the forester can give useful advice, but make themselves as familiar as possible with the aims and methods of timber extraction, and the purposes for which the timber is to be exported. While it is true that the ordinary Forest Officer has not the time to specialise in utilisation nor to give an extensive assistance to the logging companies and that the solution lies in maintaining an adequate staff of specialists in utilisation, yet it is not sufficient to leave this aspect solely to the utilisation staff. It is part of the business of a Forest Officer to grow trees for timber, and he should know a great deal more than in many cases he does about the subject. With some exceptions, co-operation with the logging companies is by no means what it should be. It has been established in the Ondo Circle,[7] and the trade speak in high terms of its value.

P.W.D. Forest Department and Trade sawmills.

25.   The Public Works Department in its well-equipped sawmill at Ijora, has wide facilities for the investigation and practical trial of the properties and uses of the various timbers, and mention has already been made of the valuable results achieved. Moreover, the Forest Department's experimental drying kiln is in operation there. It is strongly recommended that investigations concerning the characteristics, preparation for market, and uses of Nigerian timbers should form a definite function of the Public Works Department, and that financial provision should be made for it, based on a joint programme to be drawn up by a body which should at least include the Public Works Department, Forest Department, and the United Africa Company in / conference. In drawing up this programme, certain work would also be allocated to the Forest Department mill at Eba, and to the United Africa Company's mills at Koko and Degema, such as might be economically more appropriate to them.

Messrs, James Latham & Company.[8]

26.   Messrs. Latham are in a different position from the United Africa Company in that they possess their own sawmill, workshops, and plywood factory in London. It is believed, however, that they would be willing to co-operate in investigations carried out in Nigeria.

Antiseptic treatment of timber.

27.   Timber preservation has not been mentioned in the above paragraphs on preliminary investigations. At present, creosoting and other means of preservation find no place in Nigeria, and there is no experimental nor commercial treating plant in the country. Experiments in antiseptic treatment upon timbers which would have to be used for certain purposes in treated condition in the United Kingdom would at present have to be carried out at Princes Risborough. But more important than the export market is the fact that by preservative treatment many of the Nigerian timbers now subject to attack by white ant, 'worm' and decay could be brought into domestic use thus widening domestic trade and providing a market for many 'unwanted' species. Telegraph poles, sleepers, fencing, and certain requirements in dock and building construction are among the outlets for treated timber. Considerable saving would be made in the cost of replacements. The antiseptic treatment of timber is no longer in the problematical stage, either as to its technique or its value. It is widely practised all over the world. Here again, for Nigeria, perusal of the history of the development of wood preservation in India is instructive, as contained in the bulletins issued by the Forest Research Institute, Dehra Dun, recording experiments carried out of a long period of years by the then Forest Economist, Mr. R. S. Pearson, C.I.E., now

Director of the Forest Products Research Laboratory, Princes Risborough. At the outset, antiseptic treatment was by no means looked upon with favour by the majority of engineers in India, partly no doubt owing to the failure of spasmodic and ill-conditioned experiments carried out before Mr. Pearson's time. But it is now recognised practice and most, if not all of the railways, it is believed, have their own treating plants. Creosote is now in fact manufactured commercially in India. It is strongly recommended that an experimental plant of semi-commercial size should be installed in Nigeria, for the examination of the aptitude of the various species of timber for treatment, to be followed, when the requisite knowledge of the species and the skill in treating them have been attained, by a scheme of practical trials in co-operation with the Public Works, Railway and Post and Telegraph services. The best situation for such a plant would probably be the Public Works Department sawmill at Ijora. Advice on equipment, with estimates of cost could be provided by Princes Risborough. It would be necessary to procure an engineer and give him some months' training at Princes Risborough. But it is suggested that Mr. Sleigh, the Forest Engineer, should be given this duty. His assistant at Eba, is a competent man, and Mr. Sleigh could visit Eba, say, once or twice a month. Mr. Sleigh would need some special training at Princes Risborough. It is thought that the position of the Eba sawmill, as a site, is too out of the way. It is important that the investigations should be easily accessible for inspection by engineers and others interested. In view of the / character of the Nigerian timbers that it would be desired to use in the treated condition, it is probable that a small pressure plant would be necessary for the practical trials, though the initial experiments in aptitude for treatment might be carried out by the cheaper, 'open tank' method in the first instance. Since writing the above I have been informed that the Public Works Department have already purposed to erect an 'open tank' plant at Ijora.

B. – Development of a Domestic and Export Trade in Sawn Timber.

28.   I entirely agree with the views expressed by the Director of Forestry as to the advisability of fostering a trade in sawn timber rather than in timber in the round, on the grounds that –

(*i*)   much waste of timber will be saved;

(*ii*) many timbers can be exported and landed in good condition that do not travel satisfactorily in the log;

(*iii*) by far the greater part of the using trades of the United Kingdom have for years past purchased their supplies in sawn, seasoned and graded form at reasonable prices, and it is highly unlikely that they will abandon this practice for the more hazardous and troublous one of buying timber in the log;

(*iv*) it is likely to result in the use of a greatly increased number of species on the domestic market.

The point is the more important in that America, Nigeria's chief competitor, is the country supplying most of the sawn timber. The preference for sawn timber does not mean to say that shipments of sawn lumber will entirely replace shipments of logs. There will always be an export trade in prime logs for highly decorative solid work and veneers, and for cutting to special requirements.

29.   A sawn timber trade cannot however be developed all at once. Seeing that a large proportion of the cut from the average run of logs will not be of sufficiently high grade for export (for it would probably not pay to ship it, particularly in the early stages of the sawn trade), it will be necessary to develop a domestic trade in the lower grades, as a sure basis for the export trade. This the United Africa Company have started to do, and the venture deserves every encouragement. It must also be realised that there is much spade work to be done before a high quality sawn timber trade can be built up: it is essential that the product should be high quality, since it will compete with the best prepared product on the market, namely that from America. It cannot be too clearly emphasised that the United Kingdom market is in any case an exacting one. Proper seasoning is all-important and will have to be investigated for the several species; some timbers are liable to deteriorate during ocean transport, and preventive measures will have to be devised; a definite standard of quality, with equivalent marks, must be introduced; costs will have to be closely determined, together with the output to be expected from different grades of logs; many timbers will need investigation, long or short, to determine uses.

C. – Costs.

30.   The heaviest single item in the cost of placing timber on the market is freight. I received a number of complaints that the rates, both ocean and coast-wise, demanded by the Shipping Conference lines, are excessive. As far as I am able to judge, / there seems some justification for these complaints. Indeed, whether or not it be wholly for this reason, the United Africa Company now charter their own steamers and ship timber to England at considerably less cost. Competition in the timber trade is now so severe that high freight rates in comparison with those of rival countries must seriously curtail exports. I have not yet been able, since my recent return to England, to obtain all the facts necessary for examining this question, and, in order not to delay this report, those figures will

be furnished later. The subject certainly needs close inquiry. Reasonable railway freight rates, also, are an essential to the growth of domestic trade.

31.   It is recommended, as advocated by the Director of Forests, that royalties should be scaled down on the lines he suggests in his memorandum, for the encouragement of an export trade in sawn timber, but this might also apply to the domestic trade as well, seeing that this is the true foundation of an export trade. Until however a sawn timber trade is established, it is recommended that similar scaling down should apply to exports of new timbers in the log, until they are established on the market.

D. – Girth Limits.

32.   It has been observed that a considerable number of trees felled for timber have unsound hearts. In some species this is particularly prevalent and severe. Although, of course timber companies prefer the larger trees and often fell in excess of the minimum limit, there seems to be little doubt that the girth limit is in many cases too high and that the trees are over-mature, even at the minimum limit. These girth limits were arranged at a very early date on small evidence, and it is recommended that they be revised. This would not prevent the felling of over-mature trees – it is important in the interests of the forest that they be removed – for conversion in the sawmill. In fact a good trade is being done at Degema in sawn timber from such logs. Most over-mature logs are large, and produce sound, wide boards from the outer portions. Since the commercial tendency is to select the larger trees for felling, it might or might not be necessary to encourage the taking out of over-mature trees, after lowering the girth limit, by scaling down royalties on such trees.

E. – Market Extension.

33.   During the tour, some fifty probable and possible commercial timbers have been investigated as to their value, and classified. Notes on supplies and distribution have been made. A final list has been drawn up in consultation with the Public Works and Forest Departments, and the Forest Utilisation Officer, showing –

   (*i*)   timbers likely to be suitable for export;
   (*ii*) timbers likely to be suitable domestically;
   (*iii*) timbers on which further investigation is necessary in Nigeria or at Princes Risborough;
   (*iv*) timbers which either for technical reasons or shortage of supplies are of no value for export.

A descriptive list will be forwarded in due course to the Forest Department and other interests concerned.

34.   It is recommended that, of the promising species, a few, only, at a time should be selected for intensive investigation. For instance, the mill at Koko is concentrating on the local and export marketing of sawn mahogany and abura; the mill at Degema on the local marketing of black afara. For co-operative investigation, the various species of *Celtis* might take first rank in / view of their abundance and promise for export. Intensive work on this one group will not prevent subsidiary work of a preliminary character to explore three or four of the more promising timbers to determine which should be next for intensive investigation. Indeed, this is already being done. It is well again to stress the point that the domestic market is the foundation for an export trade and should not be starved of attention.

35.   The building up of local industries is of extreme importance. It is understood that the United Africa Company is about to install a box-making plant at Sapele. Mention has been made of the promising cabinet trade at Koko under native auspices. Every effort should be made to start other such local industries. The question of training native craftsmen is of importance in this connection.

36.   There is some heart-burning in the commercial timber world both of Nigeria and the United Kingdom on the contention that the Public Works Department are entering the market not only as rivals in the domestic trade but, lately, in the export trade as well. As explained in a subsequent paragraph, this contention is not justified by the facts. As a general principle, however, it is not considered that direct Government competition with the trade is conducive to the speedy and economical development of the country's timber industry, especially the domestic industry, which, as remarked above, is the indispensable foundation. The Government of India's ruling on this matter is again instructive, the result of many year's experience. The following is an extract from the quinquennial review on forest administration for the period 1909–10 to 1913–14.

'The question of the agency by which forest produce should be extracted has given rise to considerable discussion in the past and although certain general principles may be laid down, the form of agency most suited to any particular province or area must necessarily depend upon local conditions.

'In forest administration the object in view is two fold – first to conserve and improve the forests, and this is the first concern of the trained staff, and secondly to secure to the tax-payer the greatest immediate benefit from their commercial working. To obtain the best commercial results departmental or private agency should be employed as circumstances dictate, and provided always that Government receives a fair share of the profits earned, private agency should be freely employed. But when this is done the term of the contract should on the one hand be sufficiently long to enable the initial outlay to be recovered while on the other hand provision should invariably be made for a revision of the rates of royalty at stated interval so that Government may not be deprived of its share of any rise in prices which may take place. Should it be found impossible to employ private agency on these terms departmental working should be adopted, and if this cannot be undertaken by the trained staff without prejudice to the work of conservation and improvements there seems to be no reason why a separate staff specially trained in commercial exploitation should not be employed At times, indeed, departmental working is essential as for instance, in the extraction of little-known timbers other products for which it is desired to create a market when for any reason the system of extraction by purchase breaks down, or when it becomes necessary to prevent trade manipulation or the creation of a monopoly.' /

37.   Where the Public Works Department can be of extreme value in building up both a domestic trade and an export trade is in the joint exploratory work already suggested and the preparation of trial shipments of a new timber ripe for introduction to the market. The shipments, in the writer's opinion, should be in sawn form rather than in the log. Their character and quality is then readily seen; the boards are seasoned, which is of the first importance; graded; and the shipment provides its own demonstration, to a large extent, of the possibilities of the timber. In the earlier cases at least, it would be advisable for one of the Utilisation Officers at Princes Risborough to inspect the timber at the docks and, if he thought necessary, to have the consignment sent to the Laboratory for re-grading and conditioning. In the first instance it would probably be necessary to send a small, sample shipment, say 100 to 200 cubic feet, for the broker's inspection and for use as samples for his clients. According to the reception of these, the broker would then advise upon the size of the first trial shipment in commercial volume. Under the scheme of co-operation suggested, it is unlikely that a timber without any prospects would be so proposed to the market, and it therefore seems improbable that a properly prepared shipment would remain unsold. Indeed, it is possible that the broker might be able to arrange a contract in advance. If advance contracts have not been made, the timber is sent on consignment and there is delay in selling it, it might be necessary for the broker to distribute all or part of it free, in order to get it tried out by users and create a demand for it.

38.   It is recommended that pamphlets descriptive of the timber, hand samples, and samples cut to veneer thickness, should be prepared for distribution by the broker prior to the arrival of the timber. Princes Risborough would co-operate in this work. Sample planks, showing the average run of the timber, should be available for inspection in London and at Princes Risborough. In certain cases it would be advisable to have semi- or wholly-manufactured articles on display.

39.   It is suggested that the exploitation of a new timber in this manner should be continued by Government until assured that the commercial interests concerned can and will supply the export market with shipments to the standard of quality required. In the early stages it may be necessary for the Government to supply demands that are over and above the capacity of the trade to fill. Care would have to be taken that no shipments were made by Government either on contract or consignment which would compete with unsold stocks of the same timber, suitable in quality and specification for the same requirements, lying in merchants' yard at home. This is important in the case of Messrs. James Latham, who hold stocks of Nigerian timbers at their yard in London.

40.   As stated in paragraph 36, the facts do not justify the contention that the Public Works Department are competing with the trade in the domestic and export markets. I have carefully examined the system of costing employed by the Public Works Department in arriving at the sale prices of their timbers and am satisfied that these costs (*e.g.*, power and on-charges) are well above the level that a commercial firm would find necessary, at least in the early stages. But the main point is that at present the United Africa Company's mills are certainly not well enough equipped to handle the trade satisfactorily, either in quantity or quality. Further, it is certain that sales of native timbers by the Public Works Department have been very effectual in reducing the quantity of foreign softwood timber imported. Lacking this check, it is more than probable that local interests in Lagos would / go in heavily for this foreign import, as an easier trade than milling native logs. It seems to me essential that the Public Works Department should continue this work until such time as private interests have been induced to take it up and can handle it efficiently. As remarked above, care would have to be taken in regard to the export market against competing with unsold similar stocks in merchants' yards at home.

41.   A standard quality of logs for export should be maintained. The United Africa Company has in being a rigid inspection in the forest and again at the point of shipment. But the majority of native producers, owing to the difficulty of financing labour, do not deliver logs at the shipping point in 'fair average quality' condition. These logs are in many cases exported unsold, on consignment, and the market is likely to be flooded with inferior timber to the detriment of Nigerian timbers as a whole, both in reputation and price. A partial remedy would be to exact some security against the payment of labour, as in the case of European firms. This would result in speedier extraction and corresponding improvement in the condition of the logs. Bad manufacture on the other hand, it is thought, could be improved only by an export mark of quality. Some special arrangement would have to be made in this connection with Messrs. James Latham. It probably may and does pay this firm to have a certain proportion of lower grade logs,

according to the market, transported to their London sawmill to be there converted into sawn timber and sold, after grading, as such. It must also be realised that the rigidity of the standard of logs for sale will vary slightly according to the state of the market. The exact means by which this proposal should be implemented is a matter for settlement between the Government and the trade.

F. – Advisory and Co-ordinating Board

42.   It will be clear from what has been said above that many interests are concerned in the development of Nigeria's forests and that there are many matters that must be the subjects of conference. The general policy governing development is one; carefully considered programmes of research and investigation are necessary in the several directions mentioned; there will be questions as to means of expanding domestic trade, establishing new industries, and training craftsmen; the question of an export mark of quality has to be determined; and there is the need for maintaining close co-operation both between Government and the trade and between the several Government Departments concerned. It is suggested that some form of Advisory and Co-ordinating Board might be set up for this purpose. Thorough co-ordination is essential for success.

Part IV.
FINANCE.

43.   At my request, the Director of Forests has submitted figures, shown in the Appendix, setting out the financial consequence of putting the forests of Nigeria on a secure, practical and permanent basis. The figures cover the period of the next ten years. Compared with the present staff of the department, the increases that he suggests may seem unwarrantably high. This is certainly not so. The present strength of the Forest Department is very far below the strength required and bears no practical relation to the demands of the task. The basis of judgment must be the size of the forests; their climatic value and their great / commercial value, nationally and imperially; their backward state of conservation and management and the work involved in putting them on a practical footing; and that the present situation is critical and urgent. So far as the task is concerned I am therefore fully in accord with the Director of Forests in his request for ten additional Assistant Conservators a year over the next decade.

I am, however, informed that it is quite impossible for Nigeria, in the present circumstances of trade depression, to afford the financial provision required for an increase on this scale. I suggest therefore that, while that establishment should be recognised as the ideal to be attained, a modified scheme within the compass of present conditions should be drawn up to cover an agreed preliminary period, the scheme to be a definite minimum, to be expanded as and when increased revenue from development permits. In view of the need, especially in forestry, for an uninterrupted programme of development and for providing training institutions with advance estimates of staff requirements, it is suggested that the preliminary period should be not less than three years, preferably five. To arrive at the modified scheme it is suggested that two statements should be compiled: the first to show the number, distribution (including staff on leave and average number of casualties), and individual duties of the staff, with the area of the several districts; the second to show essential silvicultural work, work that could be put on a maintenance basis or slowed down, and essential work (botanical and stock-taking surveys, etc.) connected with timber trade development. These statements would show whether or no it would be possible to make temporary use of existing forestry or administrative staff for urgent development work and afford definite figures for the extra staff required. The conclusion would then be read in conjunction with the financial provision possible, taking into account the increased revenue likely to be derived from more intensive development. It is believed that the revenue from timber exports will certainly show an increase during the current year, and there seems little doubt that with stricter regulation and supervision the revenue from the local use of timber could be very materially increased.

The re-appointment of a Deputy Conservator, or at least that of a senior, experienced officer attached to the headquarters staff, is also entirely sound. To carry out effective supervision the Director must be constantly on tour. It is essential for efficiency and smooth working that he possess an officer of sufficient experience to represent him in his absence or whom, as occasion may demand, he may depute to act for him in some duty away from headquarters. The Director must not be tied to his desk.

44.   The Director of Forests has included in his estimates a figure of £1,000 to cover the cost of sending certain timbers to Princes Risborough for test and of both sample and larger scale, trial shipments to the home market. The maximum cost in 1933/34 of sending timbers to Princes Risborough would probably be of the order of £200. Particulars will be supplied to the Director of Forests, to allow him to submit firm figures, after consultation with the Director of Forest Products Research. If trial shipments of three new timbers were sent to the English market in 1933/34, the cost would be about £1,000; but, as stated earlier, it is probable that with proper organisation and care, most or all of that sum would be recovered. In addition, it was recommended earlier in this report that sawmill and utilisation experiments should form a definite function of the Public Works Department, entailing the necessary financial provision. I understand that the erection and running cost of a creosoting 'open tank' plant, which the Director of Forests / originally included in the estimates for his own Department, will now

be a charge on the Public Works Department. Recommendations as to the size and character of the plant required can be supplied by Princes Risborough. The cost, manufactured at home, would be of the order of £120 for a suitable plant.

SUMMARY.

To sum up. The large forests of Nigeria, containing a wide variety of excellent timbers, are extremely valuable from the national standpoint: from the Imperial standpoint they assume a particular value in that Nigeria is among the four Empire countries that can at present offer generous hardwood supplies for export. But the position is not safe.

The area of forest under measures protecting it from destruction is woefully small – only 6.3 per cent of the total. Of the 53,000 square miles of very valuable forest accessible for export supplies, only 9,518 square miles, or less than eighteen per cent of it, have been protected. Further delay is dangerous. At the Imperial Forestry Conference in 1920, it was reported by Mr. H. M. Thompson, then Director of Forests, that, during seventeen years, 40,000 square miles of good forest had been destroyed. The present Director of Forests estimates the annual rate of destruction at 1,000 square miles.

The size of the Forest Department staff is, and for some years has been, quite insufficient for the magnitude, difficulty and urgency of the task. Indeed, the department is entitled to great credit for the results it has achieved under this handicap. In various places in this report I have quoted India. There is nothing that renders India, as some may think, an exception in requirements. The problem and its demands for India and for Nigeria are parallel, technically and commercially. The only divergence is that, India being three and a half times the size of Nigeria, distances are greater, provincial services require to be more or less self-contained units on this account, and therefore headquarter staffs must be somewhat larger. In comparing the figures given below it must also be remembered that India, with a Forest Service established nearly a hundred years ago, is many chapters ahead while Nigeria is at the beginning of the story. Against this, Nigeria has almost the same area of forests. The staff of the two countries is:–

	India.	*Nigeria.*
Imperial (European) service	257	47
Provincial (Native) service	260	nil.
Subordinate:		
Rangers		
Deputy Rangers	15,240	237
Foresters		
Forest Guards		
	15,757	284

Making every allowance for India's extra provincial requirements and her stage of development, this great contrast is almost sufficient in itself to prove the inadequacy of Nigeria's staff for a similar task. The proposals of the Director of Forests, especially in respect of adding ten Assistant Conservators to his staff annually over the next ten years, appeal to me as entirely reasonable. Indeed, the delay has been so great that, but for the limits imposed on speed by technical and other considerations, the scale of increase might well have been greater. /

But it is vital to begin at once, and without more delay to embark on a steady uninterrupted policy of development under which all the several interests are co-ordinated. Apart from the safety of the capital resources, the development of marketing and of the consequent demands, under the impetus of the policy of Empire trade, is seriously over-running the organisation of supplies. Indeed, this was a reason for my mission. A check now may well put the clock back again. The closer the situation in Nigeria is studied, in the light of probable commercial demand in volume and character, the more justification is shown for an advance on Indian lines. India could not have achieved her remarkable results with a staff on the meagre scale of Nigeria. Indian statistics show that the rise in net revenue has closely followed the increase in superior staff. Had production been organised, Nigeria could at this present time have had a larger export trade, restricted though the market is. With improved demand and prices, even at her present stage of development she will doubtless increase her export trade, possibly from the present three hundred and forty thousand pounds a year to the half million which was the average for some years before the slump. But however good the demand becomes, she can never take full and, more important, permanent advantage of it without an adequate, skilled staff to maintain the required level of organisation, based on a steadily progressive policy. Early last year, before I had visited Nigeria, I endeavoured to review the present and probable future demands of the United Kingdom timber market and to assess the value in replacement of foreign timber that could be shared by the several parts of the Empire, in addition to their present trade. My calculations, which were carefully conservative, showed that British West Africa's share should be close on a million pounds, of which the greater proportion would fall to Nigeria. Now that I have first-hand knowledge of the possibilities, I believe that I was too conservative and moreover that the attainment of such an objective is by no means so difficult as I had feared.

Other factors beside large timber resources and a keen Forest staff are in Nigeria's favour. In the last few years, the Public Works Department, who have a well organised and equipped sawmill and wood workshops, have pursued a policy of investigating and utilising native timbers, which has brought the use of foreign timber to an insignificant quantity and placed the chances of expanding the export trade in a much more forward position. Timber traders in Nigeria are keen, and anxious to co-operate in those investigations. Of the interest on the part of dealers and users in the United Kingdom, there is no doubt.

I believe that if the commercial interests of Nigeria see that Government, on its side of the task, has determined upon an adequate policy of development, they on their part will be encouraged to incur the expenditure necessary to improve matters on their side of the task. In the past lean years, they have had to bear the whole burden, under great difficulties. They have faced cut-throat foreign competition at prices indicative of sale below cost of production. It may be argued that their own first costs might have been lowered by expenditure on improvements in extraction and sawmilling plant. Even then, to expand markets, they would have been obliged at the outset to sell at a loss, trust to an increased production to lower their overhead costs still further, and to improving trade and prices to confirm their position on a market won at a sacrifice and re-imburse them for their losses. Discouraged and uncertain, with no prospect at that date of any protective help for British production, they have not felt warranted, even if funds / allowed, in taking the risk. That situation has not only been improved but can be improved still more. And happily there are signs that trade is itself improving.

Lastly, there are many interests involved. Close, sympathetic co-operation is required, both between the various Government Departments and between Government and the Trade. Given this, which is an essential, the steady policy of development proposed should not only, in normal conditions, show ample justification financially but is one of the steps necessary to bring back these conditions. /

APPENDIX.

A NOTE ON THE FINANCIAL REQUIREMENTS FOR THE EFFICIENT DEVELOPMENT OF THE FOREST OF NIGERIA.

A. – Immediate requirements (i.e., an increase of the 1933–34 votes).

(1) Enumeration Surveys.

	£	£
Labour		800
5 African Surveyors		200
3 Forest Guards		90
		£1,090 – £1,090
(2) Increased transport vote of		3,500 – 3,500
(3) " canoe vote		600 – 600
(4) Demarcation, etc.		1,200 – 1,200
(5) Timber investigation, etc.		1,000 – 1,000
(6) Impregnating tank:		
Cost	£300	
Upkeep	£250	550 – 550
(7) Sylviculture and botanical work		600 – 600
(8) Tools, seeds, etc.		200 – 200
		£8,740

B. – Annual minimum requirements on certain votes for years subsequent to 1933–34: Other charges (actual total amounts).

	£
(1) Guaranteed minimum of Demarcation Vote (to be increased to £3,000 after five years and £4,000 after ten years)	2,000
(2) Guaranteed minimum of Enumeration Vote (to be increased to £2,500 after five years and £3,000 after seven years)	1,750
(3) Transport	7,000
(*Note:* This Vote to increase by £180 per each additional Assistant Conservator's appointment).	
(4) Canoes (purchase, hire, etc.) (to be increased to £1,500 after five years)	1,100
(5) Timber Investigation and Research (to be increased to £1,500 in three years)	1,200
(6) Sylvicultural Investigations (to be increased to £2,500 after five years)	2,000
(7) Bush Houses	500

Personal Emoluments (increases only).

(1) Re-appointment of Deputy Director of Forests at £1,100+£220 =	1,320
(2) Re-appointment of Senior Conservator of Forests at £960+ £96 =	1,056
(3) 10 Assistant Conservators at £480	=	4,800
(4) 12 Forest Guards at £30	=	360/

The re-appointment of the Deputy Director of Forests and the third Senior Conservator of Forests are obviously essential in view of the work which the Department is now doing and in view of the increased work necessary as forest development occurs. The item ten Assistant Conservator of Forests and twelve Guards to be added to annually by that amount until the European staff maximum of 125 is reached; eight is actually the figure required but the additional two allows for casualties; the number of guards should be increased yearly until the increase is 185 on the present figure.

The figures given above are based on the assumption that the reserved area of merchantable forest should be increased from the present 9,500 square miles to a minimum of 45,000, *i.e.*, the minimum which will allow for the permanency of the timber trade. This trade can neither continue to exist nor can it be developed further unless the forests upon which it is dependent are properly managed.

The minimum superior staff required for this is between 125 and 130 officers; the extra recruitment being spread over ten years.

In regard to transport the present vote, drastically cut in recent years, has reached a point which in many cases limits effective work to about three months in the year; it is vastly inadequate. The same applies to the votes for canoe-travelling, demarcation, sylviculture, tools, seeds, etc., while the timber investigation and enumeration surveys votes have ceased altogether.

Those immense reductions were the result of a definite command in the name of economy for a further total reduction of £5,000 on the 1933–34 estimates after they had been prepared and this will, as was pointed out at the time, compel abandonment of essential work, which cannot result otherwise than in loss of trade. My own view is, as I stated at the time, that these reductions cannot and will not prove economical.

The estimated development costs given above do no more than allow for the carrying out of essential work, if the forests are to be a permanency and if the export trade is not gradually to become reduced to the extent that it ceases to matter.

As shown elsewhere the value of this trade, taken over the last five years, in export alone is £340,000 annually and the total annual value (internal and export) may safely be estimated at 2 ¾ million pounds; over the previous five years the annual export value was approximately half a million pounds, the decrease in recent years being due partly to general depression but also the destruction of formerly exploitable forest areas due to lack of reservation.

It is safe to say that had it not been for the activities of the department the present value of the export trade would not have been one-eighth what it is at present; it is also safe to say that with proper management of the forests, with proper investigation and handling this trade can be increased to three or four times its present value and more.

Nigeria is still largely a forest country, its prosperity depends entirely on its forests; in addition these forests, giving as they do the direct yield recorded above and possessing such immense development possibilities, it is only reasonable, when the cost is comparatively so small, to urge that they be given every chance not only to maintain their present output standard but to be given every facility for further development.

J. R. AINSLIE,
Director of Forests.
6. 2. 1933.

J. W. Nicholson, *The Future of Forestry in Uganda* (Entebbe: Government Printer, 1929).

UGANDA PROTECTORATE.
FOREST DEPARTMENT.

THE FUTURE OF FORESTRY IN UGANDA.
By J. W. NICHOLSON,[1] *Forest Adviser.*

ENTEBBE:
[...]

Introduction.

1.   At the present time no definite forest policy is being followed by the Govern- Introduction. ment of Uganda. This report is an attempt to outline and justify a definite forest policy. As far as possible a statistical basis of justification has been avoided. Because Germany finds that 25 per cent of the total area of Germany should be maintained under forest it is not to say that other countries must also retain 25 per cent of their area under forest and that if they do not do so they cannot reach a Teutonic plane of civilisation. The Eskimo is likely to remain cold if he be informed that he is on a par with prehistoric man because his sole use for forest produce is to convert it into smoke. Similarly with regard to nomadic tribes, for nomadism, originally at any rate, was a mode of life evolved in response to the succession of a grassland over a woodland climate. The forest problem in each country must be studied in itself without undue emphasis being laid on foreign comparisons. In Uganda the main problems to be investigated are how far does the life of the people of Uganda depend on the existence of forests; how far can their progress towards a higher degree of civilisation be improved by the maintenance or extension of existing forest areas; how far are the Uganda forests a negotiable and valuable financial asset; and what is the role to be played by a scientific Forest Department. In other words I have not assumed it as a premise but regarded it as a matter to be proved that Uganda must have forests and a Forest Department.

PART I.

The Foundations of Forest Policy in Uganda.

Considerations governing general forest policy.

2.   In a previous preliminary report I referred to the fact that the forest problem in Uganda was a peculiar one in that over much of the Protectorate forests did not appear to exercise an important climatic rôle; the possibilities of exporting forest produce were limited; and the demand of the people for forest produce which they could not grow themselves was small. These three considerations have to be fully and separately dealt with before any attempt can be made to define a general forest policy.

(A) THE INDIRECT UTILITY OF UGANDA'S FORESTS.

Indirect effects of forests erosion.

3.   The most important indirect effects of forests, and the only ones which need be considered here, are their influences on (1) erosion, (2) rainfall and humidity, and (3) water supply. The importance of forest growth in preventing erosion is unquestionable, but it is not a factor which in itself constitutes a sound reason for forest conservation, for on all but very sandy soils many grasses can prevent erosion nearly as efficiently as tree growth. I have seen very few cases of serious erosion in Uganda and I impute this to the fact that now-a-days forest destruction is immediately followed by invasions of grasses. I have written now-a-days because I am of the opinion that some at least of the swamps in Uganda have originated from forest destruction and subsequent silting up of valleys through heavy soil erosion in days gone by when grassland in Uganda was not the prevalent form of vegetation that it is to-day. The main evidence in favour of this statement is that in no case, either in Kenya or Uganda, do I know of a swamp originating in virgin forest. While I do not consider that the prevention of soil erosion is a factor of material importance so far as general forest policy is concerned, I do think that caution is necessary in clearing wooded or grass-clad slopes for cultivation purposes. The most extensive examples of steep hill side clearing for cultivation purposes are to be found in Bugishu and fortunately the people have there adopted the excellent practice of planting lines of trees or bananas above each little clearing. If this practice is always followed on steep hill slopes there need be little fear of erosion and subsequent soil infertility. /

Forests and rain-fall controversy.

4.   The influence of forests on rainfall and precipitation is a much debated subject, but it is of immense importance to Uganda as I hope to succeed in indicating. It has for centuries been a popular belief that forests induced rain. In most cases this belief was undoubtedly induced by the fact that wooded areas received the greatest rainfall, but in many instances the fact was not that the forests created rain but the rain forests. This popular belief was seized on by

professional foresters as an argument in favour of that policy of conservation of forests which on direct utilitarian grounds they had had difficulty in getting adopted owing to vested rights of usage. The extravagant claims of professional foresters brought on a conflict with meteorologists who disputed their assertions. The most recent work on 'Forests and Rainfall,' by Zon (1927), gives a very large number of facts in support of the contention that forests induce rain but contradictory data are ignored. The work is in fact that of a biased author. More recently still Dr. Brooks, a meteorologist of some repute, has written a paper contradicting most of the claims about rainfall and forests. Unfortunately this paper too appears to have been written with a bias and the author's arguments are not all very convincing.

5.   In my opinion a great deal of the confusion of *ideas* on the subject of the influence of forests on rainfall is due to the fact that the source of the rainfall has generally been ignored. The two main kinds of rain* are (1) monsoon rain due to general currents passing over rising land, and (2) 'Continental' or 'Instability' rain which is induced by cooling due to convection currents. Now there is little evidence to prove that forests exert an important local effect on rainfall when the latter is monsoon in origin, but there is a certain amount of evidence to show that forests exert a regional influence on monsoon rainfall. The reason is this: The ordinary European forest (and probably all evergreen tropical forests) evaporates or transpires into the air more moisture than does a free water surface such as that of a lake. Monsoon-borne rain naturally tends to diminish as the monsoon passes into the interior of a continent. If, however, it passes over lakes or forests the tendency will be for the moisture contents of the prevailing wind to be maintained with the result that the limits of rainfall will be extended inland. As regards 'instability rain,' Mr. Walter, the present Government statistician, conducted meteorological researches on this subject in Mauritius and he found that forests increased the probability of afternoon rain. Further observations on this subject are made below.

Distinction between monsoon and instability rain.

6.   In the midst of theories I am fortunately able to give concrete facts regarding one case of the effect of forest destruction on rainfall which is personally known to me. In my last district in India (Ranchi in Chota Nagpur) several tea gardens were opened up about fifty years ago when the greater part of Ranchi district was mainly forest. During the last half century most of the forests have been destroyed in the process of the extension of cultivation with the result that not only are the tea gardens dying out but also the villagers are no longer able to grow the winter crops which they were able to do in the past. The interesting fact is that the total rainfall has hardly changed at all during the last fifty

A practical example of effects of deforestation.

---

*   Ignoring rain due to cyclonic disturbances.

years, and the real explanation of the present state of things is as follows: In the old days most of the rain, say about 90 per cent, was monsoon rain which fell in the course of three or four consecutive months. The remainder of the rain was instability rain which fell intermittently in the cold and hot weather. The monsoon rain still falls as it used to but there has been a marked decline in the fall of instability rain. From the districts point of view the change has been most adverse as it could easily spare 20 inches of monsoon rain in exchange for five inches of instability rain in the dry months of the year. But it is not only the loss of instability rain which has affected the production of crops adversely; it is also the decrease in the humidity of the air which has been caused by forest destruction. This is an aspect we have not considered so far but it is a most important aspect. Whether forests do or do not increase rainfall it is an undoubted fact that they tend to increase the humidity of the atmosphere, to condense moisture in forms other than that of rain and to act as a shelter against / desiccating winds. The most recent researches carried out at the South African Forest Research station show that the precipitation of atmospheric moisture in the form of dew, etc., amounts to 25 per cent of the annual rainfall in the case of land under forest. For many crops, particularly cereal crops, atmospheric moisture or dew is just as good as rainfall, and in a naturally dry climate shelter from desiccating winds may make all the difference between crop failure and success. It is on account of these considerations, which are often ignored by meteorologists, that the popular conception that forests induce rainfall may be regarded as fundamentally sound although inaccurately expressed in that if they do not actually induce rain they do induce conditions of moisture which economically, for cereal food crops at any rate (and it is abdominal repletion which influences the thoughts of most mankind) is almost equivalent to genuine rain.

Uganda's rainfall continental not monsoon.

7.   Let us now consider rainfall conditions in Uganda. It has generally been assumed, I do not know why, that the Uganda rainfall has a monsoon origin, and to explain the annual distribution of rain bi-monsoon and tri-monsoon theories have been advanced. The truth of the matter appears to be that by far the greater part of Uganda's rainfall comes not from some distant ocean but from Uganda itself. Mr. Walter, from data collected south of the equator in Kenya and Tanganyika, has come to the conclusion that most of the rainfall in those countries is continental and not monsoon in character. I make no claims to being a meteorologist but all the data I have seen and the observations I have been able to make go to prove that Uganda's rainfall is also mainly continental in origin. The prevailing wind throughout most of Kenya and the north-east of Uganda, and the prevailing direction of rain is from the north-east. In the south and south-east of Uganda the direction is deflected to become eastern probably owing to the influ-

ence of a south-west wind on Victoria Nyanza. In the west of Uganda the Lake Albert region is influenced by south-west winds blowing up the Semliki valley. This being the case, if the rainfall is monsoon in origin how is it that the country to the north-east and the coast line receives practically no rain at all? Another curious fact, which I have not seen commented on before, how is it that the places with the greatest rainfall in Kenya and Uganda, *e.g.*, Kericho, Kakomega, and West Elgon, are situated on the *leeward* side of the prevailing wind which is the reverse of what would be the case if the rainfall was monsoon in origin? How is it that Kakomari at over 5,000 feet near the edge of the Turkana escarpment gets far less rain than places to the south-west which are lower in altitude? How is it that except in localities where the atmosphere is thoroughly saturated, *e.g.*, Entebbe, most of the rain falls in the late afternoon, and why is the actual rainfall so extraordinarily local in character? There is only one possible reply, and that is that the monsoon is not responsible for most of Uganda's rain. It is continental in origin.

8.   In the previous paragraph I have called attention to facts which should stimulate thought. I now propose to try and clarify such thought as may have been provoked. Let us turn to the annual rainfall map of Uganda which has been compiled by the Land Office. It is a praiseworthy effort but hopelessly misleading as the available data are not sufficient to justify the drawing of detailed isohyets.[2] I will point out a few errors. On the 60' and 65' isohyet drawn round Mount Elgon the actual rainfall on the Kenya side, as recorded by two or three stations, is about 40' and 45' respectively. Lobwor and Rom fall on the 30' isohyet. These two places judging from local information and vegetation get a rainfall of at least 50' if not more. Kitgum is shown as having an average rainfall of 45.44'. I have been informed that the Kitgum fall is below the average of the immediate neighbourhood which receives much more rain. Napak hill on the border of Teso district is shown on a 35' isohyet. The average fall cannot be under 45' to 50'. These facts all concern the north-east but as the prevailing wind is from the north-east it is to the north-east that I have looked for a clue to the riddle of Uganda's rainfall. Owing to defects such as these I think it may be assumed that the rainfall map is not a reliable guide to rainfall hypotheses. It is indeed doubtful whether it will ever be possible to draw detailed isohyets as the rainfall is too local in character. /

Unreliability of Uganda rainfall map.

9.   If we cease to think of isohyets and consider the recorded rainfall for individual stations we are more likely to get at the truth. The law which in my opinion holds good generally throughout Uganda is that the places with the greatest rainfall are those that lie beside forests, swamps, or lakes or to their immediate south-west or west, subject to the ordinary meteorological law that the greater the altitude the greater the rainfall. I cannot claim that this law is absolutely true as

Factors influencing rainfall in Uganda.

I have insufficient knowledge of the climate of Uganda, but it appears to hold true for all the places I have seen. Further, when I write of forests, I am referring to forest in the larger sense of the word which includes open savannah forest such as is typical of most of the Northern and Eastern Provinces. If my observations are correct it means that forests and water surface exercise a vital influence on the rainfall. How far their influence is local rather than regional I do not know, but the fact that the rainfall to the west and south-west of Victoria Nyanza diminishes very quickly tends to show that the influence is of more local than regional importance. I spent two weeks or so on the interrupted chain of hills which divides Karamoja from Teso and Chua districts and it was instructive to watch how day after day out of a cloudless, or almost cloudless, Karamojan sky the clouds would start to gather overhead and eventually precipitate rain. It is this chain of hills which roughly divides the dry from the wet country, and the reason why it does so is that to its east there is a large tract of country incapable of supporting swamps or forests – a feature further referred to below – and of contributing moisture to the air. I do not intend to attempt a meteorological explanation of these facts. This can be left to the meteorological service about to be initiated. Sufficient to say that I think they can all be explained on the basis of a continental origin of rain theory as also can the annual distribution of rain. The run-off from Uganda as represented by the outflow of the Nile constitutes but a very small percentage of the annual rainfall. Unless most of the latter sinks through the ground to form a vast sunless sea in the underworld of Uganda it must be evaporated into the air and if the moisture so evaporated is precipitated in Uganda itself one need look to distant oceans or neighbouring countries for but a small percentage of the total rainfall. Further solar tropical movements are bound to affect the rainfall, and the coalescence of rainy seasons in the north and the divergence of rainy seasons in the south are phenomena which should be capable of interpretation on the basis of the sun's passage north or south of the equator.

A peep into Uganda's past – grassland woodland.　10.　If the rainfall in Uganda is regulated by forests, lakes, and swamps one is led to enquire what of the past, what of the future? Let the problem of the past take precedence, but before we follow in the steps of our geological friends and attempt to peep behind the veil of mystery which shrouds Uganda's past we must refer to one important feature of plant distribution. Geographical botanists distinguish between woodland and grassland climates. So far as the tropics are concerned the position may be summarised as follows:–

(*a*)　With a rainfall of over 65' high forest predominates.

(*b*)　With 35' to 65' of rainfall there is a struggle between xerophilous woodland[3] and grassland. Xerophilous woodland is favoured when greater heat and more prolonged rainless periods prevail during the vegetative season; grassland is favoured when a milder temperature, a more even distribution of rainfall during the vegetative season, and windy dry seasons prevail.

(c) With a rainfall below 30'–35' xerophilous scrub, in particular thorn forest and thorn bush prevail; both of these, if the precipitation be less, pass over into open scrub (semi desert).

A woodland climate leads to victory on the part of the woodland, a grassland climate to victory on the part of the grassland. In transitional climates the ordinary tendency is for woodland to beat grassland but edaphic[4] influences or other factors decide the victory. Now whereas India enjoys a typical woodland climate in which with decreasing rainfall woodland passes directly into desert, over many parts of Africa and over most of Uganda the climate is transitional. There are areas in Uganda where the rainfall exceeds 65' and high forest prevails; there are also areas (*e.g.*), N.-E. Karamoja) where / the rainfall is less than 30' and xerophilous scrub prevails; but over most of Uganda the climate is transitional in character.

11.   The factors which in the transitional climate of Uganda have influenced and are influencing the battle between forest and grass are the following:– Firstly, there is the edaphic factor. Neither black cotton soil nor laterite are favourable to forest formation and where these occur (*e.g.*, the black cotton soils of Karamoja, lateritic outcrops as at Entebbe) grassland prevails. Secondly, man by clearing for cultivation, especially shifting cultivation, has caused large areas of virgin forest to retrogress into secondary forest or grass. Thirdly, there is the greatest factor of all, and that is fire. Grass fires can and are started in nature but when there is man, and especially pastoral man, their frequency is greatly intensified. In a transitional climate forests can resist occasional fires but successive annual fires must lead to the ultimate complete victory of grassland. *Factors influencing struggle between grassland and woodland.*

12.   If we eliminate the direct and indirect influences of human occupation the conclusion is reached that if Uganda in the past (say *circa* 500 B.C.) enjoyed a rainfall as great as it is to-day practically the whole of Uganda was covered with dense forest. The exceptions would be the limited areas affected by unfavourable edaphic influences and parts of Mubende and Ankole districts where the climate at the present day is probably more favourable to grassland than to woodland. The advent of man has caused a striking change in the distribution of vegetation. Where the rainfall is heavy or the average humidity high dense forests have been able to resist fire and they have survived except where cleared by man. In the north and north-east where the climate favours woodland against grassland the *Probability Uganda more densely forested in past.*

virgin forests have been replaced by Sudanese savannah forests of a fire-resisting type. In the drier regions of Mubende, west Masaka, and Ankole where the rainfall is more evenly distributed and the climate more favourable to grassland the latter now dominates. (*N.B.* – Possibly the Sudanese flora would have found a footing in these districts if it had had time to spread there).

The evidence of forest destruction.

13.   The evidence in support of this conclusion is firstly* that one finds similar species, many typical of the West African flora, throughout scattered detached blocks of forest up to the foot of the Nandi escarpment. Secondly, in Ankole and in the north-east one finds patches of dense forest surviving only either where the rainfall and humidity is high or where fires have been unable to destroy them owing to the protective influence of precipices and rock outcrops. Thirdly, there is the evidence of the Sango Bay forests. These forests contain two species of podocarpus[5] which are normally never found at such a low altitude. The distribution of these species within the Sango Bay forests in belts and the fact that they are only found elsewhere on the lake shore near river mouths points to their having originated from seed brought down by a river – the Kagera. Hydrological evidence proves that the present low lake levels and therefore the forests are of recent origin. This is confirmed by the fact that under prevailing climatic conditions podocarpus would not be able for long to withstand competition from tropical species more adapted to the environment. The seed could only have been brought down when the Kagera was a swamp-free river capable of severe flooding. At the present day these two species of podocarpus are said to be non-existent or very rare in the Kagera river basin. The mother trees must therefore have been felled or destroyed by fire. The probability is that fires and possibly shifting cultivation caused the destruction of the podocarpus forests along the Kagera. Forest destruction entailed high flooding with transport of seed to the lake shore. Replacement of the forests by grass led to diminished floods, silting up, and invasions of papyrus. (*N.B.* – The suggested history of the Sango Bay forests opens up an interesting speculation. In the Geological Survey Department's report of 1927 Mr. Wayland has drawn up a hypothetical correlation table of the Nakuru – Elmenteita deposits in which he assumes a dry period between 700 – 1000 A.D. This might well be the period during which, driven out by droughts from their original homeland, the Bahima invaded Ankole district – the most suitable pastoral district in Uganda, their invasion being rendered all the easier / by the fact that the original inhabitants being of agricultural habit would have been weakened by successive failures of their crops. If so, grass fires initiated by the Bahima would gradually spread to and destroy the forests along the Kagera

---

*   Not a definite proof as the forests may have been united in pluvial periods. Detailed study of individual forests might yield indications of how long ago they were united.

river. This may be a wild surmise, but it fits in with the time factors indicated by the theory of the origin of the Sango Bay forests).

14.   The destruction of forest growth in the past 2,000 years or so must have had some effect on the climate and more particularly the rainfall of Uganda. If the rainfall is continental in origin the supersession of woodland by grassland should lead to a diminution in the rainfall as shallow rooted grasses cannot extract from the subsoil and transpire into the atmosphere the same amount of moisture that deep rooted tree vegetation can extract and transpire. On the other hand, at about the time grasslands were gaining over forest lands, and perhaps as a consequence of the destruction of forests, the formation of swamps was initiated or accelerated. Swamps evaporate even more moisture than lakes or forests. The inference is that the formation of swamps, so far as effects on rainfall are concerned, more or less counterbalanced the loss of forests except in regions where swamps were few. On the other hand, the loss of forests growth and the formation of swamps must have affected the run-off and the levels of the great lakes. This reduction in lake levels and consequently in lake surface may have affected the rainfall slightly. The general inference is that the rainfall of most of Uganda can only have been slightly affected by the destruction of forests except in the drier tracts of Mubende, Ankole and west Masaka where it may now be considerably less than formerly, in which case the climate in these districts must have been originally more favourable to woodland than it is to-day.

Effects of forest destruction on rainfall.

15.   And now for a glimpse into the future. There is considerable evidence, geological, hydrological and botanical, that parts of Africa are undergoing progressive desiccation,* and such desiccation is proceeding independently of secular variations of rainfall (*e.g.*, present dry period commenced in 1870 only). In West Africa it has been more or less definitely proved that desiccation has been progressing towards the south and south-west. The Guinea flora has been receding before the Sudanese flora, woodland before grassland. We know that grass fires have been raging for thousands of years as they were witnessed and recorded by Phoenician travelers. The conversion of woodland into grassland would undoubtedly allow the dry north wind fuller scope and affect both the humidity and the rainfall. It is therefore extremely probable that the most potent cause of progressive desiccation is the destruction of woodland both by fires and by man for cultivation purposes. In Uganda there is reason to believe that even if such desiccation has not been progressing in the dim past in the drier areas of the country as has been surmised above, it has certainly been in progress in recent times. Mr. Fiske, the late Government Reclamation Officer, has shown that des-

The menace of desication in Africa.

---

*   Desiccation, here and in the paragraphs immediately following, is dealt with from the aspect of 'loss of humidity and rainfall.' The further aspect of 'loss of water supply' is dealt with later.

iccation has occurred in recent years in Masaka district (I have not actually seen this report and do not know whether desiccation in Masaka is a consequence of a secular variation of climate since about 1870 or whether it has been a gradual process due to deforestation). In his recent 'Report on a proposed new track from Soroti district to Moroto' Mr. Wayland, the Director of Geological Survey, has shown that desiccation is occurring in Karamoja. I had independently come to the same conclusion from what I had seen in north Karamoja where the cedar forest is dying out. There is hardly any doubt but that Uganda is faced with the same desiccating menace as West Africa. I do not put down this menace to the Sudan, as has been suggested by Mr. Wayland, but to the north-east, whether that north-east lie in Kenya, the Sudan, or Uganda itself.

Causes for its existence in Uganda.

16.   The two reasons for this menace are, as in West Africa, fire and clearing for cultivation. I do not know the real cause of recent desiccation in Karamoja as I have not had an opportunity of examining conditions in detail. It may be surmised that since the advent of human tribes into the dry regions to the north-east of Uganda there has been a gradual retreat of forest growth. Since the introduction of more settled times it is likely that the / population of these tracts has increased. At any rate the cessation of tribal wars must have resulted in nature enjoying fewer respites from man's destructive activities. It is natural, therefore, that the borders of Uganda towards the north-east should be drier now than they used to be. Within these same borders the same process has been going on. Chua, Teso, and Lango districts are generally well covered with savannah forests of fire-resisting trees but owing to increases in the population most of these forests are burnt over annually. Well adapted as the component trees are to withstand fires it is difficult to see how the forest growth can survive for long when the young growth is never given a chance to grow up. It is significant that the forest growth is denser where the population is less and where fires are not invariably annual. Clearing for cultivation purposes, which is year by year being carried out on a vaster scale – in Teso alone 40,000 acres are now said to be cleared annually – is responsible for the destruction of large areas of open forest.

The tragedy of unchecked desic- cation.

17.   The disappearance of forest growth in the north and east of Uganda is bound to have an adverse effect on the climate. The humidity of the atmosphere will become less, for, as has already been pointed out, grass is not a substitute for trees as a moisture producing agent, nor can grass break up dry winds as can a forest formation. Further, almost without doubt the rainfall itself will be adversely affected. I have already indicated that the influence of forest on rainfall has not been proved. I am not biassed on the general question. Subsequent investigations may prove me wrong, but it is my strong personal conviction, based on all the data at present available to me, that the future prosperity of Uganda is dependent on a successful resistance against the enemy of desiccation which is

insidiously invading the country from the north-east. I say insidiously because not with blare of trumpet will the advance be advertised. I have been asked if the 1927 drought was due to deforestation. I doubt whether deforestation was the main cause as periodic dry years are due to solar cyclio phenomena. But deforestation will surely and inevitably cause the climate to become drier even although progressive desiccation may be so gradual and slight as to pass unnoticed by an individual generation. Nor need the inhabitants of Buganda and the Western Province flatter themselves that they are secure from the enemy behind their barrage of lakes and swamps for the latter will slowly dry up or become silted up with wind-borne sand from the wildernesses of the north-east. The fight against the enemy is Uganda's fight, and if she fail the united efforts of all her rainmakers will not suffice to restore her former prosperity.

18.   I have prophesied tragedy if the enemy emerges victorious, but the further advance of the enemy can be checked and where the advance has already proceeded too far the enemy can probably be made to retreat. The defensive and offensive measures which I consider necessary are as follows:–

Proposed remedial measures against desiccation.

(a) Defensive. –

(1) The main line of defence against progressive desiccation from the north-east should be the broken line of hills represented by Mts. Debasien, Napak, Nakwai, Lobwor, Napono, Rom, Nangeya, and (westwards) Ngora. These hills are all covered* with savannah forest which is burnt over every year. There is plenty of regeneration present on the ground and if the forest growth can be successfully protected from fire the forests would revert to their original closed type. These hills should be demarcated and constituted into forest reserves and fire protective measures should be instituted. (*N.B.* – Adoption of this line as the primary line of defence involves abandoning the Karamojan salient to the enemy. The reason for these tactics is that I have not been able to examine most of this salient and also from what I have seen of the edaphic conditions I am doubtful whether any action taken in Karamoja will materially affect climatic conditions in the rest of Uganda. The Karamojan problem requires separate investigation in conjunction with that of neighbouring Turkana). /

(2) Should the main line of defence prove inadequate it may be advisable to attempt to link up the hills, by establishing a continuous belt of forest. Such a measure would be expensive and should not be attempted unless meteorological or other observations prove that such action is required.

(3) Behind the main line of defence all scattered blocks of savannah or closed forest whose reservation is likely to have a beneficial effect on climatic

---

*   Debasien and Nakwai from hearsay evidence only.

conditions should be demarcated and protected from fire. Such blocks occur in many districts, *e.g.,* Chua, West Nile, Teso, Lango, Busoga, Mubende, etc.

(4) Steps should be taken to demarcate and reserve the mountain forests of Elgon and Ruwenzori which are being steadily encroached on by cultivation.

(5) In the regions where desiccation is most to be feared, *e.g.,* most of the Eastern and Northern Provinces, tree planting by the local inhabitants must be actively encouraged (as it is at present in the Eastern Province). The vast numbers of trees which are being felled or burnt every year must be replaced by planting either in groups or rows and to achieve the best results active co-operation is required between the Agricultural and Forest Departments and local administrative officials.

(b) Offensive. –

(1) In regions where there is reason to believe that desiccation has already resulted from past deforestation an attempt should be made to ascertain how far re-afforestation will prove a remedial measure. It is proposed that experiments should be initiated in Ankole district in co-operation with the meteorological department. If successful, action should be taken on a larger scale so that the enemy can be made to retreat.

Lakeside forests not of climatic importance. 19.   In the preceding paragraphs I have dealt with the positive aspect of the problem of the effects of forests on rainfall. There is a negative aspect, as if under certain conditions forests exercise a positive effect on rainfall there are other conditions under which they can exercise no appreciable effect. These conditions in Uganda exist along the shores of Victoria Nyanza and Lake Kioga. Any climatic effect which the lake-side forests may exercise is in my opinion negligible as the influence of such forests is completely dwarfed by that of the lakes themselves. Hence from the climatic point of view it will not matter whether such forests are destroyed or not and the question of their retention is one which must be decided on direct utilitarian grounds.

The influence of forests on water supply – General. 20.   We must now consider the third important respect in which forests exercise indirect effects and that is in connection with water supply. Until recently it was assumed that forests invariably increased the supply of water in streams and of underground water. Such assumptions have now been disproved to be of universal truth for the effect of forests on water supply depends on the character of the soil, subsoil and underlying rock, the nature of the rainfall, the slope of the land, and the composition of the forest. The reason why these factors operate are as follows:– Firstly, trees generally possess deep roots which obtain their moisture from strata lower than those from which other forms of vegetation obtain their moisture. They transpire enormous quantities of moisture into the air. If the amount of moisture so transpired exceeds the normal amount of evaporation on open ground then it is obvious that tree growth will lower the water level although the moisture of the surface soil in a forest is greater than on open ground. Secondly, certain highly fissured rocks such as some limestone formations (and possibly the Shimba grit capping the Shimba hills) are highly fissured and capable of acting as important water reservoirs. If they are penetrated by the roots of trees they will lose far more moisture than they would if covered with a shallow rooted vegetation. On the other hand the water capacity of certain types of rock is improved by the penetration of tree roots. Thirdly, the humus formed in forests tends to increase the moisture-absorbing capacity of the soil and, although on level ground this increased moisture capacity will not affect the run-off appreciably, on hill slopes it is of great importance as it / permits more rain to percolate into the soil and subsoil thereby at once reducing the extent of floods and causing the run-off to be more regular. Fourthly, it is obvious that the effect of forests on run-off must depend on the character of the rainfall in that where precipitations are light and frequent the water capacity of the soil will be of less importance than when the reverse is the case. Fifthly, the character of the forest vegetation which in itself is in part an expression of the soil factors has a great bearing on the subject. Avoiding the use of ecological terms which tend to become multitudinous and confusing (most ecologists seem to think fame depends on the number of new terms they can invent!) it may be said that on dry gravelly or sandy sites forests improve the water supply; on wet sites they reduce the water supply; while on intermediate sites they exercise little appreciable effect. This statement requires to be qualified, however, as certain trees, particularly exotics such as gums, black wattle, and to a lesser extent pines, are particularly exacting as regards their moisture requirements and in Africa on intermediate sites they would reduce the water supply. Indigenous trees are far less exacting in this respect.

21.   Consideration of the above factors will show that the whole problem of In Uganda. the effect of forests on water supply is an exceedingly complicated one. It is not one which admits of regional study but can only be studied in relation to particular individual localities. So far as Uganda is concerned I can only make a few general observations:–

(1) The rainfall in Uganda is not of a heavy monsoon type and forest cover cannot have the same influence on run-off as it would in a country of heavy precipitations such as India.

(2) The localities where forest cover has most influence on run-off is on the steeper mountain slopes of Elgon and Ruwenzori where destruction of cover is certain to have an adverse effect on the regularity of run-off.

(3) I had at one time thought it possible that forest protection or afforestation schemes in the north of Uganda might conduce to ensure a more regular supply of water in tributaries of the Nile. I am afraid this idea cannot be realized as except in times of flood there is an enormous loss of water in all the river beds I have seen by percolation underground.

(4) It is unlikely that forest destruction in the north-eastern districts has had any direct influence on the lowering of telluric waters. The influence has probably been indirect by causing a reduction in rainfall and humidity.

(5) We cannot tell what direct effects forest destruction in the past has had on water supply, but it is probable (a) that it has led to the formation of swamps, and (*b*) that it has caused a decreased supply of water in the mountain streams of Elgon and Ruwenzori, while it is possible (*c*) that it has led to a diminution of stream flow in the drier tracts such as W. Masaka and Ankole.

Limited action needed – swamp planting. 22.   From what has been written above it is clear that the effects of forests on water supply in Uganda are not such as are likely to have an important influence on general forest policy. It is only in the following respects that I think any action is at present indicated:–

(1) The steeper mountain slopes of Ruwenzori and Elgon must be conserved – a measure which has already been proposed in para. 18a (4) above.

(2) In the case of the afforestation schemes proposed in para. 18*b* (1) exacting exotics such as gums should be avoided if other equally suitable and less exacting species can be successfully introduced.

(3) Exacting exotics such as gums are likely to prove of great value for drying up swamps. I am certain that the headwaters of most swamps can be successfully planted up with gums without drainage channels. In lower areas drainage channels may or may not be necessary. The drying up of swamps is likely to confer great benefits from the point of view of public health. Further, if by planting gums the lower reaches / of swamp rivers can be confined within definite channels the consequences may be of far reaching importance as the extent of navigable water-ways may be improved, and the outflow into the Nile increased. At the same time any increase in run-off may involve a decrease in evaporation and consequently rainfall. It depends on whether the increase in run-off will be counterbalanced by the absorption and transpiration of subsoil waters which are at present not evaporated. The whole problem is one of exceedingly great importance which should be tackled by the Forest Department in co-operation with the meteorological department and a hydrological engineer.

(B) The Direct Utility of Uganda's Forests.

23.   The direct utility of the forests of Uganda is a problem which has to be investigated with reference not to the present but to the future. Forests take decades or centuries to mature and national forest policies must be based on a far-sighted statesmanlike appreciation of the requirements of the future. There are no figures available showing the present consumption of forest produce in Uganda, but we do know that Uganda is at present more or less self-supporting as regards forest produce. The question is, are her existing forests sufficient to meet the demands which are likely to be made on them in the future? It is a difficult question to answer. We do not know whether Uganda will remain essentially an agricultural and pastoral country or whether she will become industrialised. The present indications are that industrialisation will proceed further than it is to-day. Again, we do not know whether wood fuel will continue to be the main source of power. Lastly, we do not know what the future domestic requirements of the population will amount to. In almost every country progress in civilisation has involved a progressive increase in the demand for wood and in its *per capita* consumption. Will history repeat itself in Uganda? At present the domestic forest requirements of the population are more or less limited to firewood and small poles. There is hardly any doubt but that the majority of the races of Uganda will gradually adopt a higher standard of living which will involve the consumption of far higher quantities of forest products, such as timber, poles, and bamboos, than are required to-day.

General problem of Uganda's requirements.

24.   Before discussing whether Uganda's forest resources are sufficient to meet the estimated needs of the future one must deal with the possible query 'how far is it necessary that Uganda's needs should be met from scientifically managed forests rather than from extensively planted individual trees or from trees growing wild?' In reply, one may say that no country whose development is at all extensive can possibly depend on wild products and trees must be cultivated in the same way as food crops. The question narrows itself down, therefore, to whether individual tree planting will suffice. Where timber is required in large quantities for commercial purposes there is no doubt at all that it should be grown in properly managed forests as economic exploitation on a big scale necessitates exploitation of concentrated areas, and to grow timber of the best quality trees must be concentrated and scientifically treated. Uganda must therefore have definite forests from which commercial, municipal and state requirements can be met. Domestic requirements are in a different category. The native peoples of Uganda can at present obtain most of the forest produce they require from individual trees scattered outside the main defined forest areas, and there is no doubt that if they are encouraged to plant trees on their shambas they will be able to continue to do so. I have already advocated (*vide* para. 18 (5)) that local inhabitants should

Are 'forests' necessary to meet Uganda's – requirements?

be encouraged to go in for tree planting in districts where desiccation is most to be feared, and I consider that this same policy may be worth applying even in humid areas where there is little existing danger from desiccation. The people of Uganda are far more likely to adopt a higher standard of house construction and furnishing if they do not need to go far afield for the timber they require, and in any case it is inadvisable that they should not be able to obtain firewood and small poles near at hand. There is, however, another aspect to the problem. The more intensive the settlement and cultivation of the land the more likely it is that it will pay to concentrate tree growth in definite forest areas, as has been found economically / advisable in other countries, such forest areas being situated if possible on land which is of minor agricultural value. Further in the future when the people enjoy greater political freedom it may not be possible to enforce tree planting and tree preservation. In these circumstances while I think that tree planting should be actively encouraged under present day conditions, I at the same time think that it should not be assumed that individual tree planting will meet all the needs of the future but provision should be made for safeguarding such forest areas as are likely to possess a utilitarian value in the future, and in treeless tracts for establishing centrally situated plantations.

Per capita requirements of population.

25.   In estimating the future forest needs of the population of Uganda statistical computations become rather unavoidable. The estimated annual *per capita* consumption of wood in cubic feet varies greatly in different countries as the following figures indicate:– Great Britain 12, Germany 40, U.S.A. 100 to 250, New Zealand 66, Canada 200, and India 1–5. (The last figure is decidedly an underestimate – in my last district in India the consumption was at least 12 cubic feet). The principal reason for the remarkable range in the above figures is that the consumption of timber and fuel is naturally far greater where timber and fuel are abundant, accessible, and cheap.

In calculating the future forest requirements of Kenya Colony I divided the population into Europeans, Asiatics, and natives, and calculated their requirements separately. In Uganda it should suffice to lump all classes together and to estimate the future *per capita* consumption at 18 cubic feet per annum – which is the figure I adopted for the native populations of Kenya. It is further estimated, as in Kenya, that this amount of timber and fuel will be yielded by 0.15 acre. (In Germany the average yield of intensively managed forests is 60 c. ft. per annum but in Kenya and Uganda the average yield should be about 120 c. ft. per annum). The figure of 18 c. ft. applies to demands on proper forests. The total demand, which will include timber required by Europeans and industrial enterprises and for the general development of the country, is quite likely to exceed an average *per capita* consumption of 18 c. ft. but it is assumed that such excess will be balanced by the extra forest production of timber and fuel by the natives themselves. Now to get at the total forest area requirements one must multiply the figure of 0.15 acre not by the present but by the estimated future population. This introduces a further doubtful factor, but if one has any faith in the future development and prosperity of Uganda one cannot estimate her future population below 12,000,000 people. This gives us an estimated required forest area of 1,800,000 acres equivalent to about 3.5 per cent of the land area of the Protectorate. This percentage falls far below that considered as essential in European countries, but as has been stated in the introduction, statistical comparisons are misleading.

26. The figure of 1,800,000 acres which has been arrived at in the preceding paragraphs by a series of doubtful calculations is not intended to constitute the basis of any forest policy but merely to be a rough guide in estimating whether the areas of forest in Uganda will suffice to meet the future needs of the country. On page 5 of his Report on Forestry in Uganda Professor Troup estimates the area of Crown timber forests, exclusive of savannah and bush forests, to be 2,043 square miles or approximately 1,300,000 acres. This figure was a very rough estimate, but no new data are available which enable one to improve on it. In my opinion he has overestimated the areas of several forests. However, if we accept this figure as a comparative basis we find that we are 500,000 acres short of the estimated area required. From what I have seen of the savannah forests which on climatic grounds should be reserved (*vide* para. 18*a* (1) and (3)) I am of the opinion that their reservation and protection will contribute at least a further 300,000 to 400,000 acres of forests, in addition to which some native-owned forests may survive. Hence, as far as one can foresee there are no grounds for alarm regarding any serious shortage of forest in the future, although the productive capacity of many of the forest areas, particularly the savannah types, will have to be greatly increased by scientific management before they will yield any figure approaching 120 cubic feet per annum. /

Sufficiency of forest in area to meet future demands.

27. In the preceding paragraph we have considered sufficiency of forest areas on an 'area' basis but the equable distribution of forests is a factor of equal importance. Forest produce is bulky and expensive to transport and for forest areas to meet the requirements of the population they should be so distributed over the country as to enable the peoples thereof to obtain their requirements as conveniently and cheaply as possible. In this respect the existing forest areas fail as their distribution is uneven. Certain forests, *e.g.,* Ruwenzori, Semliki, West Ankole, Kabale, and the greater part of Kibale, and Mt. Elgon, are so inconveniently or inaccessibly situated that they are at present of no use for commercial exploitation and they can never serve more than a very small percentage of Uganda's population's domestic needs. The area of these inaccessible forests is nearly 1,000,000 acres. This means that when these forests become workable through an extension of communications there will be a surplus of timber available from

Insufficiency of forest in distribution to meet future demands.

them which Uganda will not want, while there will be a shortage of fuel, poles, and possibly timber for domestic consumption elsewhere. The extent of the deficiency of forest areas on a 'distribution' basis may be summarised as follows:–

(1) *State, Municipal, and Commercial Timber Requirements.* – The accessible forests which are or can be worked to meet these requirements are Minzira, Budongo, N. Kibale, W. Elgon, Mabira, and part of the lake shore belt. These forests can conveniently meet all existing State and commercial needs and yield a surplus for export. Certain townships, *e.g.*, Mbarara, Lira, and Kitgum, are somewhat remotely situated from timber supplies, but their present consumption is so small that the matter is of small account. As the number of accessible forests will increase as communications are extended or improved it may be assumed that so far as timber requirements are concerned the distribution of forests will remain sufficiently satisfactory.

(2) *Municipal and Commercial Fuel and Pole Requirements.* – Fuel and poles being of less value than timber cannot stand the same lead to markets. The present position is not satisfactory and in the future it will be less so. Townships which are now, or are soon likely to be, short of fuel and poles are: Kabale, Mbarara, Tororo, Kampala, Soroti and Kitgum. Of industries, some cotton ginneries may be short of wood-fuel (I have no proper information on this point), while the tin mining industry in Ankole is undoubtedly suffering from a shortage of fuel and poles. The main concern which is suffering from an ever-growing shortage of fuel is, however, the Kenya – Uganda Railway and its auxiliary fleet.

(3) *Native Domestic Timber Requirements.* – These are at present small but where the demand is increasing, *e.g.*, in Buganda and Busoga, supplies are easily available. Except near the main forest areas there will be a shortage in most other districts as soon as the demand for good class timber commences to arise.

(4) *Native Domestic Fuel and Pole Requirements.* – Most districts are well off but there is a shortage in some localities, *e.g.*, Kigezi, Ankole and W. Masaka.

Possibilities of export – policy *re* excess forest areas.   28.   The above review of the extent of the direct utility of Uganda's forests has shown us that although in area they should suffice to meet future requirements, their distribution is such that in certain localities there is an excess of forest; in others a deficiency. The policy in respect of these excess and deficient areas has now to be considered. If the excess forest areas are not required for climatic reasons and cannot be profitably managed as commercial forests there is obviously no justification for retaining them under forest and they should be utilised for whatever other purpose they are economically most suitable. Now although the climatic importance of forests in Uganda has been stressed in preceding paragraphs there is little doubt but that parts of the excess forest areas could be deforested without materially affecting the climate. The main problem is: Can the excess areas be profitably developed as forests? Now hitherto it has been assumed that owing to Uganda's geographical position and / distance from the sea the contingency of being able to export timber was rather remote. It has been forgotten that in other continental countries, *e.g.*, N. America, Russia and India, timber has often to be railed distances greater than separate Uganda from the coast. It is true that timber freights on the Kenya and Uganda Railway are higher than in the three countries mentioned, but with the further development of Kenya and Uganda and the adoption of a fairer basis of railway freights the present freights on timber should be capable of considerable reduction. In England high-class hardwoods such as mahogany, satinwood, and teak fetch a price of £20 to £30 per ton against a price of about £6 only for softwoods. Uganda possesses high-class hardwoods some of which should fetch £20 per ton or more. In Kenya softwoods are put on the market at £8 a ton or less and this figure includes substantial royalties to the Forest Department. If in Uganda hardwood timbers can be marketed locally at about this figure there is available a sum of £12 or more per ton to cover their export to England. This latter figure would more than cover export costs from accessible forests at present rates. The probability is that valuable hardwoods from some forests can now be exported to England at a profit and with an extension of communications the areas of forest from which exports can be profitably made will increase. This opinion is not entirely a personal one as it is shared by one or two timber dealers with whom I have discussed the question. I consider, therefore, that so long as there is a contingency that excess forest areas can be profitably exploited for export it would be a mistake to deforest such areas and put them to other uses. At the same time where there are excess forest areas which for various reasons are unsuitable for concentrated management and commercial exploitation and which are not required for climatic reasons, *e.g.*, some of the lake-shore belt forests, the policy should be to surrender them for other land developments.

29.   As regards forest area deficiencies it is obvious that such deficiencies should be made up if the general welfare of the country is to be developed. Individual tree planting will help to make up the deficiencies but as has been pointed out in para. 24 such individual tree planting cannot be relied upon as a permanent solution of the problem of meeting forest produce requirements. Concentrated plantations will be necessary and the question to be decided is whether such plantations should be established by the central Government or by local native administrations, commercial enterprises, and municipalities (*i.e.*, townships). Now in Uganda the administration of townships is bound up with the central

Policy *re* deficiency forest areas.

Government so that it is unlikely that separate municipal action in respect of establishing plantations will ever be indicated as advisable. The main commercial enterprise which is suffering from a shortage of forest produce is the railway and its auxiliary fleet, but this again is a State enterprise and the assurance of supplies of fuel to the railway becomes a matter of State policy. The railway itself is not in a position to establish plantations for its own use as the establishment of such plantations and their working requires the technical skill of trained forest officers. Such plantations should therefore be established by the State Forest Department although, as more than one State is concerned in the operation of the railway, the latter may be required to assist in the financing of the establishment of the plantations. It remains to be considered how far local native administrations rather than the central Government should attempt to meet local shortages of fuel, poles and timber. Now of the areas mentioned in para. 27 (4) as being deficiency areas Ankole and W. Masaka are dry districts in which the establishment of plantations may not prove an easy matter. In such localities it will be best for the Forest Department to initiate the work, more especially as these areas are ones recommended in para. 18(*b*) (1) for afforestation schemes on climatic grounds. In other districts in which fuel, pole and small timber plantations may be necessary I consider that as a general rule they should be established by local administrations. The advantages of getting the latter to do the work are as follows:– Firstly, it is uneconomic for the Forest Department to establish and look after numerous small scattered plantations and it is small scattered plantations which will best meet local requirements. Secondly, outside the drier localities, except under special conditions, *e.g.*, swamps, plantation work does not require much technical skill. Thirdly, the work can be more cheaply carried out by local administrations and this cheapness should counterbalance / the possibly smaller efficiency of the work done. Fourthly, it is sound to encourage local administrations to take an active interest in forest creation and preservation.

Summary of proposed forest utilitarian measures.
30.   The measures which are considered advisable from the forest utilitarian aspect may be summarised as follows:–

(1) Individual tree planting by the natives should be encouraged especially in districts where such planting will have beneficial climatic effects.

(2) The 'excess' forest areas which are not of climatic importance and which are incapable of profitable commercial development should be given up.

(3) The remainder of the 'excess' forest areas should at present be reserved for exploitation for timber export purposes.

(4) Provided suitable financial assistance or guarantees are given by the Railway, fuel plantations should be established by the central Government wherever necessary. Such plantations should as far as possible be situated in localities where they will have a beneficial effect on climate or water

supply, *e.g.*, swamps. Wherever possible they should be combined with (5) below to reduce overhead supervision costs.

(5) Township fuel and pole plantations should be established by the central Government wherever necessary. As far as possible they too should be situated in localities where they will have a beneficial effect on climate or water supply.

(6) Fuel and pole plantations to meet local domestic requirements should be established by the central Government in the drier districts, *e.g.*, Ankole and West Masaka. This recommendation coincides with that made in para 18 (b) (1).

(7) Lukiko plantations should be encouraged in all other districts in which shortage of fuel and poles is impending.

(C) NATIVE RIGHTS AND NATIVE FORESTS.

31.   The subject of native rights to forest produce has already been dealt with in my Memo No. U. 31/1 of the 20th October last, and as the question is still *sub judice* little more need here be said. In the past the Forest Department has admitted as few rights as possible and it cannot altogether be blamed for this attitude as every shilling raised in taxation of forest produce meant a shilling more for forest development. It is the tendency to regard the Forest Department primarily as a commercial money-making department which is responsible for this attitude. It must not be forgotten that in all countries Forest Departments are only *quasi*-commercial. They have protective and other duties to perform which need not bring in any revenue at all. If this point of view is fully realised and if the Forest Department is not stinted of funds for necessary developments because its expenditure exceeds its income the question of native payment for forest produce ceases to be a matter of departmental concern but becomes purely a matter of State policy. *[Native rights to forest produce.]*

32.   The future of native owned forests in the Buganda Kingdom was fully discussed by Professor Troup on page 10 of his Report on Forestry in Uganda. I am in general agreement with his views. The main points are that, as far as I know, none of the native forests are of essential climatic importance nor are they essential from the point of view of meeting State and commercial demands for timber. They are of purely local utilitarian importance and as such there is no reason why the central Government should intervene in their management. Further in some cases, as in the case of some of the Crown lake shore forests, it is quite possible that the land could be put to better purpose if deforested. The central Government's policy should be to make the native owners realise the value of their forests so that they do not waste them, and to give such free advice as they may require. Further, as has been recommended by Professor Troup, it may be *[Native forest policy.]*

sound policy to encourage the owners to replace the present growth by fast / growing plantations of fuel and poles, but inasmuch as the natives of Buganda are steadily acquiring a taste for better houses and larger sized timber I would not advocate a universal adoption of this latter policy.

(D) THE FUNCTIONS OF THE FOREST DEPARTMENT.

General functions of Forest Department.

33.   In preceding paragraphs I have dealt with the policies which should underlie the treatment of forests on climatic or utilitarian grounds. It remains to be considered what the scope of the functions of the State Forest Department should be. The considerations which govern this subject are as follows:–

(1) It is essential that all forests, the reservation or establishment of which is necessary on climatic grounds, should be under the control of the central Government exercised through its Forest Department. Although some forest areas may be of only local climatic importance it is better that they should all be subject to the safeguards of State control. Control by the Forest Department does not, however, necessarily mean direct management by the Forest Department. The protection and management of small scattered blocks of forests by the Forest Department involves a relatively costly expenditure and wherever possible the aim should be to place such blocks of forests under the management of local native administrations subject to such regulations which the Forest Department may consider necessary to impose. In the case of such forests the functions of the Forest Department become supervisory only.

(2) All forest areas which are of commercial importance or direct utility to the State should be under the control and direct management of the Forest Department.

(3) All plantations established to meet township or commercial demands should be under the control and direct management of the Forest Department.

(4) The Forest Department should act in an advisory capacity in respect of all tree planting and Lukiko plantations schemes initiated to meet local domestic demands. This advisory aspect requires emphasis. The functions of a Forest Department should be no more confined to the direct exploitation or creation of forests than are those of an Agricultural Department to the creation or exploitation of field crops. A very great deal of work can be done in Uganda by the Forest Department in the way of improving the standards of tree planting and protection.

Summary of Forest Department's general policy.

34.   The general aims of the Forest Department's policy can be summarised as follows:–

(1) To retain under forests or afforest all areas of land the retention of which under forest is considered necessary on climatic or other indirect grounds.

(2) To meet with due regard to vested rights such of the demands of the population of Uganda as cannot be met by individual or local native administration efforts.

(3) To advise individuals and local native administrations in all matters appertaining to arboriculture or forestry.

(4) In so far as is consistent with the three preceding objects to manage the State forests of Uganda so that they will give the best financial returns on the capital invested.

[...]

PART II.
Forest Organisation and Development.

(A) FUTURE DEVELOPMENT PROGRAMME.

36. The development of the forest resources of a country should normally proceed on certain successive lines. The following statement / summarises the nature of such successive lines of development and the progress already achieved in Uganda:– *Progress already achieved in forest development.*

Item No.	Lines of development.	Progress already achieved.
1.	Selection of forest reserves	A few reserves have been selected by the Forest Department in conjunction with Land Office. Other reserves have been selected by Land Office. Large tracts of forest have not been selected at all.
2.	Demarcation of boundaries of forest reserves.	Reserves selected by Land Office have been temporarily demarcated. No permanent demarcation has been done.
3.	Initiation of forest protective measures.	No work done except the appointment of a protective staff to safeguard some of the forest areas.
4.	Legislative enactments to permit of the proper conservation of forest reserve.	A Forest Ordinance was drawn up in 1913.
5.	Preparation of forest maps	The outside boundaries of reserves selected by Land Office have been surveyed. Otherwise no work has been done.
6.	Investigation of the resources of forest reserves.	The Mabria, Budongo, Bugoma, Minziro, and Lake shore belt forests have been partly investigated.
7.	Initiation of forest research work, both silvicultural and economic, to permit of the best treatment and utilisation of forest resource.	A small amount of research work, mainly botanic, has been carried out.

8.	Preparation of working plans for all areas which can be exploited or require silvicultural treatment.	A rough working scheme has been drawn up for the Minziro forest. Otherwise no plans have been prepared.
9.	Exploitation of forest reserves	Actual area of forest being exploited is not known but main exploitation is at present confined to the Maule tracts and parts of the Minziro and Elgon forests. Other forests are being exploited spasmodically.
10.	Introduction of afforestation schemes for climatic or direct utility purpose.	Afforestation has been done on an insignificant scale in several localities.

The failure to conserve forests.

37.   The sequence of development which has been indicated above may be regarded as an ideal which can rarely be carried out as considerations of staff and finance will generally necessitate the omission of some of the preliminary steps of development. It is only through exploitation that revenue can be obtained from forests and in the absence of revenue few Governments will sanction the expenditure on forests which the initial lines of development necessitate. One therefore finds that exploitation precedes instead of succeeds most development steps. Such has been the case in Uganda and for this the Forest Department cannot be blamed. The Uganda Forest Department has achieved some sound work but I do not propose to waste time in bestowing faint encomiums as where the Forest Department has failed, and failed badly, has been in its omission to take proper steps to ensure forest conservation – its prime duty, as the very titles of its officers indicate. Forest selection and demarcation does not involve a relatively large expenditure and had half the money spent on various afforestation schemes been spent on such selection and demarcation the forest position in Uganda would have been far sounder than it is to-day. In the succeeding paragraph I will indicate what I consider should be done to remedy the deficiencies of the programme of the past.

Details of future programme of development.

38.   The future programme of development is best discussed under the heads detailed in para. 36.

(1) *Selection of Reserves.* – This work should be carried out as soon as possible. Reservation should be effected in accordance with the recommendations made in paras. 18 *(a)* (1), (3) and (4), the work being done as far as possible district by district. Rejection of forests already selected by the Land Office should be carried out in accordance with the proposal made in para. 30 (2).

(2) *Demarcation of Reserves.* – All reserves should be demarcated at the time of their selection with numbered boundary posts surrounded by cairns of stone or earth. Where special protective measures are not required against

fire (*see* (3) below) it may prove a sound plan to plant exotics such as gums along the boundaries so that the latter will be readily recognizable.

(3) *Protection of Reserves.* – Protection from man should be afforded by the appointment of such protective staff as may be necessary. The co-operation of administrative officers in ensuring such protection should / be obtained in all districts where no superior forest staff is stationed. Except in the immediate vicinity of the lake shore and in the case of some of the mountain forests fire protective measures will have to be initiated. I recommend that in the more humid tracts the forests should be surrounded with belts of bananas, while in the northern and eastern districts belts of heavy shade-bearing trees such as the mango and the jack fruit should be tried. I think that belts of such trees should stop grass fires very efficiently and they will also constitute a valuable food supply in times of famine. Pending the establishment of such belts fire protection will have to be effected by cleared and burnt lines.

(4) *Legislation.* – The present Ordinance is defective. I do not propose any immediate revision as in the event of any federation of the East African forest services it will be a sound plan to have one general East African Forest Ordinance under which local Governments could make regulations to suit local conditions.

(5) *Preparation of Forest Maps.* – Intensive forest management involves the preparation of topographical maps which in the case of the Uganda forests would be expensive to produce. As the future value of most of the forests from the timber export point of view is at present an uncertain factor I am not inclined to recommend any immediate heavy expenditure on surveys and maps. For the present it will suffice if boundary surveys are carried out *pari passu* with boundary demarcation and if, in the case of forests which are due to be exploited, internal features such as roads, rivers, and main peaks are surveyed by the Forest Department. I think this work can all be done by the executive staff but this opinion may require amendment later on.

(6) *Investigation of Forest Resources.* – This should be carried out in the case of all forests which seem capable of exploitation in the near future.

(7) *Research Work.* – I have already dealt with this subject in my letter No. U. 9/1 dated 15th March, 1928. I am more than ever convinced that as far as Uganda is concerned my proposal to establish a Central Forest Research Institute is sound. Uganda has got some magnificent forests the full development of which will be quite impossible without prior research work on the properties of the timbers they contain while on the silvicultural side a large field of research work is indicated. In particular afforestation problems require full investigation. If my proposal to estab-

lish a Central Institute is not adopted it will be necessary for Uganda to have one whole-time research officer.

(8) *Preparation of Working Plans.* – There are insufficient data on which to base intensive plans of management. The present aim should be to compile rough working schemes for all forests under exploitation and to prepare more detailed plans when data have been collected. The collection of such data will form part of the duties of the research branch. Working plans must not be neglected and in the future no forest should be regularly exploited except under an approved scheme of working.

(9) *Forest Exploitation.* – Forest exploitation must necessarily depend on demand. The three main areas which are likely to be exploitable in the near future in addition to the areas now under exploitation are the Mabira and Budongo forests and a forest area on west Elgon near Bubulu. The Mabira forest should be opened to working after the Jinja – Kampala line has been built. The west Elgon forest contains the softwood – podocarpus, and as the Minziro forest cannot produce all the podocarpus ordinarily in demand in Uganda the west Elgon area may constitute a second source worth exploiting. At my request the Conservator of Forests is having this forest investigated to see whether there is sufficient podocarpus therein to justify a saw milling concession. The Budongo forest is the finest in Uganda, but in view of the shortage in forest staff and the necessity for reorganisation I am opposed to opening up new areas in localities where there is at present no superior staff. The Budongo forest must wait. Apart from the main exploitable areas reference should be made to the fact that many other forest areas have to meet small local / demands for timber. Now the aim should be to concentrate exploitation to definite forest areas as indiscriminate felling of trees over large areas does not fit in with scientific management, but at the same time such concentration of work should be done with due regard to protection of the public, and care should be taken that the public are not unduly inconvenienced. Finally, in all main exploitation areas steps must be taken to secure the regeneration of the forest.

(10)*Afforestation.* – Afforestation proposals have been made in paras. 18 (*b*) (1) and 30 (4) (5) and (6). If accepted by Government work in connection therewith should be initiated as soon as possible, but care should be taken to concentrate the work where it can be properly supervised. This consideration will mean that work to begin with must be limited to definite localities. Definite proposals for work in 1929 and 1930 will be submitted later once a definite agreement has been arrived at with the Kenya and Uganda Railway. In the meantime one need not altogether waste time in districts where there is at present no superior forest staff. I consider that it would be an excellent plan to send a European forester, when available, round the district headquarters of districts where tree planting is of importance to start nurseries on efficient up-to-date lines. All the nursery work I have seen in Uganda is poor and the wastage of plants is great. Such nurseries would be looked after by the district administrative staff who would carry out experiments in tree planting. The results of such experiments would be of value to the Forest Department when the latter is ready to undertake the establishment of larger plantations. Further, the district nurseries would serve as models for Lukiko nurseries. This proposal is favoured by such district officials as I have consulted.

(B) The Organisation of the Forest Department.

39.   In paras. 33 and 41 of his Report on Forestry in Uganda Professor Troup recommended that four main territorial divisions should be constituted and that the administrative branch should comprise of the following cadre:–

Considerations governing constitution of territorial changes.

> 1 Conservator.
> 4 Divisional officers.
> 1 Research officer.
> <u>2</u> Assistants.
> 8
> <u>2</u> Leave reserve.
> Total 10

I am not in full agreement with Professor Troup's recommendations which have been mainly based on Indian practice. In India territorial divisions have to be of such a size that the divisional officers in charge can properly control the work of native range officers – the range being the executive unit of management. As work has become more intensive the tendency has been to increase the number of divisions and ranges and to reduce their territorial size. Now in Uganda, as in Kenya, conditions differ from those in India. Firstly, there is no indigenous class of men who can undertake the work done by Indian range officers. In their place European foresters have to be recruited, and these foresters are more capable and reliable than the average Indian range officer. Secondly, efficient clerks are more expensive in Uganda than in India. These differences in conditions require that divisions in Uganda should be larger than in India, for on the one hand if the subordinate officers in charge of executive units are more reliable the divisional forest officers can control a greater area; on the other hand, if clerks are expensive the number of divisional offices should be reduced to a minimum. Once the African can be trained to become a more efficient forest officer it will probably be possible to reduce the number of European foresters, but that time is not yet within sight. In the meantime, I consider that forest stations or ranges must be of such a

size that the forester in charge can directly supervise all important work going on
therein, and divisions must be of such a size that the divisional forest officer can
control / the work carried out by foresters economically. By economically I mean
that if the divisional forest officer has constantly to travel long distances to control
work going on it may prove cheaper to subdivide the divisions into two.

Strength of
required adminis-
trative cadre.

40.   On the above basis of constitution of territorial changes I recommend that
the cadre of the administrative branch should be as follows:–

> (a) *Divisional Officers.* – There are at present two territorial divisions with
> headquarters in Jinja and Kampala respectively. These two headquar-
> ters are far too close together, especially, as on the bridging of the Nile,
> Kampala will be brought nearer to Jinja by both rail and road. The Jinja
> headquarters are fairly convenient and there is no advantage in push-
> ing them further east. There is, however, a distinct advantage in pushing
> the Kampala headquarters further west, and I propose that they should
> be moved to Masaka or Mbarara – preferably to the latter place, as it is
> more central to all the forests and will be near to the afforestation work
> proposed in Part I. There seems to me no necessity for having an admin-
> istrative officer stationed in Kampala itself, as the issuing of petty forest
> produce permits could be done by a Forest Department clerk attached
> to the District Commissioner's office. In addition to these two divisions
> I consider the formation of a northern division is essential, for as has
> been pointed out in Part I the forests of the north and north-east are
> climatically of great importance. I propose that the headquarters of this
> northern division should be at Lira which is very central to the proposed
> divisional area. Apart from these three principal divisions I propose that
> Entebbe district should constitute a minor division under the direct
> control of the Conservator of Forests. This will not involve a special divi-
> sional forest officer so in reality I am proposing three divisions in place
> of the four recommended by Professor Troup. The details of the divisions
> may be summarised as follows:–

Name of Division.	Headquarters.	Territory.
Eastern	Jinja	Mengo, Busoga, Budama, Bugishu and Bugwere districts.
Western	Mbarara	Western Province and Masaka and Mubende districts.
Northern	Lira	Northern Province and Lango, Teso, and Karamoja districts.
Direction	Entebbe	Entebbe district and Sese islands.

> (b) *Assistant Officers.* – The greater part of the work which in India is done
> by assistant forest officers can in Uganda be done by European foresters.
> I consider it is only necessary to provide for one assistant who normally
> will be a new recruit. He will be given training both by being placed in

charge of a forester's station and by being attached to the Conservator's office where he can act as a personal assistant if required as such.

(c) *Research Officers.* – If a Central Research Institute is not established one research officer will be necessary. This officer in addition to ordinary research duties can be responsible for the collection of working plan data (*see* below) and he can also be employed if necessary as personal assistant to the Conservator of Forests when an assistant is not available. Should a Central Research Institute be established the research officer will be absorbed on its staff.

(d) *Working Plan Officers.* – In India working plans used to be prepared by divisional forest officers but the tendency now-a-days is to appoint special whole-time working plan officers as this procedure relieves the divisional officer of work which he generally has no time to perform properly, and it admits of working plans being prepared by specialists on the job. Professor Troup did not propose the appointment of any whole time working plan officers and I agree with him in this matter. Exploitation operations in Uganda are so limited in scope that for the present at any rate the divisional officer can spare a certain amount of time for preparing working plans, more especially as the areas for which plans are required / are limited to areas that can be exploited in the near future. The research officer or the Central Research Institute will be able to give advice and assistance to divisional officers on the preparation of working plans, and if the collection of field data is beyond the capacity of the divisional officer or his regular staff a whole-time European forester can be appointed for this work (as has been recently sanctioned in Kenya).

(e) *Total Administrative Branch.* – The total administrative cadre will therefore consist of the following:–

> 1 Conservator.
> 3 Divisional officers.
> 1 Research officer.
> <u>1</u> Assistant.
> 6
> <u>1</u> Leave reserve.
> 7

With the possible exception of the addition of a working plans officer I consider that a cadre of this strength will suffice for several years to come. At the same time I would like to emphasise the fact that the above staff is required as soon as possible as unless the present staff is augmented it will be impossible to carry out the proposed programme of forest development.

41. The necessity for forecasting staff requirements has been emphasised by the Secretary of State and agreed to by the Government of Uganda in their Despatch

Recruitment of administrative cadre.

No. 209 dated the 25th June, 1928. I have myself recommended that officers should be recruited at school leaving age three-and-a-half years in advance of the time they are required, and trained at one institution. I have unofficially learnt that my recommendations will be discussed by the Colonial Office and the matter need not be gone into further now. In the above mentioned despatch the Government of Uganda stated they required one Assistant Conservator in 1931. This will bring the total cadre up to five officers. To complete to the proposed strength I recommend that two officers should be obtained in 1932. Thereafter no further officers will be required for some years except in replacement of retirements or casualties.*

Strength of required cadre of European foresters.

42.   The required cadre of European foresters cannot be forecasted with accuracy as its strength will depend on exploitation and afforestation developments. Assuming that the Uganda Government will agree to sharing a forester with Kenya for the supervision of work in the Suam forests (*vide* proposals made in my letter No. U. 24/1 dated the 17th October, 1928) and omitting this post from the calculations of immediate needs I consider that the cadre required will be as follows:–

Division.	Headquarters.	Nature of main work.
	(1) REQUIRED	IMMEDIATELY.
Eastern	Near Iganga	Supervision of mvule plantations and railway fuel plantations near Tororo and Namasagali.
"	Near Mabira forest	Supervision of work in Mabira forest and of railway fuel and township fuel plantations, towards Kampala.
Western	Katera	Supervision of exploitation and afforestation work in Minziro, and of afforestation work near Mbarara.
Northern	Lira and Soroti	Two foresters will be required to demarcate and protect the extensive areas of forest in the north and east of Uganda and to supervise township plantations and railway and steamer fuel plantations established north of Lake Kioga.
	(2) LIKELY TO BE REQUIRED IN ABOUT FOUR YEARS TIME.	
Eastern	Bubulu	Supervision of work on Mt. Elgon including exploitation of softwood areas near Bubulu and Suam forest area (Kenya forester's services will probably not be available beyond three or four years).
Northern	Near Budongo forest	Supervision of work in Budongo forest and of fuel plantations down the Nile.
Direction	Entebbe	One forester as assistant to Research Officer.
"	"	One forester as an Assistant Working Plans Officer. /

---

*   The recent death of one Forest Officer has involved a further vacancy which should be filled in 1933.

On the above basis the number of foresters required works out as follows:–

(1) Immediately:–

	5 foresters.
	1 leave reserve.
TOTAL	6 foresters.

(2) Likely to be required in about four years' time:–

	9 foresters.
	2 leave reserve.
TOTAL	11 foresters.

43. The recruitment of European foresters does not present the same difficulties as the recruitment of assistant conservators as generally they can be recruited at a few months' notice. At present there are two European foresters on the strength of the Forest Department and the appointment of a third forester during 1929 has been sanctioned. To complete to the proposed strength three more foresters are required and I recommend that if possible all three should be recruited during 1930.

Recruitment of European foresters.

44. I have not been into details regarding the required staff of native assistant foresters, but in view of the proposed appointments of European foresters it is unlikely that the staff of assistant foresters will have to be augmented appreciably. The assistant foresters as a class are inefficient and there is probably not one who could be entrusted with responsible work without adequate supervision. I am inclined to think that it may prove a sound plan to adopt the Kenya system of grading assistant foresters, into two grades. The first grade assistant foresters, who are on a higher scale of pay, comprise Arabs, Swahili, and Seychellese – principally the latter. They are far more responsible than the locally recruited native and do not require the constant supervision of European foresters or assistant conservators. The second grade foresters are locally recruited and they work directly under European foresters or assistant conservators. Such first grade assistant foresters would be useful in Uganda in certain circumstances. For instance, if a railway fuel plantation is established at Tororo it will be difficult for the European forester stationed at Iganga directly to supervise the planting work and in such a case a first grade assistant forester would fulfil requirements. A further instance would be the Suam forest area, as when the Kenya forester can no longer directly supervise work therein, a first grade assistant, working under him (or under a forester stationed at Bubulu), would meet the requirements of the case. However, I do not at present intend to make any definite recommendations on this subject until it is known exactly when and where railway and steamer fuel plantations are required.

Assistant foresters.

Practical training
of forest officers.

45.   Finally, I would refer to the question of the training of the staff. Assistant conservators and European foresters come out to Uganda fully trained but they have to acquire local practical experience before they can be considered fully efficient. Now in Uganda a heavy plantation programme is contemplated, as apart from railway, township, swamp, and climatic plantations all forest areas undergoing intensive exploitation will have to be planted up. In Uganda, except near Kampala where the work has been under a European forester, nursery and plantation work is of a low standard. Even near Kampala it falls below the Kenya standard. In Kenya they have been developing nursery and planting technique for over 20 years and under the efficient control of European foresters it has attained a high standard of excellence, higher in fact than anything I have seen in India. I consider that assistant conservators and European foresters would gain from a knowledge of Kenya methods and that they should be deputed there for brief periods of instruction. The best plan would be for such officers to stop a brief period in Kenya on their way back from leave or on first appointment as by doing so no expense worth considering will be incurred on their deputation. This recommendation is best considered separately for each individual officer. As regards assistant foresters they should at present receive all their training locally. I have already urged the necessity of / establishing a central training school in East Africa attached to Central Research Institute (*vide* para. 10 of my letter No. U. 9/1 dated 15-3-28) and pending consideration of my proposals the matter need now not be considered further.

(C) FOREST FINANCE.

Anticipation of
deficit on working
of Forest Depart-
ment.

46.   Consideration of the proposals made in this report must depend on the problem of finance, fundamental alike to governments and private individuals. It is impossible to estimate what the future expenditure and revenue of the Forest Department will be, but it may be taken as a certainty that for many years to come the expenditure will exceed the revenue if the requisite sums are spent on essential forest development schemes. The main reasons for this anticipated excess are as follows:–

(1) The native population of Uganda obtain their main forest produce requirements free and even if they are required to contribute to the cost of forest conservation their demands are always likely to be met at a net loss.

(2) A considerable staff will be required for purely protective duties the cost of which will not be covered by forest receipts.

(3) The Forest Department will have important advisory functions to perform for which no payments will be made.

(4) Exploitation operations are at present on too inconsiderable a scale to yield much revenue.

(5) A large amount of capital will have to be sunk in various afforestation schemes and on experimental research which will not bring in any immediate returns.

47.   There are one or two ways in which the financial burden of the central. Government in respect of the Forest Department may be alleviated. These are as follows:–

(1) As suggested in my letter No. U. 31/1 dated the 20th October, 1928, people enjoying rights to forest produce ought to contribute to the cost of forest protection either by free labour or by payments for forest produce obtained.

(2) As suggested in para. 29 the Kenya and Uganda Railway ought to give financial assistance in the case of all fuel plantations established for railway or steamer use.

(3) Wherever plantations are established by the Forest Department to meet the local domestic needs (*vide* para. 30 (6)) the possibility of assistance from local native administration funds should be considered. If the central Government establishes such plantations full fees to cover costs will have to be charged for all produce removed. Any financial assistance given by local native administrations could be passed on to the people in the shape of reduced fees.

(4) An extension of exploitation operations is not likely to alleviate the financial position at all appreciably as in most cases the revenue obtained will have to be put back in order to increase the future productive capacities of the forests exploited. Further, it is unlikely that the royalties on timber can be appreciably raised during the next few years. The case is different with firewood. In Uganda the firewood fees are Shs. 10/- per annum for a daily headload and Shs. 2/- per 100 cubic feet. In Kenya the firewood fees are based on the costs of production and they amount to Shs. 24/- per annum for a daily headload and Shs. 6/- per 100 cubic feet. The firewood fees in Uganda should undoubtedly be raised to about these latter figures. If this is done an appreciable additional revenue will be derived which will help to meet the cost of necessary capital developments.

48.   While on the subject of finance one must deal with what has been termed the 'vexed question' of payment for forest produce by Government departments. I look at the question primarily from this point of view. The Colonial Office Conference of 1926 agreed that in future Government departments should be required to pay in full for all forest produce required by / them. This being the

case it seems to me that it is less Government's duty to make out a case showing why produce should be paid for than it is to make out a case why Government departments should be exempted from paying, and in Uganda there seems to me to be no special circumstances warranting such exemption. I do not intend to go into the whole question in detail but simply to draw attention to one or two facts. In India the Forest Department is termed *quasi*-commercial for the reason that except in the case of forest produce supplied to right holders the aim is to grow forest produce with the maximum possible profit to the State and in order that the correct financial position of the Forest Department may be known all other departments are debited with the full costs of forest produce purchases. This same principle is followed in Kenya. It is exactly the principle which any big commercial firm would work on as it would debit each of its branches or departments with the cost of services rendered by another branch or department. In Uganda the system whereby Government departments obtain stores free of customs duty and reduced railway freights, and whereby they are not credited or debited with the cost of services rendered or enjoyed respectively, strikes me as wrong and uneconomic. In India the system of payment for services is adopted in the case of all departments and the result is that the departments are run with great economy. A further result is that the exact cost of each department to the State can be calculated with exactitude. I fully realise that in the pioneer stages of a country's development such intensive costing systems may not be neccessary and may even be disadvantageous, but surely Uganda has got beyond such stages and if so can a start towards a better costing system not be made in the case of one department? The opposition may say the proposal is one-sided in that the Forest Department will not be paying for services rendered them by other departments. Such an argument is unsound as the Forest Department is trying to start the ball of economy rolling and I would welcome other departments following suit and charging it for services rendered, even if the result were to show that the financial position of the Forest Department is less satisfactory than it now appears to be. In Kenya the system of charging other Government departments for forest produce was introduced in 1926 with the result that Government departments became far more economical in their use of forest products. In Uganda, as is inevitable when produce is obtained free, forest produce is wasted. Not only so, but the latitude given to Government departments and missions to help themselves has had the unfortunate consequence that other people, not entitled to free produce, have followed suit. I know, from information confidentially imparted, that many of the planters in Uganda obtain the timber they require free of charge and a case has recently occurred in which an important company* operating in Uganda was detected taking large quantities

---

*   Tanganyika Concessions Ltd.[6]

of timber free. Criminal, no doubt, but can the offenders be blamed when the general attitude of Government departments is to regard forest produce as one of nature's inexhaustible gifts? If in Kenya all Government departments and missions have to pay for forest produce required cannot the same procedure be adopted in Uganda?

49. There is one further aspect of the financial position which has to be referred to and that is the problem of the separation of capital and ordinary expenditure. Forests and forest land represent a capital asset but they are an asset which cannot be fully developed without the investment of further capital. The natural forest, or the forest which has been maltreated by man, does not produce the quantity of produce it could be made to produce under scientific management. In Kenya it has been calculated that on the average the forest could be made to produce at least five times what they are producing at present. In Uganda no data are available on which calculations can be based but without doubt the average productivity of the forests can be doubled or trebled. Expenditure incurred on maintaining a forest in its existing condition of productivity may be regarded as ordinary recurring expenditure but expenditure incurred on increasing its productivity and value should be regarded as capital expenditure. Further, all expenditure incurred on new plantations such as township or railway fuel is capital expenditure. The correct financial position of the Forest Department cannot be estimated until / some accounting system is evolved whereby capital and recurring expenditure can be separated. Such a separation is essential if owing to financial stringency it should become necessary to raise a forest loan. In India and in some Dependencies such as Australia, capital and ordinary expenditure is now separated and the results of the year's working are shown in profit and loss or trading accounts. I consider that the same accounting principles should be adopted in Kenya and Uganda but at the moment I am not prepared to make any definite recommendations on the subject as it requires a full knowledge and consideration of local conditions.

[margin note:] Separation of capital and ordinary expenditure.

Conclusion.

50. In the early stages of my enquiry into forest conditions I became rather pessimistic regarding the future of forestry in Uganda as it seemed to me that the rôle to be played by forestry and a Forest Department would remain, as in the past, an inconsiderable one. A fuller knowledge of local conditions, especially climatic conditions, has led me to change my views. It is true that forestry would fill a larger and more important place if as over much of India climatic conditions were sufficiently adverse to render the successful regeneration of forests and individual trees a problem requiring solution through technical skill, or if surplus forest produce not required by the indigenous population were

[margin note:] Conclusion.

easily exported and marketed. But, although such conditions do not prevail in Uganda, I hope that I have shown that forestry can and should play an important rôle in the life history of the Protectorate. Further, I have not attempted to claim for forestry functions which more properly lie within the sphere of other departments. There may be subsidiary lines of development which should fall to the Forest Department to carry out – the creation and tending of cinchona plantations is probably one for essentially silvicultural problems of spacing and treatment are involved – but it would be unsound to include such subsidiary hypothetical developments amongst the true foundations of any policy of forest development. We do not need to plan branch lines to justify main line construction. The Protectorate of Uganda has immense agricultural potentialities the full development of which can only be carried out with the assistance of the handmaid of agriculture – forestry. If the latter's lot be prostitution Uganda will become a sterile solitude.

J. W. NICHOLSON,
Forest Adviser.

W. G. Leckie, *The Growing of Wattle and Production of Wattle Bark in Kenya* (Nairobi: Government Printer, 1932).

COLONY AND PROTECTORATE OF KENYA

Department of Agriculture

The Growing of Wattle and Production of Wattle Bark in Kenya
BY
W. G. LECKIE,[1] B.Sc.
Agricultural Officer

BULLETIN No. 1 of 1932

[...]

INTRODUCTION

The wattle tree is of Australian origin and was introduced into South Africa in 1880 where the greatest development of the wattle-bark industry has taken place. Particularly is this so in Natal where conditions are favourable for the growing of wattle and in addition a ready market has been available for the stripped timber as pit props in the mines. This utilization of the timber is important as it gave a great stimulus to the industry. A return from one plantation in Natal showed that of the total receipts 56 per cent was obtained from the sale of bark, 33 per cent from pit props and 11 per cent from fuel. The industry has gradually extended and now many of the plantations are too far from railways for the selling of timber to the mines to be practicable. The mines also are using an increasingly large number of concrete props so that Natal is becoming faced with the same problem as Kenya, namely that of utilizing the timber.

Wattle is also grown in India but only to a limited extent, so that at present no surplus is produced for export.

Australia, too, though the home of the wattle, does not produce bark in sufficient quantities for its own requirements. This is accounted for by the fact that

Origin.

South Africa.

India.

Australia.

– 303 –

the readily accessible forests have been cut out and the cost of replanting these areas is too great owing to the high cost of labour.

Kenya. Wattle was introduced into Kenya in 1903 with a view to producing fuel for the Kenya and Uganda Railway. It was, however, found that the fuel burnt too quickly and its use was therefore unsatisfactory. The first shipment of ten tons of bark from Kenya was in 1910 and the industry showed signs of progressing until the high freights during the war made export unremunerative. In 1920 exports recommenced. /

Other tan barks. Practically all the materials with which wattle competes such as quebracho, valonia, oak, chestnut and hemlock are from wild sources. The readily accessible areas of quebracho are being steadily depleted and fresh areas will have to be planted. In this latter respect wattle has a marked advantage owing to its rapid growth.

Value of wattle bark. In the United States of America about 50 per cent of tanning materials used are from the locally grown chestnut and this supply is getting short so that the country will have to rely more on imported materials. The Tanners' Council of America point out that 'wattle bark's chief value lies in its quick penetration, good colour, capacity to blend with other tannins and tendency to dissolve insoluble tans.' Wattle is one of the most valuable and extensively employed of the tanning materials of the British Empire and is meeting with increasing popularity with British tanners.

Kenya bark. Although the cultural conditions for wattle in Kenya have proved more favourable than in Natal, trees reaching maturity about a year ahead of Natal, the industry is not so well developed and through bad harvesting and lack of grading the bark realizes lower prices in London, by Sh. 20 per ton or more. In an endeavour to improve the quality Government introduced rules under the Crop Production and Live-stock Ordinance, 1926 (Government Notice No. 726 of the 23rd December, 1930, and Government Notice No. 75 of 11th February, 1931). The application of these Rules has already effected an improvement, but the quality is still below that of other countries.

VARIETIES OF WATTLES

Four species have been imported into the Colony which are grown in other countries for the production of tanning barks, namely:–

Acacia mollissima, black wattle.
A. decurrens, green wattle.
A. dealbata, silver wattle.
A. pyonantha, golden wattle.

Black Wattle. – This species is the most extensively grown and in quality and quantity yields the best tan bark of all the wattles. The foliage is dark green and the leaflets (pinnules) are short and flat and closely crowded on the pinnæ [...]. The young shoots assume a golden tinge and the flowers when they first appear are yellow, later changing to pale cream. Trees flower from June onwards but / the main flowering is in October-December. Seeds pods are narrow and contracted between the seeds.

Acacia mollissima. Description.

The variety thrives in a fairly humid climate with a rainfall of from 30 to 60 inches. In the younger stages it is liable to damage by frost and should therefore not be planted in valleys where there is this danger. Germination of seed is difficult to obtain, necessitating burning or boiling.

Trees reach maturity in five to eight years giving an average yield of six to ten tons of green bark and twenty-eight tons of timber per acre. The dry bark for export should contain not more than 12 per cent of moisture and not less than 30 per cent of tannin.

Green Wattle. – This variety has been found in small plantations in the Limuru area but it is more commonly to be seen as single trees mixed through black wattle plantations. The foliage is a brighter green than that of black wattle and the pinnules are much longer and finer and not so closely crowded on the pinnæ. The tree has a feathery appearance and the flowers are golden yellow, appearing in July-September. Seed pods are longer and not so contracted between the seeds and are if anything narrower than those of black wattle. Green wattle appears to thrive under colder conditions and is said to be more resistant to insect attack. The bark strips easily at almost any time of the year, but it is thinner than that of black wattle and therefore gives a correspondingly lower yield of bark per acre. The tannin content is approximately the same as that of black wattle but the colour of the infusion is deeper, producing a darker tanned leather. This species grows well at elevations of 7,000 feet and over.

Acacia decurrens. Description.

Silver Wattle. – This species resembles black wattle very closely but the foliage has a bluish green tinge. The pinnules are slightly finer and are closely crowded on the pinnæ. The flowers are golden yellow appearing in profusion in June-August. The trees are most easily recognized by the seed pods which are of a brown glaucous colour and are very much broader and less contracted between the seeds than either of the previously described species. The bark is comparatively thin and of very inferior value for tanning purposes, containing only approximately half the tannin of black wattle. The colour of the infusion is dark. In view of the above and the fact that the species seeds and suckers readily. Government has forbidden its being grown in the Colony, *ride* Government Notice No. 726 of 23rd December. 1930.

Acacia dealbata.

Acacia pycnantha. *Golden Wattle.* – This species is grown mainly as an ornamental tree and is readily recognized by its entire silvery leaves, or lanceolate phyllodes, as opposed to the feathery foliage of the species already described. The flowers which / appear in May-July are yellow and larger than those of the other wattles. The seed pod is almost one inch in breadth and is comparatively slightly contracted between the seeds. The tree takes longer to mature and does not attain the size of black wattle; the bark is thin and so the aggregate yield is much less. The percentage of tannin is, however, usually higher, but the colour of the infusion is darker.

As golden wattle thrives on poorer soils and under much drier conditions than are required for black wattle it would appear to be well worth a trial in those parts of the Colony which are unsuitable for black wattle.

BLACK WATTLE – ACACIA MOLLISSIMA.

As black wattle is the main source of tannin and produces the best returns it is proposed to go into its cultivation and harvesting in Kenya in some detail.

Soil. This wattle prefers deep red chocolate soils with a rainfall of between 30 and 60 inches. With a rainfall under 30 inches the tree makes but slow growth and when over 60 inches the bark is apt to become lichen-clad, which is detrimental to quality.

Black wattle belongs to the family Leguminosæ and shares the family's faculty of fixing nitrogen. With this and the large amount of organic matter it adds Soil improver. to the soil, it may be counted as a valuable soil renovator. On account of this fact it is quite a usual custom with natives to plant their trees on worn-out arable land. After a period of five to seven years the humus content of the soil is considerably increased and together with the addition of nitrogen the land is again capable of supporting seasonal crops.

The establishment of wattle plantations may solve the problem of renovating worn-out maize lands which would otherwise require a prohibitively large expenditure to bring them back to a productive condition.

Preparation of the land for sowing. In thick bush country where there is little or no mat of grasses it is usual to establish plantations simply by clearing the bush and cultivating by hand small patches about 18 inches square and 6 feet apart, on which the seed is sown. In country where there is a mat of grasses it is wise to plough and harrow the land down to a good tilth. If the land is worked up clean during the dry months it saves much hand weeding later on and gives the seedlings a good start. Given the same conditions of soil and climate the latter method gives by far the better stand and trees reach maturity earlier. /

SEED.

Good seed is produced locally and can be purchased from estates having a permit from the Department of Agriculture.

Black wattle seed on account of its very hard coat needs special treatment before sowing. If mature seed is sown in the usual way it may remain lying in the ground for many years. Seed should be immersed in water which has been brought to the boiling point and left in the water until cool. It is ready for planting when the seed is soft enough to be easily dented by the finger nail and should be planted immediately. In order to make planting easier, seed may be mixed with sand or soil until dry enough to handle.

Seed treatment.

SOWING.

The operation is best carried out during the long rains when the soil is thoroughly moist. After the seed has been treated as prescribed above, it may be broadcast at the rate of 6 to 10 lb. per acre, drilled in rows 3 to 12 feet apart or sown at stake at the rate of 1 to 2 lb. per acre. The last method is cheapest in seed and entails least thinning later on and is therefore to be generally recommended. The area is laid out in rows 6 feet apart and six to twelve seeds are sown at intervals of 3 to 6 feet apart in the rows and buried to a depth of not more than half an inch. Germination should take place in seven to ten days.

Broadcast.
Drills.
Sown at stake.

The amount of seed required varies naturally with the condition of the land and method of sowing. The less seed the less the thinning; on the other hand, it is easier to thin than to resow. One must also bear in mind that the wider the spacing of plants the more cultivation will be required to keep the land clean until a canopy is formed.

Taking everything into consideration the spacing recommended is 6 feet by 6 feet with subsequent thinning to 6 feet by 12 feet.

Spacing.

CULTIVATION.

As a rule two cultivations are necessary during the first year in order to keep the land moderately clean. If for reasons of economy, it is impossible to hoe the land, weed growth will have to be cut by hand, as otherwise the young trees will be overgrown. On large plantations it is economical to cultivate by tractor, but tractor work is necessarily limited to plantations situated on reasonably level land. /

Two further cultivations are required during the second year from seed. At the end of this period and if the spacing has not been too wide, a canopy is formed and weed growth smothered.

A very troublesome weed, *Ipomœa* sp., belonging to the convolvulus family, which climbs up the trees and seriously affects their growth, is difficult to eradicate when once established.

Weeds.

THINNING.

First thinning. The first thinning should be carried out when the plants are about 12 inches high, leaving only the strongest plants in each hill.

Second thinning. The second thinning should be carried out at between 2 ½ and 3 ½ years from the time of sowing, resulting in a final stand spaced 12 feet by 6 feet. This wide spacing will be found to repay the loss of trees by the rapidly increased growth, making it economical to strip the trees at from five to six years old.

A fair market is obtained for the poles from this thinning, which are used as drop posts in fencing and in the erection of rough huts, etc.

STRIPPING.

Since the thickness of the bark, providing it has not become corky, is generally taken by the trade as a good indication of its maturity and market value, it is unwise to mix strippings from thinnings with bark from older trees. These strippings should be bagged separately and sold in one consignment.

Age. Trees are ready to strip at from five to eight years old depending on the climate and the cultural and thinning methods employed. As already mentioned, the thicker the bark the higher the tannin content, so that the bark near the foot of the tree is the most valuable. In order to obtain this bark horizontal cuts are made on the standing tree about three feet from the ground and the bark is stripped off from these cuts to the base. The trees are then felled and the branches are cut off leaving any of 2 ½ inches diameter and over.

The bark is then stripped from the whole tree and should be tied in bundles and carted off to the extract factory, if one exists in the area. The best returns are usually obtained from the sale of green bark, as on drying it loses approximately 48 per cent of its weight, so that a price of Sh. 45 per ton, / green bark is equal to about Sh. 90 dry bark. If the bark has to be railed to the factory it is essential to obtain wooden trucks as otherwise the bark sweats and is spoilt.

Stripping should be carried out immediately after the rains cease. If left too late the bark becomes difficult to strip and if carried out in the rains it is damaged by moisture.

DRYING.

This is the most important of all the operations as, if improperly carried out, the bark is worthless on the market. Heavy losses have been borne by exporters and others through bark reaching European markets in poor condition, the result of bad drying.

Rains in the dry- As soon as stripping is completed the green bark should be spread out in thin ing period. layers, preferably off the ground, or may be carted to the choppers, chopped into small pieces 1 ½ to 2 inches long and then spread out in thin layers to dry. Power-driven chaffcutters are used in chopping large quantities of bark. The time taken in drying naturally depends on the weather but usually about 15 days are necessary. Heavy rains during drying do a lot of damage to quality, but provided the bark is spread thinly, off the ground, showers will not do any material damage. The aim should be to produce a sample of uniform thickness, of a light colour on the inner surface and free from mould growth. When dry the bark should split between the fingers and should show a light-coloured fracture.

Too often bark is seen which has been stripped, dried, tied in bundles and left in heaps exposed to the weather for a number of months. These heaps get wet and the inside becomes heated and mildewed, while the bark on the outside is of such a dark colour that it can only be sold subject to arbitration. Producers must make sure of a market before beginning to strip and the bark should be dried and sold as quickly as possible unless suitable sheds for storage are available.   *Damaged bark.*

Bark which is mildewed and of a dark colour is worthless and if the Colony is to produce bark of similar quality to that of other countries, this must be avoided.   *Mildewed bark.*

On large estates it would be well to develop a mark for export which would soon be recognized by buyers. If such was done the bark would have to be roughly graded at stripping, the bark from the lower half of the trees being kept separate and when bagged marked 'A' or 1st Grade. The / 2nd Grade would come from the upper part of the tree and thicker branches, and the 3rd would be strippings from thinnings and discoloured bark.   *Grading.*

In districts where there is no dry season in which the drying of bark can be successfully carried out, it is necessary to erect drying sheds. These may have thatched or corrugated iron roofs and should be open at the sides. A large number of horizontal poles are slung from the rafters inside the shed, so that the strips of bark may be hung over these poles, or a system of overhead rails may be erected, so that the poles carrying the bark can be run in and out of the shed as weather permits. Under the latter system the bark dries much faster and smaller sheds are required to handle the same quantity of bark. When the bark is thoroughly dry, that is when it can be broken by the fingers, it may be bagged ready for export. By tamping the bark with poles, bags can be made to hold 140 to 150 lb. making fifteen to sixteen bags to the ton.

ROTATION.

If plantations are kept moderately clean, crops of wattle may be grown successfully for at least four rotations without manuring the land. In order to obtain a continuous supply of bark and firewood the plantations must be divided into five to seven blocks, blocks being cut out and regenerated each year in a rotation of five to seven years.

Regeneration.   Regeneration of plantations may be economically brought about by laying the branches and twigs, from the previous crop, in rows on the top of the old stumps, and burning them when sufficiently dry, immediately before the rains. After this has been done a good germination will be found to take place from seed dropped from the old trees in the lines of the burnt brush. A fair amount of thinning is required to keep the lines and proper spacing.

UTILIZATION OF TIMBER.

This presents the most serious obstacle to the economic development of wattle in the Colony. Up to the present, a local market has been found for the timber as firewood, but if the number of plantations is increased to any extent this market Buildings. will be flooded. Unfortunately wattle will not stand for more than six years when Fencing. placed in the ground, so that it is ruled out for any but very temporary buildings. Boxes. Charcoal. Thinnings and smaller trees may, however, be used as drop posts in fencing or for the rafters in huts. etc. The timber splits / when made into boxes unless holes are first drilled to take the nails. Fair quality charcoal may be produced, but here again the local market is limited.

The Imperial Institute has carried out numerous experiments with the wood and have reported as follows:–

Paper-making.   'Suitable for the cheaper grades of wrapping paper.

DESTRUCTIVE DISTILLATION

Charcoal	605 lb. per ton.
Acetate of Lime	139 " "
Wood Spirit	3.7 gallons per ton.
Tar	134 lb. per ton.

MANURIAL VALUE, WATTLE WOOD ASH

Matter Soluble in Water		Insoluble in Water	
	Per cent		*Per cent*
Potash K2O	6.98	Potash K2O	0.78
Soda Na2O	1.24	Phosphate P2O5	2.11
		Lime CaO	45.80

One hundred pounds of wattle wood ash would therefore equal about 30 lb. of muriate of potash. The phosphates are negligible from a manurial point of view. Owing to the lime and potash being principally in the form of carbonates the ash is particularly suited for applying to sour soils, but less suited to alkaline soils for the same reason.'

For plantations situated at some distance from a market, charcoal at Sh. 20 Charcoal. per ton would give the best return per acre, an acre of mature wattle yielding about 7 ½ tons of charcoal.

Destructive distillation would mean the formation of a company handling large quantities of timber and having sufficient capital to push the products of Distillation distillation on to the market.

PESTS.

Of late years some damage has been done, especially to young trees, by insect pests. The damage is probably due to the frog hopper which sucks the young shoots causing stunted growth resembling 'witches broom.' This stunted growth is most noticeable in February and March each year. The only treatment which can be recommended at present is the pruning of the affected shoots, but further investigations by / an entomologist are expected to be undertaken. Although the growth of the trees is checked by these pests, they quickly recover after the rains.

COST OF PRODUCTION.

The costs naturally vary greatly with the district and methods of cultivation employed. The following figures are only meant to give a rough guide to those intending to take up the growing of wattle:–

Expenditure per Acre	Sh. cts.	Receipts	Sh. cts.
1. Clearing Bush	5 00	Thinnings bark, 2 tons at Sh. 40	80 00
2. Ploughing and Harrowing	25 00	Thinnings poles, 800 at 3 cents	24 00
3. Seed	2 00	Mature bark, 4 tons at Sh. 55	220 00
4. Sowing at Stake	2 50	Timber as firewood, 28 tons at Sh. 5	140 00
5. Four cultivations	16 00		
6. Felling and stripping thinning	12 00		
7. Drying, chopping and bagging bark from thinnings	6 00		
8. Bags	16 00		
9. Felling and stripping main crop	24 00		
10. Drying, chopping and bagging bark	12 00		
11. Bags	32 00		
	Sh. 152 50		*Sh.* 464 00

This gives an annual return per acre on a six-year rotation of approximately Sh. 52. In future rotations the return would be higher owing to the economical method of regeneration described above.

When plantations are situated close to Native Reserves it is possible to have the felling and stripping carried out for the wood of three or four trees out of seven.

No capital value has been given for wattle land, as this must vary greatly according to its proximity to a railway and its amenity from a residential point of view. Suitable land may be purchased at from £3 to £10 per acre.

Green bark.   The price of green bark delivered to the factory has not been lower than Sh. 40 per ton during the past year. Considering that the loss on drying is approximately 48 per cent it will be obvious that a much better return is obtained from the sale of green bark, providing the factory is within reasonable distance of the plantation. /

Prices.   At the time of writing the price of fair average quality dry chopped bark is
Rail freight.   Sh. 100 per ton at Mombasa. From this must be taken the cost of transport to the railway and the cost of railing. The latter is Sh. 17/92 per ton in 10-ton lots, for export, on main lines. Local freights are 9 cents per ton mile.

Conclusion.

In considering the growing of wattle, one may expect a small annual return per acre little affected by periodic droughts and locust ravages. As already mentioned, tan barks with which wattle competes are from trees making much slower growth and therefore costing more to produce. Future prospects are therefore reasonably good, unless some non-vegetable tan is produced cheaply, other than that used in the chrometanning method.

A. Moloney, *West African Produce (Indigo &c.). Letters from His Excellency Sir Alfred Moloney, K.C.M.G (Governor of Lagos), to the Secretary of the Chamber* (Liverpool: Lee & Nightingale, 1890).

AFRICAN TRADE SECTION
OF
THE INCORPORATED
CHAMBER OF COMMERCE OF LIVERPOOL.[1]

WEST AFRICAN PRODUCE.
(INDIGO, &c.)

LETTERS
FROM HIS EXCELLENCY
SIR ALFRED MOLONEY,[2] K.C.M.G.
(GOVERNOR OF LAGOS),
TO THE
SECRETARY OF THE CHAMBER.
LIVERPOOL:
[...]

AFRICAN TRADE SECTION OF THE INCORPORATED CHAMBER OF COMMERCE.

ELMINA CHURCH ROAD,
RICHMOND, SURREY,
17th May, 1889.

DEAR MR. BARKER,

With a view to their full advertisement, I left in your charge at Liverpool some Museum Specimens of products of Yoruba, which I brought from Lagos last month.

I now hasten to give you a few particulars thereon. Please utilise my remarks as you think fit and best.

GUM.

Specimens about half cwt. each. These are really resins. Much inferior samples have been valued in England at £96 to £120 per ton. Trade has made a start at Lagos in this commodity – small consignments having realised from 40s. to 50s. per cwt.

There is room for a considerable development of this industry Yoruba abounds in the article.

The native name '*ogea*' is generally applied to gum, as is '*ibo*' to rubber.

The tree yielding this resin has been given by Professor Oliver,[3] of the Royal Gardens, Kew, as a *Daniellia*, and will probably prove a new species.

You have also with you two or three small samples of Gum I got at Benin; it is deeper in colour and somewhat different in smell from the Yoruba 'ogea.' /

RUBBER.

Rubber is in its infancy in the Colony of Lagos. We have there several *Landolphias*, which yield the best white rubber of commerce. In view of the success of this industry in the Gold Coast Colony within six years, Lagos bids fair to rival the sister colony before long.

Interesting experiments on the *Abba* juice have been made by Mr. Alvan Millson, Commissioner of Badagry, which were fully published in the Government *Gazette*; he deserves considerable credit for his efforts in the direction of promoting the economic botany of his district. This industry requires greater attention and persistent efforts put forth.

COCOANUT INDUSTRY.

Lagos offers a fair field for the establishment of an oil-crushing business, conducted on a small scale at first. The yield of foresent-bearing trees is sufficient; the yield in the future will be considerable. Cocoanuts can be there purchased *as they fall from the tree* at 2s. to 2s. 6d. per 100.

In connection with any Cocoanut Crushing business, an addition with profit might be made by associating with it the preparation of fibre, in which Yoruba is rich. As examples – *Coir:* You have some samples roughly prepared in the Lagos gaol; it has been divided in England into three samples, as is required by the trade, which have been valued respectively at £10 to £11 per ton, £18 to £19 per ton, and £29 to £31 per ton.

SANSIVIERA GUINEENSIS.[4]

The Yoruba name for this commodity is *'ojaikoka,'* which is generally indeed applied by Yorubas to *Sansiviera* fibre. West Africa is rich in species. I had some fibre roughly prepared in the gaol from the *Sansiviera Guineensis;* it unfortunately arrived damaged, and notwithstanding has been valued at £15 per ton. I am informed that if properly prepared, and carefully shipped, it should realise from £20 to £30 per ton. Samples are at Liverpool.

HONCKENYA FICIFOLIA (Tiliaceae).

This is a Jute-like fibre, and might be cultivated to any extent in Yoruba. Samples sent to England have been valued at £16 to £17; it compares favourably with Indian jute. The native name of this plant is *'bolobolo'* in Popo, and in Yoruba *'Agbonrin Ilasa.'*

You have also another Tiliaceous fibre, native name Toja, closely allied to the *bolobolo*, which has been valued at £17 to £18 per ton: this plant is capable of extensive growth and deserves attention. /

The vast of both these Tiliaceous plants is used generally all over Yoruba for rope and TIE-TIE.

Next you will notice a large bunch of grass-like fibre, composed of epidermal strips of the leaves of the *raphia vinifera*, or what is commonly called *bamboo*. In 1886 Messrs. Cross and Bevan, consulting chemists, London, called special attention to this yield, and said it should command a high price amongst gardeners and nurserymen, as did Madagascar *Rafia*. I left with you a bunch of West African *Rafia* dyed black.

The *white clay* (used for personal adornment – I should say disfigurement – in Yoruba) comes from Okeodan, behind Badagry, and may deserve attention.

Could it be put profitably to any use at home? The leguminous pods are seeds used medicinally by the natives.

There are also samples of camwood and barwood *(baphia nitida)* from Benin river, and a native mangle of country wood sent to me as ebony (?)

INDIGO.

Yoruba land is famous among West Africans for its blue dyeing: over it are found many botanical species that yield the Indigo of commerce. Some time back, through the courtesy of Kew, I had some specimens, prepared on the Niger, analysed. The report was that it was worth 4/- to 4/6 per lb. If prepared with care, it might compete with Bengal. A large field here offers for development.

In connection with what I write, Lagos (as do I) owes much indeed to the Director and authorities of Kew. I view the Royal gardens as the mother of botanic enterprise in our colonies; may the bond grow and endure; and may we continue to show proper filial affection and just appreciation.

In conclusion, allow me to acknowledge here your invariable kindness and courtesy on the occasion of my visits to Liverpool, and to say how indefatigable you always seemed to me in your exertions to promote the interests of the position you represent and so ably fill.

I am, Dear Mr. Barker,
Very faithfully yours,
ALFRED MOLONEY. /

AFRICAN TRADE SECTION OF THE INCORPORATED CHAMBER OF COMMERCE.

LAMARSH HOUSE,
RICHMOND HILL, S.W.,
3rd December, 1889.

DEAR MR. BARKER,

I referred in a letter I addressed to you a short time back to the indigo industry at Yoruba. For exhibit at Liverpool and such later disposal as may seem best for British and Negro interests, I now send specimens of that commodity which I had prepared at Lagos by a Nupe-man.[5]

In Western Africa this industry is, I may say, almost entirely confined to women, and is co-extensive with the cotton manufactured by the natives. Its range may be gauged when we remember the millions of cotton cloths that are there turned out annually, for home consumption and export, from the crude hand looms of the country. The cloth export in the direction of Brazil is of special interest and of growing importance; their use has become a fashion there, where such cloths are employed for decorative and other purposes.

The fashionable colour of native cloths is blue, from the dye to which I now invite attention. The special Commissioners who were sent into Yoruba in 1886 by the Government of Lagos saw repeatedly indigo under cultivation, and thus remarked upon its use in the town of Ibadan, the estimated population of which is 150,000:– 'Nearly all the people wearing blue cloths, the market-place was quite a study in blue.'

Within my own experience the industry proceeds extensively on the banks of the River Gambia, where indigo is called in Mandingo *karro*, and in Volof *n'gangha;* in Yoruba, where *elu* is given to it, and in Houssa where it is known as *suini, suni,* or *zuni,* and the plant as *baba.* I give the following translation of a saying in Houssa in explanation of the interest taken in this industry, Schön's 'Dictionary of Houssa Language':– 'The place where indigo is growing is good land; its leaves are small and its seeds are small, but when it is ripe it turns red, and its mouth is pointed; my country is full of indigo, and of cotton.'

Along the valley of the Niger we come across the pure precipitate – the only form in which it is of marketable value. On a sample, which contained unfortunately a good deal of earthy matter, I brought home some time ago, Dr. Hugo Müller, F.R.S., Foreign Secretary to the Chemical Society, reported that it was worth 4s. to 4s. 6d. per lb. It / must be remembered that the manufacture at best is a very crude preparation; but, if in the process such earthy matter can be excluded, the return would be greater – indeed it should compare favorably with Bengal indigo.

In the Gambia and in Yoruba we come across it in the form of balls of decomposed or fermented leaves of indigo plants generally mixed with cowdung, and of no commercial value in foreign markets.

Plants classified botanically under the genus *indigofera* are mainly confined to the Tropics, and are generously represented in West Tropical Africa, where we find of wide range under cultivation, also indeed wild, the species *I. tinctoria* and *I. anil* which chiefly yield the indigo of commerce; the former is much grown in the upper Gambia by the Mandingos and Volofs. Of this genus, only the growth of those species most productive and profitable need be encouraged.

In Oliver's 'Flora of Tropical Africa,' no less than 155 species are detailed, most of which are found in Western Africa. Repeatedly in my country rambles in Lagos I came across wild *I. anil.*

The Niger is not excluded from the world's vanity, for there indigo mixed with animal or vegetable butter is used as a dye for grey hair, antimony for colouring the eyelids, and *lali, Lawsonia alba* (henna) for the disfigurement of the toe and finger nails.

The process of extraction of indigo is as follows:– In an earthenware pot of a capacity of 15 gallons, an extract by soaking the leaves is made and fermentation allowed to follow when the liquid is poured off, and aerated so far as the rapid withdrawal and restoration from a height of 2 or 3 feet of a portion by means of a calabash or some other vessel will allow. Precipitation follows, and when all the dye matter *(fecula)* has sunk to the bottom of the pot the supernatant fluid is poured off. The precipitate in the form of powder is then mixed with a little gum and shaped into small balls, cones, &c., such as you find in the jar I send.

Dyeing process: A cloth is soaked in the extract, unaerated, and then freely exposed to the air to dry; the process is repeated until the depth of colour desired is reached. When stripes or other shade designs are desired, patterns are secured by stitching up for process of dyeing portions on which colours are to be lighter; such confined parts are less affected by the dye, and thus fancy is indulged in.

Of dye stuffs imported into the United Kingdom in 1888 I notice foreign countries supplied indigo to the value of £244,708, of which Central America took £200,034, whilst British Possessions gave us to the extent of £1,457,524, of which Bengal took £1,012,161, and Madras £394,503. From the supply markets Africa is excluded, and why? /

When we remember the interesting leather work, in various native colours, of Western Africa, we have proof of other valuable vegetable dyes there which demand attention. Again, the arnatto *(bira orellana)* of commercial value, grows luxuriantly in West Africa, and will soon be added to the exports, through Lagos, from that continent.

On such a wide and well established basis to work as I have here briefly sketched, surely there is room for further enterprise and hope in indigo, as an addition to our exports from West Africa, especially when so often so much comes from so little, for as an instance you know that from the bird lime of the Tchis of the Gold Coast, the coagulated juice of the landolphia and wild fig, there has resulted since 1882 a rubber industry of the value to that Colony of £244,177, or nearly a quarter of a million of money.

I hope in a few days to fulfil my promise to Liverpool, by sending off my contribution of Gambia and Yoruba, lepidoptera, to your interesting and valuable Natural History Museum.

> Allow me to remain, my dear Mr. Barker,
> Very faithfully yours,
> ALFRED MOLONEY.
> T. H. BARKER, Esq., Secretary,
> Incorporated Chamber of Commerce of Liverpool,
> Liverpool.
> [...]

Report of the Tobacco Advisory Committee, 1936 (Entebbe: Government Printer, 1936).

UGANDA PROTECTORATE.

Report of the Tobacco Advisory Committee, 1936.

ENTEBBE:
[...]

NOTE.

The [...] government is, generally speaking, in agreement with the recommendations of the Committee, but final decisions cannot be taken until the Report has been considered by the Secretary of State for the Colonies. /
[...]

History of the Industry.

5.   Although a tobacco expert was engaged by the Government in 1907, and although there is constant reference to tobacco experiments in the Annual Reports of the Department of Agriculture, the commencement of the native tobacco industry really dates from 1927 following upon a visit of Mr. Philpott to Nyasaland in 1925–26.

6.   On the recommendation of the Director of Agriculture this crop was purchased by Government at 30 cents and 20 cents per lb. for 1st and 2nd grade leaf respectively.

7.   In the United Kingdom market this tobacco was reported upon very favourably and it was sold for 1s, 8 ¾d. per lb. Consequently it was decided to increase the acreage to about 90 acres of varieties suitable for fire curing in the following year.

8.   Development so far had been based upon the possibilities for export although the Director of Agriculture was not overlooking the possibility

– 319 –

of developing a local cigarette and tobacco industry designed to replace the imported article. /

9.   It had been the intention for Government to purchase the two 1928 crops and to export the leaf. At the end of April, however, the British-American Tobacco Co., Ltd.,[1] became interested and made proposals to purchase the Bunyoro crops and to erect a cigarette and tobacco factory at Jinja. Both proposals were accepted by Government.

10.   In 1929 and 1930 two crops were grown each year in Bunyoro and the entire production was purchased by the British-American Tobacco Co., Ltd. From the middle of 1928 the Company had employed Mr. T. R. Hayes in Bunyoro who was of great assistance in fostering the growing of useful types of tobacco.

11.   In 1931 a spring crop only was grown and while the bulk of the crop was purchased by the British-American Tobacco Co., Ltd., a new feature was introduced in that local planters began to purchase small quantities of leaf.

12.   In 1932 and to date (August, 1936) a spring crop only has been grown in Bunyoro. In that year (1932) Messrs. Stafford and Margach purchased between them some 200,000 lbs. of leaf and on representations being made that an export business could not be built up on the basis of 30 cents and 20 cents being paid for the two grades of leaf, the prices for the entire crop were lowered to 27 and 17 cents per lb. respectively. In this year it became apparent that orderly development could not continue without control by legislation and the Native Produce Marketing Ordinance was passed for the purpose of regulating the marketing of tobacco and certain other crops grown by Africans. This system of control has remained without important modification.

13.   In addition to tobacco grown by Africans a few acres were grown by Europeans in 1927; the quantity increased in the next few years to a peak of about 400 acres and declined again to a negligible quantity in 1935. To-day the industry is based in Uganda entirely upon native agriculture.

14.   In 1931 experiments were conducted in the West Nile area in growing tobacco and continued in 1932 on a larger scale when some 30 acres were planted but without much success. In the following year some 20,000 lbs. were produced and this was increased to 159,000 lbs. in 1934 and reduced to 88,000 lbs. in 1935. On the whole, however, fair progress has been made in the West Nile area but progress has been more erratic and less substantial than in Bunyoro District.

15.   In 1934 a number of small cigarette and tobacco factories came into being, and as it was necessary to maintain close control from an excise duty point of view the Excise Duties Ordinance (1931) was amended so as to bring these factories within its scope.

16.   In terms of production of leaf the history of the native tobacco industry is as follows (*vide* Annual Reports Department of Agriculture for 1932 to 1935 inclusive and corrected to-date):–

			lbs.		Totals.
1927	Bunyoro 1st crop		1,631		
"		2nd crop failure	–	–	1,631
1928	Bunyoro 1st crop		5,377		
"		2nd crop	55,979	–	61,356
1929	Bunyoro 1st crop		89,316		
"		2nd crop	48,656	–	137,972
1930	Bunyoro 1st crop		112,919		
"		2nd crop	70,093	–	183,012
1931	Bunyoro 1st crop		367,041		
"		2nd crop	36,467	–	403,508
1932	Bunyoro 1st crop		622,166		
	West Nile		7,007	–	629,173
1933	Bunyoro		768,804		
	West Nile		21,421	–	790,225
1934	Bunyoro		1,469,142		
	West Nile		159,830	–	1,628,972
1935	Bunyoro		825,048		
	West Nile		88,821	–	913,869 /

17.   During the period of development prices paid to the growers have been as follows:–

	1st Grade. Bunyoro. Cents per lb.	West Nile. Cents per lb.	2nd Grade. Bunyoro. Cents per lb.	West Nile. Cents per lb.
1927	30	–	20	–
1928	30	–	20	–
1929	30	–	20	–
1930	30	–	20	–
1931	30	–	20	–
1932	27	20	17	10
1933	25	25	15	15
1934	26	25	16	15
1935	27	26	17	16

NOTE. – In 1927 there was an additional grade purchased at 25 cents per lb.

18.   In addition to the above prices licensed buyers have been required to pay the following cess charges:–

1927 – 1932 inclusive		Nil.
1933	Bunyoro	2 cents per lb.
1934	Bunyoro	2 cents per lb.
1935	Bunyoro and West Nile	3 cents per lb.

19.   Cigarette and tobacco factories holding a licence for 1936 under the Excise Duties Ordinance, 1931, are as follows:–

Name.	Date of first operation of factory.
The British-American Tobacco Co., Ltd., Jinja	November, 1928.
The East African Tobacco Co., Ltd., Kampala[2]	February, 1935.
The Nile Industrial & Tobacco Co., Ltd., Arua	November, 1933.
The Colonial Tobacco Co., Ltd., Kampala	November, 1933.
Messrs. Jamal Ramji & Co., Kampala	October, 1935.

The Present Position, its Difficulties and the Need for Re-organisation.

20.   The historical review has shown that the growth of this industry has been rapid. In less than ten years it has grown from nothing to the million pound stage and it will become apparent later in this report that practically two million pounds of leaf are now required to satisfy all demands. With such rapid growth difficulties of various kinds have made themselves apparent and the time has come to review the position and if possible to make suggestions for removing them. The main difficulties centre in the two points that there is not sufficient tobacco grown to meet all requirements and that the exporters of leaf cannot afford to pay as high prices for leaf as can the local manufacturers. The detailed discussion of these matters will be found in the following pages of this report.

The Local Industry Regarded as a Third Prop in the Economic Structure.

21.   One of the difficulties would be removed if it were decided to discourage exports and to provide tobacco only for the local manufacturers. It is necessary, therefore, to consider the implications involved.

22.   The local manufacturing industry has been built up behind customs barriers and high railway freight rates on the imported article and, without the customs barrier deliberately erected by the Governments concerned, it could not have come into being. In this process the Uganda Government as will be made clear in the discussion of customs and excise duties has lost substantial revenues, and in this way has contributed something like £115,000 toward the development of the industry. The position is changing as excise duty collections increase and from the point of view of cash receipts from the industry the Uganda Government now obtains an annual revenue at least approaching that obtained before the local industry commenced and this is at least reasonably satisfactory.

23.   From the point of view, however, of this manufacturing industry being a prop in the economic structure the position is not at all satisfactory. The industry caters almost entirely to the native trade and the native in Uganda / obtains his cash almost entirely from the sale of cotton or coffee. The outlook for coffee on the

world's markets is becoming more and more difficult; and while the cotton posi-tion in the world's markets has improved somewhat in recent years the position is by no means secure, and any country based upon a single crop runs the perpetual risk of unforeseen damage of the first order by some insect pest or plant disease. It is apparent that if things do go awry with either cotton or coffee there will be little cash wherewith to purchase cigarettes or tobacco and the industry would suffer in direct proportion to the damage done to the two cash producing crops.

24. The only possible method of converting the industry from a dependent one to a supporting one is to build up the export of cigarettes, tobacco and leaf to a volume which would enable the local industry as a whole – the growers are as directly concerned with this as exporters, manufacturers, and Government – to withstand the shock that would result from major or minor disasters to coffee or cotton.

25. While the views in this section have been put forward by the Chairman, the Committee sees no reason to disagree with them and accepts the view that it is necessary for all concerned to do everything possible toward developing the export side of the industry. There can be no possibility, however, of developing a large export of leaf because most markets are already over-supplied and develop-ment can only take place slowly and as opportunity may occur. From the prop point of view, however, exports of cigarettes and manufactured tobacco to such places as the Belgian Congo are as useful as exports of leaf to Europe.

26. In considering various proposals for re-organisation, therefore, the Com-mittee has had in mind that in the above sense and for the above reasons it is desirable to afford every possible assistance to the development of exports.

The Position in Regard to Customs and Excise Duties.

27. The following table shews the approximate revenues collected by the Uganda Government from customs and excise duties on cigarettes, manufac-tured and unmanufactured tobacco. The figures for 1927 to 1930 inclusive have been obtained by multiplying the poundage imported as shewn in the Annual Trade Report by the duty as shewn in the Blue Book for the appropriate year. This method involves an inaccuracy in 1930 as the rate of duty was changed on April 17th, and it was certain, therefore, that the figure given of £74,819 is too high. From 1932 onwards the information is taken from the analysis of customs and excise revenues published in the Annual Trade Report. The figures are not strictly comparable because they include duty on snuff and cigars; the amounts are very small, however, and may be safely ignored. While not absolutely accurate the table may be taken to reflect correctly the true position in regard to the collection of customs and excise duties from the commencement of the industry to date:–

		Lbs. Imported.	Duty. Sha.	Yield. £
1927	Cigarettes	74,380	2.00	7,438
	Manufactured Tobacco	496,324	2.00	49,632
	Unmanufactured Tobacco	940	0.50	23
	Total Revenue			£57,093
1928	Cigarettes	142,276	2.00	14,227
	Manufactured Tobacco	606,132	2.00	60,613
	Unmanufactured Tobacco	12,332	0.50	308
	Total Revenue			£75,148
1929	Cigarettes	131,429	2.00	13,142
	Manufactured Tobacco	664,078	2.00	66,407
	Unmanufactured Tobacco	70,719	0.50	1,767
	Total Revenue			£81,316 /
1930	Cigarettes	112,040	2.40	13,444
	Manufactured Tobacco	484,813	2.40	58,177
	Unmanufactured Tobacco	63,978	1.00	3,198
	Total Revenue			£74,819
1931	Cigarettes	91,158	2.40	10,938
	Manufactured Tobacco	546,616	2.40	65,593
	Unmanufactured Tobacco	65,631	1.00	3,281
	Total Revenue			£79,812
1932	Customs			59,673
	Excise 75 cents per lb. on cigarettes			5,491
	Excise 50 cents per lb. on other tobacco			
	Total Revenue			£65,164
1933	Customs			40,974
	Excise rate same as in 1932			11,654
	Total Revenue			£52,628
1934	Customs			23,024
	Excise rate same as in 1932	}		19,178
	Total Revenue			£42,202
1935	Customs			21,037
	Excise rate changed on June 27th to Shs. 1.25 per lb. on both cigarettes and other forms of tobacco			29,364
	Total Revenue			£50,401

28.　Customs revenues were increasing steadily between 1927 and 1929 and would in all probability have continued to do so had there been no local industry. In 1930 imports of manufactured tobacco and of cigarettes dropped with the rise of sales of the local article and thereafter there is a steady drop to the low water figure of 1935. In order to remedy the revenual position an excise duty was introduced in December, 1931, of 75 cents per lb. on cigarettes and of 50 cents per lb. on manufactured tobacco other than cigarettes. As the decline in revenue continued the excise duty was increased on 27th June, 1935, to Shs. 1.25 per lb. for both cigarettes and tobacco other than cigarettes, and on the same date the customs duty on both cigarettes and tobacco other than cigarettes was raised from Shs. 2.40

per lb. to Shs. 2.65 per lb. As these changes were made in the middle of the year the full effect of the new rates is not reflected in the final figure in the table for 1935.

29. It is impossible to say with any degree of accuracy what the Uganda Government has contributed in cash toward the development of the local industry. Had there been no local industry it is reasonably certain that customs revenues would have shown a steady increase from 1929 to 1935. Had there been no increase since 1929 and taking normal revenue at £80,000 the losses would have been as follows:–

				£
1930	Difference between actual revenue and £80,000			5,181
1931	do	do	do	188
1932	do	do	do	14,836
1933	do	do	do	27,372
1934	do	do	do	37,798
1935	do	do	do	29,599
Total Loss				£114,974 /

30. As a set-off against this substantial sum, customs duty has been paid on factory equipment, money is kept in circulation that would otherwise have gone out of the country, and natives in certain areas of the Protectorate have a crop that it pays them to grow.

31. Some members of the Committee expressed the view that the rate of excise duty was somewhat high. On the other hand it was felt that a small reduction could not be passed on to the consumer; that the Government revenual position was still well below the level of 1929; that the industry was at least able to carry on and even to expand at this level; that it had been given additional protection by raising the customs duty from Shs. 2.40 per lb. to Shs. 2.65 and that no changes could be recommended without going more carefully into the matter than had been possible in the time available to the Committee, particularly in view of the fact that other territories in the Customs Union were equally concerned. It was decided, therefore, to make no recommendation in regard to the rates of customs and excise duties.

32. Arising out of this discussion it was represented by the manufacturing Members of the Committee that the arrangements for collecting excise duties were not sufficiently proof against fraud. It is considered, therefore, that the attention of the Commissioner of Customs should be drawn to the position with a view to the arrangements being tightened up.

Crop Requirements.

33.   Without allowing any margin for the building up of stocks to enable manufacturers to carry on in a year of crop shortage and to enable them to blend one year's crop with another so as to minimise the effect of seasonal changes in the quality of the crop, the following is estimated to be the amount of tobacco required in 1937. This is given in pounds of bought wet weight, or in other words in terms of the leaf as purchased from the growers at the markets. For the purposes of this report it has been assumed that there is a loss in weight of 30% between the bought wet weight and the manufactured article:–

FIRE CURED LEAF.			*Lbs.* *(bought wet weight)*
Required in 1937 for the local East African market			1,000,000
Do	do	Congo market	1,00,000
Do	do	United Kingdom (Messrs. Stafford & Margach)	180,000
Do	do	United Kingdom (British-American Tobacco Co., Ltd.)	75,000
Do	do	expansion	200,000
		Total fire cured	1,555,000
AIR CURED LEAF			
Required in 1937 by Mr. Busby			250,000
Do	do	Messrs. Stafford & Margach	50,000
Do	do	The East African Tobacco Co., Ltd.	100,000
Do	do	The British-American Tobacco Co., Ltd.	50,000
do	do	for normal expansion	100,000
	Total air cured		550,000
	Total fire and air cured leaf required		2,105,000

34.   Reference to the table at paragraph 16 shews at once that production has not nearly reached the 2,000,000 lb. level and that it is necessary to increase production. Having come to this conclusion it was necessary to consider whether the required increases could be obtained in Bunyoro and the West Nile or whether it would be necessary to open up a new area elsewhere.

35.   The table at paragraph 16 also shows that tobacco growing in the West Nile District is still in an experimental stage and those field officers best able to judge are agreed that no rapid expansion can be anticipated. Moreover this district is now devoted almost entirely to the production of air cured leaf and cannot be expected to assist to any considerable degree in solving the fire cured leaf problem. /

36.   Bunyoro in 1934 produced the amount of fire cured leaf now required but this was a record crop much above the average. It is agreed that by giving such encouragement as the payment for total or nearly total damage by hail (referred to in the discussion of cess at paragraph 72), by keeping prices up as high as possible and by giving encouragement in numerous smaller ways, it may be possible to increase production slightly in Bunyoro. Those best qualified to judge are of opinion, however, that no great increase can be expected and the Committee accepts that view.

37.   It is necessary, therefore, to open up a new area somewhere in the Protectorate. Experimentally tobacco has been grown by the Agricultural Department in almost if not quite every possible area in the Protectorate. On experimental grounds and with due regard to the fuel situation Busoga, Lango and the Kagade corner of Mubende all have possibilities. The Chairman explained, however, that it had been the accepted policy so far to encourage the growing of tobacco in areas where other cash crops were difficult to grow and said he was very anxious if possible not to depart from this policy at least until tobacco supplies could be obtained in no other way. The Committee accepts this policy and because there is no satisfactory alternative crop recommends that an area in Ankole between Bushenyi and Kichwamba should be opened up experimentally. It was explained by the Chairman and noted with satisfaction by the Committee that an experiment was being conducted in this area at the present time in collaboration with Messrs. D. N. Stafford and the East African Tobacco Co., Ltd. The experiment is in connection with air cured leaf and may not be very satisfactory on account of the late arrival of seed from Nyasaland. If successful, however, and particularly if the natives concerned take to the crop it would be possible to grow up to 500,000 lbs. of fire cured leaf in the area which would meet requirements for the next few years.

38.   It was considered that a small market might be developed for flue cured leaf but on account of the difficulties of the process it was agreed that the leaf would have to be grown and cured by Planters.

39.   An experiment that gave quite good results was conducted by Mr. Philpott (Tobacco Officer) in 1927 but the matter had been carried no further. At the present time an experiment was being conducted by the Department in collaboration with Mr. D. N. Stafford. The Committee considered that such experiments should be continued at least until it became certain that there was no future for locally produced tobacco of this type.

The Present System of Marketing and its Difficulties.

(a) THE PRESENT SYSTEM EXPLAINED.

40.   Since 1932 the marketing of native grown tobacco has been done under the provisions of the Native Produce Marketing Ordinance by the issue of exclusive licences to selected individuals or firms in respect of a market or markets, the area selected for the encouragement of the crop having been gazetted as a declared area within which only licensees under the Ordinance have any legal rights to purchase tobacco leaf.

41.   By notice in the *Official Gazette* applications are invited each year well in advance of the planting season for tobacco requirements. At the end of the statutory time limit the Governor-in-Council then allocates exclusive buying rights at the various markets in such a way as to meet insofar as may be possible the quantity requirements of each applicant and with due regard to equity. Licences are then issued and the licensee is required to purchase at prices fixed by Government all the tobacco that can be described as grade 1 or 2 offered for sale at his market or markets.

42.   In practice the system worked reasonably well so long as there was sufficient tobacco to satisfy all requirements, and it has had the outstanding merit of ensuing an orderly growth in the size of the crop in that the crop under the system is virtually sold before it has been planted. It is perhaps due to the system that no unsold stocks of Uganda tobacco have accumulated in London or elsewhere and that no licensee so far has been unable to dispose of his purchase.
43.   While the system has much virtue in it, however, there are difficulties in working it which may now be described. /

(b) DIFFICULTIES DUE TO LACK OF TIME.

44.   Under the Ordinance as it stands prior approval is obtained each year from the Secretary of State to the limitation of licensees in the declared area or areas and while this is a routine matter it takes time and no steps can be taken until the approval has been obtained. The publication of notices of intention and of the allocation of areas is sometimes delayed because the *Gazette* is published only twice a month. There is a statutory delay of three months required after the notice of intention to issue licences has been published. The dates of Executive Council meetings may not fit in conveniently with the requirements of tobacco licensing. None of these causes of delay are of any great importance in themselves but taken together they have in practice created substantial difficulties.

(c) Difficulties of Government in Making Allocations.

45.   In recent years the demand has been greater than the supply. In respect of the present crop applications were made for 3,100,000 lbs. of leaf, whereas the actual crop was estimated to produce less than half this amount. To allocate on a *pro rata* basis would be commendably simple but would in fact have done grave injustice this year to established manufacturing firms who had applied for the amount of tobacco really required. If the allocations cannot be made equitably on a *pro rata* basis it becomes necessary to lay down principles upon which the allocations can be made. Among the applicants there are the established factories doing an expanding volume of business; the new factories that cannot gauge requirements on the basis of business done in past years; the exporter of leaf who has built up a connection that should not be broken, and the middleman.

(d) Difficulties of the Leaf Exporters.

46.   Under the existing system the price paid to growers for tobacco is based upon the local manufacturing industry and is substantially above Nyasaland prices which are based on the export market. Exporters can only hope to dispose of a high grade of leaf on the overseas market and must, therefore dispose of the balance locally. Only 25% of the leaf purchased can be exported under this system and in seasons – as in 1934 – when there is a plethora of tobacco the problem of disposing of the remaining 75% may become extremely difficult.

(e) Difficulties of the Local Manufacturers.

47.   So long as the local manufacturers can obtain adequate supplies of good leaf the present system works reasonably well in so far as they are concerned. If, however, a system were developed of exporting most of the top grade, which would amount to approximately 25% of the entire crop, then the local manufacturers would find themselves in difficulties because some of them at least consider that the top grade is required in the locally manufactured article. These manufacturers would object to purchasing rejects from the exporters.

Examination of a Pool System.

(a) Based on Tobacco Leaf.

48.   With a view to finding some plan under which the disabilities referred to above could be removed the Committee examined various systems the first of which was the leaf pool. Two full days, with a Sub-Committee at work in the intervening evening, were spent in an endeavour to work out a pool system designed to meet the somewhat peculiar conditions obtaining in Uganda. In

the end it was decided that such a system would be unworkable on account of the necessity for exporters to dispose of their non-exportable leaf locally, and because of the fear of local manufacturers that their purchase of such leaf would inevitably lower the standard of their products and ultimately affect sales.

(b) BASED ON AREAS.

49.   Having given up the idea of a tobacco pool with a single buying organisation, control of all conditioning and baling plants and control of the issue of tobacco to members, the Committee then considered a modification more like the existing system but operated under a separate Ordinance and based upon areas rather than upon tobacco. In the end it was decided that such a system would be unworkable for the same reason that a leaf pool would be unworkable. /

Examination of the Open Market System.

50.   The Committee understands that in Nyasaland the open market system with no price fixing is satisfactory. Messrs. Foster and Georgiades informed the Committee that to the best of their knowledge and belief the buying in those markets was done by four or five exporting firms or their agents and that because rubbish could not be exported buying was done carefully and with due regard to quality. In Uganda on the other hand such a system would open the door to hosts of irresponsible middlemen buyers whom it would be undesirable to introduce into the system. In Nyasaland also the native growers have now learned to grade quite well into two grades prior to offering their tobacco for sale whereas in Uganda this primary grading is far from being satisfactory, and buying in an open market would be far more difficult than in Nyasaland. In Nyasaland also, the price that can be paid is based upon the export market prices and with 15,000,000 lbs. or so of leaf to dispose of the price relation must be very close. In Uganda a higher price can be paid for the one and a half million lbs. or so used locally than can be paid for leaf to be exported, and under an open market system exporters would have great difficulty in obtaining leaf at a price at which business could be done.

51.   The Committee came to the conclusion, therefore, that it would be very unwise to apply the open market system to the purchase of tobacco leaf under Uganda conditions.

The Real Difficulty is the Position of the Exporters.

52.   An examination of various possible systems for re-organising buying and marketing arrangements has served to emphasise the fact that no system is likely to be successful that omits to take into consideration the peculiar position of the

leaf exporters whom Government up to a point is particularly anxious to encourage. It has become evident that the only solution is to place the leaf exporter on an equal footing with the Nyasaland exporter by enabling him to purchase the run of crop at comparable prices, and to export the lot without having to sell rejects locally to manufacturers who do not really want them.

Proposals in Regard to Exporters of Leaf.

53.   In order to remove one of the main difficulties and to give practical effect to the encouragement of exports, the Committee considers, therefore, that it would be in the best interests of all concerned to give a rebate of cess plus a bounty on exports of leaf equivalent to the difference between prices paid to growers in Nyasaland and Uganda. In 1935 the Nyasaland price in the Northern Province is understood to have been approximately 18 cents per lb. for the run of crop. In the same year Uganda prices were 27 and 17 cents or approximately 22 cents for the run of crop. In addition, buyers paid into revenue a cess of 3 cents making the average price paid for leaf 25 cents. After giving a rebate of the 3 cents cess on exports there would be an additional 4 cents to provide. On the crop exported in 1935 – 63,262 lbs. – this bounty of 4 cents would have amounted to £126 and such a sum could have been provided from the Cess Fund with no difficulty.

54.   In the event, however, as a result of a stimulus of this kind, of exports rising to half a million pounds the 4 cents bounty to be found would represent £1,000 and such a sum could not be found conveniently from the Cess Fund. In this event it might be necessary to reduce prices to the growers by a cent or even by two cents as it is now apparent that they have been set considerably above the economic level. It has been mentioned in the historical notes that the prices of 30 cents and 20 cents were set in respect of tobacco which sold in the overseas market from Is. 8 ¾d., whereas the present price is nearer 10d. for the run of crop. It has also been mentioned that the Uganda Government has sacrificed more than £100,000 in customs revenues in order to assist the local industry to stand on its own feet.

55.   If the prices to the growers were lowered to 26 cents and 16 cents, the bounty would be reduced to 3 cents per lb. and the cess fund, on the basis of a 3 cent cess, could provide the sum required to make exports economical up to 500,000 lbs. By reducing the prices to 25 cents and 15 cents, the bounty would amount to 2 cents only, and the cess fund could then provide for much larger exports. /

56.   As the proposed payment would be made by the industry itself it cannot be called a subsidy and is rather in the nature of a device for maintaining a rea-

sonable balance between the export and the local market, designed primarily to remove or lessen the inherent economic weakness of the industry as now developed.

57.   The Committee recommends that this system of cess rebate and bounty be adopted, if possible, in respect of the 1936 crop as the amount involved will be so small and that it be applied only in respect of exports of leaf to points beyond Kenya, Tanganyika and Zanzibar.

Proposals in Regard to Exports of Manufactured Tobacco.

58.   In order to remove the objection that the local tobacco industry is dependent on cotton and coffee, it is as desirable to encourage exports of manufactured products as to encourage those of leaf. Rebates of excise duty are already provided for in the Excise Duties Ordinance, 1931, and the Committee considers that partial rebate of cess should be made if possible in respect of cigarettes and tobacco made wholly from locally produced tobacco and exported to any country other than Kenya and Tanganyika Territory. The cess fund cannot be raided indefintely, however, and the manufacturers have received substantial encouragement from the low duty on imported leaf, the protective duty on tobacco and cigarettes and from the rebates of excise duty in respect of exports. The Committee feels, therefore, that the case is not nearly so strong for granting rebates of cess on manufactured products as on leaf, and consider that it should be granted only after noting the position of the cess fund and should be fixed to 1 cent per lb. in respect of 1936.

Railway Freight Rates.

59.   It is considered that the railway freight rate on tobacco leaf from Masindi Port to Kilindini Harbour is fair and reasonable, and that no change is required.

60.   An adjustment is required, however, in respect of the export rate on manufactured cigarettes and tobacco. At present, class 6 rate is charged in respect of exports via Mombasa while the very high rate of class 2 is charged in respect of exports via Butiaba. In view of the fact that 46,738 lbs. of locally manufactured cigarettes were exported to the Belgian Congo in 1935 it is evident that there are possibilities of developing a substantial business in this direction, and the Committee considers that class 6 rate should be applied in respect of locally manufactured tobacco for export irrespective of the port or station of exit.

The Allocation of Areas.

61. Without for the moment going into the question as to who should issue licences, it is extremely desirable at this stage when there is a crop shortage to recommend the broad principles on which allocations should be made. In suggesting principles it is realised that no section of the tobacco industry can be entirely satisfied until production increases so as to approximate the demands, and the industry recognises that production is being actively encouraged, and that the gap will of necessity have to be bridged by allocating the available areas in as fair and reasonable a manner as can be devised.

62. So long as there is a crop shortage the Committee considers the following principles to be fair and reasonable:–

(a) For manufacturers in Uganda already in business the allocation to be based on sales on which excise duty was paid during the previous year plus 10% for expansion and 15% for the accumulation of stocks to provide against irregularity of supplies.

(b) For manufacturers in Uganda who have not yet done any business 100,000 lbs. of leaf until such time as the crop shortage has been remedied.

(c) For established exporters the allocation to be based upon the maximum amount exported in any one year or upon actual contracts.

(d) The above three groups to be regarded as having prior and equal rights and in the event of the crop being insufficient to meet their requirements a *pro rata* reduction to be made all round. /

(e) In respect of any balance, nothing less than 100,000 lbs. to be allocated to any one applicant. Exporters to be given prior claims to middlemen selling leaf in the East African Territories and Zanzibar.

(f) When allocations have been arrived at on a poundage basis, the available markets to be allocated by the licensing authority in such a way that on the basis of average yields the applicants should obtain reasonably close to the poundage allocated.

Review of Position in Regard to Conditioning Plants.

63. There are three conditioning plants in Bunyoro and after inspecting them it was agreed that fullest possible use should be made of all three and that for the time being at any rate the Government plant at Masindi should continue to be operated by Government. It was agreed, therefore, to recommend that the three existing plants should all be permitted to condition and bale tobacco for the local market or for export.

64. It was represented by Mr. Busby that an additional plant was urgently required for the West Nile and it was agreed to recommend that arrangements should be made for its erection. The Committee holds no strong view as to whether the proposed plant should be erected by Government or by private enterprise. The Committee recommends that the question be gone into further by the Director of Agriculture and Mr. Busby.

65. It is considered that it would be unwise to permit unregulated development of conditioning plants, and that as from the date of the publication of this report no such plant be permitted unless licensed.

66. In regard to the Government factory it was considered that, as the establishment is very different from most Government buildings, it was desirable to insure and to take out a policy to cover any tobacco that might be involved in a fire in any part of the buildings. The Chairman explained that he had taken the matter up with Messrs. the British-American Tobacco Co., Ltd., and that in due course he hoped to be able to put a concrete proposal to Government.

67. In regard to the recent fire the Committee considered that as the building had not been insured because in the long run Government found it cheaper not to insure, it would be inappropriate to charge the cost of repairs against the cess fund and that the cost should be met by Government.

Review of Position in Regard to Tobacco Factories.

68. Licences to manufacture tobacco are taken out under the Excise Duties Ordinance, 1931, as amended in 1934, and the Governor-in-Council may limit the number of licensed factories for any good and sufficient reason. At the date of this report five factories are in operation and there is not sufficient tobacco to meet their requirements. In view of the crop position and of crop prospects, the Committee considers that no new licences should be granted for three years from the date of publication or issue of this report, and that the position should then be reviewed.

The Position in Regard to the Cess Fund.

69. The cess fund account to December 31st, 1935, as laid on the table of Legislative Council is attached as an appendix to this report. Of the £3,596 collected, £3,469 was collected in Bunyoro and £127 in the West Nile. Most of the expenditure from cess funds to date have been in respect of the Government conditioning factory at Masindi which was a service to the whole of the industry. The balance of the expenditure was spent in Bunyoro. For 1936, £75 has been authorised to be spent in Bunyoro and £50 in the West Nile.

70.   Members of the Committee expressed surprise at the rapidity with which the Government conditioning and baling plant at Masindi was being paid for, and noted that except for any improvements which might be made the buildings and equipment would be practically paid for during the current year. When that has been done there will be more available for services required by the industry.

71.   It has been recommended in this report at paragraphs 53 and 58 that full rebate of cess should be given in respect of leaf exported; that a partial rebate / should be given if possible in respect of manufactures exported, and that a bounty paid from the cess fund be given in respect of exports of leaf so as to relate the price paid by exporters to Nyasaland prices.

72.   It was represented to the Committee that growers were frequently discouraged by hail damage particularly when the damage was total or almost total, and that it would be much appreciated if compensation could be paid from the cess fund for this type of damage. On ascertaining that the total amount of damage of this type represented a very small proportion of the total crop and that the financial commitment was not likely to be a large one, it was agreed that compensation should be granted from cess funds for total or practically total damage by hail to native grown tobacco in the declared areas. It is recommended that the damage should be assessed by the District Commissioner as soon as possible after its occurrence and that payment be made by the District Commissioner at the end of the picking season. It is considered that the damage should be assessed on the basis of the average crop yield over the last five years and that for 1937 compensation be paid at the rate of 15 cents per lb. for total damage down to 10 cents per lb. for damage that might be somewhat less than total, and that in the event of funds being available, compensation be paid at the same rates in respect of the 1936 crop.

73.   A Factory Manager has been appointed this year at Masindi and it is intended that he shall spend part of the year supervising the growing and curing of the crop. The sum of £300 in respect of salary is being paid from cess and Government is providing quarters, motor mileage allowance and passage when due for leave which will amount to a sum estimated at £113 per annum. The Committee recommends that in future a proportion of this Officer's salary should be met from the charge made for conditioning and baling of tobacco at the factory.

74.   In view of the additional services now suggested the Committee is unable to recommend any change in the rate of cess. This is a matter that should be reviewed from time to time but the Committee see no early prospects of a reduction.

Grading of Leaf by Natives.

75.   The Chairman raised the question of the initial grading of tobacco leaf offered for sale and wondered if it was worth continuing. The Committee was informed that in Nyasaland where the growers had now had a long experience the system worked quite well and that the initial rough grading was of great assistance to the buyers. All members considered that sufficient improvement had been made to justify the continuation of the system.

76.   It was considered, however, that it would facilitate the sorting of the two grades to open the markets at first for the purchase of grade 1 only. The period in which grade 1 only could be bought would have to be varied by order of the District Commissioner according to the amount of tobacco available at each centre.

Control of Tobacco Development in Non-Declared Areas.

77.   Control of development has been limited so far to areas declared under the Native Produce Marketing Ordinance and it has been completely effective. It is possible, however, for a quantity of tobacco that cannot be estimated and of varieties that may not be desirable to be grown in non-declared areas. In the event of a substantial development along these lines it would become impossible to estimate with any degree of accuracy the quantity of tobacco required in the declared areas. It is considered, therefore, that legislative power should be taken to control and regulate and if necessary to limit this development by introducing a system under which growers in non-declared areas would be licensed.

78.   In order to make such legislation effective it would also be necessary to provide that tobacco factories licensed in Uganda under the Excise Duties Ordinance should be permitted to purchase only tobacco leaf imported, leaf grown in a declared area, or leaf grown under licence in a non-declared area.

Liaison Between the Industry and Government.

(a) TOBACCO ADVISORY BOARD.

79.   It is considered that the industry has now reached the stage at which it is desirable to set up a Tobacco Advisory Board along the lines of the Coffee / Board to advise Government from time to time on all matters connected with the growing and marketing of tobacco and with the welfare of the industry generally. At this stage a statutory body is not required, and as a safeguard to avoid friction and to make for amicable and smooth working it is felt that the Board should not be a licensing authority or assist in allocations further than to recom-

mend the basic principles upon which it considers allocations should be made. In the initial stages at least the Board would be an experiment, and in order for it to become a successful medium of liaison it is essential that its deliberations be conducted in the friendliest possible atmosphere, and that the number of personal axes capable of being ground be reduced to a minimum.

80.　It is recommended that the membership of the proposed Board should be the same as the *ad hoc* Committee now sitting together with Africans as members when in the opinion of the Provincial Commissioner any item or items on the agenda called for African representation.

(b) AN ADVISORY PRICE FIXING COMMITTEE.

81.　The ultimate authority for the fixing of prices to be paid to the growers for their leaf must be His Excellency the Governor. At the present time His Excellency is advised by the Director of Agriculture who has previously consulted the various sections of the industry and obtained a responsible opinion from London regarding the state of the overseas market. An Advisory Committee of three persons and Native Observers appointed by the Governor with the Director of Agriculture as Chairman and the other two members representing the manufacturers and exporters might be worth trying as an experiment. It may be observed, however, that the growers will naturally wish for higher prices, the exporters for lower prices, and that the manufacturers are not greatly concerned so long as customs and excise duties are adjusted from time to time to enable them to function satisfactorily. Whether a Committee representing these diverse interests, would be an improvement on the existing system may be open to question and on balance it is considered that the existing arrangements should stand and that the matter be reviewed from time to time by the proposed Tobacco Advisory Board. On first consideration the Committee now sitting came to the tentative conclusion that an advisory price fixing Committee should be set up. On re-consideration, however, it is felt that the time is not quite ripe for taking this step.

How Best to Give Legal Effect to the Major Proposals Contained in this Report.

82.　The Committee had considered the question of submitting a rough draft bill designed to give effect to the principal proposals in this report involving legislative sanction but came to the conclusion that the preparation of any legislation that might be required would better be left to Government after decision had been reached on the various recommendations.

83.　For reasons that have been set out it is felt that the existing system of granting licences for the purchase of tobacco leaf is unnecessarily cumbersome, and it is suggested either that the procedure as laid down in the Native Produce Marketing Ordinance be simplified or that tobacco matters be dealt with in a new ordinance on the lines of the Cotton Ordinance, 1926.

84.   In addition to the matters now dealt with in the Native Produce Marketing Ordinance it is desirable to provide:–

(*a*) for a preliminary season in which first grade tobacco only may be purchased at markets;

(*b*) for the licensing of tobacco growers outside the declared areas.

(*c*) for the control of purchases of tobacco leaf in respect of origin;

(*d*) for preventing the export of the leaf that might be described as rubbish unless appropriately marked; and

(*e*) for the licensing and control of tobacco conditioning and baling plants.

85.   New proposals are almost certain to arise in the course of drafting and no doubt the draft bill would be sent to the proposed Tobacco Advisory Board for comment prior to introduction in Legislative Council. /
       [...]

Conclusion [...].

87.   The main conclusion reached after the most careful examination of possible alternatives and after studying the legislative arrangements in force particularly in Nyasaland, Mauritius and Cyprus, is that no fundamental change is desirable in Uganda. The system that has been developed and which has enabled the industry to attain its present stature is felt to be fundamentally sound and in spite of all the difficulties has worked well and with little or no friction. It is felt and has been recommended that we should build on and improve the existing system and at this stage introduce such changes as may be required in order to remove from the system the difficulties adumbrated in the body of this report.
       [...]

DEPOSITS: TOBACCO CESS.

Statement of Transactions from the 1st April, 1934, to the 31st December, 1935.

1st April, 1934, to 31st December, 1935:–
£ s. cts.

Cess received in respect of the 1933, 1934 and 1935 crops 3,596 7 61

TOTAL £3,596 7 61

1st April, 1934, to 31st December, 1935:–
£ s. cts.

Amount paid to Government being 70% of the cess collected during the period 2,517 9 31

Amount paid to Government in respect of interest at 2 ½% per annum on the outstanding monthly balances 51 7 18

Payments to sundry natives for erection of tobacco buying posts 48 2 98

Payments to sundry natives as compensation for barns destroyed by fire 68 15 75

Cost of materials for use in the factory 25 0 00

Refunds of cess in respect of tobacco leaf exported 115 16 16

Balance 769 16 23

TOTAL £3,596 7 61

MONTHLY TOBACCO FACTORY BUILDING ACCOUNT.

£ s. cts.

Expenditure incurred by Government during 1934 and 1935 3,222 4 25

TOTAL £3,222 4 25

£ s. cts.

Payment to Government of 70% of the Cess received during 1934 and 1935 2,517 9 31

Balance due to Government 704 14 94

TOTAL £3,222 4 25

A. E. FORREST,
Treasurer.
ENTEBBE,
9TH MAY, 1936.

J. H. Holland, *Rubber Cultivation in West Africa* (London, 1901).

RUBBER CULTIVATION IN WEST AFRICA
BY
J. H. HOLLAND,[1]
[...]

For some years past the question of how to increase the supply of rubber and at the same time preserve the industry has been one of considerable moment. It is still a much discussed and undecided problem. As with all products of vegetable origin, success, if at all attained, will only be by slow and steady progress.

Rubber from West Africa, up to the present, has been purely a forest product. Prior to the discovery of the tree rubber in the Lagos Colony (1895), and elsewhere on the Coast, it was obtained chiefly from Landolphia vines and Ficus.[2] The supply on the discovery of the new plant rose considerably for a few years and then began to decline, owing principally to reckless cutting of the trees, which resulted in their death. This somewhat broke the faith in the vastness of West African forests, and showed that it was not possible to gut them with impunity. It would appear that totally different conditions prevail in the Amazon regions. For 50 years at least the forests there have yielded large supplies of the Para rubber,[3] and still show no signs of exhaustion; attributed not to any special care, but mainly to the fact that the trees are being constantly reproduced by nature. It is very probable that the West African tree rubber does not exist in the same quantity, and that they do not reproduce themselves so readily. The seeds of both trees rapidly lose their vitality on exposure, but those of the Para, being larger, are not so apt to get destroyed by birds or insects, as it is possible the small and delicate seeds of the West African tree do. The Landolphias have a much better chance of being reproduced naturally; the seeds being hard and bony, and the young plants of a more vigorous habit.

The result of the contracted supply from West Africa has been serious restrictions on the gathering, and an impetus to the general desire for increase by cultivation.

Rubber cultivation anywhere can hardly be said to be established as a system, and in West Africa the experimental stage is barely initiated.

Taking six of the principal rubbers of the world, we have Para, Ceara, African Vine, African Tree, Central American and Assam; representing the three natural orders, Euphorbiaceae, Apocynaceae, and Urticaceae. To introduce /

There are a few enterprising firms who have made a beginning in the right direction, and deserve every success. Cacao has been cultivated with profit, and there might be considerably more of it. Coffee it is true has not been an unqualified success, but this is due more to fall in price, a circumstance it was impossible to foresee, than to any other cause.

Concluding then, that the Native tree (Funtumia elastica) is the safer investment, a description as to its Botanical characters, Distribution, Cultivation, and the Extraction and Preparation of the latex, may be of use.

BOTANICAL CHARACTERS.

The tree belongs to the natural order Apocynaceae; to the genus Funtumia; and to the species Elastica, There is one other well known species of Funtumia (F. africana) which does not produce rubber. These two trees grow practically side by side, and with a cursory glance they can scarcely be distinguished from each other. The following table shows in brief the principal points of distinction that are likely to present themselves to anyone in the bush.

	True Rubber. (Funtumia elastica.)		Spurious Rubber. (Funtumia africana.)
1.	Leaves somewhat coriaceous (leathery), with small pits or shallow depressions in the axils of the midrib and lateral nerves on the under side.	1.	Leaves somewhat charactaceous (papery,) with no depressions.
2.	Latex tested on the finger tips coagulates readily, and comes away quite cleanly from the skin.	2.	Latex sticks to the finger with no evident appearance of coagulation.
3.	Flowers whitish.	3.	Flower yellowish.
4.	Fruit or follicle woody (4 mm. thick), broad (2 in. approx.).	4.	Fruit or follicle slightly woody (2 mm. thick), narrow (1 in. approx.).
5.	Fluff on the seeds white.	5.	Fluff on the seeds cream coloured.

DISTRIBUTION (Hooker's Icones Plantarum, Feb., 1901).

Gold Coast:–	Sierra Leone:–
Mampon Hills.	Near Kukuma on the Scarcies River.
Sefewohi and Wam Dist. Coomassie.	Bagroo River.
Lagos:–	Ivory Coast:–
Ibadan.	Dobou.

Shagamu. / when being put out in the plantation; they may be easily made by the native, and if the plants do not turn out properly from them they can be readily split with a hatchet. It is most important to keep the plants growing without a check until they are established in their permanent places, otherwise they are liable to become stunted and useless. As regards soil; in both low damp ground and in ground high and dry. I should say the medium of these conditions would be the most desirable. Under favourable conditions the young trees flower when about four years old and the seed pods take six months to ripen.

EXTRACTION OF THE LATEX – The method of Tapping usually practised on the Coast [...], is not the best one, being detrimental to the tree. The incisions are much too wide, and it would be better to have a greater number of narrow cuts than a few broad ones. The usual width is about half an inch, cut with an ordinary gouge. The bark averages in thickness about one-fifth of an inch, and it seems to me that there can be no object in having a cut wider than the depth of the bark.

[...] For cutting, a V shaped chisel is recommended in preference to the rounded gouge. It is clear that perpendicular cuts, not wider than the depth of the bark, would be safer for the tree, but I have no data to prove whether perpendicular or oblique incisions yield the most milk.

It would be a great advantage if the collector cleaned all loose bark and dirt from the trunk before making any incisions, otherwise the friction of the rope he uses to climb the tree with does this, and the dirt then mixes with the milk as it flows. It will be understood that the upright cuts are made from below upwards.

Trees should not be tapped until they are at least 8 inches in diameter.

If the tree is tapped properly and without cutting into the wood, no dressing or styptic will be needed, as there will be no flow of sap to hurt the tree, but where a wound is made, tar is a convenient and reliable dressing. Clay should not on any account be used; it is of no value as a styptic, and would do more harm than good by retarding the healing process. The principal point to be observed is the keeping out of excessive moisture to prevent decay. It will be evident that clay in the wet season (the period recognised as the best for tapping) could not well have the desired effect. /

[...]

ROYAL BOTANIC GARDENNS
KEW.
March 7th, 1901.
[...]

Report on the Tobacco Industry, Union of South Africa, Office of Census and Statistics, Special Report no. 4 (Pretoria: Government Printer, 1924).

[...]

PRETORIA.

1924. /

UNION OF SOUTH AFRICA.
OFFICE OF CENSUS AND STATISTICS.

MANUFACTURING INDUSTRIES.

NO. 4. Tobacco, Cigars and Cigarettes.

INTRODUCTORY NOTE.

In connection with the reports on the annual censuses of factories and productive industries issued by the Census and Statistics Office, it has been suggested that a useful purpose would be served by the publication of short reports dealing in summary form with the development of the more important industries carried on in the Union. The Statistical Council approved of the suggestion and the following report is one of a series which is being prepared on the lines suggested. It is hoped that manufacturers and others interested in the various industries will find these summaries useful for purposes of reference.

Full details regarding each industry were published in the annual reports on the industrial censuses covering the years 1915–16 to 1918–19, but in later years considerations of expense led to the curtailment of detail to some extent. Certain particulars not published in these later reports will be found in the statements embodied in this survey.

The particulars regarding imports and exports have been taken from the annual statements of trade published by the Commissioner of Customs and Excise. The trade statistics relate to the calendar year, whereas the statistics of production cover the year ended 30th June.

It should be noted that the definition of a factory given in the regulations under the Statistics Act was altered in 1917 to include establishment employing three hands, which were not enumerated in connection with the first (1915–16) census.

C. W. COUSINS,
DIRECTOR OF CENSUS.
PRETORIA.
JANUARY, 1924.
[...]

1. NUMBER OF FACTORIES. – The following table shows the number of tobacco, cigar and cigarette factories enumerated in the various Provinces and the principal industrial centres at each census since 1915–16.

NUMBER OF FACTORIES, 1915–16 TO 1921–22.

| Year. | PROVINCES. | | | | UNION | PRINCIPAL INDISTRIAL CENTRE | | | |
	Cape	Natal.	Transval	O.P.S.		Cape Peninsula.	Port Elizabeth.	Durban	Wit waters rand.
1915–16	36	8	13	1	58	x	x	x	x
1916–17	36	9	21	1	67	12	4	9	10
1917–18	32	9	21	1	63	10	3	9	9
1918–19	31	8	20	1	60	10	3	8	10
1919–20	33	8	22	3	66	11	3	8	14
1920–21	34	6	21	3	64	11	4	6	15
1921–22	37	2	19	3	61	11	4	2	13

x Not Available.

The increase between 1915–16 and 1916–17 is due to the enumeration in the latter year of a few small factories employing three hands which were not included in the previous year. Since 1916–17 the number of establishments has decreased slightly, mainly owing to a falling off in Natal. More than half of the tobacco factories in the Union are situated in the Cape Province.

2. FIXED CAPITAL. – The amount of fixed capital, i.e., value of land, buildings, machinery and plant, is given in the subjoined table. The total amount of capital invested is also shown in respect of the years 1915–16 and 1916–17. The inquiry regarding total capital was not repeated in subsequent years.

FIXED CAPITAL, 1915–16 TO 1921–22.

Year	Value of Land and Buildings.	Value of Machinery and Plant.	Total Fixed Capital.	Total Capital Invested.
	£	£	£	£
1915–16	158,709	90,604	249,313	1,328,814
1916–17	199,167	90,597	289,764	1,382,474
1917–18	205,117	85,902	291,019	x
1918–19	222,522	90,489	313,011	x
1919–20	264,436	104,484	368,920	x
1920–21	284,974	148,655	433,629	x
1921–22	321,644	221,069	542,713	x

x Not Available.

Between 1915–16 and 1921–22 the total amount of fixed capital increased by 118 per cent, the percentage increase in the case of land and buildings being 103 and for machinery and plant 144. The average amount of fixed capital per factory in 1921–22 was £8,897 as compared with £4,298 in 1915–16. /

3. NUMBER OF EMPLOYEES. – The number of employees classified according to race and sex, the average number of employees per factory and the respective proportions of European and non-European workers are given below for each year since 1915–1916.

NUMBER OF EMPLOYEES, 1915–16 TO 1921–22.

Year	EUROPEAN		NON-EURO-PEAN.		TOTAL.	Average Number of Employees per Factory.	Proportion per cent of Total Employees	
	Male	Female	Male	Female			European.	Non-European.
1915–16	350	369	741	481	1,941	33	37	65
1916–17	400	368	955	518	2,241	33	34	66
1917–18	365	374	999	564	2,302	37	32	68
1918–19	362	394	1,020	786	2,562	43	30	70
1919–20	373	391	1,111	787	2,662	40	29	71
1920–21	422	511	1,149	928	3,010	47	31	69
1921–22	397	411	789	806	2,403	39	34	66

The number of employees increased annually till 1920–21 when a total reached 55 per cent. above the number in 1915–16. The number of employees in 1921–22 was the lowest recorded since 1917–18. In 1921–22 the number of Europeans was 12 per cent. and the number of non-Europeans 31 per cent. above the corresponding figures for 1915–16.

The proportion of females employed in this industry has increased appreciably. In 1915–16 44 per cent, of the total employees were females; in 1921–22 the percentage was 51. European females increased by 11 per cent. and Non-European females by 68 per cent.

The ratio per cent. of European employees to total employees decreased annually up to 1919–20 when 2.40 non-Europeans were employed to every European. Since then the proportion of European employees has increased, the figure for 1971–22 (34 per cent.) being identical with the percentage for 1916–17.

4. SALARIES AND WAGES PAID. – The total amounts and average amounts of salaries and wages paid to European and non-European employees are given hereunder for each year since 1915–16.

SALARIES AND WAGES PAID, 1915–16 TO 1921–22.

Year	TOTAL AMOUNT PAID TO			AVERAGE AMOUNT PAID TO –.		
	Europeans.	Non-Europeans.	All Races.	Europeans.	Non-Europeans.	All Races.
	£	£	£	£	£	£
1915–16	57,713	36,237	93,950	80 x	30 x	50
1916–17	75,837	39,781	115,318	99 x	27 x	53
1917–18	81,154	44,116	125,270	110 x	28 x	56
1918–19	80,158	83,865	144,023	113	35	57
1919–20	107,251	57,515	184,766	149	41	71
1920–21	172,890	108,545	281,435	193	52	95
1921–22	172,686	83,831	266,517	226	59	113

x In these cases Working Proprietors have been included with employees in calculating average amounts paid. In all other cases they have been omitted. /

The total amount paid out in salaries and wages in 1921–22 was 184 per cent. above the amount in 1915–16. The amount paid to Europeans increased by 199 per cent. and the amount paid to non-Europeans by 159 per cent.

Between 1915–16 and 1921–22 the average annual wage paid to employees of all races increased from £50 to £113 representing an increase of 126 per cent. The average amount paid to European employees in 1921–22 was 100 per cent. above the figure for 1918–19. The increase during the same period in the case of non-Europeans was 69 per cent. As separate particulars regarding the number of the European and non-European working proprietors are not available for the years 1915–16 to 1917–18 comparative figures for average amounts in these years cannot be given.

5. CLASSIFICATION OF FACTORIES ACCORDING TO NUMBER OF EMPLOYEES.

– The following table shows the number of factories of various sizes, together with the number and percentage of employees in establishments of each size.

CLASSIFICATION OF FACTORIES ACCORDING TO NUMBER OF HANDS,
1915–16 TO 1921–22.

Year.	Under 4 Hands.	4 Hands.	5–10	11–20	21–50	51–100	101 and over.	Total
NUMBER OF FACTORIES								
1915–16	3	2	18	10	14	9	2	58
1916–17	5	2	20	16	12	9	3	67
1917–18	5	2	19	14	9	9	5	68
1918–19	5	1	15	16	8	11	4	60
1919–20	3	5	16	17	10	11	4	66
1920–21	2	7	15	14	11	9	6	64
1921–22	3	6	15	15	11	5	5	61
NUMBER OF EMPLOYEES.								
1915–16	8	8	121	143	453	595	613	1,941
1916–17	13	8	139	223	455	641	762	2,241
1917–18	14	8	147	203	337	578	1,015	2,302
1918–19	14	4	104	262	297	683	1,198	2,562
1919–20	9	20	112	246	377	763	1,135	2,662
1920–21	4	28	103	203	366	583	1,723	3,010
1921–22	8	24	110	219	379	337	1,326	2,403
PERCENTAGE OF TOTAL EMPLOYEES.								
1915–16	0.41	0.41	6.23	7.37	23.34	30.56	31.58	100
1916–17	0.58	0.36	6.20	9.95	20.31	28.60	34.00	100
1917–18	0.61	0.35	6.38	8.82	14.64	25.11	44.09	100
1918–19	0.55	0.15	4.06	10.23	11.59	26.66	46.76	100
1919–20	0.34	0.75	4.21	9.24	14.16	28.66	42.64	100
1920–21	0.13	0.93	3.42	6.75	12.16	19.37	57.24	100
1921–22	0.33	1.00	4.58	9.11	15.77	14.03	55.18	100

The most noticeable feature of the above figures is the increased proportion of workers employed in factories of the largest size.

6. MOTIVE POWER. – The cost of fuel, light, and power and particulars of the class of motive power used are given in the subjoined table. /

COST OF FUEL, LIGHT AND POWER AND ANALYSIS OF POWER USED,
1915–16 TO 1921–22.

Year.	Cost of Fuel, Light and Power.	ELEC-TRICITY		STEAM		OIL		GAS		WATER	
		Fac-tories	H.P.	Fac-tories	H.P.	Fac tories.	H.P.	Fac tories	H.P.	Fac tories.	Total Horse Power.
1915–16	£4,652	20	238	10	259	12	65	1	20	3	582
1916–17	5,470	21	249	8	277	16	93	4	23	2	642
1917–18	5,445	23	251	7	267	15	81	3	21	2	620
1918–19	6,075	24	231	5	245	15	92	3	22	1	590
1919–20	7,910	24	242	6	257	18	96	3	23	1	618
1920–21	8,860	27	272	7	254	16	88	2	14	1	638
1921–22	9,787	28	549	9	272	14	92	1	10	2	923

The use of electric power extended considereably during the period under review. In 1921–22 the horse power of electric motors represented almost 60 per cent. of the total horse power used as compared with 41 per cent. in 1915–16.

7. MATERIALS USED. – The subjoined table gives particulars of the quantity and value of tobacco leaf and the value of other materials used during the years 1915–16 to 1921–22.

MATERIALS USED, 1915–16 TO 1921–22.

Material	1915–16	1916–17	1917–18	1918–19	1919–20	1920–21	1921–22
QUANTITY							
Tobacco Leaf –	1000lb.	1000lb.	1000lb.	1000lb.	1000lb.	1000lb.	1000lb.
Union of S.A.	7,992	9,622	9,584	10,347	12,490	10,972	7,860
Rhodesian.	x	x	1,195	1,303	1,501	1,877	2,181
Other Imported.	466	451	372	368	211	118	87
TOTAL	8,458	10,073	11,151	12,013	14,202	12,967	10,078
VALUE							
Tobacco Leaf –	£1,000	£1,000	£1,000	£1,000	£1,000	£1,000	£1,000
Union of S.A.	248	312	307	318	476	452	326
Rhodesian.	x	x	65	84	108	161	199
Other Imported.	134	95	98	101	65	42	35
TOTAL	382	407	470	503	650	655	570
Packing Materials		143	160	270	324	349	414
Other Materials.	124	10	17	9	16	15	13
GRAND TOTAL	506	560	647	782	990	1,019	997
S. A. Materials.	267	336	381	439	598	564	447
Imported Materials.	239	224	267	343	392	455	550
Proportion per cent. of S.A. Materials to Total Materials.	53	60	59	56	60	85	45

x Included with imported materials. Included in 'Other Materials'.

The following table gives particulars regarding the area under tobacco in the Union and the quantity of tobacco leaf produced. /

TOBACCO GROWN IN THE UNION, 1911 AND 1918 TO 1922.

Year.	Cape	Natal.	Transvaal.	O.F.S.	Native Locations, Reserves, etc. (1)	Union.
AREA.						
	Acres.	Acres.	Acres.	Acres		Acres.
1911	4,411	1,062	11,495	2,396	–	19,364
1918	7,427	1,096	13,569	1,033	–	23,125
1919 (1)	–	–	–	–	–	–
1920	6,367	1,729	16,733	980	–	25,809
1921	8,121	1,740	15,711	990	–	26,562
1922	5,619	468	12,428	809	–	19,324
YIELD.						
	1000lb	1000lb	1000lb	1000lb	1000lb	1000lb.
1911	3,767	2,685	7,702	807	(2)	14,961
1918	4,467	515	6,929	591	2,429	14,931
1919	4,776	614	8,122	671	–	14,183(3)
1920	3,602	730	6,924	388	–	11,644(3)
1921	5,008	911	8,462	625	1,614	16,621
1922	3,404	221	5,830	358	–	9,813(3)

(1) Areas not enumerated.
(2) Included in Provinces.
(3) Exclusive of tobacco produced in Native Locations, etc.

The quantity of Turkish tobacco produced in the Union since 1918 was as follows:– 1918 – 280,000 lb.; 1919 – 450,000 lb.; 1920 – 306,000 lb.; 1921 – 650,000 lb.; 1922 – 590,000 lb.

8. OUTPUT. – The quantity and value of articles manufactured or produced during the years 1915–16 to 1921–22 are given below.

OUTPUT, 1915–16 TO 1921–22.

Product.		1915–16	1916–17	1917–18	1918–19	1919–20	1920–21	1921–22
QUANTITY.								
Tobacco	1000lb	6,452	7,994	8,441	8,677	10,093	8,590	6,596
Cigars & Cheroots No.	1000	10,480	12,624	12,481	12,228	16,105	11,448	2,326
Cigarettes No.	1000	959,343	990,978	1,160,052	1,334050	1,517,157	1704388	1441,348
Snuff	1000lb.	x	203	215	158	130	129	111
VALUE								
		£1,000	£1,000	£1,000	£1,000	£1,000	£1,000	£1,000
Tobacco.		265	399	421	432	660	629	508
Cigars & Cheroots.		26	34	36	40	46	31	10
Cigarettes.		735	745	940	1,051	1,231	1,698	1,500
Snuff.		x	18	18	14	14	12	11
Other Products.		25	16	2	1	–	1	1
TOTAL.		1,051	1,212	1,417	1,538	1,951	2,371	2,030

x Not Available. /

The output of manufactured tobacco in 1921–22 (6,596,000lb) was made up as follows:–

	lb.	£
Roll Tobacco	2,749,000	94,000
Proprietary Brands packed in containers.	2,640,000	289,000
Loose Cut.	1,207,000	125,000

Practically the whole of the roll tobacco was produced in the Cape Province and over 2,000,000 lb of the proprietary brand tobacco in the Transvaal.

The following table gives indexes of value and volume of output, value of output per £1000 expended on salaries and wages, volume of output per head of employees, and ratio per cent. of 'Value Added' to total valus of materials used.

Year.	GROSS VALUE OF OUTPUT.			VOLUME OF OUTPUT.			Percentage of 'Value Added' to Total Value of Materials Used.
	Total Value.	Index.	Per £1000 expended on Salaries and Wages.	Total x	Index.	Per Head of Employees.	
	£		£	1000lb.		lb.	%
1915–16	1,050,748	1000	11,184	9,740	1000	5,018	108
1916–17	1,212,320	1154	10,486	11,422	1173	5,097	117
1917–18	1,417,408	1349	11,315	12,386	1272	5,381	119
1918–19	1,537,911	1464	10,678	13,081	1343	5,106	97
1919–20	1,951,236	1857	10,561	15,096	1550	5,671	97
1920–21	2,370,515	2256	8,423	14,061	1444	6,672	133
1921–22	2,029,638	1932	7,615	11,077	1137	4,610	104

x Tobacco, cigars, cigarettes and snuff.

The indexes of value and volume of output show that a considerable proportion of the increased value of the output was due to the rise in prices. Except in the year 1916–17 the index of value was higher than the index of volume the difference being especially marked in 1920–21 and 1921–22.

9. SALARIES AND WAGES, COST OF FUEL, LIGHT AND POWER, VALUE OF MATERIALS USED AND BALANCE EXPRESSED AS A PERCENTAGE OF GROSS VALUE OF OUTPUT.

– The following table shows the ratio which the more important items of expenditure bear to the gross value of output. It must be noted that the heading 'Balance' covers certain items of expenditure which are not detailed on the industrial census form, e.g., interest, depreciation, repairs and maintenance, insurance, advertising, etc.

SALARIES AND WAGES PAID, COST OF FUEL, LIGHT AND POWER, VALUE
OF MATERIALS USED, AND 'BALANCE' EXPRESSED AS A PERCENTAGE OF
GROSS VALUE OF OUTPUT. 1915–16 TO 1921–22.

Year.	Amount of Salaries and Wages Paid.	Cost of Fuel, Light and Power.	Value of Materials Used.	Balance – other Expenses and Gross Profit.	Gross Value of Output.
1915–16	8.94	0.44	48.17	42.45	100
1916–17	9.54	0.45	46.15	43.86	100
1917–18	8.84	0.38	45.67	45.11	100
1918–19	9.36	0.40	50.87	39.37	100
1919–20	9.47	0.41	50.75	39.37	100
1920–21	11.87	0.37	42.99	44.77	100
1921–22	13.13	0.48	49.12	37.27	100 /

10. IMPORTS – The following statement gives the quantity and value of
tobacco, cigars and cigarettes imported into the Union during the years 1913,
1916, 1918 and 1920 to 1922.

IMPORTS – TOBACCO, CIGARS AND CIGARETTES, 1913 TO 1922.

Commodity.	1913	1916	1918	1920	1921	1922.
QUANTITY						
	1000lb.	1000lb.	1000lb	1000lb	1000lb	1000lb.
Tobacco, Unmanufactured.	2,104	2,164	1,600	2,597	3,336	3,082
Cigars.	112	117	64	135	48	41
Cigarettes.	316	117	58	116	80	68
Tobacco, Manufactured.	75	56	74	52	15	12
VALUE.						
	£1,000	£1,000	£1,000	£1,000	£1,000	£1,000
Tobacco Unmanufactured	100	75	94	203	245	169
Cigars.	50	56	45	140	45	37
Cigarettes.	86	40	28	81	51	42
Tobacco Manufactured.	7	6	7	8	4	3

11. EXPORTS. – The exports of tobacco, cigars and cigarettes from the Union during the years 1913, 1916, 1918 and 1920 to 1922 are given below under the headings (a) South African Produce and (b) Imported Goods re-exported.

EXPORTS – TOBACCO, CIGARS AND CIGARETTES, 1913 TO 1922.

Commodity.	1913	1916	1918	1920	1921	1922
QUANTITY						
S.A. Produce. –	1000lb	1000lb	1000lb	1000lb	1000lb	1000lb
Tobacco Unmanufactured	123	332	386	1,047	233	1,373
Cigars.	5	19	15	11	3	1
Cigarettes.	110	253	396	365	300	284
Tobacco Manufactured.	506	899	1,332	871	477	556
Imported Goods Re-exported.						
Tobacco Unmanufac-tured.	71	–	138	188	1	119
Cigars.	9	19	13	14	8	8
Cigarettes.	51	57	22	36	28	17
Tobacco, Manufactured.	27	33	32	23	19	10
VALUE.						
S.A. Produce –	£1,000	£1,000	£1,000	£1,000	£1,000	£1,000
Tobacco Unmanufactured	4	9	14	60	11	21
Cigars.	1	5	5	5	1	–
Cigarettes.	43	95	135	177	154	144
Tobacco, Manufactured.	34	60	83	65	54	61
Imported Goods Re-exported, –						
Tobacco Unmanufac-tured.	5	–	5	19	–	2
Cigars.	3	11	11	12	6	5
Cigarettes.	10	12	8	17	13	9
Tobacco, Manufactured.	2	3	4	5	4	2

E. D. Rutherford, *Sisal in Kenya* (London: Jas. Truscott & Son Ltd, 1924).

KENYA
[...]

SISAL[1] IN KENYA
BY
E. D. RUTHERFORD
[...]

The Sisal hemp plant in Kenya Colony is probably Agave Rigida Sisalana. In Mexico, its home, the plant generally lives, according to reports, twenty-five years, but in the forcing climate and fertile soil of Kenya Colony it lives its life in from five to eight years.

When the plant is about to die a pole grows out from the centre like in appearance to gigantic asparagus. This pole then branches out, blossoms and seeds, after which little plants called bulbils form where the seed boles fall off. One pole yields about 2,000 bulbils. The pole grows to about 25 feet high in three months.

When dry the poles are very useful for hut building, fuel and other purposes.

The industry was started in German East Africa (now Tanganyika Territory) in 1893, when 1,000 bulbils were imported into that country from Florida. Only a very small number of these bulbils survived, probably on account of having heated on the journey. From these few plants enough were propagated to start the whole industry in German East Africa. From German East Africa in 1907 bulbils were imported to British East Africa and planted at Punda Milia and also at Gazi.

In 1908 the Germans put a prohibitive export duty on bulbils and suckers, probably to prevent the industry going ahead in British East Africa.

In this way they were too late to attain their purpose, for the Punda Milia plantation was well established, and was soon after able to supply all the plants needed to start other plantations.

In German East Africa and at the Coast in Kenya Colony very little cultivation is done before planting. The land is usually only cleared of vegetation. This method of planting has to be adopted on the Coast partly on account of the difficulty of keeping oxen, and because on the coral land no other method is possible.

In the Highlands the land is thoroughly well ploughed, cross / ploughed and harrowed. Recently a number of Fowler's double engine ploughing sets have been imported, which prepare the land rapidly and perfectly. Planting can be done either in the rains or in the dry weather, and need not be done with great care except to alignment, as the plants are very hardy. Either suckers which come out from the parent plant, as they do from rose trees, or bulbils, previously mentioned, can be used for planting.

Suckers can be planted when detached, but bulbils are generally nurseried, because they are too small to plant out when they fall from the pole.

The spacing of the plants varies a good deal. Forty-eight square feet is about the average given to each plant in the Highlands, and about thirty-two square feet at the Coast. The first cutting is generally taken at about three-and-a-half years old in the Highlands, and at under three years old at the Coast. During the first two years after planting catch crops such as maize and beans can be grown with profit, between the plants, and at the same time they help to keep the land clean

When ready the bottom leaves are cut with large butchers' knives, then tied in bundles and carried to trucks running on the trolley lines laid through the plantation. As about eighty tons of leaves are cut in the day, it is necessary to lay the lines at near intervals to avoid long carrying by hand. One man will cut and carry out one thousand five hundred leaves per day. Practised men will more than double this quantity.

The first cutting yields about 70 leaves per plant, or about one ton of clean fibre per acre. After this two cuttings of twenty to twenty-five leaves are taken per annum.

A plantation yields about three-and-a-half tons of fibre per acre in its lifetime of seven or eight years.

The factory should be situated near the middle of the estate, and in such a position as to allow the trucks loaded with leaves to travel to it down hill, having regard also to the source of the water supply.

At the same time, there should be a good fall from the factory into a convenient gully so that the water-borne waste may be easily disposed of. /

CUTTING AND TRUCKING SISAL LEAVES. /

The factory consists of a shed about one hundred feet by forty, containing a decorticator,[2] usually made by Robey, of Lincoln, or by Krupp, driven by an engine or by electricity.

Brushing and beating machines, of which there are many types, are necessary to dress the dry fibre.

A press, usually by Shirtliff,[3] driven by power, is used to bale the dry fibre. These bales are usually of two cwt. each, and of a density of eighty cubic feet to the ton.

The leaves are taken from the trucks and fed regularly into the decorticator by means of a conveyor table.

In the Robey machine the leaves are gripped and conveyed through by a phosphor-bronze chain. In the Krupp machine they are gripped by ropes.

In both machines the skin and fleshy parts of the leaf are torn away from the fibre by steel knives bolted to revolving drums as the leaf passes over concave saddle plates. During this operation water flows through the machine and washes the fibre white as it is being decorticated.

This water also washes all the waste matter down a drain, generally made of wood, into the adjacent gully.

The clean wet fibre is then carried out to the lines to dry, after which it is brushed and baled.

Formerly the fibre was hung out to dry on ropes, but latterly sisal poles have been used for the purpose with a considerable saving of labour. At most factories ropes made on the spot are used for tying up the bales of fibre.

Wires is sometimes used, but it is, of course, more costly.

In Kenya Colony sisal thrives at all elevations from the coast up to over 6,500 feet.

At the Coast it thrives on sandy soil, red soil and coral rag. Plantations on the red soil of Masongaleni, Kibwezi and Voi at from 2,000 to 3,000 feet are also successful. The biggest centre of the sisal industry is at present in the Thika district, at an elevation of about 5,000 feet; but, as can be seen by its success in other districts, there is every reason to believe that much increased development may be expected elsewhere. Round Thika most of the sisal is grown on deep red soil, but a very fine plantation has recently been started on black soil, /

INTERIOR OF FACTORY: LEAVES ON TRAVELING TO DECORTICATOR. /

At Longonot, at an elevation of nearly 7,000 feet, there is a very fine sisal plantation on volcanic ash soil, where hardly anything else will grow. When the rainfall is plentiful, sisal grows more rapidly, but it can withstand long periods of drought without sustaining harm. A water-logged soil is about the only land in which sisal will not thrive.

The sisal business in Kenya Colony has had many vicissitudes during its short life. Before the War the price averaged about £29 per ton, and at this price, with the lower cost of machinery, lower wages to Europeans and natives, lower land values, the business could, with care, be made to pay.

During the War sisal was eventually controlled at £99 per ton, a quite unnecessarily high price, in spite of sea freights of over £25 per ton. This high price led to somewhat extravagant methods of production; and after the War, when prices fell rapidly and freights fell slowly, few, if any, plantations could make a profit.

The fixing of the rupee at two shillings coming at the same time was probably the severest setback the industry had to contend with. The price of £36 a ton in London leaves a working profit, provided the price paid for the estate does not over-capitalize the business, and provided the shipping freights are not raised.

Sisal, so far, in this country has suffered little from any insect or animal pests, probably on account of the amount of acid contained in the leaves. Porcupines occasionally pull out young plants, but the damage they do is negligible.

In some parts of the country herds of game passing over a new plantation knock out the plants, but the damage is rarely serious.

When the sisal industry started in Kenya Colony, about four hundred natives were employed on the actual production of two tons of fibre in the day. At the present time 200 natives can, and do, produce about three tons in the same time. This reduction in numbers has been brought about by labour shortages on various occasions in the past, which have stimulated the planter to get the best out of his labour, and to employ labour-saving devices. /

There is still great scope for intelligent effort in the same direction.

The present methods of decortication are somewhat primitive, with the result that some 25 per cent. of the fibre contained in the leaf is lost. The use of a crusher before the decorticator reduces this loss considerably, but the loss is still too great.

The world's consumption of hard fibres, under which sisal is classed, was, before the War, about 350,000 tons annually. About half of this was sisal hemp, chiefly the product of Mexico. East African sisal is of considerably better quality than that of Mexico, so there is no fear of over-production from this country for many years to come.

No practical use has yet been found for the by-products of sisal. Sisal juice contains a small percentage of saccharine matter, and therefore alcohol can be made from it, but it has yet to be done on commercial lines.

Reports have come from America that suction gas-engines have been run on wet vegetable waste. A sisal factory produces 80 to 100 tons of this matter per day.

The chief use of sisal hemp is for binder twine, but it is also used for making ropes of various kinds, both by itself and mixed with Manila hemp. It is usually considered that 2,000 acres of arable land are necessary for a one-unit plantation in order to plant 250 acres annually with an eight-year rotation. To this should be added about 1,000 acres for grazing, etc.

Land of this kind could probably be bought at present in certain districts for about £2 per acre. A factory completely equipped with new machinery, the necessary rails and trucks, can be erected for about £8,000. It would be necessary to allow about £6,000 for planting 1,000 acres in four years, when production should begin. During these four years returns from catch crops could be expected. From the above figures £20,000 would be sufficient capital to start a sisal plantation on which a good return can be made.

It is hardly necessary to add that some successful sisal businesses have been started with much less capital, and others at a much higher figure.

W. L. Speight, 'Big Game Hunting in South Africa', *South African Railways and Harbours Magazine* (Christmas 1926), pp. 23–9.

BIG GAME HUNTING IN SOUTH AFRICA.
By W. L. SPEIGHT.

AFRICA is the paradise of the big game hunter. It contains more game than any other part of the world; and now happily denizens of the wild are being preserved in great reserves of our land completely closed to the hunter, who, however, has a wide and wonderful field in other parts of the country.

Of all big game animals, the most dangerous is undoubtedly the buffalo, an animal confined to Africa and India, and, in spite of all America's 'Buffalo Bills' and other hunters, it has never existed in that country. It is a sturdy and heavy beast that cannot be tamed. It is so vindictive that it will attack a man, at whom it readily takes offence, without any provocation. Once on the trail of a man it will persevere until it has found its victim, and, having overcome him, will not leave him while there is even the tiniest spark of life in the human body. Sometimes it will pound its prey with its stamping hoofs until not a particle is remaining. No other animal will carry its enmity to these lengths.

There are many stories which illustrate this traditional hatred for man. On one occasion four hunters were to work together in a large stretch of jungle into which a wounded buffalo had gone. The men paired off and entered the jungle from different directions. The first pair met the animal unexpectedly. Before they had time to defend themselves, it charged, and, after knocking down the first man, attacked his comrade. The first hunter was practically unhurt and quickly regained his feet. His rifle was gone and the infuriated animal had already killed his companion.

There was nothing for it but to climb the nearest tree, and from there he saw the buffalo pound and stamp his comrade until not a fragment of him remained. It was only when the other hunters came up, and, having been warned by the man up the tree, wounded the beast again, that it stopped pounding the spot. A second shot killed the animal.

Buffaloes will mingle readily with elephants, either animal seeming indifferent to the other, which proves a great nuisance to elephant hunters. The buffalo is a little afraid and jealous of the other animal, but this very rarely leads to fights between them.

It is the experience of every big game hunter that the animals he seeks are by no means easy to shoot. The inexperienced hunter is always tempted to aim at the head of an animal such as the buffalo, hippopotamus, or elephant. Any of these animals would treat a score of head shots as nothing more than the stings of a number of bees, and they would fail to make the slightest difference to the express-train-like onrush. The elephant is not such a clumsy brute as it may seem, but a bullet in the knee will bring it down, and the hunter then has time to fire a vital shot. /

In much big game hunting the hunter seeks first to incapacitate the animal and then to kill it. One of the best hits that a hunter can hope for when firing at an elephant is one midway between the eye and earhole, or one in the third wrinkle from the top of the trunk. These invariably bring down the animal.

The herd of elephants in the Addo Bush, not far distant from Port Elizabeth, was considerable. These animals comprised a variety peculiar to the Addo Bush. They were broad and heavy, with a bulk that made light of the thick barriers of bush and thorn. The hide, too, was so thick that thorns and sharp branches had no effect upon it. Thousands of years must have gone to the development of this species, which is shorter and broader than the average species of elephant. The Addo herd was slowly becoming tuskless, for in the Addo Bush food was not obtained by tearing the bark from the trees, as elephants have to do elsewhere in South Africa.

Major Pretorius was faced with a hazardous task when, with the 'passport' of the Union authorities, he set out not long since to exterminate this herd, due to its damage to neighbouring farms. No less a hunter than the late Captain F.C. Selous once said that the man who went to the Addo Bush to hunt elephants for pleasure was a 'suicidal ass.'

Frequently the hunter of elephants becomes the hunted. An old rogue elephant lurking behind a screen of dense bush might get the scent of the hunter and force its huge bulk silently to some spot where it could ambush the human foe, and unless he was quick to act he could not escape being overcome by the animal.

The black rhinoceros is still found in some parts of South Africa. The white rhinoceros, however, is represented only by the few in the Zululand game reserve. The white is the largest variety of rhino. Its front horn, sometimes three feet in length, is set tightly between tiny eyes, and behind it there is usually a smaller horn. This huge mass of horny fibre must prove a nuisance to the animal. From certain angles its sight is unavailing, due to the horn's interference; but the rhinoceros has / little use for its small, weak eyes, the inefficiency of which is amply compensated for by its acute sense of smell.

It is easy for the hunter to draw very close to this animal without being seen, and by keeping to the leeward he can avoid being detected by the animal's sense of smell. The massive horn is a formidable weapon. When the animal rushes through the long grass it may lay a tree flat with a blow from this rapier-like weapon. With its horn the beast thrusts and tosses, and it is the physical characteristic that distinguishes it from all other mammals. The short, unproportional tail, which curls into a knot when the animal is angry or about to charge, is a danger signal well known to hunters.

The rhinoceros on the whole is an inoffensive kind of animal, though it is extremely dangerous when molested. But being a dull-witted creature it is easy to outwit by a display of swiftness. The natives chase it with spears, which have little effect on the animal's tough hide. The spear-thrower has to hurl his weapon with such force that frequently he is overturned.

White hunters have often managed to approach so near to the animal that it can see them. It will then take fright, and, with a toss of its ungainly head, flee. Any obstacle in its path will be charged at, and this has sometimes resulted in the head of the animal being caught in the gnarled roots of a tree and held in a temporary grip. But although such a tree may be deep-rooted and firm, once the beast begins to lever it up it gives way sooner or later.

One story about a rhinoceros hunter is that of the sportsman who, when he wounded the animal, thought he had killed it. Greatly to the man's consternation, when he reached it it rose and attacked him. The only place to which the hunter could run was a tree which looked ridiculously frail. The animal charged this and gored at it with blind force. And while it was doing so a fellow-hunter of the man up the tree arrived and fired a shot which proved mortal only after the rhinoceros had broken away from the tree and charged far into the bush.

The wild pig is a very difficult animal to kill. It is a brave fighter and the dogs fear it more than either the lion or the leopard. They will chase it vigorously, but they draw back from its fierce and terrible methods of defence, from the slash of cruel tusks. The dogs are often caught by these, and, if they are not thrown heavily, their bodies may be ripped by a gash extending from head to tail. A couple of well-placed shots, unless through the heart, fail to despatch the tough beast. Some boars are so strong and tenacious in their hold on life that they will give up the struggle only after their heads have been almost severed from their bodies. They are the toughest and ugliest creatures that the hunter has to face. Some of them are over / nine feet in length, with a head over two feet long, huge ten-inch tusks, and wide ears. This bulk is so heavy that at least six natives are required to carry the prize.

Hippopotamus hunting, especially as practised by the natives, is very exciting. The river where these hunts take place will have all the vivid colouring of the sub-tropics. The dark green reeds along the bank and the tall trees on the little islands dotted about the broad river are reflected in the placid water. The dug-outs steal over the water towards the unconscious animal. As the quarry is quick to attack once it has been alarmed, the paddlers are ready to retreat immediately. False alarms are frequent. The dug-outs retreat swiftly several times, but at last they approach near enough for their crews to put down their paddles quietly and take up their assegais.

With remarkable stealth the hunters rise to their feet and stand erect in the unsteady-looking dug-outs. They raise their assegais and hold them ready to throw. Very slowly now the boats draw nearer and nearer. But still the unsuspecting prey sleeps on. Will he, before the assegais are hurled, awake and upset the boat? As the suspense becomes more intense that question runs recurrently through one's mind.

The huntsmen in all the different boats throw their assegais at a given signal, and this is no sooner done than another flight of spears is on the way. Stirring shouts rise from the hunters and mingle with the excited cries of the spectators on the shore. The river now is disturbed by wild splashings, the rapid movement of canoes, some of which are overturned, and the struggles of the hippopotamus, which is so full of assegais that it is almost dead.

More hunters dash in and more assegais are thrown at the beast. Then some of the bolder men paddle up to the hippopotamus and announce that life is extinct. The cry is taken up on the bank and it passes from mouth to mouth like some charmed chant. The hunters shout and sing. Their dug-outs are formed in a sort of line, which, when a rope has been fixed to the carcass of the prize, drags the animal to the shore.

In the Kalahari Desert and elsewhere in South Africa one may find the oryx or gemsbok. This is quite as noble and fine an animal as either the sable ante-lope or the roan. It is a courageous fighter, unafraid of any animal, including the much-vaunted lion. Many big game hunters relate how the two have died together in a combat, the lion usually being impaled on the buck's horns.

These antelopes offer a large target, but in spite of that it is difficult to get in a vital shot. Those who know little about these animals usually fire at the great head, but as its brain is so small, and the bones that protect the brain are so large, a head shot generally has the effect of sending the beast careering over the veld. The only really certain shot seems to be one placed near the / shoulder blade. This enters the heart of the animal and brings it to its knees. F.C. Selous always aimed at this spot, and probably for this reason the shot has been named after him.

When wounded, all these large antelopes are dangerous to approach. The cautious hunter makes a rule of putting in a second shot, into the heart if pos-sible. The gemsbok has a very light skin that is marked very beautifully. The head, with its long straight horns, with their pointed ends, has an impressive beauty.

Some of these species of antelope have had to withstand over-strenuous activities of hunters. But there are still thousands of the animals that wander alone, or in troops, like the sable antelope, with its fluted horns that curve in a graceful semi-circle from its head.

Out on the bush veld the long-limbed impala leaps marvellously, rising like a bird over high bushes and alighting easily and gracefully. Zebras are still plentiful in South Africa. During 1923 and 1924 about a hundred of them were caught and taken overseas to restock some of the zoological gardens of Europe and America. When these animals become too plentiful they are a nuisance to farmers. They break down fences, invade lands and root up crops. If much of such damage is done the animals have either to be herded into a reserve or shot. But to export them is the more profitable and humane expedient.

The district around the Magalakwin River, in the Transvaal, is one of the best hunting places in South Africa. It is beyond the Blaauwberg Mountains and some miles south of the Limpopo River. In the season people from all over the country travel up there with the object of shooting as much game as their permit allows. These permits allow each hunter to shoot a certain number of animals of different breeds. There is a charge for each animal killed, and these charges vary according to the breeds, those which are rare calling for a much higher fee than the plentiful.

The colouring of most wild animals is protective, and they use it so cleverly that until one knows what to look for they are difficult to find. The trained hunter employs all his senses, and not merely that of sight. He listens for the snorts of the sable antelope, the roan, or the wildebeest. He watches closely for the large ears of the koodoo, which sooner or later are sure to move. The rooibok betrays itself by the white of its tail, while the unpleasantly strong smell of the waterbuck warns one of proximity to it. And in other ways, by smell, sight, or hearing, spoor or sign of movement, the hunter is able to locate his prey and take a shot at it.

There are many lions in this region. In the past these beasts must have been grander animals than they are now, for there are many proofs in support of the belief that they have deteriorated both in size and strength. But the modern lion is a formidable foe. It weighs about five hundred pounds and measures nearly nine feet from the nose to the tip of its tail. Its roar is so loud that when it is over two miles away it seems to be quite near.

Lions are nocturnal in their habits. During the day they will sleep, but at night they steal forth in search of antelopes and those other beasts on which they feed. They lie in wait for the quarry at the drinking places. Lions generally hunt in pairs. It is the lioness that does most damage, for she is fiercer than her mate and is the first to attack. These animals rarely turn man-eating, and the popular stories about man-eating lions are mostly exaggerations. A lion, in fact, will rarely attack a man unless the beast is provoked or wounded.

A lion will charge at twenty yards and within two seconds will reach its objective. The only shot that can save a hunter in a predicament of that sort is that known as the 'stopping' shot, which must be placed in the beast's chest. It is a fatal mistake to aim at a charging lion's head. The front of the head is so well protected by the thick bones of the skull that a bullet would be deflected upwards without doing any damage or in any way stopping the furious rush of the animal.

The lion does not charge forward by leaps or bounds, but keeps low on the ground. Even when it is attacking an animal it does not jump or climb, but fights with its forelegs, keeping its hind legs on the ground the whole time. When it has reached its prey it strikes / it to the ground with its paws, using one in quick succession to the other.

One of the most successful methods of hunting lions practiced by hunters today is that of shooting the animals from tree-kraals built for the purpose while they are gorging themselves with an antelope or other animal that the hunter sets as bait for them. The bait is dragged over the country for several miles and then placed about twelve yards from the thorn-tree kraal wherein the hunter waits for the animals. They arrive well after dark and while they are feeding the hunter watches for his opportunity and obtains his 'bag.' Thousands of lions have been shot in this way, and, so far as can be judged, not a single hunter has lost his life following this method. The reverse was the case when hunters used to erect high platforms in the jungle with the intention of shooting the animals from the elevations. From above, the lions presented a difficult mark, and sometimes, when they had been wounded, they sprang on to the platforms and made short shrift of the hunters. F. C. Selous recounts some instances of this in his foreword to Lieut.-Colonel J. H. Patterson's 'The Man-Eaters of Tsavo.'[1]

If a lion is fired at and not wounded it will retreat, but within half an hour will return to its prey; and it will continue to do this so long as it remains unwounded. If one lion is killed, the others will return in the usual way, and sometimes they are joined by other lions. Frequently a wounded lion will disappear into the bush, where it may be difficult to locate it, and when found may have been partly eaten by hyænas. Hyænas have spoilt many fine lion skins and they are also a nuisance while one is waiting for the lions to come to the kraal.

Lion hunters also experience a great deal of excitement in following up wounded animals. There is much more danger in this than in shooting the beasts from the kraal, for when wounded a lion will always show fight. Hunting lions from horseback, too, is exceedingly exciting, but this sport is not practised as much as it used to be. When a lion has been chased by a man on horseback it becomes far more savage than when pursued on foot. It will charge from a considerable distance, generally without being wounded. The most effective way of hunting lions, however, is with the aid of a pack of dogs.

P. Lyttelton Gell, *The Rubber Industry in the British South Africa Company's Territories* (Salisbury: British South Africa Company, 1900).

The
Rubber Industry
in the
British South Africa Company's
Territories.

By
P. Lyttelton Gell.[1]

BRITISH SOUTH AFRICA COMPANY,

15 St. Swithin's Lane, E.C.

DEPARTMENT OF AGRICULTURE,

Salisbury, Rhodesia

1900. /
[...]

Introductory Note.

IN THE following pages I have endeavoured to summarise the main points relating to the Rubber Industry, so far as they are important to the Administration of the British South Africa Company's territories. In many directions our knowledge is partial and imperfect, and I should suggest that the memorandum might be circulated to the Company's District Officials, to Industrial Missions, etc., and that their observations may be invited. A proposed form of enquiry is annexed, which they may be requested to fill up.

The conclusions arrived at may be briefly stated as follows:–

(1)   All Rubber extracted should contribute to the revenue; but different principles will apply to the product of wild Rubber and of cultivated Rubber in reserved areas.

(2)   Wild Rubber trees should be regarded as a capital asset of the Company, and as an important source of future revenue. Rubber areas should not be alienated, but should be worked as a branch of Forest Administration, either (*a*) directly, by the Company through a Forest Department, or (*b*) by Subsidiary. Companies in which the British South Africa Company retains a controlling interest, or (*c*) defined areas may be let for an annual revenue on terminable leases under strict covenants to responsible parties undertaking the systematic *cultivation* of Rubber. /

I. *The Sources of Rubber.*

IT IS now ascertained that extensive tracts in North-West and North-East Rhodesia produce natural Rubber of high commercial value, while in Southern Rhodesia indigenous Rubber is reported in abundance in the Sabi Valley and along the Zambesi. There is also good ground for believing that various foreign species of a yet more valuable character can be gradually established throughout the territory, and there are certain kinds which may be expected to thrive even in the dryer climate of the Southern Rhodesia plateau.

On the other hand, the native methods of extraction are very destructive, and, in the absence of protective Regulations, the opening of markets will inevitably tend to the rapid extirpation of indigenous Rubber trees.

Further, the existing methods of preparation are faulty, and impair the market value of South African Rubber.

The Board has more than once been urged by its local officials to consider how this highly profitable industry may be preserved from exhaustion, and be made a source of wealth to the territory, and of revenue to the Company. Overtures have also been received for the exploitation of the industry, which are generally associated with demands for grants of land of a quite unnecessary magnitude, as well as for a monopoly of the production and trade over large areas. /

It therefore becomes necessary for the Board to consider its whole policy in regard to the question, so as to determine the principles upon which protective regulations should proceed, revenue be raised, and applications from external capitalists be dealt with.*

The Administrative problems being closely bound up with scientific questions, it may be useful at the outset to summarise the elementary facts of the Rubber Industry.

Rubber, or Caoutchouc, is the product of no one species, but may be procured from an extensive variety of trees and creepers of quite different characters. It is a hydrocarbon (which, chemically, can be derived from turpentine), and is found in minute agglutinative particles held in suspension in the 'latex' – *i.e.,* the milky fluid (not the sap) – secreted in a special tissue which permeates the cortex and the leaves of the Rubber trees and plants.

There are two stages in the production of Rubber before it acquires any commercial value:–

(*a*) The extraction of the latex from the tree (p. 377).
(*b*) The extraction of the rubber from the latex (pp. 377–8).

The latex of different plants, and of the same plants under different conditions, exhibits varying degrees of fluidity, and contains varying proportions of Rubber, up to 40 per cent. A. result of 30 per cent, is excellent. Species in which the proportion of rubber falls below 15 per cent. may be dismissed as commercially unimportant. /

Again, the other constituents of the latex which accompany the rubber particles vary considerably, and the processes of eliminating these elements vary also, Most native processes are very imperfect, leaving the rubber seriously depreciated by injurious or useless matter. Other processes, especially chemical ones, impair the character of the rubber itself. Moreover, it is believed that some kinds of rubber may owe their valuable characteristics to the retention of small proportions of some other constituents of the latex.

The fundamental commercial value of a Rubber plant would, therefore, depend on the following points:–

(1) The yield of latex.
(2) The percentage of rubber in the latex.
(3) The facility with which the rubber can be separated, without detriment to itself, from accompanying constituents of the latex.

* NOTE – It may be assumed that the Company has already parted with its interest in extensive Rubber-bearing areas under concessions of various kinds.

(4) The inherent character of the product, the value of which varies in different plants, and even in the same plants, according to climatic conditions.

(5) The market for the ultimate product. At present this appears to be only a question of degree. All East African rubber, *if properly prepared*, is in demand in London at 2*s*. 6*d*. to 3*s*. 6*d*. a lb., while inferior products will fetch 1*s*. to 2*s*. a lb., and are not always saleable.

The essential conditions for the development of the Rubber latex appear to be tropical or sub-tropical heat, accompanied with shade and with varying degrees of moisture. Some Rubber trees / develop also useful timber; others resemble the cactus in form; others are gigantic creepers. Some flourish only in absolute marsh; others thrive on stony soil, provided it receives ample though intermittent rainfall.

The profitable Rubber-bearing plants appear to belong to the following four families:–

Family	Species indigenous to Central and Southern Africa.
(1) Euphorbiaceae (Spurges)	Euphorbias (various).
(2) Arto-carpaceae ('Bread-fruit' order)	None in Africa.
(3) Apocynaceae	Vahea Madagascariensis.
	Urceola Elastica
	The Landolphia Florida.
	Landolphia Foreti (Congo).
	Landolphia Hendeloti (Guinea)
	Landolphia Kirki (Mozambique).
	Landolphia Owariensis (West Coast).
	Landolphia Watsoniana (East Coast).
	Carpodinus Acida.
	Carpodinus Dulcis.
	Kickxia Africana (the Lagos tree), though akin to the Landolphias, is a valuable tree and not a creeper.
(4) Asclepiadeae	Callotropis – a shrub 6 to 10 feet high, bearing large red flowers. /

The indigenous rubber, which (so far as our official information goes) has at present been identified in the B. S. A. territories, belongs chiefly to the third of these classes – gigantic creepers scattered amongst other growths.

In the Mweru district, Mr. Blair Watson has reported, amongst other species not described, a Landolphia with pink flowers, which possibly is the 'Landolphia Florida,' well known in the Niger district. The latter is a large creeper, sixty or seventy yards in length, which thrives in marshy and tropical surroundings, entangled amongst forest trees. It does not produce the very best rubber, but ranks high.

A Euphorbia was identified by Dr. Gray, while accompanying Mr. Sharpe and Mr. Codrington on their expedition against Kazembe in 1899, while other rubber-bearing plants were observed by him, but not identified.

The rubber plants of North-West Rhodesia also seem to include Euphorbias*[....]

The policy towards proposals of exploitation.

i. PROTECTION OF WILD INDIGENOUS RUBBER.

It is the universal experience in countries producing Rubber and Gutta-Percha that the energetic intervention of the Government is required to prevent the extirpation of the trees whence the latex is derived, – to secure replanting, and to penalise destructive methods of extraction; whilst it is also found desirable to forbid methods of preparation which depreciate and discredit the product by the incorporation of valueless or detrimental substances.

The systems established in other Territories have been of the following types:–

(*a*) Forests, including rubber trees, are reserved as State property; they are directly administered, and the rubber is collected, by a Forest Department.

(*b*) The Forests are retained as State property, but private enterprise is permitted over specified areas under terminable leases and strict conditions.

(*c*) Tracts of Forest are transferred to private or joint stock ownership, and the development is left to individual action under some degree of legislative regulation. /

(*d*) Forests are abandoned to the first comer, subject to more or less effective regulations as to methods of extracting or trading rubber; this appears to be the usual British principle outside India, and the least wise of any.

---

*   NOTE. – Since writing the above I have received the following from Sir W. Thiselton Dyer:– '... In the North-West I expect there is little but Root-Rubber. The most important seems to be a 'Carpodinus.' The Rubber is got from the underground stem or rhizome. It consequently cannot be collected without more or less destroying the plant. But it is possible that enough may be left in the ground to renew the plant ... In the North-East you have the Rubber Vines (species of Landolphia). Though the stems are destroyed in collecting the Rubber, the roots remain and are said to produce fresh stems in a few years ...'

With regard to the Root-Rubber (which I understand is obtained by boiling the roots), this product is usually forbidden in the neighbouring territories. It is of poor quality, and is so depreciated by the presence of dirt and extraneous matter, that in any case it discredits the trade. [...]

The regulations existing in other African territories afford some useful suggestions, though, speaking generally, they appear to be very imperfectly enforced.

CONGO STATE. – (*a*) No unauthorised extraction of Rubber is permitted.

(*b*) The industry is largely worked by the State, but concessions for extracting rubber within fixed areas and for limited periods are also granted, the lessees being bound to conform to the regulations applicable to the State Forests.

(*c*) In each year the Department of Forests or the lessee must plant a number of new trees, bearing a fixed proportion to the weight of rubber extracted. If lessees neglect to keep up plantations, the Government may intervene and charge the expenses to the lessee, or may cancel the license to collect rubber.

(*d*) The felling of Rubber trees is forbidden under heavy penalties.

(*e*) Extraction of Root-rubber is forbidden, and no method but that of incision may be used.

Penalties of from Frs. 100 to Frs. 10,000 and imprisonment of ten days to six months may be imposed, Employers, Directors / of Companies and State Agents being liable for the payment of fines incurred by their servants.*

LOURENCO MARQUES. – A monopoly of the production and trade in rubber for twenty-five years has been granted over the unoccupied State lands. The concessionaires pay a rent of 200,000 Reis (= £44 7*s*. 11*d*) per annum, and undertake to plant 20,000 trees in two years. They further pay a duty of 50 Reis (= 2.65*d*.) per kilo. for seven years; rising to 75 Reis (= 4*d*.) per kilo. for the remaining eighteen years. They are exempt from all other imposts. They have the option of retaining the land at the same rent at the expiration of the monopoly.

The monopoly does not restrain the *cultivation* of rubber on private property and its export by private persons.

THE MOZAMBIQUE COMPANY[2] forbids any individual to purchase rubber from natives, or to extract it through agents, without a special annual license, extending only from February 1st to August 31st, which costs £3 per annum. Thirty Reis (= 1.6*d*.) per kilo. must be paid before rubber can leave the district in which it is collected, and a receipt for the tax must always accompany the goods. Every person purchasing rubber or collecting it must keep books showing the amount received daily, / and report it once a month to the District Official.

---

* Export duties on Rubber are fixed at 10 % by Treaty with France and Portugal. There is apparently an additional duty of 50 centimes per kilo. fixed in February, 1898, and a fee of £200 is charged for every license to establish an India-rubber warehouse. Natives who hold licenses to collect rubber apparently have the option of compounding for their fees by paying one-fifth of the rubber collected to the State.

All warehouses, and consignments of rubber in transit, whether by river or land, must be open to inspection on demand.

LAGOS. – The system in Lagos is based upon a theory, apparently of purely British origin, that the ownership of Forests is vested in the local tribes, under their 'Native-Authorities,' *i.e.*, Chiefs. Within districts under the control of such 'Native Authorities' no person may collect rubber without a license, for which he pays £5 to the 'Native Authorities' and 2*s.* for each load of rubber. No tree of less girth than 3 ft., at a distance of 3 ft. from the ground, may be tapped. It may not be tapped more than once in eighteen months, and only in the manner prescribed by the 'Native Authorities.' The preservation of the protecting timber is also provided for. No tree of a girth less than 9 ft. at a point 10 ft. from the ground may be felled, and a similar tree must be planted in the nearest suitable spot within seven days. A permit must be obtained from the 'Native Authorities' for all trees felled, and a fee of 5*s.* a tree must be paid.

I understand that this system, resting upon a British conception of Tribal Property in Forests, which has no root in the native mind, proves ineffectual. The fees are cordially received, and the licenses are cheerfully handed over, but the sense of responsibility which in theory was to result, is not evoked.

THE BRITISH CENTRAL AFRICA PROTECTORATE has not yet established any adequate system for preserving the rubber industry and deriving substantial revenue from it. The British Central Africa Protectorate does, however, forbid the destructive traffic in Root-rubber and rubber obtained by boiling bark, and / it levies a 5 per cent. transit duty on rubber for the maintenance of roads, etc., which produces about 1 ½*d.* a lb. Regulations against frauds in rubber have been also promulgated.

There will probably be no hesitation in recommending that immediate Regulations should be framed for North-West, North-East and Southern Rhodesia for the protection of *Wild Rubber*, which should embody certain well-ascertained principles, *i.e.*:–

(*a*) A minimum age and girth should be established, below which a tree must not be tapped. The exact measurements must be adapted to different species and localities, so that legislation should only establish the principle, empowering our officials to promulgate the precise regulations for each district, after reports have been received as to the nature of the Rubber plants there prevailing.

(*b*) The intervals at which trees may be tapped should also be regulated. Subject to local modifications, it would be safe to forbid tapping the same trees, or the same area, in two successive years.

(c) A general regulation will be required that rubber may only be collected by tapping; that no tree may be cut down, and no roots grubbed up and boiled. On the other hand, to avoid unreasonable rigidity, or to deal with exceptional conditions, a local official should be empowered to modify this regulation.* /

(d) A general regulation is desirable, providing for the plantation of young rubber trees in forest-land by persons extracting rubber, in some proportion to be fixed by the local official, and a small reward for every tree planted should be paid.† If in special districts the extraction of Root-rubber is permitted, the rate of replantation must be high – not less than two to one.

(e) The forest trees which provide the indispensable shade must also be protected from destruction.

(f) Powers should be taken to forbid absolutely the extraction or sale of rubber in a district for a fixed period; as a penalty for breach of Regulations, or merely as a protective measure.

It is obvious that such a system would only gradually come into practical effect, and that for the present it would be inoperative in many districts. The protection of Rubber, however, presupposes the possibility of eventually establishing control over forest areas, and this object must be kept in view, even if at the present stage such a step may appear visionary. Probably the most satisfactory course would be, that whenever there was a strong headman or Chief, he should be experimentally recognised as the Warden of a limited area; that his people should have the sole right of collecting rubber within that area; that he should be responsible for their compliance with regulations, being fined in rubber for damage done, and rewarded in truck for all trees planted. In order to encourage careful preparation, / rubber might be accepted in payment of Hut Tax or other dues, provided it was of unimpeachable quality.

Wherever the system of salaried Indunas[3] is established, such an experiment may be worth trying, but I am informed that in North Eastern Rhodesia the tribal Chief rarely possesses sufficient authority for the purpose. The ultimate control must rest in the hands of the Company's District Official, who will be directed to exercise it either personally, or through a local Chief, as he may think

---

* Root-rubber is reported in North-West Rhodesia as a special product of the country. Unless it differs from other rubber extracted from roots, the process is not to be encouraged – See note, page 371.)

† In Indian forest districts the systematic plantation of any trees which it is desired to establish is secured by paying the Natives trifling rewards for sowing seeds distributed to them during the last season before they migrate from exhausted clearings to take up fresh ground. Small further payments are annually made for three or four years as a reward for weeding, etc., until the new trees can protect themselves. This system has proved effectual and cheap.

fit. In any case, control will be impossible unless it is ordained that the trees in a given area must only be tapped by the people of the locality, or by outsiders specially licensed by the District Official.

Doubtless, in large tracts in North Western Rhodesia, no such administrative control can be established for some time to come. If that be so, we cannot help the rubber being destroyed there. As in many matters, the regulations must be pushed as far as the Company's Officials have influence with Native Chiefs, and nothing more can be done.

Other conditions will also vary. In one district the rubber may be collected in the locality; there, outsiders can be excluded; and the tapping can be controlled by authority, native or British. Elsewhere, the rubber will be collected by an expedition to some place at a distance. In that case only the man in charge of the expedition can be held responsible.

ii. – *Sources of Revenue.*

As already indicated, it is reasonable that the largest possible proportion of the wealth latent in *wild rubber*, after remunerating / the extractor, should be appropriated for the Administration. This may be effected in the following ways, for all of which parallels may be found in other Rubber countries:–

(*a*) The Company may itself trade in rubber, either employing natives in its preparation, or purchasing it from them, or accepting rubber in payment of hut-tax, etc.

(*b*) The Company may lease the rubber in assigned areas to subsidiary Companies, receiving an adequate rent or share in the profits.

(*c*) Fees on licenses to extract and trade rubber may be required, and fines for breach of regulations may be imposed.

(*d*) An Excise or Export Duty may be levied.

The conditions of the Company's territories are so varied that none of these methods need be excluded, with one important exception. Other Administrations which have reserved Rubber as a source of public revenue have injured the trade by setting up a monopoly in *extraction*, by leasing this monopoly, and by levying duties on the extractor. This policy should be avoided. It should be the object not to restrain local natives from extracting rubber, but to offer them every encouragement to do so, subject to proper regulations enforced by penalties for the destruction of trees, and rewards for replantation. *The native who extracts the Rubber is the man who gives negotiable value to the Company's property in Rubber*, and so long as he obeys regulations he should be encouraged in every way. The attempt to levy revenue upon the local *extraction* of rubber necessarily discourages native effort, which is already far too lax. Some revenue may be legitimately raised from strangers entering a district to extract / rubber by requiring them to take out licenses, but as a main principle it is the Trader from whom Revenue should be collected.

(1) The first proposal, that the British South Africa Company should trade in rubber, is worthy of consideration in the more remote districts. No Capital is required, except the cost of truck for payment to the natives, and the cost of carriage to the point of sale. Rubber can with great advantage be accepted as currency for fines or hut-tax, though to secure care in preparation, only first-class qualities should be recognised. The trade would fall in with the general supervision of Forest areas, and the Company's acceptance of the product at its current local value would keep out undesirable traders in guns, etc.

(2) If the trade in special districts is delegated to subsidiary Companies, it should be only as part of an undertaking to introduce the *cultivation* of rubber on an adequate scale. It will be essential that the British South Africa Company's interest in such Companies should represent the fact that it is the owner of the raw material; that so far as indigenous rubber is concerned a very small proportion of subscribed Capital is required for mere trading expenditure; and, further, that the Company's interests must be strongly represented on the subsidiary Board.

(3) No one should be allowed to trade rubber without a special license, and no strangers should be allowed to extract rubber without a license.

(4) An Excise or Export Duty should be levied on rubber, to be paid by the trader, the amount approximating to the margin between the London price and the sum of the three items:– Cost / of preparation*, cost of carriage, and trader's fair profit. 3*d*. a lb. is suggested as a commencement, which may be taken as representing 10 per cent.† of the value of second-quality rubber on the London market.

In any Ordinance powers should be reserved to responsible officials to abate the duty locally if it seems advisable. Our experience with the British Central Africa Protectorate in the effort to protect young elephants by increasing the duties on immature ivory, shows that along our Eastern frontier our tariffs must always be dependent upon those of our neighbours. The imposition of the duty would be facilitated by the encouragement of local markets to which rubber would be brought for sale, of licensed storehouses†, and, if possible, by the imposition of similar duties in the British Central Africa Protectorate.

---

*   NOTE. – The cost of production in Liberia has been stated to me as about 1*s*. per lb. in truck. It pays a duty of 2*d*. per lb. The cost in North-East Rhodesia is at present 3*d*. to 6*d*. per lb., which would admit a far higher duty. The duty paid in India is about 2 ½*d*. per lb. The duties in Brazil, federal and local, vary between 18 and 29 per cent. *ad valorem*.

†   See Congo Regulations, p. 372 Note.

The tariff on cultivated rubber will not arise for some years. There would not be the same *political* justification for a high tariff upon a product due to the application of intelligence and capital. Still, in practice, the higher market value and the greater economy in the collection of cultivated rubber will probably support the tariff established for wild rubber.

iii. – THE FUTURE DEVELOPMENT OF THE INDUSTRY.

The important points are as follows:–

(*a*) The steady replanting of indigenous trees, and the preservation of the shade trees in Forest areas. /
(*b*) Improved methods of extraction and preparation.
(*c*) The introduction of superior species in cultivated areas.
(*d*) The formation of a small Forestry Department, a member of which would have special experience of Rubber.

(*a*) REPLANTATION. – This has already been touched on (see p. 374). It should be a condition of all future leases or concessions of Forest Areas, and be obligatory in areas not thus appropriated, being encouraged by small rewards. If the rewards prove ineffectual, all extraction must be prohibited from time to time whilst the trees are recuperating.

(*b*) The question of EXTRACTION, though highly important, appears to be simple. The African native injures his product by the incorporation of dirt and by cutting too deeply, thus penetrating the vascular tissue. He increases the proportion of useless or even injurious substances, which have subsequently to be eliminated.

Speaking generally, the objects to be inculcated are these:–

(1) Exclude the extraneous juices which result from over-deep incisions.
(2) Exclude all dirt and foreign substances.
(3) Evaporate all moisture as immediately as possible after extraction by spreading the latex as it exudes over extended and warm surfaces.
(4) The latex of different species must never be mixed.

The methods of PREPARATION must vary according to the nature of the tree, and be a matter of local observation and training. Native methods are numerous, and usually quite unscientific. The fundamental object is to separate the Rubber / particles from the resinous and albuminoid matters in the latex. Even assuming that care in the process of extraction has excluded everything but the pure latex, the albuminous elements in the latter produce a general coagulation after contact with the air, and the complete elimination from the coagulated mass of all that is not rubber, without injury to the rubber itself, is the fundamental problem of the industry.

The methods used fall under the following heads:–

(1) Evaporation of moisture, and decomposition of extraneous matter by heat and exposure to the air.

(2) Elimination of extraneous matter by dilution, washing, skimming and pressing.

(3) Chemical removal of extraneous matter, a process often injurious to the rubber. (It is believed that the use of all substances inducing fermentation, and all mineral and vegetable acids and alum must be regarded with great suspicion.)

Recent chemical researches appear to suggest that the ideal method would be one which suspended the coagulation of the albuminoids until the separation of the Rubber particles can be effected. This has been successfully accomplished by centrifugal force (*Kew Bulletin*, August, 1897, and *Biffen's Annals of Botany*, June, 1898), and such a method might become practicable on organised rubber plantations.* In the meantime it seems that of the native methods employed none is superior to that pursued in Gambia (Ivory Coast). The essential point in the Gambia method is the constant application of salt water to the / incisions†, which secures the separation of the serum from the rubber particles as the latex exudes, before general coagulation has taken place. On the other hand, a peculiar dexterity is required to handle the rubber at the moment of separation, and it would be well worth while to make enquiries in Gambia, and possibly to import some skilled manipulators from that district to establish their method in Rhodesia. In any case, the methods of preparation must be matters of instruction and not of legislation, though adulteration and fraud (*e.g.*, the concealment of stones or dirt in rubber) should be forbidden by Ordinance, as in the British Central Africa Protectorate, where it is checked by inspection when the transit duty is levied.

The special attention of Industrial Missions should be invited to this branch of the subject, and skilled manipulators might be sent to instruct them.

(*c*) THE INTRODUCTION OF SUPERIOR SPECIES, in cultivated areas, selected according to the varieties of the soil and climate, and the demands of the London market.

---

*   NOTE. – Separators have been recently tried in Brazil. They have failed with the *Hevea* latex, but have succeeded with the *Castilloa*.

†   NOTE. – In Ceylon the same result is secured by placing a 1 per cent. solution of ammonia and water in the collecting cups (Ceylon Circulars, 12, 13, 14, June, 1899, p. 127).

The introduction of cultivated rubber implies conditions totally different to those which apply to wild rubber. It requires capital, superintendence, and sufficient labour. There can be no effective return for five years, and no full return for ten years. Afterwards the result should be exceedingly remunerative to the proprietor, the Revenue being benefited by a progressive rent,* to / be paid for the lands planted, and by the duty on the rubber produced.

There are several foreign species of trees, which, *primâ facie*, may be expected to thrive in Rhodesia. The following seem most suitable for experiment:–

The *Hevea Braziliensis* (Euphorbiaceé). – This tree, which produces the valuable Para Rubber, flourishes alike at the sea level and up to 3,000 ft., requiring a heavy soil. The damp and marshy borders of streams and rivers suit it particularly well. It grows to a height of about 70 ft., and at five years old is already 40 ft. high, and can then be utilized for rubber. It should be set out in plantations with about 10 to 12 ft. between the trees, as it is important that the roots should be shaded.

A tree which should be tried in Southern Rhodesia is the *Manihot Glaziovii* (Euphorbiaceæ), which produces the Ceara Rubber. This flourishes in Brazil, in mountainous and dry situations, 6,000 ft. above the sea, upon stony soil. It must be sheltered from wind. It requires a hot, but not tropical, climate (77° to 86° Fahr. average), and it is well adapted for climates where the soil does not remain saturated with water. It requires a full rainfall, but it can stand periods of drought. At the end of three years it is about 15 ft. high, and begins to be productive.

The Panama Rubber, *Castilloa Elastica*, might be possible in other situations. It thrives at an altitude not exceeding 3,000 ft., but it requires a hot and not too changeable climate, 60° to 95° Fahr. The soil must be good and fully watered, but not swampy. This tree is also valuable for its timber, reaching about 60 ft., with a / diameter of over a yard. Its product is not so good as the Para, but is high-class.

The *Landolphia Kirki*, which produces the Mozambique rubber, is also indicated as a plant worth trying. It grows naturally about 2,000 ft. above the sea. It is a vigorous and hardy creeper, and can stand occasional cold. It requires very little cultivation, and has been found exceedingly profitable.

The *Sapium Tolimense* – a South American tree, growing to 100 ft. – is highly commended by the Brussels 'Horticole Coloniale,' as suitable for temperate climates up to 6,000 ft.

The *Kickxia Africana* should undoubtedly be introduced, if it is not indigenous.

There is a promising tree, the *Minusops globosa* (Balata), which flourishes in tropical America, the product of which forms a link between caoutchouc and

---

* The Reports of the Rubber Government Plantations in Assam by Mr. H. C. Hill, 1896, and Mr. E. G. Chester, 1899, and also the detailed Reports as to the establishment of State Plantations in Burmah (1899–1900), are full of valuable information and suggestions.

gutta-percha. It is also a valuable timber tree, which has been used for railway sleepers and bridges, and is not attacked by insects.

Amongst gutta-perehas (which have not yet succeeded outside their original habitat), the most hopeful tree for Rhodesia is, apparently, the *Palaquium oblongifolium*, which thrives in hot climates in situations which are raised above the level of the sea and are not liable to flood.*

It should be noted, however, that experiments in the naturalisation of Rubber trees have occasionally resulted in a / distinct deterioration in the product. The wholesale plantation of foreign rubbers on theoretical grounds is therefore inadvisable, but specimens of the trees above-named should be distributed to various stations and reports be obtained, the indigenous rubber being cultivated in the interval.

(*d*) From this brief investigation of the many ramifications of the Rubber question one conclusion emerges clearly; – that not merely in the interests of rubber, but on much wider grounds, the very first step should be the organisation of a FOREST DEPARTMENT to exploit, or, if that is too great an undertaking, at least to control wild land not at present alienated; and that to this Department an official having special experience of rubber should be attached. Such a Department would collect information as to indigenous rubber, analyse specimens, give advice as to methods of extraction and preparation, and advise the Government as to regulations, and as to areas suitable for reservation for rubber culture. It would establish small rough-and-ready nurseries at the police posts and elsewhere, and send out specimens for experimental plantation.

It would also advise private and joint stock owners, earning fees in this way.

On the other hand, the full development of a Forest Department, so as to become a source of revenue, requires large capital, or, at any rate, a serious annual expenditure in its earlier stages, which neither the Company nor the local Rhodesian revenue is in a position to provide. /

The difficulty might possibly be met in the following way:– A general scheme for the organisation of such a Department might be prepared, and general regulations be laid down, full advantage being taken of the experience acquired in other countries, especially in India and Ceylon, while an official familiar with the Forest System of those countries might be usefully enlisted.† When once the general principles had been established, a small defined area (probably in North-East Rhodesia) might be reserved by the Company, to be worked by the Department as the nucleus of larger operations hereafter, while subsidiary Com-

---

*   All the trees named are supplied by 'L'Horticole Coloniale,' Parc Leopold Brussels.

†   Experienced men will frequently be lent for a time by the Indian Government, whilst others, in the prime of life, who have taken their pension after 21 years' service, can often be engaged.

panies might be formed to lease defined Forest Areas (including the Rubber) in other districts. The B. S. A. Company's Regulations and general scheme of development would form part of each subsidiary Company's contract. It would be the duty of the B. S. A. Company's local officials to inspect the operations of the subsidiary Companies, and to report negligence of Regulations to the Board. The Chartered Company must be effectively represented upon the Boards of such Forest Companies, so that no divergence of policy should be possible.

Finally, in case new conditions arise under which it becomes desirable to resume direct control, it may be agreed that, upon certain terms of bonus to Shareholders, the B. S. A. Company may terminate the leases. /

iv. – POLICY TOWARDS PROPOSALS FOR THE EXPLOITATION OF RUBBER.

Large areas, which probably contain quantities of indigenous rubber, have been already granted away, and in regard to these, the Company's action is doubtless limited to the preservation of rubber by Legislative action, and to its taxation by means of duties and Traders' licenses.

As regards future proposals affecting rubber-bearing areas still retained by the Company, there seems to be *no ground whatever for entertaining applications for wholesale land grants*;* or for granting a monopoly of extraction, or of trade. So far as wild Rubber is concerned, its exploitation is properly a branch of Forest Administration. Concessions in fee-simple are absolutely unjustifiable and injurious, though, as above suggested, rubber areas may be legitimately worked by subsidiary Companies acting under the control of the B. S. A. Company.

The *cultivation* of Rubber stands on a different footing. This is undoubtedly a matter for private enterprise, and for the concentrated application of brains and capital. All applications for defined areas of moderate extent from responsible persons may be cordially received. These areas will, in all probability, contain a certain amount of wild rubber, which may thus pass into private ownership and help the enterprise during the early years of cultivation. / No large areas should be appropriated offhand. Every grant should be conditional on the plantation of a fixed number of trees in each year, and options might be properly given to increase the area so soon as the first grant was fully planted.

Such grants would be on long leases, which might be renewable, the rent being at first nominal, but rising at the end of six years, by yearly increments, to a maximum at the end of twelve years, At the latter stage, under good management, a substantial income ought to be accruing from a plantation. The carefully

---

* NOTE. – The area reserved by the Indian Government in Burmah for Rubber cultivation is only 10,000 acres. The estimated expenditure on this is Rs. 2,10,000, spread over twelve years. The anticipated revenue after twelve years is Rs. 1,10,000 per annum.

considered estimates for the Government Plantation in Burmah point to a profit of about 50 per cent. upon the Capital from that date.

It might be admissible to associate with leases of moderate areas thus reserved for cultivation, the exclusive right to collect wild rubber in a larger adjacent district, subject always to strict covenants as to replantation. This right would be limited to a few, say twelve, years, being only conceded as an assistance whilst the cultivated area is developing. After that transition period, the retention of exclusive rights over such land should only be permitted upon condition of extended cultivation.

All permanent concessions of land which do not result in early cultivation must be regarded as impolitic, and unprofitable alike to the Territory, the Company, and the Concessionaire. /

Suggested Form of Enquiry to be issued to all Local Officials and Mission Stations.

INDIGENOUS RUBBER IN B. S. A. CO.'S TERRITORIES.

1. Have any Rubber-bearing trees or plants been identified in your District? If so, in what locality, and in what numbers? Describe their general character and appearance, size, girth, bark, leaf and flower, if any. (Photographs or rough water colours would be much valued.)

2. Is there any Rubber-production in your District? If so, is it confined to special seasons? What is the local method of extraction and preparation? How is the Rubber disposed of and at what price?

3. Have you any proposals as to the best methods of preserving and replanting wild Rubber trees?

4. If there is no local production, is there any knowledge or tradition of Rubber-production amongst the Natives? If so, can it be traced to any adjacent territory?

5. Are there any unidentified trees or plants in your District which give promise of Rubber? If so, give details as in section 1.

6. Are there any areas in your District suitable for reservation for the cultivation of Rubber? /

The following additional information has been received in a letter from Sir W. T. Thiselton Dyer:–

'The Euphorbias said to yield Rubber in N.W. Rhodesia are *probably* similar to those existing in Angola. These produce 'Almeidiria' or Potato Gum. The value of this is very small ...

'The produce of "*Kickxia Africana*" is worthless. The valuable Lagos Rubber is now known to be the produce of "*Kickxia Elastica.*"'

'Root-rubber* ... the produce of '*Carpodinus Lanceolatus*' ... is of inferior quality ... Any attempt to protect it would not be worth the cost.'

Regulations Established in German East Africa, June 16th, 1897.

SECTION 1. – Every preparation of rubber otherwise than by the legitimate process of extraction, and every adulteration thereof by the admixture of water, sand, small stones or scraps of rind or wood is hereby prohibited.

SECTION 2. – Rubber may be brought into the market on the coast and exported, only if packed in bales which are cut open at least down to the centre.

SECTION 3. – The so-called Pira ya chini (root-rubber) and Pira ya kuponda (rubber prepared by the boiling down of peeled rinds) must not be brought into the market.

SECTION 4. – Adulterated rubber, uncut bales when brought into the market on the coast and exported, root-rubber and boiled rubber will be confiscated, wherever they are found, by the authorities, and will be handed over to the chief or local district administrations, or to the stations in the interior, and there publicly destroyed.

SECTION 5. – Persons who carry on a regular trade by the purchase or sale of the rubbers enumerated in Section 4 will be punished by a fine not exceeding one thousand rupees, or, in default of payment, by imprisonment.

SECTION 6. – Infringements of Section 1 of the present Decree will incur a fine not exceeding one thousand rupees, which may also be accompanied by imprisonment not exceeding two months.

---

* N.B. – This must be distinguished from Rubber extracted from the roots of *Landolphias* – a product which is fatal to those valuable plants, and must be suppressed.

EDITORIAL NOTES

Thomas, 'On the Oil Rivers of West Africa'

1. *F.R.G.S.*: Fellow of the Royal Geographical Society, which was founded in 1830 under the name Geographical Society of London as an institution to promote the 'advancement of geographical science'. It later absorbed the African Association (1788), the Raleigh Club and the Palestine Association.

2. *King George Pepple and Oko Jumbo*: George Oruigbiji Pepple (1849–88) ruled the Kingdom of Bonny, an independent trading state in the Niger Delta, between 30 September 1866 and 14 December 1883, when he was deposed. After the British signed a treaty making the state a protectorate, he was restored on 22 January 1887 and ruled until his death. Oko Jumbo was an important chief in the Kingdom of Bonny and died in 1891. See S. J. S. Cookey, *King Jaja of the Niger Delta: His Life and Times 1821–1891* (London: UGR, 2005).

3. *Ju-Ju*: Ju-Ju, a word of West African origin derived from the French *joujou* (toy), referred to the supernatural power ascribed to an object.

4. *a son of Oko Jumbo ... superior education*: This was presumably Herbert Jumbo, who later quarrelled with his father and was forced to place himself under the protection of the British consul.

5. *'Where the fever ... shivering chill'*: Thomas Moore, 'Song of the Evil Spirit of the Woods', ll. 1–6.

Despatches relating to the Sierra Leone Oil Palm Industry

1. *experiment of Messrs. Lever Brothers ... proved a failure*: For a discussion of this episode, see K. D. Nworah, 'The Politics of Lever's West African Concessions, 1907–1913', *International Journal of African Historical Studies*, 5:2 (1972), pp. 248–64.

2. *pericarp oil*: The pericarp forms the edible tissue around the seeds. It is made up of the exocarp, which is the external layer or peel; the mesocarp, the middle layer or pith; and the endocarp, the inner layer containing the seeds.

3. *Depericarper*: The depericarper separates the nuts from the fibre.

West Africa. Palm Oil and Palm Kernels

1. J. H. THOMAS, M.P.: James Henry 'Jimmy' Thomas (1874–1949) was a British trade unionist and Labour politician.

2. *pericarp*: see note 2 to *Despatches relating to the Sierra Leone Oil Palm Industry*, above.

Middleton, *Report on the Ground-Nut Trade in Kano Province*

1. H. H. Middleton: H. Hale Middleton was the District Officer in Hadejia Emirate in the Kano Province.
2. W. F. Gowers: Sir William Frederick Gowers was born in 1845. After working for the British South Africa Company, he became Governor of Northern Nigeria and Uganda before returning to London to serve as a crown agent. He also compiled the *Gazetteer of Kano Province* (London, 1921). He died in 1945. See R. Scott, 'Gowers of Uganda: The Public and Private Life of a Forgotten Colonial Governor', *Australasian Review of African Studies*, 30:2 (2009), pp. 1–22; M. Critchley, *Sir William Gowers, 1845–1915. A Biographical Appreciation* (London: William Heinemann Medical Books, 1949).
3. *Beri-beri*: Beri Beri, a Hausa name, refers to the Kanuri ethnic group who reside in south-eastern Niger.
4. *Mangawa*: The Mangawa are found in northern Jiwawa State, northern Nigeria.
5. *Fulani*: The Fulani are a nomadic group found throughout West Africa.

Penzer, *Cotton in British West Africa*

1. *Federation of British Industries*: Founded in 1916, the Federation of British Industries (FBI) sought to promote the interests of British industry and was the forerunner of the Confederation of British Industry.
2. *N. M. PENZER*: Norman Mosley Penzer (1892–1960) was the author of *The Mineral Resources of Burma* (London: George Routledge, 1922); *An Annotated Bibliography of Sir Richard Francis Burton* (London: A. M. Philpot Ltd, 1923); and *The Harēm* (London: G. G. Harrap & Co., 1936).
3. *VISCOUNT MILNER*: Alfred Milner, the first Viscount Milner, was born in 1854. He was successively Governor of the Cape Colony and High Commissioner for South Africa (1897–1901); Administrator and later Governor of the Transvaal and the Orange River Colony (1901–2); and Secretary of State for the Colonies (1919–21). He died in 1925.
4. *Leo Africanus*: see P. Masonen, 'Leo Africanus. The Man with Many Names', *Al-Andalus Magreb*, 8–9 (2001), pp. 115–44.
5. *Thomas Clegg ... supply of raw material*: Clegg also grew arrowroot, coffee, indigo and tobacco; bought saw gins and set up workshops for carpentry and brick-making among other manufactures. In 1863, he helped to establish the West African Company. See J. F. Ade Ajayi, 'Crowther and Trade on the Niger' (Henry Martyn Lectures 1999, Faculty of Divinity, University of Cambridge).
6. *Macgregor Laird ... native opposition*: Macgregor Laird (1808–61) was a Scottish merchant. After his ill-fated expedition, he never returned to Africa, but devoted himself to the development of trade with the area that later became Nigeria. He was also one of the main promoters of a company formed to operate a steamship service between England and New York.
7. *Benjamin Crapper ... Lancashire cotton trade*: see K. Dike Nworah, 'The West African Operations of the British Cotton Growing Association, 1904–1914', *African Historical Studies*, 4:2 (1971), pp. 315–30.
8. *Mr. Bonar Law*: Andrew Bonar Law (1858–1923), a British Conservative Party statesman and later Prime Minister.

9. *black-water fever*: Blackwater fever is a complication of malaria and frequently leads to kidney failure.
10. *Gustav Nachtigall ... West Africa*: Gustav Nachtigal (1834–85), a doctor and traveller, was appointed Consul in 1882.
11. *Dr. Oudney ... Captain Clapperton and Major Denham*: Walter Oudney (1790–1824) was a Scottish physician and African explorer. In early 1822 he departed from Tripoli with explorers Dixon Denham (1786–1828) and Hugh Clapperton (1788–1827), reaching Bornu in February 1823. They were thus the first Europeans to complete the north–south crossing of the Sahara Desert.

The Cotton-Growing Industry in Uganda, Kenya, and the Mwanza District of Tanganyika

1. *Empire Cotton Growing Corporation*: The Empire Cotton Growing Corporation was established in 1921 under Royal Charter to extend and promote the growth and cultivation of cotton within the British Empire. It was funded by a levy on cotton imports and windfall tax surpluses extracted from African and Egyptian cotton producers. It controlled all cotton research and propaganda within the empire. It was the publisher of a large number of reports including G. F. Keatinge, *Cotton Growing in South Africa* (London, 1923); J. W. Munro, *Cotton Pest Control Work in Southern and Central Africa and the Rhodesias* (London, 1937); and H. Horne, *The Extension of Cotton Cultivation in Tanganyika Territory Report of Major Hastings Horne to the Committee on a Tour Undertaken in Tanganyika Territory November 1920–July 1921* (London, 1922).
2. *Training College of Makerere*: The college later became Makerere University.

Addison and Jefferys, *Cotton Growing in Southern Africa and the Rhodesias*

1. *EMPIRE COTTON GROWING CORPORATION*: see note 1 to *The Cotton-Growing Industry in Uganda, Kenya, and the Mwanza District of Tanganyika*, above.
2. *G. F. Keatinge ... view of the prospects*: G. F. Keatinge, *Cotton Growing in South Africa* (London: Empire Cotton Growing Corporation, 1923).

Simpson, 'Report on the Cotton-Growing Industry'

1. *Dr. Livingstone ... production of cotton*: David Livingstone (1813–73) was a Scottish Congregationalist missionary with the London Missionary Society and an explorer in Africa. For a description of his career, see A. C. Ross, *David Livingstone: Mission and Empire* (London: Hambledon, 2002).

Oliphant, *Report on the Commercial Possibilities and Development of the Forests of Nigeria*

1. *Empire Timbers Committee*: The Empire Timbers Committee was appointed in 1929 to determine ways in which the forests of the empire could be best developed.
2. *Forest Products Research Laboratory*: For more on the work of the Forest Products Research Laboratory, see *Fifty Years of Timber Research: A Short History of the Forest*

Products Research Laboratory, Princes Risborough (London: Building Research Establishment, 1977).

3. *F. M. OLIPHANT*: F. M. Oliphant was the assistant director of Forest Products Research at the Forest Products Research Laboratory, Princes Risborough. He also authored *The Air-Seasoning and Conditioning of Timber* (London, 1927).

4. *the Andamans*: The Andaman Islands are a group of archipelagic islands in the Bay of Bengal.

5. *the Experimental Station at Sapoba*: The station was established in 1926.

6. *the Indian Forest Act*: The Indian Forest Act, 1927, sought to consolidate and reserve the areas that had forest cover or significant wildlife and to regulate the movement and transit of forest produce.

7. *the Ondo Circle*: The Ondo Circle is in the Western State of Nigeria.

8. Messrs, James Latham & Company: The company was formed in Liverpool in 1757 by James Latham. It is still trading.

Nicholson, *The Future of Forestry in Uganda*

1. *J. W. NICHOLSON*: John Wilfred Nicholson was born in 1893. He spent several years in the Indian Forest Service, before becoming Forest Advisor to the Governments of Kenya and Uganda (1927–30) and Conservator of Forests in Orissa (1936). He died in 1949.

2. *isohyets*: An isohyet is a line on a map connecting points having the same amount of rainfall in a period.

3. *xerophilous woodland*: woodland that is adapted to a very dry climate or habitat, or to conditions where moisture is scarce.

4. *edaphic*: a general term referring to characteristics of the soil.

5. *podocarpus*: a type of conifer.

6. *Tanganyika Concessions Ltd*: Tanganyika Concessions Ltd was a British company established by Robert Williams which started prospecting for minerals in 1899 and was granted mining concessions in 1900. In 1906 it merged with Société Générale de Belgique, Belgium's largest holding company, to form the Union Minière du Haut Katanga (UMHK).

Leckie, *The Growing of Wattle and Production of Wattle Bark in Kenya*

1. *W. G. LECKIE*: W. G. Leckie was Agricultural Officer of Kikuyu Province and later a Senior Agricultural Officer. He also wrote, with R. W. Thornton, *The African and his Live-Stock* (Oxford: Oxford University Press, 1946).

Moloney, *West African Produce*

1. *AFRICAN TRADE SECTION ... CHAMBER OF COMMERCE OF LIVERPOOL*: The Liverpool Chamber of Commerce was established in 1850 and its African Trade Section represented those members of the Chamber with trading links with West Africa.

2. *SIR ALFRED MOLONEY*: Sir Cornelius Alfred Maloney was born in 1848 and was Secretary of the Gold Coast in 1879–84 and Administrator of the Gambia in 1884–6 and of Lagos in 1886–90. He also authored *West African Fisheries, with Particular Reference to the Gold Coast Colony* (London, 1883) and *Sketch of the Forestry of West Africa:*

with Particular Reference to its Present Principal Commercial Products (London, 1887). He died in 1913.

3. *Professor Oliver*: Daniel Oliver FRS (1830–1916) was librarian of the Herbarium, Royal Botanic Gardens, Kew, in 1860–90 and Keeper in 1864–90. In 1861–88, he was also Professor of Botany at University College, London.

4. *SANSIVIERA GUINEENSIS*: also known as bowstring hemp. Although not a true hemp, its fibres are high in xylan.

5. *Nupe-man*: The Nupe, also known as the Tapa, are an ethnic group located primarily in the middle belt and northern Nigeria. They are the dominant group in Niger and an important minority in Kwara State.

Report of the Tobacco Advisory Committee

1. *the British-American Tobacco Co., Ltd.*: British American Tobacco was formed in 1902, when the United Kingdom's Imperial Tobacco Company and the United States American Tobacco Company founded the company as a joint venture.

2. *The East African Tobacco Co., Ltd., Kampala*: The East African Tobacco Company was founded in Tanganyika in 1934 and operated its own factory in Kampala. It was taken over by British American Tobacco in 1949.

Holland, *Rubber Cultivation in West Africa*

1. *J. H. HOLLAND*: J. H. Holland (1869–1950) was the curator of the Calabar Botanic Gardens and a former curator of Kew Gardens, London. His other publications include *The Useful Plants of Nigeria* (London: HMSO, 1922) and (co-authored with H. A. A Nicholls) *A Text Book of Tropical Agriculture* (London: Macmillan, 1929).

2. *Landolphia vines and Ficus*: The rubber obtained from Landolphia plants is known as 'landolphia' or 'Madagascar' rubber. Ficus is a genus of about 850 species of woody trees, shrubs, vines, epiphytes and hemiepiphytes.

3. *Para rubber*: The Pará rubber tree (Hevea brasiliensis) belongs to the Euphorbiaceae family. It is the primary source of natural rubber.

Rutherford, *Sisal in Kenya*

1. *SISAL*: In 1907 Rutherford introduced sisal plants into Kenya from Tanganyika, and, in the same year, established a sisal plantation with R. Swift at Punda Milia near Thika. See *Kenya's Sisal Industry* (Nairobi: Export Processing Zones Authority, 2005).

2. *a decorticator*: a machine for stripping the skin, bark or rind off nuts, wood, plant stalks, grain, etc, in preparation for further processing.

3. *Shirtliff*: F. R. 'Dick' Shirtliff, a well-known Kenyan manufacturer of machinery.

'Speight, 'Big Game Hunting in South Africa'

1. *J. H. Patterson's 'The Man-Eaters of Tsavo'*: published in 1907 by Macmillan & Co.

Lyttelton Gell, *The Rubber Industry*

1. P. Lyttelton Gell: Philip Lyttleton Gell was born in 1852. He was a director of the British South Africa Company and a member of the 1917 Empire Settlement Committee. He died in 1926.

2. *The Mozambique Company*: The Mozambique Company was a royal company that operated in the Portuguese colony of Mozambique. It was established in February 1891 with a capital stock of approximately $5 million obtained from financiers from Germany, the United Kingdom and South Africa, and possessed a fifty-year concession to large areas of Mozambique. The concession allowed it to exploit the resources and existing manpower of the region, to grant sub-concessions and to collect taxes.

3. *Indunas*: An induna was a black adviser or overseer.